RUSSIA'S FAILED REVOLUTIONS

From the Decembrists to the Dissidents

ADAM B. ULAM

Basic Books, Inc., Publishers

NEW YORK

Library of Congress Cataloging in Publication Data

Ulam, Adam B., 1922–
  Russia's failed revolutions.

  Includes bibliographical references and index.
  1. Russia—Politics and government—19th
century. 2. Russia—Politics and government—20th
century. 3. Revolutions—Russia. 4. Dissidents—
Russia. I. Title.
DK189.U43   947.08   80–50534
ISBN: 0–465–07152–X

CONTENTS

PREFACE

THIS BOOK does not purport to be a systematic history of the Russian revolutionary tradition. Rather it seeks an answer to the question: What was it that at decisive moments has frustrated or flawed the libertarian intentions of Russia's revolutionaries and reformers? Beginning with the Decembrists, it concludes with a discussion of the meaning and prospects of contemporary dissent and its implications for the future of freedom in Russia and elsewhere.

This work, like several of my previous ones, owes a great deal to the pleasant and intellectually bracing atmosphere of Harvard's Russian Research Center. Among my many friends and associates there I must express special thanks to my assistant Mrs. Christine Balm, and also to Bill Fierman and Misha Tsypkin, both of whom helped with research for this volume.

ADAM B. ULAM
Cambridge, Massachusetts

Russia's Failed Revolutions

Chapter 1

HESITANT REBELS:
THE DECEMBRISTS

THE MOURNFUL CEREMONY had been planned by Nicholas I with the same meticulousness which was to characterize his administration of the empire during his thirty-year reign. This was to be the epilogue of the story of the Decembrists, who on Nicholas's accession to the throne had attempted a military coup with the aim of overthrowing him and ending autocracy in Russia. In the course of one day, December 14, 1825, the badly prepared uprising was suppressed. Now the rebels already sentenced were to be publicly disgraced in front of their former comrades and soldiers. On the night of July 13, 1826, at two o'clock, more than one hundred ex-officers were brought from their cells into the courtyard of the Petropavlovsk fortress, which was surrounded by detachments from all the regiments of the St. Petersburg garrison. Each prisoner in turn was made to kneel in front of his former regiment. A noncommissioned officer broke a sword over the prisoner's head and ripped off his epaulets and decorations. Then the convicts were stripped of their uniforms and clothed in prison smocks. As of now they ceased to be officers and noblemen and became criminals with no civic rights. The erstwhile rebels were then marched back to their cells to await a long journey in chains, in most cases to Siberia.

Five of the conspirators were exempted from the opprobrious ceremony and would not set out on the long journey. Theirs would be but a short walk across the courtyard to the gallows erected the preceding day on the edge of the enclosure. Before it, they attended their last religious services, and at 4:00 A.M. they were ready for the final act.

Though the death penalty had been abolished in Russia, the guilt of those five had been judged so great that they had been sentenced to be drawn and quartered. The emperor, who had been discreetly managing the court's proceedings behind the scenes, then ordered that the manner of the execution be changed in accordance with the enlightened spirit of the age: death by hanging.

The five young men had quite different backgrounds and had played different roles in the events which now brought them to the scaffold. In fact, each of them could serve as an exemplar of a distinct kind of rebel, each in his own way a progenitor of one of the breeds of revolutionaries who would crowd the Russian political scene through 1917.

Peter Kakhovsky came closest to the pathological type of revolutionary, inwardly driven to embrace an extreme cause, whether on the left or on the right, who in its service would not hesitate to kill. Kondrati Ryleyev, poet and dreamer, was one of those people who are always ready to combat social injustice, even to the point of plunging into a madcap adventure and who through sheer enthusiasm are able to overcome their comrades' scruples and hesitations. Michael Bestuzhev-Riumin was the youngest of the lot, twenty-two years old at the time of the insurrection. Hotheaded and childishly enamored of conspiracy and intrigue, he was not popular with his fellow rebels.

The other two stood out among the whole crowd of the Decembrists, Serge Muraviev-Apostol by virtue of his moral principles, Paul Pestel through his intellectual qualities. Muraviev fits that often abused epithet: idealist. Heir to great wealth and bearer of a famous name, he was set on the path of conspiracy and rebellion through his revulsion at the treatment of the common soldier in the Russian army. After the fiasco of December 14, and with the attempted coup clearly a failure, Muraviev Apostol still tried to stir up a mutiny, leading his own regiment in a suicidal venture. Paul Pestel has been considered the outstanding but also the most enigmatic figure among the Decembrists. Of German descent, a brilliant officer, once thought to be slated for highest military preferments, Pestel chose instead the road which would lead him to the gallows. Thinker and writer, as well as a practitioner of the conspiratorial craft, he stands first in the long line of revolutionaries who were both activists and theorists—the tradition which one day would produce Lenin. And with his penchant for egalitarianism and authoritarianism, of all the Decembrists Pestel comes closest to being a precursor of bolshevism. His comrades, not without reason, suspected him of harboring dictatorial ambitions.

With the doomed men facing the gallows, their sentences were read once more. Except for Bestuzhev-Riumin, who had to be forcibly hoisted onto the scaffold, all faced their ordeal calmly and with dignity. They embraced, were blindfolded, and the executioner started his task. Then an accident occurred which compounded the frightfulness of the occasion. When the trap was sprung, three of the condemned proved too heavy for their ropes and, still alive, fell into the ditch. An apocryphal tradition insists that Muraviev, one of the three, called out, "What a wretched country. They don't even know how to hang properly." It took some time before new ropes could be fetched; this time the executioner, prompted by the curses of the commanding officer, did his job, and the savage rite was concluded. Tsarist justice transformed five unsuccessful conspirators into martyrs whose legend would inspire and sustain future generations of Russian revolutionaries.

What had led all these men, most of them nobly born, quite a few with brilliant prospects, to start on the road which would lead to the scene in the Petropavlovsk fortress? One answer was suggested by Pushkin in the verses intended for his *Eugene Onegin* but for obvious reasons never included in the published version. He wrote of the Decembrists, many of whom were his close acquaintances and boon companions, ". . . Those were plots hatched between claret and champagne to the accompaniment of satirical songs and friendly arguments. [But] deep in their hearts, there was no revolutionary intent. It all came out of boredom, out of their young minds [chafing under] idleness. [Though] grown-up men, they plunged into the madcap games of adolescents."[1] This was not to be the poet's last word on the significance of the drama of the Decembrists.

But even in the beginning, there was more to the story than just "madcap games." True, what triggered it was this craving for action which often seizes young men when, after being through exciting times, they find themselves pushed back into a humdrum, daily routine. The epic of the Napoleonic era had just concluded, and the elite of the Russian youth had experienced the elation first of defeating the hitherto invincible foreign enemy on their native soil and then of the triumphant march across the Continent. For them, as for the rest of the Russians, the emperor, Alexander I, had embodied the people's resolve to repulse the invader and to end Napoleon's tyranny over other nations. He had been acclaimed as Europe's liberator and the arbiter of her fate. Yet, upon returning among his own people, Alexander reverted to the role of autocrat. The same man who had insisted that the Bourbons, whom he had restored to the throne, grant a constitution to France, who was about to bestow representative institutions on his Polish subjects, continued to rule Russia as an absolute monarch. Nor did the emperor show any signs that he proposed to deal with the country's pressing social ailments. Most of Russia's peasants were serfs, the servile status of the majority of the nation being both a symptom and the prime cause of its backwardness. With the war's end, the young officers' professional life reverted to the routine of endless parades and drills. The more intellectually minded among them had been deeply affected by what they had seen in the West. They could not help reflecting how for all of its military might, the empire, when it came to its political and social institutions, economy, and education, everything which meant civilization, lagged behind France and England and even the petty German principalities.

A sensitive man could not remain indifferent to one of the most depressing aspects of Russian life: the draconic discipline prevailing in the tsar's army, where even for minor transgressions or faults of deportment, soldiers would be whipped, the victim occasionally dying under the lash.

It was a fervent desire to cure Russia of such ills that led six young officers of the Imperial Guards in February 1816 to form a secret society. Called at first the Union of Salvation, it soon acquired a supplementary name, Society of True and Faithful Sons of the Fatherland. The initiative came from Alexander Nikolaye-vich Muraviev, at twenty-three years of age already a colonel and much decorated veteran of the Napoleonic wars. His associates, all under thirty and also of noble birth, were Prince Serge Trubetskoy, Ivan Yakushkin, and three of Alexander's kinsmen and namesakes, among them Serge Muraviev-Apostol. Four Muravievs on this historic occasion! But then few names appear as frequently in the annals of nineteenth-century Russia as that of the famous clan. They were among the country's leading generals, most distinguished imperial proconsuls, high civil and judicial officials, ambassadors, as well as among its famous rebels. The political ambivalence of the Russian ruling class is most vividly illustrated by the career of Michael Nikolayevich Muraviev (Alexander's brother). An early adherent to the secret society, imprisoned after the coup along with other Decembrists, he managed to clear himself and was exonerated. The erstwhile conspirator lived to become a classical example of the brutal and reactionary tsarist bureaucrat, and his exploits in suppressing the Polish insurrections of 1830–31 and of 1863 made him pass into history as Muraviev the Hangman.

By the end of its first year, the Union of Salvation had fourteen members, whose backgrounds were similar to those of the original six. Among them was Paul Pestel. In its organization and structure, the secret society was modelled after a Masonic lodge, reflecting both its members' Masonic affiliations and an attempt to provide a protective coloring to what was already a budding political conspiracy. Freemasonry was then quite fashionable among Russia's upper class. It was viewed indulgently, if without enthusiasm, by the government, tradition-ally suspicious of any private organizations not of a purely social nature. Masonic lodges, the authorities believed, provided relatively safe surrogates for political clubs, their usually bland and vague moralistic creed and rhetoric never quite reaching the level of concreteness and activism which would make them a source of danger to the established order.

At the end of its first year of existence, the society acquired a statute. Its members pledged to work for the introduction of a constitutional monarchy, for the abolition of serfdom, and to limit the influence of foreigners in the government. This was something new in Russian life: a formal program of political action developed not by the authorities, but by a group of private persons. As such it was hardly sensational. Constitutional ideas and aspirations were frequently voiced in the more progressive drawing rooms of St. Petersburg and Moscow, and during the earlier liberal phase of Alexander's reign, such discussions went on within the government itself. There was also fairly universal and public grumbling that so many high positions within the civil and military administrations were occupied by foreigners, mostly Germans, not only those from the Baltic provinces who had been Russian subjects for generations but also recent expatriates, some of whom never bothered to master the language of their adopted country.*

But the statute went beyond mere aspirations and formulated a program which clearly smacked of subversion. The Union of Salvation was to expand greatly its membership and to infiltrate the higher ranks of the military and civil bureaucracy. Upon the emperor's demise, the conspiracy would come into the open, and its members would refuse to swear allegiance to the new monarch until and unless he abolished autocracy and introduced a system of national representation.

If in the eyes of the law this program was clearly subversive, by twentieth-century standards it was not terribly revolutionary. At the time, Alexander I was thirty-nine years old and in apparently good health. The conspirators thought they would have to bide their time until they reached middle age.

Quite moderate in their political views, at least in the beginning, temperamentally these young men were a hotheaded lot, and it is not surprising that some of them would chafe under the injunction that they wait twenty to thirty years to see the fulfillment of their dreams. There was one obvious way of shortening the interval. Already in the fall of 1816, Michael Lunin, the most mercurial of the original band, "a devotee of Mars, Bacchus and Venus,"[2] as Pushkin described him, had proposed that the emperor should be kidnapped and assassinated. But his comrades unanimously rejected the idea, arguing that Russia was far from ready for a revolution. Furthermore, the secret society, fourteen strong, would have to seize power in the wake of the emperor's death. One suspects that this was, indeed, a case of too much claret and champagne rather than a serious proposal for political terror. Lunin did have a more serious side to his character: He was a man of great

---

*A classical example was the current foreign minister, Count Karl Nesselrode, born an English subject, whose father was German and mother Jewish.

chivalry and of deep religious convictions. Thus, it is almost impossible to visualize him as a participant in or planner of an actual assassination.

That the idea of regicide should appear among the Decembrists, as members of the secret societies and their associates are generally referred to, so early is a testimony to the essential ambivalence of the movement. Its members viewed themselves, justifiably, primarily as reformers attuned to the political realities of Russian life. But this moderation was combined with a certain revolutionary impatience and desire for violence. It was not mere theatricality inherited from the Masonic formulas which led to the inclusion in the statute of the Union of Salvation the following ominous injunction: "Any betrayal of the organization, revealing of its secrets, the slightest indiscretion, will be punished by death. No traitor will escape the dagger or poison." A correct reading of the actual situation in Russia instructed that the country was not ready for drastic changes, that it would take time and much patient work through infiltrating the state machinery and educating what there was in the way of public opinion to prepare Russia for free institutions. There was, on the other hand, the existentialist spirit of the age which proclaimed that the contest between freedom and autocracy can never be resolved through political bargaining and constitutional reforms but only through struggle and an act of will. Intellectually, the leading Decembrists, like most young Russians of aristocratic background, had been brought up in the rationalist spirit of the eighteenth century; they had been brought up in the belief that man was shaped by his environment. Human progress depended on wise institutions and laws mandated by an enlightened ruler or legislature. But emotionally the young would-be-reformers found themselves more and more under the spell of romanticism, whose writers such as Byron and Schiller, both avidly read in Russia, extolled innate wisdom and the virtues of the common people, told stories of the constant struggle between liberty and tyrannous rulers, and showed how a heroic act by an individual or a handful of people could affect decisively that struggle.

It is thus understandable that the idea of regicide would continue to tantalize and haunt the conspirators' minds. Its first reappearance in their deliberations took place almost exactly one year after Lunin's outburst. Most of the Decembrists were then in Moscow, where their regiments had followed the emperor on his extended visit. During one of their meetings, Alexander Muraviev read aloud a letter from St. Petersburg in which a fellow member reported sensational news: he had learned from authoritative sources that Alexander I was to detach some provinces from the empire in order to turn them over to the Poles.*

*After the Congress of Vienna, the central part of the prepartition Polish Commonwealth had been erected into the Polish kingdom to be in perpetuity under the scepter of the Russian tsar. Alexander had promised to rule it as a constitutional monarch, and on several occasions he hinted to the Poles that some day he would return to them the provinces which Russia had annexed in the partitions of 1772 and 1793.

The conspirators were outraged. It was bad enough for Alexander to deal a blow to Russian national pride by bestowing a constitution on Poland, but the provinces in question, despite the prevalence of the Polish element among the landowners, were overwhelmingly Ukrainian and Byelorussian insofar as the mass of the peasantry was concerned and hence, by contemporary criteria, essentially Russian.

Much later Ivan Yakushkin was to describe what happened after the report of Alexander's alleged betrayal of Russia's national interest.

> Having heard the contents of the letter with its fatal news for Russia, I asked those present if they believed it. I was assured that indeed they did and were convinced that it would be disastrous for the country to remain under the rule of the late emperor. I then announced to them that I was ready to sacrifice my own life to save Russia and would attempt to assassinate the Emperor. They demanded that they be allowed to share the risk and that the assassin be selected by lot from all of us, but I declined their proposal, not wanting to subject them to so great a danger.[3]

The next day his comrades informed Yakushkin that they realized that the news was completely false, but the young man was so upset, both by having been misled and by his self-sacrifice having been refused, that he broke off his relations with them and for the next three years would not have anything to do with the secret society.

The idea of regicide exercised a strong attraction for the minds of the conspirators; yet they would never be able to bring themselves to attempt it. The reasons for this go far to illuminate certain basic characteristics not only of the Decembrists but also of the entire Russian revolutionary movement during the balance of the century.

Fascination with political terror reflects more often than not the revolutionary's awareness of his weakness and a frustration at his obvious inability to achieve his aims through any other means. And so with the Decembrists. Eventually they would be able to enlist hundreds of confederates and sympathizers. But even then the hard facts of politics would mock their dreams and plans. Political power and authority still reposed entirely in the hands of the emperor. There was currently in Russia no body similar to the French General Estates in 1789, whose conversion to the cause of reform could impart momentum to revolution. Institutions such as the Senate, the highest judicial and administrative court of the empire, and the State Council were entirely creatures of the tsar and had no independent power or prestige. There was no class interest which could be summoned against autocracy and in favor of political change. If in some ways the Decembrists represented the elite of their class and of the officer corps, they were also but a small fraction of both, with the great majority of the nobility adhering to the old ways and fearful of any change which might affect their rights over the serfs. Russia as yet had no middle class in the Western sense of the word. The vast mass of the peasantry was sunk in ignorance and hence assumed to be unresponsive to political ideas. The absence of any source except one of political authority was epitomized by the mad emperor Paul I, Alexander's father, who, when asked by a foreign ambassador which one of his ministers was especially important, replied, "Whoever happens to be talking to me and only while he does!" Russia was not only an autocratic state but also a servile society, and the very extent of this servility, while it bred revolutionaries, made their task almost hopeless.

Paradoxically, while the country seemed immune to political change, it was very vulnerable to revolutionary violence. Most of the rulers between Peter the Great's death in 1725 and the accession of Alexander I in 1801 reached the throne as a result of a plot, usually carried out by a handful of officials and Imperial Guards' officers. Several monarchs were deposed by force; two, Peter III and Paul I, were murdered. This sequence of violence failed, however, to alter the character of the monarchy; the new ruler might be more liberal and enlightened than the predecessor, but he or she would rule just as autocratically, either directly or through favorites.

In addition to palace revolutions, Russia had been afflicted by popular revolts. The lower classes' essentially apolitical mentality did not mean that they always remained passive under a system which economically, socially, politically, was based upon their exploitation. Their ignorance and sufferings made it occasionally possible for an impostor posing as a recently deceased tsar to trigger a popular uprising. A wave of anarchy would sweep through the countryside, and armed bands would roam, looting and killing indiscriminately, especially landlords and government officials, until the revolt could be suppressed, often by means as barbarous as those used by the rebels. Pugachev's rebellion in 1773 was led by an illiterate Cossack claiming to be Peter III, spread over large areas of the Urals and lower Volga and was only put down by a large army. Pushkin summarized every educated Russian's feelings when he wrote of the event, "God spare us from ever witnessing again this kind of Russian revolution with no thought behind it save that of wanton destruction."[4]

But the Decembrists' principles and background inhibited them from seeking power through a palace revolution or through setting a match to the ever present combustible material of the misery and sufferings of the Russian countryside. The coup of December 14, 1825, would partake of elements both of imposture and of palace revolution, but it would be done in a halfhearted way and hence be doomed from the beginning.

Thus the idea of regicide, for all its attraction, was recognized by the Decembrists in their more sober moments as futile: by itself it would just replace one autocrat with another. The tsarist officials presiding at the trial of the Decembrists fastened on their alleged plans for assassinating Alexander I as the most heinous of their crimes. But a longer perspective shows all that was much more in the nature of talk than of a terrorist design. Had the Decembrists been in earnest, they would have had innumerable opportunities to strike at the monarch. They moved, at least some of them, in the highest circles, encountered Alexander at the court, army maneuvers, and social functions. Most of these rebels had neither the cold-blooded cynicism of the courtiers who had carried out the previous palace revolutions nor the ideological fervor which would persuade revolutionaries of later generations that the end justifies any means, including terror.

Alexander I began his reign in an aura of great expectations. The young emperor, twenty-three years old at his succession, was reputed to be a friend of reform and determined to tackle the basic ills of Russian society. The first few years of his reign to be sure saw the abolition of the most barbarous forms of corporal punishment, efforts to ameliorate the conditions of the serfs, and a thorough reorganization of the by-then-unwieldy and inefficient machinery of administration. Many hoped that these were but preliminaries to the establishment of a system of national representation as proposed by the ablest of his ministers, Michael Speransky, and of the eventual abolition of serfdom. But in 1812 Alexander abruptly dismissed Speransky. Following the epic of national resistance and victory over Napoleon, the emperor's policies took an increasingly reactionary turn. Abroad he sponsored the Holy Alliance, a sort of trade union, of Europe's absolutist monarchs, designed to maintain legitimacy, that is, to preserve their powers and to quell any popular challenge to the status quo. In domestic affairs, Alexander's chief adviser after 1815 became Alexis Arakcheyev, a narrow-minded and brutal reactionary. The educational establishment, which the emperor had earlier expanded by chartering three new universities and other schools, was now subjected to strict thought control aimed at eradicating any progressive ideas and echoes of the French Revolution. For the regime higher education became, and would remain for the rest of the century, the main potential source of subversive ideas and hence an object of constant suspicion and chicanery. To be sure, public education was as yet on so small a scale that it could contribute little, whether good or bad, to national life. What the government spent on schools amounted to about one-fifth of what it cost to support the imperial family and court. It is unlikely that more than 2 or 3 percent of the population of Alexander I's Russia could be described as literate.

The emperor's turn toward conservatism paralleled his growing preoccupation with religion. He had always displayed a great interest in mystical cults, ranging from varieties of sectarianism condemned by the Orthodox Church to Protestant pietism. Alexander had known and authorized the conspiracy against Paul I, and it is likely that with the passage of time the thought that he had been responsible, even if indirectly, for his father's murder, preyed increasingly on his mind. This, as well as other personal and family sorrows, possibly enhanced the tsar's absorption in spiritual meditation, bringing him under the spell of obscurantists and alleged holy men while the actual management of domestic politics was left in the hands of reactionary bureaucrats.

Not only religious resignation but also other more prosaic reasons prevented Alexander from pursuing the path of reform. His liberal notions, instilled in him by his early immersion in the ideas of eighteenth-century Enlightenment, clashed with an essentially autocratic nature. "A crowned Hamlet" was to be Herzen's apt description of him. Most fundamentally, the emperor's dilemma was similar to that of many of Russia's rulers down to the present: desirous of bestowing on their country free institutions, they would at some point recoil from the immensity and apparent impossibility of the task. This point was reached often when it became a question of surrendering or weakening the autocratic power. The very absence of free institutions in Russia meant that any genuine effort to emancipate society had to be a leap into the unknown, the end result of which might be not an orderly system of constitutional government but anarchy, an explosion of the pent-up popular grievances and aspirations which could destroy not only autocracy but also the unity and greatness of the Russian state.

Alexander's hesitations sprang from the same source as those of his conspiratorial opponents: both sides were fearful of striking a resolute blow at the existing system because they could not really visualize how Russia could be ruled differently. Autocracy had served the Russian state well: under its aegis the empire had grown into a world power and had come to occupy one-sixth of the world's land surface. Some rulers had been imbeciles, some outstanding statesmen. There had been among them tyrants as well as humanitarian reformers. No matter who the occupant of the throne, the process of expansion and of foreign conquest went on almost uninterruptedly. Autocracy was then the key to Russian national greatness at the same time that in the modern age it had to be acknowledged as the main source of her people's oppression, backwardness, and poverty.

The conspirators, much as they shared Pushkin's scathing verdict of Alexander as "a weak and perfidious ruler, an aging fop and idler,"[5] could not disregard the fact that for the vast majority of their countrymen, Russia was inconceivable without the autocratic tsar and the very concept of constitutionalism incomprehensible. Much as they fantasized about regicide and even about slaughtering the whole imperial family, they could never quite abandon the hope that the emperor would revert to the reforming zeal of his earlier years and do what they themselves did not quite know how to accomplish: give freedom to the people.

Whether sincerely or not, Alexander kept encouraging such notions. In his speech opening the Polish Diet on March 15, 1818, he hinted that sometime in the future he might introduce representative institutions in his Russian dominions.[6] The paradoxical hope-despair complex of progressive Russians about the ruler is again well illustrated by Pushkin. In 1819 he wrote a poem denouncing serfdom which concluded with the passage, "Shall I see, oh friends,/The people freed of oppression,/And serfdom struck down by the emperor's hand?/And will the glorious dawn of freedom/Eventually rise over our Fatherland."[7] Alexander, to whom the poem was presented, instructed the intermediary to convey to the poet his warm thanks for the noble sentiments. This, however, did not save Pushkin from being exiled a few months later for writing some verses less loyal in their tone.

The convoluted problem of regenerating Russia was further complicated by the fact that there were people who recognized unflinchingly the abuses of the autocratic system and of serfdom and yet for whom both institutions were necessary and salutory not only because the country was not ready for their abolition but also because they accorded with the Russian national character. Proponents of this view, such as the famous contemporary historian Nicholas Karamzin were not mere reactionaries. They admitted that constitutional systems could work well in the West, but not in Russia. In a historico-political essay written in 1818 and intended for the emperor's personal perusal, Karamzin criticized Alexander's reforming tendencies and warned him against any tampering with the principle of autocracy. Were he to do so any patriotic Russian would have the right and duty to say, "Sire, you're transgressing your authority. Russia, taught by previous disasters, had before the holy altar delivered absolute power to your ancestor and demanded that he rule her alone, with no limitations or hindrance. This mandate is the foundation of your power, you have no other. You may do anything except limit your powers by law."[8] Similarly, Karamzin believed that it would be disastrous to tamper with serfdom. Freed, the peasants would take to drinking and crime.[9] Under the current system landowners, by virtue of their power over serfs, helped the government to keep peace and order. The state alone could not expect to cope with the inevitable disorders among the peasants in the wake of their emancipation. "The first duty of the sovereign is to preserve the internal and external unity [and security] of the state. *Solicitude for the welfare of social classes and individuals must come second.*"*[10]

It is not known whether Alexander ever read the *Memoir.* Certainly it contained much which would have been very painful to him, such as the very pointed references to his father's tyranny and murder, the debauched life of the emperor's

*Italics mine.

grandmother, Catherine the Great, et cetera. As a result, the book could not be published unexpurgated until after the revolution of 1905. It was never easy for a Russian historian, and it would be even more difficult in the Soviet period, to write truthfully about his country's recent history even if the general thrust of his work was strongly proregime. While defending autocracy, Karamzin was scathing in his references to practically all of Russia's past rulers, and there was unwitting irony in his condemnation of palace revolutions. "What will happen to autocracy if some lords, generals, and guardsmen usurp the power to kill in secret or to remove our monarchs? It would become a plaything of an oligarchy that soon would turn into anarchy, which is worse than the most evil ruler for it threatens all, while the tyrant kills only some."[11] A strange apology for autocracy which comes so close to being its indictment. But perhaps this is not so different from those official eulogies of the Soviet system which claim that only Communism could have overcome the evils of Stalin's "cult of personality."

Except to a handful of people, the existence of the *Memoir* remained unknown until 1836. Yet its ideas expressed well what the contemporary Russian conservative firmly believed and what his liberal counterpart feared, even if for the most part he would not admit it: Russia's history and actual condition did not offer much hope for freedom. The Union of Salvation had been created in a fit of youthful exuberance. By 1818 its members were a bit older and much wiser. They had realized the immense complexity of the task they had set for themselves two years before, and now they would seek a firmer foundation for their enterprise.

In the course of its members' deliberations in Moscow early in 1818, it was decided to dissolve the old secret society and to burn its papers. In its place the Decembrists created a new organization, the Union of Welfare. The element of continuity between the two unions was very strong, twenty-two of the twenty-nine founders of the new one had belonged to the old one. But the Union of Welfare was to eschew the explicitly conspiratorial and political character of its predecessor. Dropped were the quasi-Masonic language and rituals. Instead of the old oath with the fearful sounding sanctions, a new member was now required simply to give his word of honor that he would not reveal the society's secrets nor work against its interest. Nothing in the aims and laws of the Union of Welfare, the formula asserted, could be taken to imply disrespect for the faith, patriotic feelings, or social obligations of the Russian.[12]

The statute of the union was drafted by a committee of three, one of whose members was Michael Muraviev (the future "Hangman"), and modelled after the constitution of Tugendbund (Union of Virtue), organized in Prussia in 1808. Tugendbund, impeccably monarchist in its sentiments, sought to reform and modernize Prussian society with the ultimate aim of enabling Germany to throw off the French domination. Insofar as its declaration of principles was concerned, the Union of Welfare could thus point to a thoroughly respectable and unsubversive prototype.

But the Decembrists did not abandon their revolutionary dreams in order to concentrate on educational and philanthropic activity, as a superficial reading of the statute would have suggested. The proposed structure of the Union of Welfare featured an inner group composed of its original founders, which, under the name of the Basic Union, was to run the affairs of the secret society as a whole. Each member of the inner body was to organize a branch cell of at least ten, but not more than twenty, members. Only after the total membership of the Union of Welfare had grown considerably would nonfounder members become eligible for election to the Basic Union and thus fully privy to the organization's policies and plans. The Decembrists' Basic Union then designated six of its members as its executive branch, called the Basic Council. The whole Union of Welfare was to be organized upon hierarchical and elitist lines with a pyramidlike arrangement. This is a pattern similar to that found in the Populist conspiracies of the 1860s and 1870s, and it is fairly analogous to the clandestine Marxist cells in pre-1917 Russia. What the founders obviously intended was that only the core of the union, that is, themselves, should be privy to the ultimate political aims of the secret society; new members would acquire that knowledge only after a period of indoctrination. There was, thus, at least temporarily, a conspiracy within a conspiracy with the larger body serving as a front for a group of veterans of the old Union of Salvation, who were still determined to force basic changes in Russia's political and social system.

The founders believed that those hundreds and indeed thousands of potential adherents who might at first hesitate to join would become reassured by the apolitical and humanitarian character of the union's ostensible program. This being Russia, the government could not and would not license a public organization on this scale; the emperor guarded jealously not only his prerogatives but also his claim to be the sole benefactor of his people. But should the regime learn, as it was likely to, about the existence of the Union of Welfare, it could not but privately approve its goals and efforts. They were to be concentrated in four major areas. One was philanthropy. People working in this field were to sponsor, as well as to join, the already existing organizations intended to relieve poverty, take care of the sick, improve the lot of prisoners, et cetera. Special attention was to be given to protecting peasants from rapacious landlords and in general to relieving the condition of serfs.

Associates of the union assigned to work in the field of public enlightenment were charged to seek to control and give direction to the educational institutions. Many of the leading Decembrists had been brought up by foreign-born tutors and/or studied abroad. Yet they firmly believed in a nationalist orientation in education. The young were to learn first about their own country, were to be taught to be proud of their national heritage and to avoid aping foreign ways. The field of public enlightenment included what we would call today propaganda and indoctrination. The Union of Welfare proposed to sponsor journals, newspapers, and books advancing its aims. It would attempt to impose its moral and artistic standards on society as a whole. Literature and the arts, it believed, were to be judged not primarily by aesthetic criteria but by the degree to which they inculcated socially useful ideas and patriotic feelings. "The strength and charm of poetry" should consist mainly "in the liveliness of its style and the decency of the language and above all in its unambiguous advocacy of high minded and altruistic principles." Or, "it is unworthy of poetry to deal with a subject or to depict feelings which weaken rather than strengthen the striving after moral good."[13]

Ironically, these precepts of the opponents of the regime came quite close even in their language to the rationale behind the imperial regime's supervision of literacy and artistic activity. For all the progressive and liberal intentions behind their proposed guidelines for the arts, the Decembrists' moral and patriotic censoriousness suggests more than just a hint of that intellectual intolerance which would afflict future generations of Russian revolutionaries and which would find its fullest expression in the Communist system of thought control.

The third broad aim of projected activity was law and order. Those delegated to work in this area were instructed to watch for, expose, and combat official abuses. If employed as judges (Russia at the time had no professional lawyers nor was there a clear-cut distinction between the executive and the judicial branches), they were to observe the strictest standards of probity and efficiency. Brisk propaganda was to be directed against officials who took bribes, neglected their duties, oppressed their subordinates, and otherwise abused their powers. In brief, this segment of the Union of Welfare had as its goal to instill efficiency and humanity in the administration of justice and civil affairs and put the fear of God in the corrupt and indolent Russian bureaucrat. In this way, the union also undertook to educate society that something can and must be done to make officials, from the lowest to the highest level, live up to their responsibilities.

National economy was the fourth major division of the union's activity. To work in it, the Decembrists hoped to enlist not only people from the appropriate branches of the government and landlords with special knowledge of agronomy but also those from the lower orders, such as tradesmen and craftsmen. Yet this effort at broadening the social base of the secret society was to prove signally unsuccessful. The economic part of the program of the Union of Welfare was to remain largely in the realm of good intentions. Russia was still some decades away from the Industrial Revolution and had but the merest rudiments of the middle class in the Western sense of the term. But it is a testimony to the breadth of the authors' views that the program stressed the need for sponsoring industrial and commercial development, improving communications, and establishing insurance companies. Conspicuous by its absence was any explicit reference to the abolition of serfdom. This was in line with the studied moderation of the public part of the program of the Union of Welfare.

Yet the program, known as the Green Book from the covers of the original copy, was unrealistic. Though the Union of Welfare would have a membership running into the hundreds, it would still prove grossly inadequate for the task specified in its program. It would have taken the full resources of a modern, well-organized, and disciplined party to achieve the Green Book's goal: for the Decembrists to become a power in Russian society rivalling that of the actual government. Despite all the provisions for centralized direction of the Union of Welfare and its successor societies, their activities would never be successfully coordinated; until the end the Decembrists would remain a loosely connected network of separate cells rather than a disciplined unitary organization. The modern political party is, among other things, a product of modern technology, and the vast distances of the pretelegraph and prerailway Russia made the ambitious designs of the Green Book quite impractical.

But the moderate and seemingly noncontroversial program of the Union of Welfare did not express the whole of its aims. There was another and more secret part of the Green Book known to the inner core of the union's membership which spelled out its political goals, reaffirming the secret society's determination to introduce representative institutions and to abolish serfdom.[14] Nor was the society completely committed to a peaceful pursuit of its aims: it did not preclude the possibility that the regime would have to be overthrown by force.

As of 1818 the Decembrists remained undecided as to the path they would pursue, revolution or peaceful reform, conspiracy against or cooperation with the government. Just as there was something Hamlet-like about their emperor, so there was about this first generation of Russian revolutionaries. The former's liberal convictions were held in check by his authoritarian temperament; in the case of the Decembrists, their revolutionary impatience yielded to the fear that by striking at the hated political system and its embodiment, the emperor, they might hurt Russia. After all, as its statute proclaimed, the ultimate aim of the Union of Welfare was to bring the country "to the level of greatness and well being for which it had been destined by the Creator." But the question was whether this could be furthered by internecine struggle, assassinations, and perhaps a civil war. The Decembrists would never bring themselves to strike at Alexander, and he, for all the frequent reports about the secret societies' activities, would not, until the very last days of his life, contemplate measures against them. In 1821 Count Ilarion Vasilchikov, then the commanding officer of the Imperial Guards, reported to the emperor at length about secret societies among his officers. "Dear Vasilchikov," replied the tsar, "you have served me a long time. You must know that I myself once shared and encouraged similar illusions and errors. It is not up to me to punish them."[15] It was not mere fatalism or a sense of personal guilt which explains this attitude of the emperor's. Alexander was quick at forestalling what he considered a real danger to his person or power and quite ruthless in punishing those who defied him. But he knew the Decembrists and felt that it was unlikely that they would ever bridge the gap between subversive talk and revolutionary action. There was no imminent danger, and in due time the young zealots would realize, as he had, that one could not move Russia or change her immemorial ways.

Indeed, during the three years of its existence, the Union of Welfare did not come even close to achieving any of the objectives it had set for itself. It expanded in membership, but some of the older members departed, whether because of a change of heart, like Alexander Muraviev, increasingly engrossed in religion, or on the grounds of prudence: it was clear that the government had been apprised of their activities. New branches sprang up in St. Petersburg, Moscow, and in several garrison towns, the most notable one, Tulchin, where Paul Pestel, increasingly acknowledged as the society's leading intellect, served at the headquarters of the Second Army. But the sum of the society's activity was rather meager. The Basic Union, as well as the individual branches, would hold their meetings, discuss the deplorable state of the country, debate and quarrel about what should be Russia's political system once autocracy had crumbled, and then raise without answering the inevitable and as yet unanswerable question: when and how?

Little or no progress was made toward achieving the Green Book's ambitious plan of the secret society, making its influence felt in the most important spheres of national life. The Decembrists promoted some literary and economic societies and discussion groups, they castigated and wrote opprobrious poems about the main pillars of official reaction, notably Arakcheyev, subjected to criticism such historical and literary apologies of autocracy as Karamzin's famous *History of the Russian State*. All those activities fell considerably short of the original goal: the creation and control of public opinion in the true sense of the word. Liberalism, as promoted by the Union of Welfare, could achieve only the status of one of several fads currently in vogue among the upper classes. But it failed to become a powerful force which could impose policies upon the government or through its own efforts promote desired reforms and attitudes.

Some results, truly microscopic when measured against the magnitude of the problem, emerged from the Union of Welfare's activities in education. Several decades would have to pass before progressive landowners would organize and finance from their own pocket schools for their peasants and before there was to be a rapid growth of Sunday schools for the urban lower classes. As long as serfdom persisted, it would have been impractical, perhaps cruel, to promote literacy on a mass basis, and it is at least doubtful that the government would have sanctioned such a plan.

What little could be done in that direction took the form of the so-called Lancaster schools, an idea imported from Britain. In these schools the more advanced pupils were employed in teaching the beginners. The Decembrists helped organize and run The Free Society for the Establishment of Schools Based upon the Method of Mutual Instruction, which was licensed by the government in 1819 and which set up Lancaster schools for children of the poor. Obviously this method could be employed also in adult education and especially for the purpose of reducing the appalling illiteracy rate among the soldiers. Not surprisingly, it did not take long for at least one Decembrist to realize the propaganda potential inherent in this method of education.

Because of events later in his life, Count Michael Orlov is not usually listed among the leaders of the Decembrists, but he was undoubtedly one of the outstanding personalities among them. His family's fortune was made by an uncle, one of the earlier official lovers of Catherine the Great, who along with his brothers assisted her in seizing the throne. Orlov gained great distinction during the Napoleonic wars, both on the battlefield and as a skillful diplomat and negotiator. He was instrumental in arranging the capitulation of Paris in 1814. Major general at the age of twenty-six, a favorite of the emperor, he seemed destined for a brilliant career. But Orlov was not made for a courtier, and his very closeness to Alexander proved fatal to his further advancement. He made clear to the latter his opposition to the granting of a constitution for Poland, a measure he felt was injurious to Russian national pride and interests. The independent-minded officer then sponsored a petition by a number of landlords in which they asked the tsar to abolish or at least to reform serfdom. It was his and not their business, Alexander coldly informed the petitioners' representative, to devise measures for his subjects' welfare. Orlov, now in disfavor, was relegated to a succession of provincial commands, first in Kiev, then still further from the capital in the Bessarabian backwater town of Kishinev.

Thwarted in trying to influence the emperor, the young aristocrat became one of the founding members of the Union of Welfare and one of the most active propagators of its ideas. Both in Kiev and in Kishinev he organized Lancaster schools for his soldiers, with the number of pupils running into the hundreds. Upon assuming the command of an infantry division, Orlov announced that he would not tolerate unfair treatment of soldiers, and he kept his word. Officers accused of abusing their authority or of undue severity toward their subordinates would by his order be brought before the military court. Even more unusual for the Russian army of his period, Orlov encouraged soldiers to report any transgressions of their superiors.

The man charged by him with the supervision of educational activities in the division was a fellow member of the Union of Welfare, Vladimir Rayevsky. To the latter belongs the distinction of being the "first Decembrist," that is, he was the first among the secret society's members to be charged and sentenced for subversive activities long before the actual revolt. Rayevsky was arrested in February 1822, and the investigation established that he used his position to spread constitutional and egalitarian ideas among his soldier-pupils. There is no question that he did it with Orlov's knowledge and encouragement, but his court connections protected the young general from a fate similar to that of Rayevsky's. (The latter was kept imprisoned and then sent to Siberia.) But in 1823 Orlov's division was taken from him, and though retained in the army, he was not given another command.

The Orlov-Rayevsky affair is the only case until the fatal day of December 14, 1825, when the Decembrists resorted to large-scale agitational activities among the rank and file of the army. And the uniqueness of the attempt underlines the truth of Pushkin's insight that the Decembrists lacked the true revolutionary's resolve, that self-assurance and passion which persuades the conspirator that the end must justify any means.

The scheme then propounded by the Union of Welfare, its commitment to achieve revolutionary changes through gradualist tactics, could not work under the conditions of an authoritarian society. The very sentiment, their patriotism, which turned them into conspirators inhibited the Decembrists' effectiveness as revolutionaries. They could not, in pursuit of their aims, seek power by stirring up peasants' and soldiers' revolts and plunge their beloved country into a civil war and anarchy.

Had they felt differently there would have been countless opportunities for the conspirators to exploit growing social tensions. Among the greatest sores of Russian life were the so-called military colonies, an idea which belonged to Alexander I, though somewhat unfairly it became identified with Arakcheyev whom the emperor put in charge of them. In theory the plan was both humane and sensible. These colonies were rural settlements whose adult male inhabitants combined agricultural labor with military service. It had been expected that the soldier-peasants themselves would realize the obvious advantages of the system: though in uniform, except in wartime they were not separated from their families and villages. Strict supervision and discipline would assure greater labor productivity and healthier and more orderly living conditions than those prevailing in an ordinary village. In brief the colonies would set an example for the rest of rural Russia, and the agrarian soldiers would be self-supporting, thus reducing the enormous expense which went for the maintenance of the armed forces.

But, like many schemes of social engineering, while enticing in theory, this one proved to be disastrous in practice. Except when owned by the most tyrannous of landlords, peasants, even when unfree, still enjoyed a degree of privacy in their lives which was entirely missing under the regime in the military colonies where even family relations were subject to rules and regulations. Hence for all the alleged advantages of the new settlements, their inmates came to feel that they were living under a particularly vicious form of slavery, combining the worst features of both serfdom and soldiering. Many villages petitioned to be allowed to resume their normal peasant existence, but their pleas were in vain. Exasperated, the peasant soldiers erupted in a number of riots and mutinies which had to be suppressed by the regular army. Alexander's stubborn streak exploded: he would persevere with his idea and he would be obeyed even if it took a wholesale massacre of the settlers. This was the emperor's reaction to one such occurence. A Decembrist was to write of the ill-begotten experience: "The forcible imposition of the so-called military colonies was received with amazement and hostility . . . does history show anything similar to this sudden seizure of entire villages . . . this taking over of the houses of peaceful cultivators, expropriation of everything they and their forefathers had earned and their involuntary transformation into soldiers?"[16] But much as they sympathized with the sufferings of the unfortunate settlers, the Decembrists as a body remained both unwilling and incapable of assisting their cause or of exploiting the situation for their own purpose.

Even more characteristic of the Decembrists' inability to pass from revolutionary talk and proposals to revolutionary deeds was their complete inactivity during the disturbances in the Semyonovsky Guards Regiment. The incident, which took place in the fall of 1820, is usually described as a mutiny, but since it involved no violence, the protest by the regiment rank and file was, in fact, more in the nature of a strike.

It is difficult for the modern reader to understand why mutiny was not a frequent occurrence in the Russian army of the period. The soldier was conscripted for twenty-five years; the slightest infraction of discipline, fault in deportment, or a misstep during the endless parades and drills could lead to his being whipped. It was a common practice for officers to supplement their meager salaries by diverting into their own pockets some of the money allotted for their soldiers' subsistence. Still, in the vast majority of cases, the Russian soldier endured the ordeal and indignities of his everyday existence with the resignation and submissiveness inherited from generations of his peasant ancestors.

Conditions were somewhat better in the elite corps of the Semyonovsky Guards. Here officers were usually of a much higher caliber, morally and intellectually, than those in the regular army as can be seen in the number of Decembrists among them. The enlisted men expected to be, and were usually, treated more humanely. Their term of service was less—a mere twenty-three years—decorated veterans were supposed to be exempt from corporal punishment, and quite a few of the soldiers could read and write. Insofar as it was possible in a class society and army, there existed a certain bond of regimental solidarity and camaraderie between the men and their superiors.

It was therefore resented in the Semyonovsky Regiment when an outsider, a Colonel Shvartz, was appointed to its command. He was a protégé of the omnipotent Arakcheyev, who had felt for some time that the regiment needed a strict hand in view of the officers' lax treatment of their soldiers and some regrettable lapses on the parade ground.* Of German descent, Shvartz spoke Russian ungrammatically which, added to his atrocious manners, outraged the officers' mess. Also, like his sponsor Arakcheyev, the new commandant was a sadist, ever devising new chicaneries and punishments for the soldiers. Soon several officers put in for retirement or transfer, and there were cases, previously unheard of in the proud regiment, of desertion among the lower ranks. The actual crisis was set off by a particularly brutal act by Shvartz. The guardsman's uniform was designed with an eye to its aesthetic effect rather than comfort or battle conditions: his torso was held in a viselike grip by the jacket, and the trousers were so tight that they gave the appearance of the ballet dancer's accoutrements. Hence dressing was a torturous and time-consuming operation. Espying a private who had several buttons undone, the infuriated colonel struck him and then, dragging the culprit in front of the platoon, ordered every soldier to spit in his face. The next day soldiers of the company refused to assemble for field exercises, and their example was soon followed by other units. At unauthorized meetings, the Semyonovsky officers' pleas to the enlisted men to return to duty were met with shouts that they would rather die than serve under Shvartz. Eventually the whole battalion in which the incident took place was imprisoned in the fortress, and the rest of the regiment sent out of the capital. There were rumblings in other Guards' regiments and the garrison of St. Petersburg was put on the alert.

News of the disturbances reached the emperor in the West where he was attending a diplomatic conference. He was both incensed and frightened. The

---

*Both Alexander and his two brothers, the future emperor Nicholas I and Grand Duke Michael, had an inordinate passion for military reviews and drills. A soldier's fitness and morale were thus held to be secondary considerations as against his blind obedience, the ability to keep his uniform and equipment spotless and to blend in harmoniously with his unit during the intricate maneuvers on the parade ground.

Semyonovsky, of which he himself was the honorary colonel, had been his favorite regiment. He must have reflected on how in the past the Guards had been instrumental in the palace revolutions, including the one which brought him to the throne. There seemed to be ominous parallels with the current revolutionary stirrings in Italy and in Spain where there had been a military coup. To Metternich, who was with him at the time, Alexander confided his belief that there must be some international revolutionary organization behind all the troubles. Three thousand Russian soldiers, with the habit of obedience bred into them from their childhood, could not mutiny without some pernicious outside influence and instigation.

By today's standards the whole affair was fairly tame: no physical violence and, after their noisy protestations, the culprits meekly let themselves be marched to prison. But the emperor demanded and exacted severe punishments. The entire personnel of the dishonored regiment was ordered dispersed among the regular army units; its officers and men, the great majority of them not involved in the protest, were reassigned and, in addition, forfeited the right to leaves. The alleged instigators of the disturbances drew draconic penalties: six thousand lashes for nine soldiers, for hundreds of others hazardous service in Siberia and on the Caucasian front. Three officers found guilty of sympathizing with the protestors were stripped of their rank and imprisoned. Shvartz, the real culprit, though sentenced to death for cowardice (he hid during the disturbances) due to Arakcheyev's intercession, was not only pardoned but appointed to command another regiment.

The Union of Welfare's passivity during the Semyonovsky affair was all the more striking in view of the fact that several of its members, including the future leader of the mutiny in the south, Serge Muraviev, served at the time in the regiment. Yet none of them was linked to the disturbances, and Muraviev did everything in his power to try to persuade soldiers in his company to stay out of trouble.

But Alexander's equanimity about the secret activities among the officer corps was now replaced by apprehension and watchfulness. He authorized the use of political informers within the army and ordered special surveillance over the soldiers who had been taught in Lancaster-type schools. In May 1821 the whole Guards' corps was sent out of St. Petersburg for field maneuvers in Byelorussia, and it did not return to the capital until the following summer. By that time the revolutionary stirrings in Spain and Italy had been suppressed. In 1822 there followed an imperial rescript dissolving the Masonic lodges and reemphasizing the ban on all secret associations. By then the Union of Welfare was also a thing of the past.

23

Its demise reflected not only the realization that the government was privy to its activities but also recognition of the fact that the whole concept of the union was unrealistic.

The union had tried to follow two parallel but not necessarily compatible programs at the same time. It hoped that although illegal in the eyes of the law, its program of reform would be tolerated if not assisted by the government. Nevertheless members of the inner core of the secret society did not foreswear revolution should an appropriate occasion present itself. Were the government to remain tolerant of the activities of the union, about which it inevitably would and did learn, the fond and thoroughly utopian expectations of its founders was that in twenty years' time Russian society through the very momentum of reform would rid itself of the autocratic system and serfdom. But this schizophrenic nature of the conspiracy—revolutionaries planning the overthrow of the autocracy or reformers succoring the regime—obviously could not endure. Many Decembrists were growing impatient. In January 1820 the movement's high command, the Basic Council of the union plus a few other members, held a meeting in St. Petersburg, the main item on the agenda being a discussion of the relative advantages of the monarchical versus republican forms of government. Pestel argued fervently in favor of a republican constitution and his eloquence carried the day. All those present voted for a republic. It was only subsequently that some of them, reflecting on the implications of such a step—it was an unambiguous commitment to revolution—severed their connections with the secret society. Though perhaps another plot conceived "between claret and champagne," the resolution, communicated to all the members, meant a rupture with the whole gradualist philosophy of the Green Book. And in the wake of the Semyonovsky affair, the government no longer proposed to remain indulgent toward the not-so-secret society.

Revolution or dissolution were then the two alternatives confronting the leading Decembrists as they assembled in the beginning of 1821 in Moscow to consider the future course of the movement. One of them, Ivan Yakushkin, subsequently wrote, "The Union of Welfare was, it seemed to us, asleep. Because of its structure, it was too limited in its activities."[17]

The case for revolution was argued by Michael Orlov. He proposed that the society should prepare to carry out an armed coup d'etat. The first step would be to step up a clandestine press to print revolutionary proclamations and issue false money. But this was too radical for his fellow conferees. Rebuffed, Orlov announced that he was leaving the society. The conference then decided to dissolve the Union of Welfare. But this was meant as a ruse designed to deceive the government which, as those present realized, had its agents within the society. The conspiracy was to go on in a different guise, and its goal was to be clearly revolutionary: the introduction of representative institutions through forcible means.

But the results of this Moscow conference as presented by Soviet historians on the basis of rather skimpy and often confusing evidence is somewhat oversimplified.[18] It errs insofar as it imparts a too clear-cut and overly definitive character to what in fact were rather chaotic and not fully conclusive deliberations. A Soviet historian tends to view the Decembrists through the prism of the history of the Communist party. But these people were inexperienced and unskilled in the revolutionary craft, a politically heterogeneous collection of individuals rather than an ideologically homogeneous party. And so perhaps terms like *attitudes* and *impulses* should be used rather than *ideologies* and *decisions*. As Pestel was to testify before the commission investigating the December 14 uprising: "From the very beginning of the secret society not a single one of its rules would be consistently observed throughout its activities . . . very often something decided at one time would the very next day be again questioned and argued about. . . . Everything would depend on the circumstances."[19]

Formal dissolution of the Union of Welfare was intended to fool not only the government and its agents within the secret society. It was desirable, the Moscow conferees felt, to rid the movement both of people like Pestel, suspected of dictatorial ambitions and committed by now to republicanism, and those too conservative and unwilling to resort to forcible means for the overthrow of the absolutist system. People in both categories were not to be informed that the conspiracy was still active. But this attempt at a purge foundered from the very beginning. Pestel, as might have been expected, simply refused to heed the Moscow decision and instead of ceasing, intensified his conspiratorial activities. Through the force of his personality, he was able to carry with him the majority of the Decembrists in the south.

Thus, in expiring the Union of Welfare gave birth not to one, but to two new secret societies, the Northern Society, centered in St. Petersburg and led at first by Nicholas Turgenev, a high official of the Ministry of Finance, who had presided over the Moscow conference, and Captain Nikita Muraviev; and the Southern Society, dominated by Pestel. The charade about the dissolution of the conspiracy had to be given up, and the two branches of the Decembrists continued to maintain contacts. Unlike their common progenitor, the Union of Welfare, both secret societies were clearly dedicated to the overthrow of the autocratic system, though differing in their ideas as to what should replace it. The Northerners favored a constitutional monarchy, Pestel and his companions were firm proponents of a republic.

Since they now had definitely abandoned their dream of changing Russia through peaceful means, logically both Decembrist groups should have embarked upon concrete plans of revolutionary action. Yet this did not happen. As had been true ever since the beginning of the movement, the problem of how to seize political power continued to baffle the Decembrists. The first step seemed obvious: one would have to seize the tsar and constrain him to agree to a constitution or to do away with him. The discussion among the Decembrists of how to do this bore a tragicomic character, testimony to the fact that they were psychologically incapable of performing the deed. Who would get hold of and guard Alexander? The Russian soldier could under the most extreme provocation turn against his commander, but even in the Semyonovsky affair no one actually laid his hands on the hated colonel. Was it then conceivable that some conspirator officer could persuade his men to seize and physically constrain "The Sacred Person of the Emperor," as the soldiers heard him described every Sunday in the liturgy of the Orthodox Church? There were frequent proposals to kidnap Alexander during one of the field maneuvers he attended annually, but invariably something would happen which persuaded the conspirators to stay their hand and to postpone the action until the next year.

Inevitably many Decembrists, especially in the south, reverted to considering a more drastic solution: assassination. But killing Alexander would not automatically annihilate the monarchy nor secure a constitution. Some Northern members entertained ideas of replacing him on the throne by his wife, Empress Elisabeth. But it was fantastic to believe that the dreamy and ailing German princess, though long estranged from her husband, would either agree or be capable of emulating the example of Catherine the Great.

In their depositions before the tsarist investigators, several of the Decembrists later were to reveal that Pestel considered an even more radical way of solving the problem: the wholesale slaughter of the imperial family. He urged that not only Alexander but also all conceivable heirs to the throne, women and children included, must be killed. And it is undeniable that with his fatal manner, designed both to impress and to mystify his fellow conspirators, Pestel at times intimated to them that he was about to assemble, or had already, a team of assassins, each of them ready to lay down his own life in order to kill one of the Romanovs, with the number of victims to be at least thirteen. In his own deposition the unfortunate man insisted that it all had just been talk: "I was never committed to it [the mass assassination]. Any fair-minded man who knows me even slightly will grant that I would not have been capable of such a deed. It is quite far from words to acts."[20] All he had meant was that following the coup the imperial family should be sent abroad. The emperor's brothers were unpopular with the Guards, hence they would not have presented any danger to the republican regime. And no foreign government would have dared to intervene to restore the monarchy in Russia. They would be afraid to provoke revolutions in their own countries.

It is difficult to decide what was really in Pestel's mind when he unfolded his terrorist designs. As an intelligent person, he must have known that mass killings would compromise the whole revolutionary enterprise. This was not yet 1918 when the imperial family could be liquidated in a wholesale fashion without stirring up much trouble among the people brutalized by four years of foreign and civil wars. In the 1820s this would have been impossible. Before their eyes the Decembrists must have had the example of the Jacobins who had failed precisely because of the revulsion engendered by the mass terror of the French Revolution. This was Russia, not France. But there was a streak of the doctrinaire in Pestel, and it is not difficult to believe that given the chance he would have approved of terrorist means.

Even though their revolutionary resolve hardened, the Decembrists between 1821 and 1825 made but little progress toward their goal. Unlike most of those who would succeed in the endeavor to liberate the Russian people, they did not think of revolution as a continuous process. Everything was to depend on a single event. And until that fateful day the secret society was not going to be too noticeable. Hence the conspirators felt inhibited from carrying out propaganda among the masses and fearful of staging public demonstrations. They consciously forsook those means through which a modern radical movement seeks on the one hand to undermine the self-assurance and prestige of the regime and on the other to preserve its own morale and dynamism. There were exceptions, as in the Rayevsky case. But there the initiative for propaganda among the soldiers came from an individual rather than from the conspiracy as a whole. And Rayevsky's fate was bound to discourage similar attempts.

Unwilling and/or unable to carry revolutionary agitation to the masses, the Decembrists still gave considerable thought to how one could reach the common man's mind and undermine his allegedly blind trust in the tsar. Nikita Muraviev believed that this had to be done by striking at the religious underpinnings of political obedience. Found among Muraviev's papers following his arrest was a brief catechismlike document: *A Curious Conversation.* This is the earliest example of the type of propaganda which would become quite widespread in the hands of the next revolutionary generation—the Populists. Religious arguments and historical examples are used here to buttress the case for freedom and against autocracy:

God granted freedom to man. . . . Should all men be free? Yes, without doubt. Are all people free? No, a small number of them enslaved the rest . . . [because] the former have unjustly aspired to rule, while the latter have meanly acquiesced in the loss of natural human rights given by God Himself. . . . One should establish rules or laws the way it was of old . . . [when] there were no autocratic sovereigns. . . . The Monarch usurped absolute power, step by step, employing all kinds of deception.

RUSSIA'S FAILED REVOLUTIONS

The document stresses how unique and evil is Russia's autocratic system.

> Are there Absolute Rulers in other countries? No, everywhere else autocracy is considered stupid and lawless, everywhere else you have firm rules or laws. . . . Autocracy . . . cannot tolerate permanent laws. It feeds upon lawlessness and constant [arbitrary] change* Today the Monarch will want one thing, tomorrow another. He has little consideration for our good, hence the proverb "If you're close to the Tsar, you're not far from death."[21]

Old Russia, the document asserts, enjoyed representative institutions. Its princes were freely elected and subject to the popular assemblies. It was the Tatar yoke which instilled servility in the people and made them forget their ancient rights.

Muraviev's pamphlet was presumably a sample of the propaganda technique the Decembrists expected to use on their soldiers after the revolutionary tocsin had sounded. A similar catechism, composed by Serge Muraviev Apostol, was read to the soldiers of the Chernihov Regiment after it rose in mutiny in January 1826. The Decembrists were clearly influenced by the example of the Spanish guerrillas in their war of national liberation against Napoleon. Assisted by Catholic priests they had used a similar religious motif in arousing their people to fight the French. But it is one thing to mobilize national and religious sentiments against a foreign invader and another to try to exploit them effectively when the enemy is your own government and the person who your church teaches is God's anointed.

Thus the dissolution of the Union of Welfare did little to impart fresh vigor to the conspiracy. But the conspirators felt differently. They had now definitely committed themselves to a revolutionary solution. They were busy recruiting new members and drafting legislation for postrevolutionary Russia.

Unlike most revolutionaries who seldom bother to work out a detailed blueprint of their utopias, the Decembrists invested a great amount of time and energy in drafting and arguing about constitutional projects. Some of it reflected undoubtedly the conspirators lingering hesitations and inner doubts about whether and how to proceed with the actual coup. But there was another, weightier reason. They were idealists enough, or visionaries, to reject the thought of seeking power for its own sake. They had to prove to themselves and to the world that their goal was a genuinely new social and political order which would guarantee Russia's freedom and greatness. Infused by the romantic spirit, the rebels were also children of an age which believed that man is shaped by his environment, that the secret of individual and collective happiness reposes in wise and humane laws. The intellectuals among the Decembrists imbibed deeply of

*While not quite just in relation to the old-fashioned autocracy, this *dictum* of Muraviev's anticipates the restlessness of modern totalitarianism.

the writings of Montesquieu, Destutt de Tracy, and Adam Smith and studied the laws of England and the United States Constitution. The very word *constitution* suggested to many some miraculous blueprint which of and by itself could save Russia from the usual pangs of a political upheaval and would usher in an era of freedom and prosperity. That the Decembrists were allegedly in possession of this magic formula was a strong selling point of the conspiracy. When soliciting new members for the Southern Society, Bestuzhev-Riumin exploited the constitutional theme constantly and rather unscrupulously. He would brazenly assure the would-be-neophytes that as early as 1816 the secret society had formulated the future fundamental laws, and this project had then been shown to and approved by the leading Western philosophers and legislators:[22] "Our constitution will secure forever the people's freedom and prosperity."[23] To be sure, such arguments could persuade only the very young and naive, and Bestuzhev, rather untypically for the Decembrists, was quite irresponsible in his proselytizing. But even the most sober-minded and sophisticated of the conspirators believed that before destroying the old, they must set on paper a clear and definitive blueprint of the new.

"The experience of all nations and all times has proved that Autocratic Power has fatal consequences both for the rulers and the ruled. It is repugnant to the teachings of our holy faith and to the precepts of common sense."[24] Thus began the preamble of Nikita Muraviev's proposed constitution. Originally drafted by him in 1821, it subsequently underwent several modifications designed to meet the criticisms of his fellow Decembrists. But basically it remained unchanged and reflected the dominant political orientation within the membership of the Northern Society.

Every other European country, maintains Muraviev in his preamble, has already achieved, or is in the process of achieving, freedom under the law (a considerable exaggeration when speaking of Europe of the 1820s). Russians, he proudly asserts, are more deserving of constitutional liberties than any other people. But this outburst of national pride is tempered by historical realism, as demonstrated in his discussion of the most appropriate form of government for his country. A small state, he writes, will often become the prey of an aggressor. A large state conversely tends to oppress not only its smaller neighbors but also its own people. "Vast territories, and a huge standing army are in themselves obstacles to freedom." It is because of her vast size, Muraviev implies, that Russia has been both imperialist and autocratic. But the nationalist in him cannot accept the logical conclusion that the empire should then disgorge its foreign conquests and non-Russian territories. He thus opts for a federal system as one which reconciles "national greatness with civic freedom."

Along with federalism the author is a strong proponent of the separation of powers. Indeed, the document bears a strong imprint of the United States Constitution, especially when it comes to the mechanics of its federal structure. While the monarchical form is preserved in name, Muraviev's Russia would be in effect a crowned republic. "The Russian nation is free and independent. It cannot be the property of a person or of a family. The people are the source of supreme power. And to them belongs the sole right to formulate the fundamental law." Muraviev's emperor, though hereditary and endowed with an enormous income, is, insofar as his powers are concerned, modelled after the United States president. He is the commander-in-chief but cannot declare war or conclude peace without the legislature's concurrence. He conducts foreign affairs, but treaties must be approved by the Supreme Council, which corresponds to the American Senate. Judges and high officials can be impeached by a two-thirds vote of the House of Representatives. They are then subject to suspension by the Supreme Council but are to be tried in an ordinary court of law. Even within the executive branch, the emperor's power is subject to limitations, and he has but a suspensive veto over legislation. The most piquant detail of all is that the tsar is to be denied a right enjoyed by the humblest of subjects: he is not allowed to go abroad. It is easy to surmise what must have been the feelings of Nicholas I upon reading this provision of the rebel constitution.

Muraviev's advocacy of federalism was not to be echoed by any major political movement in Russia until the twentieth century. The empire was to be divided into fourteen states and two districts, each with its own legislature (bicameral) and executive. Though a federalist, the author did not propose national autonomy for non-Russian ethnic groups, even though some national and territorial divisions coincided. There was a Ukrainian and a Caucasian state. As for most of their countrymen, so for the Decembrists, The Little Russians, as Ukrainians were known at the time, were not a separate nationality any more than the Don Cossacks, who were assigned a separate district, and their language was considered but a local peasant dialect.

The Northern Society, which was scandalized by Pestel's readiness to grant independence to Poland, certainly was not going to sanction anything which might have undermined the unity and greatness of Russia. Yet, paradoxically, unlike Pestel's constitutional project, this one was not imbued with Russian chauvinism and probably unwittingly opened the door to national autonomy for such major ethnic groups as the Ukrainians and the Georgians.

Muraviev's choice of the capital for his Slavic Russian Empire was a good proof of his fervent Russian feeling. St. Petersburg, by its very name, suggested foreign influence and was associated in the people's mind with the authoritarian bureaucratic government devised by Peter the Great. Moscow recalled the Mongol overlordship of the country and its grand dukes' despotic usurpations. Hence the new capital was to be Nizhni-Novgorod, the cradle of the modern Russian nation. In 1612, with Russia in the throes of anarchy, the people of Nizhni-Novgorod organized the army which freed the country from foreign invaders and domestic warlords. The initiative for this national revival came not from any noble, but from a local butcher. Hence the historic appropriateness of this Volga city to be the seat of government of new Russia.

"All Russians are equal before the law." Yet the constitution made it quite clear that some were to be more equal than others. While it would have abolished all class distinctions and made every Russian free to choose any profession he wished, Muraviev's charter set very stiff property qualifications for voting and office holding. To be classified as a citizen, one would have to possess at least five hundred rubles or personal property worth at least one thousand, more if one was to be able to vote for various offices, still more to be eligible to be elected to them. To be a member of the federal Supreme Council one would have to be very rich indeed, owning an estate bringing in one hundred twenty thousand rubles per annum or having personal property worth twice as much. In the second version of his draft Muraviev abandoned the property requirements for citizenship and lowered those for holding various state and federal offices. But still his Russia would be ruled by the rich.

Equally unsatisfactory from the egalitarian viewpoint was his proposal concerning the peasants. Serfdom was to be abolished, but privately owned peasants were to be liberated without land, which was to be retained by their former masters.* Here again pressure was brought on the author by some more liberal members of the Northern Society, and in the second version Muraviev modified his land reform: the peasant would get the title to his dwellings and his household plot.

It is easy to criticize Muraviev's proposals as reflecting the class point of view, as well as the fact that he himself came from one of the richest landowning families in the country. But at the time there was no state in Europe which adhered to the principle of universal male suffrage. Even in the United States most states still had property qualifications for voting. The most radical democrat would have hesitated to entrust political power to the overwhelmingly illiterate peasant masses. (Muraviev's project stipulated that twenty years after its adoption, the constitution would require literacy as a condition for citizenship.) Had Muraviev and most other Decembrists been motivated by the narrow class interest they would not have joined the revolutionary movement in the first place. The question of peasant land would bedevil Russia's statesmen and reformers for the rest of the century. And if Muraviev resolved it in accordance with a principle enunciated in his constitution, "property rights are sacred and inviolable," this

---

*The military settlements were to be abolished, and their inhabitants were to be given land upon being emancipated, as were the peasants belonging to the imperial family's estates.

is not because of his "class limitations," a standard phrase of the Soviet historians when they choose to criticize the Decembrists' social and economic views, but because few educated Russians could as yet envisage a different solution to the damnable problem of serfdom.

The egalitarian and democratic rhetoric of Muraviev's project clearly clashes with its prescription of an essentially oligarchic political system. But then, not many political doctrines and constitutional documents succeed in being entirely consistent. Consistency is not a key to political success. In fact, if anything makes the constitution less than completely utopian under the conditions of Russia in the 1820s, it is precisely its nondoctrinaire character and the recognition of the fact that the Russian people must be prepared for the exercise of political responsibilities rather than to have them suddenly thrust upon them. What distinguishes Muraviev's project from that of Pestel is its thoroughly liberal orientation. It eschews the latter's national and religious intolerance and is much more solicitous of the citizen's liberties. Unlike the ideologist of the Southern Society, Muraviev does not dwell at length on the need for, and the organization of, the secret police. He proposes trial by jury and the writ of habeas corpus and is an uncompromising advocate of the freedom of speech and the press. While struggling against an oppressive and intolerant system, many Russian revolutionaries ultimately exhibited just those characteristics in their own thought and in their prescriptions for the future of the country; Nikita Muraviev was one of the few who did not.

The same cannot be said about Pestel. If Muraviev's nationalism was tempered by liberalism, then Pestel, who was of German descent, Lutheran in his religion, and had spent his formative years in Saxony, was the quintessential Russian nationalist. It would be difficult to ascribe to him, any more than to his fellow Decembrists, a consistent ideology. But a convenient label for the general assemblage of his political ideas, one which would fit best is national socialism if it is dissociated from recent historical connotations. Radicalism on social issues was combined in Pestel with an aggressive nationalist spirit, and it is startling how in some ways he anticipated the mentality of Soviet Communism.

It was still some years before the term *socialism* would come into use. Yet, in describing his political views to the investigating commission, Pestel used a formula quite similar to Marx's definition of class war: "It seemed to me that the main political tendency of our age is the struggle between the masses of the people and Aristocracies of all kinds, whether those based upon wealth or hereditary ones."[25] The same theme appears frequently in Pestel's writings, and of course this contributes to his popularity with the Soviet authors. Thus his criticism of bourgeois constitutionalism: ". . . in many states which have representative institutions the right to vote belongs to the rich while the majority of the citizens are excluded. This way the aristocracy of wealth has simply replaced the feudal one, and the people in some ways are politically worse off than before because they are forcibly dependent on the plutocracy."[26] It would be a gross oversimplification, however, to see Pestel as a "premature Marxist," or a socialist in the modern sense of the word. He was not an *economic* egalitarian. "The rich will always exist, and it is highly beneficial that they should."[27] But, fairly unique for his time and society, he wanted political power and rights to be completely separated from any criteria of wealth and property. All class distinctions were to be abolished, everyone was to be equal before the law. There was to be an aristocracy in Pestel's Russia, but one of merit; people would be ennobled for distinguished services to the state and society.

Radical as he was on social and political questions, Pestel found it difficult to come up with a forthright solution of the enormously complex peasant-land problem. The first variant of his constitutional project prescribed a gradual abolition of serfdom over a ten- to fifteen-year period. Insofar as the privately owned peasants were concerned, the details of their emancipation and land allotments would be worked out by the landlords' committees, on the principle that "freeing the peasants from serfdom should not deprive the nobility of its income from the estates."[28] The reason for this seemingly incongruous, by his egalitarian premises, solution becomes apparent in another of Pestel's injunctions. "Emancipation should not be allowed to lead to riots and disorder and therefore the Supreme Authority is to employ the most severe measures against those who threaten law and order." No social or political good was to be allowed to jeopardize the security and unity of the Russian state. The social reformer in Pestel was subordinated to the nationalist.

In the second version of his project, written in 1824–25, the leader of the Southern Society evidently moved toward a more radical solution. Serfs would now be emancipated immediately, and their allotments would come from the estates of their masters, with the wealthiest among the latter required to turn over half of their land *without compensation.* To add to the confusion, in both versions of his constitutional project, Pestel advocated what might be called seminationalization of land. All the agricultural area of the country would be divided in two parts, one-half to be owned by the district (the lowest territorial division of the state). This land would be parcelled out among individual cultivators, who would not be allowed to sell, lease, or bequeath their share. The other half of the country's land could be owned privately without any restrictions. The underlying theme is, however, the opposite of that inherent in the usual socialist opposition to private property. Everybody should be a proprietor. Every Russian who desires it had the right to claim a land allotment in his commune, which would be sufficient for the maintenance of a family of five. And of course those able to afford it could always buy and freely dispose of the land reserved for private use. The plot of land which became the share of every Russian would provide, Pestel hoped, not only a kind of social security and eliminate pauperism but also a bond of social solidarity since every adult citizen would be guaranteed that "wherever he was or [at whatever profession] sought his fortune . . . he could always find refuge and sustenance within his political family—the district."[29]

Pestel's approach to the peasant-land problem was, by the standards of the time, quite revolutionary. His views were often inconsistent and showed but little awareness of the enormous technical, political, and economic difficulties attending any resolution of this problem, a quandary which would perplex everyone—governments, reformers, and revolutionaries—until the end of the tsarist era and which, in fact, is still with the Soviet government of today. Private property, he asserts, is sacred, yet the very rich are to have half of theirs expropriated. Every lot-holder's record as an agriculturist is to be reviewed at the end of each year, and if he is found incompetent, his lot would revert to the district—provisions which showed Pestel's lack of understanding of the technical side of agriculture. The peasant commune and its place in the new order of things was not dealt with by him at all.

There is, however, no ambiguity in Pestel's approach to the state-national issue. "Russia is one state indivisible." His passion for russification goes beyond anything that even the tsars or Stalin aspired to. There is to be only one Russian nation in the state, and all other ethnic groups are to be assimilated. The very names *Ukrainian* and *Byelorussian* are to be banned since "there are no genuine differences between various divisions of the basic Russian nation, and the small ones which exist should be eradicated."[30] The non-Slavic nations are to be subjected to the same, though more gradual, assimilationist process. The most peremptory is the procedure recommended for the nations of the Caucasus. "They are to be divided into categories: peaceful and turbulent, the former to be left in the homelands, but to be organized according to the Russian model, the latter to be forcibly resettled in the interior,"[31] that is, presumably in Siberia or Central Asia. The brutality of this recommendation brings to mind Stalin's notorious punishment of the allegedly disloyal Caucasian nationalities, who in 1944 were torn away from their native lands and deported en masse to Kazakhstan. Russian colonists are to be settled in the territories inhabited by other ethnic groups in order to strengthen the process of assimilation and the unity of the state. Another and unpleasant resemblance to the Stalinist methods and mentality is that all those brutal and chauvinist measures are rationalized in the name of progress and civilization. A Lutheran, Pestel had no compunction in advocating that all churches are to be tolerated only if they give up their allegiance to any foreign authority, which of course would banish from the country all the Roman and Greek Catholic clergy and monastic orders.

After all that, it is not surprising to discover that this Decembrist is strongly anti-Semitic. The Jews' "religion teaches that they should subjugate and rule all other nations . . . makes them despise other peoples."[32] They avoid manual labor, tend to monopolize any profession into which they have gained entrance, lower public morality by bribing officials, and so on in the all-too-familiar way. The postrevolutionary government should adopt some measures to put an end to the Jews' anti-social and anti-Christian *(sic)* behavior, though Pestel perhaps mercifully does not specify what those measures should be. But one tentative plan which he advances is to collect all two million Jews from the Eastern provinces and Poland* and push them through the Turkish frontier to let them settle down in their own state, somewhere in Asia. But, alas, avers Pestel, this plan presents some practical difficulties and would require "special circumstances and genius-like ingenuousness." The overwhelming mass of the empire's Jews were at the time miserably poor, and unlike the West since the French Revolution, there had been no movement to remove their legal and civil disabilities. Yet for Pestel the little tolerance shown to Jews by the tsarist government already went too far: "They enjoy more rights than the Christians," he states unabashedly. His anti-Semitism is clearly religious rather than racial in its character. He would not bar a converted Jew from his national community, and in fact there was one such among the Decembrists.

At first glance it might seem surprising that this rabid nationalist and xenophobe was willing to grant Poland independence and would, to the horror of his fellow Decembrists, allot her some Russian (in fact, predominantly Byelorussian) lands, specifically parts of the provinces of Vilna and Minsk which had belonged to the old Polish-Lithuanian Commonwealth. But upon closer examination, this independence appears very restricted, considering the conditions Pestel attaches to his offer. Poland must be bound to Russia by a perpetual alliance. Her political and social system must be identical with that of her powerful neighbor. "Russia takes Poland under her protection and will guarantee her existence and security."[33] In brief this is the type of tutelage the USSR exercises today over its East European satellites, including Poland.

It comes as no surprise that Pestel was an advocate of imperial expansion. Many of his territorial goals were in fact to be reached by Russia later in the century: the rounding out of the Caucasian conquests, Central Asia, the Far East, where in 1860 a Muraviev was to annex from China the area around today's

---

*Very few Jews were at the time permitted to reside in Russia proper.

Vladivostok. And, of course, it was incumbent on Russia to liberate its mostly Orthodox and Slav population from the Turkish yoke. Pestel's Russia, even more so than the tsar's, would have been a martial and aggressive state.*

The authoritarian who abides within so many revolutionaries is most discernible in Pestel's discussion of the secret police. This constitutes a separate chapter of his *Notes About the System of Governance*, written before his main constitutional projects and probably as early as 1818. With an Orwellian touch he names the secret police The Department of High Order of Benevolence. "Secret investigation or espionage is not only permissible and lawful, but the most dependable, one might say the only, means through which the Authority can achieve its aims."[34] Hence the Department of Order's activities were not to be subject to the courts. It was to operate in utmost secrecy, nobody but its officials to be aware of its existence. Among some of its duties were (1) supervision of other branches of the government (2) spying on private people, so as to catch at an early stage any subversion, secret societies, and illegal assemblies; (3) intelligence gathering about foreign envoys and foreigners in general. Officers of the secret police should all be men of high intellectual and moral qualifications. And to attract such people, wrote Pestel with unwitting humor, they should be paid much more than the rest of the government employees and be guaranteed anonymity. Were their profession to become known to their fellow citizens, not only their efficiency but also their reputations would be impaired![35]

Like the Jacobins of the French Revolution, Pestel saw no inconsistency between democracy and political intolerance and repression. There would be no room in his Russia for political parties or, in fact, for any associations not sponsored by the government. "All private societies . . . should be strictly forbidden, be they public or secret, since the former are useless and the latter harmful."[36] And there was quite a bit of the puritan in him. "Amusements and games of all kinds, whether private or public, are permissible as long as they don't clash with strictest morality."[37]

Pestel's is a welfare state. Its orphans, indigent, and disabled are to be cared for by the community, more specifically their particular districts, whether in special institutions or through subsidies. A nationwide network of banks was to provide interest-free credit up to a certain limit to anyone who required it. There was to be one such bank in each district, with all of its citizens providing the necessary capital through contributions. Each district was to have a population of between five thousand and thirty thousand, which made this a fairly unrealistic scheme for rural Russia, most of whose population was living close to the subsis-

---

*Strangely enough, the only real concession he urged was that of Alaska, which he proposed to turn loose.

tence level. Russia was to have, as we would say today, a mixed economy. The state was to encourage private enterprise and promote inventions, industry, and private banking.

His proposed constitution Pestel entitled *The Russian Justice* (Pravda). Neither of its two variants is too explicit about the actual structure of government. By 1822 when he wrote the first draft, Pestel was already a staunch republican and rejected the idea of property qualifications for voting. In 1825 he sketched a brief paper called "Mandate for the State Constitution." Here he prescribed a thoroughly democratic structure. The legislative power was to be vested in the universally elected National Assembly, one-fifth of its members renewable annually. There was to be a sort of collective president, the State Council of 5 members, also elected nationwide for five years and each of whose members would take turns as Head of State. The State Council would exercise most of the usual functions of the executive. There was to be, in addition, the Supreme Council, composed of 120 members elected for life, which would not have any legislative or executive powers of its own (except for appointing the commander-in-chief in wartime) but would watch over the constitutionality and execution of the laws.

Pestel was an indefatigable writer, and among his surviving papers are notes, fragments of treatises, and sketches on a most varied collection of subjects: the military, economics, judicial affairs, science, economy. He had a pedantic streak. Nowhere is this more evident than in his obsession to remove foreign terms from the military vocabulary and to replace them by Russian-sounding words, whether borrowed from the Muscovite past or some Slavic neologisms of his own. Similar fastidiousness made him condemn the docking of horses' tails, which he maintained ought to be forbidden as it originated in England and mars the beauty of the Russian horse. Granted that the current uniform of the Russian soldier was cumbrous, it is still peculiar that he should take time from his conspiratorial and constitution-making activities to sketch in detail the future infantryman's dress (for the constricting jacket and tight white knee breeches he would substitute a long blouse and loose green pantaloons as in the warrior of old).

But amusing as it may be, Pestel's passion for details and regulations is not unimportant or merely incidental to his thinking. At one level he sought for his beloved country what he believed was freedom, the rule of law, and democracy. But in fact, like some French Jacobins, he was unconsciously groping for what today would be described as a totalitarian society. It is not only his immoderate nationalism which was bound to make his Russia more oppressive (certainly for a non-Russian) than that of the tsars. His citizen would be constantly watched, admonished, and regulated. Those who would stray from the extremely straight and narrow path of civic virtue as prescribed by him could not expect any indulgence: ". . . if there be such unworthy sons of the Fatherland they [the authorities] should take against them resolute measures so as to tame their savage behavior and to render them incapable of harming the Fatherland, by the means employing the most summary and ruthless severity."[38] In the premier political thinker and theorist among the Decembrists can be found much of the feverish taste for violence and coercion which will mark the path of the Russian revolutionary movement.

It is not surprising that Pestel's views both fascinated and repelled his fellow conspirators. It is difficult to judge how much of him is expressed in his writings. Even Pestel was not free from those inner doubts and contradictory impulses which affected his fellow Decembrists, from the feeling that all their revolutionary plotting and writing was somehow taking place in a different dimension of reality from that in which they were actually living as officers and loyal subjects of the emperor. Before his conversion to republicanism, Pestel had been among those who clung to the hope that the tsar might yet be induced to turn reformer and to free the country from the evils of serfdom and absolutism. Alexander, while aware of Pestel's suspicious associations and views, still esteemed him as a brilliant officer and military thinker. In Tulchin, where he served at the headquarters of the Second Army, Pestel became close to its chief of staff, General Paul Kiselev, the future minister of Nicholas I, and one of the few enlightened and reform-minded officials of that era of dark reactions. A general adjutant (one of the chief aides-de-camp to the tsar) Kiselev was one of those dignitaries under Alexander who also maintained personal contacts with some of the future rebels, and there is little doubt that he had an inkling at least of what they were up to. In 1821 it was finally felt desirable to detach Pestel from the staff, and he was appointed commander of the Viatka Regiment, then considered one of the most poorly run and disorderly in the whole army. The twenty-seven-year-old colonel soon brought his unit up to such a level of efficiency and battle readiness that Alexander I, after witnessing its performance at maneuvers, pronounced it the equal of the Guards. But in order to instill discipline, Pestel showed himself ruthless; his soldiers were whipped for the slightest misdemeanor or ineptitude during the drill.

At once martinet, careerist, idealist, this strange man was widely suspected, especially by the Decembrists of the Northern branch, of harboring dictatorial ambitions. To be sure, in his constitutional project he comes as close as one could at the time to prescribing popular sovereignty, and his Russia would not even have a single head of state but a collective presidency of five. But there was a catch. *The Russian Justice* was in his conception *not* to be applied immediately after the revolution. Its subtitle proclaimed it to be a *Mandate for the People and the Provisional Supreme Government.* The latter was to be a dictatorship and would last some ten years. In expounding his ideas in 1824 to some members of the Northern Society which he wanted to merge with the Southern, that is, under his leadership, Pestel was quite specific:

> The principle of the constitutional projects should be known only to the leaders of the Society and ought not to be [widely] circulated. . . . The leaders should first liquidate members of the Imperial family and compel the Holy Synod and the Senate to proclaim them as the provisional government which will dispose of unlimited powers. . . . The provisional government, having distributed ministries, military commands, etc., among the society's members, would then gradually over several years introduce the new order. All that time the society would continue to function and receive new members, and none but a member could hold a [high] civil or military office.[39]

This is then a blueprint for one-party dictatorship, and it is doubtful as to how "provisional" this setup was intended to be.

Pestel in private conversations often expressed his admiration for Napoleon and did, at least occasionally, think of himself as dictator. His closest collaborators in the Southern Society were for the most part people under his spell. He wooed energetically the Northern Decembrists, trying to undermine there the influence of Nikita Muraviev who, following the coup, envisaged the summoning of a constituent assembly which would adopt a constitution. Pestel felt Muraviev to be the main obstacle, both politically and personally, to his designs. His approach was often quite disingenuous. As Ryleyev, a Northern Decembrist, was to testify:

> I remember how Pestel tried to smoke me out. During our two hours' conversation he was in turn an admirer of the United States, of Napoleon, an advocate of terror and a partisan of the English constitution . . . but after a while he agreed with me that the English system was obsolete; the current level of enlightenment among nations calls for more progressive institutions and greater freedom . . . but if we have to have a dictator, let him be like Napoleon. To what heights did he raise France.[40]

Pestel's ascendance over the Southern Decembrists was based not only on his personal charm, as described by Pushkin among others, but also on that air of self-assurance and mystery surrounding him, which is so often an important ingredient in the making of a political leader. Though well educated by the standard of the time, his associates were for the most part politically unsophisticated and except for their conspiratorial activities, carefree souls in the traditional manner of young officers and aristocrats. In contrast was this man who seemed to live for the cause and who, in addition to being a brilliant military administrator, possessed the gifts of the legislator and political philosopher. But in the Northern Society there were people like Nikita Muraviev and Nicholas Turgenev who were Pestel's intellectual equals and who opposed his ideas and saw through his Machiavellianism. Rebuffed in his efforts to seize the leadership of the whole movement, Pestel became prey to doubts and hesitations. He thought that perhaps the future constitution of Russia might have to be an amalgam of his and Muraviev's projects. Yet it is difficult to see how a compromise could be effected between such diametrically different philosophies. As for himself, Pestel intimated to a friend, he would after the revolution retire to a monastery.[41] Again a paradoxical thought expressive of a troubled mind: a Lutheran becoming an Orthodox monk. But this was not mere posturing, as Pestel's letters to his family in 1825 bear witness. His thoughts more and more turned toward religion, and after a five-year lapse he went to confession and took communion. He was to testify following his arrest, "Having fully and frankly admitted my liberal and radical ideas, I must add that in the course of 1825 their hold on me weakened and I began to see things differently but it was already too late to turn back."[42]

As the catastrophe of December 14, 1825, approached, the two leading theorists and moving spirits of the conspiracy became disheartened. Nikita Muraviev retired to his wife's estate some weeks before the fatal date. A kind of apathy seized Pestel. "The writing of *Russian Justice* was not going as easily as before. They wanted me to hurry up with it, but it simply did not work and in the course of the whole year I could not add anything new to it. . . . I would occasionally become excited again in conversations, but not for long and it was not the same thing as before."[43]

The course of events moved, albeit in a manner wholly unanticipated by its actors, toward the grim *dénouement* of the drama of the Decembrists. Between 1823 and 1825, there had been a considerable amount of *talk* about capturing the emperor and either forcing him to issue a constitution, as most Northern confederates would have preferred, or doing away with him, the latter at least ostensibly the position of Pestel and his partisans in the south. The constitutional dispute within the secret society could only have further hampered the development of any concrete plan of action. Thus, though in 1825 it was definitely decided to capture Alexander during his expected attendance at the field maneuvers of the Third Army Corps in the fall of 1826, it is unlikely that had he been spared until then the conspirators would have found enough resolution or resources to carry out their plan. As Pestel was to confess: "I firmly believe that if the Emperor Alexander Pavlovich continued to live, then for all the advances of the secret society, the revolution would not have begun till after his natural death."[44] At any rate, the plan provided for killing the emperor and then for the Third Corps, led by the Decembrists, to march on Kiev and Moscow. Other army units, it was expected, would join them. In the north the revolutionary confederates would seize the capital, send other members of the imperial family abroad, and compel the Senate to issue a proclamation legalizing the new regime. Pestel was probably right when, in telling this story to the government investigators, he stressed the utter unrealism of the plan: "In viewing this plan as against the resources of the Southern Society . . . one can see clearly that it [the plan] did not have the slightest chance of success. It simply reflected rashness and impatience [on our part] which as the time for its execution approached would have undoubtedly yielded to reason."[45] It is probable that Pestel's deprecating remarks were made with the aim of minimizing his guilt in the eyes of the tsarist judges. There is evidence, however, that practically on the eve of the fatal events, the leader of the Southern Society did indeed grow more and more irresolute and hesitant. He confessed to a confederate that he contemplated going to see the emperor, confessing all, and begging him to grant the needed reforms.

In the meantime the doomed conspiracy widened its sphere of activity. For some time the Southern Society had had contacts with a clandestine Polish organization seeking full independence for Poland. In January 1825 Pestel and Prince Serge Volkonsky met with its emissaries to see if they could work out a common plan of action. Both sides characteristically tried to impress each other by what charitably can be described as embellishing the truth about their resources and connections. The Poles let it be known that not only did they have connections with revolutionary bodies in the major European countries but also that "the English government has contacts with the Polish secret organization and has been furnishing it with money and promises to provide arms."[46] (When this information was imparted to the tsarist officials following the failure of the insurrection, it set the government on a frantic search for any evidence linking Britain with the revolutionary movement in the empire, probably the earliest example of the traditional Russian belief that domestic dissent has its roots in foreign influence. But there is no question that while the Polish cause had many friends among liberal English politicians, there was not the slightest connection between the British government and the contemporary revolutionary movements, whether in Russia proper or Poland.) On their part the Russian representatives gave their Polish interlocutors to understand that if they hoped for the new Russia to grant independence to Poland, they had to synchronize their activities with those of the Decembrists. Specifically, Pestel desired that upon the outbreak of the revolution in Russia, the Poles would stop any attempt by Grand Duke Constantine* to come to the help of his brother. The Poles were to "take care of" the grand duke (that is, presumably to kill him) and otherwise to link their revolutionary movements with those of the Russian rebels. With both sides being less than frank with each other, the discussions were inconclusive.

---

*He was the commander-in-chief not only of the Polish army but also of the so-called Lithuanian Corps, consisting of troops in Russia's western provinces neighboring on the Kingdom of Poland.

RUSSIA'S FAILED REVOLUTIONS

In their march toward doom the Decembrists managed to absorb and drag down with them yet another organization. This was the United Society of Slavs, which quite independently of the Decembrists and unknown to them had existed among officers of the Second Army since 1823. It is not surprising that this body, yet another example of the craze for secret societies among the youth of Russia, indeed of the whole Continent,* did not at first attract attention either from the government or their predecessors in conspiracy.

Members of the United Slavs were young officers interspersed among garrisons in the Ukraine, often in the very same regiments as members of the Southern Society. But they were for the most part junior in rank and, insofar as their background and economic status were concerned, quite different from the Muravievs, Trubetskoys, and other ancient nobility and substantial property owners found among the older Decembrists. These were generally sons of impoverished landholders and petty officials and instead of being educated by foreign tutors and in special academies, the United Slavs' members had been taught by their parents or in the wretched local schools of the period. Where could they then have imbibed the ideas of dissent? This question obviously puzzled the tsarist investigators of the Decembrist uprising who considered liberalism, constitutionalism, and similar forms of subversion as foreign importations. One of their standard questions to the accused was "Where were you educated and from whom did you learn the subversive ideas which led you to the criminal intent of changing the established order of things?" To which one of the founders of the United Slavs, Peter Borisov, answered:

> I was educated at home by my father. . . . Already in my youth the readings of Greek and Roman history filled my mind with the love of democratic government. And this feeling was subsequently strengthened in me [by observing] the cruel treatment of their subordinates by some commanding officers, the sufferings imposed upon the peasants by so many landlords, as well as by the injustices which I have personally experienced in service.[47]

But apart from such simple and noble sentiments, the United Slavs' program was a hodgepodge of fantastic ideas. Somehow (unlike the older branches of the Decembrists, they never considered how and when) Russia was going to be turned into a republic and serfdom was to be abolished. Then, also in some unspecified way, the other Slav nations were going to be liberated from their

---

*What accounts for the sudden mushrooming in the post-Napoleonic Europe of this type of organization? Very likely the following: the breakdown of the pattern of society, with its traditional, mostly religious, outlets for the need for participation; the intellectual ferment stirred up by the French Revolution; and, finally, the attempt of most European governments after 1815 to turn the clock back to stem intellectual curiosity and the new political consciousness of the nineteenth-century man.

foreign and domestic oppression, and they were all going to form a federation of free republics.

The young men's zeal for the unity of the Slavs was much greater than their knowledge of their history and geography. Thus they included among them the Hungarians, assumed that the inhabitants of Bohemia and Moravia belonged to separate nationalities, seemed oblivious to the existence of the Bulgarian nation; and, most puzzling of all, since some of the United Slavs were natives of the Ukraine, they did not consider her people as distinct from the Great Russians.

The existence of the United Slavs became known to some members of the Southern Society during the summer maneuvers of the Third Army Corps in 1825, and by the time the exercises were over in the middle of September, the two secret societies coalesced. Some of the younger conspiracy's members were reluctant to become submerged in the general movement of the Decembrists. But they were swayed by the eloquent, if unscrupulous, arguments of Bestuzhev-Riumin, who acted as the chief prozelytizer: the Decembrist movement was already a powerful force which was about to deal a mortal blow to the autocracy. The projected coup d'etat could not fail if among the conspirators were not only most of the regimental commanders in their region but also such renowned military figures as General Paul Kiselev and General Alexis Yermolov, command-er-in-chief in the Caucasus. The young neophytes could not but be impressed by this galaxy of princes, generals, and colonels whom they would be joining in a common revolutionary enterprise. Bestuzhev was equally untruthful in assuring them that the constitution which his secret society would bestow on Russia had been in existence since 1815 and that it had been seen and approved by the leading minds of Europe. All this was quite exciting for those inexperienced and naive lieutenants and ensigns. But, Bestuzhev-Riumin almost overdid it when he outlined the list of honors and riches with which the grateful Fatherland would compensate its saviors: "The reward for your sacrifices will not be death but high honors and dignities. You're young and what is ahead of you is not the crown of martyrdom, but fame and fortune."[48] At which point there were angry mur-murs among the young idealists and shouts that it was insulting to suggest that they would even consider a reward for their patriotic labor. Bestuzhev-Riumin hastily changed the subject.

This juvenile Machiavellianist could not have inspired much confidence: he was twenty-one years old, brash, and garrulous in his manner. But Serge Mura-viev, whose personality and record compelled respect, confirmed his intimate friend's story. Consequently, the United Slavs decided to dissolve their own organization and to submit themselves to the direction of the Southern Society. Almost immediately there were clashes between the impatient neophytes and their new associates. When would the coup take place? Muraviev explained that it was planned for the next summer. Why wait so long, and in any case, should they not start revolutionary agitation among their soldiers? Their seniors were scandalized. No such agitation was necessary, the Russian soldier did not understand politics but he would always obey his commanding officer. If he would still have scruples about rising against his emperor, the officer would explain it in terms of a religious duty. "Our soldiers are good, simple folk. They don't think much and hence should serve merely as instruments in attaining our goals."[49] That Muraviev, well known for his humane and considerate attitude toward soldiers, could express himself in such unceremonious terms is good evidence of how much he was under the spell of Bestuzhev. Indeed it was a mystery to most people who knew both of them what accounted for their intimacy and for the influence which the young braggart and intriguer exercised over the older man.

In reflecting much later on the merger, Gorbachevsky, a member of the United Slavs, wrote rather bitterly about the Southern Society:

[Its members] were for the most part people from the upper classes. They planned to carry out the *coup* through purely military means with no participation of the masses. [But even] to the officers and the lower ranks they could not reveal in advance their ultimate goals. The former it was hoped to enlist by the sheer enthusiasm of the movement and various promises, the latter . . . by bribery and threats. In addition . . . members of the Southern Society were mostly of mature age, people in fairly important positions. . . . As against them the United Slavs were without an exception young, passionate, naive, and impatient. It was not in their nature to confine themselves to pious wishes. They craved action, wanted badly to see their dreams fulfilled. They did not balk at being considered unequal by others or at suppressing their personal aspirations for the sake of the cause because they had never tasted of the proverbial fruits of power.[50]

For all the class and temperamental differences between the old and the new members, the accession of the United Slavs should have brought the Southern Society a considerable infusion of strength: some fifty young and energetic men. Yet what was true of the Decembrist movement as a whole would also be true of the Southern Society during the few remaining months of its existence: there was no catalyst, no leadership capable of transforming revolutionary ideas and plans into revolutionary action. The new members indeed injected some life into the secret organization. Some of them agitated among the lower ranks. But in the absence of an overall plan of action the agitators were incapable of effectively indoctrinating the soldiers. The latter listened attentively when told what they already knew, that life was hard and unjust for the majority of the Russians, but they did not know what exactly was expected of them. "Their hearts and minds were agitated by a vague feeling that the existing order of things must be changed. They wanted something new, but what precisely? To that question they could not give a clear answer."[51]

But the days of the conspiracy were counted. All along government officials had had intimations about the existence of the secret societies. However, it was only in 1825 that informers within the Southern Society gave the regime a fuller picture of the conspiracy. Had the tsarist regime been more efficient it could have moved against the plotters long before the uprising of December 14. But it is also certain that except for a peculiar turn of events, the totally unanticipated death of Alexander in November, there would have been no attempted coup d'etat: the conspirators would have been arrested long before August 1826, their target date for the uprising. If the conspirators had been arrested when the scope of their activities became known, the new regime of Nicholas I would have been spared the traumatic shock of the revolt. The new tsar, while not a man to inaugurate constitutionalism, would quite likely have undertaken to solve some of the country's outstanding social ills, such as serfdom. Thus Russia might have been spared the thirty years of reaction and stagnation, and without December 14 the conspirators probably would have been dealt with much more leniently and would have passed into history as noble dreamers and amateurish revolutionaries, but without that aura of romance and martyrdom which has clung to the Decembrists. As it was, the events of December 14, 1825, were to open a chasm between Russian society and the imperial government, one which would never be bridged.

In 1823 the Northern Society acquired a new member who was to play a decisive role in the events which triggered the uprising. Kondrati Ryleyev was a poet of rather modest endowments, but his poems were widely read because of their patriotic and radical themes. The son of an impoverished officer, he was constrained to leave the army early with the rank of sublieutenant to seek more remunerative civil employment. Eventually he became an official of the Russian American Company which administered Alaska. The young poet was a man of action, who, unlike the majority of his confederates, could not be satisfied with endless discussion about what should be done after the revolution. He also knew how to impart his enthusiasm and impatience to others. The government commission investigating the abortive coup would summarize Ryleyev's contribution to it as follows:

The Committee knows that by 1823 the Northern Society was composed of relatively few people who were active, and was about to cease to exist. But you having joined it became one of its most fervent and active members, and with the help of some people in the south instilled in it fresh order, enlisted new associates whom you dominated and indoctrinated with liberal ideas. . . . Thus enlarging the sphere of subversive activity . . . and that finally you became the main catalyst of the events of December 14.[52]

Though the statement exaggerates the extent of the conspirators' demoralization prior to his joining them, its assessment of Ryleyev's role does not. His position within the Northern Society paralleled that of Pestel in the south. But the sources of their influence were quite different. Pestel's was grounded in his intellectual domination over his followers, their awe at his erudition and ability to spin out elaborate theoretical plans. But he was devoid of that self-confidence and that ability to capture men's hearts as well as their minds, important attributes for a revolutionary leader. Ryleyev, on the contrary, by his gift for friendship, his enthusiasm, and sheer vitality was capable of dissipating his comrades' doubts and hesitations and thus to propel them into action. But he was also prone to recklessness and not a good judge of people.

A man made for sociability, Ryleyev turned his modest apartment into the center of St. Petersburg's revolutionary activity. There was a constant stream of visitors: Guards' officers, literary luminaries, liberal-minded bureaucrats. With but little concern for conspiratorial precautions, veteran Decembrists mingled and talked radical politics with the host's casual acquaintances whom he hoped to recruit for the cause. If hospitality was effusive, the fare was rather primitive; but the young poet's "Russian luncheons" soon became celebrated throughout the capital precisely because of their exciting and innovative simplicity insofar as St. Petersburg salons were concerned. Unlike the homes of the more opulent Decembrists, here the guests were served not champagne, but vodka, and the main course was cabbage soup, supplemented by generous portions of rye bread. And a lot of singing. Ryleyev believed that subversive songs were a very effective means of revolutionary propaganda. He himself composed one which derided the tsar's mania for military parades and drills and made indelicate references to the imperial family's German background and mannerisms. But some of the songs had more serious themes. The paraphrase of one popular ditty recounted how a smith was sharpening three knives: one for the magnates, one for the clergy, and one to strike down the tsar. The guests, who included scions of the noblest families in Russia, most of them officers on active service, would join delightedly in the singing. This bracing atmosphere was quite different from the somber arguments about the future constitution which preoccupied so many of Ryleyev's fellow conspirators. He was one of those who live for the revolutionary moment and are not overly concerned with what happens afterward.

As such, he had to consider various contingencies. Among his acquaintances were high government officials such as Michael Speransky, once again occupying an important position in the imperial administration, and Admiral Nicholas Mordvinov, senator and former minister of finance, one of Russia's earliest writers on economics. While neither of them could openly advocate it, both were believed to be partisans of reform and of weaning Russia from autocracy. Speransky retained much of his earlier liberalism, while Mordvinov, married to an Englishwoman, was a great admirer of the British constitution. Such notables,

Ryleyev and his associates believed, could not, of course, be expected to support openly the conspiracy, but there was little doubt that they had an inkling, at least, of what was going through the minds of the young men whose acquaintance they cultivated. And at a decisive moment the support of people like Speransky and Mordvinov, should they be persuaded to throw their great prestige behind the revolutionary cause, could prove most helpful.

Ryleyev was not a fanatic. His model for Russia's future government was the American constitution. The country, he once explained to Pestel, needed a Washington, not a dictator like Napoleon, a role to which he believed his interlocutor aspired. But one could not exclude the possibility that the overthrow of the regime would require drastic means and the assistance of people quite different from senior statesmen like Speransky and Mordvinov. Therefore, he was also looking for potential assassins. And it was best that they should not be too closely associated with the secret society. The Russian people might not take too kindly to a new regime whose leaders' hands were stained with the blood of God's Anointed. There were two men in his entourage whom he thought might serve the purpose of removing the emperor without the blame falling on the Decembrists. Peter Kakhovsky, though received in the society in 1825, was not privy to its plans. The twenty-eight-year-old ex-lieutenant was in many ways the prototype of the future long line of Russian terrorists. Brooding and emotional, his entire life had been replete with personal misfortunes and professional disappointments. To Ryleyev, who despite his own straitened circumstances supported him financially, Kakhovsky more than once declared his intention of striking down the tsar. But it was not yet the right moment, and Ryleyev managed to dissuade his friend, pointing out that his apprehension would be followed by the destruction of the secret society.

Another self-declared candidate for tyrannicide was Captain Alexander Yakubovich. Unlike Kakhovsky, Yakubovich had a personal grudge against the tsar. For having been a second in a duel, Alexander I had him dismissed from the Guards and transferred to a regular regiment in the Caucasus. Here Yakubovich distinguished himself by all kinds of heroic deeds in the fighting against the tribesmen, but he also confirmed his reputation as a brawler who would challenge his fellow officers at the slightest provocation and in actual duel would invariably try to cripple his opponent. Wounded in the head, the choleric officer was invalided out of the army. Tall, with a martial air, with his skull, which never fully healed, covered by a black bandage, he was at the time a colorful figure in St. Petersburg society. A braggart and loudmouth, Yakubovich would tell any and all who would listen about his unmerited slight at the hands of the monarch and how he proposed to avenge himself. The Decembrists showed some residue of common sense in that they never formally admitted Yakubovich into the secret society, but for Ryleyev he was another man who might be "unleashed" should the occasion warrant it.

Would such an occasion ever come? For all his revolutionary enthusiasm and schemes, Ryleyev, who in 1825 became one of the three-member directorate of the Northern Society, was still far from formulating an actual blueprint and timetable of the uprising. Since by the end of the year the government was ready to arrest the leaders of the Southern Society, there is little doubt that before too long this would have been the fate of the Northern Decembrists. But just as the conspiracy was being unravelled, on November 19 Alexander I expired in the southern city of Taganrog.

News of his illness had been trickling into the capital for some time, but no one expected its fatal conclusion—the emperor was but forty-eight years old. The announcement on the twenty-fourth of his death struck St. Petersburg like a thunderbolt. There ensued two weeks of utter confusion during which Russia was without a ruler and the government paralyzed. Out of this chaos came the revolt. The indecisive, disorganized conspirators were propelled by the course of events and almost against their will into action. Such was the weakness of the rudderless ship of state that this hastily improvised, half-hearted, and amateurish rebellion almost succeeded in bringing down the autocracy.

The cause of the confusion lay in the tangled question of succession to the throne. As Alexander was childless, his heir, as everyone assumed and the law prescribed, should have been his brother, next in age, Grand Duke Constantine. Only within the imperial family was it realized that Constantine was both temperamentally unfit and unwilling to rule.

The grand duke's aversion to the crown dated from the trauma of his father's murder. He feared that the same fate was in store for him were he ever to succeed to the throne. For almost ten years now he had resided in Warsaw as commander-in-chief of the Polish army and the virtual viceroy of the country. His preference for the Poles over his own countrymen was not unconnected with the fact that Polish history does not offer a single case of regicide. Constantine inherited his father's unbalanced mentality with intermittent moods of chivalry and brutality. For all his liking of the Poles, he would on occasion abuse his officers in public, several of whom felt constrained by the code of honor, then prevalent, to commit suicide. Rumors of those and other excesses reached Russia, but since Constantine was only two years younger than Alexander, no one gave much thought to the possibility of his becoming emperor.

In 1822, now married to a Polish commoner, Constantine wrote a private letter to Alexander offering to renounce his right to succession. The latter then took a very strange course of action. His brother's letter was never made public. Instead, in 1823 in a document which also remained secret and of which but three copies were deposited, the tsar designated his next and much younger brother Nicholas, who was then twenty-nine, as his heir. For reasons which have never been clarified, Alexander thus chose to dispose of the empire as if it were his private estate. Not even Nicholas was told in so many words that the succession would skip Constantine, nor was he being prepared for his future responsibilities, his occupations having remained purely military.

A few days after the announcement of Alexander's death, the secret document became known to the empire's dignitaries. But in the meantime they, as well as the army, had sworn allegiance to Emperor Constantine I. So did Nicholas, fearful of the slightest appearance of trying to snatch the crown from his elder brother. The latter then behaved in line with his unhinged character: he would not for a moment acknowledge that he was emperor, and he refused to budge from Warsaw or to make a public renunciation of the throne. Thus, as messengers were speeding back and forth between St. Petersburg and Warsaw, the whole government machinery ground to a standstill.

For all their years of planning for the eventuality of the emperor's death, when it did occur, the Decembrists were unable to act—vivid proof of the chimerical and daydreaming quality of all their revolutionary plans. The Southern Society, its members far from the main scene of action and dispersed completely, remained quiet. Their St. Petersburg comrades plunged into feverish discussions: all the revolutionary scenarios of the past nine years were now revived and heatedly debated. It was only the very length of the crisis, the seemingly complete disarray into which the regime had been plunged, which imposed upon the indecisive and quarrelling conspirators the conviction that something had to be done.

That something was constructed of odds and ends of the previous plans for an uprising. This was going to be essentially a palace revolution with units of the Guards, officered by members of the secret society, carrying out the coup. However, the objective was not going to be to dethrone one man in favor of another but to install a provisional regime which would summon a national assembly which in turn was to proclaim Russia a republic or a constitutional monarchy. As it became clear that Nicholas finally was going to be installed as emperor, an element of deception stole into the plan. They would exploit Constantine's silence and persuade the soldiers that Nicholas was a usurper trying to wrest the crown from its rightful owner. There were other variants discussed and rejected: to proclaim a regency in the name of Nicholas's seven-year-old son, the future Alexander II; to proclaim the late emperor's widow Elizabeth as monarch and then to persuade her to abdicate. In brief the conspirators had but little faith in the effectiveness of revolutionary or constitutional slogans: initially at least, the Russian people had to be won over through deception. Ryleyev and his associates carried out last minute investigations as to whether the trick would work. By mingling with soldiers and street crowds they established that the people were completely befuddled with all sorts of fantastic rumors circulating: Nicholas had imprisoned his brother; the real will of Alexander was being withheld, et cetera.

To be fair, while trying to conquer through a ruse, the Decembrists, nevertheless, were not about to forget their ideals once in power. Simultaneously with the coup it was proposed to publish a manifesto instituting far-reaching reforms, even before the summoning of the national assembly.* The manifesto would immediately abolish serfdom, disband the military colonies, and eliminate taxes and monopolies especially burdensome to the lower classes. All citizens were to be equal before the law, trials with juries were to be made public, the length of military service was to be reduced from twenty-five to fifteen years, a provision expected to gain wide support for the coup among the soldiers. While some of these measures had obviously not been thought through, for example, it was not specified whether the peasants, upon their emancipation, were to be given land or not, the proclamation constituted a clear commitment to a new and vastly different Russia, and a proof that the Decembrists were not seeking power for its own sake.

Doubts and hesitations returned when it came to the mechanics of the uprising. No one opposed the Constantine gambit, but it was questionable whether by itself it would guarantee success. Some, notably the irrepressible Yakubovich, disconsolate that by dying Alexander had robbed him of his vengeance, urged drastic steps: one had to stir up the masses, exploit those anarchic instincts lurking beneath the surface of Russian life. Hence soldiers ought to be permitted to loot liquor stores and not be unduly restrained from other forms of violence. But such arguments were found to be both reprehensible and unreasonable. An appeal to the basest instincts of the mob would not only besmirch the revolutionary cause, but also make the majority of the nation recoil in horror from it. Should the mutineers try to seize the Winter Palace? This too was unacceptable to many of the conspirators. Any violence done to the imperial family was bound to destroy the fiction that the coup was being carried out on behalf of the legitimate emperor.

No plans for a revolutionary uprising are ever worked out to the last detail, and few revolutions have ever adhered exactly to a previous blueprint. But with the Decembrists there was not only a divergence of opinion as to the best way to go about it but also as the day of decision approached, increasing and searing doubts about the whole venture. That which they had so often and confidently planned before now loomed as an almost insurmountable task with snares and dangers on

*It was not specified who would be eligible to vote for it.

every side. Would they not in fact be unleashing a wave of anarchy and mob violence which might submerge them as well as the government? Were they justified in precipitating what might turn into a civil war that might damage irreparably their beloved country's greatness? How substantial and reliable were the forces at their disposal, and would the officer-conspirators be able to carry along their soldiers? Last minute apprehensions assailed Ryleyev who, in view of his position, should have been setting an example of resolution and confidence. At times the leader of the Northern Society breathed optimism: such was the existing confusion that one resolute blow was sure to topple the regime, and other actions would be taken as needed. But in his less euphoric moments he recognized the fantastic nature of the enterprise. With some fifty officers, mostly of junior rank, and a handful of civilians they proposed to bring down an edifice which had existed for centuries. There were, of course, many others who were ready to join the revolution once it scored an initial success. But as its hour approached there were defections from the revolutionaries' ranks. On December 9 the plans became known to the high officials, and the news reached the Decembrists through their sympathizers within the bureaucracy that Nicholas would be proclaimed emperor within a few days. Constantine had now definitely, though still not publicly, renounced his rights. Many members of the secret society, some longstanding, now professed their unwillingness or inability to assist in the rising against the rightful tsar. Ryleyev's mind groped for new stratagems. Perhaps he could "unleash" Kakhovsky against Nicholas with the conspirators disavowing responsibility for the assassination. But Kakhovsky, when the idea was broached to him, refused. He was ready to sacrifice himself for the cause but only if his comrades would not repudiate him.

On the eve of the portentous undertaking, it was a fatalistic rather than confident mood which characterized the Decembrists. They had to go ahead, said Ryleyev at one point, because even if they failed, their sacrifice would inspire future fighters for freedom. The conspirators now were holding almost continuous sessions at Ryleyev's apartment (the poet, who had been spending much time in agitated consultations with his associates and days in wandering through St. Petersburg to gauge the mood of the masses, finally fell ill and had to stay home) where young Prince Alexander Odoyevsky, cornet in the Guards, kept repeating, "We shall die, but die gloriously." Such sentiments did not augur well for the rebellion.

Indeed, the final plan of action adopted by the insurgents appears to have been programmed for disaster. They kept debating and procrastinating until it was almost too late. On December 13 it was learned that the next day officials and the army would be required to swear allegiance to Nicholas. Now or never! It seemed imperative to act the same night and to make the seizure of Nicholas's residence and of his family the central feature of the coup. Instead, it was decided that the insurrection was to begin the next morning. Decembrist officers were to explain to their soldiers, when they assembled in the barracks for the oath, that Nicholas was a usurper, and then they were to lead them in full battle array to the Senate Square. The Senate was scheduled to meet at seven o'clock in the morning. The rebel units were to occupy the building and to coerce the assembled dignitaries to issue the revolutionaries' manifesto. Some elements of the plot have never been clarified. Thus it is not possible to determine whether the manifesto would have been issued in the name of the alleged emperor Constantine, or whether the Senate was simply to pass over Constantine as having abdicated and to proclaim the regime in its own name. If the latter, it is difficult to see how the Decembrists could have hoped to retain the allegiance of their soldiers, who quite conceivably might have turned against their officers for so blatantly deceiving them. Neither before or after the uprising did any of its instigators seem to feel any compunction or scruples about exploiting these simple men's trust and habit of obedience and thus exposing them to death and draconic penalties on behalf of a cause they did not understand.

Compounding their other errors, the conspirators entrusted the command of the military operation to the one person in their midst who was perhaps least suited for the task. Prince Serge Trubetskoy had shown himself to be quite dubious about the whole venture. As the events of the fourteenth were to show, he neither believed nor really wished for the revolution to succeed. There seemed to be plausible reasons for designating him as the dictator which was his official title: bearer of a historic name, colonel in the Guards, and thus senior in rank among the conspirators, Trubetskoy had also been one of the founding members of the secret society. But his comrades should have recognized that in view of his irresolute character, though a brave soldier, he was not suited for an independent command, let alone for the task they thrust upon him. He accepted the charge, Trubetskoy was to state later, because he hoped to be able to negotiate some sort of agreement with the government and to avoid bloodshed, odd feelings in a man who agreed to lead a revolution.

The story of the fateful day itself will always be accompanied by the historians' conjectures, "What might have happened if only . . ." and "It could not have happened otherwise." What if the rebels had chosen a different type of man to lead them; if more soldiers had come over to their side; if they had had the foresight to equip themselves with a few pieces of artillery? And most basically, what would have happened had the rebels, having brought out their soldiers in revolt, been able to act speedily and resolutely rather than stand and wait for something to happen: something which in the end was to be their doom?

On the side of "it could not have happened otherwise" there is the argument that based on the planning and execution, the insurrection had been programmed for disaster. Its instigators were filled with doubts and apprehension, virtually conceding a defeat from the very beginning.

Early in the morning of the fourteenth, civil and military personnel of St. Petersburg were assembled in various locations for the ceremony of swearing the oath to the new emperor. This was the moment for the conspirators to act. Their script called for officers privy to the plot to call upon their soldiers not to swear allegiance to the usurper but to remember their oath to Constantine and to lead the troops out of the barracks, allegedly to protect the rights of the legitimate emperor. The Decembrists hoped that they could thus subvert and gain at least six regiments and that the other units would then refuse to fire upon their brother soldiers. All hinged on the initiative, persuasiveness, and popularity among their men of a relative handful of mostly junior officers. From the beginning things began to go wrong. In most regiments, loyal (that is, pro-Nicholas) officers were able to persuade the soldiers that Constantine had in fact renounced the throne. In the end the conspirators were able to carry with them but parts of three units: the Moscow, Grenadier, and Marine Guards regiments, some three thousand instead of the hoped-for twenty thousand men. More catastrophic than the numerical weakness of the forces of the insurrection proved to be its leaders' indecision and inability either to adhere to the plan or to improvise new and bold measures. An essential part of the plan had been that the mutineers seize the Senate while it was in session and compel its members to issue the revolutionary manifesto which would formally institute the new regime. They had known that the Senate's session was scheduled for 7:00 A.M. But it was 10:30 before the first of the mutinous units, the Moscow Guards Regiment, its flags unfurled, drums beating, entered the square. The senators, having taken the oath to Nicholas, were long gone. Finding the square empty, the regiment arranged itself in battle formation and stood in the piercing December cold, occasionally raising a cheer for Constantine. (A story, possibly apocryphal, claims that the soldiers shouted, "Long live Constantine and his wife, Constitution!") In the next two hours they were joined in the same posture by the other mutinous detachments. The revolution stood and waited.

It was also headless. Trubetskoy, panic striken at the last moment, could not bring himself to join the men whom he should have been leading. Instead, after wandering for several hours through the streets of the capital, he sought refuge in the home of his brother-in-law, the Austrian ambassador. Equally prominent by his absence from the square was the man the Decembrists had designated as second-in-command to the dictator, Alexander Bulatov. Ryleyev, as a civilian, could not take part in the military activities. Exhausted from his exertions of the last few days, he spent the morning trying to whip his officer associates into action and then returned home to await the bitter end. By default, the command should have fallen upon the chief-of-staff of the uprising, Prince Eugene Obolensky, but he was only a lieutenant and could carry little authority with the soldiers.

Even more damaging for the prospects of the revolution than the inability to capture the Senate was the rebels' failure to seize the Winter Palace, where Nicholas and high dignitaries assembled in the morning. The occupation of the imperial residence had been finally agreed upon by the Decembrists the night before, but again they seem to have planned this all-important operation so as to assure its failure. The palace was supposed to be occupied by the Marine Guards, led by Yakubovich, which was a strange choice in view of his well-known unreliability and the fact that as an army man he was a stranger to the men he was expected to lead on that very delicate mission. As might have been predicted, Yakubovich, entirely oblivious of his responsibility, joined with the Moscow Guards Regiment, while the Marine Guards, whom he should have been commanding, bypassed the palace and joined the other mutineers standing in the Senate Square.

While confusion and panic afflicted the revolutionary leaders, the picture was somewhat different on the government side. To be sure, many senior officials and generals were afflicted by a paralysis of will as the turn of events brought home their negligence in not having taken proper precautions to stave off the mutiny. In the last analysis, however, all depended on the new tsar, and he kept his head. Nicholas had known for some time that there might be trouble on his accession. A martinet and of an irritable disposition, he knew that he was not popular in the Guards, where as grand duke he had long served as an officer, lately a division commander. Just two days before he had been informed that an insurrection was in the offing. A young officer, Jacob Rostovtsev, had been told of the secret plans by his Decembrist friends, and he felt it his duty to divulge the information to the emperor-to-be, stipulating, though, that as a man of honor he could not reveal any names. Nicholas, though acquiescing in his informant's scruples and thus unable to move against the conspirators, still gained the invaluable advantage of having been prepared for the dramatic events which would usher in his reign.

Now he acted with considerable resolution. Having provided for the protection of the Winter Palace and his family, the tsar personally assumed the command of the loyal forces. Gradually the latter surrounded the Senate Square, barring access to any further reinforcements for the mutineers. The government side enjoyed a clear superiority: some twelve thousand troops against three thousand, and unlike the rebels they had artillery and cavalry. But the situation still remained explosive. Nicholas could not bring himself to order an attack upon his enemies and so the two almost immobile masses of soldiers confronted each other for several hours. The tsar was loath to inaugurate his reign in bloodshed; perhaps a more important consideration was the fear that the loyalty of his men would waver if they were ordered to charge and kill their fellow soldiers. Several emissaries were dispatched to the rebels to urge them to lay down their arms. One of them, the city's governor, General Miloradovich, well known and popular among the soldiers, started addressing them about the senselessness of their adventure, and how he, as a personal friend of Grand Duke Constantine, could vouch that he had in fact resigned the crown in favor of his brother. But his harangue was cut short by a bullet from Kakhovsky's gun, and Miloradovich fell mortally wounded. There were other shots and a few casualties in the government ranks. Indeed it is remarkable that for all the previous talk of regicide and despite the fact that the emperor, mounted on his horse, presented a clear target, no one attempted to take his life.

Remarkable also was the hardiness of the Russian soldiers. On both sides they stood without budging for some five hours, in full battle array and in subzero temperature. But the Decembrists, abandoned by their leaders, most of their calculations exposed as false, persisted in their suicidal stance. In a sense this final act of the conspiracy epitomizes its whole history. The Decembrists dreamed, prayed, and worked for a new Russia. But they could never quite believe that they had the right to seize their country's destiny and to strike down the man who, while a despot, by virtue of his office still represented Russia and her greatness. Patriotism drove them toward revolution, patriotism kept them from carrying it out.

It was three o'clock in the afternoon and growing dark. Officers in Nicholas's entourage now felt they could wait no longer. There might be, once the night came, defections from the government's ranks, a sudden spurt of activity from the rebels. The mob composed of the city's proletariat which had invaded the square for the spectacle and along with the mutineers was cordoned off by the loyal troops was growing restive; stones and bricks were being hurled at the emperor's soldiers. He must make up his mind, declared a general to the tsar, either to disperse the rebels or to abdicate. Let his artillery sweep the square. Twice did Nicholas command, "Commence firing," and twice he countermanded his orders. The third time he let the order stand. A few salvoes of grapeshot into the serried ranks of rebels, and the hitherto disciplined phalanx became a panic-stricken fleeing mob. There was no attempt at resistance. The uprising was crushed.

The same strange fatalism which had kept them from storming their way to victory now kept the Decembrists from trying to escape apprehension and prison. In some cases they voluntarily surrendered to the authorities. Courageous as well as solicitous to spare his subjects' blood during the confrontation in the square, the emperor, now that victory was his, displayed another side of his character.

As one by one the main figures of the rebellion were being brought before him to be questioned, the Emperor of All Russia turned into an inquisitor. With some he tried cajolery and persuasion: they had nothing to fear if they sincerely repented and divulged all they knew about the conspiracy. With others he burst out in threats and insults, his hitherto repressed fear now finding an outlet in rage and bullying. After their questioning the prisoners were conveyed to the grim cells of the Petropavlovsk fortress. The tsar personally prescribed the kind of regimen to which each one was to be subjected, some to be treated leniently, others to be kept in strict isolation and in chains. That night the main facts about the plot became known to the authorities. Completely broken in spirit, begging the tsar for his life, the unfortunate dictator, Trubetskoy, provided most of the information needed to unravel the history of the secret societies, their chief members, and other details. Imperial aides were soon racing to all corners of European Russia and Poland with orders to arrest and bring back under guard any and all who had had any connections with the Decembrist movement from the very moment of its inception.

In the south the arrests had begun even before, with Pestel being taken on the thirteenth. But before expiring, the Southern Society signalled its end by one last desperate act.

It is interesting to speculate what might have happened in St. Petersburg had Serge Muraviev Apostol been there among the leaders of the uprising instead of being confined to his regimental duties in the Ukraine. After receiving the news of both Pestel's arrest and the catastrophe in the capital (the latter reached the Southern Decembrists on the twenty-third) Muraviev at first considered suicide but then decided to act. Placed under house arrest on instructions from St. Petersburg, Serge and his brother Matthew soon regained their freedom with the assistance of their associates from the United Slavs. The latter had several members among the officers of the Chernihov Regiment where Muraviev himself was second-in-command and very popular among his men. It was thus not difficult for him to make some eight hundred soldiers follow him in his suicidal venture. The argument used by Muraviev was at first similar to those of the St. Petersburg rebels: the soldiers were told that Constantine was the legitimate emperor and Nicholas a usurper.[53] They were also promised that their term of service would be reduced. In addition, Muraviev had composed and ordered read by the regimental chaplain a short catechism which instructed how autocratic power was incompatible with Christianity and how the tsar in usurping it acted against the teachings of Jesus Christ who preached freedom and equality. Fortified by this teaching and by the extra rations of vodka issued to them, the mutinous part of the regiment set out in the direction of Kiev. It was Muraviev's desperate hope that other Decembrist officers, still at large and presumably with little to lose, would emulate his example and that his force would grow to a sufficient size to occupy Kiev and confront the government with the specter of civil war. But it was too late. His former conspiratorial associates were fearful and no reinforcements were coming. On the contrary, several officers and men deserted from the ranks of the mutineers. Wandering more or less aimlessly through the countryside, the rebel column found itself confronted on January 3 by much superior government forces which included cavalry and artillery. As on the fourteenth of December, it was no contest. The mutineers were dispersed by cannon fire. Most of the rebels were captured on the battlefield, among them the severely wounded Serge Muraviev. There were no casualties on the loyalist side. The whole Chernihov affair took four days.

Thus what had started as a revolution resolved itself into what might be called an armed demonstration in the north, followed by an equally abortive mutiny in the south. Yet despite its ephemeral character, the Decembrists' effort illuminated the glaring weakness of the regime. The rebels had come from the midst of the ruling class. Had by some miracle the initial attempt by the conspirators succeeded, it is quite likely that a substantial part of that class, and even of the bureaucracy, would have ranged itself on their side. Never again would the tsarist government be able to count on the unquestioned allegiance of its people. To secure its allegiance it would have to resort to creating an elaborate machinery of repression and that in turn would increase the alienation of society and set the stage for the almost uninterrupted struggle between reaction and revolution which would be the main feature of Russian history until 1917.

For those officers who at the critical moment took his side, the emperor displayed great generosity, showering them with orders, promotions, and honors. Twenty of the senior loyalist officers were promoted to the rank of adjutant general, a position which assured its holder of personal access to the monarch and virtually guaranteed a brilliant military and civil career. Among the junior officers, forty were appointed aides-de-camp, a lesser but still important step on the ladder to honors and preferment. More prosaic were the rewards to the lower ranks, money to noncommissioned officers, and to every private who on the fourteenth had the luck to find himself on the right side merely a present of two rubles, two glasses of vodka, and two pounds of fish.[54]

For the defeated there was to be little mercy. From the strictly legal point of view, the Decembrists had been guilty of treason, and thus those who had been officers on active service should have been judged by military courts and presumably sent before firing squads. There were on the other hand voices in Nicholas's entourage pleading for a lenient treatment. It would be politic, it was argued, for the emperor to begin his reign in a spirit of generosity and forgiveness. The whole affair had after all been a failure, as much on account of the conspirators' scruples as their ineptitude. They were mostly young men, some of them descended from the noblest families of Russia. Yet Nicholas chose to apply the full vigor of the law, showing himself neither merciful nor forgiving. In a way the punishments he was eventually to mete out to the unfortunate men were to be for Russia's future more opprobrious and more fateful than would have been a wholesale execution. Few would be punished by death, but many more, including some whose connection with the uprising itself was quite tenuous or nonexistent, would be disgraced and exiled for life, their infamy and suffering in distant Siberia serving as a warning to any who might be tempted to follow their example to defy the rightful authority and to indulge in the "mad lust for novelty," as the court was to characterize one of the main sources of the Decembrists' treasonous design. In fact Nicholas's decision, the result of the trauma he received on the day of the uprising, led the judges to devise the manner of punishment which would secure the Decembrists' place in history and the revolutionary legend. The memory of how amateurish was their rebellion and how undignified their behavior after the defeat became blurred, and what the future generations would remember would be mainly their self-sacrifice and martyrdom.

How deeply mistaken was Nicholas I when he thought that he could shape posterity's judgment on the Decembrists is well illustrated in the words of his official biographer.

> But whatever one's opinion about the movement represented by the Decembrists, however one might consider it as a mistake or a result of delusions, one cannot deny them one general characteristic. That characteristic was their readiness for self-sacrifice in the broadest sense of the word. Here [were people] . . . who already had or were about to have brilliant careers . . . people who when it came to their professional duties acted according to their convictions, were full of humanity and fairness, and who were deservedly trusted both by their subordinates as well as by others who depended upon them. . . . The self-sacrifice of the leaders [of the Decembrists] is all the more striking because hardly anyone among them counted on success, on the contrary they all were prepared to die for their convictions.[55]

This passage from the pen of a conservative writer, published when Russia was still an autocracy, speaks for itself.

On December 17, 1825, took place the first session of The Secret Committee Appointed by His Majesty for the Purpose of Investigating Members of the Subversive Society. This cumbrously titled investigating commission was composed of various high dignitaries, some of them personal friends of the emperor. Neither the investigation nor the subsequent so-called trial bore the slightest resemblance to what even by contemporary Russian standards could be described as judicial procedure. The whole spirit of the proceedings was epitomized by the imperial decree setting up the special high court to try the Decembrists. "The court's function will be to pass judgment on the state criminals," a remarkable foresight since all 121 were found guilty.

It proved fortunate for the legend of the Decembrists that the full texts of their depositions before the investigating commission did not come to light until after the revolution of 1917 when the archives of the imperial government were opened. The great majority of the rebels hastened to express repentance, gave the authorities full details of their conspiratorial activities and those of their associates, and begged for mercy, often in a most craven way. Colonel Vasili Tisenhousen wrote to Nicholas:

> Allow your very unfortunate loyal subject, oh Most August Majesty, to express his devout thanks for Your magnanimity in letting me write to you; condescend to listen to a repentant sinner. I would not dare to try to justify my behavior which through sheer faintheartedness on my part led me to crime . . . but I swear that I never intended to violate the law. . . . Sire, be merciful and magnanimous. . . . You will not find a more faithful servant than myself among your most loyal subjects.[56]

Pestel, who before being arrested had told an associate that he would let himself be torn to pieces rather than to confess or provide the authorities with any information, soon was telling them everything. On December 3, the now utterly broken erstwhile leader of the conspiracy wrote a pathetic letter to one of his inquisitors: "You can have no idea how terrible is the anxiety one experiences at being in prison and at not knowing one's fate. His Majesty had commanded that I tell all and so I have, fully, without concealing anything." He had been crying thinking of his aged parents and how they must suffer. Let the emperor, for their sake, pardon him: "I shall forever be grateful and devoted to His Sacred Person and to His August Family. I realize that I cannot remain in the army, but at least let me be free. . . . Perhaps God in His infinite mercy will incline the Emperor's heart in my favor."[57]

Soviet historians have for the most part attributed the behavior of the imprisoned Decembrists to their class origins: "The brittle revolutionary spirit of these rebels from the gentry would break easily under the impact of the full victory of the autocracy, the collapse of their own movement and plans and the mass arrest."[58] But this is a great oversimplification. In the years to come there would be many other Russian revolutionaries from the nobility, including Vladimir Ulyanov-Lenin, and their behavior when questioned by the authorities or facing the gallows would for the most part be quite different. The Decembrists were the first. Just as the soldier's tenacity under enemy fire, so the revolutionary's endurance, whether in the struggle or in defeat, is not so much the function of his innate courage, still less of his class origins, as of his training and experience. Just as the rebels had been unprepared to carry out a revolution, so there was nothing in their background to teach them how to endure the consequences of its failure. Many of them would not have hesitated to give their lives for the cause, as some did, but they did not know how to cope with the loneliness of the prison cell, the sufferings and reproaches of their relatives, and the intermittent cajolery and threats to which they were being subjected by the tsar and his inquisitors.

It was not so much the brittleness of their revolutionary spirit, but their deep ambivalence about Russia which led many of them to indulge in self-accusations and repentance and to prostrate themselves before the man they had aimed to dethrone. Now that their cause had lost, Nicholas loomed again as the rightful ruler, the arbiter of Russia's fate, and as such was to be revered. From his prison cell, Peter Kakhovsky, perhaps the most turbulent among the Decembrists, kept bombarding the emperor with letters imploring him to become a reformer: "Sire, I am not your enemy. . . . I love passionately my country. Its happiness is bound up with Your fate. . . . On you depend the fortunes of fifty million people."[59] Brought into the emperor's presence, Kakhovsky was completely conquered by the man he had offered to assassinate when he heard Nicholas say, "I, too, am a Russian." This was enough to throw his prisoner into transports of rapture. He would die happily, he wrote subsequently to the emperor, having heard from his own mouth of his love for Russia. Less unbalanced but also repentant was the tone of another would-be-assassin now a prisoner, Yakubovich, who also addressed his imperial jailer with a letter suggesting various reforms and assuring him that if he should adopt them "the malcontents . . . will vanish like fog before the sun and You will be the savior of the fatherland . . . with the love of fifty-two million of Your subjects being the harbinger of Your immortal fame."[60]

To be sure there were individuals who refused to join in the attitude of contrition and servility. One of the standard questions posed to the accused ran "Since when and from whom did you imbibe liberal ideas? Was it from your acquaintances, or through reading books, and if so, which ones? And who is responsible for your final conversion to them?" To which Michael Lunin proudly answered that he had believed in freedom from the moment he could think for himself, and nothing else but reason's own dictates had led him to become a convinced liberal."[61] Of Peter Borisov, a cofounder of the United Slavs, his investigator wrote: ". . . He stated that having sacrificed himself for the fatherland, he awaits joyfully whatever might be in store for him."[62]

These are but isolated voices in the general chorus of mutual recriminations, self-accusations, and pleas for mercy which issued from the imprisoned Decembrists. Many blamed Ryleyev especially for seducing them from the path of duty. The tsar showed himself a talented inquisitor. Some who displayed initial defiance he ordered to be kept in chains until they confessed with "heartfelt candor," as the official phrase went, and they invariably did in the end. With others he played a more subtle game: how could they, his old comrades-in-arms from the Guards, have fallen in with the men who wanted to slaughter the whole imperial family? They could still expiate their sins by telling all. He relieved the financial distress of Mrs. Ryleyev, who had found herself without any means of support, and when he learned about it, the poet wrote to his wife asking her to pray for the imperial house. And so the accused betrayed to the authorities not only their coconspirators but in some cases men like Lunin, who for years had had nothing to do with the secret society.

The main concern of the emperor and his agents was to uncover the full scope and background of the conspiracy. The prisoners were questioned endlessly about their knowledge of not only their own but also any other secret societies and dissident groups in Russia and Poland. A theme which would continue to reverberate through similar proceedings down to the present was the authorities' curiosity about any possible links between the Decembrists and revolutionary movements abroad, and the official incredulity that on their own and without some foreign provocation Russians could have revolted against their government. Or perhaps even some foreign power, notably Great Britain, had been behind the plot? The belief that "perfidious Albion," envious of her greatness, was bent upon stirring up trouble in Russia would endure into the Soviet period, when in the Moscow purge trials of the 1930s, the accused would be made to confess their complicity with the British intelligence service.

Equally insistent was the investigators' search for any high officials who might have known of or sympathized with the seditious plans. But here again the accused could offer nothing concrete to justify the emperor's suspicions. True, among themselves, they had discussed people like Speransky, Mordvinov, and the commander in the Caucasus, General Yermolov, as possible candidates for the provisional government after the coup, but they offered no information linking them to the plot.

The emperor's inquisitorial tactics are understandable in view of his not unfounded suspicion that had the revolt succeeded, a large part of Russia's elite would have hailed it and that perhaps some two or three thousand had known of and sympathized with the secret society's goals. If he wanted to stamp out dissent, one of the imprisoned Decembrists told him, he would have to destroy the whole generation which had grown up during his brother's reign. But this was something Nicholas would not and could not attempt: it was not within the power of a nineteenth-century autocracy to rule through mass terror. Speransky and Mordvinov would be allowed to retain their high offices. Yermolov was soon removed from his command but not otherwise punished. Of the approximately five hundred arrested, many who had been on the periphery of the conspiracy or who had detached themselves from it in time and convinced the authorities of their "heartfelt repentance" would be released, some of them like Michael Muraviev eventually to reach high posts in the military and civil hierarchy. The revolutionary spirit in Russian society had not been exorcised by the catastrophe of December 14, but for the balance of Nicholas's reign it would be held in check by another social characteristic, that of servility toward the powers that be. It is strange to the point of obscenity that one day after his brother's execution, Vladimir Pestel could be offered and would accept the post of an aide-de-camp to the emperor.

The regime showed itself assiduous in trying to track down the intellectual sources of the rebellion. The questionnaire to be filled in by all Decembrist prisoners contained several items bearing on their upbringing and education. Whence came the "ill intentioned" ideas which inspired their seditious doings? What books, teachers, or experiences first cast the seeds of treason in their minds? Were they practicing Christians? (Quite a few were.) The interrogation reflected the questioners' genuine incredulity: surely a Russian gentleman and officer could have never on his own conceived the absurd idea of betraying his emperor or that his country needed or was fit for constitutional government! If not suborned by some foreign power or revolutionaries, they were plunged into their fatal delusion through the influence of noxious foreign ideas. But the impression which emanates clearly from the answers is that it was not French or English thinkers but the appalling reality of Russian life which in the main inspired the Decembrists in their undertaking.

The most morally dubious aspect of the uprising was hardly touched on in the investigation. At no point were the Decembrists asked how they could justify the gross deception they used on their soldiers in stirring them to rebellion. Nor did any of the main actors of the drama see fit then or subsequently to express contrition for the hoax. Yet those deceived, unsophisticated men paid dearly for their trust in their officers. Perhaps two hundred were killed on December 14 and January 3. Others, though also mere tools in the struggle and for the most part completely ignorant of its real purpose were punished with inhuman severity. The lash, in a number of cases twelve thousand strokes (incredibly some survived), lifetime exile, and hard labor in Siberia were the lot of those found to have been especially active in the events. Practically all the soldiers who had followed their Decembrist officers were discharged from their regiments and reassigned to the units in the Caucasus, there to be decimated by disease and the tribesmen's bullets.

The emperor's decree of June 1, 1826, setting up the special High Court for the so-called trial of the rebels named to it seventy-two judges from among the realm's notables, among them, as a test of their loyalty, Speransky and Mordvinov. The court's only function was to determine the *degree* of guilt and to settle on the extent of punishment of *all* 121 Decembrists whose cases had been turned over to it by the investigating commission. Even so the word *determine* is too strong, since it was Nicholas who in fact was the judge, the court expressing his will in legal formulas. It is then not surprising that what would appear to have been an extremely complicated case involving so many people should have been settled in five weeks, the speed of the proceedings facilitated by the total absence of the accused and of any defense. It was Speransky's cruel duty to formulate the language of the verdict spelling out the doom of the men, many of whom had been his close friends. Only one judge showed himself worthy of the name: Admiral Mordvinov voted against the death penalty for five of the accused, correctly pointing out that the existing law banned capital punishment. But Nicholas had long decided that the five he considered the main culprits must die, while the others, whatever the degree of their guilt or the technicalities of their sentences, must be exiled for life to Siberia or as privates to the Caucasian front and never allowed in his lifetime, at least, to return to European Russia. And so it was.

But the ceremony in the courtyard of the Petropavlovsk fortress on July 13, 1826, and the five hangings did not mark the end of the story of the Decembrists. It ushered in its most important phase. The same men who had shown themselves inept in conspiracy and pitiful in defeat, now through their courage in the face of adversity and the dignity with which they bore their sufferings redeemed their sins of omission and commission. There were to be the usual exiles' squabbles, some became disheartened and demoralized, but for most of the Decembrists, their Siberian exile was the period of spiritual and intellectual reflections and growth. Freed from prison and allowed to become settlers, many engaged in humble but essential social and educational activities, becoming pioneers of culture in the hitherto wild land. Its population soon grew to consider them not as political criminals but as representatives of what was best and most humane in Russian life.

In stripping the Decembrists of their titles and estates and in forbidding their wives and children to follow them, except if they also chose perpetual exile, the regime hoped to exorcise dissent from society and to teach a lesson to the educated class. But in fact throughout the thirty years of reaction which was

Nicholas's reign, the dwindling band of exiles in distant Siberia continued to weigh heavily on the nation's conscience, serving as a constant reminder for those at home that there could be a different Russia. If the pre-1825 period of the Decembrists' activity partook often of "adolescents' madcap games," then the effect of the legend into which they grew is also well expressed by Pushkin in his poetic message to them:

> Your mournful toil and high-minded aspirations will not have been in vain . . .
> [Once your] heavy chains drop off and crumble the dungeon's walls,
> Freedom will greet you joyfully.[63]

Alexander Odoyevsky, the same Odoyevsky who on the eve of the uprising had talked about dying gloriously and who during the investigation completely broke down, writing Nicholas that he wanted to throw himself at the feet of his Most Merciful Sovereign, answered Pushkin in a poem of his own:

> Bard rest assured, we're proud of our fate and chains. . . .
> Though locked in cells, as of old we laugh at the Tsar.
> Our mournful toil will not be in vain.
> Out of this spark will come a conflagration
> And our people, their eyes opened, will gather under freedom's sacred banner.[64]

In 1900 a group of Russian Marxists, which included Lenin, chose *The Spark* as the name of their revolutionary journal, and it would justify its device "out of this spark will come a conflagration."

Yet if they ignited the spark, the Decembrists also retained to the last one trait which would reappear in those who followed them on the revolutionary path and which would be responsible for the fact that when the great conflagration came, it did not bring freedom to the Russian people. This trait is illustrated vividly in the story of Serge Volkonsky. For his participation in the Southern Society Volkonsky, prince and major general, was stripped of his titles and estates and sent for life to Siberia. His wife, one of that heroic band of women who chose to share their Decembrist husbands' exile, could do so only at the price of also never returning to European Russia. She had to leave behind their infant son, who died soon afterward. But when the then aged Volkonsky heard in 1855 of Nicholas I's death, he broke down and cried disconsolately. His grandson and biographer explained this strange behavior. No, those were not tears of joy or for his own blighted life. The prince cried *for* Nicholas, because he was afraid of what would happen to Russia no longer run by his iron hand. He, like many in his own and the succeeding generations, saw in external power and domestic order an evidence of national strength.

And when will our national consciousness be rid of this fatal confusion [between power and national welfare] that has brought so much falsehood into every sphere of national life, falsehood which has colored our politics, our religious and social thought, our education. Falsehood has been the principal ailment of Russian politics along with its usual companions, hypocrisy and cynicism. They run through our whole history. Yet surely life's goal must be not just to exist, but to exist *with dignity*. And if we want to be frank with ourselves, then we must admit that if Russia cannot exist otherwise than she did in the past, then she does not *deserve* to survive. And as of now we have had no proof that the country can be run along different lines.[65]

Bitter words, as relevant now as when they were written.

Chapter 2

THE
IMPERFECT FREEDOM:
THE 1860s AND 1870s

TO THE FUTURE GENERATIONS, the thirty years of Nicholas I's reign, 1825–55, were to appear as a time of unrelieved oppression and national humiliation. Backward in its beginning, Russia was at the conclusion of the reign even farther behind Europe* insofar as her social, political, and economic condition was concerned. The government was not only tyrannical but preposterous in the way it suppressed anything even vaguely resembling intellectual, as well as political, dissent and tried to isolate the country from whatever might conceivably threaten the autocratic status quo. A system like that, historians almost unanimously conclude, could be maintained only by a most thorough repression, the best proof being that with the death of the emperor and with the demise of the method of governing he had created and epitomized, Russia entered upon a period of social turbulence and revolutionary ferment which was to conclude with the revolution of 1917.

His thoroughness in practicing the despot's craft does account largely for Nicholas's success in preserving his country from the winds of change which during those years were blowing all over the Continent and, assuming the intensity of a storm, in 1848–49 toppled or transformed practically every other Euro-

---

*It was a peculiarity of the Russian political terminology of the nineteenth century that *Europe* was taken to mean the leading countries of the West, rather than, for example, contemporary Spain or Italy.

pean government. By contrast, Russia remained an oasis of political tranquility and reaction. Unlike his predecessor, the emperor practiced repression in a consistent and systematic way. In 1826 he created the first modern political police, a prototype of similar institutions which have flourished on Russian soil ever since, down to the Soviet KGB. Like them, this Third Department of His Majesty's Chancery was not limited to fighting subversion but had wide-ranging functions, making it in effect the guardian of morals and culture and the instrument for the detection and suppression of nonconformity and disloyalty in all areas of public life. The intellectual community, then as now the object of special concern to the rulers, was severely restrained. How ubiquitous, to the point of absurdity, was the effort to muzzle this community is well illustrated by the reaction of a high official to a thoroughly innocent literary essay which had passed a censor: "One should only display some attention to perceive that the author, while pretending to consider literature, insinuates in fact something quite different: by the word *enlightenment* he means *freedom,* the *mind's* activity is to be read as *revolution,* and the *skillfully contrived middle ground* is nothing else but a *constitution.* "[1] The writer, in fact a firm believer in autocracy, was banned from publishing books and articles, a prohibition which stood for eleven years; the journal which published the article was shut down; and the negligent censor fired from his job. Even though his famous essay, though critical of Russia's past history and culture, was devoid of political allusions, Peter Chaadayev was by the tsar's personal order declared mentally ill and placed under house arrest. The Petrashevsky circle, a group of young intellectuals who gathered to discuss political ideas au courant in the West, such as socialism, but who never got to the point of doing anything about them, was after its denunciation to the police in 1849 dealt with as if it had been a conspiracy like the Decembrists. Several of its members, including Dostoyevsky, were sentenced to death, actually arraigned for execution, and only then informed that their sentence (as had been prearranged all along) had been commuted to exile and hard labor.

Yet this view of the Nicholean regime as resting solely upon force is certainly oversimplified. Nicholas I was able to rule the way he did very largely because for most of his reign he successfully appealed to Russian nationalism, and unlike Alexander with his cosmopolitan ways, he fit the popular image of the Russian tsar. What the future generations would see as the greatest blot on Nicholas's reign—his cruel treatment of the defeated Decembrists—awed rather than repelled the majority of his contemporaries. The emperor's prejudices not infrequently coincided with those of his subjects. Alexander had been widely criticized for favoring Poles; Nicholas, after crushing the Polish rebellion of 1830–31, stripped the "ungrateful" nation of its autonomy and representative institutions, which in view of their absence in the empire proper were felt to be a standing insult to the Russians' national pride. An educated Russian knew that for a liberal Westerner his country was synonymous with political tyranny and servility, yet whether consciously or not he drew comfort from the fact that it was Europe's greatest military power and as such was universally feared. The empire expanded its frontiers during the reign and again those external manifestations of Russia's power and greatness tended to compensate many of Nicholas's subjects for that exasperating feeling of inferiority which involuntarily gripped them whenever they looked at the West.

This identification of autocracy with the national tradition and interest was also based on two assumptions which, as the reign progressed, were increasingly seen as having been fallacious. The first to go was the hope that Nicholas would be an autocrat in the mold of Peter the Great, a crowned revolutionary who by his very despotism would be capable of pushing Russia into the nineteenth century, to modernize and civilize her backward society. Even some of the imprisoned Decembrists, as is clear from their depositions and letters, fell prey to the illusion that this narrow-minded and badly educated young man would become a reformer, something which the first few years had proved Nicholas was not. His naturally conservative inclinations were reinforced by the trauma of the uprising which had ushered in the reign, by the conviction that his elder brother had helped to bring this about through his irresponsible talk about reforms, and that the latter, under Russian conditions, were bound to lead to further hopes and demands, eventually incompatible with the institution of monarchy and social order. The tsar was not devoid of intelligence nor in his view of solicitude for his subjects. He saw the evils of serfdom, but how could one tamper with this very fundament of the country's social fabric without stirring up that revolutionary and anarchist virus which he and his advisers believed was latent in Russia's body politic and could be kept from breaking out in an epidemic only by the most thorough vigilance and repression. The regime gradually abolished the military colonies and in the 1830s and 1840s adopted some measures designed to improve the condition of state-owned peasants. But the latter, as is usually the case when palliatives are employed to deal with major social problems, led to disorders and large-scale rioting among the peasant masses, thus confirming the government's fears that any prospect of change in his status serves only to arouse the peasant's anarchic instincts. Therefore, when the government set up a committee in 1839 to consider the situation of the landlords' serfs, it did so in strictest secrecy, members of the committee being forbidden to reveal its true purpose and deliberations even to their fellow officials. But the committee did not lead to any meaningful change in the status of privately owned serfs.

The same fear of reform characterized the government's attitude on other social issues. There was no significant (as compared with the West) industrial growth during those thirty years: a large middle class, not to mention an urban proletariat, is conducive to political unrest as events in the rest of Europe were amply demonstrating. It would have been out of character for Nicholas's regime to encourage unduly education at any level: universities were potentially the hotbeds of seditious ideas, and after 1848, when German and Austrian students showed themselves especially active in the revolutionary disturbances in their countries, the teaching of philosophy was banned in Russia's institutions of higher learning. A widespread system of elementary education was obviously impractical, in fact would have been cruel as long as serfdom persisted, so the little that was done at that level was left to church schools. The Industrial Revolution, with its social corollaries, was firmly refused entry at the border posts of the empire. As against the creative turmoil which seized the rest of Europe, Russian society seemingly slumbered.

His sins of omission on the domestic front would not have perhaps proved as damaging to the autocratic principle had the tsar been able to advance effectively Russia's power abroad. But toward the end of the reign it became increasingly clear that here, too, he was far removed from Peter the Great. With the Habsburg Empire on the brink of dissolution, the tsar in 1849 sent his armies into Hungary to crush its national uprising against Austrian rule. This step, which in the West earned him the sobriquet of "Europe's gendarme," could not be pleasing to many of his subjects for whom the Habsburg state represented German oppression of millions of fellow Slavs and Russia's rival for hegemony in southeastern Europe. By helping a fellow autocrat, Nicholas demonstrated that he put considerations of monarchical legitimacy over what Russia's elite considered her national interest.

The final blow to the nationalist mystique of the Nicholean system was rendered by Russia's defeat in the Crimean War. The war brought out vividly all the consequences of the reactionary regime under which the country had suffered for a generation: its isolation in European politics, its economic and social backwardness, which now translated into military weakness. The army was incompetently led, its supply system was shot through with corruption, and the failure to develop an adequate communications system (in the 1850s the empire had barely entered the railway age) meant that no adequate reinforcements could be brought to avoid the ultimate defeat, the fall of the fortress of Sevastopol. Thus the Russian army, which had been absorbing a major share of the state revenues, proved incapable of coping with the numerically inferior French and British forces. The Habsburg Empire, which Nicholas had helped save only a few years before, adopted a menacing attitude toward its benefactor. This, combined with defeats and a desperate economic situation, forced Russia to sue for peace. On February 18, 1855, the tsar died after a brief illness, and many quite well-informed people were firmly convinced that faced with the bankruptcy of his system, Nicholas took his own life.

Even in old Muscovy the Russians usually greeted the death of their ruler with a mixture of trepidation and hopeful anticipation, a telling testimony to how little faith they traditionally had in the essential strength of the fabric of national life and how everything was thought to depend on the personality of the monarch. Such was the anxiety of the moment that it was hardly noticed at the time that Alexander II was the first tsar since 1725 to ascend the throne without the drama of a palace coup or usurpation attending or shortly following his enthronement. By Russian standards he was well prepared for his awesome responsibilities. Despite all that might have been expected to the contrary, Nicholas was a loving and enlightened parent, and Alexander, though a dutiful son, soon demonstrated that he wanted to be quite a different ruler from his father.

Even before the political complexion of the new reign could be discerned there was an electrifying change in the atmosphere. It was as if the door to a prison cell were suddenly thrown open, and the prisoners, while still constrained and unsure of their fate, could for the first time in a long while breathe fresh air. The coronation of the new monarch in 1856 was followed by a deeply symbolic act: the handful of the Decembrists who had survived in their Siberian exile were pardoned and allowed to return to European Russia. This act of clemency was marred by a reservation, also in its way and, less happily, symbolic: the returning exiles were banned from residing in either of the two capitals, the government thus seemingly fearful that these people, most of them now in their sixties and seventies, were still potential carriers of political subversion. Society received them with reverence; for Russians of almost all political persuasions these erstwhile participants in youth's "madcap games" and amateurish conspirators were now martyrs and their release a harbinger of a better future for their country.

As for the shape of this future, all thinking people shared a feeling of urgency about political and social change, but few were able to express it in some concrete idea. Official censorship still banned public discussion of politics, but even in their private correspondence and opinions most leading representatives of society, some of whom would soon be found among dissenters and revolutionaries, were as yet extremely unsure about the kind of laws and institutions which were needed to enable the country to reach that "level of greatness and well being for which it had been destined by the Creator." Its long slumber under Nicholas having atrophied what little sense of practical politics Russia's elite had been allowed to develop prior to 1825, it was as yet incapable of giving specific suggestions as to how the Creator's design was to be fulfilled. Its leading representatives tended to view the most pressing issues of the day through the prism of moral imperatives and philosophical absolutes. Vissarion Belinsky, who by combining literary and social criticism became the progenitor of the Russian radical of the 1860s, had written in 1847, "The most pressing national problems in Russia now are: the abolition of the right to own serfs, the abrogation of corporal punishments, the introduction as far as possible of a strict fulfillment of at least those laws which already exist."[2] Implicit in this list of social priorities was the assumption that it was up to "them"—the government—to attend to those evils of Russian life. Since the letter, though private, was intended to become widely circulated, the writer could not or would not specify how the reforms were to be accomplished. Even so, only his death soon afterward saved him from the Third Department. Even in 1855 few Russians were as yet ready to offer practical suggestions for solving the enormously complex problems attendant on the abolition of serfdom, and still fewer could see clearly what it would take to reform the fantastically anachronistic and corrupt judicial and bureaucratic system.

But if not prepared to become the government's partner in reform, Russian society was both ready, and to some extent allowed, to be its critic and judge. The striking thing about Russia between 1855 and 1905 was that while it remained an absolute monarchy and a police state, her political life was greatly influenced and in many ways shaped by public opinion. Political ideas and passions denied their natural outlets flowed into and at times dominated the nation's cultural and intellectual life. Still subject to occasionally rigorous censorship, Russia's literature and press would acquire political significance surpassing that of the most influential authors and journals of the liberal West. In writing about the period it is in a way imprecise, though at times unavoidable, to use the term *dissent.* Attitudes critical of Russian reality, hostility toward the government (again with the caveat that the emperor in this connection was often, as during this period, thought of as being somehow apart from and above the government, somewhat in the manner that an American draws a distinction between the President and the bureaucracy), were the rule rather than the exception among the educated class. The term *intelligentsia,* which comes into use under Alexander II, denotes not only a social stratum, members of the free professions, and people who, whether for livelihood or by choice, engage in intellectual pursuits but also an attitude of alienation from and opposition to the existing system. In the virtual absence of the middle class in the Western sense of the term, it is the intelligentsia which will arrogate to itself the right to speak for society; in fact most of the prerevolutionary writers from its midst would use the two words interchangably. Going beyond such terms, the radical component of the intelligentsia would soon claim that it represented the true interests of the people, the inarticulate mass of the peasants held in bondage not only because of serfdom but also psychologically by their superstitious veneration of the emperor, whom in their ignorance they saw as their protector from the officials and landlords, rather than in his true light as the landlord as well as bureaucrat-in-chief.

Conspicuous by his absence in this cast of main characters of the drama of Russian history during the second half of the nineteenth century will be a figure now frequent on the European political stage—the liberal. Ideologically, Western liberalism was based on the assertion of the individual's fullest freedom—political, economic, religious, social—vis-à-vis the state. Historically, its appearance was made possible by conditions peculiar to Western Europe, existence of a sizeable business community, at least rudimentary parliamentary and libertarian traditions, et cetera. In Russia of 1855 those were absent. A progressively minded Russian could not endorse the concept of sanctity of private property, a cardinal tenet of liberalism, if his most urgent demand was the abolition of private ownership of serfs. He could not believe in freedom of enterprise if seemingly only the state would be equal to the enormous task of social engineering required to lift the country out of its appalling situation. The intelligentsia thirsted for many freedoms it saw in the West, and progressively minded bureaucrats realized the necessity of introducing some Western institutions, if only to enable the state to function more efficiently. But it was mainly nationalism which proved to be a psychological barrier to Russian society becoming infused with the ethos of liberalism, as against its various segments endorsing liberalism's select features. National pride bridled at the idea that Russia should merely learn from and imitate Europe. The Decembrists' realization of their country's backward and servile condition by way of compensation made them dream of a Russia which, while having utilized what was best in the thought and institutions of the West, would far surpass it insofar as freedom and social justice were concerned. This idea would be taken up by the circle of the so-called Westernizers in the 1840s and 1850s and would become the leading motif of the radical part of the intelligentsia.

For a conservative Russian the vision of his country's unique destiny, while equally pleasing to national amour propre, was based on a different premise. What was needed to heal Russia's body politic was not a more perfect version of foreign institutions but a reform which would purify national life and politics of alien excrescences. The Slavophiles, as followers of this intellectual fashion called themselves, sought their inspiration in Russia's past, or rather in what was their mostly fictitious picture of her history before Peter I warped the fabric of national life by forcing the government and society into a foreign mold. In that golden age, the tsar had ruled absolutely and yet in perfect concord with the people, heeding the advice proffered by the Assembly of the Land (a sort of General Estates which in seventeenth-century Russia in fact met extremely infrequently) and solicitous of his subjects' welfare. Deeply spiritual in their nature, the Russian people scorned the false idols of the contemporary West, materialism and individualism, and they yearned not for such new fangled devices as constitutions and parliaments but for the restoration of the good old times when perfect harmony prevailed between the tsar and his nation with no meddlesome and venal bureaucracy separating them.

Very revealing of the educated Russian's frame of mind is the memorandum presented to Alexander II at the beginning of his reign by a prominent author and Slavophile, Constantine Aksakov. Before 1855 no one would have dared to express such sentiments in writing, let alone address them to the monarch:

> The current state of Russia is one of internal disorder and dissension, masked by a veneer of unconscionable lying. The government and the upper classes have become strangers to their own people. . . . Not only are the people not asked for their opinion, but every honest man is afraid to open his mouth. The people do not trust the government and vice versa. The former in every act of the regime tends to see a new form of oppression, the government is ever fearful of revolution and in every independent expression of opinion sees subversion.[3]

What is most striking in the writer's complaints, of which the above are but a small sample, is first of all the extreme vagueness of his political nomenclature. Usually *the people* stands for all classes below the ruling elite, sometimes, as in its customary contemporary meaning, for *the peasants*. The writer does not include the emperor in his indictment of the government; for him the emperor stands above the bureaucracy, yet he has harsh words to say about the "cult of personality" of the tsar "that unmeasured unconscionable adulation . . . which has turned the respect owed the Tsar into idolatry as if he were a god." As for the ruling class and bureaucracy: ". . . all lie to each other, know it and continue lying. . . . Bribery and systematic plunder by officials have reached frightening proportions. And it is not only dishonest people who steal, some fairly honest are (out of necessity) thieves. . . . This is inherent in the condition of society, in the nature of the political system."[4]

Furthermore, the writer of this diatribe does not then come up with some revolutionary conclusions or at least drastic remedies. Far from it. Faithful to his Slavophile creed he does not believe that the people are capable of, or desire, self-rule. "The Russian nation is not politically minded, it does not seek power over the state, it does not clamor for political rights." In view of the general thrust of his argument it is astounding, at least for anyone brought up in the rationalist tradition, that Aksakov can continue: "Absolute monarchical power is for the Russians not an enemy or antagonist but a friend and the guarantor of freedom, that true spiritual freedom." Look at the West! "Its nations having abandoned the path of religious and spiritual development have fallen prey to the impulse of selfish political vanity. . . . They have created republics, have tinkered with all sorts of constitutions and have [thus] become spiritually impoverished."[5] Besides, despite all the claims of superiority on behalf of such systems, they are subject to constant political and social convulsions. God save Russia from such freedom!

In his summary judgment on Russian history, the writer concludes that the source of all trouble lies in the "un-Russian" reforms of Peter the Great, for whom his nation was but putty to be molded according to a foreign model rather than a living organism. All the evils which had befallen the state and people since his times had been the consequences of the work of this misguided genius, not excluding even the Decembrists uprising, a "revolt of the upper classes which had become estranged from the people, since the soldiers who were involved in it had, as is well known, been deceived [by their officers]."[6] In view of his scathing verdict on contemporary Russia, there is unwitting irony in Aksakov's outrage at the fact that "since Peter's time" it had become almost obligatory for a Russian to despise his country and its people.

To achieve salvation, one must "understand Russia and return to principles compatible with her national spirit."[7] It should not try to revive the old Assembly of the Land. That repository of folk wisdom consisted of representatives of the various estates. But, alas, the later (i.e., estates) degenerated from the pre-Petrine times and can no longer be depended upon to give sound advice to the sovereign. There is something pathetic in the way Aksakov assesses various social strata of the nation, which he believes are still spiritually superior to all others. According to him, Russia's nobility was corrupted by Western philosophies and manners, and her merchant class aped foreign ways: witness their dress, an incongruous mixture of the traditional and the western—a vest worn over the Russian long blouse, native boots, but a foreign tie! It is better not to speak of artisans, "the most miserable class in all of Russia." Of them all, it is the Russian peasant who has best retained the old national virtues, "but what could the peasants say, having been silent for so long?"[8]

To change this deplorable state of affairs the writer proffers to the emperor one concrete suggestion: let him allow the fullest possible freedom of speech and of the press. Here an apologist for autocracy reverts to being a typical *intelligent*, with the difference that his plea for free speech is grounded in Aksakov's deep religious feeling. This feeling enables him to disregard any possible incompatibility between the freedoms he urges and an autocratic system, makes him pass over the reservations even the most thorough liberal would have in advocating them for a society still predominantly illiterate where a demagogue or a fanatic could exploit the masses' ignorance and superstitions. "When freed from all constraints, truth is always strong enough to crush falsehood. . . . it would be a sin to believe otherwise."[9]

The Imperfect Freedom: The 1860s and 1870s

The Slavophiles, for all the anachronistic and semimystical cast of their thinking, cannot be considered as reactionaries. They sought a different Russia. They believed that serfs must be emancipated. They wanted the government to heed the free voice of the nation. But their uncritical nationalism contributed to the intellectual atmosphere which made Russian politics of the second half of the nineteenth century a stage of conflict between revolution and reaction, with reform coming in as a poor third, with what there was of Russian liberalism lacking both the power of reaction and the passion of radicalism. Reaction would fasten on the negative part of the Slavophiles' argument: Russia did not need representative institutions which reflected the moral decadence and composition of the West. The left, for its part, would find the French or British constitutional model grossly inadequate for expressing the inherently democratic spirit and aspirations of the Russian people. Alexander Herzen, who epitomized the Westernizer tendency within the intelligentsia and who at the same time was one of the progenitors of modern Russian revolutionary thought wrote, as early as 1851, after four years' exposure to the West:

> Our laws begin with the overwhelmingly true formula "The emperor has been pleased to order." Your laws begin with a shocking untruth: a derisive invocation of the authority of the French nation, with the words "liberty, fraternity, and equality." . . . Russia will never be protestant [moderate and materialistic]. She will never be mediocre [prosaic and middle class]. Russia will never make a revolution just to get rid of Nicholas and to replace him by tsar-representatives, tsar judges, tsar policemen.[10]

It was not a good augury for the future of freedom in Russia, that its representative thinkers, both on the left and on the right, could dismiss so contemptuously what had been achieved in its pursuit by Europe's most civilized nations.

There was one problem facing the country which most people agreed could not await the settlement of a philosophical dispute as to Russia's true destiny and to whose solution the currently fashionable Western philosophies could contribute but little.* This was the peasant-land question.

In 1856, addressing a gathering of noblemen, Alexander II gave a rather ambiguous picture of his intentions on the subject.

> Gentlemen, I have learned that there are stories circulating among you that I plan to abolish serfdom. To prevent the spreading of such unfounded rumors on so important an issue, I deem it necessary to tell you that for the time being I have no intention to do that. But of course, you yourselves realize that the current state of affairs cannot continue.

---

*If the Decembrists hearkened to the voice of British and French social thinkers and constitutional theorists, then the first generation of the intelligentsia was, especially when young, literally captivated by German idealistic philosophy. For all their "nativism," the Slavophiles, even when they stressed the uniqueness of Russian historical experience, echoed the organic theories and politics of Hegel and Schelling.

RUSSIA'S FAILED REVOLUTIONS

It is better to begin abolishing serfdom from *above*, rather than to wait [the moment] when it will become undermined from below. I ask you gentlemen to consider how to put it into effect.[11]

The emperor's words, though uttered at a closed gathering and intended for the time being only for the nobility, became of course widely known.

The task of emancipation of the serfs had to be the most extensive and complex piece of social legislation and engineering in nineteenth-century Europe and would remain so for all of Russian history until the 1930s when Stalin, by imposing collectivization on Soviet peasantry, would in effect create a new form of serfdom. What centuries of history had accomplished in Western Europe would in Russia be done within a few years. The task loomed enormous: it involved in the first instance the lives, the legal and economic status of some forty-three million peasants. It touched on the property rights of thirty thousand landowner families. It affected the entire development of Russian society in a way almost as fundamental as would the revolution of 1917. Yet the main features of the reform would be worked out in the course of four years, 1857–61, and would be put into effect within the next nine.

The problem involved in freeing some nineteen million peasants who belonged to the state and the two million who were the property of the imperial family was relatively simple. The chief difficulty turned on the twenty-two million who were under private owners. Though not slaves in the literal sense of the word, their persons, as well as their land, belonged to their masters. The latter could order them whipped and confined to correction houses for up to three months. In fact, though not in law, the owner of the serfs could order them to marry against their will, select the ones who were to serve in the army, strip a serf of his land, make him his domestic servant. Yet the landlord had certain obligations toward his peasants, which though often honored in the breach, could not be entirely disregarded. He was obligated to preserve them from destitution. A notoriously vicious master could be warned by the authorities and in extreme cases be imprisoned or exiled. Mostly, however, it was self-interest and prudence which made the average landowner observe a measure of humanity and restraint in dealing with his charges. They had before their eyes the not-too-infrequent examples of those proprietors who had been assassinated or whose residences had been set on fire by their exasperated serfs. It was advisable to allow peasants a modicum of self-government and to take the advice of village-commune elders to settle disputes, which village lads should be sent for military service, and so on. With all that, peasant disorders triggered by some especially onerous demands upon them were a fairly regular occurrence, and in the 1850s they grew in frequency. Owning serfs was becoming a bit dangerous, and as the more intelligent landlords realized, like most unfree systems of labor, it was not conducive to efficiency, hence in a way an economic burden to the proprietors, as well as their unfree tenants.

It was the tsar's hope that the general outlines of reform could be worked out jointly by the government and the serf-owning landlords. Hence his appeal to the nobility to suggest proposals for emancipation. But for all the presence of enlightened and patriotic individuals who saw the necessity of emancipation, the gentry as a whole could not be expected to take a dispassionate and disinterested view of the reform which, quite apart from depriving it of its feudal rights, affected so fundamentally its economic interests. Few were ready to defend serfdom as such, though here and there a die-hard reactionary might still represent it as a patriarchal relationship, which in many ways was more advantageous to the serf than, say, the landlord-peasant tenant situation in Ireland, or the condition of the industrial proletariat in the West—an argument strikingly reminiscent of that used by apologists for slavery in the pre-Civil War United States. By and large everybody agreed that personal bondage had to go.

The main difficulty touched on the land aspect of the landlord-serf relationship and how this Gordian knot could be untied in a way which would be fair and equitable to the peasant and his master, as well as conducive to social stability and material progress. The economic side of serfdom was a vastly complex mosaic of laws and customs. The great majority of serfs held land which provided them with livelihood and for which they paid their masters either in money and kind or by working some days of the week on the land owned directly by the latter; or sometimes it was a combination of the two. Some serfs worked in cities and towns as craftsmen, industrial workers, or even entrepreneurs, paying a part of their earnings to the landlord from whose village they had come. The most fundamental issue before the planners of reforms was whether the peasant was to be liberated with or without the land he considered his, and not surprisingly, most landowners would opt for the latter.

Yet to free the peasants without giving them land was unacceptable to the more enlightened of the tsar's advisers, both on the grounds of equity and of social stability. To turn the serf into a landless agricultural worker who would have to make the best deal he could with his former master, or be cast adrift from his village and forced to seek work elsewhere would have meant to deprive him of that small element of material and psychological security which he had enjoyed even while unfree. The peasants would very likely reject such freedom and see it as a much more vicious form of oppression. "We are yours, but the land is ours" was the typical and immemorial peasant definition of his relationship to his master. Then how much land was each peasant household to receive upon emancipation? Exactly as much as he had had before, or what the statisticians decided was needed, granted regional variations, to secure the livelihood of the average family?

Equally tangled was the problem of compensating the landlords. Would they be paid just for the land which was ceded to their former serfs, or for their "baptized property," as Herzen described the serfs, as well? Who should shoulder the cost of the entire operation and how?

Had the determination of these issues been left to the serf-owning nobility, it would have undoubtedly come up with answers predicated upon its self-interest, or what it assumed to be such. The peasant would have been given little or no land beyond his household plot (and some landlords even begrudged him that, holding that only his dwelling should be liberated along with his person), thus making him economically even more dependent upon his master. Government committees, for their part composed largely of conservatives fearful of alienating the class from which they came, would have continued to exchange countless memoranda proposing half-way measures, et cetera. But for once the autocratic principle was vindicated as an instrument of public welfare. Alexander II was determined to emancipate the serfs. And the power of the autocrat was strong enough to prevail over the interests of the ruling class and the principle of the sanctity of private property. Not completely, to be sure, for the tsar was a conservative and far from wishing to preside over a social revolution or to despoil the nobility. But he would not let it stand in the way of his ideas on how the reform was to be accomplished.

The way he forced the issue into the open was in itself revolutionary. Tradition required that any major social or political reforms should be discussed without publicity in officials' closed committees so as to avoid agitating the people's minds, giving rise to unfounded and extravagant expectations or fears. Here, in a step which in itself marked a drastic departure from the system epitomized by his late father, the emperor broke with the tradition that matters of high policy were not something with which the public had any right to be concerned. In a rescript to the governor-general of Lithuania, dated November 20, 1857, and made public shortly afterward, Alexander II called upon the nobles' committees of the region to prepare plans "for the improvement of the condition of landlords' peasants," the main feature of this improvement to be the abolition of serfdom and the securing for the liberated peasant of adequate land for his and his family's needs.[12] Similar messages were then addressed to other provinces of the empire ordering their nobility to proceed likewise. In brief, the landlords were required to become an instrument of the curtailment of their own privileges. Since the tsar's intentions were now public knowledge, there was no turning back, and the autocracy's power and prestige were behind the vast social change. The reactionary part of the nobility and officialdom could now only delay and obstruct the reform, but they would not be able to stop it. In society at large the emperor's action led to great jubilation and enthusiasm: "What for long has been awaited is finally to be realized, and I am overjoyed to have lived to see it," wrote Ivan Turgenev to Leo Tolstoy.[13]

That the Russian monarchy in the nineteenth century could have become an agent of social change is something of an embarrassment to Soviet historians, who find it rather difficult to fit this fact into their Marxian categories. "How can one explain that the government undertook the reforms against the wishes of the majority of the gentry?"[14] They tend to give two answers to this question. In the first place the government understood the real class interests of landowners better than they themselves and realized that serfdom had to be abolished if large-scale peasant revolts were to be avoided. In the second place the more enlightened part of the nobility saw clearly that it would be profitable to substitute hired labor for serf labor or, to use Marxian terminology, to replace the feudal pattern of a rural economy by a capitalist one. But such explanations, reasonable up to a point, still miss the main impulse behind the drive for reform, the conviction that both on moral and patriotic grounds it was imperative to put an end to the system under which most Russians were unfree. This Soviet authority quotes the words of one who probably more than anyone else was responsible for formulating the general principles of the law on emancipation: "No thinking, enlightened person who loves his country could be against making the peasants free. A man ought not to belong to another man. Man is not a commodity."[15]

The writer of these words was General Jacob Rostovtsev. It was he who as a young officer with friends among members of the secret societies had warned Nicholas I on the eve of December 14 that an insurrection was imminent and begged him to resign the throne to spare Russia from an upheaval. Some of his former Decembrist friends subsequently gave credence to Rostovtsev's version of the interview with the tsar: he acted out of a patriotic impulse and refused to give names of the plotters. But for others he carried the stigma of an informer. He was a high and, to all appearances, very conservative official under the late reign. As inspector general of officer training, he issued an order which contained this remarkable statement: "Conscience should guide a man in his private and domestic behavior, while when it comes to professional and civil duties he must conduct himself according to orders from his superior." But after 1856 Rostovtsev became a staunch and indefatigable worker on behalf of the peasant reform. Personally close to Alexander II, he fortified his resolution to disregard the malcontents among the gentry. Appointed chairman of the drafting commission on the emancipation law when he was already ill, he pressed on with the task until the very day of his death on February 5, 1860. It is not unusual under an authoritarian system, be it tsarist or Soviet, that a high dignitary should take on the political complexion of the ruler, a reactionary under one tsar or general secretary becoming a liberal under another. But in Rostovtsev's case this transformation was due neither to servility nor cynicism; along with other leading men of the time, he saw in the emancipation the promise of a new and glorious era for his country.

The duration of this patriotic elation can be dated with some precision. It lasted from November 1857 when the nation learned about the tsar's resolve to February-March 1861 when it was enacted into law.

Never before or again would Russian society acclaim its ruler with such enthusiasm and repose such confidence in him as it did during those four years. Peter the Great's reforms were imposed by force upon an uncomprehending nation and recalcitrant nobility. Alexander I's popularity was but a brief reflection of the national victory over Napoleon. The jubilation which would greet the February 1917 revolution was followed immediately by social chaos and partisan strife. It would be distorting the meaning of the term to speak of Stalin as popular. Even at the end of World War II he would be the object of slavelike worship, compounded of awe and fear. For most of their history the Russian people have found it difficult to respect a ruler whom they did not fear. It is as if they have learned to suspect that government and freedom are really incompatible. They have craved freedom, but no more than they have feared anarchy. But at the time of the emancipation, for a few years one could have the illusion of living in the best of all possible Russian worlds: autocracy was very much alive, and it was an agent of freedom.

These paradoxical emotions were the rule not only among the intelligentsia at home; they reached to distant London where two political refugees had started a tradition of dissent which was the source of all subsequent Russian revolutionary and radical movements. It was in London in 1853 that Alexander Herzen established the Free Russian Press, dedicated to the struggle against tsarist despotism. The son of a rich nobleman, Herzen in his boyhood dedicated himself to following in the footsteps of the Decembrists. In 1856 he was joined in London by his childhood friend, Nicholas Ogarev. One year later the two of them began to publish the famous *Bell*, "devoted to the task of Russian freedom and to propagating within Russia free ideas." A writer of genius, Herzen employed his pen to excoriate the evils, injustices, and absurdities of contemporary Russian society and government. Soon he became and remained for several years the spokesman of most that was progressive and radical among the intellectual community in Russia. It was as if he were their leader. *The Bell* was regularly smuggled into the country, where it acquired a very wide circulation for those days, as well as a body of clandestine correspondents who furnished Herzen with political news and stories of official malfeasance, which of course could not be broadcast at home. The slim (usually eight to ten pages) bimonthly thus became a more reliable chronicle of what was going on in Russia than any journal published there and as such would be surreptitiously sought even by officials. Herzen considered himself a socialist and his detestation of Nicholas I, as well as of practically all contemporary rulers, left him with little sentiment for the institution of monarchy. Occasionally *The Bell* would carry most irreverent stories about some members of the imperial family. The government in St. Petersburg viewed Herzen as what he in fact was—even if intermittently—a revolutionary advocating the overthrow of the existing political and social system.

And yet the great exile, the self-acknowledged heir of the revolutionary legacy of Pestel and Ryleyev, spoke at times, especially between 1857 and 1861, as if he were a firm believer in autocracy. Even before then, he, an avowed opponent of the Slavophiles, greeted with rapture the accession of Alexander II, "You truly love Russia and You can do so much for the Russian people." There had been as yet no indication that the new tsar would be a reformer, in fact his views were believed to have been shaped by his father whom Herzen loathed. Still, unlike his Decembrist predecessors and models, Herzen did not demand from the monarch a constitution or representative institutions but only that he should use his autocratic powers for public good. "Sire, give us freedom of speech. . . . We have so much to say to the world and ourselves. . . . Give land to the peasants. . . . remove from Russia the fearful blot of serfdom, heal the lash wounds on the backs of our brothers. . . . "[16] The first intimations of peasant reform by the tsar brought from the democrat and socialist an even more Slavophile-sounding eulogy of the autocrat: "No other monarch in Europe is in as favorable a situation as Alexander II. . . . Having all power in its hands, supported on the one hand by the masses of the people, and on the other by all thinking and educated persons in Russia, the present government could, without the slightest danger to itself, perform veritable miracles."[17]

The emperor's rescript of November 1857 was rather ambiguous and vague as to the eventual solution of the peasant problem. Still, since it meant that the regime was now publicly committed to reform, Herzen might have been expected to greet it with approval. But his reaction surpassed mere satisfaction. It found its expression in a euphoria turning into a cult of personality of the tsar, who for all his promises to abolish serfdom had given every indication that he intended to cling to his autocratic powers, and he retained such of its appurtenances as the secret police, censorship, et cetera. He was now seen as the answer to the people's age-long prayers, an embodiment of both the autocratic and the revolutionary traditions. "We have before us not an accidental successor of Nicholas, but a mighty statesman who has opened a new era for Russia. He is as much the heir of December 14 as of Nicholas. He is working with us for the greatness of our future." There was still no assurance, the writer must have known, that the emancipation would not end up with the peasants being landless, more at the mercy of his former master than before, but Herzen was already convinced that "the name of Alexander II, from now on, belongs to history; were his reign to end tomorrow, were he to fall under the blows of some rebellious oligarchs, defenders of serfdom and of the lash, this would still make no difference. He has begun the work of freeing the serfs. Future generations will never forget it." On behalf of the radical intelligentsia, Herzen assured the monarch that they were all now his allies and that this homage came from the people "who have no reason to fear him, who do not want nor ask anything for themselves." The article begins and ends with the famous invocation: "Thou hast conquered, O Galilean."[18] No Slavophile would have dreamed of using such ecstatic language; Alexander II compared to Christ, and that from the mouth of an atheist!

It was not only the passion for social justice, the joy that forty million of their countrymen would have their human dignity restored by being made free but also national pride which dictated these radicals' professions of loyalty, just as it did the imprisoned Decembrists who psychologically prostrated themselves before their imperial jailer once they heard from Nicholas I's mouth, "I too am a Russian." Their ideological descendants now also spiritually capitulated to the autocrat, since he assumed the leadership in the sacred cause.

The very extravagance of their tributes, however, carried with it portents of future troubles. Had Alexander II combined the qualities of Peter the Great and Abraham Lincoln, he still could not have satisfied the excessive hopes reposed in him. While eulogizing the tsar, the radicals still execrated the government and Russia's social system. The dichotomy, good tsar-evil counsellors, which allegedly characterized what there was of the peasant's political thinking, captivated for the moment the minds of the country's most sophisticated men. But no nineteenth-century monarch could single-handedly transform Russian society. Determined as he was to accomplish the emancipation, the tsar still could not ignore the interests of the class which was the mainstay of the throne and the whole system. When the inevitable disillusionment came, the tsar would be seen not as a flawed reformer but as a betrayer of the nation's trust. It did not occur to anybody, not even the most radical Russian of the period, to urge that the party most vitally interested in the emancipation, the peasants, should have a share in the preparation of the reform, even in an advisory capacity. But once the faith in the tsar would crumble, it was the peasant who would become the object of the radical's worship and repository of his unrealistic hopes.

Alexander II was eulogized not only by those Russian radicals who had come from the gentry and who, because of their roots in eighteenth-century philosophies, might have been accused of harboring an anachronistic belief in enlightened absolutism. The 1850s brought to the fore another strain in Russian radicalism, one which would lead directly to scientific socialism and Lenin. The man who stood at the threshold of this tradition was Nicholas Chernyshevsky, a priest's son, representative of the new group of "plebeians," people from the nonprivileged classes, who intellectually had their roots in the contemporary Western social and economic thinkers, among them the British Utilitarians, rather than in German idealist philosophy. Their radicalism was more activist in nature, tinged by a feeling of personal and class hostility and hence more prone to violence than the philosophy epitomized by Herzen. The relaxation of censorship after 1855 made it possible—to be sure this had to be done in a veiled form —to write about politics within Russia. Hence Chernyshevsky and his group could advocate their views in what became the country's leading literary and social journal, *The Contemporary*. Published by Nicholas Nekrasov, the outstanding exponent of the progressive tendency in Russian literature and the most popular poet of his generation, *The Contemporary* achieved what was for the time a huge circulation. By 1861 it had more than seven thousand subscribers. Part of this success was due to the presence in its pages of such luminaries as Ivan Turgenev and the then quite young Leo Tolstoy. But increasingly it was Chernyshevsky's long and, by today's standards, ponderous essays on social and philosophical questions which made each monthly issue eagerly awaited by the intelligentsia. He and his acolyte, Nicholas Dobrolyubov, who joined the journal in 1857 and who picked up Belinsky's tradition of using literary criticism as a political weapon, acquired enormous influence, especially among the young. If Herzen hated the existing system because of its injustices and corruption, then Chernyshevsky's and Dobrolyubov's veiled attacks upon it soon disseminated a more straightforward revolutionary message: a government like Russia's could not be healed or reformed, but because of its class character had to be destroyed. Much as he still acknowledged Herzen's authority over the dissidents, Chernyshevsky already in 1858 had revealed certain reservations, if not indeed animosity, toward the older noble-born generation of radicals: "Look more carefully at your [alleged] cosmopolite and he will turn out to be a Russian with all the usual ideas and habits of the nation he belongs to, in fact a nobleman, official or merchant with all the prejudices of the social class to which he belongs."[19] The unspoken inference, usually easily deciphered by the reader accustomed by now to this kind of Aesopian language, was that one could not expect genuine revolutionary feeling from a man like Herzen, who was not only a self-proclaimed cosmopolite but also a nobleman and very rich.

The emperor's public intimation of his resolve to liberate the serfs brought from Chernyshevsky, however, an equally enthusiastic response as from Herzen. His article on the question, published in the February 1858 issue of *The Contemporary*, begins with a biblical invocation which has always been troublesome to his Communist admirers: "Thou hast loved truth and hated injustice; and that is why thou hast been anointed by the Lord."[20] And while the Soviet commentators try, rather lamely, to justify this outburst by alleging that Chernyshevsky used this device to enable his article to get through the censorship, this is certainly refuted by other passages in the essay, such as "The blessings promised to the peacemakers and the meek crown Alexander II with a felicity which none of Europe's sovereigns ever achieved—the happiness to be one both to begin and to complete the freeing of his subjects."[21] Again a striking Russian incongruity, a revolutionary eulogizing the autocrat. But in the case of Chernyshevsky this seeming incongruity is perhaps more easily explained than in Herzen. The latter saw in Alexander a genuine reformer, motivated by humanitarian impulses. Chernyshevsky saw the tsar as another Peter the Great, a crowned revolutionary. Most of the radicals of the older generation, going back to the Decembrists, were indeed very far from eulogizing Peter: for them, as for the Slavophiles, he was the man who had destroyed Russia's ancient freedoms, made serfdom more oppressive than before, and forced the country into that bureaucratic-militarist mold which had been its curse ever since. His reforms benefited the state but hardly the people. Yet for Chernyshevsky, "the glittering achievements of Peter the Great's era and the colossal personality of Peter himself overwhelm our imagination."[22] It is not unfair to assert that what Chernyshevsky—in the Soviet classification scheme described as "the great revolutionary democrat"—admired in Peter was his dictatorial talent: he did not negotiate or play politics with his nobles; he cut off their heads if they opposed his schemes of modernization. In the impassioned words of the Slavophile Constantine Aksakov, "The state that is Peter assaulted the nation, broke into the people's private lives, tried forcibly to change their tastes, customs, even their dress. . . . [At first it was ordered that] no peasant should dare to appear in a town if he wore a beard," and only when the peasants showed themselves intransigent in the defense of their traditional facial adornment were they allowed to retain it if they paid a special tax![23] For all his rough handling of the nobility and his preference for advisers from among the low born, Peter could hardly be considered as a benefactor of the common people. His was the type of revolutionary which recurs throughout Russian history: enemy of privilege, but equally impatient and ruthless when it comes to popular resistance against progress and modernization.

How uncompromising a revolutionary Chernyshevsky already was when he wrote his paeans to Alexander emerges in his polemic against one of the few contemporary publicists of note who can be classified as a liberal, Boris Chicherin.

The latter published a book which, under the guise of observations on British and French politics, advocated moderation and gradualism in approaching Russia's political and social problems. Chicherin was a resolute opponent of both serfdom and autocracy. But he viewed with great misgivings the feverish excitement and excessive expectations in which Russian society, and especially its younger segment, was plunged following the demise of the old system. To a man of Chernyshevsky's convictions, Chicherin's urgings of caution were intolerable and in a publicist a betrayal of his mission. "What should be the main quality of a publicist? . . . He must express and clarify those tasks which are of concern to his society at the time. It is not his business to be a dispassionate scholar. He must be a tribune and a propagandist." His polemic is vitriolic, interlaced with personal attacks on the man, who on most substantive issues was on his, Chernyshevsky's, side, and who simply urged prudence and the realization that the existing system could not be changed overnight. One might think, he noted with heavy sarcasm, that Chicherin was writing for a society "which is ruled by ultra-republicans, and when anyone who as much as mutters one word in favor of monarchy is put in jail."[24] And while seemingly just ridiculing his opponent, Chernyshevsky manages to slip through the censor his own profession of faith:

And so it would seem that the greatest vice of our society consists in the fact that it advances its aspirations, hostile to the existing order, too abruptly, uncompromisingly and passionately. . . . We are now at work in ruthlessly demolishing this order [Chicherin would makes us believe] and hence it is the duty of every publicist to instruct us, to preserve some remnants of our traditional institutions. . . . How truly amazing.[25]

In fact it was Chernyshevsky who would ruthlessly demolish the existing order, even if for the moment he would have the tsar as the main instrument of that demolition.

How he could select the emperor for that role is all the more mysterious, since as one of the founding fathers of what would become known as Russian populism, Chernyshevsky was a resolute enemy of bureaucracy. He reacted angrily to Chicherin's assertion that democracy, like autocracy, leads to the proliferation of bureaucracy and to centralization.

Democracy, by its very nature, is antithetical to bureaucracy. It requires that every citizen be independent when it comes to his personal affairs, and every village and town, every district free to manage its own business. Democracy requires that the administrator be fully accountable to the inhabitants of the constituency with which he is concerned. . . . Democracy means self-government and implies a federal system.[26]

Russia then should presumably have become the loosest of all federal states, a voluntary association of self-governing units all the way down to the village community. This notion contradicts the vision of a benevolent autocrat using the state to smash privileges and particularities and thus ordain a new and more just society. Peter the Great, after all, did not strive to transform Russia into an association of free communes; he made her the most bureaucratic and centralized state in Europe.

But this is a paradox which is inherent in the whole history of Russian revolutionary thought. From Pestel to Lenin, its leading exponents found little incongruity in espousing on the one hand the most far-reaching personal freedoms, and on the other craving a powerful centralized state to act as an instrument of social justice and progress. Pestel's Department of High Benevolence was a remarkable preview of the Third Department and the subsequent organs of secret police in both pre- and post-1917 Russia. "All power to the soviets," Lenin's slogan would be, he thus seemingly endorsed a virtually anarchic system of government, and his Communist state would become a hitherto unsurpassed model of centralization and bureaucratic power. Like them, Chernyshevsky sought to overcome the inherent difficulty in his political philosophy by a fanciful use of political semantics, and to his satisfaction he succeeded. Chicherin pointed out, for his time very perceptively, that the very pressure for social reform was inevitably leading to centralization and the growth of bureaucracy. As an example there was the factory legislation in England: the recent laws prohibiting certain types of industrial labor for women and children, various sanitary and hours of work regulations, et cetera. They all required that the state must interfere with the individual's freedom, as well as expand its legislative and administrative apparatus and functions. This was not, said Chernyshevsky, palpable proof that as a society grows more democratic and bent upon social reform, it inevitably becomes more centralized, more bureaucratized. What Chicherin saw as a trend toward a more powerful state, that is, its regulatory activities in economic life, is in fact something very different; it is socialism. And socialism, since it serves the interests of the masses cannot, by definition, lead to the individual being less free and the state and bureaucracy growing stronger and more ubiquitous. Here is a preview of that revolutionary logic which would lead apologists for the Soviet state, even under Stalin, to claim that for all the appearances to the contrary, it was the world's freest and most democratic society. By being socialist it had to be.

Democracy, socialism, parliaments legislating for the people—it now could be discussed, if circumspectly, in the columns of a journal appearing in Russia, whereas only a few years before the mere mention of such subjects, if by some quirk it got into print, would have earned the writer years in exile or jail. One can begin to appreciate how intoxicating must have been the effect of Chernyshevsky's articles, especially on the young, and how they could overlook the illogicalities of his arguments and the vagueness of the message they tried to impart. There was as yet no revolutionary organization nor even a program to which a young enthusiast could pledge his adherence. Born in 1828, Chernyshevsky, because of his age, had a much closer rapport with the new generation than Herzen, then in his mid-forties, but he was in 1858 still some distance from advocating revolutionary action. Nonetheless, the logic of his argument pointed unmistakably in that direction: it was not only serfdom which had to be abolished; the whole political system ought to be changed since it was based upon exploitation and oppression. For the moment he still exempted the emperor from his critique. But his writings and those of his followers contributed to the changing mood of the radical intelligentsia, its earlier gratitude to the regime for its promise of reforms beginning to be replaced by a feeling compounded of impatience and growing distrust.

A university student of the time, Panteleyev, who was soon to become a conspirator, describes this mood:

Only three and a half years separated the famous [imperial] rescript of November 27 from February 19, 1861 [when the Emancipation Law was signed], but this relatively short period appeared to the majority of the intelligentsia to be unbearably long; to the impatience for the reform there soon joined apprehension as to its fate, the fear lest the forces hostile to the emancipation prevail. . . . The shame at twenty million people being without any rights was present in everyone's mind, all the more so because before Russian society had been almost unmindful of the fact. Of course all people of progressive views, even the followers of *laissez faire* thought it imperative that the reform should provide freed peasants with economic security. But the main thing was to return to them their human rights—this above all focused on the peasant emancipation society's passionate interest, the like of which it never felt before or after about any other social question. . . . Up to that time Russian society had lived under conditions where there could be no question of free and spontaneous activity, and now it saw in the mere word "freedom" a magic elixir which no social ailment would be able to withstand.[27]

And these feelings, Panteleyev adds, agitated all the students, whether princes' sons or those who came from the lowest social strata.

Freedom and *liberation:* these are very suggestive words. Just as in America of the 1950s and 1960s the course of civil rights for the blacks triggered liberation movements in other social and ethnic groups, so in Russia one century before these terms led to similar reverberations. Before 1855 every social institution down to the family and the elementary school had mirrored the authoritarian pattern of the whole, and now with the autocracy relaxing its grip on public life, a similar transformation was taking place at every level. Women's rights, autonomy for universities, greater freedom for students—these became fashionable causes. In the Kingdom of Poland, nationalist agitation was gaining momentum.

There was talk about emancipation of the Jews. Suddenly there was a strong urge on the part of the advanced segment of society to reexamine and restructure every form of authority and obligation. With the edifice of autocracy still intact, with society still in its traditional mold, much of the psychological underpinning of the old order had already collapsed. In three brief years the educated class had emancipated itself from that fear and awe of authority which for a generation had held Russia sealed off from revolutionary stirrings bursting out all over the Continent. What still remained as the crucial element of social cohesion was the emperor's personal popularity and would it survive the almost inevitable disappointment when the actual details of the emancipation law were announced?

The government's apprehensions touched not so much on the state of mind of the intelligentsia as that of the two classes directly affected by the proposed reform: landowners and peasants.

Had he been endowed with all the despotic instincts and skills of Peter the Great, Alexander would still have had to take into account the views of landowners. First of all, he was deeply conservative and did not want a social revolution to turn into an economic one. But some form of cooperation by the nobility was imperative for putting the reform into effect. It would require a large body of arbitrators to adjudicate the respective claims of the peasants and their former proprietors. It seems strange that these arbitrators of peace, as they were called, should have been selected from the very class which was an interested party. But nineteenth-century Russia did not have at its disposal a body of administrators numerous and expert enough to perform this necessary function. Even the most propeasant advocate of the reform allowed that for a time, at least, the landowner should retain some residual authority over his former serfs. After centuries of slavery, the peasants, whether individually or collectively, could not be suddenly entirely left with no assistance, and there were not enough officials to watch over every village and hamlet in the vast country. It was hoped that enough landowners would be able to rise over their class interests and accept the government's design of how to help the freed peasants establish themselves and how to keep the rural economy going.

Hence the tsar felt that he had to mollify the landowners at the same time that he kept before their eyes the fatal consequences of undue delays and obstructions. Addressing a deputation of nobles on February 21 he stressed both themes:

The law must not be a mere declaration of good intentions. It must result in real improvements, insofar as the peasant's way of life and work is concerned. It will mean an upheaval, but this upheaval need not bring with it violence and disorder, if the landowners make real sacrifices. I do not want these sacrifices to be too onerous. . . . There have been rumors that I no longer trust the nobility. . . . That is false and slanderous. . . . I hope that you will demonstrate by deeds that my trust in you is not misplaced.[28]

The Imperfect Freedom: The 1860s and 1870s

While the nobles' reaction could be anticipated and they could be maneuvered accordingly, nobody was sure about the behavior of the peasants when the great day would come; whether the very word *freedom* would act on them like a spark in a powderhouse. Nobody knew how they would feel and what they would do when instructed about the complex technicalities of the law, that there had to be a transition period before the landlord's authority over them lapsed, that a number of obligations toward their former masters must continue for years, that in some cases they would be getting less land than they had cultivated as serfs, that they would have to shoulder onerous financial burdens. This was to be a leap into the unknown. It might set Russia on the path toward prosperity and modernity, or it might trigger peasant uprisings like that of Pugachev's in the last century.

What for those in authority was a grim possibility—peasant uprisings—was beginning to loom as a tantalizing prospect for people on the left. *The Bell* on March 1, 1860, printed an anonymous letter from Russia in answer to a previously published editorial by Herzen. Its author remains unknown, but there are strong indications that it was either Dobrolyubov or Chernyshevsky. If the latter, then he had certainly changed from his appeal of two years ago to the tsar to follow in the footsteps of Peter the Great. For the letter is an uncompromising attack not only upon autocracy but on the person of the autocrat himself: Alexander II was deceiving the nation. How could Herzen continue to burn incense before him, addressing public letters to the empress as to how the heir to the throne should be brought up, et cetera, while the tsar's power was the main cause of Russia's misfortunes. Herzen has a great responsibility: "In distant England you first raised your voice on behalf of the suffering Russian people ground down by the tsar; you showed Russia what free speech is. All that was vital and honest in society hailed you with joy and admiration." How then could he fail to unmask the inanity of the slavelike worship of the tsar, that main source of the people's sufferings? Obviously he does not fully realize what is happening at home, has been listening to fables conveyed by "liberal writers, landowners and professors" about the government's alleged benevolent intentions.* The truth is that the people—peasants—are fed up with the government's promises and believe that emancipation will be a hoax. "No, our situation is desperate and insufferable. Only the axe can save us and nothing else. . . . Call upon Russia to raise the axe. . . . remember that for hundreds of years the belief in the tsar's good intentions has ruined Russia; it is not the likes of you who should try to perpetuate such illusions."

*Liberal was now beginning to be used by radicals as a catchall term for all those who believed in the possibility of peaceful, gradual reforms; it would continue to be used by the left as a pejorative term.

The letter may be taken as the first harbinger of the revolutionary movement of the 1860s. As such it is an eloquent testimony of that elemental lusting for revolution which would inspire this movement. There is as yet no political program, no concrete vision of what should replace the old order once the axe has done its work. Equally characteristic is the writer's scorn for moderation for all those liberals who advocated "caution, gradual progress and God knows what else" while the people suffered. If the masses rise they might destroy not only the regime, but the liberals as well, and it would not be such a bad thing: "Why regret those fops in yellow gloves chattering about *democracy* in America while incapable of doing anything at home, those dandies filled with contempt for the common man, convinced that you can do nothing with the Russian people."[29] And still the writer was rather ambivalent about the liberals—here a synonym for the moderate part of the intelligentsia. He granted that the task of overthrowing the regime would be accomplished more purposefully and easily if some of those liberal professors and landowners lent their hand to it and assured the leadership of the revolutionary masses. Like the Decembrists the new type of revolutionary showed himself to be something of an elitist. The peasants would be amply justified if they rose and swept away the whole rotten system, but to build a new and just one they needed guidance from the educated class. This idea of *directed spontaneity,* the belief that the revolutionary potential was ever-present in the masses of the people, but that to carry out a successful revolution the masses must be provided with a sense of direction and leadership which only an elite of professional conspirators can give, would play an increasingly important role in Russian radical thought, culminating in Lenin and the Bolsheviks.

The "Russian from the provinces," as the anonymous correspondent called himself, also touched on another theme which would be explicitly stated by the maker of the Bolshevik revolution once World War I broke out: Russia's defeat at the hands of a foreign foe may turn out to be a victory for her people. He disputes Herzen's assertion that the Crimean War had brought a surge of patriotic feeling on the part of the nation. Herzen was then abroad, hence he could not know what his correspondent saw and heard at the time: "When the British and the French landed in the Crimea, the nation expected that they would help liberate them; the peasants from the landowners' yoke, the Old Believers from the religious persecution from which they have been suffering." Apart from being palpably untrue, this statement represents the first appearance of the antinationalist motif in Russian thought. And insofar as this theme will be taken up by the succeeding generations of Russian revolutionaries and reformers, it will prove until the very day of the revolution the greatest obstacle to their strivings and the greatest source of strength to their opponents and the defenders of the autocratic order.

The Imperfect Freedom: The 1860s and 1870s

Herzen's response to this vitriolic declaration bares another weakness of the radical camp, one which was to persist until October 25, 1917. Those within it who hoped for a nonviolent solution of the social and political problems of Russia would always be put on the defensive and grow unsure of themselves when attacked from the left. A man of deep humanitarian impulses as well as revolutionary convictions, Herzen could not bring himself to condemn outright the appeal to violence. He was apologetic about his praise of Alexander II: ". . . I ask you, have I been entirely wrong? Who of late has done something useful for Russia except the monarch? Render unto Caesar that which is Caesar's." He could not endorse a call for bloodshed: "The blood spilled during the June revolution [in France] has affected my mind and nerves, and ever since then I feel revulsion at bloodshed unless it is absolutely necessary." He grants that such a necessity might arise, but says, "Having called for the axe, one must be able to control the [revolutionary] movement; one must have an organization and a plan, be ready for sacrifices, not only when wielding the axe, but when it becomes necessary to grasp its sharp edge if the axe strikes too widely. Do you have all that?"[30] Yet in a few years Herzen would be ready to foresake his scruples and to lend his prestige and assistance to those who would call for a violent uprising.

There was already an undoubted ferment among the younger generation. Unencumbered by his elders' memories and cautions, the Russian student, whether from the university, the military, or theological academy, or even high school, now made his appearance on the political stage and would remain its most revolution-prone actor until the end of the century, when he would be superseded in that role by the industrial worker. Nowhere else did partial liberalization of an authoritarian regime have as far-reaching effects as among the young. It almost inevitably radicalized them and induced a spirit of skepticism and alienation from the existing political system. No other area of Russian life underwent as much of a change between 1855 and 1860 as that of education. The number of students in institutions of higher learning more than tripled. With the quantitative came also a social change; there was a considerable influx of youths from the lower classes, Jews were now permitted to enroll, and beginning in 1860 women appeared in lecture rooms, as yet only as auditors. The strict discipline and supervision of educational institutions of the Nicholean era had given way to much more indulgent attitudes on the part of the authorities. Students no longer were required to wear uniforms, the poorer among them were exempted from paying tuition. Professors, though still well advised to behave circumspectly, no longer had to fear that a mere allusion to politics or social issues threatened instant dismissal, if not something worse. Where the local head of the university (appointed by the government from outside the faculty) was particularly indulgent, the students enjoyed freedoms still not open to their elders. They could organize their own associations, libraries, collect funds for their impecunious colleagues, enjoy a virtual self-government. Within what was still the police state the universities, and even to some extent theological and military academies, became little enclaves of intellectual freedom. Hence it is not surprising that the kind of discussion which a few years earlier earned members of the Petrashevsky circle years of hard labor in Siberia now was carried on almost openly and with impunity at various gatherings of the young. There was still an element of risk involved in such activities, but just enough to make it more exciting. In 1856 some students at Kharkov and Kiev universities organized circles, members of which compared and circulated parodies of imperial manifestoes, as well as leaflets reproducing the more radical themes from Herzen's editorials in *The Bell*. When their activities came finally to the attention of the police in 1860, the culprits were dealt with, certainly by comparison with what would have happened to them in the previous reign, quite leniently. Though expelled, they were allowed to settle down in other cities of European Russia. And the professor who the authorities believed was among the instigators of such pranks was merely required to exchange his chair at Kiev for one in St. Petersburg; in fact a promotion!

Gratitude is not a striking characteristic of the young, and of course though they were freer than their fellow citizens, the university students were still subject to bothersome regulations. The argument that things were so much better than they used to be could not be as convincing to them as to their elders. What they read somewhat clandestinely in *The Bell*, and quite openly in *The Contemporary*, was bound to have a powerful impact on the minds of the young. If, like the "Russian from the provinces," one despaired of educated society as a whole and was disgusted by its still worshipful attitude toward the emperor and its readiness to accept with gratitude whatever the regime would bring in the way of peasant emancipation, then he had to be heartened when looking at the young. They had but little of that awe of authority and reverence toward the throne which even the quite radical among the older generation found it so difficult to shed. Thus, it was hoped that peasant disorders would lead to a revolution, and the students would turn what might be called the casual radicalism of the young into revolutionary activity.

Now came the testing time for all such hypotheses and scenarios. On February 19, 1861, the emperor signed the Edict of Emancipation. As it was bound to be, the law was very complex, its technical details difficult to understand for an educated man, let alone an illiterate peasant. As was almost equally inevitable, it was not fully satisfactory either to the radical or to the conservative. The latter had to feel that it sanctioned a gross violation of property rights. The serfs were liberated without the government compensating the landowners for their loss. The regime also decided that the peasants were subject to special and involved arrangements with their former masters, to be given land along with their personal freedom. For this land the state was to compensate the landlords in interest-paying bonds with the peasants in return repaying the treasury. This repayment was to be spread over forty-nine years, with the peasant purchaser annually paying 6 per cent of the price of his allotment.

In addition to this onerous burden placed upon the rural masses, a radical critic had to be displeased by another feature of the law. Many of the peasants' allotments were to be smaller than the ones they had cultivated for themselves as serfs. This was especially true in the fertile south where the landlords found farming profitable, and the government appeased them for the loss of free labor by increasing their land share at the expense of their former serfs.

Another momentous provision of the law was its retention of the communal system of land tenure. In Russia proper and in the easternmost Ukraine, peasant land had traditionally been pooled, except for serfdom one might almost say "owned," by the village community as a whole rather than individual households. It was the village assembly, *mir* (the word which significantly means in Russian also "peace" and "world"), which in addition to its other functions would periodically redistribute it among the peasant families according to their size and needs. The most advanced among the Westernizers had long considered this communal system of ownership as equally anachronistic as serfdom itself: for them it meant a brake on social mobility and economic progress since it usually worked to the disadvantage of the more efficient producers, and its retention after the emancipation was bound to delay the creation of a rural middle class. But the *mir* was much beloved by the Slavophiles, who saw it as conducive to social harmony and as being in line with the inherently democratic spirit of the Russian people. And for those who, like Herzen, believed in socialism, the commune embodied not only the wisdom of the ages and the egalitarian instincts of the masses but also a safeguard against Russia acquiring a large industrial proletariat and falling prey to other evils of capitalism. But the government's reasons in retaining the communal system were based neither on its alleged antiquity nor its equally questionable democratic and socialist virtues. With all the upheaval to take place in the countryside, the commune was the most convenient way to make sure that the peasants would meet their financial, military, and other obligations.

The law was to take effect in several stages. There was to be a two-year transitional period, during which the new economic arrangements were to be worked out by agreements between the ex-serfs and the landlords, helped by the arbitrators selected from among the latter. The landlord was not required to sell the land, but then the peasant became its leasor, bound to his ex-master by a contract specifying his rent or other obligations. (It was correctly expected that most landowners would be eager to sell, now that they could no longer enforce the peasants' obligations with the lash.) Then there was a seven-year period, only at the end of which would the peasant, if dissatisfied with his situation, be free to leave the village and seek his luck elsewhere. Thus though personally free in other respects immediately upon the promulgation of the law, the villager would still be tied to the land for nine years.

But what the small print said would become important a bit later on. The immediate reaction to the edict among the educated Russians was one of deep thankfulness. Meeting in the street, acquaintances greeted each other with the traditional salutation and response of Easter Sunday "Christ has risen—Verily he has" and would embrace. And in London, one who was an agnostic, as well as a republican, found his joy at the event overcoming his earlier doubts about the emperor. "Alexander II has done much, very much; his name already stands higher than that of any of his predecessors," Herzen wrote in *The Bell* on April 1, 1861. He eulogized not only "the Tsar-Liberator" but his brother Grand Duke Constantine, credited with a large share in the defeat of the final efforts by the reactionary part of the gentry to block an effective reform. There was one group for whom the event had special meaning: the aged survivors of the Decembrists greeted the edict as the fulfillment of their dreams and a vindication of their youthful strivings.

While for the moment society applauded, the government had serious apprehension about the reaction of the people, whether the mostly illiterate masses would greet the edict as a boon or be outraged by all the *buts* and *not yets* attached to their freedom. Though the law was signed on February 19, its nationwide promulgation was prudently delayed until March 5, which fell during Lent, thus minimizing the chance that the peasants would greet it, whether in approval or from disappointment, by the greatest alcoholic explosion in the history of Russia. Throughout March the emperor's manifesto was read before village assemblies. It did trigger quite a number of peasant disorders, since many serfs could not understand why, if they had been liberated, they would have to go on discharging their obligations to their former masters as of old for two more years. Rumors were current that the tsar would soon grant his peasant subjects a second, "real" freedom or that the landlords and officials were deceiving the people about his benevolent intentions. But while the disturbances were widespread, they were far from reaching the proportions of anything resembling a nationwide uprising. Where it took place the peasants' resistance was passive in its nature, refusal to go on working for the landlord, demonstrations with speakers calling for the officials to produce the tsar's real charter of freedom, et cetera. It was while trying to disperse one such demonstration that an irresponsible officer ordered his troops to open fire on an unarmed crowd in the village of Bezdna, which led to more than one hundred casualties. Elsewhere recalcitrant peasants were subdued by the lash and imprisonments. But despite such brutal measures, the Russian people did not attempt "to raise the axe." Suspicious of the landlords and officials, the peasants retained their faith in the tsar, and it gradually percolated down to the masses that the emperor wanted them to submit and that there would be no so-called second freedom. The peasant accepted his new status, not with enthusiasm but certainly as an improvement upon the past. In spirit rural Russia might have still been of the sixteenth century, as is well illustrated by a typical harangue of the tsar to a group of peasant elders:

> I welcome you children. . . . I have granted you freedom, but mind you well, it is freedom according to the law and not the right to be disobedient. That is why I require you above all to submit to the authorities I myself have established. You must scrupulously fulfill your obligations. I desire that where the agreements [between the peasants and the landlords] have not yet been reached, that they be so promptly by the date set by me. After they have been concluded . . . do not expect any new freedom or further concessions. Do you hear me? Do not listen to any rumors, or what others may try to persuade you. Believe only in what I have told you. And now go in peace. God be with you.[31]

The fact that such speeches were effective testifies how hopeless it was to try to turn the rural masses against the tsar. Even more disheartening to a radical must have been the response to the emancipation of the city proletariat with its roots still in the countryside and many of the worker-serfs indentured to industrial labor. In both St. Petersburg and Moscow there were mass demonstrations in honor of the ruler, and while many suspected behind them the discreet hand of the police, the fact is the urban masses would remain loyal and hostile to anything smacking of revolutionary propaganda until the very end of Alexander's reign.

In the face of such unpromising attitudes, from their point of view, the would-be-revolutionaries refused to lose heart. Their optimism touched on two premises, one which was to prove largely fallacious and the other largely justified. The first one was based on the belief that the peasants' acquiescence in their very imperfect freedom was based on their ignorance and could not withstand the test of time. Surely by 1863, when the land agreement would have come into force, the rural masses would have come to realize that they had been cheated and that the vaunted Emancipation had imposed upon them a heavier economic burden while at the same time giving them in many cases less land than they had held as serfs. Perhaps Russia would raise the axe in the spring of 1863.

The other premise behind revolutionary optimism was more involved and at the same time quite perspicacious: the alliance between the regime and the intelligentsia was by its very nature temporary. It had been based upon the educated Russians' belief that as long as the emperor was working for the reform, however flawed its concept, to oppose him would have meant to play into the hands of the reaction. But now that the common objective had been achieved, the intelligentsia, its outlook shaped by the repression and humiliations the intellectual community had endured for thirty years before 1855, had to revert to its natural posture, that of dissent. Gratitude is a rare commodity in politics. What educated Russians really desired in the way of further reforms was incompatible with the autocratic nature of the system. To men like the "Russian from the provinces," only a revolution could cleanse the nation. The very acquiescence with which the masses received their phony emancipation showed how necessary was a violent upheaval to shake the people out of their servile stupor. One could not continue to live calmly in a society where millions accepted scraps of freedom instead of demanding the real thing and where they found it quite natural that the head of state should address grown up men as "Children." He was sure that with the alleged emancipation on the statute book, the youth would become further radicalized and Russian society revert to that deep feeling of shame and humiliation it experienced during the last years of Nicholas's reign. Then it was accompanied by a feeling of impotence, but now, with the government itself having destroyed the foundation of the old order, society's rage would no longer be stifled by fear.

Insofar as the young were concerned, this was sound psychology. And the older generation of radicals was soon ready to sound the revolutionary tocsin. Six weeks after Herzen had hailed Alexander as the Tsar-Liberator, in the June 15 *Bell*, Ogarev struck a very different note: "The Emancipation law was written for the officials. . . . It was written for the robbers and not for the robbed. . . . The peasants *have not* been freed. . . . old serfdom has given way to a new one, in fact serfdom has not been abolished. *The people have been deceived by the tsar.*"

In April 1861 Michael Shelgunov, a thirty-seven-year-old official of the Ministry of State Lands and in his free time a radical journalist (the bureaucrat part-time revolutionary figure was not too rare in those days), wrote with the help of a friend, poet Michael Mikhailov, an inflammatory political pamphlet. Printed by Herzen's Free Russian Press in London, some six hundred copies of the pamphlet found their way to Russia in July, and in September they were distributed through the mails as well as by hand. Entitled *To the Young Generation,* this was one of the first revolutionary appeals to appear in major Russian cities in what would become in the next two years a veritable flood of underground pamphlets against the government. *To the Young Generation* was probably the longest of these proclamations and most revealing of the mentality of those radicals who were now ready to grope their way toward a conspiracy to overturn the regime.

Significantly it began by quoting some revolutionary verses by Ryleyev. Then the authors explained why the moment was propitious for a revolution: "The regime has not realized that by abolishing serfdom it has undermined the imperial system. The emperor was strong only as long and insofar as he could depend on the landowners. . . ." With its social and political basis gone, the imperial regime would try to appease the growing dissatisfaction by some temporary concessions, but in fact it cares nothing for the people: ". . . for its own interests it is ready to ruin the future of the entire country. Some hundreds of scoundrels don't care a hoot for the happiness of sixty million!"

And so the authors addressed their appeal to the young.

Only in you we see the people ready to sacrifice their own interests for the good of the country. . . . We consider you as the only ones who can save Russia. You are her real strength, you are the natural leaders of the nation. It is you who should explain to the people and the army the evil and harm being done to us by the emperor's power.

The peasant reform, the broadside asserts, was of course a fraud.

In proclaiming it the tsar has shown his contempt of the whole nation and of its most advanced element, that is, the best educated, most honest and able part of Russian society, the national party. The whole business was done in deepest secrecy. The reform was decided upon by the tsar and the landlords. The people had no share in it, the press was not allowed to breathe a word on the subject. The tsar gave the people this [alleged] freedom, the way one tosses a bone to an ill-tempered dog, to distract it so it would not bite.[32]

Of course, as with most revolutionary propaganda, certain inconsistencies and liberties were taken with the facts. The Emancipation was a fraud according to the authors, but elsewhere they asserted that by adopting the edict the regime had sounded its own death knell. Also, it was more than questionable whether the national party of which the proclamation spoke ever existed and did really comprise what was best in society, the young intelligentsia. Moreover, it was simply untrue to say that the drafting of the Emancipation law took place completely in secrecy and that the press could not write about it.

When it comes to raising the axe the authors are quite matter of fact: "We will not hesitate if in order to achieve our goals and to distribute land among the peasants it should become necessary to cut the throats of one hundred thousand landowners." In any case the landed gentry were parasites and Russia would be better off without them.

While *To the Young Generation* is unambiguous about the necessity of overthrowing the regime, it does not offer any concrete proposals about the type of government Russia should have following the revolution. Of one thing its authors are sure: her political system should not imitate that of Europe. "We are a backward nation, and therein lies our salvation. We ought to bless destiny that we have not lived the life of Europe. . . . Why cannot Russia create something quite new, something unknown even to America? We not only can but must. There are elements of our national life entirely unknown to Western Europeans." And the main element of this alleged originality of Russian national life was, of course, the peasant commune. In new Russia, there should be no private owners of land. Every citizen, and here was an unmistakable variant of Pestel's idea (though the writer could not have been acquainted with his *Pravda*), should be inscribed in one of the rural communes, having a share of the land it owns collectively. But other than that and beyond saying that government should be elective and limited, the proclamation was extremely vague on the constitution of postrevolutionary Russia. And for all of its detestation of hereditary monarchy, it was not clear that it would disappear, for there is a puzzling postulate: "We demand that the expenses of the imperial family be reduced."

Their formula for the revolution was quite simple. When the people rise and the regime sends it troops against the peasants, the army should turn its weapons on the oppressors, rather than on their brothers. Let the "national party," now defined as "the young generation of all the classes" agitate among the peasants and soldiers and persuade them how easy it would be to overturn the established order: "There are millions of us against a few hundred scoundrels." Let the young form clandestine circles to prepare for the struggle and, if need be, to die for the cause in the manner of their predecessors of December 14, 1825.

By the time *To the Young Generation* began to circulate in St. Petersburg and Moscow there were already other illegal pamphlets being passed from hand to hand among the young intelligentsia and students. Most of them indeed were the work of small clandestine circles and printed in Russia, where and by whom has never been established in some cases. The publication called *The Great Russian* (Velikorus) appeared in three separate installments between July and September 1861. Though its tone in general was more moderate than that of *To the Young Generation, The Great Russian* must have been, from the point of view of the authorities even more alarming.

Its first issue struck the already familiar theme that the Emancipation was fraudulent unless corrected and would lead to a vast peasant uprising. Society must undertake the task of reform by itself, since the government "does not understand anything, being stupid and ignorant."[33] If the educated classes prove impotent, then the patriots would be constrained to call upon the people to rise with all the lamentable consequences which must follow.

The second broadside filled in some details of the above analysis: the peasants are currently divided into two groups. One would be content to receive the land which they had cultivated as serfs, if they were freed from the necessity of paying for it and other obligations. As against this moderate element, the other group wanted not only their allotments, but the land which had belonged to the landowners, that is, the latter are to be completely expropriated. This division among the peasants was duplicated by one among the patriots. Some wanted to preserve the hereditary monarchy, provided it became constitutional and granted representative institutions and full civic freedom. Others demanded the overthrow of the system and a republic, "an easy task in view of the frustrations of the peasants, dissatisfaction among the landlords, the disenchantment of the educated class and the financial bankruptcy [of the state]." The committee responsible for *The Great Russian* was willing to give the emperor a chance: let him summon the people's representatives to adopt a constitution. If he refuses, he must go!

These two features, a handful of people professing to speak for an allegedly widespread movement and the call upon the emperor to summon a constituent assembly, would be quite common with revolutionary organizations for the rest of the century.

What makes *The Great Russian* fairly unique in the revolutionary literature from the time of the Decembrists to that of Lenin is its stand on the national issue. It demands the *unconditional* liberation of Poland, something which even Pestel was unwilling to concede. "Our rule over Poland is maintained only by armed force." This leads to ruinous expenses on the army, but above all it is immoral and covers Russia with dishonor in the eyes of Europe. "The Poles will be satisfied by nothing less than complete independence. . . . And our own national pride, love for our people, and financial considerations also demand this."

There were other Russians at the time, not exclusively among the radicals, who were friendly to the Polish cause, but then the anonymous authors adopted a position which no other Russian opponent of the imperial system, whether of the tsarist or Soviet variety—not even Lenin and not in our days Solzhenitsyn—would be willing to endorse without *buts* and *ifs:* they are ready to grant independence to the Ukraine.

. . . The population of southern Russia [should] be given full freedom to dispose of its destiny by its own will. . . . If it wants to separate itself completely, let it be so. . . . We Great Russians are strong enough to live by ourselves. Proud of our might we have no need ignobly to seek artificial greatness by retaining within our state by force other civilized nations.

By the fall of 1861 the clandestine pamphlet campaign was in full swing. When writing about a minor character in his *Possessed,* Dostoyevsky was to recall the scene: "In his youth through his hands passed whole packages of *The Bell* and of the proclamations, and though he would have been scared even to open them, he would have considered it utterly base to refuse to circulate them."[34] Most of the revolutionary proclamations repeated familiar themes: the fraudulent character of the Emancipation law, the imminence of a peasant uprising, the need for Russia to become a constitutional state and/or a republic. The furthest escalation of revolutionary rhetoric was reached in a bloodcurdling broadside issued in the spring of 1862, by a body calling itself grandiosely The Central Revolutionary Committee, in actual fact a group of four young students. Entitled *Young Russia*, it was written by nineteen-year-old Peter Zaichnevsky. It included a withering critique of all the past and current recipes for political change. They were branded as being pusillanimous and falling short of what was actually required. In their place *Young Russia* offered one solution: revolution. "A bloody and ruthless revolution which must drastically change all the existing social institutions and eliminate partisans of the present order." It goes without saying that the goal of the revolution would be a socialist and republican Russia with communal ownership of all the means of production. But the revolution must also destroy marriage, "an institution thoroughly immoral, contrary to the principle of sexual equality," and the family "which is an obstacle to the development of mankind." Also to be eliminated are, of course, churches, monasteries, "those dens of dissipation, shelters for all sorts of bums and parasites."[35]

In retrospect it is clear, as it could not be to the imperial authorities, appalled and bewildered by this sudden explosion of anonymous subversive literature, that most of the pamphlet campaign represented a fad, revolutionary excitement among the young, rather than serious conspiratorial activity. As the Decembrists in their earlier phase, so these young men spun their plots largely out of "boredom, their young minds chafing from inactivity. Though grown-up men, like adolescents they plunged into madcap games." Behind the inflammatory rhetoric it is easy to discern a feeling of frustration: the expected vast peasant uprising failed to materialize and the peasants' faith in the tsar stood like an iron barrier between Russia and revolution. Those grandiose designs for widespread agitation among the peasants and soldiers would remain for the time being on paper.

Yet these symptoms of revolutionary excitement among the young were bound to radicalize the older generation of the intelligentsia and make it shamefaced about its initial enthusiasm over the Emancipation. Insofar as they had a serious content, some of the proclamations expanded on themes dear to the leaders of the radical cause, such as Herzen and Chernyshevsky. Thus there was the obvious fear of the authors of *To the Younger Generation* that for all of its iniquities the emancipation law might work and Russia would be propelled onto the path of peaceful and prosaic reform already traversed by the West. And inevitably this peaceful evolution must end in capitalism and the rule of the bourgeoisie, with its hateful materialistic outlook on life. The Russian peasant, with his instinctive craving for socialism and democracy, would then be transformed into the worker, and as Herzen had already gloomily opined, "the worker of all countries will grow into the bourgeois."[36]

It is therefore not surprising that the volatile patriarch of Russian radical thought (all of forty-nine, he was nevertheless viewed as such by the young) would by the summer of 1861 repudiate his spring enthusiasm for the Galilean and Tsar-Liberator. He now exclaimed,

> Oh, if my words could reach you, tiller and sufferer of Russian soil, you whom that Russia, the one of lackeys holding you in contempt. . . . If you could hear me I would teach you to despise the [alleged] spirtual shepherds put over you by the Petersburg Synod and the *German tsar.* . . . You hate and fear your landlord and your priest and you are right. But you still believe in the tsar, and the bishops. . . . Don't! The tsar is on the side of the landowners. They are his kind of people. . . . Through his phony emancipation the emperor has shown himself in his true light to the people . . . [and then ordered] shootings and floggings.[37]

Quite an evolution within four months in Herzen's views.

Some manifestoes (obviously not those like *Young Russia*) mirrored, even if in extravagant form and brazen language, the hopes and aspirations of the more progressive elements of society, thus *The Great Russian* with its plea for a constitution and representative institutions. Even its stand on the Polish issue, though extreme, reflected the spirit of the times, one of those rare and brief periods when Russian chauvinism appeared to have been subdued in the general striving for freedom.

Perhaps even more important than its effect on society was the impact that the outburst of revolutionary literature had on the regime. The authorities refused to panic; from their point of view the turbulence among the youth was not viewed as seriously as would have been more violent disturbances among the peasants. It was the case of a handful of agitators, influencing at most a few thousand immature minds, as against riots and uprisings which might have affected millions.

From the conservative point of view, it was the universities, which in view of the scandalous license prevailing there were obviously the main source of social malaise. In May 1861 the government decided to restore some semblance of discipline among the students. It banned unauthorized student assemblies; the self-help societies and libraries were henceforth to be controlled by faculty councils; and a limit was put on the number who were to attend institutions of higher learning without paying tuition. The result was predictable: when the fall semester opened Moscow and St. Petersburg universities became scenes of student disorders. These developed along the lines all too familiar: tumultuous meetings where the speakers demanded the abolition of the repressive rules, boycotting the lectures of unpopular professors, and finally mass demonstrations both within the precinct of the schools, and in front of the homes of academic and government officials. In St. Petersburg there was a march on the residence of the university curator, in Moscow on that of the governor general. The authorities' and some professors' attempts to mollify the frenzied young men also met the kind of reactions one might expect. A very popular St. Petersburg professor remonstrating with the demonstrators that they were doing great harm to their school and to the cause of learning received this classical answer: "What does learning have to do with this, Alexander Vasilievich? We are deciding important social issues of the day."[38] The students were finally required to sign declarations pledging good behavior, the majority of them did so. Thereupon three hundred or so diehards ". . . decided to march *en masse* to the university building, attack those who signed pledges, seize from them those documents, and tear them up right on the premises."[39] Here the police and the army intervened. There were mass arrests, and some hundreds of rioters found themselves in the Kronstadt and Petropavlovsk fortresses. Thereupon, in a gesture of solidarity a number of young professors offered their resignations. A very similar sequence of events took place in Moscow. The two universities were ordered closed for the balance of the academic year.

The government soon recovered its sense of proportion. The emperor was displeased by the clumsy handling of the young men's grievances. Several of the responsible officials, including the minister of education, were dismissed and replaced by men who were progressives and would confirm their reputations as such. The arrested students were soon released, and the poorer among them granted subsidies to enable them to continue with their education. It was noticeable that the attitude of the urban masses during the disturbances was distinctly hostile toward the students, with rumors circulating that the "young gentlemen" wanted to restore serfdom. Even if the riots were an indirect expression of political dissent, quantitatively they were very far from posing a real threat.

But that in itself was a challenge to the radical camp. The government, wrote Herzen on November 1, 1861, in *The Bell,* had shown itself to be a "gang of scoundrels, robbers, and male prostitutes." And he continued with what was both wishful thinking and a preview of things to come:

From all parts of our enormous country—from the Don and the Urals, from the Volga to the Dnieper—one hears groans, one hears the growing murmur. This is just the beginning of the roar of a tidal wave which after that oppressive period of calm, boils up, pregnant with storm. *To the people, to the people*—there is your place, you exiles from seats of learning. Show that you will become fighters for the Russian people. You have begun a new era. You have understood that the time of whispers, discreet criticisms and [of reading] forbidden books has passed. Glory to you our young brothers and our blessings. Oh, if you only knew how our hearts beat excitedly! How we were close to tears when we read about the *student days* in Petersburg.

As yet few of the young rebels were ready to heed Herzen's call. Unlike the 1870s when there would be a mass movement of students and young intelligentsia to the people, most of the contemporary radicals were extremely diffident about their ability to communicate with the peasant masses. Still, their brief detention in prisons like the Petropavlovsk fortress, with its suggestive memories of the Decembrists who had been held there, acted upon the students like an intoxicant. Also there were other arrests. In its pursuit of the instigators of the campaign of subversion, the government was providing the radical camp with its first martyrs. The poet Michael Mikhailov who circulated and possibly contributed to the writing of *To the Young Generation* was denounced by an agent provocateur. A general's son and himself a former officer, Vladimir Obruchev was caught distributing *The Great Russian.* Both were sentenced to terms at hard labor and Siberian exile, where Mikhailov was to die before long. Their fate aroused sympathy not only among the intelligentsia but also within official circles, especially in view of the young men's gallant behavior in refusing to name their accomplices. This was in telling contrast to the attitude of the masses as displayed during the public degradation—the so-called civic execution of Obruchev prior to his being dispatched in chains to Siberia. The prisoner, kneeling in front of the gallows, had his sentence read to him, and then the executioner broke a sword over his head. The crowd which witnessed this barbarous rite was composed mostly of workers and artisans of St. Petersburg and was in an ugly mood. There were shouts that the culprit for his disloyalty to the tsar should be hanged or at least flogged; another vivid demonstration of the chasm separating the radicals from the object of their hopes and solicitude—the people.

But far from discouraging them this fact only strengthened the determination of those who believed in the necessity of a violent solution. Obviously the longed-for revolution would not come of itself—for the moment the masses had refused to raise the axe. All the more reason to create a clandestine organization which must hasten and prepare for the day when the scales would fall off the eyes of the peasants and they would be able to see how grossly they had been deceived.

This logic was expanded in an article in *The Bell* of September 15, 1861, signed by "one of many," its anonymous author almost certainly the twenty-seven-year-old Nicholas Serno-Solovievich. A man made in the mold of the more radical Decembrists, Serno had resigned from government service and was currently the proprietor of a Petersburg bookstore and rental library which was the gathering place for young political malcontents. In his article, he admitted that the current flurry of political excitement among the educated class was largely deceptive. In fact, most of its members were filled with servility toward the government and cared only for their own selfish interests and careers. There was a small minority among society which held with the people, but alas, it did not have any ties with it.

Good intentions of the minority are ineffective in view of its weakness, and the people [peasants] lack any initiative. . . . For a nation which has been enslaved from time immemorial, there is no other way of overthrowing oppression than through secret societies. They bring up fighters, unite dispersed [revolutionary] forces, prepare the general movement. Without them the masses will not rise, or if they do they would do so unprepared and could not prevail against the enemy who is organized.

The Decembrists, continues Serno, made the cardinal error of not involving the people in their activities. The new revolutionary conspiracy must be nationwide:

One must use propaganda, write a lot, and in a way which would be understood by the people. One must have clandestine presses, circulate printed stuff among the peasants and soldiers . . . have secret cells in the regiments . . . establish ties with the Old Believers, Cossacks, monks . . . influence above all the military, gain adherents among the civil servants. . . . [The conspiracy] ought to have its own commercial and industrial enterprises and accumulate financial resources.

It was in 1861 that there first germinated on Russian soil the idea so essential to communism of a revolutionary party; one which not only seeks political and social change but also believes in and works for revolution as a goal in itself; a party that not only professes to speak for the people but also endeavors to activate and mold the masses and lead them in the ultimate struggle. In Serno's manifesto is also a preview of the concept of permanent revolution which Trotsky formulated and Lenin applied in 1917. Serno rejected out of hand the idea that his camp should strive for just a constitution for Russia. Certainly, a constitution would make the revolutionaries' task easier. They could carry on their conspiratorial and propaganda activities more easily, but "we know that a constitution is not our final goal nor the last word."

What in the twentieth century would become possible seemed for the 1860s a fantastic dream, a product of its proponents' frustration that the masses had not risen rather than of sober political thinking. Therefore, one had to find people and recruit them for the kind of conspiracy Serno had in mind. Here again his and his fellow zealots' concept was to influence profoundly the future of the revolutionary movement: what was important was to have a revolutionary organization no matter how numerically weak it might be in the beginning. The rest would largely take care of itself. The mere existence of an underground group and its subversive activity, even if at first on a small scale, would have a disproportionately significant effect on the regime. It would have to abandon its phony reforms and have recourse to repression. And so let it increase repression tenfold. Let it press harder on the universities, intensify censorship, proclaim martial law, practice terror! It would thus alienate and exasperate ever larger strata of the population: "The experience of ages teaches that a [revolutionary] party becomes stronger the more it is persecuted. Those who fall in the struggle become [in the eyes of society] martyrs and saints. Their suffering is a hundredfold more valuable for the cause than their actual achievements." Besides, adds the author, remembering perhaps that that was hardly the case under Nicholas, the present regime is so inept that it could never apply repression systematically and effectively.

By the time this fiery manifesto was printed, there was already in existence a nucleus of the conspiracy which would try to put its preachings into practice, with Serno-Solovievich one of its members. It called itself Land and Freedom. In the course of its brief existence, Land and Freedom fell quite short of the ambitious goals its founders set for themselves. They never quite succeeded in making it more than a loose confederation of conspiratorial circles, most of which engaged in discussion and pamphleteering, rather than in effective revolutionary activities. Nor did Land and Freedom ever surface in a major insurrectionary coup such as December 14. As the wave of revolutionary excitement began to abate after 1863, most of its members abandoned conspiracy and turned to more prosaic occupations and in due course some of them achieved high position in the official world. Quite a few of the alumni of the revolutionary classes of 1861 to 1863 would become eventually ministers, generals, and senators. But others paid for their youthful beliefs with years of imprisonment, exile, or even their lives.

The device-name of the conspiracy came from an editorial by Ogarev in *The Bell.* Having asked in its title, "What Do the People Want?" he answered, "Land and freedom." The gist of his argument was not nearly as uncompromising as that of Serno-Solovievich's. Ogarev's was essentially a prospectus for a revolutionary party which aimed to enlist radicals of all varieties, ranging from constitutional monarchists to those who wanted a republic and agrarian communism. While its political program was not clear-cut, there was an unmistakable revolutionary flavor to its conclusion which called upon the masses not to waste their strength in sporadic rioting, but to "collect forces, seek out dependable men who will help with advice and will lead in word and deed . . . [men] ready to sacrifice their fortunes and lives. This way we shall be able to stand up calmly and firmly . . . against the tsar and nobles, and for communal land, national freedom, and human rights."[40]

The budding conspiracy centered around two focal points, Herzen's circle in London and that of Chernyshevsky's in St. Petersburg. Herzen, the most humane of revolutionaries, was hitherto opposed to violence and plots but now lent his enormous prestige to the undertaking. Apart from personal reasons, such as the influence of his friend Ogarev, he was increasingly disenchanted with Alexander II. This change began with the floggings and shootings which ushered in the emancipation and reached the point of revulsion at the news from Warsaw, where on several occasions Russian troops fired upon demonstrating Polish crowds. The Polish issue would now assume crucial importance for the Russian revolutionary movement.

As for Chernyshevsky, he was now a fervent proponent of a violent solution. It is not clear when, or even whether, he actually joined Land and Freedom. But then Gandhi was never formally a member of the Congress party, and Chernyshevsky's role in the Russian revolutionary movement became by 1861–62 somewhat similar to that which Gandhi would play in the struggle for Indian independence. This quite bookish man was enormously popular among the youth, young officers, and university students. They all read tremulously his lengthy disquisitions in *The Contemporary*, seeking and usually finding between the lines the desired message: the existing system, the entire reality of Russian life, was intolerable and only a revolution could regenerate the country.

Apart from propaganda, Chernyshevsky tried his hand at agitation. (The classic statement about the two given by Plekhanov which speaks volumes about the Russian revolutionary movement, and especially Communism, makes a sharp distinction between the propagandist who tries to explain many and complex ideas to a few and the agitator whose task was to infuse many with a few ideas.) It was he who undoubtedly wrote a broadside to be read among the peasants, which began with *Greetings to the Landlords' Peasants from Their Well-Wishers*. Written in a somewhat strained folksy language and quite demagogic in its content, the pamphlet listed all the real and alleged deficiencies of the Edict of Emancipation, though it also added a palpably untrue charge that under the law the landowner could chase the peasant off his allotted land. What could you expect from the tsar: he himself was a landowner! Apart from the land question, why should the Russians be denied those freedoms which all civilized nations enjoy? Elsewhere you don't have compulsory military service, the poll tax, and other burdens borne by the peasant in this country. There the people decide everything. If the English or French become displeased with their tsar, they simply tell him, "You, tsar, stop being over us; you do not please us. We are replacing you. Go in peace . . . but far away, otherwise we shall put you in jail and place you on trial for disobedience."[41] Such wonderful things could also happen in Russia too if the peasants would only unite, and once the signal was given by their well-wishers, do what they told them.

Unlike the Decembrists, who at most dabbled in it, the Land and Freedom partisans put great stress on agitation and into efforts to wean the masses from their uncritical faith in the tsar. In retrospect it is clear that such efforts had to be futile. Even had the would-be-revolutionaries disposed of a well-organized network of underground presses and been able to circulate their agitational literature on a mass scale (many of their pamphlets, like Chernyshevsky's, were intercepted by the police before they could be printed), its message would have been incomprehensible to the average peasant of the time. Perhaps he was both too uneducated and too sophisticated to heed the revolutionary appeal. Whatever grievances he had against the actual form of Emancipation, they were not connected in his mind with politics. And the villager would naturally grow suspicious when addressed in an exaggeratedly folksy language by someone who was obviously a gentleman. The same held true, though perhaps less so, of the agitation aimed at the soldiers. One of the first organizers of Land and Freedom was Nicholas Obruchev, colonel of the General Staff, who would end his career as the head of the Russian army. It was Obruchev (cousin of Vladimir) who co-authored with Ogarev an appeal to the army. Printed in the November 8 issue of *The Bell*, it urged soldiers to mutiny if and when they were called upon by the authorities to suppress peasant uprisings. "The tsar has signed an order on how and when to repress the people. Why did he get the idea to issue the order and to have it printed? It is clear he fears the people. And if a man is frightened, he is weak." What are the soldiers to do? They should refuse to obey the orders. "What will the tsar do when the soldiers refuse to put down the people? Obviously he will have to give the people land and freedom and that is all the people want. And so if the army does not turn on the people, they will get land and freedom without massacres, without a drop of blood being spilled."[42] The authors went to great lengths to examine and refute all the possible objections to disobedience. The soldier's oath could not bind him to do something inherently immoral or evil, such as shooting peasants who want their land or Poles who want national freedom. Here again more than fifty years and two disastrous wars would have to intervene before the Russian soldier would heed his rebellious countrymen's "Brothers, don't shoot" and would refuse to fire on his own people.

Equally imaginative, though also much, much ahead of their times, was the revolutionaries' overall strategy. For all of its outward might, its apparent ability to stand like a granite rock amidst surging social forces, there must come a moment when the tsarist regime would become susceptible to a frontal attack. The imposing edifice of the Nicholean system had been shaken to its foundations by the defeat in the Crimean War. Autocracy itself must then become vulnerable in the case of another foreign threat, especially if it coincided with a critical period in domestic politics. Here again Land and Freedom pioneered the idea which would become of crucial importance to Lenin and his followers: a revolutionary party must not strike at its enemy haphazardly on the spur of the moment, the way the Decembrists did and which brought them disaster. It must husband its forces and make the move only when the time is ripe, when the government, its prestige and self-assurance already undermined, finds itself on the defensive, both at home and abroad.

Such a time, the conspirators believed, would come in the spring of 1863. It was then that the two-year period of transition prescribed by the Edict of Emancipation expired, and the peasants' new status as landowners or tenants and their obligations to their former masters would have been formalized. Surely by then the peasants would see how cruelly they had been deceived, how the alleged emancipation meant less land for many, heavier financial or working obligations for all. And so Russia would finally raise the axe. In envisaging the dimensions of the uprising, the conspirators had before their eyes the tantalizing visions of the great *Jacqueries* of the past, the one led by the Don Cossack Stenka Razin in 1670–71 and especially that of Emelyan Pugachev in 1773. Both encompassed huge areas, the latter especially spreading over the lower Volga region and the Urals. In both cases regular army forces had to be brought in to suppress the rebellions and to restore order.

But, there was another reason for the revolutionaries pointing to the spring of 1863 as their target date; by that time the imperial army would be preoccupied elsewhere. There was bound to be a rebellion in Poland, and quite likely on this account a general European conflict with the empire facing, as in the Crimean War, the great powers of the West. This unabashed premise of a national disaster as a precondition of revolution is another point of similarity between Land and Freedom and the Russian Marxists of the twentieth century, who both in 1905 and in 1914 would hope for their country's defeat, considering it a lesser evil than the perpetuation of the autocratic system. Such calculations were in line with the internationalist creed of those who pursued them, the creed that proclaimed that "workers have no country" and that could be rationalized by the belief that a Russian revolution would be a prelude to a general European one. However, in the 1860s the ideas of Karl Marx were virtually unknown in Russia and played no role in radical thought. When the moment of national danger came, there would be no ideology readily available to offset the pull of Russian nationalism on the emotions of not only the masses of the people but also of the revolutionaries themselves.

In theory, the conspiracy's expectations of an upheaval in Poland and of its political consequences on Russia appeared to be well founded. The Kingdom of Poland, ruthlessly repressed under Nicholas, became after his death once again a scene of political turmoil with nationalist agitation once more in the open and demands first for autonomy and then for full independence gaining the adherence not only of the upper classes, as had been the case in 1830, but also of Jews and of the urban proletariat. As in Russia proper, the imperial government relaxed its grip and promised reform. But just as in Russia Alexander II was determined that the scope of reforms should stop short of a constitution, so in his Polish domains he would not grant what was the minimal demand of the moderate patriots: restoration of the kingdom's legislature and its internal independence, the union with the empire to be maintained as theoretically it had been before 1830 merely through the common sovereign. In addressing a gathering of nobles in Warsaw in 1856, Alexander called such aspirations "idle dreams." Instead he tried a series of palliatives, staffing the administration with natives, reopening the institutions of higher learning closed by Nicholas, and allowing greater freedom to the Catholic Church, then as now the standard-bearer of Polish nationalism. But instead of stemming the rising tide of political discontent and agitation, such measures had the opposite effect. Soon the authorities had to cope with the growing incidence of nationalist demonstrations and with assaults upon Russian officials and officers. As in the empire itself, the government's response vacillated between further concessions and repression, the difference being that in Poland revolutionary fervor was not confined to small circles of conspirators but had gripped the urban population as a whole.

The attitude toward the Polish problem had often been the litmus test of the Russian revolutionaries' real devotion to freedom. For most of the Decembrists the idea of complete Polish independence was not at all popular, and even Pestel would have Poland a satellite of Russia. But now, rather miraculously in view of the centuries' old unhappy relations between the two nations, Russian progressive opinion, not merely of the revolutionary variety, appeared friendly to the Polish cause. No one represented this attitude more strongly and genuinely than Herzen. On April 10 he had arranged a banquet in London to celebrate the proclamation of the Emancipation at which he proposed to drink a toast to the man who in his eyes was still the Tsar-Liberator. But before the guests sat down, the news reached them of the bloody events in Warsaw: a crowd of demonstrators had grown unruly; soldiers had fired on it, causing a number of deaths and other casualties. Denouncing the emperor, Herzen then raised his glass "to the full unconditional independence of Poland."

A perceptive observer of contemporary Russian society could not, however, have helped noticing that there was something quite superficial about this apparent polonophilia of its educated class. It sprang from a generally critical attitude toward the government rather than from a genuinely liberal sentiment on the national issue and the repudiation of the country's imperialist past. Chernyshevsky, who in view of his social origins and lack of an extended immersion in the West was a much better judge of his countrymen than Herzen, wrote words which are as relevant today, if not more so, than they were in 1862:

> Russia's policies until recently have been directed mainly toward expansion, and this task, which has been carried out very successfully, has weakened the real strength of our own people. We have never been able to become really civilized, nor even to have sound economic conditions, because we never had any time or resources for our domestic affairs. . . . With us the materials needed for ploughs and sickles have always been used to forge swords and spears, and that is why up to now we have not been able even to cultivate our land properly.

This imperialism and militarism was not just the result of the government's policies. Here, as contrasted with many of his social and political ideas, Chernyshevsky was brutally realistic:

> It would be incorrect to ascribe this absorption of all of society's thoughts and resources on conquest to previous governments. *Society itself* called for and supported those [expansionist] policies of the government. . . . Let us recall how in the beginning of the late [Crimean] war, ninety-nine out of one hundred supposedly educated people exulted at the thought that we would soon capture Constantinople.[43]

Of what use could Constantinople be to Russia—he asked and, answering his own question, notes, again very astutely, that it was sheer irrational emotion rather than any idea of material gains for themselves or for their country which had turned his fellow nationals into chauvinists. Had Russia in fact won the war, she would be poorer than she was, she would have had to expend huge sums to maintain a large army in the Balkans, this leading to further troubles and wars, and so on ad infinitum. But even Chernyshevsky was not entirely realistic in analyzing this root cause of his nation's historical predicament; he believed that the high point of Russia's imperialism and of its popular acceptance had passed.

It was this belief which led the conspirators to postulate the feasibility of synchronizing the Polish uprising with a peasant one at home. In the October 1, 1861, issue of *The Bell* Ogarev wrote:

> We beg the Poles not to start things prematurely [just] with their own forces, which would prove insufficient. Such a harmful step would deprive Russia of the help she expects from Poland and would for long postpone their common liberation. . . . The Polish [secret] society and [similar] Lithuanian, Ukrainian and Russian societies should be parts of a common front and should act together.

It was perhaps rather naive on the part of a conspiracy thus to advertise publicly its strategy, enabling all, including the government, to know in advance its plans.

The Imperfect Freedom: The 1860s and 1870s

But then Land and Freedom was a revolutionary party which never succeeded in fully organizing itself—a conspiracy which never carried its conspiratorial activities to the point of planning, let alone attempting to seize power. Despite its activist philosophy and ambitious designs, Land and Freedom waited on events somewhat in the manner of their revolutionary predecessors who, having brought their forces to the Senate Square, on December 14, then proceeded to wait for something to happen. Unlike the Decembrists, the revolutionaries of the early sixties knew what they were waiting and hoping for: the simultaneous peasant and Polish uprisings. But until these uprisings in fact materialized, their activities were to be confined to the recruitment of members, propaganda, and agitation. Here then was the inherent paradox, one which would beguile Russian revolutionaries until 1917: they proclaimed the tsarist regime to be iniquitous, decadent, and inept; yet somehow they also regarded it as almost immune to a direct assault. It was only a foreign defeat, a spontaneous popular uprising, or a self-inflicted wound, such as the granting of a constitution, which could make the autocracy vulnerable and clear the path for a revolutionary party. Until then its role remained that of a prompter, rather than a main actor. This attitude would of course clash with the revolutionary zealot's passion for action *now*. And this clash in turn helps explain why beginning with 1866 the conspirators would increasingly be tempted to resort to individual terror as a means of resolving both their political and personal dilemmas. The revolution-in-waiting model as developed first by Land and Freedom would not lack its critics, such as Peter Tkachev who wrote in the 1870s: "To prepare a revolution is not up to the revolutionary. It is being prepared all the time by exploiters, capitalists, landowners. . . . The revolutionary does not *prepare* but *makes* the revolution. Then make it. Do it right away. It is criminal to be indecisive, to delay."[44]

Land and Freedom proposed to wait. Quite apart from its premises, it had no choice, for it never achieved the political and organizational cohesion and enough members which would enable it to move beyond blueprints and propaganda and into action. Theoretically its structure was built upon interconnecting cells, each with five members. Every member in turn was supposed to recruit four more, his identity thus to be known by only eight people. The directing group, which rather grandiosely called itself the Central Committee, was composed of brothers Nicholas and Alexander Serno-Solovievich, Colonel Nicholas Obruchev, Alexander Sleptsov, an official of the Imperial Chancery, and the poet-journalist Vasili Kurochkin. Total membership of the conspiracy was never impressive, somewhere between one and three thousand, the bulk of it recruited from the young, alumni of the university disorders of the fall of 1861, students in military academies, junior officials, this time not from the elite Guards, as with the Decembrists, but mostly from the army's specialized branches, notably artillery. Since Land

and Freedom was never destined to stage a major revolutionary coup, most of its rank-and-file members were never unmasked by the police, and even some of its notables, on whom there were extensive files in the Third Department and who were kept under its secret surveillance, escaped harm, probably because they found influential protectors within the government. As in the case of the Decembrists, there were people of high standing in the regime who tended to look through their fingers at the subversive activities of their young subordinates and acquaintances, viewing them as the results of misguided idealism and youth's natural ebullience. "Such a small group," an indulgent police official was to say in 1895, after the arrest of a number of St. Petersburg Marxists, Lenin among them, "something might come out of it in fifty years." In addition, in the early sixties, there was a certain bond, if not of sympathy then of understanding, between the more moderate of the revolutionaries and the progressive element within the imperial bureaucracy. Both shared the desire to keep Russia moving along the path of reforms and ultimately toward a constitution. The latter group included such high-ranking officials as the emperor's brother, Grand Duke Constantine Nikolayevich; Minister of War Dmitri Milyutin, who must have known at least about some of the extracurricular activities of Nicholas Obruchev, one of his most promising officers; Prince Alexander Suvorov, governor of St. Petersburg and in his youth a Decembrist, now very much au courant with what was going on in the radical circles of the capital. Under an autocracy the line separating the revolutionary from the reformer became at times somewhat blurred, and the latter would often feel that political dissent, if kept within certain bounds, could be of great help to his own cause.

However, for all of its numerical weakness, Land and Freedom could damage, and perhaps fatally, the cause of reform. In view of the open advertisement of its existence and inflammatory goals by *The Bell* and by underground pamphlets in Russia, the government might have decided that it faced a really well-organized and dangerous conspiracy, that political discontent among the educated class could never be appeased through further concessions but had to be dealt with by police measures. Political repression in turn was bound to widen the gap between the regime and society. This was of course what the extreme among the radicals hoped for, and in the course of 1862 they were to get their wish.

In April of that year three Russian officers stationed in Poland were apprehended for spreading revolutionary propaganda among their soldiers, court-martialled, and sentenced to death. One month later disaster struck St. Petersburg. There was a series of fires of unexplained origin which raged in the poorer districts of the capital, where workers, artisans, and petty tradesmen had their living and business premises. On May 28 a huge conflagration consumed the Apraxin market, with its more than two thousand shops, warehouses, and stalls.

Immediately there was an outcry among the lower classes that this was arson perpetrated by the Polish revolutionaries and/or their Russian associates. What the government subsequently felt constrained to do is succinctly and characteristically described by the official tsarist historian of the period:

> The investigating commission appointed by His Majesty did not succeed in tracing those directly responsible for the arson. But through the depositions before the commission it was established that the [adult education] schools conducted by various literary people and students for workers and artisans tried to instill the latter with subversive teachings. These Sunday schools established within the past two years in great numbers by private persons were run without any official supervision whatsoever. What was also established were the links between the London [political] emigrés and collaborators of several St. Petersburg journals. Therefore His Majesty was pleased to decree: pending a review of their status, all Sunday schools to be shut down and the publication of *The Contemporary* and of *The Russian Word* to be suspended for eight months. Simultaneously there was organized within the Third Department of His Majesty's Own Chancery a special commission for tracking down the disseminators of underground pamphlets and other revolutionary literature. This commission ordered the arrest of a few people, among them Chernyshevsky, the most influential publicist of the so-called "progressive camp." . . .[45]

Obviously, it need not have been arson. Fires in the lower-class districts, with their incredibly crowded conditions and utter neglect of any precautions, were a frequent occurrence. Someone has estimated that the typical wooden building of those days would be accidentally set on fire on the average of once every eight years. And if it was arson, it is hardly likely that it would have been revolutionaries who put the torch to the dwellings of the poor. In part the radicals were victims of their own scheme: the masses, on behalf of which they professed to speak and work, vented their rage and frustration against them rather than the authorities. The latter felt that finally they had a pretext, as well as the sanction of public opinion, to proceed against those who they believed were behind all the revolutionary agitation of the last two years. But while the government's suspicions were well founded, no evidence could be found to incriminate seriously Chernyshevsky and Serno-Solovievich, who was arrested with him on July 7 and lodged in the Petropavlovsk prison. All that could be genuinely established was that they had been in contact with Herzen and his group, something which was true of most prominent Russians of the period, including some highly placed personages. They remained confined in the fortress for two years, awaiting trial by the Senate, while the Third Department was forging proofs of their guilt.

The arrests, especially Chernyshevsky's, aroused great indignation among the educated. To many, even quite conservative people, he was Russia's leading social thinker, and no one could impugn the genuineness of his idealism. This was another reason why the authorities would not try and condemn him until the radical cause had been discredited, even within the intelligentsia.

Brutal as it occasionally was, political repression under Alexander II never could reach the degree of efficiency it had achieved under Nicholas. So it should be no surprise that the novel Chernyshevsky wrote while in prison was routinely passed by the censor and published quite legally and under his own name. Even more than his explicitly social and political writings, *What Is to Be Done?* would become the bible and inspiration of whole generations of radicals, and its title would be borrowed by Lenin for his most important work, where he set the foundations of Bolshevism. Its bracing, if naive and artistically inept, story of the new men and women, their rejection of the stifling social conventions, and of their search for self-fulfillment would be deciphered by the young as a call for revolution. For all his disenchantment with the people, Chernyshevsky reaffirmed here his faith that soon the handful of apostles of the new order would succeed. "We did not see these men six years ago . . . but it matters little what we think of them now; in a few years we shall appeal to them. We shall say, 'Save us,' and whatever they say will be done by all." And so it would be, though not in 1870, which Chernyshevsky set as the new date for the expected revolution once it had failed to materialize in 1863, but in 1917.

The mood of panic occasioned by the fires passed, and for the time being the government would not try to turn the clock back. Beginning with the spring of 1862, there was a significant change in the tone of the regime's pronouncements and attitudes. What returns in the ruling circles is a certain mood of exasperation: would reforms ever be able to exorcise the revolutionary virus from Russian life! The more conservative of the emperor's advisers would never get rid of the conviction that the country was menaced by a widespread conspiracy, of which the arrested intellectuals and the banned journals constituted but a small part. This latent conspiracy, they felt, had as its fellow travellers practically the whole educated class, for which every reform became but an occasion for fresh demands on the government, demands which eventually would threaten the regime's and the country's survival. Hence the tendency to lash out at the slightest manifestations of open dissent. This was vividly demonstrated in the case of the assembly of nobility of the Tver province when it respectfully petitioned the tsar that the financial burden of the serfs' emancipation should be shared by all classes rather than just the peasants. This proposal was accompanied by a humble request that the regime should seek the advice of elected representatives of the nation concerning further measures of reform. Perfectly legal in its form and loyal in its tone, this petition was answered by the imprisonment of thirteen of its proponents, all substantial landowners who were kept in jail for five months and then exiled to their estates.

The Imperfect Freedom: The 1860s and 1870s

The government now tended to sniff treason in the most moderate and innocuous form of political dissent. As a consequence society was bound to grow skeptical of the government's ability to regenerate Russia. This mutual disenchantment set the stage for the ultimate tragedy of the reign which had begun so auspiciously. Unlike the old regime whose treatment of its subjects had in it something of a jail warden's attitude toward his charges, Alexander's expected to earn the people's trust and gratitude, and naturally it became first puzzled and then enraged when its reforms were rewarded by a growing wave of disaffection and sedition. The government failed to perceive one basic flaw in its behavior: it was similar to that of an indulgent but not overly sensitive parent who while ready to lavish gifts on his adolescent child, refuses him what the latter desires and needs most, freedom. The tsarist government also failed to understand that for most educated Russians this freedom was not necessarily or mainly synonymous with a constitutional system and representative institutions. What comes out from the pronouncements and aspirations of representative men of the period, including the most conservative among them, is their craving for *glasnost'*, the term best, if somewhat freely, translated as "open society." *Glasnost'* implied a government which, even if its form was autocratic, would operate in full view of society and with due regard for public opinion rather than having its policies formulated in secrecy by a small clique of officials, in its own way a sort of conspiracy. Open society meant also that what a person could and could not do, say, and write would be determined by the law and not the tsar's or some bureaucrat's whim. It might seem that the concept of *glasnost'* as such was incongruous, if not naive: how can personal liberty be safeguarded except through constitutional guarantees; how can the government pay heed to the people's needs except under democratic institutions? However odd the idea may strike someone brought up in the Western tradition, that freedom and authoritarianism need not be mutually exclusive has been a persistent motif in Russian political thought. It has been encountered with the Slavophiles. It is found today in Solzhenitsyn when he writes: "It is not authoritarianism itself that is intolerable but the ideological lies that are daily foisted upon us. Not so much authoritarianism as arbitrariness and illegality, the sheer illegality of having a single overlord in each district, each province and sphere whose will decides all things."[46] In 1862 an average intelligent did not worry unduly about official ideology. Unlike now he did not even have to pretend that he believed in it. But he did chafe under "arbitrariness and illegality" and loathed the "often brutal and ignorant bureaucracy." Had the government understood the psychology of its moderate critics, had it understood that they wanted it not to abdicate its authority but above all to rule in a humane and civilized way, it would have made a giant step toward social reconciliation. There were enlightened officials who were aware of what was needed to pacify society, but they were unable to offset the influence of the tsar's reactionary advisers. And the latter had unwitting allies in the revolutionaries.

Then an event took place which was to deal a crippling blow to the cause both of revolution and of reform and to endow autocracy, at least temporarily, with new vigor and popularity. The long-awaited Polish uprising erupted in January 1863. From the point of view of the Russian revolutionary camp the uprising was premature. Representatives of the Polish nationalists had established contacts with Herzen's group in September 1862 and with the Central Committee of Land and Freedom in December and laid plans for synchronizing revolutionary activities in both countries. The Russian side insisted on both occasions that the Poles delay their move until the spring when they hoped for peasant uprisings. But the Poles refused to wait. By their precipitate action, they weakened the liberal element within the imperial administration. Its leading spokesman was Grand Duke Constantine Nikolayevich, the current viceroy of Poland, who had pleaded for a policy of moderation and reconciliation both there and in Russia. Now his counsel was no longer heeded by his brother. The government knew about the links between the Russian radicals and the Polish insurgents. On receiving the news of the rebellion, Alexander II declared, "It is the work of the revolutionary party, striving everywhere to subvert the legal order. I know this party counts on traitors within our own ranks."[47]

Without outside help the rebellion was a hopeless enterprise, much more so than the one of 1830–31. Then the Poles had a regular army and controlled at the outset the territory of the kingdom. Now they had to resort to guerrilla fighting in the countryside and some twenty to thirty thousand poorly armed partisans could hardly expect to hold out for long against over one hundred thousand regular troops. Land and Freedom had had high hopes of the insurrection triggering if not a mutiny, then large-scale desertions among the Russian garrisons in Poland, more than four hundred of whose officers were on its list of members and sympathizers. Such hopes were soon exposed as illusory. Nationalist fervor prevailed even with those who had been affiliated with the revolutionary cause. There were only a few cases of Russian soldiers and officers going over to the enemy. Land and Freedom's proclamation to the soldiers fighting in Poland "Instead of killing . . . Poles, turn your sword against the enemy—leave Poland with her stolen freedom restored and come here to the fatherland to free it from the cause of all national miseries, the imperial government" fell on deaf ears.

Even more cruelly disappointed were the expectations of large-scale peasant uprisings which were to take place following the second anniversary of the emancipation. Again the revolutionaries should have known better. In 1862 the number and intensity of disorders in the countryside was substantially lower than in the preceding year. And now rural Russia remained quiet. How ineffective Land and Freedom proved during what was to be the year of revolution is best attested to by the fact that the authorities had little occasion to search for and apprehend its members. In the province of Kazan there was an attempt to stir up the local peasants by printing a fake imperial manifesto which urged them to seize all land and fight the landowners and officials. But before the phony proclamation was even distributed, the plot was denounced to the authorities and the conspirators, among them Polish-born officers and local students, were arrested.

Conspiracies which fail leave behind them a trail of futility and appear in retrospect pathetic and amateurish. It was not only its numerical weakness which condemned the conspirators of Land and Freedom to failure. Certainly Lenin's party on the eve of the February revolution was hardly more sizable in proportion to the population of the major urban centers, although the Bolsheviks would be incomparably stronger insofar as their ideological and organizational cohesion and leadership were concerned. But the inability of the 1863 revolutionaries to make more of an impact on the events of that year can be mainly traced to one basic error in their calculations: they failed to make an allowance for the explosive force of Russian nationalism, now rekindled by the news of the Polish insurrection. The threat to the empire's power and prestige muted political and social disaffection and tended to turn even the most radical critics of the regime into its supporters. Stories were widely circulated of Polish partisans slaughtering unarmed Russian soldiers whom they surprised in their barracks. Equally jarring to the man in the street was the rebels' demand that in addition to independence Poland should recover the western provinces of the empire proper, where for all the predominance of the Polish element among the gentry and in the cities, the bulk of the population was Ukrainian and Byelorussian, hence in the contemporary view essentially Russian. Social and religious antagonisms served to exacerbate the chauvinistic reaction. It was the Polish landowners and clergy who turned the masses of their nation against the benevolent rule of the tsar and their fellow Slavs; so ran the official Russian version of the causes of the uprising. The ungrateful people, who had proved in the past incapable of governing themselves, now sought not only to revert to their anarchic ways but also to seize and rob millions of Orthodox Russians of their national and religious birthright.

The extent of this jingoistic explosion astounded the radical circles. Even Chernyshevsky, who understood his countrymen's imperialist longings, believed that in the post-Nicholas era there had been a great and salutary change in this respect. Educated men had begun to realize that Russia's greatness depended not on how many foreign lands she could conquer and dominate but on the solution of pressing domestic problems. In general, he held, nationalism, except for the peoples seeking independence and unity, was a largely spent force. The great issue of the day in Europe was that of social justice.

When it comes to material conditions, Europe is divided into two parts: one lives off the other's labor, the second by its own. It is in the interest of the first to preserve the existing order of things. . . . The other, consisting of ninety percent of the people, has an interest in effecting a change so that the laborer would enjoy all the fruits of his work, rather than seeing them enjoyed by someone else.[48]

This Marxist sounding statement bespoke a strong belief that reasonable men everywhere had come to understand that militant nationalism, militarism, et cetera, could not be genuinely popular with the masses, much as they are artificially fostered by governments to distract the people from their real needs and to perpetuate economic and social injustice.

In 1863, and in Russia, Chernyshevsky's analysis was belied by the events. The mass of the intelligentsia now ranged itself with other classes in supporting the government in the hour of national danger. Nationalist fervor was enhanced by the threat of a general European war with the empire, as in 1854–56, facing the main powers of the West. Early in the year Britain, France, and Austria addressed notes to the St. Petersburg court urging it to restore Poland's autonomy and constitution which Russia, in violation of its international obligations, had abrogated thirty years before. The imperial government's defiant answer that the rebellion must be crushed and only then might the emperor deign to examine his Polish subjects' grievances was widely applauded by public opinion and raised the patriotic fever to its highest pitch. Progressive journals, like *The Contemporary*, were now allowed to resume publication, competing with the reactionary press in professions of loyalty to the regime and in denouncing the "perfidious Poles" for their "jesuitic" designs. From London Herzen watched this chauvinist epidemic—he called it "patriotic syphilis"—with loathing and disgust. His continued pro-Polish stand cost him and his cause dearly. *The Bell*'s circulation within Russia fell precipitously, and he himself would never recover his mastery over the minds of the intellectual elite in whose eyes he was a friend of his country's enemies.

His and Chernyshevsky's place in that respect was taken over by Michael Katkov, a firebrand journalist whose attacks on the Poles and their Russian allies fit the current mood of his countrymen. One-time liberal, and in his youth a companion of such luminaries of radicalism as Belinsky, Michael Bakunin, and Herzen himself, a man of wide erudition and wide intellectual horizons, Katkov now attacked the radical cause with the violence and conviction which only one who used to be its adherent could find possible. It was not only the Poles and a few deluded Russian youths who threatened the fatherland. Russia was the target of an international conspiracy that intended to use her for its war against European civilization:

> Our foreign refugees find that Europe has passed its revolutionary apogee, that revolution there cannot succeed because of such obstacles to progress as science, civilization, freedom expressed in the rights of property and person. . . . Hence the blessed thought to choose Russia for their experiment, where in their opinion those obstacles are not strong enough or do not exist. . . . [They believe] she will let be done to her what one wills, will submit to anything that would be insufferable in any other society.[49]

This was a clever polemical thrust quite likely to sway the minds of wavering intellectuals. Instead of the now stale charges of subversion, lack of patriotism, et cetera, the radicals were identified as enemies of progress, cynically hoping to exploit Russia's backwardness for their own purposes, which in fact were quite hostile to progress.

But Katkov also engaged in outright demogoguery, exploiting the rising tide of xenophobia and religious intolerance. For the average Russian the word *Jesuit* carried much the same connotations as did *Communist* to the Americans of the 1950s. Katkov saw the Jesuits' hand in all the troubles which had afflicted Russia of late. (How the Jesuits and the Catholic Church found themselves in an alliance with an international anarchist conspiracy was never elucidated.) Those sinister, clandestine powers were also responsible for the lamentable state of Russian education and public morals, for young men were being brought up in the spirit of "atheism and cosmopolitanism," for the absurd notion that there was such a thing as the Ukrainian nation, for anything and everything which might contribute to Russia's downfall. Katkov's chauvinist preachings were so extreme that they aroused displeasure in official circles. Yet for the time being he was enormously popular, even among the groups which had traditionally suffered under official policies. In its revolutionary scenario, Land and Freedom had assigned a prominent role to the Old Believers, a schismatic offshoot of the Orthodox Church, and as such, suffering from legal disabilities and official chicaneries. Now the Old Believers, for all their grievances, hastened forth with expressions of loyalty, and their Moscow community commissioned Katkov to draft a patriotic address to Alexander II.

Even when it became clear that there would be no foreign war—the Western powers, as they had in the past and would in the future, confined their exertions on behalf of Poland to diplomatic protests—virulent nationalism kept its hold on public opinion. This was amply demonstrated in the reception accorded General Michael Muraviev. Imprisoned in his youth for membership in secret societies, he barely escaped the fate of his martyred kinsmen. Since then Muraviev had earned the reputation of a brutal and reactionary bureaucrat and in 1863 was assigned to Lithuania where the rebellion had spilled over from the Polish kingdom. Even against the general picture of ruthless severity with which the authorities had dealt with the insurgents, Muraviev's behavior stood out for its wanton barbarity.

As military governor of Lithuania, he ordered captured partisans be treated as criminals rather than prisoners of war, with many ending on the gallows or before firing squads. He also applied the policy of forcible russification: Polish landowners, even if uninvolved in the uprising, had their estates sequestered, peasants of the Catholic rite were often compelled to convert to the Russian Orthodox Church. He was of the Muravievs who hang rather than those who are hanged, boasted the brutal satrap, and history appropriately immortalized him under the name Muraviev the Hangman. Having suppressed the rebellion in his province, Muraviev upon his return to Russia was greeted as a conquering hero. Public acclaim lavished upon this victor over partisan bands and civilian population surpassed anything accorded in the past to Russia's most eminent military leaders. There were high-ranking officials, like Grand Duke Constantine and Prince Suvorov, who refused to join in the homage to "the Hangman," but they in turn were widely castigated for their unpatriotic fastidiousness. He himself, resenting such snubs, characterized the people who criticized his conduct as "cosmopolite followers of Western ideas."

Michael Muraviev's personal career epitomizes that Jekyll-and-Hyde characteristic of Russian society so apparent in 1862–63. In his youth he was a revolutionary and talented intellectual. He had shown considerable scientific ability and had been one of the authors of the statute of the Union of Welfare. Transformed in his middle years into a faithful servant of autocracy, at the crest of his career he became a brutal oppressor and xenophobe. The government itself, hitherto so hesitant and vacillating in its policies between appeasement and repression, now turned to the latter. By the summer of 1864, the rebellion had been crushed. Hundreds had been executed, thousands sentenced to hard labor and exile. And shortly after the pacification of Poland, the government, in flagrant violation of its previous assurances to the Western powers, stripped the unhappy country of the last remnants of its autonomous status.

Beyond its immediate and disastrous consequences for the radical cause in Russia, Poland's travail was also to have long-lasting effects on the future of the revolutionary movement. Its vision of revolution proved to have been a mirage, the remaining members of Land and Freedom dissolved their now-moribund organization early in 1864. Brief and ineffective as its existence had been, its legacy was to prove of great importance. Various ideological and tactical components of the defunct organization—conspiracy, socialism, populism—remained deep within Russian radicalism to re-emerge in different amalgams in future revolutionary enterprises. Lessons drawn from Land and Freedom's failure would influence those who followed in its footsteps. For a long time the revolutionary movement would eschew explicit endorsement of national self-determination for non-Russians within the empire. The hope for a spontaneous peasant uprising would die hard. It would be a recurrent theme of the Populist movement in the 1870s. At the same time, future conspiracies would tend to be both more radical and more activist than their prototype. For all of its violent rhetoric, Land and Freedom never excluded the possibility that it might accept the constitutional monarchy as an intermediate stage toward its ultimate goal of a socialist and republican Russia. Subsequent conspiracies would reject the possibility of any compromise with the existing system. They would also be more impatient in their revolutionary fervor, would carry out more direct and intense propaganda, and when that failed, would resort to terrorism.

Though it now could feel more secure and could afford to be more generous, the imperial government decided to teach the intellectual community a lesson it would not forget. Having kept him in prison for two years, the authorities finally sentenced Chernyshevsky to seven years at hard labor and thereafter to lifetime exile in Siberia. Since the Third Department had been unable to secure any proof of the writer's guilt beyond the fact that he had corresponded with the London exiles, his conviction was secured on the basis of forged evidence. Like other political criminals of the time, Chernyshevsky, before being dispatched to Siberia, had to undergo in public the savage rite of civic execution: kneeling in front of the gallows, the prisoner had a sword broken over his head, and then his sentence was read to the assembled crowd. On hearing the news, Herzen exploded with a malediction not only against the government but also against the society which now so supinely accepted the martyrdom of its erstwhile idol:

> May the crime bring a curse on the government, on society, on that vile pack of journalists who applaud persecutions . . . be they the killings of war prisoners in Poland, or those sentences meted out in Russia by the brutal judges and gray-haired scoundrels of the State Council. . . . Our congratulations to Katkov and Co. But how does their conscience feel now? Chernyshevsky was placed in the pillory for fifteen minutes, but you, and all Russia, how long will you have to live in shame? . . . And think, ten years ago we hailed the beginning of this reign.[50]

In fact, by punishing so harshly the man whom it held accountable for subverting the young generation, the regime committed not only an injustice but also a political mistake of the first magnitude. Like Herzen's, Chernyshevsky's great popularity would not have survived the patriotic frenzy of 1863, and if left at large and allowed to publish he could have hardly preserved his hold over the minds of the young. Now the story of his martyrdom would sustain and fortify the resolve of the little underground circles which survived the crash of the revolutionary cause and from one of which would come the first attempt on the life of Alexander II. *What Is to Be Done?* would become the veritable bible for successive generations of Russian radicals who would scan rapturously its veiled hints of the inevitability of revolution and of the joyful liberated life following it. It was undoubtedly the author's fate which influenced this reception of the artistically inept novel. At the end of the century which had seen the appearance of *Eugene Onegin, War and Peace,* and *The Brothers Karamazov,* George Plekhanov, father of Russian Marxism, would be able to say that "we all have drawn [from the novel] moral strength and faith in a better future. . . . From the moment when the printing press was introduced in Russia until now, no printed work has had such a success as *What Is to Be Done?*"[51]

Chernyshevsky's case is a good example of how much Russia's fate at this crucial period of her development was affected by a peculiar configuration of events and personalities. It was not only the proverbial grim forces of history, but the imperial government's clumsiness which barred the path to social reconciliation and instead propelled the country on the road to revolution. Instead of rewarding society for its support and patriotic mood in the moment of national danger, the regime chose to remind its citizens once more that Russia was still, and very much so, a police state.

Ironically, at the same time the authorities were putting the last touches on two reforms which under different conditions could have had far-reaching effects in dispelling the intelligentsia's antagonism to the regime. Prior to 1864 Russia could hardly be said to have had a judicial system in the proper sense of the word. Now in one swoop her legal institutions were brought from a state which would have been deemed anachronistic and intolerable in the sixteenth-century West to the modern age. The scope of the reform is indicated by the following succinct summary:

> The judicial branch was separated from the executive. . . . In civil suits judicial organs were separated from the administrative ones, in criminal suits from the prosecution. . . . Trials became public both in criminal and civil cases. Judges were made irremovable. . . . The institution of the prosecutor was established as was the Bar, that is, independent advocacy. . . . Also introduced were trials by jury, and new appellate courts.[52]

Juries, independent judiciary, open trials—it is difficult to think of another authoritarian system which on its own initiative so curtailed its own prerogatives and powers. It is fair to add that the government retained the power to banish by administrative fiat people it deemed dangerous to the public order to different parts of the empire. Also in dealing with political crimes it would occasionally resort to emergency legislation and special courts. After 1864 the judiciary, unlike that in the Soviet Union, would for the most part be genuinely independent of the political authority, and even under darkest reaction the Russian Bar would remain notable for its high professional standards and liberal spirit.

Less sensational, but in its potential implication even more momentous, was another law of 1864, which introduced local self-government in the ethnically Russian parts of the country. Provinces and counties received elective assemblies, which though weighted in favor of the gentry included representatives of the peasants and townsmen. These *zemstvos,* as they were called, were endowed with considerable competence in matters affecting education, communications, and health services.

In the opinion of most educated Russians of the time, a constitutional system would have been a fitting culmination of the reforms. In 1865 both the assembly of the Moscow nobility and the St. Petersburg zemstvo passed resolutions urging the summoning by the emperor of a national assembly. But having presided over the liquidation of many attributes of authoritarian society, Alexander II would not surrender its most indispensable feature. He said, undoubtedly sincerely, to a dissident nobleman that he would authorize a constitution and a parliament that very day if he was not convinced that it would result in "Russia falling into pieces."[53] Here was a variant on an old theme: Russia could not be free and yet remain united and great. What would be the effect of constitutionalism on Poland and on the growth of national consciousness among the Ukrainians, which already was alarming the imperial authorities and Russian nationalists of the Katkov persuasion?

If the conservatives believed that a constitution must lead to Russia's disintegration, both nationally and socially, the revolutionary camp feared it for exactly the opposite reason. Were the liberals to prevail, said Nicholas Ishutin, head of an underground group which called itself simply Organization,

The people's condition will become a hundred times worse than now because they will devise some sort of constitution . . . and will make Russian life like that of the West; this constitution would find support among the middle and upper classes because it would guarantee personal freedom and prompt the growth of industry and commerce, but would not prevent, but rather facilitate the growth of the proletariat and pauperism.[54]

Organization, situated in Moscow, was part of the flotsam and jetsam left behind by Land and Freedom. Its fifty or so members, all very young, most of them former students who had left university for one reason or another, were busy organizing workers' cooperatives and Sunday schools where they carried on radical propaganda. But during its heated discussions, the circle also debated the possibility of more direct revolutionary action, some associates advocating assassination of officials, armed robbery, and blackmail of the rich.

On April 4, Dmitri Karakozov, Ishutin's cousin, shot at Alexander II as he was taking his daily walk in a St. Petersburg public garden. What followed was a period of nationwide hysteria and persecution of anyone even alleged to have been connected with the radical cause, the period which subsequent historians dubbed with some exaggeration as white terror. Members of the Ishutin circle were arrested, and thirty-five of them were subsequently convicted though it was never established that they had been privy to Karakozov's deed. The would-be-regicide, though mentally deranged, was executed. Detained for varying periods were several people with radical connections from the St. Petersburg and Moscow literary and journalistic fraternities. *The Contemporary* was permanently shut down. Its erstwhile guiding spirit had been idolized by the zealots of the Ishutin circle. In the course of the investigation it was also established that its members had discussed how to rescue Chernyshevsky from Siberia and that they had planned to spirit him abroad.

The single shot by an unbalanced man also had more enduring effects. If the Decembrists' abortive coup had ushered in thirty years of reaction, then the Karakozov affair tilted the scales in favor of Russia remaining a police rather than becoming a constitutional state. Prior to it, for all the emperor's obduracy and other forces standing in the way, an enlightened Russian still could hope that the very momentum of reform would carry the country to the threshold of freedom. Now the hand of the conservative element within the regime was considerably strengthened, and that of the liberal one curtailed. The investigations and trial of Karakozov and his comrades did demonstrate the existence of what might be called a revolutionary counterculture among some marginal groups of intellectuals and the young. Certainly the bulk of the intelligentsia and university youth reacted with horror to the assassination attempt and hastened with professions of loyalty to the emperor. Still the regime would persist in viewing the intelligentsia as a potential reservoir of subversion and as such requiring firm handling. Loyalty to the regime became equated with the acceptance of the status quo. The underlying philosophy of the ruling establishment was well expressed by Katkov when he wrote, "Wherever in our national life something is up to the people, then with God's help we accomplish veritable miracles. But once our intelligentsia speaks and acts we begin to totter."[55]

The intelligentsia, for its own part, if it could speak with one voice would have reciprocated Katkov's compliment: it was the inept and oppressive government which stood in the way of the Russian people realizing its wonderful potentialities and which was responsible for the heavy, claustrophobic quality of Russian life.

The Imperfect Freedom: The 1860s and 1870s

Wherever one looked, except in politics, one saw enormous progress. The Emancipation had finally brought Russia into the industrial age. There was a railway boom, foreign capital was pouring in, banks and factories were springing up all over the country. Culturally the nation was experiencing its most glorious period, its literature and arts indisputably in the forefront of those of Europe. All the more poignant was the fact that this talented people was not allowed a voice in the governance of its own country, that Russians lacked those freedoms and rights which were taken for granted in the West, and which even a country as primitive as Bulgaria, liberated by Russian arms, bestowed on its citizens. These startling contrasts explain why the average educated Russian now felt more acutely a sense of political alienation than he had even under Nicholas. All the enormous social advance of the preceding decade did not add up to civic freedom; in fact it made its absence more glaring and humiliating. Russia seemed condemned forever to remain outside the mainstream of political progress, always a foster child of European civilization.

The intelligentsia's frustration tended to make it tolerant of the extremists and to endow them with a significance far transcending their numbers and what they represented. Respectable lawyers, professors, doctors, even some bureaucrats, themselves far from wishing an overthrow of the regime, nevertheless could view indulgently the revolutionaries and their activities. Perhaps an occasional act of violence was the only way of shaking the government out of its complacency and of making it responsive to society's aspirations. Some would push this toleration to the point where they half-excused actions which clearly crossed the line separating political fanaticism from wanton criminality, as in the case of Nechayev and his circle.* Nobody portrayed and criticized this attitude of the liberal intelligentsia as perceptively and scathingly as did Dostoyevsky in his *Possessed,* which purports to be a fictional account of the Nechayev affair. Yet the great writer himself once confided to a friend that he would find it impossible to denounce a revolutionary even if he knew that he was about to dynamite the Winter Palace.

The mainstream of Russian radicalism of those years was populism, a catchall term embracing both the advocates of peaceful propaganda among the peasants and those who would combine this propaganda with the instigation of revolutionary action. The basic ideas of populism were found already in Herzen and Chernyshevsky: agrarian socialism based upon the peasant commune, the desirability of saving Russia from passing through the capitalist phase, egalitarianism. But now there were new prophets. Peter Lavrov, a former artillery colonel,

---

*As leader of a group of revolutionaries called The People's Justice, Serge Nechayev, in November 1869, ordered and participated in the murder of one of the group's members. The crime led to the sensational trials: of Nechayev's accomplices in 1871 and his own in 1873.

enormously influential in the early seventies, urged the younger generation to become "activists for progress": people from the upper classes had the moral obligation to go among the peasants to teach and help them, so that they could be made to understand that they must take their destiny into their own hands.[56] More directly revolutionary was the message of another exile in the West, the veteran anarchist Michael Bakunin: the peasants were to be stirred into an active struggle against the government. On the periphery of populism were others such as Peter Tkachev, who rejected the notion of preparing a revolution through propaganda, peaceful or otherwise. The regime must be overthrown by an organization of professional revolutionaries, and only after the coup the time would come for indoctrinating the masses in socialism.

The effort to uplift the peasantry was of course not confined to the radicals. Ever since the Emancipation, men and women of all political persuasions had sought to help the underprivileged and, often abandoning their promising and remunerative careers, had been settling in the countryside to work as teachers, doctors, midwives, et cetera. But the crescendo of the movement, the so-called Pilgrimage to the People in 1874, was undoubtedly politically inspired. Over one thousand young people from the upper classes and intelligentsia went to live in the villages. Their goal was not only to serve the peasants in no matter what humble capacity but also by working alongside them to gain their trust and to instruct them in the inequity of the existing social and political system. For most the experience proved disheartening. Whether because of his traditional belief in the tsar, or his distrust of gentlemen, the average peasant did not prove susceptible to propaganda. "You may have thousands upon thousands of propagandists; all the same you will not win over the people, will not budge them" was the verdict of one of the pilgrims.[57] The government would have been well advised to heed this lesson. Instead the authorities, in many cases with the peasants' cooperation, arrested over seven hundred of the young idealists; some two hundred were eventually brought before courts.

It was from veterans of the movement to the people that revolutionary organizations of the next few years would draw their cadres. In 1876–77 several of them coalesced under a familiar name, Land and Freedom. While its namesake had been still born, the second Land and Freedom, though even less impressive in its numerical strength with probably never more than some two hundred members and fellow travellers, certainly made its impact on the political scene. Its program reiterated the traditional Populist goals and methods, such as communal ownership of all land, propaganda among the peasants, et cetera, but the new conspiracy soon turned to terror as the main means of political struggle. For all the isolated incidents in the past, such as the Karakozov affair, Russia's politics had hitherto, and remarkably so in an autocracy, been free of terrorism. Now

Land and Freedom, though professing to use violence only in self-defense, carried out a series of assassination attempts, some successful, against government officials and agents. In the process the conspirators discovered that a few acts of violence were more effective in making their presence felt than all the previous propaganda and agitation activities of populism. "Propaganda by deed," the revolutionary's euphemism for terror, seemed easier than trying to overcome peasant indifference and inertia. The new tactics presented the regime with an almost insuperable dilemma. It is not easy for a nontotalitarian state to deal effectively with terrorists. Arrests were depleting their numbers, but short of raising repression to a level which after 1855 was simply inconceivable, the tsarist government could not hope to eliminate a revolutionary group which, though numerically small, could count on steady replenishment from the ranks of alienated youth.

Disputes within Land and Freedom as to the role terrorism should play in its activities and the propriety of the populists advancing political demands as against propaganda among the peasants and workers led in 1879 to it splitting into two groups. One which took the name of The People's Will adopted explicitly terrorist tactics and set before itself the ambitious goal of compelling the regime to grant a constitution. (The other, which called itself Black Partition, adhered to the original Populist program, but its main importance lies in the fact that some of its members became eventually the pioneers of Russian Marxism.) On its formation The People's Will issued an ultimatum: unless the government summoned a constituent assembly, the conspirators pledged a campaign of violence, its goal to kill the emperor. The next two years witnessed a fantastic duel between The People's Will and the government of a mighty empire, which for all of its vast resources could not prevent several successive attempts on the emperor's life. Actually, the active nucleus of The People's Will consisted of only about forty members, though in order to create the myth (widely believed) that the membership of the organization was much more numerous, this tiny group called itself the Executive Committee. Neither the exertions of the Third Department nor the liberal direction given to his administration by Alexander II in the hopes of winning over public opinion and of undercutting the covert sympathy with which part of the intelligentsia viewed the revolutionaries' professed goal could stop the relentless hunt. It is at least problematic how much the conspirators believed in the desirability of bourgeois parliamentarism for Russia, or the possibility that the constituent assembly, which if democratically elected would reflect mainly the peasants' views, would endorse their republican and socialist ideas. In any case there was no chance of the regime summoning such an assembly. All that the tsar was finally ready to agree to was the introduction of some elected representatives into the State Council, which itself had mostly

127

consultative functions. On March 1, 1881, in their seventh attempt, the terrorists finally cornered their quarry; the bomb squad of The People's Will inflicted mortal wounds on the tsar as he was passing along a street in St. Petersburg.

Here is yet another example of how much the course of history is determined by fortuitous events and personalities. The late tsar's proposed modest opening toward representative government was cancelled by his successor Alexander III. It was not only the course of reform which suffered a setback through the assassination. During the next two years the remaining members of The People's Will were hunted down by the police. The absolutist-bureaucratic regime gained another lease on life, and in the next twenty years it would not be seriously challenged either by revolution or reform. Much as the aura of the Tsar-Liberator had been tarnished by the events since 1863, society reacted to his murder with revulsion and to the conservative, indeed retrograde, character of the new reign with resignation. "Russia is an autocracy tempered by assassination," went a famous saying. In fact terror helped to prolong the anachronism of autocracy.

Yet, as the story of 1855 to 1866 suggests, the most basic obstacle to an advance toward freedom was then, as it is now, the peculiar nature of Russian nationalism, that nationalism compounded of psychological traits of both an oppressed and an imperial nation. And so at decisive moments it was not only the government but also Russian society which found itself unable to opt clearly for freedom if its price seemed to involve a threat to the country's unity and greatness.

Chapter 3

THE SORCERER'S APPRENTICES: THE 1905 REVOLUTION

REVOLUTION, according to Webster's Dictionary, means "a fundamental change in political organization, or in a government or constitution; the overthrow of one government or ruler and the substitution of another." When it comes to Russia, this definition hardly helps in understanding what happened in 1905 and 1917. The revolution of 1905 was the most elemental and all-encompassing of the three the country was to experience in this century. The volume and ubiquity of revolutionary turbulence surpassed anything which was to be witnessed either in February or in October 1917. But it all did not add up to "the overthrow of one government and the substitution of another." When in 1907 the revolutionary tide receded, Nicholas II was still on the throne, and the autocratic system, embellished with a parliamentary veneer, seemed unimpaired in its essentials. To a perceptive observer it was clear, however, that the sources of the strength and prestige of the autocracy had been irreparably damaged. The monarchy in its discredited and anachronistic form survived because of the discord among its enemies, some of whom feared that in pulling it down they would destroy the Russian state, while others aimed their blows with precisely that intention. There was as yet no force capable of completing the revolutionary process in the way the dictionary defines it, by overthrowing the existing government and creating a new one.

Paradoxically, throughout their modern history, Russians have found it difficult to think of revolution in terms of a struggle for power. If autocrary were overthrown, then it would be replaced by a constitution or by the people, rather than by a specific group of men exercising (even if in outward forms) the same functions as had the emperor and his ministers. Centuries of authoritarian rule had eroded the society's understanding of practical politics so that "power" was felt to be if not synonymous with repression then at least peculiar to the autocrat. "No one who has not been in jail knows what the state is," said Leo Tolstoy, a sentiment that was shared by many Russians and not just by those who followed his brand of Christian anarchism. This prudish attitude toward government often reflected a fear of responsibility as much as a hatred of autocracy and was not uncommon even among rebels and radicals. It is suggestive how in the eighteenth century a group of nobles after forcibly deposing a ruler who had displeased them would then, usually without any preconditions, turn over full autocratic powers to his or her successor. In the nineteenth century we do find individuals, witness Pestel and Tkachev, who thought in terms of the coup d'etat and at least a temporary revolutionary dictatorship. But more typical was the behavior of the Decembrists who tried to endow their rebellion with spurious legitimacy and who after bringing out their troops, just waited for the government to collapse of itself. Somewhat the same mentality pervaded the Populists, except that most of them looked for a nationwide peasant uprising that would result in the collapse of the state as well as the autocracy, with both being replaced by a loose federation of socialist communes. Even a group in many ways as hardheaded as The People's Will did not conceive its mission as wresting power from the imperial regime but rather of compelling it through terror to become an instrument of its own demise, to summon a democratically elected constituent assembly that would legislate a new people's Russia. Incongruously, most of the revolutionaries knew that such an assembly, elected mostly from the peasant masses, was unlikely to endorse their own socialist and anarchist ideas. After the assassination of March 1, 1881, The People's Will addressed a letter to the new emperor asking him as "a citizen and honest man" to give freedom to the people. "We declare before our country and the whole world that our party will submit unconditionally to the decisions of the Constituent Assembly." A simultaneous declaration directed to "honest members of rural communes, Orthodox peasants, all Russian folk" urged them to send their representatives to "His Majesty the Emperor in St. Petersburg. . . . Open the eyes of our Sovereign Lord to how the peasant suffers in this Russian land. . . ."[1] Even if conceived as a political ruse, these documents are psychologically revealing. The very same people who had just killed an emperor still felt that his successor was the legitimate wielder of the nation's power, still seen as the father of his people by the peasant masses. If the late tsar was killed it was because he had been a bad father rather than an autocrat was the gist of another pamphlet issued by the assassins for popular consumption: "The tsar ought to be a good shepherd, ready to die for his flock. Alexander was a wolf."[2]

The autocracy then had to destroy itself before there could be a real claimant for the role it occupied. But even then most Russians would find it difficult to visualize somebody rather than some constitutional or ideological formula replacing it and governing the land. At the All-Russian Congress of Soviets in June 1917 one of the speakers mentioned that of course everybody understood that no single party could or would want to rule by itself. Lenin produced a shock and then general merriment by shouting from his seat: "There is such a party." He proceeded to astound the incredulous audience still further by specifying that the Bolsheviks "were ready to take over power in its entirety."[3]

But if revolution couldn't and wouldn't seize power, then the autocracy found it increasingly difficult to exercise it. The twenty years prior to the revolution marked a growing paralysis of the imperial regime. Ideologically it was an anachronism and felt to be such by some of its most devoted servants. In his recollections, Serge Witte, Russia's only real statesman at the turn of the century, stated his conviction that autocracy had been the cornerstone of the country's greatness: "If you did not have autocracy, you would not have the great Russian empire." Yet there was no doubt in his mind that the system could not endure:

That is the clear and inevitable conclusion to which both history and the order of things on our planet draw us. . . . All countries have come to adopt constitutional government. It is hard and under [our] circumstances impossible to hold on to a political system which has been rejected not only by all more or less civilized nations but even by those whose general level of culture is much below our own.[4]

Interestingly, Witte, who at crucial periods in 1905 helped save the regime, evidently did not count Russia among those "more or less civilized nations."

The only rationale for preserving the status quo was the by now slightly shop-worn argument that in view of her history and mission in the world, Russia was somehow different. But this argument could become a weapon in the hands of the extreme left, as well as that of the right. It was a revolutionary of the 1860s who wrote, "We ought to bless destiny that we have not lived the life of Europe."[5] An assertion of spiritual superiority is a frequent compensatory mechanism for societies that are politically and economically backward. Even the intelligentsia could occasionally be susceptible to the appeal of messianic nationalism, as was vividly demonstrated at the great commemoration of Pushkin in 1880. Dostoyevsky, who was the main speaker on that occasion, turned his eulogy of the great poet into a passionate panegyric to the Russian nation. According to Dostoyevsky, what endowed Pushkin with a genius surpassing that of such supreme artists as Shakespeare and Cervantes was his ability to express the soul of his people and thereby the universal yearnings of mankind. For "what is the strength of the Russian national idea but its striving toward the ultimate ends of humanity, what is our nation's destiny but to lead the world toward a universal union of all branches of the Aryan race."[6] The poet's life and work was a lesson that "to be really and truly Russian one must become a brother of all men," concluded the orator, forgetting for the moment his own distinctly unbrotherly feelings concerning the Jews and the Poles.

The scene which followed this impassioned address would have pleased a believer in the Russian soul. The audience was thrown into a frenzy of rapture: people wept, strangers embraced each other. There were voices acclaiming Dostoyevsky himself as a national prophet and saint. And this audience was composed of the elite of the country's intellectual and literary community.

But once the moment of exaltation passed, it is quite likely that most of those present reverted to their more customary reflections on the unfree and uncivilized condition of their society and on those quite unmessianic and nonhumanitarian features of Russian life which Pushkin and Dostoyevsky himself had so often depicted. What a thoughtful witness would have deduced from the scene was that Russian society was yearning for an ideology that would not only explain but point a way out of the depressing reality.

After 1881 the regime had proved itself incapable of producing or associating itself with such an ideology. The brief reign (1881–94) of Alexander III appears deceivingly as a time of political calm and stability. But beneath the placid surface of national life pressures were building up and forces ripening which would usher in a new period of revolutionary turbulence. The government's policies assisted unwittingly in creating an atmosphere which would result in a challenge, the most fundamental yet, to autocracy. Constantine Pobyedonostsev, the new emperor's erstwhile tutor and now procurator general of the Holy Synod (minister of church affairs), his most influential adviser, set the tone of the reign by decrying the idea that Russia should evolve toward a constitutional government. The experience of the West, proclaimed this ideologue of reaction, demonstrated that constitutions promoted social strife, public immorality, and intrigue. There was no place for such contrivances in Russia "which has always drawn her strength from the unlimited confidence which prevails between the tsar and his people."[7]

This confidence notwithstanding, the regime did not trust the people with the rights and social advances secured in the previous reign but tried vigorously, if clumsily, to undo the effects of the Great Reforms. The limited system of local self-government instituted by Alexander II was subjected to stricter controls by St. Petersburg and the franchise in elections to provincial, country, and municipal assemblies, already weighted in favor of the propertied classes, made more restrictive. Though the peasant's financial burdens were somewhat lightened, he was still treated as the ward of the state; indeed, his status as such was reinforced in 1889 when village affairs were placed directly under the control of the bureaucracy, rather than, as hitherto, with the zemstvos—elected organs of local government.

Russia was going through a period of rapid economic and population growth. From every point of view it seemed imperative to enlarge educational facilities and promote social mobility. Instead, the government under Alexander III tried, by raising fees and other measures, to minimize educational opportunities for children from the lower classes. It was foolish and dangerous to encourage them to acquire ideas and aspirations not appropriate to their station in life, wrote Ivan Delianov, a minister of education, to his subordinates. Institutions of higher learning were subjected to new and stringent regulations that limited the autonomy of their faculties and further restricted the freedom of the students who were required to pledge not to join unauthorized associations and to wear uniforms. It is hardly surprising that, even more than during the sixties and seventies, the university of the period became the training ground for future radicals.

But it was the official nationality policy which would have the most far-reaching, and for the regime disastrous, results. Russian nationalism and Orthodoxy could be expected to be the chosen ideological props of the regime which held on tenaciously to autocracy. Yet in fact the government's russification and, when it came to the Orthodox faith, proselytizing policies were to prove a source of weakness rather than strength to the very institution they were supposed to preserve. In Poland, prostrate after the rebellion of 1863, official attempts at russification were carried to the point of absurdity. By banning the use of the native tongue in the country's schools and offices, Poland's Russian overlords only enhanced the smoldering nationalist resentment and hatred of their rule. Crude xenophobic policies were also creating malcontents even among those ethnic groups, such as the Baltic Germans and Armenians, who in the past had displayed staunch loyalty to the throne and eschewed separatist tendencies, as well as the Ukrainians whose freshly emerging intelligentsia only sought recognition of their linguistic and cultural distinctiveness. Traditionally Russian nationalism had been a powerful shield of the autocracy, but the policy of narrow-minded jingoism and russification ran counter to the true national interest of the empire, half of whose population was non-Russian.

The oppressive nationality policy was compounded by chicaneries and legal disabilities suffered by the non-Orthodox. This again was bound to prove a source of disunity and antigovernment feelings, for the empire comprised not only a great variety of religions and cults but many Russians, especially among the peasantry who were Old Believers and sectarians and who rejected the authority of the established church. Tsarist Russia contained the largest Jewish community in the world. Its legal and social status, never enviable, was improved somewhat under Alexander II, with Jews gaining access to universities and the free professions and the government in general looking leniently at their settling outside the Pale. Here again the situation sharply deteriorated after 1881. Vicious pogroms erupted in the Ukraine in the spring of 1881 and were to recur in the fall and in 1882. While undoubtedly spontaneous, triggered perhaps by the presence of a few Jews among the "tsar killers" of The People's Will, some of the concerned officials displayed less than exemplary diligence in trying to prevent the outrages and punishing the culprits. Ironically, in some of its publications The People's Will adopted an "understanding," if not approving, attitude toward the anti-Jewish excesses on the ground that they represented the kind of popular uprising against the public order and economic exploitation which a revolutionary had no right to censor. "In the depths of my soul" he could sympathize with those who beat the Jews, wrote Alexander to Minister of the Interior Dmitri Tolstoy.[8] While neither the tsar nor his ministers would license mob violence because of its implications for law and order, official prejudice was reflected in the new residential and economic restrictions on the Jews and further curbs on their access to schools and professions. There were high dignitaries, such as Witte, who expostulated that even on purely political grounds, anti-Jewish measures were ill conceived and bound to do harm to the state. They antagonized a community of over five million and made it inevitable that many of its younger and culturally assimilated members would be attracted to the revolutionary cause. They tarnished the reputation of the imperial government throughout the civilized world, and they made it more difficult to secure foreign loans and attract foreign capital. For the most part such arguments proved unavailing. Challenged by forces it did not understand, the authoritarian state often came to resemble an irrational and vindictive mob, its grievances and fears blamed on outsiders and on traitors within its midst.

In brief the era of apparent normalcy and political stability was to prove disastrous in its consequences. "It was the reign of Alexander III which set Russia on the road which led to the ultimate catastrophe," V.A. Maklakov, a contemporary, was to write.[9] As under Nicholas I, the emperor's firmness and the awe surrounding the figure of the Autocrat obscured for most of his subjects the ultimate implications of the policies of his reign. For all his rather coarse, peasant-like appearance, which was the subject of jokes (the sculptor of the emperor's equestrian statue, when asked why he presented his subject with a rather unflattering realism, answered that he hoped he had succeeded in portraying one animal astride another) Alexander III fitted the popular stereotype of the tsar. "His personal qualities gained him the sympathy even of those who criticized his policies. He was not brilliant or dashing, but gave the impression of being a modest, simple-mannered and devoted servant of the fatherland."[10] The emperor was a beneficiary of the revulsion and guilt feelings produced by the assassination of his father and by society's exhaustion and disenchantment in the wake of the era of reforms and revolutionary stirrings.

Nevertheless, the greater the feeling of disenchantment and resignation under one ruler, the more the Russian people had come to expect in the way of freedoms and innovations from his successor. It was inherent in whatever remained of the mystique of autocracy that each tsar should in the very beginning stamp his own distinctive mark on his reign.

Nicholas II was to do so but in a most unfortunate manner. Hated or feared as the institution of autocracy might have been in the eyes of many Russians, few had ever thought of it as ridiculous. But that was precisely the effect produced by one of Nicholas' first public pronouncements. Among the loyal addresses presented to the new tsar on the occasion of his ascent to the throne and subsequent marriage was one from the zemstvo of the Tver province. Some thirty years before, representatives of the Tver nobility had petitioned Alexander II to crown his reforms by endowing Russia with a nationwide assembly. On the surface, at least, their successors' request in 1895 was much more modest. All they pleaded for was that their zemstvo and similar elected bodies throughout the land be allowed to voice their opinions on matters of public policy. "We look forward, Sire, to it being possible and right for public institutions to express their views on issues concerning them so that expression of the needs and thoughts of the representatives of the Russian people, and not only of the officials may reach the heights of the throne."[11] A wise ruler would have welcomed such a petition, which, even if one read between the lines, asked at most for a national representative body to *advise* the tsar and whose implied criticism touched not on his powers but was directed against the bureaucracy. Had the emperor felt that the address somehow challenged his prerogatives, common sense would have urged a noncommittal answer and awaiting further public reactions. But the twenty-six-year-old tsar was as inept politically as he was incapable temperamentally and intellectually of fulfilling the role of either a reformer or an iron-willed autocrat. Unsure of himself and stubborn, a dangerous combination for one in his circumstances, Nicholas had the answer drafted by one of the court camarilla, allegedly his uncle, Grand Duke Serge, widely known and disliked as a reactionary. With an equally poor sense of timing he chose to read it at a great reception for notables and public representatives from all over the empire. Gathered to offer their monarch felicitations on his marriage, the assembled were told that he meant to preserve autocracy in full and that those who thought the zemstvos should be free to intervene in national affairs had been carried away by "senseless dreams."[12] The few nervously and haltingly read sentences were not only an undeserved slap in the face to those who considered themselves, and in fact were, loyal subjects but also ludicrously inappropriate. No one had questioned the autocratic principle; all that the Tver address urged was that the government be purified of bureaucratic excrescences, thus to reassert that "trust between the tsar and his people," which was supposedly the cornerstone of the system. Now all these reputable landowners, lawyers, et cetera, who had hoped to reform the monarchy in order to strengthen it indeed had reasons to believe that theirs had been "senseless dreams." The phrase itself reverberated from one end of the country to the other and became a derisive battle cry of those who would bring a new order to Russia.

The attrition of the emperor's prestige played a crucial role in the crisis which would produce not only 1905 but also the delayed last act of its drama, February 1917. For most educated Russians, "The Sacred Person of His Majesty," as official liturgy termed him, was now but the apex of the official hierarchy, the man himself but a tool in the hands of whichever court or bureaucratic camarilla had his ear. Short in stature and otherwise unimpressive in appearance, Nicholas had the makings of a conscientious Guards officer but hardly of an autocrat—its Russian equivalent meaning literally "sole wielder of power." How personally insignificant he was considered is perhaps best attested by the fact that during a twenty-three-year-long reign, when ministers, governors, and other high officials were frequent targets of bullets and bombs, there is not a single verified instance of a plot against his life. Revolutionary propaganda naturally enough tried to portray the tsar as a willful despot, Nicholas the Bloody, but the revolutionaries' real feelings were reflected by Lenin when he referred to him as "the idiot Romanov."

Incapable of ruling, or even of appearing to rule in the traditional manner, Nicholas II was nonetheless jealous of his prerogatives; hence he was an undependable ally of those officials willing and capable of shouldering the burden of power. The autocracy arrived in the twentieth century poorly equipped ideologically and administratively to deal with the complexities of the modern state and politics. There was no prime minister, in fact no council of ministers as such. The only thing resembling a central legislative authority was the Council of State, composed for the most part of superannuated bureaucrats. Policies and laws emanated from a cumbersome maze of ad hoc official committees and individual ministries, high officials usually and strenuously intriguing against each other. There was no clear-cut apportionment of responsibilities and authority among the various departments of the government. The Ministry of Finance warred constantly with that of Interior over who should be in charge of industrial regulation and labor legislation. Pobyedonostsev, as the guardian of Orthodoxy, and by his own lights and not only the religious one, kept a wary eye on the Ministry of Education, as well as on censorship, the latter technically under the Ministry of the Interior. In the Far East where Russia was competing with other Great Powers in trying to carve up the Manchu Empire, her policies reflected conflicting pressures by rival coteries of officials, some of whom had a direct financial interest in territorial expansion.

At the local level this part feudal, part conspiratorial pattern was paralleled by what might be described as bureaucratic anarchy. Subject to some theoretical limitations, almost invariably disregarded in practice, a local governor or chief of police could detain or banish from his jurisdiction any citizen, shut down an educational institution or industrial enterprise, and suspend or dismiss elected or appointed officials. One governor general, his tolerance reinforced by bribes, allowed Jews, who except for those in privileged occupations were prohibited from living there, to settle in Moscow. His successor had some thirty thousand of them thrown out of the city.

The secret police at all levels often acted with but scant supervision by other authorities. The Third Department had been abolished in 1880, a gesture of conciliation toward a society which had come to loathe its very name. But though its functions were then transferred to the Ministry of Interior, the organ of internal espionage not only preserved its autonomy and powers but became under its new name, Okhrana, even more ubiquitous and notorious than before. What was perhaps the last creative contribution to the ideology of autocracy came from a police chief, who conceived and sponsored a scheme which was to have nation-wide reverberations. To undermine the influence of the revolutionaries, he had the police organize labor unions and assist them in their disputes with employers. The workers, it was hoped, would thus recognize that the tsar and government were their protectors and benefactors and would reject the noxious intellectuals with their socialist ideas. Ironically, the practical application of this plan was to trigger the first act of the revolution of 1905.

Suddenly in 1900 the atmosphere of puzzled exasperation on the part of Russian society was replaced by frantic activism. Almost simultaneously there arose several movements and parties ready to take on the regime. Populism, its conspiratorial side destroyed in 1881–83 and its theory seemingly discredited, was now revived in the form of the party of Socialist Revolutionaries (the SRs), which like its predecessors would employ terrorism as a political weapon and would seek to instigate peasant revolts. The gentry and intelligentsia proponents of a peaceful transformation of Russia into a constitutional state would coalesce in what would become known as the Liberation movement, out of which would be born the party of Constitutional Democrats (Kadets). And the most portentous development of all: meeting clandestinely in the dingy provincial city of Minsk, nine delegates proclaimed in 1898 the foundation of the Russian Social Democratic Workers Party.

This party consisted of a few clandestine workers' circles, an underground newspaper, and a number of intelligentsia disciples of the teachings of Karl Marx, some in the West and some in Siberian exile, as well as in Russia proper. Until 1905 its membership probably never reached ten thousand. But the appearance of Marxism on the scene was bound to have immediate and far-reaching effects on the country's political and intellectual life that were quite out of proportion to the number of its original adherents.

Western ideologies when transplanted to Russian soil would often be received with a passion and intense excitement they could no longer arouse in their place of origin. It is a startling paradox of this intensely nationalist society that it had always looked abroad for an analysis of its problems and ways of solving them. Upon closer scrutiny, even such nativist creeds as slavophilism and populism can be seen to have their intellectual roots in a theory or philosophy developed in the West. The impact of a fashionable intellectual trend could not be measured merely by the number of its devotees. It immediately entered the mainstream of society's unending inquest upon itself, about the meaning of Russia's historical experience and what was to be done.

So with Marxism, except that its explanations were more explicit, its answers more forceful than those offered by the philosophies that had beguiled the intelligentsia in the past, such as Hegelianism, utopian socialism, utilitarianism. Russia's present condition was not due to a particular tsar, not to some peculiar virtue or deficiency of her people. If she differed from the West, it was only because her economic development had been delayed and she had entered the Industrial Revolution much later. Having started on the capitalist path, the country was now bound to follow it to its inevitable conclusion, socialism, shedding on the way such relics of the feudal past as still coexisted incongruously with the Russia of factories and railways—autocracy, the peasant commune, et cetera. The capitalist phase could not be bypassed for all the increasing economic exploitation and the hateful bourgeois rule that it was bound to bring. The peasant commune, so dear to the right and to the Populists who saw it as the foundation of agrarian socialism of the future was viewed by Marxism quite unsentimentally: like serfdom it was an anachronism and an impediment to social and economic progress.

What was to be done was equally clear, though because of the inherent contradictions between the country's political system and its economic development, the strategy of class war had to be different in Russia than in the West.

The Sorcerer's Apprentices: The 1905 Revolution

There political freedom had been won largely through the exertions of the middle class, which then found itself constrained to give political rights to the workers. But Russia's middle class, which in 1898 was the intelligentsia, found itself unable even to budge the autocracy. "The further East in Europe, the weaker in the political sense, the more cowardly and vile becomes the intelligentsia. . . . It is upon the stout shoulders of the Russian working class that must and will rest the job of conquering political freedom," proclaimed the first manifesto of the Russian Socialists.[13]

The opening sentence was pregnant with meaning and prophetic of much of the sense of Russian history of the next twenty years. To be sure, the intelligentsia, because of circumstances over which it had no control, had hitherto been unable to change the political system, but they were hardly "cowardly and vile." The intelligentsia had been in the forefront of every progressive and revolutionary movement in Russia and would continue to be so until a socialist party, led by a man in many ways a typical intelligent, would destroy not only the old Russian state but also the class from which he himself had sprung. The author of the manifesto with its memorable phrase was Peter Struve, descended from a family of scholars and professional men, a distinguished writer on social and economic problems, who would soon abandon socialism for liberalism.

In referring to the revolutionaries of the past, the manifesto was more complimentary, but still a bit condescending:

[Insofar as political liberty is concerned] Social Democracy aims at the goal, already clearly indicated by the famous fighters of the old People's Will. But the means and paths which Social Democracy chooses are different. Its choice is dictated by the fact that it consciously aims to be and remain the class movement of the organized labor masses. It is firmly convinced that the liberation of the working class can only be achieved by its own effort![14]

In its very first pronouncement Russian socialism breathed self-confidence and defiance.

As a theory Marxism had been known in Russian intellectual circles for quite a long time. Its propagation had been facilitated by the fact that tsarist censors tended at first not to interfere with its literature, feeling no doubt that its abstruse philosophical and economic content was unlikely to turn its readers into conspirators and bomb throwers. Revered as a theorist of revolution, Marx was, however, not thought to be relevant to the Russian scene since the dominant radical ideology, that of populism, rejected his emphasis on industrialization as the instrument of social change and of the industrial proletariat as the revolutionary class. (On occasion, in his correspondence with some Russian radicals, Marx allowed that in Russia the peasant commune might become the instrumentality of a direct transition from a precapitalist phase to socialism, but the logic of his entire system argued otherwise.)

But the influence of Marxism extended beyond the avowed Marxists. It affected the Populists, some of whom claimed that they understood Karl Marx better than those who would apply his teaching literally under the uncongenial conditions of Russia. And it affected the liberal intelligentsia, which having given up on the peasant, now looked more and more to the industrial worker to become a valuable ally in the struggle for freedom. Unlike the peasant, the industrial proletarian was not given to the extremes of servility and apathy on the one hand and uncontrollable anarchy on the other. He tended to be better educated, and factory and city life made him more amenable to political organization and discipline. A peasant riot would usually end with its leaders sent into exile and the participants whipped. The industrial strike, on the other hand, had already proven its effectiveness as the tool of economic struggle. Massive strikes of the mid-1890s in St. Petersburg extracted concessions from the manufacturers and induced the government to introduce regulations, even if rudimentary, protecting the worker.

Puny in its membership, Social Democracy assumed crucial importance in Russian life from the very beginning because of its ability to address itself to and influence practically every major political issue and social force in the country. For all of its revolutionary rhetoric, its initial demands were of a kind that every progressive intelligent could subscribe to: freedom of speech, press, and assembly, representative institutions. As for the worker, Social Democracy did not try to proselytize by teaching him the theoretical intricacies of Marxism but by endorsing and assisting him in the never-ending struggle to secure better working conditions and higher wages. For those longing for revolutionary activism, the Social Democrats offered a new type of conspiracy, one which would not risk everything on a coup d'etat or a spectacular assassination but which would work patiently, husbanding its resources, trying to acquire a mass basis, striking when a crisis of special circumstances warranted it, rather than dissipating its forces in terrorist heroics.

At the time it would have required great perspicacity to identify the Socialists as the most dangerous of the forces then challenging the traditional order. The most dramatic symptom of this challenge and of the feverish condition of society was the revival of political terrorism. Even before the formal creation of the Socialist Revolutionary party at the end of 1901, assassination reappeared on the political scene. Disorders in a number of Russian universities during the past two years had induced the authorities not only to sanction mass expulsions but also to conscript a large number of culprits into the army as privates. Early in 1901 the minister of education was shot and killed by a former student. A lineal descendant of The People's Will, the Socialist Revolutionary party could be expected to resume its terrorist tactics. But whereas the former pursued them for a specific and stated purpose, to force the regime to summon a constituent assembly, the Fighting Organization of the SRs would carry on the assassination campaign as a kind of revolutionary ritual. Its first major victim was Minister of Interior Dmitri Sipyagin, killed in 1902. Only several years later did it become known that Yevno Azev, the head of the Fighting Organization, which enjoyed virtual independence from its parent body, was simultaneously a trusted agent of the Okhrana. Azev, while masterminding the killing of high dignitaries, at the same time had betrayed several of his comrades to the police. The history of the Socialist Revolutionary party was to offer further examples, as suggested already by the fate of The People's Will, that terrorism tends to demoralize and then destroy the revolutionary party which resorts to it. Conversely, the authorities' excessive reliance on double agents and similar dark forces within the police apparatus was to have similar effects on the entire machinery of the government.

Terrorism was something the regime had learned to live with before. In fact it was not the extremists who, in its estimation, posed the biggest threat to the existing political order. The greatest danger, it was believed, originated within the ranks of the Establishment itself. Ever since the emperor's offensive response to the humble supplication of his faithful Tver subjects, a number of zemstvo officials from several provinces, all of them noblemen and substantial landowners, had taken to conferring periodically on matters of common interest—shades of the Union of Welfare of the Decembrists. In any previous reign the government would have put a quick end to such consultations, their participants placed under house arrest or worse. But the autocracy no longer had the self-assurance to deal with men of high social status in such a peremptory way. In 1900 the dissident noblemen had organized what in the eyes of the law was a conspiratorial circle. Called Symposium, it was devoted to discussing ways and means of changing the political system. Some of its fifty-or-so members still dreamed of the Slavophile ideal: the autocracy purified of its bureaucratic excrescences in close communion with the nation. But the majority felt that only an end to autocracy and the granting of a constitution and civil freedoms could heal Russia and avoid, as one put it, the otherwise inevitable "crumbling of the existing regime amidst blood-shed." The liberal-minded noblemen, along with some sympathizers among the intelligentsia, decided to found a journal, of necessity located abroad, which would mobilize society behind the struggle for constitutionalism. On July 1, 1902 (w.s.) there appeared in Stuttgart the first issue of *Liberation*. Its editor was Peter Struve, now disillusioned with Marxism or more properly with the Russian Marxists.

In his first editorial, he stressed the link between the Liberation movement and the revolutionary traditions of the past. Russian constitutionalists had, it was true, chosen a different path from that followed by those who in their struggle against autocracy preached and practiced violence: "Our organ is not 'revolutionary' . . . but it demands a wholesale transformation of Russian life, the replacement of the lawlessness of the autocratic bureaucracy by the rights of individuals and society."[15] Struve rejected revolutionary violence as a means of overthrowing the autocracy. But he was far from condemning movements and persons who had resorted to terrorism and armed struggle against tsarism. They deserve, he stated, the profound respect of every lover of freedom. In a way the violence was not of their own making. It was really the ministers and officials under Alexander II who were the culprits of the bloody events of the seventies and eighties and not the terrorists of The People's Will, for whom no other way had been left to pursue their ideals. There is here that embarrassment over its own moderation and sense of inferiority vis-à-vis more extreme movements which was to prove such a heavy, eventually fatal, burden to Russian liberalism.

Like every Russian émigré journal, down to the present, *Liberation* aspired to emulate the example of Herzen's *Bell:* to become a mighty voice of freedom within Russia. The journal did not quite live up to that role, but it was the first step in the creation of the political movement which took its name. In 1903 some of its aristocratic sponsors travelled to Switzerland where they were joined by a group of intelligentsia publicists, most, like Struve, with socialist or Populist antecedents, and laid the foundation of the Union of Liberation, which sought to unite people of different ideological persuasions to work for a peaceful end to the autocracy. Back at home they succeeded in recruiting a number of adherents and the Union of Liberation was formally organized on Russian soil at a clandestine meeting in January 1904. It was attended by fifty delegates from twenty-two localities.[16] More than eighty years after the formation of the Union of Welfare, the cause of liberalism in Russia still had to be pursued through a conspiracy. But from this point the decline of the autocracy was to be precipitous.

While liberalism was martialling its supporters, so was Russian Marxism. It was still the beneficiary of the government's belief that the followers of this esoteric cult were a lesser danger than the throwers of bombs, or those aristocrats, lawyers, and writers who wanted a constitution. Thus the police offered no objections when, after completing their three years of free exile in Siberia, two alumni of a St. Petersburg Marxist circle, Vladimir Ulyanov-Lenin and Julius Martov repaired in 1900 abroad. Here they joined forces with the veterans of Russian Marxism, headed by its patriarch (all of forty-four years old), George Plekhanov, and established another would-be-successor to *The Bell,* the socialist democratic journal, *Iskra* (The Spark); its title commemorating the Decembrist Odoyevsky's famous promise to Pushkin: "Out of this spark will come a conflagration." In this case the promise was to come true, far beyond the Decembrists' dreams. The movement represented by *Iskra* was to start a worldwide conflagration to which, eighty years later, the end is still not in sight.

But before lighting the fire, the Russian Socialists fell to quarrelling among themselves. The natural advantages Marxism possessed to become the vanguard of the revolutionary movement in Russia were offset somewhat by certain handicaps it suffered in what was rapidly becoming an arena of feverish political activity both at home and among the exiles. It lacked the romantic existentialist appeal of the Socialist Revolutionaries who were not just expounding theories but were doing things. It grated especially on the younger generation of radicals that Marxism seemed to promise the socialist paradise in Russia only for a fairly distant future after capitalism had run out its full cycle.

More basically, like every highly doctrinaire movement, Marxism was vulnerable to ideological splits and schisms. In his Siberian exile, Lenin and his fellow exiles had become highly incensed by the news of one such heresy they dubbed economism. Its few proponents, soon to follow Struve on the primrose path to liberalism, argued that socialist intellectuals should take a back seat in the movement. Karl Marx clearly taught that the emancipation of the working class must be accomplished by the workers themselves. The intellectuals should thus merely second the proletariat's economic struggle and in politics assist the liberal bourgeoisie in securing constitutional institutions. Lenin's violent response to this alleged attempt to emasculate Russian Marxism of its revolutionary meaning was entitled *A Protest of the Russian Social Democrats,* and was subscribed to by seventeen fellow exiles. Socialism, he maintained, dare not become an auxiliary of other movements. It must whiplash other movements into revolutionary action and quite apart from its attack upon the autocracy, must keep a militant attitude toward its temporary allies, the liberals.

In 1902, now in the West, Lenin developed his views more fully in what was to become the bible of Bolshevism, and hence Communism, *What Is to Be Done?* That the title was borrowed from Chernyshevsky's novel was indicative not only of Lenin's veneration of the great radical publicist but also of his conscious effort to erect a socialist party which would combine the theoretical and internationalist premises of Marxism with the conspiratorial militancy of Russian populism. Temperamentally Lenin was never at ease with the "democratic" part of his party's name and its implications. Now, though professing strict orthodoxy, he expressed startling reservations about the "workers" part of its title.

Socialist consciousness cannot exist among the workers. This can be introduced only from without. The history of all countries shows that by its unaided efforts the working class can develop only a trade union consciousness, that is a conviction to form labor unions, struggle with the employers, obtain from the government this or that law required by the workers, and so on.[17]

The true socialist party under Russian (after 1919 it will become under any) conditions must be like an army or a religious order, centrally controlled, hierarchical, and disciplined in its organization, composed of professionals rather than part-time revolutionaries and sympathizers. Some forty activist members of The People's Will managed for two years to defy the forces of a powerful government. How much more will be accomplished by a cadre of revolutionary fighters based upon a mass movement!

The party thus becomes a political perpetuum mobile: conscious of the historical inevitability of its cause, unaffected by the vicissitudes of politics and economics and of changing moods of the proletariat or the population at large, it carries on. Its alliances with other parties and classes must always be temporary in their nature. It knows how to accept concessions and not scorn them out of misplaced ideological scruples, but it never rests content with them, just as it is capable of enduring defeats, only to regroup and prepare for further assaults. Consciously, until 1914, Lenin was still far from rejecting the social democratic premises of his movement; not until 1917 would he try explicitly to seize "power in its entirety." But in *What Is to Be Done?* there is already an inkling of his essentially undemocratic temperament and of his future bid to create a Communist autocracy.

The dazzling success which Lenin's organizational and tactical blueprint was to bring him in 1917 and 1918 ought not hide the fact that its formulation in 1902 was a serious blow to Russian Marxism. The Bolsheviks' attempts to put this blueprint into effect between 1903 and 1914 were to bring them to the verge of extinction as a serious political force and did considerable harm to the unity of the Russian working class, as well as the cause of political freedom in Russia. The name Bolsheviks ("Majoritarians") originated at the Second Congress of the Russian Socialist party held in Brussels in 1903. On a seemingly minor organizational issue Lenin's followers there were able to outvote (twenty-four to twenty) their opponents, who from that moment on pass into history under the ill-omened name of Mensheviks ("Minoritarians"), one which they themselves would resignedly accept and use, even though on several subsequent occasions it would be the Mensheviks rather than their opponents who commanded majority support. Formally, the two factions would coexist within the same party until 1912, and in some ways the Russian Marxists would not be definitely split into two openly hostile parties until 1917. But in fact one man's personality and policies made the division real and fundamental from 1903 on, and all efforts at a genuine reconciliation were to prove unavailing.

That there had been fundamental ideological differences between the two socialist groups is very largely a legend, or rather an optical illusion, since we tend to view the history of Russian Marxism through the prism of what happened in 1917 and afterward. But from the beginning there was also a significant difference in the ethnic composition of the competing factions. As one might expect, ethnic minorities were represented in all the revolutionary parties of the period, quite out of proportion to their share in the total population. This was especially true of Jews, Poles, and Georgians. And there were quite a few of these among the Bolsheviks, yet not nearly as many as among the Mensheviks and the Socialist Revolutionaries. In their membership the Bolsheviks were the most "Russian" of the radical parties. Was it simply an accident or did their authoritarian pattern of organization and leadership hold a greater appeal to a Russian radical than to his Georgian or Jewish counterpart?

What was the tsarist government doing in the face of this sudden efflorescence of revolutionary and liberal activism? Superficially, at least, it responded, as of old, with repression. Arrests and exile continued to be the fate of active political malcontents. Through its political espionage and double agents the police could follow the subversive groups, as well as the "respectable" kind of opposition to the regime as was represented by the activist zemstvo leaders. Yet the time-honored ways of dealing with political and social disturbances and with the rising tide of organized subversion, now served merely as additional irritants, rather than as effective means of protecting the regime's power and prestige. As in the wake of Nicholas I's death, so following that of Alexander III, the regime had largely lost its ability to inspire fear. But unlike that previous occasion, society's grievances and aroused aspirations were not being appeased by the hope of far-reaching reforms.

It was now the twentieth century, and the traditional authoritarian methods of securing political conformity and obedience were becoming unthinkable and impractical even in Russia—and modern totalitarianism was still far in the future. An active revolutionary, unless arrested for an act of violence, no longer faced the prospect of the gallows or of years in a fortress or at hard labor. Lenin's case is not atypical of the treatment meted out to an avowed revolutionary under Nicholas II. Arrested for socialist agitation among workers, he spent fifteen months in jail where he received frequent visits from relatives and friends. He was then sentenced to three years' exile in Siberia. Prior to setting out there he was given several days' freedom to arrange his personal affairs. Lenin travelled to Siberia by train, unguarded. Once in his place of exile he was subjected to no restrictions on his activities and movements. He could and did visit fellow exiles in neighboring areas, was free to send and receive mail, including political literature, go on lengthy hunting expeditions, et cetera. Compared to what a political prisoner could expect under Nicholas I, or his treatment in today's (not to mention Stalin's) Russia, this must appear as almost a vacation! Police supervision of exiles tended to be lax, and several people, including such future celebrities as Trotsky and Stalin, found it easy to escape and regain European Russia. Lenin chose to complete his prescribed term and upon his return had little difficulty in obtaining a passport to go abroad, though the authorities could have entertained few illusions as to what he proposed to do there.

Of course there were cases of political prisoners being treated much less leniently or being unable to endure the solitude and monotony of exile. But the once dreaded words *Siberia* and *exile* no longer inspired the same fear nor had the same power to deter would-be-revolutionaries. One engaged in conspiratorial activities of a liberal variety had even less to fear; for his participation in the Union of Liberation a prince, like Paul Dolgorukov, risked at most an order confining him to one of his estates, a professor perhaps the loss of his chair. It was difficult for the government to cope with the impression produced on society by Leo Tolstoy, who as everybody knew abominated autocracy and on occasion supported what we would call today civil disobedience. The great writer's moral authority was probably no greater than had been Chernyshevsky's on the intelligentsia of the sixties. But then the government had had few compunctions about imprisoning and exiling the dissident, while now it was obvious to the authorities that Tolstoy could not be touched or silenced.

Tolstoy was a world figure; Chernyshevsky had been little known outside his own country. For all the stir created by radical ideas in the 1860s, they were of passionate interest to perhaps a few thousand. But in the early 1900s the number of professional men in Russia ran into hundreds of thousands, not all of them sharing the traditional antiautocracy posture of the intelligentsia, but a substantial majority convinced that for one reason or another, the old system could not continue. Throughout most of the nineteenth century the strength and self-confidence of the autocracy reflected very largely the country's backward condition, and to the great bulk of Russians the tsar was the only recognizable national figure. The masses, especially in the urban centers, were becoming educated; one-fourth of the population of the empire was literate. The regime's relative leniency in dealing with outright subversion, and its diffidence in the face of nonrevolutionary dissent, was an inevitable corollary of the changed social scene. Now that much of the fear that the government had once inspired was gone, it appeared to growing numbers of Russians as not only oppressive but inefficient, and even preposterous. Economic and educational changes were undermining its traditional source of strength—the loyalty of the rural masses to the throne.

Given rudimentary education, the peasant no longer took for granted that his status should be different from that of the other classes. It was not so much radical agitation as the facts of economic life, the growing pressure of population upon arable land and continuing agricultural depression which had been arousing the peasant out of his age-long political apathy.

There were people among the ruling bureaucracy who saw that the autocratic system could be given another lease on life only if it, as it had forty years before, became once more an agent of social change. Outstanding among these was Serge Witte, minister of finance between 1893 and 1903 and a vigorous sponsor of industrialization both through government spending and by attracting foreign capital to Russia. High tariff walls protected native industries, and the introduction of the gold standard acted as an incentive to foreign investors. A self-made man, with a background as an industrial manager, Witte was a novel type of high official: a manager and social engineer in a bureaucracy whose upper ranks were drawn mostly from the nobility and those with a military background. His horizons went far beyond industrialization. He saw that the country's overall economic and social progress was hampered by the status of the peasant and Russian agriculture. Three-quarters of the population lived (though no longer unfree serfs) as wards of both the state and the rural commune. The peasant's spirit of enterprise, his longing for private property, and his productivity were all inhibited by the commune. (Most communes were of the repartitional type, that is, the individual member's share of the land was usually in several parcels, and they were periodically redistributed in accordance with the size of the household, quality of the soil, etc. All of which interfered with efficient cultivation.) Hence, as Witte never ceased to argue in his memoranda to the emperor and his ministerial colleagues, economic progress and therefore the nation's and monarchy's interest required that the peasant be given full civic rights and be freed from the shackles of this obsolete institution. It should be made easy for the individual peasant to opt out of the commune, to consolidate his holdings and thus to become an efficient producer. This would then lead to the growth of a vigorous rural middle class, with a stake in economic and political stability. As it was, the poverty of the rural masses was a brake on industrial development, and a festering sore on the body politic.

Paradoxically, for much of his official career, Witte had appeared to be a staunch proponent of autocracy. But it was not so much a belief in the viability of the institution as his personal attachment to Alexander III, who had brought him from the obscurity of a railway manager to the ranks of high bureaucracy and eventually to be minister of finance and virtual director of the country's economy, which tinged his earlier attitudes. (The emperor disregarded such compromising facts—for official Russia of the time—as that his protégé's wife and some of his closest associates were Jewish.) But with the advent of the indecisive Nicholas II, Witte's support of the political status quo gave ground to growing doubts, and he eventually came to the conclusion that autocracy under modern conditions was incompatible with the national interest. Even in the memorandum he wrote in 1899, where he had opposed the extension of local self-government to the western provinces (from which it had been withheld because of the strong Polish element among the local gentry) there were veiled hints of the need for reform along constitutional lines. "Only in abstract theory can one postulate a state in which all free social activity is replaced by the activities of bureaucrats, and where the whole sphere of private and legal needs and aspirations is regulated by organs of the state."[18] Though this was designed to remain an intragovernment memorandum, Witte could not have been unaware that the abstract theory came close to describing the Russia of the day.

Witte, who for all his undoubted patriotism had a strong element of the careerist in him, continued to serve Nicholas, even though he had come to despise him and to loathe his neurotic and domineering wife and the parasitic imperial family. Several of the grand dukes held high military and civil offices, for which most of them were utterly unqualified. After 1900 Witte grew increasingly convinced that the system faced a catastrophe if it were not reformed. For a man with his bureaucratic temperament, the greatest danger of revolution came not so much from the revolutionaries themselves as from the government's sins of omission and commission. Timely reforms and efficient administration, if supplemented by a modicum of repression, could still avoid a violent upheaval.

But like most doomed regimes, Nicholas's was not only insensitive to the needs of the hour and incapable of developing coherent policies, it was prone to adventurist initiatives, both on the domestic and foreign fronts. Russia's foreign policy followed its traditional, and currently fashionable, pattern of imperial expansion. Witte himself was a cautious imperialist. As minister of finance, he took the lead in procuring economic concessions and special privileges in Manchuria, which from the mid-nineties became a virtual protectorate of the empire, with a sizable Russian military force "temporarily" stationed there. In 1898 Russia had wrested from the helpless Manchu Empire the Liaotung peninsula and Port Arthur. This increasingly blatant policy of trying to turn north and east China into a Russian dependency put St. Petersburg on a collision course with Japan, the newcomer to the ranks of great powers, which resented especially Russian efforts to secure domination of Korea.

A variety of factors were pushing Russia on its dangerous course of expansion in the Far East. Russia had wrested vast territories from China ever since the seventeenth century; it seemed, to paraphrase the rationale of another imperialist seizure, to be her manifest destiny to secure hegemony in the area. Her other traditional outlet of expansion, southward and at the expense of Turkey, was being blocked by the opposition of Britain and Austria, the latter now an ally of Germany. There were influential courtiers and officials who hoped to fill their pockets through various commercial enterprises in Manchuria and Korea. Japan, for all her rapid military and industrial modernization, was lightly regarded as a potential enemy. How could a small Oriental state prevail in a military conflict with the vast power of Russia! Moreover, such a conflict and its inevitable conclusion would have a salutory effect on the domestic situation. As Vyacheslav Plehve, who after a long service in the secret police became in 1902 minister of the interior, observed lightheartedly "a small victorious war" was exactly what the regime needed to stem the rising tide of political unrest.

To Witte, as to the more thoughtful members of the ruling bureaucracy, it was obvious that Russia could not afford a war, no matter how short or even victorious. Her finances were in a deplorable state, her army ill prepared to wage a campaign thousands of miles from the homeland, in an area connected with European Russia by a single railway line. Simple knowledge of history should have convinced the government how foolish it was to expect the war to have a tranquilizing effect on domestic politics. Even the great victorious war of 1812–15 brought in its wake increased political unrest and the Decembrist movement. The Crimean War buried the Nicholean system of autocracy. True, a threat to the motherland had never failed to produce an effusion of patriotic feeling, which on occasion, as in 1863, did help to unify society behind the regime and to destroy the nascent revolutionary movement. But this war would be fought entirely in a foreign and distant land, and for reasons incomprehensible to the average Russian. Witte spoke for a number of more realistic public officials when he declared that the last thing the world's largest country, with vast areas still undeveloped, needed was more territory. Yet an economic crisis and intrigues among his fellow bureaucrats (including Plehve) combined to topple him from his position of power. In August 1903 Nicholas II dismissed him suddenly as minister of finance. The most prescient of the empire's servants was promoted to a mainly honorific position which stripped him of any opportunity to arrest the further drift toward war and revolution. The Russian government continued on its reckless course, rejecting several chances at accommodation with Japan, while doing little to prepare society and its armed forces for war. Tokyo, its diplomatic position strengthened by an alliance with Britain, signed in 1902, decided upon the ultimate step. With little regard for the punctilios of Old World diplomacy, the Japanese on February 8, 1904, without a prior declaration of war, suddenly attacked with their warships the Russian base of Port Arthur.

What followed was an uninterrupted series of Russian military and naval defeats. Geography certainly played a key role in Japan's successes. But the decrepitude of the imperial regime was now vividly confirmed by its lamentable management of the war effort. Russia's military and naval forces were poorly commanded, and their supply system broke down. The pathetic incompetence of the St. Petersburg government was epitomized by the tragicomic saga of Russia's Baltic squadron. Eight months after the start of war, it was dispatched on a mission to relieve Port Arthur, now besieged and blockaded by the Japanese fleet. The journey was to take the mostly obsolete and badly maintained Russian warships on a trip around the world and lasted seven months. In the North Sea an incident occurred which brought Russia to the verge of an armed clash with Britain. A Russian commander mistook English fishing trawlers for Japanese torpedo boats and opened fire, sinking some of them. With the incident finally submitted to international arbitration, the ill-omened fleet lumbered on, arriving in the China Sea after Port Arthur had capitulated and the Russian armies in Manchuria had been repeatedly trounced. Then, on May 27, 1905, the Japanese navy fell upon the dispirited and incompetently officered Russian force in the Straits of Tsushima, and annihilated it in the most one-sided major naval battle since Trafalgar. The war had been lost, and the main problem was now not how much of Russia's position in the Far East could be rescued in a humiliating peace settlement but whether the tsarist regime would be able to survive the short and disastrous war and the revolution it had helped to ignite.

To be sure the actual beginning of the war prompted a surge of nationalist feeling. It was aroused by the manner in which the Japanese opened the hostilities and then by the tenacity of the Russian soldiers in the besieged fortress of Port Arthur. In *Liberation* Struve at first struck the patriotic note; the fatherland was in danger and it was the duty of every Russian, no matter how oppressive and inept the government had proved, to support it in the struggle against the country's enemy. But very soon this qualified support for the regime was replaced, even among the moderates of the Union of Liberation, by seeing the war as yet another reckless adventure by the ruling bureaucracy, and the determination to exploit it as such for the struggle against the autocracy. Symposium, that half-conspiracy and half-pressure group of liberal noblemen and intelligentsia, had initially decided to suspend its political agitation for the duration of the war. But by August 1904 it shifted its attitude: the war must be ended by a compromise settlement, and the regime, having demonstrated its ineptitude in the military sphere, could not be trusted to secure an honorable peace. Hence the pressure for a representative assembly must be revived and intensified.

The Russo-Japanese War has traditionally received but little attention from either Soviet or Western historians, who are usually eager to rush on to the greater dramas of the first and second revolutions. Yet it was a vital link in the chain of events which produced the two. It loosened and thus made easier the definite severance in 1916–17 of the traditional bond between the autocracy and Russian nationalism. The Crimean War had discredited one particular type of autocracy, that practiced by Nicholas I. This war went far in demonstrating the incompatibility of the institution itself with the national interest. The regime had shown itself to be a poor custodian of the country's greatness and power and thus had damaged irreparably the last rationale which could be used in its defense. In the Crimean War Europe's major powers were united against Russia. Now, for no cogent reasons, Nicholas II exposed the country to a humiliating defeat at the hands of an Oriental nation whose population was less than one-third of Russia's. It became almost inevitable that political change would come not through reform, but through revolution.

Political dissent and conspiratorial activity had been steady companions of the autocracy since 1815. Yet for all the profusion of revolutionary groups, plots, et cetera, such groups had always been small in numbers, their membership almost exclusively limited to the upper classes: the nobility and intelligentsia. Peasant uprisings had never been focused around politics in the proper sense of the word. Much as they had tried, revolutionaries of various persuasions had never succeeded in creating anything resembling a mass movement against the autocracy. Hence the paradox that while in no other country on the continent did the idea and possibility of revolution preoccupy so much the attention of both the government and society, Russia alone among the major European states failed to experience a mass revolt against the established order throughout the nineteenth century. It had been the hope of the Social Democrats that the rapidly growing urban proletariat would provide the fulcrum for such a revolt. But four years after the formation of their party, Lenin admitted in *What Is to Be Done?* that it was hopeless to expect the workers by themselves to take up the political struggle. It would have to be a fairly long-drawn process to build the kind of party which he believed could prepare for and lead the working class in this struggle. Thus, for all the inflammatory rhetoric, not even the revolutionaries really believed that the decisive blow leading to the downfall of the autocracy would be struck by the people. Rather, it would be an unremitting pressure by society which would make the initial and decisive breach in the system. Pressured and ostracized by the progressive elements within the gentry and the intelligentsia, the government would have to grant a constitution.

Yet history was to confound both those tsarist bureaucrats who saw the revolutionary danger as coming from the intelligentsia and the Jews rather than from the masses, and people like Lenin, who had abandoned hope of a spontaneous rising by the Russian proletariat against their rulers. It was a peculiar irony, if not retribution of fate, that it should have been the tsarist government which unwittingly taught the Russian worker how to organize for such a struggle. Whatever the success of socialist and other radical groups in organizing Russian workers and in instilling in them class consciousness, the major step in that direction came, in the first years of the twentieth century, from seemingly the most unexpected source—the secret police.

The idea originated in the twilight world of the Okhrana, with its highly refined techniques of political espionage and provocation, an official underworld whose tentacles gripped not only the entire governmental machinery during the last years of the regime but also, through its double agents, the radical camp. This in many ways symbiotic relationship between the secret police and revolutionaries was to affect profoundly the psychology of both and would leave indelible traces on the mentality of the future Communist rulers of Russia. Much of what might be called the practical political philosophy of people like Stalin had been forged through the experience of years of political underground work where one could never be absolutely sure that one's closest collaborator was not a double agent, and where conversely one knew and depended on secret sympathizers within the police apparatus.

Serge Zubatov, who initiated what became known as police unionism, had been in his early youth a member of one of the offshoots of The People's Will. From a genuine revolutionary he soon turned into a police informer, later becoming a regular official of the security organs and advancing rapidly to become a colonel and chief of the Moscow Okhrana at the age of thirty-two. His professional success reflected his skill in fighting subversion; he introduced scientific methods of police detection and insisted that his agents study the ideologies and history of the revolutionary movements which they combated. Zubatov was a worthy successor of another master spy, George Sudeykin, who by infiltrating his men into the high command of The People's Will managed to destroy its terrorist organization in the early 1880s.

Yet Zubatov was far from being a mere cynical manipulator. Unlike most of his fellow bureaucrats, he saw clearly that the autocracy could not be saved through sheer repression. It needed popular support, and under modern conditions this had to be sought elsewhere than in traditional reliance on the passive loyalty of the peasant masses. The most dynamic factor on the social scene was the growing labor movement. The most acute and present danger therefore was that the workers' unceasing striving for the improvement of their economic lot would be utilized by the revolutionaries for their own purposes, and that the Russian proletarian, though he cared little and understood less about Karl Marx or a constitution, would be turned into a fighter in their cause. Zubatov then developed a modern version of the thesis of the tsar and his people: the government should win the workers' support not only by protecting them through labor legislation, but also by encouraging and guiding workers' associations that protected their interests and sought concessions from employers. In this way the autocracy would demonstrate to the urban masses that unlike those radical intelligents, it had their real interest at heart, and that it was the Russian tsar, rather than some esoteric and alien ideology, who would protect them from exploitation and stand behind their efforts to obtain higher pay and better working conditions.

The policeman-social philosopher launched his experiment in 1901. A number of Moscow working-class converts to his ideas, some of them alumni of clandestine socialist circles, were encouraged to organize workers' mutual aid societies and associations—in fact labor unions, though the name itself, because of its militant connotations, was usually eschewed. Imitating, for a time very successfully, the socialists' propaganda and agitation techniques, Zubatov supplemented his organizational efforts with a many-sided campaign of indoctrination. The more advanced among his adherents, the officer corps of his movements, were instructed in social and economic subjects. He himself "lectured on the history of the labor movement in Western Europe . . . discussed the history, tactics, and programs of the revolutionary movements," with of course the appropriate conclusion that it was only through peaceful and legal means and with the government's help that the worker could realize his aspirations.[19] Members of the Orthodox clergy and conservative journalists preached on the virtues of autocracy and the established church and on the evils of alien ideologies.

To the horror of the Socialists and other opponents of the regime, *Zubatovshchina,* the Zubatov system, was proving a huge success. On February 19, 1902, on the anniversary of the Emancipation, Zubatov was able to muster some fifty thousand Moscow workers in a patriotic ceremony before the monument of Alexander II. The number of participants in Zubatov's unions dwarfed that of Moscow's social democratic workers' circles. Impressed by such hopeful developments, Zubatov's superiors licensed police unionism in several other urban centers, notably in the great Black Sea port of Odessa. What was especially hopeful from the authorities' point of view was that Zubatovshchina was even gaining hold among the most class-conscious element of the working class, the Jewish proletarians of the western and southern regions, who because they were subjected to ethnic discrimination as well as economic exploitation, were most likely to become recruits of the radical cause.

Yet it should have been obvious from the beginning that under the actual conditions of Russia in the beginning of the century, the Zubatov scheme had no chance of success and, in the long run, was bound to accentuate the revolutionary danger it had been designed to eliminate. Both in substance and spirit the police chief's ideas were more in tune with the modern totalitarian state than with an old-fashioned autocratic one. Indeed, Zubatov himself possessed many qualities which would have made him an ideal Soviet official under Stalin and his successors. The imperial administration in its senescence was incapable of either following any consistent social policy or sponsoring a bold and unprecedented experiment in what, to use an anachronistic term, would have been a variety of national socialism. Police unionism caused dismay not only on the left. The factory owners besieged their protector, the Ministry of Finance, with complaints: it was certainly an odd way for the government to promote foreign investments and industrial growth by officially sponsoring unions and taking their side in industrial disputes. The issue was aggravated by an intrabureaucratic rivalry, and Witte's struggle with Zubatov's ultimate superior, Minister of Interior Plehve.

Moreover, unless it was carried out systematically and consistently, the government's sponsorship of unions was bound to have dangerous consequences. The workers were learning to organize and becoming aware of their power to exact concessions from the factory owners; in brief they were losing their passivity and enlarging their sociopolitical horizons. Once learned, such habits and attitudes would remain, and find other expressions than through patriotic demonstrations.

By the summer of 1903 Zubatov's enemies both on the left and the right had finally a cause for rejoicing. What began as police unionism in Odessa led to a general strike which for several days paralyzed the great port. Soon afterward Plehve unceremoniously fired Zubatov. Like a true revolutionary, he was sent into administrative exile and never again held an official position. For all the government's ingratitude, the inventive policeman remained a fervent nationalist. In 1917, hearing of Nicholas II's abdication and convinced that the demise of autocracy spelled the end of Russia's greatness, Zubatov committed suicide.

His dismissal did not mean a complete end to his experiment. Plehve himself, whose work with the secret police antedated Zubatov's, also believed that the revolutionary danger had to be fought by securing popular support for the autocracy. This now was a situation reminiscent of the tale of the sorcerer and his apprentice. Plehve's policies were as ill conceived as they were reprehensible. We mentioned his fatuous belief that a war would have a salutory effect on the political situation. Appeals to anti-Semitic prejudice were another element in Plehve's design to turn the masses against the revolutionary movement. The minister of the interior, the official guardian of law and order, did little during his tenure of office (1902–04) to restrain anti-Jewish agitation and riots, the most notorious of which, the Kishinev pogrom, was widely believed to have been caused and aggravated by the passive attitude of the local police. To police unionism Plehve attempted to impart a narrow monarchist and chauvinist character and was hardly discriminating in examining the credentials of individuals charged with its guidance.

The Sorcerer's Apprentices: The 1905 Revolution

It was thus ironic that it fell to Plehve to receive and submit to the tsar a loyal address of the St. Petersburg Association of Russian Factory Workers. This branch of police unionism had been in the planning stage prior to Zubatov's fall. Following it, and with most of his working-class agents themselves suspect, the project fell into abeyance. Finally, in February 1904, the association was approved by the authorities and held its organizational meeting. Its head, though a former associate of Zubatov, was still believed by the police to be reliable, and indeed his background was such as to inspire official confidence. He was George Gapon, a young priest of Ukrainian extraction, currently serving as chaplain of St. Petersburg transit jail, and highly recommended by various influential dignitaries of the church. In brief he was not the kind of person to let the organization he headed stray from the straight and narrow path. The initial meeting was also reassuring. The assembled, it was noted in the press, sang "God Save the Tsar" not once but three times, listened respectfully to the speech by the local chief of police, and passed a resolution asking the minister of the interior "to lay at His Majesty's feet their loyal assurances of love and devotion."[20] Speedy communication was not characteristic of the imperial government, and it was only on May 20 that Plehve discharged that errand, whereupon the tsar deigned to express "His Most Gracious Thanks" and best wishes for the success of the enterprise.

Not long afterward, on July 15, 1904, Plehve was blown up by a bomb thrown by a Socialist Revolutionary, the assassination prepared by one of his own agents, Yevno Azev. Few political assassinations, even in Russia, have been greeted by society with such general approval. A contemporary would recall that he was conversing with a prominent nobleman and landowner when the news was brought in. His companion crossed himself, was obviously about to say, "Thank God," but seeing his interlocutor's shocked expression said feebly, "Heaven have mercy." The disastrous war, Plehve's shocking use of his powers—he not only appealed to the lowest instincts of the masses but also employed chicanery in dealing with liberals and his intrabureacracy rivals—all produced a situation where society virtually rejoiced at his murder.

The moral bankruptcy of the regime tended to attenuate the differences between revolutionaries and moderates. The autocracy's last line of defense, its hold on nationalism and the conviction that only the traditional system could preserve the unity of the country was crumbling. In October an unprecedented event occurred in Russian politics: a conference of liberals and revolutionaries. Also represented, in addition to Russian enemies of the regime, were representatives of several national groups seeking autonomy or independence from Russia. The participants ranged from Azev, representing the terrorist Socialist Revolutionaries (and on the side the secret police) to Prince Dolgorukov of the Union of Liberation. On the national issue those present ranged from Professor Paul

Milyukov, who combined liberalism with a strong belief in the unity of the empire, to delegates of the revolutionary and separatist parties of Poland, Georgia, and Finland. The Union of Liberation participated despite the rumors (which were largely true) that some of their Polish and Finnish fellow conferees had contacts with the Japanese intelligence. On the other hand, the Russian Social Democrats rejected the invitation to join this Conference of Opposition and Revolutionary Organizations of the Russian Empire, allegedly because of the involvement of some of the participants with the Japanese but most likely because of the current split within their party. It was the fact that such a conference could be held at all—believers in a peaceful evolution toward a constitutional monarchy sitting down with terrorists and anarchists, partisans of Russia great and united along with the fighters for Polish independence—which endowed it with historical importance.

There are several ways of looking at the willingness of representatives of the Union of Liberation to associate with and to subscribe to a joint declaration with the people whose ideologies should have been as alien to them as that of autocracy. Viewed through the prism of 1917, the event can be seen as a symptom of the Russian liberal's fatal weakness, his lack of self-assurance and his sense of guilt about his moderation, which repeatedly made him yield and at the decisive moment rendered him helpless before the left. To a contemporary, however, the picture looked quite different: it was the incredible obtuseness and incompetence of the tsarist regime which narrowed the gap between the people who ten years before had humbly petitioned for a surrogate of parliamentarianism and those who would destroy the entire social order, between the fervent nationalists and those for whom any Russia, be it autocratic or democratic, was alien and hateful.

From yet another point of view the Russian moderate of the time worked under a considerable psychological handicap. He was deeply conscious, even embarrassed by the fact, that he was a member of the privileged class. The social antecedents of his Social Democratic or Socialist Revolutionary counterpart were for the most part very much like his own, and yet the Russian liberal saw in the latter not Vladimir Ulyanov-Lenin, hereditary noble and lawyer, but a spokesman for the people. Therefore, one could not go too far in criticizing the radical's methods and goals. This attitude also reflected the intellectual's traditional feeling of inferiority vis-à-vis a man of action. The revolutionaries were fighting the regime with bombs, trying to stir up local insurrections, the liberals with speeches, writings, and resolutions.

Yet objectively it was the latter technique which in the fall and winter of 1904 promised to bear fruit. The government was clearly in retreat; society, that is, the forces for reform, on the offensive. Plehve's successor, Prince Peter Svyatopolk-

Mirsky, abandoned his predecessor's reactionary and repressive course and sought to appease public opinion. The campaign for reform and a constitution could be conducted without undue interference by the police. Thus a meeting of zemstvo representatives from all over Russia voted in November by a large majority in favor of a representative assembly with full legislative powers. (It was characteristic of the government's pusillanimity that this meeting was first authorized, then banned, and then finally permitted, provided it would preserve the appearance of a private gathering.) Spokesmen for traditionally the most conservative element in Russian society demanded unambiguously an end to the autocratic system. A minority opted for a national council with purely consultative functions, but there were also voices suggesting that it was not sufficient to press the tsar to grant a constitution and that the decision as to how Russia was to be ruled should be entrusted to a constituent assembly elected by the people. But the general orientation of the zemstvo leaders, reflecting that of their principal constituents, the gentry, was still monarchist. The memorandum embodying their views which was handed to the government urged the tsar to follow in the footsteps of his reformer grandfather. Let him immediately issue a manifesto asserting, even if only in principle, his will "to abolish the police bureaucratic system and to assemble for creative work the elected representatives of the land."[21]

By the time the memorandum reached the tsar at the end of November, its reverential tone toward the monarchy seemed somewhat anachronistic, so fast were events moving. The Union of Liberation, though in a kind of symbiotic relationship with the zemstvo people, was ideologically—or perhaps it would be more precise to say emotionally—more radical than the progressive gentry. The government's indecisiveness now emboldened the union to emerge from its semiconspiratorial status and to launch a public campaign for basic political reforms. Somewhat in the manner of the ancient Hebrews before Jericho, the Union proposed to bring down the walls of autocracy by making a lot of noise. This took the form of a series of mass banquets organized in the main cities of the country, supposedly to celebrate the fortieth anniversary of the great judicial reforms, but in fact to denounce the regime and pass resolutions calling for a constitution. (This hitherto taboo word had not actually been used in the statement of the zemstvo representatives.) These were huge affairs; the initial dinner in St. Petersburg gathered 676 intelligentsia notables and that number was soon surpassed by similar events in other cities, the record set by Saratov with 1500! The fact that the government did not dare to interfere with this sedition by conviviality led to the inevitable escalation of political demands. At first their language was circumspect, echoing that of the gentry leaders. But soon the resolutions grew more radical and specific, including such items as the demand for a constituent assembly to determine the future form of government (i.e., free presumably to proclaim a republic) and elected on the basis of universal, equal, and direct vote, for the responsibility of the executive to the legislature, and for an unconditional amnesty for all political crimes (including, one assumes, political terrorism).[22]

Such demands went far beyond the original intentions of the sponsor of the campaign—the Union of Liberation. Rationally, the average liberal could hardly believe that Russian society was capable, in one leap so to speak, of traversing the enormous distance between autocracy and popular sovereignty. But emotionally the intelligentsia had been gripped by an irresistible and exulting feeling of its own importance.

A contemporary Cassandra, himself a firm believer in constitutionalism, noted the irresponsible and superficial aspect of the banquets: people who went to them to wine, dine, and sign resolutions did so in many cases "out of curiosity, snobbery, following a fashionable fad. Some had never been interested in politics, but now they discovered that it was a very agreeable way of spending time."[23] In view of what happened subsequently, it is easy in retrospect to be censorious. But a more balanced judgment must acknowledge how hard it must have been for the Russian intelligent to restrain his euphoria and impatience and to view the situation soberly and with proper misgivings. For the first time in Russian history he did not have to be the least bit afraid to say and write openly what was on his mind. It was the bureaucracy which was scared and at its wits' end about what to do with this liberal version of St. Vitus's dance. One could not very well pack off to jail or into exile thousands of professional men and leading landowners. And to compound the trouble, the libertarian and reform epidemic, as a reactionary had to view it, had also afflicted the main beneficiary of the government's recent policies: the capitalist. Prominent industrialists joined their voices to those of their gentry and intelligentsia counterparts in demanding representative institutions.

Thus a revolution had already taken place. Within ten years society, so supine prior to 1894, had emancipated itself of the awe of the autocracy. What a progressive had barely dared to ask for in the beginning of the reign—that the tsar grant a consultative assembly based upon and composed of the upper classes —ten years later would satisfy only a staunch conservative. Now it was a senseless dream to believe that the autocracy could continue unimpaired. For most thinking Russians the only remaining question was when and how the absolutist system would be transformed into a constitutional one.

The awareness that something had to be done finally reached the emperor. Largely under the pressure of Prince Mirsky, and in the face of stubborn opposition from such relics of the past as Pobyedonostsev, still in office though with a shadow of his former influence, he issued on December 12 a rescript which promised a number of reforms. One year earlier they would have gone far in meeting the aspirations of the progressive gentry and intelligentsia, but now they were bound to be found inadequate. Whatever good the rescript might have produced by at least lowering the revolutionary fever was completely undone by a simultaneously issued government announcement. Once again the regime displayed its fantastically poor sense of timing and insensitivity to the popular mood. The tone of the announcement would have been appropriate in the reigns of Alexander III or even Nicholas I; under the actual circumstances it sounded preposterous. The government haughtily condemned all the recent expressions of political activism, from the moderate demands of the zemstvo representatives to street demonstrations:

> Such agitation against the existing order is alien to the Russian people, which remains faithful to the immemorial foundations of the state. . . . The people participating in this agitation movement are unmindful of the heavy trials which Russia is currently undergoing [the Japanese war], blinded by the illusory boons they expect from subverting the ages-long traditions of Russian political life. They are thus, if unwittingly, rendering help not to their Fatherland, but to its enemies.[24]

But was there a real chance of the revolution continuing and prevailing through peaceful means? Again our outlook tends to be shaped unduly by what was to take place in the immediate future and, later, in 1917. Is it really conceivable that Russia could have evolved peacefully into a constitutional monarchy and a free society and functioned happily ever after? Perhaps not. But chances for such a decisive turn of events loomed stronger in 1904 than ever before. Paradoxically, the revolution up to now had been nurtured and led by nonrevolutionaries, people with impeccably liberal ideals, nationalists who retained at least a sentimental attachment to the monarchy as an institution, if not to the actual occupant of the throne. The government could fume, threaten, and occasionally repress, but short of instituting a reign of terror against the intellectual and social elite of the nation, could not have withstood this veritable siege by its own society. The extremists themselves accepted for the time being the initiative of the liberals, some of them joining in the banquet campaign and subscribing to its constitutional slogans. Even the Marxists found it difficult to swim against the current. After all, their own program proclaimed that a "bourgeois democratic" revolution must precede the socialist one.

Temperamentally, however, many socialists, especially but not exclusively those in Lenin's camp, could not relish the prospect of those liberal princes, professors, and lawyers cheating them out of a real revolution and shuddered at the vision, for them a nightmare, of Russia's politics becoming assimilated to the Western pattern. Their ideology might be that of Karl Marx, but in their psychological makeup they were heirs of those earlier revolutionaries who proclaimed that "we ought to bless destiny that we have not lived the life of Europe." The most efficacious way of saving Russia from such a grim fate was to play upon the intelligentsia's traditional phobia: that any moderation in the struggle with the government might be a betrayal of the cause of the people. The liberals would have to be pushed into more and more radical positions, thus making unlikely a peaceful accommodation between society and the regime. No one knew better how to play that game then Lenin, who throughout kept denouncing the liberals as pusillanimous and insincere, hardly better than the tsarist bureaucrats against whom allegedly they were fighting. These attacks from the left seldom failed to have at least partially the desired effect and needless to say, the liberals rarely, if ever, replied to the socialists in their own language.

This psychological malaise of liberalism may have contributed to the drama which opened 1905 and which changed drastically the character of the revolution. The St. Petersburg Assembly of Factory Workers had been organized by the young priest Father Gapon, who had a special gift for gaining the workers' confidence, and his union grew rapidly. The chief of police reported smugly to his superiors that Gapon's union provided "a firm barrier against the spread of subversive socialist ideas among the workers" with its members "spending their free time wisely and soberly." But Gapon's influence spread also far beyond the union. By the end of 1904 he was the best known and most influential person among the lower-class population of St. Petersburg. Such success might have turned the head of a much sturdier personality than the "little father" (the common appellation for a parish priest) with his adventurous and ambitious disposition. He began to establish contacts with radicals of various persuasions, and he obviously began to develop political ambitions. His disillusioned associates were subsequently to claim that Gapon had told them that sooner or later the tsar would summon him to his side and make him virtual ruler of Russia. This would not have been out of character for the good father, who was also inordinately fond of women, gambling, and strong spirits. It is that ambitious drive rather than, as some historians assert, Gapon's genuine concern for the workers which probably explains his subsequent actions. (If he was really and truly converted to the cause of social justice, whether before or after the Bloody Sunday, how can one account for the fact that after returning from his flight abroad in 1906, he once more offered his services to the police?)

Gapon's real role may have been a secret to the more naive among his followers, but not to anybody else. Even so the Union of Liberation established close relations with his organization and tried to use the group for its own purposes.

Eventually even the socialists, while denouncing Gapon as a provocateur, decided to turn tables on the government by infiltrating the Assembly.* A minor dispute in the Putilov factory where four members of his union were fired gave Gapon a pretext for calling a strike which spread to other enterprises. (Disorders in the same plant would play a similar role in triggering the February 1917 revolution.) By January 7, 1905, practically the whole working force of the capital was immobilized. Simultaneously the horrified authorities learned that Father Gapon was organizing a mass procession to the Winter Palace to lay before the tsar a list of grievances and demands of his faithful and suffering people.

Subsequent events reflect little credit on any of the parties concerned. The government clearly lost its head. Belatedly an order was issued for Gapon's arrest, but the police did not dare to drag him out from the midst of one of the mass meetings he was almost continuously haranguing. Both the Union of Liberation and the socialists were to claim credit for inspiring the political demands Gapon would present to the tsar; both, less convincingly, were to allege that they tried to dissuade him from leading the manifestation on the grounds it would lead to mass bloodshed. There must also remain some doubt as to how peaceful and loyal in its character the march was supposed to be. One version of the petition has in its concluding section the following appeal to the monarchy: "Deign to order [what we ask for] and then Thou will make Russia happy and glorious with Thy name forever in our hearts and our descendants'. If Thou don't, we will die on this very square in front of Thine palace."[25]

The petition itself, which Gapon would recite at the workers' gatherings, is a curious document, obviously a composite of several drafts from several sources. The original version stressed mainly economic demands, higher pay, et cetera. It also contained what, for the time, was a strikingly advanced idea: all factory disputes should be arbitrated by a joint management-labor committee, without whose permission no worker could be fired. The final draft, which leaped boldly into politics, came obviously from the suggestions by Gapon's friends among the radicals. It urged nothing more or less but that the tsar turn Russia into the most democratic and most socially progressive state in Europe. The Union of Liberation's hand is evident in the plea for a constituent assembly, elected by universal, equal, direct, and secret vote—something which went beyond the official program of the union but of late had been endorsed by its left wing—as well as in the points about freedom of speech, press, assembly, et cetera, all of which were needed to save the people "from the corrupt and stifling bureaucratic government." Then there was a series of demands clearly emanating from various socialist teachings: land to the people, replacement of all indirect taxation by

*It is not clear whether the initiative for such contacts came from Gapon or from the other parties.

progressive income tax, separation of church and state, an unconditional amnesty for all political and religious offenders. For all such contributions to its authorship, the petition is expressive of the deeply felt sense of grievance and hope of the common Russian man. "Here our Sovereign Lord are our chief needs which we place before thee."[26]

For some the whole business must have appeared as a bad joke history was about to play upon the traditional rationale of autocracy: "The people's unshakable trust in the tsar." From being an abstraction the people were suddenly to materialize, come to the tsar, and demand that he carry out a revolution.

The government's paralysis was now interrupted by a violent convulsion. It announced that the procession would not be allowed to reach the palace square. On Sunday, January 9, as huge crowds estimated at one hundred fifty thousand, carrying icons, portraits of the tsar, and national flags (Gapon had forbidden any would-be-socialist marchers to carry red flags or other revolutionary signs) began to flow from several directions toward the Winter Palace, they were met by the Cossacks and other army detachments. When they pressed on, the troops opened fire. According to the government, one hundred twenty-eight people were killed. Other estimates of the casualties varied from a realistic several hundred to five thousand. Whatever Gapon's ultimate designs had the procession reached the palace, it was admitted by everybody, including the government, that the demonstrators were unarmed and their behavior generally peaceful. (It was only following the dispersal of the crowds that some revolutionary hangers-on tried to throw up barricades.) Gapon, who had led one of the crowds in his priestly robes, escaped unscathed. He received a temporary refuge in the home of Maxim Gorky, already famous as a writer and soon to be close to Lenin. The same night his host escorted him to a protest meeting of the intelligentsia. There the "little father" read a proclamation denouncing "the beast-tsar and his thieving officials" who showed themselves "killers of our brothers, women and children."[27] Reverting to his priestly identity, he pronounced his "pastoral curse" on officers and soldiers who shot unarmed people, as well as "his pastoral benediction and absolution" of all those who should renounce their oath of allegiance and take up arms against the tsar. Not long afterward Gapon was spirited abroad. Such was the mood of the hour that nobody among the regime's critics and enemies, from the liberals to the Bolsheviks, was inclined to blame him even in part, for what had transpired. On the contrary, to the dissident Russian the erstwhile and soon-to-be-again police agent was a national hero. Once in the West he became the object of a brisk competition among various revolutionary parties, each of them eager to enroll this prestigious leader of the working class in its ranks. "Facts have decided in favor of Gapon," wrote Lenin,[28] and even more revealingly, "Can the Social Democrats seize this spontaneous movement [of Gapon's followers]." Accepting his new role, Gapon presided at a meeting of representatives of several revolutionary organizations. Here this strange man revealed yet another side of his personality: police agent and unwitting revolutionary, he was also a Russian patriot. After listening to the spokesmen for the Polish and Armenian socialists he exclaimed that they wanted to break up the country. "They are all for themselves and nobody cares about Russia."[29] He also astounded those present by objecting to the resolution urging the expropriation of landowners' property and the free distribution of their land to the peasants: it would demoralize the latter and plunge Russia into anarchy.

Such apprehensions did not seem to affect the attitudes of the antiregime forces, whether at home or abroad in the wake of January 9. The events of Bloody Sunday set off a wave of strikes and disorders throughout the empire. (Indeed, there were manifestations against the Russian government in many of Europe's capitals.) The intensity of the strike action during the next three months was unprecedented as was its character, now mainly political—an expression of solidarity with St. Petersburg workers and of execration of the government's actions. Some half-million workers put down their tools in January, and only by March had the number of strikers declined below one hundred thousand. In places, notably Poland and the Caucasus, the strikes were accompanied by mass meetings and demonstrations advancing not only economic demands but also displaying antigovernment and revolutionary slogans: Down with autocracy; Down with the war. On January 15 barricades went up in the streets of Warsaw, and at the end of three days' fighting there were four hundred killed and wounded. The coming of spring touched off equally widespread riots in the countryside, with the peasants seizing the landlords' estates and residences, attacking police and government offices. This first revolutionary wave of 1905 was essentially a spontaneous response to the news from St. Petersburg, with the revolutionary parties, socialists of several labels in the cities, and the Socialist Revolutionaries in the countryside hastening to catch up with and then to get ahead of the masses of workers and peasants, in the spirit of Lenin's words just quoted.*

The St. Petersburg tragedy and its corollaries were, of course, grist for the extremists' mill. But another result was to turn the intelligentsia liberals, at least temporarily, into outright revolutionaries. Having to some extent inspired the Gapon venture, the Union of Liberation was in a better position than most to know the full complexities of the January 9 drama and by virtue of its principles and goals ought to have been more inhibited in trying to exploit it for political purposes. It is understandable how in the first flush of emotion at the news, the official organ of the union should have denounced the tsar as "an enemy and

---

*Needless to say, in the more uninhibited Soviet accounts, the whole upsurge is attributed to the leadership of the Bolsheviks.

executioner of the people" and called for revenge, though it must have appeared probable even then that the primary responsibility for the shootings lay with the local officials, the tsar not having interfered with their disposition. However, even after its leaders had had time to reflect, the Union plunged deliberately into revolutionary agitation. Its local branches distributed inflammatory pamphlets, one being Gapon's proclamation calling upon the army to mutiny.[30] Nor did it condemn antigovernment violence. Terrorism intensified, its most notable victim being Grand Duke Serge, long considered the most reactionary figure in his nephew's entourage; he was killed in February by a member of the SR Fighting Organization. (Its head and the planner of the assassination, Azev, was at the time in Paris entertaining Gapon.)

For obvious reasons the people who had pledged themselves to work for a peaceful transformation of Russia now felt constrained to abandon their moderation. There was their fear of being left alone and behind with the entire society being gripped by the revolutionary fever. The liberals' enemies had always denounced them as an insignificant group of troublemakers, while the people stood firmly behind the tsar. It would have been less than human to resist the temptation to exult in and exploit the discomfiture of the camp of reaction. Their initial contacts with Gapon had been inspired by the hope that the masses would come to understand and trust the liberals and realize that no matter what the socialists were saying, they were solicitous of the people's interests, and not just seeking some fancy freedoms and new privileges for their own class.

The fable of the sorcerer's apprentice is as applicable to the liberals as to the government; both unwittingly helped release forces which they would be unable to control. Autocracy had been crumbling under the peaceful siege of society; but now faced with a frontal assault, it would recover some of its former vigor and identification with the national interest and thus gain another lease on life. History was to show that this was but a short reprieve. The real, violent revolution would undermine the foundations not only of the autocratic system but also of the Russian state. When eventually both would collapse, they would also bury Russian liberalism under their debris.

The regime's first steps after the January catastrophe indicated that it had begun to recover from its paralysis. The capital was placed under martial law. Its new governor general was General Dmitri Trepov, whose influence with the tsar was to become so great that for a while he was called, with some exaggeration, Russia's dictator. His philosophy for dealing with demonstrations was simple. One of his orders to the troops was to pass into history: "Bullets ought not be spared; blank cartridges are not to be used."[31] In the short run such methods proved effective in preventing what would happen a few months hence, when St. Petersburg passed under virtual control of the revolutionaries. Simultaneously there were efforts to improve the tsar's popularity among the working class. Some of these efforts obviously were, especially to the radically minded of the time, ridiculously transparent, yet no doubt they were at least temporarily effective in lowering the revolutionary fever. One rather humorous episode involved thirty-four St. Petersburg workers hastily collected by the police and after having been searched for weapons, dispatched before the tsar in a much, much belated effort to demonstrate how the monarch was accessible to his working-class subjects. Conceivably Nicholas I or Alexander II might have been successful with this ploy. For their descendant it was the first such encounter, and to compound the awkwardness of the occasion he read his speech from a prepared text. He was solicitous of their interests, he told the workers, but they should not have tried to approach him in an "unruly mob." However, "I believe in the honest sentiments of the working people and in their unshakable loyalty to Myself, so I forgive them," concluded the unfortunate man, his utter insensitivity to the public relations aspects of his office not the least of his shortcomings.[32] For all the contrived character of the meeting, much as it was sneered at by the radicals and the intelligentsia, it probably had a soothing effect on the mass of the workers.

Ironically, a more serious attempt to open a dialogue with the workers backfired, and its ultimate consequences were indeed to be fateful, not only for the regime. The authorities announced a plan for a commission composed of officials, industrialists, and representatives of labor that would attend to the causes of social strife and economic distress in the capital and suggest remedial measures. Workers in each factory were to select delegates, in numbers proportionate to its working force, who then would constitute a sort of electoral college, which would send employees' representatives to the commission proportionately. The elections were to be run entirely by the workers. All this must have seemed like a heaven-sent boon for radicals, notably the Bolsheviks and the Mensheviks. Though constituting but a fraction of the total working force, they could now, due to their organizational cohesion and training, compensate for their numerical weakness and turn the elections into a political campaign.

The first round of voting produced four hundred representatives (one for each five hundred workers). Socialists from both factions accounted for less than one-fifth of the total but still were a force quite sufficient to sway the attitude of their politically unsophisticated fellow electors. Before proceeding with the second round of elections, the workers' representatives, under the pressure of their Social Democratic colleagues, faced the government with a number of preconditions, partly political in their nature and which those who inspired them knew the government had to reject. Thus the socialists accomplished two goals; they used the elections for radical propaganda and for expanding their influence among the masses, and at the same time they frustrated the regime's attempt to conciliate the workers and to show itself solicitous of their needs. The Shidlovsky (from the name of the official designated as its chairman) commission and its fiasco was yet another example of the regime unwittingly presenting the revolutionaries with the very weapons which it would use against their donor.

Zubatovshchina had hastened the development of labor unions and of their class consciousness. Now the government once again impelled the workers to organize, this time on a mass scale and without the tutelage of the police. Unlike the Zubatov and Gapon unions, government agents stayed away from the workers' meetings and elections, which enabled the radicals to turn the whole affair to political use. In its essentials the citywide gathering of workers' representatives was already a preview of the *soviet.* The word is simply Russian for *council,* but as soviets would by the year's end proliferate in Russia's urban centers and even among the peasants and some mutinous army units, it would acquire a specific revolutionary meaning. The circumstances of this first experiment with workers' representation set the pattern for future soviets. They too would offer an opportunity for a well-organized and purposeful minority to dominate the proceedings. Workers' deputies were elected at factorywide meetings, with no strict procedural rules, amidst passionate oratory, some of it provided by outsiders, usually socialist agitators. It would thus be appropriate for the Bolsheviks—Communists—to acknowledge their debt to the institution which would have served them so well by incorporating its name in that of the state they conquered and by baptizing the amalgam of nationalities over which they rule the *Soviet* nation. The whole train of events leading to this institution which changed the course of Russian and world history began with an idea of a tsarist bureaucrat!

The grandiose perspectives that were being opened by soviets and the burgeoning revolution were as yet but dimly realized by those on the left. Lenin's first reaction to the post-January 1905 developments at home was one of caution. In March a proclamation by the Bolsheviks warned that "the revolution is strong morally, but not physically. The basis of that strength is the sympathy and support of all the classes, save a handful of reactionaries. Consequently one should not overlook the interests of those classes. One should protect private property from *aimless* looting and damage."[33] Lenin saw how counterproductive it was to frighten the liberals through undue violence by the left, yet obviously he and his followers chafed under such self-imposed restraints, for the declaration left open the possibility of violent measures should the circumstances warrant them: "Under certain conditions all means become permissible . . . arson . . . terrorist acts. . . . *As a general rule such means are to be avoided."* Here was a preview of the eternal dilemma of Communism when struggling for power: how not to lose its sympathizers and allies among the middle class and yet at the same time not to allow itself to be outbid by another force on the left, in this case the SRs who uninhibitedly preached and practiced violence.

The Sorcerer's Apprentices: The 1905 Revolution

For all their subsequent misrepresentations on the subject, the Bolsheviks were at the time well aware that the leading role in the revolutionary drama unfolding at home belonged to the liberals, with socialists of all varieties playing but a secondary, though increasingly active, role. As Lenin said candidly in April, "If we were now to promise to the Russian proletariat that we can seize full power, we would be repeating the error of the Socialist Revolutionaries."[34] What compounded the Social Democrats' problem was, of course, the split in their ranks, which among other things affected their attitude of how far they should collaborate with the liberals in their joint struggle against the autocracy. To confound the legend that the Bolsheviks were consistently more radical than their opponents, Lenin at the time was quite willing to support a liberal bourgeois regime should such emerge from the revolution, while the Mensheviks thought it inconceivable that true socialists should agree to share ministerial portfolios with bankers and landowners. In April both factions held separate meetings abroad, the Bolsheviks with their customary gall proclaiming their gathering of some thirty delegates the Third Congress of the Social Democratic Workers' Party, and informing the International Socialist Bureau that it spoke for the party as a whole.

There were other equally brazen efforts by Lenin to create the impression of widespread popular following for his group. He let the assembled in on the secret that "Comrade" Gapon told him ". . . that he shares the viewpoint of the Social Democrats but because of certain reasons cannot reveal it openly." Some of his more fastidious followers, who may have seen the little father getting drunk in a Paris café, or at a gambling table, loudly objected: "How come he is a comrade; when did he join the party?" They were hardly convinced by their leader's assurance that Gapon gave him the impression of "a man fully devoted to the revolution, clever and full of enterprise."[35] In fact, as Lenin must have known, Gapon had been captured by the competition; finding Marxism excessively bookish, and the Social Democrats' doctrinal discussions and quarrels reminiscent of his seminary days, he fell in with the Socialist Revolutionaries whose agents abroad were in constant attendance on him, lest this prize slip from their hands.*

The congress was hardly gracious in its resolution concerning the liberals, though indirectly it could not but acknowledge their leading role in the political

---

*For all the enticements of the West, Gapon felt there like a fish out of water. In January 1906 he returned to Russia, and in a letter to Witte, then prime minister, expressed his contrition and his readiness once more to place his talents at the government's service. What happened then throws a glaring light on the morals of both the regime and the revolutionaries. Rather than have him arrested and tried, the secret police were ready to have Gapon resume his former role. The SRs, whom Gapon kept informed of his contacts, assuring them that once again he would fool the government, did not believe the fickle priest and were afraid of him once more casting a spell on the masses. They decided to get rid of him. The task was entrusted to one of their members whom Gapon had long befriended and trusted, and who after luring his friend to a suburban cottage had Gapon garroted. The SR Central Committee then compounded its sordid role by issuing a public denial of its complicity in the murder.

struggle at home. It welcomed "the awakening of political consciousness of the Russian bourgeoisie," and promised it the Bolsheviks' support whenever "for all the limited and insufficient character of its demands" it attacked the regime. At the same time, and rather incongruously, party organizations in Russia were instructed to open the eyes of the masses to the "anti-revolutionary and anti-proletarian character of bourgeois liberalism in all its shades, beginning with the moderate liberalism of the landowners and industrialists, and ending with more radical ones, as represented by the Union of Liberation and the numerous groups of people in free professions."[36] This was an unwitting tribute to the almost complete hold that Russian liberalism had now obtained on the intelligentsia, as well as an expression of real fear that it might extend its influence to the working class. Similar fears dictated the resolution's stance on the Social Revolutionaries, whose activity was described as doing harm not only to the political development of the proletariat, but also "to the overall struggle of democratic forces against the autocracy."[37] This was quite true. Terrorism was bound to strengthen the case for law and order as preached by the regime. But Lenin's objections were based not so much on the Socialist Revolutionaries' methods, as on the apprehension that their militancy was proving attractive, especially to the young. The Social Democrats, some were beginning to say, were passing resolutions from afar, while the Social Revolutionaries were doing things at home and risking their lives. Hence Lenin's haughty dictum about his rivals on the left. Their socialism, he said, is not revolutionary, and their revolutionary methods have nothing to do with socialism.

In fact the situation in which both wings of Russian Marxism found themselves was downright embarrassing. Their followers, still not very numerous in Russia, found it difficult to understand how at this moment of crisis and opportunity Lenin, Plekhanov, and other prestigious leaders should remain abroad and continue to quarrel about abstruse doctrinal issues. The Social Revolutionaries were really fighting the regime through terror and incitement of peasant insurrections. The liberals, though also unduly addicted to passing resolutions, were at least doing it under the very nose of the authorities. They opened another front in the war on the regime by organizing nationwide professional unions, ranging from those of doctors and lawyers to railway workers. (This one made the socialists especially nervous since they felt it was unfair poaching on their territories.) These organizations were then to be joined in the Union of Unions, a united front of professional Russia which confronted the regime with demands parallel to those of the "liberationists."

In truth what various parties and their leaders were doing did not, at the moment, seem of overwhelming importance. The revolution had developed a momentum of its own, political groups could initiate protest movements and armed actions, but as 1905 progressed they seemed less and less capable of controlling or steering them in a definite direction. This runaway tendency of the revolution was most evident in the non-Russian parts of the empire. Strikes and armed clashes became endemic in Poland. The Caucasus had been stirring even before Bloody Sunday; the great Baku strike of 1904 concluded with the first collective agreement between workers and employers in the history of Russia.

Now the Georgian countryside exploded in violence. In several regions governmental authority completely collapsed. In one district officials were presented by the peasants with a list of demands to be met within one week: the government's and large landowners' estates to be distributed to the peasants, excise taxes abolished, army recruits not to serve or be stationed outside the Caucasus. In the Guria district during the first four months of 1905 there were 111 attempts on the lives of local officials. Georgia was one place where a single party did play a dominant role in the revolutionary events, the Georgian Mensheviks combining nationalist slogans with social and economic demands on behalf of the peasants and workers. Such was the prestige and power of this native variety of Marxism that in some rural areas priests would omit the traditional prayer for the emperor and his family and invoke instead God's blessing on His servants, the local committees of the Social Democratic Party.[38] Terrorism was rife in Finland, where shortly before the government had suspended the national autonomy that, alone of the tsar's dominions, the Grand Duchy had preserved throughout the nineteenth century.

It was as yet a piecemeal revolution, national and political heterogeneity of the forces participating in it precluding a coordinated effort to overthrow the regime through violent action. Not that the idea was entirely absent. A Bolshevik was to recall being invited in March to a conspiratorial meeting held in a private room of one of St. Petersburg's luxury restaurants. While partaking of a sumptuous lunch with vodka and champagne, those present, who included Socialist Revolutionaries, liberals, and some Guards officers—shades of 1825—discussed the feasibility of a coup, which would include seizing the tsar.[39] But the classical palace revolution was outmoded, and it was a peculiarity of this revolution that there were no real attempts to seize power. Whether the liberals with their manifestoes, the Social Revolutionaries with their bombs, or the workers by their strikes, they all sought to make the autocracy do their bidding rather than to bypass it. Paradoxically, no matter what they said about him, however discredited and hateful the tsar might be in the eyes of various revolutionary camps, he was for them still the only legitimate source of authority, and hence the only conceivable instrument of the country's political transformation.

Today it is possible to perceive that the real sense of the revolution was not so much a contest between autocracy and freedom as another even more fundamental question: would autocracy in its death throes still be capable of giving birth to an institution which could hold the Russian state together, be it a republic or a constitutional monarchy? Without it the eventual fall of the autocracy was bound to be followed by an ever-deepening anarchy, and with anarchy there could be no freedom under the law.

Some of the contemporaries, notably among the more moderate liberals, could see the problem, much as nobody could forecast the exact scenario of 1917. But not within the regime. Two magic words, if spoken early enough by the government, could have alleviated the situation: *constitution* and *parliament.* The longer the delay, the greater the probability that the right wingers' objections to them would turn into self-fulfilling prophecies that the government's belated concessions would lead only to ever-more radical demands and a challenge to the social as well as the political system; that the Russian people, having never had a Western-type parliamentary system, would not be able to operate one; and that any elected legislature would be in constant conflict with the executive.

The return of outward calm to the capital in the wake of January 9 reinforced the tsar's reluctance to contemplate major reforms. His current favorite, Trepov, argued that a combination of firmness and a few sops to public opinion would enable the government to ride out the storm. Under the latter heading came an imperial manifesto calling upon public institutions and citizens to address the tsar directly with petitions and proposals touching on political and social problems. This, it was hoped, would have a positive effect, especially on the peasants, demonstrating once more the "unlimited confidence which prevails between the tsar and his people," his readiness to listen to their voice without any need for an intermediary. As the Soviet writer Chermensky admitted, faith in the tsar, despite all that had been happening, was still not dead among the masses. Sixty thousand petitions from peasants were received during the next few months.[40] Along with this gracious permission for the people to bypass bureaucratic channels and to address him on subjects hitherto assumed to lie beyond the competence of private persons, the emperor called upon his subjects to help him in the fight against both the foreign and the domestic enemy and to offer prayers "for the strengthening and perfecting of true autocracy."[41]

For the more realistic members of the regime, this old-fashioned rhetoric fell short of what was required if the wave of disorders was to be halted. The country, they pleaded, needed and expected concrete political acts. One might think they were afraid of a revolution, said Nicholas reproachfully. "Sire, the revolution has already begun," replied a minister. It was also argued that the country was on the verge of financial bankruptcy and foreign bankers would not grant loans unless the government through timely reforms restored political stability. Such arguments finally swayed the reluctant monarch. Alongside the manifesto he issued a rescript to the new minister of the interior,* Bulygin, charging him with preparing a law setting up an assembly "composed of the nation's most distinguished and trustworthy men, elected by the people, whose task should be to participate in the preliminary drafting and assessment of legislative proposals." This would be the fulfillment of what reformers both within and outside the government had dreamed of for much of the nineteenth century: a nationwide elected body with advisory powers. By now the promise of such an assembly, the Bulygin Duma, as it was promptly dubbed, could no longer calm the feverish mood of the country and lead to a detente between the government and society. To the revolutionaries the Bulygin Duma was, of course, unacceptable; whatever its eventual shape and functions, they would have nothing to do with it. And even those liberals who welcomed the rescript did so with the expectation that it represented but the first step in the government moving on to meet what was now their minimal demand: a real parliament with full legislative powers.

The revolutionary scene in the spring of 1905 resembled a stage with actors on three tiers, intermittently aware of what was going on at the other levels, but concentrating mainly on trying to impress the audience—the Russian people—that their own performance was the only significant one. The government's was an old-fashioned morality play with the traditional themes of patriotism, loyalty, faith, law and order. The villains were also traditional: the revolutionary—an accomplice of the Japanese enemy—and the liberal, the latter's unwitting helper, the stock figures of the perfidious Pole and the seditious Jew (under the original plan the Jews would not have been allowed to vote in Bulygin's Duma). It could not escape attention, however, that the main heroes lacked the imposing presence of their predecessors and that their lines no longer had the same conviction and firmness as of old, and at times they faltered under the burden of their roles.

The liberal sector of the stage was filled with a most heterogenous cast of characters: professors, lawyers, progressive and not-so-progressive noblemen, all indulging in long perorations around the one theme of constitution. Constant variations on the latter might leave some of the audience bewildered as to what exactly this term was to convey. There was little action. Some of the actors seemed to display considerable uncertainty as to whether they were in the right play, rather than being part of one or the other of the competing performances.

There was finally, and increasingly preempting the attention of the viewers, the revolutionary melodrama. Here one's attention was riveted not so much on individuals as on crowds which dominated the spectacle, erecting barricades, charging the police, being dispersed by the Cossacks, the volume of the noise— shots, chanted slogans, and curses—rising to a crescendo, threatening to drown

---

*Mirsky had to resign after Bloody Sunday.

out the sounds from other parts of the stage. Behind the turbulent masses one could discern, but dimly, some shadowy figures who whenever the noise died down could be heard reciting ideological incantations and denouncing in violent language their fellow performers, as well as those of the other dramas.

By the summer the separate components of the political crisis merged into a general melee. The government's attempt to gain control of the situation was visibly collapsing. In May news of the naval disaster at Tsushima raised revolutionary excitement to the point where, in addition to civil disorders, there arose the specter of widespread mutinies among the demoralized armed forces. In June came the most celebrated one, which through the cinematic genius of Eisenstein was to become the most universally known incident of the revolution. Radical agitation was gaining a special foothold in the fleet, both because of the sailors' resentment over their comrades having been dispatched to a slaughter in Tsushima and because, unlike the army, sailors were recruited predominantly from among the city workers and craftsmen. All the more striking that the first major naval mutiny occurred on the battleship *Potemkin,* whose crew was mostly of peasant background.

The sequence of events on this most powerful warship of the Black Sea fleet epitomized in a way the course of the whole revolution. The uprising was spontaneous. Provoked by the insensitive and harsh treatment of sailors by their superiors, the men seized the ship, shot or imprisoned their officers, and raised the red flag over *Potemkin.* How close to the surface was the mutinous feeling in the fleet at large was soon demonstrated by the fact that sailors on other ships refused to fire on the rebel vessel and, in some cases, overpowered their own officers, one other warship trying to duplicate *Potemkin's* feat but running aground and eventually surrendering. Disturbances seized the naval base of Sevastopol; in Odessa the presence of *Potemkin* in the harbor turned the already explosive situation, and street fighting in the port changed into an uprising which claimed several thousand casualties before it was put down by the army. The whole Black Sea region seemed ripe to burst into an insurrection with armed sailors in the vanguard of the fighting as they were to be in 1917. But the crew of *Potemkin* lacked leadership and political sophistication. There were a few politically literate sailors (all of them Mensheviks), but they could not impose revolutionary discipline upon the unruly company. Instead of becoming the flag bearer of an armed revolt which might have spilled into other parts of Russia, the warship sailed to a Rumanian port. There the sailors scuttled it and sought refuge on foreign soil.

As it had on *Potemkin,* so all over the country the government's authority was crumbling, but its enemies were disunited and unsure of their goals, their followers too undisciplined even to think of replacing the tottering regime with another. "Down with autocracy," was a frequent chant of the demonstrating crowds, but few if any slogans specified what was to take its place. *Constitution* might no longer have been confused with, as in the story of the Decembrists, *Constantine's wife,* but for the masses (especially in the countryside) it was still an alien and incomprehensible concept.

In June the government decided to avail itself of President Theodore Roosevelt's offer of mediation and to seek peace with Japan. The unenviable task of negotiating it was entrusted to Witte, the only major regime figure who in the eyes of the public and of foreign bankers, also of vital importance at the moment, was free of the responsibility for the catastrophic policies of the last two years. For all of Witte's diplomatic skill, the final agreement had to be hurtful to national pride: Russia had to abandon her sphere of interest in Korea, pull out her troops from Manchuria, and for the first time in a long while the empire had to cede a part of its own territory to a foreign power, Japan annexing southern Sakhalin.

But the end of the war also spelled fresh trouble: the army of several hundred thousand strong had to be brought home from the Far East, some of its units having already mutinied, and the general morale of the troops, which had seen their exertions wasted, often because of the inefficiency and corruption of their commanders, was known to be dangerously low. The government's own morale, as well as intelligence, was best characterized by a suggestion of one of the ministers that the soldiers should not be allowed to return to what was becoming the revolutionary cauldron of European Russia but be forced to settle on virgin lands in Siberia. For once common sense prevailed in the councils of the empire, and forced mass resettlements of that kind had to await Stalin's time.

Insofar as the overall crisis was concerned, the regime still clung to the notion that palliatives, combined with an occasional show of force, would enable it to keep the situation under control. This policy, however, was proving counterproductive and occasionally ludicrous. On August 6 the tsar finally issued the manifesto detailing the constitution of the State (Bulygin's) Duma. The details confirmed the worst apprehensions of reformers; not only was it to be purely advisory in its functions but the franchise was to be so limited by class, property, and even geographic criteria (many border and non-Russian areas as well as most city dwellers were to be disenfranchised), that it would have been but a mockery of a representative body. Still some liberals were willing to participate in the elections to this misbegotten body in the hope that the Duma might be of use in leading to further reforms and a real legislature. One of them was Paul Milyukov, a leading figure both in the Union of Liberation and the Union of

Unions. Outvoted on the question in the latter, Milyukov proceeded to try to organize the proelection minority. But simultaneously with the manifesto of August 6, the government revoked its previous authorization of meetings dealing with political questions, on the assumption, evidently, that because the tsar had granted so great a boon, private citizens no longer had any business to debate high matters of state.

Milyukov invited his political friends to discuss in the privacy of his residence how to dissuade their fellow liberals from boycotting the election, something which would have been very much in the government's interest. Nevertheless it was an illegal political meeting, and the police raided the apartment and arrested the conferees. The comedy was compounded by the fact that the first jail to which they were marched proved to be overcrowded, and it was only after wandering through the streets of St. Petersburg that one was found which was ready to receive them. All this while passersby were treated to the spectacle of a number of distinguished and well-known citizens, professors, lawyers, and some state councillors among them, being marched under guard like a group of common criminals. Once in jail, their treatment continued to point up the tragicomic incongruity of contemporary Russia. Prisoners they might be, but also gentlemen, and the spirit of liberalism had of late invaded even the penal institutions. The jail's superintendent took every care to make his distinguished inmates comfortable, letting them use his own office for receiving visitors and for an occasional game of chess. As was the case with many tsarist prisons, this one had an excellent library, and Milyukov, who had been feverishly busy with politics, now had the time to catch up on his reading, going through the collected works of several recent authors, including Emile Zola. In retrospect, he found the whole experience not too unpleasant: "I had an opportunity to rest and reflect."[42] After one month of this involuntary vacation, the notables, who during their imprisonment were never charged with anything nor interrogated, were released as suddenly as they had been arrested. The tsar's officials could be brutal, as in their treatment of the *Potemkin* sailors, which sparked off the revolt, or relatively civilized, as exemplified by the tale of Milyukov and his friends. In both cases their behavior was equally arbitrary and unintelligent, the behavior of a regime digging its own grave.

While a group of liberals was being detained for holding an innocent gathering, the government once again demonstrated its genius for inconsistency by issuing an ordinance which virtually guaranteed that public meetings of the most unrestrained kind would spread all over Russia. It restored the universities' autonomy, which barred their premises to the police unless summoned by academic authorities. Overnight the lecture rooms became open to mass meetings, where orators of the most radical political orientations could in perfect safety advertise their respective wares to crowds of outsiders and students. This inevitably led to the escalation of political unrest. By October the alternatives ranged beyond the survival of autocracy. The question had become whether *anything* would be able to save Russia from anarchy and civil war.

The impetus to the ominous turn of events came from organizations and initiatives originally developed by the liberals but which by now were out of control, not only by the intelligentsia-progressive gentry core of the Union of Liberation but also by any single political movement. Strikes, usually triggered by economic issues, but inevitably assuming a political character, became endemic by September. The biggest one came early in October, when the huge railway network of the empire was entirely shut down, at which point other unions and white-collar workers, as represented by the Union of Unions, issued appeals to their members urging them to follow the example of the railway workers. The letters of Nicholas II to his intimates usually bear witness to his, at times incredibly so, phlegmatic attitude to political events. But in the one to his mother describing the situation in mid-October, there is a note of almost despair. St. Petersburg and Moscow had been cut off, and he himself was isolated in Peterhof, unable to reach his capital by train.

> After the railroads, the strike has spread to factories and even to municipal institutions and to the clerical staff of the ministry of communications. . . . One is simply nauseated reading the news, nothing but stories of school strikes . . . assassinations of policemen, Cossacks and soldiers, of the most varied types of disorder and uprisings. And the ministers have been acting like wet hens, that instead of acting with firmness, they are holding meetings and discussions. . . .[43]

While the autocracy tottered, an institution was being born which upon the imperial regime's fall would claim and usurp its role as the source of political legitimacy and would in another October succeed briefly and ephemerally in attaining this end, only in turn to pass itself from the political scene in everything but name: the Soviet. The Soviet's foster parents, so to speak, were the government itself by its sponsorship of police unionism and the Shidlovsky commission and liberals from the Union of Liberation who helped politicize the workers' organizations. It was some veterans of the latter who on October 13 organized the Petersburg Soviet of Worker's Deputies. This body, which soon grew to about three hundred members, came to represent virtually the entire working force of the city, two hundred fifty thousand factory and clerical employees. As of that date, and for fifty days, the capital found itself under two authorities. The tsar's (Nicholas II himself was away from the city in Peterhof) had not disappeared.

Ministries (except those whose employees were on strike) continued to function. There were ample police and army forces in the capital, occupying strategic locations, but how their loyalty would stand up in the case of a direct confrontation with the workers and prolonged street fighting was something the government was loath to put to a test.

The Soviet, for its part, could and on occasion did paralyze the entire economic life of the city. Also, and increasingly, it arrogated to itself political functions. It proclaimed that the printers' union would not allow the publication of any bourgeois papers unless they dispensed with government censorship and banned entirely those whose editorial policy was deemed reactionary. On a "borrowed" bourgeois press, the Soviet printed its own official journal, *Izvestia* (News). For political reforms, the workers' council demanded, as the first installment, a full political amnesty, evacuation of the city by the army, and creation of an armed proletarian militia. In *Izvestia* were more far-reaching slogans calling for a constituent assembly and a democratic republic. On the economic side, this second government requested an eight-hour working day and that city funds be used to support the strikers and the unemployed, as well as to purchase arms for the people's militia.

For a time an uneasy equilibrium established itself between the two governments, with neither ready for an armed confrontation. For all his blood and thunder proclamations (it was then that the famous "bullets will not be spared, blanks will not be used" order was issued and publicized), the city's governor, General Trepov, allowed the Soviet to use municipal buildings for its meetings. For its own part the latter kept its followers from storming jails and releasing political prisoners and likewise abandoned its plans for staging a mass demonstration commemorating some rioters killed by the police. Such demonstrations, it was realized, could have led to bloodshed dwarfing that of January 9.

Apart from humanitarian reasons, the Soviet's restraint was due to its uncertainty, whether it was possible and/or proper for the workers to try to seize power through violent means. No single party dominated the revolutionary council. Of the fifty members of its Executive Committee, nine were Social Democrats, and their own internal split, Mensheviks versus Bolsheviks, hampered the party from giving the Soviet a clear ideological direction. The very birth of the Soviet movement had been seen by the Bolsheviks with some misgivings. Lenin, they knew, distrusted "spontaneity." And what their absent leader—he returned to Russia only in November—feared even more was that the Bolsheviks, by joining any revolutionary enterprise not tightly controlled by themselves, might lose their past cohesion and identity, or to put it more bluntly, might slip from his grip.

The leading roles in the Soviet were played by two men then close to the Mensheviks. Its chairman was a previously obscure young lawyer going under the name of Nosar-Khrustalev.* The vice-chairman and real moving spirit was another nonproletarian, Leon Trotsky. With the revolution heating up in April, Trotsky virtually alone among the foreign-based luminaries of Russian Marxism hastened back to the country (others remained abroad until the proclamation of political amnesty). In a preview of his 1917 activities he was the chief strategist of the striking workers' movement, editor of *Izvestia,* and main author of the Soviet's fiery manifestoes.

Soviets were springing up all over Russia, and in many places they failed to observe their Petersburg prototype's caution. Prisons were being stormed and the police assailed. Local governors' reports stressed that the situation in the provinces was getting out of control. Anxious courtiers were considering contingency plans for evacuating the imperial family abroad. The full dimensions of the threatening disaster were finally grasped by the emperor's sluggish mind. There were two alternatives, Nicholas II was told by his ministers. He could institute a military dictatorship and thus risk a full-fledged civil war, or he must agree to fundamental reforms, which would spell the end of autocracy. There was no volunteer for the role of dictator, but there was one man, it was felt, who, if entrusted with the overall direction of the government, could arrest the momentum of the revolution and convince society of the genuineness of the regime's commitment to reform. Witte was appointed prime minister, the office previously unknown and thought alien to the spirit of Russian autocracy. Simultaneously, the Imperial Manifesto of October 17, 1905, promised a basic transformation of the political system, which in its essentials had remained unchanged since Peter the Great. It was, the emperor proclaimed, "our firm will . . . that no law may go into force without the consent of the State Duma," which in addition would have the power to supervise "the legality of the actions performed by Our officials." Instead of a mock parliament, like Bulygin's, Russia was promised a real one with full legislative powers. Without going into the details, the manifesto promised also that the franchise to the State Duma would be much broader than that envisaged by the August rescript, including "those classes of the population which are now completely deprived of electoral rights" and that "the further development of the principle of universal suffrage" would be up to the legislature itself. It was likewise "our firm will . . . to grant the people the unshakable foundations of civic freedoms on the basis of genuine personal inviolability,

*The story of how he became chairman throws some light on the condition of the Russian workers' movement. Nosar was his real name, and the Union of Liberation originally held his political allegiance. To infiltrate the Shidlovsky Commission, on its behalf he procured for himself the credentials of a bona fide worker named Khrustalev. After his brief moment of glory in 1905 Nosar-Khrustalev became involved in a series of personal scandals and earned his livelihood by writing for the reactionary press. When the Petrograd (as the city was then called) Soviet revived in 1917, Nosar-Khrustalev surfaced again in radical circles and claimed as his right the chairmanship of the new soviet. In 1918 this embarrassing relic of the past was shot by the Bolsheviks' secret police.

freedom of conscience, speech, assembly, and association."[44] Russia was to have a government of laws and not of men; for the first time in her history she would cease being a police state.

The autocracy had surrendered only partially and on paper. But this surrender could become effective only if there were a party ready to accept it and to enforce its provisions. Theoretically there was such a force at the time, the Liberation movement, that combination of the intelligentsia and progressive gentry which under various names in different permutations had long conducted the struggle against the autocracy and for a constitution. Its latest emanation was the party of Constitutional Democrats, from their initials Kadets for short.* At the time the manifesto was announced, the party was holding its founding congress in Moscow. As in the case of the Union of Liberation, its parent, the new party's program went far beyond the reforms promised in the emperor's proclamation: it demanded a constituent assembly elected by universal (including women's), equal, secret, and direct vote and took for the day a fairly radical stand on economic and social issues. The main goal of the Liberation movement had been a constitutional monarchy, and for all of its omissions and nonspecificity, the manifesto should have been greeted by the Kadets with enthusiasm as a giant step in that direction.

In fact its reception was quite different. The first reaction was one of sheer amazement. "No one amongst us had expected such unprecedentedly sensational news, no one in fact was ready for it."[45] This in itself is quite revealing. These liberals evidently still remained somewhat in awe of the autocracy, battered, decrepit, and in retreat though it had been during the last few years. And their amazement was perhaps tinged by fear: soon they might be called upon to make decisions and even shoulder legislative responsibilities, rather than just pass resolutions and adopt programs. In the wake of amazement came a negative reaction. "In our current mood the text [of the manifesto] made a sad and unsatisfactory impression on us."[46] This mood found its expression in Milyukov's words at the banquet concluding the congress: "Nothing has changed. The struggle must continue."[47] Nothing had changed, even though the proposed legislature would be an enormous advance on the Bulygin Duma, in whose elections he and his friends had been quite ready to participate.

What had changed, of course, was the quickened tempo of the revolution, which in turn intensified the liberals' traditional fear that by showing the slightest

---

*As in the case of the Mensheviks, the name proved to be something of a psychological handicap to its bearers. The term evokes the youthful sprightliness, ingenuity, and self-discipline of the military student. The Kadets were, if not by age then by temperament, middle-aged, often loquacious, and addicted to intellectual and political hairsplitting.

inclination for a compromise with the regime, by giving any sign of satisfaction over its latest concessions, they would be seen as betraying the people. This attitude was reflected in the fulsome tribute the Kadets hastened to pay to the St. Petersburg Soviet and the striking workers whom they acknowledged as the real heroes of the hour, who through their actions forced the regime to beat a retreat. ". . . The founding congress of the Constitutional Democratic party expresses its fullest solidarity with the strike movement."[48]

The Kadets should have exuded self-confidence, proclaimed their determination to make the regime keep its word. Instead, by their nitpicking, by insisting in advance that the manifesto would not do, they were bound to strengthen both the reactionary element within the regime and those forces which for all their lip service to constitutionalism and freedom sought in fact to promote chaos and anarchy. The right would have a plausible cause for arguing that no reforms could appease the Moloch of the revolution. The left seemed to act in accordance with the famous device of nineteenth-century Russian Jacobinism: "The worse it is, the better."

The immediate consequences of the October 17 Manifesto appeared to confirm the right's prognosis and the left's hopes. The proclamation was widely interpreted as an admission of the government's impotence and hence a signal that all forms of illegal activities could now be pursued with impunity. Prisons were being stormed and their inamates released, or in many cases local authorities, utterly befuddled by the news, let political prisoners go. In Tiflis the viceroy of the Caucasus ordered arms issued to the local Menshevik organization so that its workers' militia could patrol the city and prevent looting and hooliganism. In the provinces the situation was often more chaotic than in the two capitals. Neither the population at large nor the lower ranks of officialdom could understand the fine legal distinctions of the manifesto: what was the basis for any kind of authority, if the emperor was no longer to be absolute? Government officials in order to travel had to seek authorization from the strike committees of railwaymen. The governor general of Moscow would appear on the balcony of his residence during revolutionary manifestations and remove his hat at the passing of the red flag. In Kutais, in Transcaucasia, the local governor travelled throughout his province haranguing the rebellious peasants with quotations from Marx allegedly proving that Russia was not ready for a socialist revolution and hence they should turn their dissent into constructive nonviolent channels.

Even the intelligentsia was seized by a kind of aimless revolutionary euphoria. There are several accounts of meetings of lawyers, engineers, et cetera, where those present were solicited to contribute money "for the armed uprising," without it being specified by whom and against whom that uprising would be conducted. On October 18 a prominent lawyer found himself at a public meeting where one of the subjects under discussion was whether the Mauser or the Browning was more suitable for street fighting.

Instead of "putting an end to these unprecedented disturbances," as was the stated purpose of the manifesto, it seemed to push Russia ever deeper into anarchy. The "days of freedom," as the post-October 17 period quickly became baptized, brought back the memories of The Time of Troubles in the seventeenth century, when following the extinction of the legitimate dynasty, various impostors appeared to claim the throne, the state virtually disintegrated and the country fell prey to the marauding bands of foreign mercenaries and domestic rebels and bandits. Now in the twentieth century there seemed to be no end to troubles and challenges to the crumbling order. One nationwide strike would end only to give way to another one. The naval mutiny in Kronstadt threatened to enflame still further the situation in the neighboring capital. It was put down on October 28, but within days there was a fresh uprising of sailors and soldiers in the Black Sea base of Sevastopol. The government finally found the courage to deal decisively with the St. Petersburg soviet: its chairman was detained at the end of November, and on December 3, as many of its members as the police could get their hands on, some 190, were arrested. Almost immediately the other capital exploded. Moscow's soviet lacked a man as prudent and skillful as Trotsky at its helm. Unlike that in St. Petersburg, here the Bolsheviks played a more prominent role, and their current policy was to provoke rather than try to eschew armed confrontation with the government. At the news of the suppression of the St. Petersburg soviet, its Moscow counterpart proclaimed a general strike. Soon it led to sporadic fighting and then turned into a full-fledged uprising. The local garrison proving insufficient and unreliable, reinforcements, including the Semyonovsky Guards Regiment, had to be brought in. Artillery was used to clear the streets of the barricades and to push the soviets' fighting squads from factories they had turned into strongholds. About one thousand people were killed, including unarmed civilians and prisoners.

Yet, paradoxically, the very ubiquity and intensity of the violence proved to be one of the main factors in the ability of the government eventually to master the revolution. There was no plan and no intention even on the part of the extreme revolutionaries to seize power. There existed no single blueprint, no directing force behind the whole plethora of revolutionary outbreaks and strikes. They tended to erupt spontaneously because of specific causes or local conditions: demonstrators shot by the police, mistreatment of sailors or soldiers by their officers. Once the given revolutionary action had begun, political parties would attempt, not always successfully, to seize control and to turn it to their own purposes. In most cases even they or their local leaders were not quite certain what that purpose was beyond lashing out at the hated regime and demonstrating to the people the emptiness and hypocrisy of all those manifestoes and constitutional paraphernalia. There was no unity, even among the most extreme parties, as to what the revolution was about. Some Mensheviks had what under the circumstances and from the revolutionary point of view was a sensible idea: all the existing factions of the socialist movement should unite in one workers' party, which would set up their own representative organs, culminating in an all-Russian workers' congress.

But this was anathema to Lenin. The revolution was viewed by him not so much as a struggle against the regime for some parliament or a constituent assembly but principally as an opportunity for his party to achieve the dominant position among the workers and the whole revolutionary movement. Therefore, the soviets were of limited usefulness and, if too successful, might become a source of danger to the Bolsheviks. "The soviets," he wrote in January 1906, "serve as temporary nonparty organizations which at times can assist but in no way replace [the need for] a cohesive, disciplined, and militant party," that is, his own. The main sense of the revolution, with all its human and material sacrifices, lay for Lenin in the education it provided for the masses.

The arrests of the soviets' members have furnished an important lesson for the workers. They taught them how dangerous it is to believe in phony constitutionalism, how impermanent must be this "revolutionary self-government" [that is, soviets] without a victory of the revolutionary forces, how insufficient an ad hoc non-party body, which may sometimes help but never replace an organized cohesive and militant party.[49]

It was thus quite logical for Lenin to hold that for such pedagogical purposes the story of the Moscow soviet was much more useful than that of St. Petersburg. The latter in order to avoid bloodshed let itself be arrested without offering resistance. The thousands of casualties in Moscow, the devastation of its workers' quarter were on the other hand a small price for the lesson in street fighting and for widening the chasm between the workers and the government and teaching them the folly of any constitutional solution.

The same attitude emerges in the Bolshevik attitude toward the Sevastopol mutiny. The man who led it was an officer, Lieutenant Peter Schmidt, who, subsequently sentenced to death and shot, passed into the official Soviet hagiography. Schmidt had warned his men against needless violence and stressed in his speeches that the main goal of the revolution should be to force the tsar to summon the constituent assembly. Hence a Soviet historian's less than gracious tribute: "This man, who died heroically for the revolution, was still alien to its spirit. His sentimental and liberal outlook could not be reconciled with the real tasks of the struggle nor with the truly revolutionary way of achieving them."[50]

The standard accusation against the Russian liberals and moderates, that in their hatred of the autocracy they overlooked the danger from the left, is *insofar as 1905 is concerned,* wide of the mark. The left was then too much divided, too much engrossed in its internal squabbles to be taken seriously as a pretender to power. The revolution did bring a great increase in the membership of the Social Democrats. At the time of its Fourth Congress, held in Stockholm in April 1906, the party had probably about one hundred thousand members,* and with their sympathizers, they could be said to represent the majority of politically conscious industrial workers of the empire. But for all the formal unity proclaimed at the congress, they were split into a number of factions and national groups almost as antagonistic toward each other as they were to the regime. The Polish Socialist Party (PPS) was interested mainly in the struggle for Polish independence. Its rival, the Social Democracy of Poland and Lithuania (SDPL), held the national issue to be unimportant, thereby incurring the wrath not only of the PPS but of the Bolsheviks, for Lenin believed that for tactical reasons socialism, in spite of the fact that Marx said "workers have no country," should place national self-determination among its postulates.

The Mensheviks and Bolsheviks were split on practically every issue: the land-peasant one, their attitudes toward the middle-class parties, terrorist and guerrilla activities, et cetera. Issues apart, the problem of personalities was insurmountable. To say that the luminaries of Russian socialism were difficult people to work with would be an understatement, and the idea of Lenin collaborating loyally and on equal terms with someone like Trotsky, Plekhanov, or the fiery Rosa Luxemburg of the SDPL was as ludicrous as his working amicably with Pobyedonostsev. Without unity at the top, with its great potential strength being frittered away in separate and uncoordinated strikes and uprisings like the purposeless Moscow slaughter, the socialist movement could not be thought of as a serious contender for power. What was true of the Socialists was even truer of the Socialist Revolutionaries. Their program and tactics were a curious blend of old populism, Marxism, and outright anarchism. The very notion of centralized political power was alien to those spiritual descendants of Land and Freedom. In the eyes of the regime, the SR were the most dangerous of the revolutionary parties† because of their wholehearted commitment to individual terrorism and instigation of violence in the countryside. But it was one thing to kill ministers, governors, et cetera, and to incite peasants to burn landlords' residences (some

*A Soviet source gives the number of Bolsheviks as 13,000, the Menshevks 18,000. *The Proletarian Revolution,* No. 5 (1922), p. 75.

†The Bolsheviks were viewed by the secret police rather indulgently since they stood in the way of any meaningful unity of the workers' movement.

two thousand were thus destroyed in 1905–06) and another to pose a basic challenge and alternative to the existing political system.

There was thus no threat of a revolutionary movement of one sort or another seizing power and supplanting the tsar's government. Rather the main danger confronting Russia in the weeks immediately following the October Manifesto was one of progressive disintegration of all central authority. Either the government would find enough strength to restore some semblance of order, or Russia, as it had for years in the beginning of the seventeenth century, as it would again during some months in 1917, would be plunged into anarchy, until some yet unforeseen force or leader emerged capable of imposing a new, most likely autocratic, pattern of authority.

At the moment the problem of society (that is, the educated class) vis-à-vis the government centered around the figure of Serge Witte. The first official prime minister in modern Russian history,* he was in the anomalous position of being at once the repository of great hopes and the object of general distrust. Widely disliked in court circles for extracting the manifesto from the emperor and for his domineering ways, Witte was still in their opinion the only man capable of stemming the tide of revolution and preserving what was salvageable of the autocracy. For its part, society did not believe in the sincerity of Witte's conversion to constitutionalism, but at the same time he was felt to be the only figure in the regime who could turn the promises of October 17 into reality. It was under such unpromising auspices that this rough-hewn man entered upon his task of saving the tsar, whom along with most of the imperial family he personally despised, and of appeasing the intelligentsia, for whose leading representatives he had but little respect.

For all his bureaucratic background and temperament, Witte had a sense of public relations and tried to work through persuasion, as well as repression. He addressed an appeal to the strikers, calling them "brothers" and urging them to put an end to anarchy and to return to work. This unprecedented manner of addressing them on the part of a tsarist dignitary did have some soothing effect on the workers' mood; nonetheless the St. Petersburg soviet in its answer stressed that the proletarians did not feel themselves related in any degree to Count Witte. Turning further in this effort at what we would call today a dialogue with society, the prime minister invited representatives of the press to listen to an explanation of his policies, again a startling departure from the established custom, when such a dialogue took the form of the authorities banning troublesome journals and putting their editors under lock and key. How times had changed

---

*The autocratic principle precluded anyone but the tsar heading the executive as a whole.

was vividly demonstrated when one of the invited, an editor of a most influential and hitherto moderate paper, told the prime minister to his face: "The point is we simply don't believe anything the government tells us." The man in question, notes Witte bitterly, had been before the revolution a humble and assiduous seeker of his favor. And though a staunch enemy of anti-Semitism, his wife, as well as the proverbial some of his best friends being Jewish, Witte could not refrain from adding that the statement was in line with "that impudence which characterizes one type of the Russian Jew."[51]

The most important part of Witte's design to appease society was the attempt to draw its representatives into the cabinet over which he was to preside. This in itself was a revolutionary idea. As a rule the tsars' ministers had been drawn almost exclusively from the ranks of the civil and military bureaucracy, with an occasional lawyer or professor of unblemished political orthodoxy providing a rare exception. Now the prime minister was ready to bring into his cabinet not only people outside the charmed circle but also some of those who had participated in the Liberation movement. In October and November he held discussions with a number of leading representatives of constitutional dissent with an eye both to inducing some of them to accept ministerial portfolios and to securing the support of the liberals for his government. His efforts met with complete failure. Some of the invited declared that they could never participate in a government which was not truly representative, that is, responsible to a democratically elected assembly. Others would not serve with the bureaucrats that Witte proposed to retain in his cabinet. Milyukov, whom Witte consulted as the most influential leader of the Kadets, advised him that the government should jettison the October Manifesto and proclaim a real constitution, only then would he and his friends be ready to talk about ministerial portfolios, et cetera. It could not be done, explained the sorely tried prime minister. The very word *constitution* was intolerable to the tsar, but surely his interlocutor must understand that he, Witte, was striving for a constitutional order? ". . . It is useless for us to continue this discussion. I cannot give you any advice," replied Milyukov.[52]

Witte's initiative very probably threw the Kadets into a kind of panic. Their whole mentality, as was that of the intelligentsia in general, was predicated upon opposition to the regime. Suddenly there arose the danger of their becoming a part of it. There were some cogent reasons for their hesitations and scruples. Even if Witte himself was acting in good faith, the same was much less certain of the emperor and the court camarilla. The latter could use them as hostages to appease society, and then with order restored drop them and revert to its old ways. But the main reason lay elsewhere, in the Kadets' liberal fastidiousness and fear of bearing partial responsibility for solving tasks which appeared insoluble, of entering a government which fell short of the democratic ideals. If partners in governing the country, they would have to lend their hand to the suppression of the revolution they themselves had instigated, approve all those court martials, death sentences, et cetera. Already sensitive to criticism from the left, they dreaded the prospect of being vituperated and derided by socialist propaganda as accomplices of Nicholas the Bloody, traitors to the people's cause. "I wanted a minister, they sent me a Hamlet," observed Witte after a conference with a liberal nobleman.

With no power base of his own and with the liberals unwilling to lend their support, Witte embarked on his mission with the melancholy knowledge that the closer he got to success in mastering the revolution, the more likely became the prospect of his dismissal by the tsar. Once the tide of violence began to recede, the very same people who had implored him to take on the impossible task would argue that he had tricked the emperor into surrendering his prerogatives, that this ambitious and masterful man would never be satisfied until he became a constitutional prime minister, if not indeed president of the Russian republic. His cabinet had to be composed of bureaucrats, some of whom did not take kindly to the notion that there was now somebody who stood between them and the emperor. Gone to be sure were such relics of the past as the aged Pobyedonostsev, who left office with the same conviction he had held on assuming it twenty-five years before: any departure from the narrow path of autocracy was bound to end in a disaster. Another man loathed by public opinion, General Trepov of "bullets must not be spared" fame was also dropped. But Trepov, whose modest title of deputy minister of the interior had concealed his dominant role in the ministry, was immediately given a court appointment and retained his personal influence over the tsar. For all such changes, the new cabinet was met with a chorus of disapproval from liberal circles. The man felt to be particularly objectionable was the minister of the interior, Paul Durnovo. As head of the police under Alexander III, Durnovo used his agents to spy on men whom he suspected of sharing his girl friend's favor. One of them turned out to be the Spanish ambassador, who lodged a protest against this unheard-of violation of diplomatic immunity. "Let this swine be dismissed forthwith," was Alexander's curt order when the affair was brought to his attention. Now this man was placed in charge of domestic security, a job, to be sure, not tailored for a man of high moral sensitivity.

The ambivalence which characterized the attitude of society on the regime vs. revolution issue was demonstrated anew at the November congress of representatives of zemstvos and city councils. The zemstvo and Liberation movements had maintained a symbiotic relationship, the two representing in varying degrees the constitutional aspirations of the intelligentsia and progressive nobility. Now both were to vacate the national political scene in favor of the parties to which they had given birth. The minority at the congress expressed the view of what was to become the policy of the Octobrist party: the government ought to be supported by society in its struggle against anarchy as long as it meant to fulfill faithfully the promises of the Manifesto of October 17. But such a clear formulation was not to the liking of the mostly Kadet majority of the congress. Their fears and hesitations were most vividly revealed when after a unanimous vote in favor of the abolition of capital punishment, a delegate moved that the congress simultaneously condemn "violence and assassinations as means of political struggle." After some embarrassed circumlocutions the motion was rejected.[53]

The predicament of the Kadet party, the standard bearer and conscience of Russian liberalism, was well and sardonically analyzed by one of its own members. Unable to resolve their inner conflict between democratic virtue and fear of anarchy, the Kadets, he wrote, in effect proposed to wait out the revolution and only then engage in practical politics:

> But who will guarantee the outcome of the revolution, what can assure us that at its end the peasants and workers will follow the wise and beneficial advice of the Constitutional Democratic Party, rather than some dictator or a new Pugachev? And what by that time would remain of the party which will have waited passively for the revolution to stop by itself, rather than being willing and able to direct or influence the course of events?[54]

Though politicians might hesitate and temporize, society at large by December 1905 was showing signs of exasperation over the unending cycle of violence. The psychological break in the atmosphere came with the arrest of the St. Petersburg soviet and with the bloodshed in Moscow, which for all the wanton cruelty displayed by the government forces made even some socialist leaders have second thoughts about armed uprisings. Emboldened, the regime now embarked on a systematic course of repression. Armed expeditions were dispatched from both ends of the Trans-Siberian Railway to break the strike of the railway workers, clear its major terminals of the revolutionary soviets, and thus restore the great road to government control so that the restive troops from the Far East could be brought home. The methods used were brutal: strikers and rioters were often shot without the formality of a court martial. Similar punitive expeditions were dispatched to other trouble spots, with the greatest ferocity displayed in putting down revolutionary disturbances in Poland and the Baltic region. In Latvia the countryside was ravaged by the so-called pacification, and it was not a coincidence that twelve years later soldiers recruited from there would become the vanguard of the revolutionary movement within the army and later would constitute the elite guards of the Bolsheviks.

But for the time being such methods brought the desired effect. "Thank God, the situation in general has grown much calmer," wrote Nicholas II to his mother on January 12, 1906. Rather complacent in the face of his subjects' sufferings (most of the troublemakers he believed had been Jews and Poles), the emperor still tried to place the responsibility for the atrocities on his prime minister: "Witte has changed completely since the events in Moscow. He would have hangings and firing squads everywhere."[55] True, Witte did not balk at harsh repression when it came to the armed uprising. But most of the excesses against the unarmed population were due primarily to the savagery of some local commanders, such as the notorious General Orlov in Latvia, who was barely dissuaded from putting whole quarters of Riga to the torch.

In addition to terror as practiced both by the revolutionaries and the government, there now appeared on the scene another movement bent upon violence. One of the aftereffects of the October 17 Manifesto was the emergence of the force always latent, below the surface, of Russian life, the most primitive and destructive form of nationalism, with its inborn xenophobia, anti-Semitism, and hatred of the intelligentsia for its foreign ways. This reactionary populism now crystallized in several right-wing organizations, the most prominent of them the Union of the Russian People. Some of the ethos of the revolution affected even this reactionary movement. Officially it endorsed the idea of national representation and advocated measures for the improvement of the lot of peasants and workers. But its emotional appeal was to those who felt Russia's salvation was bound up with autocracy and who considered constitutionalism as a foreign and evil invention. Its activity at its most innocent was to stage popular manifestations, with crowds carrying icons and portraits of the imperial family, parading to the tune of "God Save the Tsar" and other patriotic and religious chants. But in addition the Black Hundreds, as the mobs became known, would at times turn to looting and violence directed mainly against the Jews, their patriotism expressed succinctly in the slogan: "Beat the Yids and the intelligents; save Russia." Not a few high-ranking personages found such sentiments highly appropriate for the times. The most lamentable example was set by the emperor himself, who had the imbecility to grant an audience to the leaders of the Union of the Russian People and to accept its badge. The public message Nicholas II saw fit to send to that congregation of fanatics and hooligans makes the liberals' squeamishness about becoming his ministers understandable: "May the Union of the Russian People be My trusty support, serving for all and in everything as an example of lawfulness and [a force] for civic order."[56] Local authorities not infrequently looked the other way when the Black Hundreds were instigating the pogroms and other outrages.

In general the Union of the Russian People and similar organizations played but a marginal role in the events of 1905–07. It was beyond the capacity of Nicholas II either to draw strength or to impart real political significance to this protofascism, just as he was incapable of a consistent stance on any political issue, save for his persistent feeling that by granting even the externals of constitutionalism he would be somehow repudiating the legacy of his ancestors. By the beginning of 1906 it already appeared unlikely that extremism of any variety, whether of the left or the right, could emerge victorious. The central issue during the final stage of revolution was legitimacy. Would society tolerate the effort of the autocracy to resume the prerogatives it had in principle given up by the Manifesto of October 17? Would the liberals be strong, united, and skillful enough to establish that only a constitutional government could be a legitimate source of authority? Revolutionary violence, which until the end of 1905 had indirectly helped the liberals by frightening the regime into concessions, would thereafter be increasingly harmful to their cause: it was society which in turn grew frightened and weary of violence and ready to acquiesce in any formula which promised to restore law and order, be it a modified autocratic system or a genuinely constitutional one.

The first was obviously the preference of the tsar and his courtiers. Without repudiating explicitly the manifesto, they proposed before the Duma appeared on the scene to limit as much as possible its competence and to safeguard the major share of the autocratic prerogative. Pursuant to that purpose, the regime between February and April 1906 enacted a number of laws defining the nature and powers of various organs of the state. (The word *constitution* still stuck in the tsar's throat.) The emperor was to retain complete authority over the executive, with ministers remaining responsible to him and not to the legislature, the power to declare war and peace, the right to veto any legislation. An additional curb on the Duma was the creation of another second legislative chamber, the State Council, half of whose members were to be nominated, the others selected by the various privileged classes and institutions, predominantly by the gentry. This was then to be a kind of House of Lords. When it came to the people's representatives, most of them were to be elected through a cumbersome, indirect voting system based on separate class and property constituencies. Still the allotment of seats to various classes did not, except in the case of landowners, depart significantly from their proportion to the population as a whole. It would then be a largely peasant-elected Duma, a reflection not of the regime's concern for democracy, but rather of its belief, greatly overoptimistic as the elections would show, that for all the recent rural disorders, the mass of peasants remained conservatively minded. There were a number of other provisions and devices which could enable the government to bypass or check the popularly elected body when it came to legislation and the state budget.

For the more radical liberals, as well as the revolutionary parties, the above added up to a caricature of a constitutional system. The moderates, however, had to feel that for all the regime's chicaneries, Russia for the first time in her modern history was to have a parliament of sorts and a system of popular representation.

The Sorcerer's Apprentices: The 1905 Revolution

Few Russians really believed that their country was ready for pure democracy. In fact many of the Kadets, while loudly complaining that the scheme fell so lamentably short of their program with its postulates of universal, equal franchise et cetera, and ministerial responsibility, were privately worried by the weight of representation accorded to the peasants.

Having presided over the birth of Russian constitutionalism, Witte, for all his love of power, hastened to resign before he would have to defend that sickly and misshapen child from attacks by both the right and the left. His real standing in the regime never corresponded to the title he bore. Members of his cabinet intrigued against him and his policies. With the most critical phase of the revolution over, the emperor's eagerness to get rid of him had been restrained by the knowledge that Witte's prestige in international financial circles made his continuance in office necessary for the government to secure a foreign loan, without which it would go bankrupt. All the more so because the opposition loudly warned that the government had no longer the right to borrow abroad without the concurrence of the Duma. With the negotiations for a huge loan from French bankers successfully concluded, Nicholas II with unconcealed relief accepted his prime minister's resignation.

The elections were boycotted by the radical parties, allegedly because the electoral law made the whole business a farce, in fact because the Social Democrats and Socialist Revolutionaries feared they could not make a respectable showing. Only in Georgia, where they justifiably felt confident of being successful, the Mensheviks chose to run for the Duma. The overall results confounded the government's expectations. The peasants may have remained loyal to the father-tsar, but their economic distress made them vote for candidates with radical views, especially on the land question. The Kadets scored a triumph surpassing their fondest hopes: one third of all seats. The largest peasant group, the so-called Trudovik (Labor) faction, ranged themselves left of the Kadets; some of them were close to the Socialist Revolutionaries in spirit, some of them politically quite moderate, but all demanded the expropriation of state and landlords' estates to appease their constituents' hunger for land. The most ominous sign, from the conservative's point of view, was the numerous representations of various non-Russian ethnic groups: Poles, Ukrainians, Moslems, et cetera, all of them clamorous for their national rights. There was only a sprinkling of conservatives. The Octobrists, the one respectable party on which the government could count for a modicum of support, elected but 17 deputies as against over 150 for the Kadets.

Under the circumstances the emperor's words on his opening of the Duma on April 27, 1906, sounded unwittingly humorous: "I greet in you the [nation's] very best people, precisely the kind I had wished My beloved subjects to choose."[57]

The ceremony, obviously copied from the British opening of Parliament, was under the current Russian circumstances somewhat incongruous. The emperor entered amidst a procession of notables: high dignitaries carrying the imperial regalia, the two empresses bedecked with jewels, serried ranks of officials, civil and military, accoutred in resplendent uniforms with epaulets and gold braid. The whole assembly redolent of the past and privilege faced the crowd of deputies, very bourgeois in their garb, except for the peasants with their long blouses and boots, and some non-Russians sporting ostentatiously their national dress.

Immediately after electing their officials, all Kadets, the country's best people, plunged into a petulant brawl with the government, which with few interruptions was to last for the entire seventy-three-day life of the First State Duma. In answer to the Gracious Speech, as it is termed in the British usage, the Duma presented the emperor with a rather ungracious Address specifying various sins of the government, such as "the officialdom's arbitrariness" and listing a number of demands, foremost among them a general amnesty for political crimes. Speeches on the subject were tempestuous. One deputy stated that Russia was currently being ruled more despotically than at any time since the Mongol yoke. Another, a socialist, refused to have anything to do with an address to the tsar, and as to the amnesty, it was ridiculous to demand it for a few hundred people, martyrs though they were, since the whole country was one vast prison with one hundred fifty million inmates. The emperor refused to accept the Duma's diatribe, personally sending instead his new prime minister, Ivan Goremykin, to explain to the deputies how several of its demands clashed with his prerogatives. The Duma received the tsarist satrap with contempt and with shouts of "Resign." There was only one solution, said the Kadet V. Nabokov (father of the writer): "The government must submit to the legislature."[58] The chamber then almost unanimously voted nonconfidence in the government, which of course not being within its powers, could have no legal consequences.

The clash, which in intensity surpassed their fondest anticipation, was followed and commented on with keen enjoyment by the revolutionaries. For Lenin especially it brought relief from his fear that the Kadets and the government would strike a bargain, thus putting a definite halt to further revolutionary developments. At times he would denounce the liberals for agreeing to participate in the whole comedy of phony elections and pseudoparliamentarism. Then intermittently he would call upon the Duma, that assembly of "liberal cowards" and turncoats, to seize power from the tsar and the minister. For the time being all such propaganda could be carried out quite openly with the police not daring to interfere. On May 9, speaking to an audience of thousands, Lenin attacked the Kadets for their shameless conciliatory policy toward the oppressors. The meeting then called upon the Trudovik group to stick staunchly to its uncompromising stand on the land question, and not to fall for the Kadets' wiles and constitutional illusions. The Bolsheviks' tactics were transparent: the peasant group, without any clear ideology of its own, was very susceptible to pressures from the left. The Trudoviks' radical stance was in turn bound to inhibit any moderation on the part of the Kadets, who needed them to command a majority in the Duma. Under such conditions the latter's life was bound to be brief and its end violent, a consummation devoutly wished for by Lenin and his friends.

The antigovernment and revolutionary rhetoric spouted by the Duma was in fact a source of secret embarrassment to its Kadet leaders. In a way they could not help themselves: this was an almost inevitable psychological reflex of the intelligentsia, a legacy of its past when it had felt both impotent and oppressed and humiliated by all those pompous bureaucrats whom now it could pay back if not by imprisonments and exile, then by verbal abuse. Yet being men of intelligence, the leaders realized that they had a unique opportunity and a duty to the nation, of which with more reason than anyone else they could claim to be the spokesmen. They had been elected not to castigate the regime for its past and present sins, but to change it. Nothing they could say or do, the more perspicacious liberals realized, would ever appease the extreme left.

The main dilemma of the liberals was well illustrated in a pamphlet published by the Kadets in 1906 under the title *Accusations Against the Party of National Freedom* (this was the Kadets' official name).[59] It is a compilation of various arguments brought against the Kadets' program and tactics both by the left and by the right and of their responses to them. Most of the polemic consists of a rather self-conscious attempt to rebut various charges advanced by the socialists. Their party, asserted the authors, is not a class party representing the class interests of the bourgeoisie. Compare its program with those of the middle-class parties in the West, and you'll see that it is permeated by solicitude for the people as a whole.

The Party of National Freedom accepts extensive government intervention in the sphere of capital-labor relations as well as extensive curbs on private ownership of land (it demands compulsory breakup of large landed estates). Such policies are certainly not compatible with any selfish interests and claims of the property-owning classes, and could never be included in the program of a party which represented just them.[60]

In principle the party had nothing against socialism, but even its leftist opponents admitted that Russia as yet was not ready for it.

Apart from such excessively painstaking pleadings with the left, the pamphlet addresses itself also to a reproach from the right, that by proposing to make the executive responsible to the people's representatives, the Kadets were seeking power for themselves. The rebuttal is, alas, only too convincing: "It should not be difficult to prove that it is much easier and convenient for our party to criticize [the government] than to assume the burden of responsibility associated with power. It is clear that any regime which would replace the present one would be confronted with all kinds of demands, that it will become the object of excessive hopes. Its political enemies would gleefully exploit not only its [unavoidable] accidental blunders, but also and above all the fact that under the circumstances no conceivable government could change overnight the whole pattern of Russian life." The party then bearing that cross would be accused of betraying its principles and the people through cowardice.

> And if the Party of National Freedom has still been prepared to shoulder this burden . . . it has thereby demonstrated its willingness to sacrifice itself for the sake of the fatherland, its readiness to bare its breast to the blows of malicious and ruthless criticism and its awareness that [by assuming power] it would risk losing most of the prestige it had accumulated by its unyielding struggle against the old order.[61]

For some, at least, among the Kadets the prospect of wielding power appeared as one of virtual martyrdom. It is not surprising that the subsequent history of this party which embodied much that was best, most civilized, and humane in Russian life was to be so tragic.

The tantalizing yet frightening prospect of power did glimmer once more before the Kadets' eyes in the waning days of the First Duma. Its continued coexistence with the ministry of bureaucrats was rapidly becoming impossible. Its dissolution, on the other hand, was feared by the regime, since it might be attended by fresh dangers—and besides, what hope could there be of new elections bringing a more cooperative chamber? Hence the sudden inspiration of General Trepov, still a confidential adviser to the tsar: why not try, since half measures had failed, a drastic one? The emperor should appoint a wholly Kadet ministry, headed by the Duma president Professor Serge Muromtsev. Trepov expounded his scheme to the most influential Kadet, Milyukov, who hastened to lay down preconditions: his party would consider the possibility of forming a cabinet provided that it would be free to carry out an extensive plan of reforms. Suffrage would have to be made universal and direct. It must be allowed to carry out an ambitious land reform by parcelling large estates (with the landowners receiving "just" compensation) among the peasants. An amnesty would be proclaimed for all political crimes, including assassinations. The upper ranks of bureaucracy would have to be purged of its most retrograde members. Trepov listened patiently and took it all down in writing.

Trepov's was not an isolated initiative. Some other regime figures held talks with the Duma and other political leaders discussing a more moderate version of his plan: a coalition ministry, part Kadet, part bureaucrat in its composition. One of them was Peter Stolypin, the new minister of the interior.

In court circles Trepov was believed to have gone mad. This feeling was reinforced when the general gave an interview to a British journalist and laid out his scheme, which thus became public knowledge. A Kadet ministry was the only way out of the present deadlock. "If that does not work, we shall have to resort to extreme measures." His enemies perceived ulterior motives behind his plan. He counted on the Kadets proving utterly incapable of governing, and then he, Trepov, would be appointed dictator and tackle the crisis in the traditional way: "bullets are not to be spared, blank cartridges are not to be used." But it is possible that his scheme was not meant as a ruse. The autocracy had gone, palliatives were not working. The only way to save the monarchy and Russia without further massive bloodshed was to turn to those who might appease public opinion.

To their mixed disappointment and relief, the Kadets were spared the ordeal-by-power. Nicholas II would not hear of a wholly Kadet ministry, and the party leaders balked at participating in a coalition. The Duma continued upon its collision course with the government. It went ahead with drafting an agrarian law providing for compulsory acquisition and redistribution of landed estates, even though the government publicly warned that forcible alienation of private property was not within the legislature's competence. The Duma's response was a proclamation to the nation that it proposed to go on with the law in defiance of the government. Both sides denounced each other as acting illegally and provocatively.

On July 9 came the inevitable: dissolution of the Duma. The decree specified that its successor was to be elected and convoked by February 20, 1907. The emperor's action was thus fully within the letter and spirit of the law. Still the government thought it prudent to have the Tauride Palace, the Duma's place of assembly, surrounded by troops lest the deputies, following the example of the French Estates General of 1789, refuse to disperse and proclaim themselves responsible only to the nation.

This was a shrewd guess. There were calls from the left for an armed uprising or, at least, a general strike. But again the Kadets opted for a revolutionary gesture rather than action. On their initiative 180 members of the defunct body crossed over to Finland, where because of the grand duchy's autonomy they could be safe from arrest. From Vyborg they issued a manifesto declaring the dissolution a violation of the constitution and calling upon the nation to respond by refusing to pay taxes and by withholding recruits from the army. The appeal proved totally ineffective. The only tangible result was the indictment of the signatories, thus making them ineligible to run in the new elections. The government was sensible enough to bring them to trial only many months afterward and to punish them leniently: three months in prison.

The revolution had passed its zenith and entered its final phase. Except for two quickly suppressed naval mutinies in the summer of 1906, there would be no more armed uprisings. In 1905 the revolution had fed upon the strike movement, unprecedented in its intensity. In 1906, while strikes were still numerous, they largely lost their political character, and the number of strikers amounted only to 40 percent of the previous year's figure. Terrorism continued unabated, as did the armed expropriations, seizures of government funds for revolutionary purposes. In the course of 1906, 768 officials were assassinated, 820 wounded, targets for such attempts ranging from the prime minister to local policemen, but in a sense this was a testimony of the revolutionaries' having despaired of the possibility of mass insurrections.

Stolypin, who was installed as the prime minister simultaneously with the dissolution of the Duma, prepared to use both repression and social reform as the means to beat down the revolution. An able administrator, the new head of the government was an updated version of a Slavophile, his belief in autocracy coupled with the conviction that it could not dispense with a system of national representation and that Russia's economic and social life must be modernized. In his first circular to his subordinates, he stressed both points:

> The government is firmly determined to abolish and modify in an orderly way those laws and institutions which have become obsolete and no longer serve their purposes. . . . Public order must be restored at all costs. . . . A strong and resolute authority acting accordingly will not fail to find support among what is best in society.[62]

He no longer would play games with the Kadets. But upon his appointment he did try to bring into his cabinet some representatives of the more moderate constitutionalists. When they in turn attached conditions to their acceptance he rejected them. No government worth its mettle, said Stolypin, could agree to have its hands tied by a political bargain; it must formulate its own policies and carry them through, no matter what.

His program, publicly announced on August 25, 1906, envisaged both the most ambitious social and economic reforms since the 1860s and police measures of unprecedented severity. Under the first, the government promised to enact far-reaching land reforms, introduce health insurance for the industrial workers, remove the civil disabilities and restrictions on worship which had been the lot of the religious minorities, including the Jews, extend local self-government to the provinces, where it had previously been absent, and to Poland. On the other hand, the government was to institute courts-martial to deal with the perpetrators of revolutionary violence. The courts were to render their judgment within two days: those sentenced to death would be executed within twenty-four hours.

Stolypin proposed to utilize the seven-months' interval before the convocation of the new Duma to legislate by decree. This was to be done through the use, in the eyes of the opposition abuse, of the notorious Article 87 of the Fundamental Laws, which empowered the government, when the Duma was not in session, to enact on its own emergency legislation. The autocracy was to demonstrate its willingness and ability to remedy the outstanding social and economic ills, in contrast to the First Duma, which during its very brief existence passed but one insignificant law.

Thus by decree the government abolished most of the restrictions on the peasant's personal freedom and rights, ending his status as the state's ward. More fundamentally by the law of November 9, Stolypin struck at the fetish of conservatives and (except for the Marxists) radicals alike, the peasant commune. The law allowed individual peasants to opt out of their communes, and if their holdings were in separate strips, to demand that they be consolidated. This the government hoped would enhance agricultural productivity, as well as lead to the emergence of a prosperous rural middle class, which as in other countries should become a force for political stability and economic well being of the country as a whole. Needless to say, such objectives could not be achieved overnight; the breakup of the commune was bound to be a slow and painful process. In the meantime in order to alleviate the economic distress and overpopulation of the countryside, the government proposed to encourage and help migration to areas thinly settled and suitable for cultivation, in Siberia and elsewhere. The state would also provide financial assistance for the peasants purchasing land from the gentry and the imperial domain.

Under Article 87 Stolypin also carried through legislation bestowing the freedom of worship on the Old Believers and removing the restrictions on admission of Jews to institutions of higher learning. But when it came to freeing the latter from all legal disabilities, the emperor balked at relief. His conscience, wrote Nicholas II to Stolypin, would not allow him to grant the Jews full citizenship.

Stolypin could not and did not expect his energetic measures to bring him popularity. The right was scandalized by his efforts on behalf of the Jews and the religious dissidents were fearful that his vigorous sponsorship of individual peasant proprietors would ruin the gentry. On the extreme left his attempts to strengthen the social base of the system brought undisguised alarm. Stolypin's social engineering, Lenin was to write, might immunize rural Russia against revolution for a long time to come. For the liberals the prime minister's undoubted solicitude for the underprivileged could not outweigh the revulsion produced by his authoritarian methods. Repression of revolutionary activities was now systematic and ruthless. During the first six months of their existence court martials passed 1,042 death sentences. The hangman's noose became known as "Stolypin's necktie." Though he escaped one attempted assassination—his villa was dynamited, killing more than thirty people and injuring his children—and though he knew that eventually his life was forfeit, Stolypin would not deviate from his course. All the revolutionary activities and propaganda, he was to declare in the Second Duma, amounted to saying to the authorities, "Hands up." The government's answer was, "You will not frighten us." Nor did his exertions earn him the gratitude of the sovereign, who as usual was ill at ease at having a strong-willed man as his minister and who was to display remarkable equanimity when Stolypin did meet his end from an assassin's bullet.

The volatility of the political situation was demonstrated by the results of the elections to the Second Duma. When it assembled on February 20 its membership, which fluctuated as independents and representatives of the minorities would join or leave the major blocs, was much more polarized than that of the first. The left had elected two-fifths of the total, among them 65 Social Democrats, and 37 Socialist Revolutionaries. (Both parties had recognized that their boycott of the First Duma had been a mistake and participated vigorously in the new elections.) There was a sizable bloc of deputies on the extreme right, and the Octobrists, now in effect a progovernment party, increased their membership to about 50. The liberals suffered a severe setback, the Kadets and their allies falling from 180 to 99. Ideologically it was thus a veritable tower of Babel. Neither the extreme left nor the extreme right took the parliamentary business seriously; for both the Duma offered an opportunity to deliver inflammatory speeches under the cover of parliamentary immunity. Deep cleavages ran even within the individual parties, the Social Democratic faction, which included 18 Bolsheviks and 36 Mensheviks finding it difficult to keep an appearance of unity, the Kadets, as always divided between those flirting with the left, and the ones willing to extend qualified support to government legislation. The life span of the ill-omened assembly was not much longer than that of its predecessor. In May the government brought up the charge that members of the Socialist parliamentary group were actively engaged in subverting the armed forces, which if not accurate in the specific instance was undeniable in principle, since the official position of the Social Democratic party committed it to revolutionary agitation among soldiers. Confronted with the demand to lift the accused deputies' immunity, the assembly launched on a passionate debate. Perceptively, though hardly in a manner to disprove the charge, one of the accused declared that the real plot was not by the left, but by the government. "The plot consists in the attempt to destroy national representation and to put in its place a bureaucratic-feudal

Duma. . . . But you will either have a national representative body or a revolution. . . . If they will chase us out with bayonets, let them. They cannot chase out the people." The stenographic record notes at this point "deafening applause from the left and the center."[63]

On June 3, 1907, the Duma was dissolved. Simultaneously the imperial manifesto proclaimed a new electoral law which, as an apologist for the regime disarmingly put it, "violated slightly the existing laws so as to make sure that the representative body would in the future work conscientiously within the framework of legality."[64] The slight violation of the Fundamental Laws consisted in a drastic revamping of the franchise, thus virtually making it certain that the next Duma would have a pleasing right-wing complexion. Representation of the lower classes was sharply reduced, as was that of the non-Russian areas of the empire, for as the manifesto forthrightly stated, "The State Duma must be Russian in spirit, the other nationalities ought not and shall not be represented in numbers giving them the power to have the deciding voice on purely Russian issues." It was all right for the Russians to sit in judgment on purely Polish, Georgian, et cetera, issues. The edict was equally honest in explaining why the tsar broke the Fundamental Laws he himself had proclaimed. The way the parliament was constituted, the right kind of electoral reform of the Duma could not be carried through. So "in order to complete the great task begun by Us aimed at reforming Russia, We bestow upon her this new electoral law."

Had the makeup of the Second Duma reflected faithfully the mood of the country, the outrage of June 3 should have been followed by a wave of revolutionary violence and general strikes dwarfing those of the fall and winter of 1905. Nothing of the kind happened. The revolution had been conquered, or more precisely the regime had outlasted it, primarily because it proved to be the sole force on the Russian scene ready and willing to govern. The only coup d'etat during the revolution was carried out by the government itself, when in flagrant violation of the constitution and of the emperor's solemn pledge, it promulgated the law of June 3. Confronted by this act, society not only submitted, but appeared relieved. The Kadets would run for the new Duma, though not only the fraudulent electoral law but also the government's subsidies to the right-wing parties and other chicaneries had made the election a farce. Nor would the Bolsheviks and Mensheviks scorn to compete for the handful of seats reserved for the workers. As long as Russia had any system of national representation, said Milyukov sometime later, his party would remain "His Majesty's opposition rather than in opposition to His Majesty." The implied analogy to Great Britain was not apt; there the opposition periodically gets the chance to become the government, something no Kadet could dream of after 1907. While the liberals repented of their revolutionary rhetoric, Lenin was constrained to explain to his followers that the time for armed uprisings had passed. Soon he and the other revolutionary luminaries who in 1905 had come home with such high hopes would again be forced to flee abroad.

The revolution withdrew, liberalism was defeated, the autocracy, though left in possession of the battlefield, had been weakened and discredited. Mao notwithstanding, political power in Russia did not come "out of the mouth of the gun." Guns had not been able to stop the sequence of events leading to October 17, 1905. In 1904–05 it was liberalism which became the beneficiary of Russian nationalism, of society's seeming determination to be done with the regime which had brought Russia' defeat and which would not alter the intolerable social and political system. Since then, as the very foundations of the state were threatened, the autocracy began to look more and more as the only safe haven of Russian nationalism. It was the nationality issue which significantly contributed to the split within the constitutional movement. The Kadets' platform promised autonomy to Poland, and its other postulate, decentralization of the empire proper, seemed to open similar possibilities for the Ukraine, Transcaucasia, et cetera. This to the more conservative constitutionalists represented a major threat to Russia's unity and greatness. They in turn, by lending their support to the regime, provided it with at least a semblance of popular support among the respectable elements of society, in addition to that extended to it by the rabble enlisted in the Black Hundreds. There could no longer be any question of resurrecting the myth of "the unlimited confidence which prevails between the tsar and his people." By the end of the revolution, however, many Russians, and not solely on the right, were ready to accept the modified autocracy as the only viable alternative to anarchy and the only system capable of preserving Russia's unity and national interest.

An eloquent speaker and fervent nationalist himself, Stolypin knew well how to exploit the patriotic argument in the defense of the regime. What its opponents needed, he threw in their face during a debate in the legislature, were continuous national crises; what the regime stood for was Russia's greatness. What better salve for the recent wounds and humiliations than the vision of the still backward Russia one day shaking the world. "Believe me, let the foundations of our political life heal and become firm, and what the Russian government says will have to be listened to by Europe, by the whole world." But first the country needed twenty years of internal stability and of peace. "Then you will not recognize Russia."[65]

Chapter 4

PRELUDE TO

CATASTROPHE: 1907~1914

WHAT HAPPENED TO RUSSIA between 1904 and 1907 was a kaleidoscopic preview of many of the developments of not merely Russian but also world politics during the subsequent decades, some of them still not fully unravelled. For the first time in modern history, a major European power was defeated in a full-fledged war by an upstart Oriental state, an event of vast importance in stimulating burgeoning nationalism all over Asia and of ominous portent for Western imperialism. The pattern of the political and social struggle in Russia in those years was to inspire rebels against other authoritarian and traditionalist regimes. Most of all, though few in Russia or elsewhere could recognize it at the time, the revolution was a warning signalling the fragility of the whole system of values the nineteenth century had enthroned in the West, one which most middle-class Europeans confidently expected was bound eventually to become the norm for the whole civilized world. It was liberalism and its carrier, the intelligentsia, which had triggered the revolution against the autocracy. Unlike what the script of such struggles had hitherto demanded, liberalism proved incapable not only of carrying it to a successful conclusion but also of controlling what it had begun. Instead of achieving their goal of constitutionalism and a government of laws, the Russian liberals unwittingly helped unleash forces as, if not more, antagonistic to what they stood for than the old-style autocracy. This drama, with an even more harrowing ending, would be replayed not only in Russia but in other societies down to our day.

"Neither of the two revolutions of 1917, the bourgeois one of February, the proletarian one of October, would have been possible without the 'general rehearsal' of 1905," Lenin was to write;[1] a rather startling admission for a Marxist, whose ideology teaches that revolutions are produced by inexorable economic forces rather than by chance configurations of historical events. A historian will question his characterization of what happened in February 1917 as a bourgeois revolution, even more so the description of the seizure of power by the Bolsheviks as a proletarian one. Yet in its essence Lenin's statement is correct: 1905 prepared the ground for 1917, and it was Lenin who alone among the major figures of the first Russian revolution would realize what had been its lesson and put it to good use during the second and more momentous cataclysm.

Prospects of another revolutionary upheaval seemed quite distant after Stolypin's bold coup of 1907 and his ruthless repression of terrorism. Russia seemed to settle down to a prolonged period of political calm. The wave of industrial unrest had receded to the point where by 1910 the number of those participating in strikes was but 6 percent of the figure for 1905. Membership in the revolutionary parties fell catastrophically: by Lenin's own estimate, in 1910 it was about thirty thousand for all the factions and national groups in the empire compared with one hundred fifty thousand in 1907, and the former figure is very likely an overestimate.[2] Everywhere, except in the Caucasus, both Bolshevik and Menshevik organizations were in shambles. The situation was not much different with the Socialist Revolutionaries, though they still carried out occasional acts of terror. The revolutionary leaders, generals with dwindling armies, now warred energetically against each other.

From Geneva and later from Paris Lenin renewed a vigorous campaign against the Mensheviks. The already extensive vocabulary of Marxist vituperation was enriched by a new term: *liquidators,* applied by Lenin to those Mensheviks, who having allegedly given up all idea of underground revolutionary organizations, were meekly confining themselves to those activities permitted by the law. In his more unrestrained moments he called the Mensheviks "Stolypin's labor party."

In fact the tactics Lenin prescribed for the Bolsheviks were hardly different from those followed by his opponents: both continued to participate in the elections to the Duma, even though the new electoral law allotted but a handful of seats to the urban working class; both exploited the now considerable opportunities for propagating their ideas through legal means, such as publishing newspapers and books (Lenin's own theoretical writings appeared quite openly under his name in Russia), trying to influence unions and other professional organizations, et cetera. Conversely, since officially all socialist parties were illegal, neither branch of Russian Marxism could dispense with conspiracy, and the activists of both risked arrest and exile. What made the situation even more poignant was that many of Lenin's disciples took issue with his own liquidationist attitude, clamored for a renewal of armed activities, and advocated the recall of the Bolshevik deputies from the fraudulent parliament. When he in turn tried to expose the unreasonableness of their demands—militant action no longer found any support among the workers and led only to further attrition of the valuable cadres; the few Duma deputies, in view of their parliamentary immunity, represented a political and propaganda asset which could not be matched by hundreds of clandestine activists—many of his former chief lieutenants left the Bolshevik ranks, some left politics altogether. For Lenin the epithet "liquidators" was not only a convenient war cry against the Mensheviks but also served to obscure similar charges made against him. Through sheer repetition and insistence he made the term and its allegedly opprobrious connotations stick in the pages of history and managed to convince not only his followers but also many future historians, even some Mensheviks themselves, that the latter lacked in revolutionary spirit.

Political vilification had already proved an effective weapon in the hands of the Russian Marxists. They employed it in political struggle the way an army uses an artillery barrage before launching an offensive. During the first phase of the revolution the innocent sounding term *bourgeois reformers* made the Kadets cringe, be ashamed of their alleged pusillanimity in fighting the regime, and it brought them farther left than they had intended to go. Among the Marxists it was Lenin who raised the art of ideological vilification to the status of veritable political magic. No matter what the merits of the dispute, you keep assaulting your opponents with contemptuous terms: revisionist, left-wing sectarian, imperialist. After a while this ceaseless verbal bombardment will wear him out, break his self-confidence, and force him to divert his energies from opposing your policies to trying in vain to mollify you and refute the charge. This skill in the art of political vilification and its obverse side, the Bolsheviks' ability to clothe their authoritarian objectives with a vocabulary of freedom and democracy, was one of the main reasons which would enable them, a small and isolated group in the beginning of the 1917 revolution, to emerge seven months later its master.

For the time being Lenin's ill-tempered abuse of his fellow Marxists was but part of the usual recriminations which follow a political defeat. The Mensheviks, though incapable of matching their tormentor's style of vituperation, were still paying him back in kind. It was Lenin and his followers, they claimed, who through their divisive tactics had disunited the Russian working class and rendered them ineffective in the revolutionary struggle. The Bolsheviks compounded their sins, the charge went on, by indulging in terrorist activities which discredited all of Russian Marxism before the people at home and in the eyes of international socialism.*

The liberals for their part also had second thoughts following the collapse of their high hopes. They had been ill advised, confessed the Kadets' leader, Professor Milyukov, in embracing the extremists as their allies. "Our record gives us now the right to say, that to our great regret, we and Russia as a whole, have enemies also on the left. . . . Our enemies are those people who appeal to the lowest instincts of human nature, who would turn political struggle into an attempt to undermine society itself."[3] In a few years, in another period of revolutionary excitement, Milyukov and his allies would forget his own warning and would again disregard the possibility of danger coming from the left.

However, whatever their immediate reactions, none of the main protagonists of the turbulent events of 1905–07 had reasons to be unduly depressed or exultant over their outcome. For the liberals the bitterness of defeat was softened by the fact that Russia, after all, still had a parliament of sorts. They adapted easily, too easily in fact, to the role of permanent parliamentary opposition, to criticizing the government from the rostrum of the Duma; questioning the ministers about the latest bureaucratic abuse or scandal was more congenial to them than an outright struggle against the autocracy. For the left, particularly for the Bolsheviks, there was the consolation that what they had feared most from the revolution had not come to pass: a constitutional state, a development which would have postponed a real revolution to the distant future, if not indefinitely. Their few representatives in the parliament could now spout propaganda to their hearts' content and for all Russia to hear. The working masses had for the time become disenchanted with political struggle and the Marxist slogans; but undeniably the Russian worker had been transformed by the revolution. He was no longer, as he had been before 1904, a peasant who happened to live and work in the city, politically illiterate and still tending to look at the tsar as his benefactor and protector against the capitalist. Though he still retained some traits of his peasant past, the industrial proletarian had acquired some of what the Marxists call class consciousness, and with it came, if not the kind of militant hostility

---

*While *for the most part* eschewing the SRs kind of political assassinations, the Bolsheviks until 1908 freely engaged in expropriations, armed seizures of government and private funds. The 1907 London congress of the Russian Social Democratic party definitely banned such activities. Most Bolshevik delegates joined the Mensheviks in voting for the ban, with Lenin casting his vote against it. Undaunted, three weeks later, on June 13, the Caucasian Bolshevik organization pulled the most notorious armed robbery of all, with Stalin as one of its masterminds. Most of the proceeds of the robbery were delivered to Lenin, then in Finland. Unfortunately, since the serial numbers of high denomination notes had been registered, the Bolshevik high command had to try to exchange them abroad. This led to arrests of several Bolshevik couriers with the whole affair leading to an international scandal.

toward the authorities which the socialist intellectuals had tried to instill in him, at best a new awareness of his own strength and interests.

There could be little elation at the outcome of the struggle among its apparent victors: the regime and the right. Superficially the autocracy had retained its essential attributes. The tsar kept not only the plenitude of executive powers but also a clearly dominant hand over the legislature. He had changed the electoral law by a fiat once, and obviously he could do it again, by "bestowing as a free gift" (the literal, if awkward, translation of the announcement of the new electoral law in the June 3 manifesto) a still more restrictive franchise to his subjects.

For the moment there appeared to be no necessity for such a step, for the composition of the Third Duma was such that it would have reconciled even the late Pobyedonostsev to parliamentarism. On its extreme right was a group of deputies so reactionary that its professed aim was to put an end to even this emasculated form of parliamentarism. Then there was a sizable faction of the Russian Nationalists, who while acquiescing in the existence of the institution of which they were members, were equally staunch in their loyalty to the principle of autocracy. The Octobrists, the Duma's largest bloc, with over 150 deputies and pledged to the support of the regime as long as it permitted some scraps of constitutionalism to remain, appeared now almost radical when compared to their colleagues on the right. The left had been decimated: some 18 Social Democrats, among them 5 Bolsheviks, a sprinkling of the Trudoviks. Considering the restrictive franchise and the fact that the government did not spare money and chicaneries in assuring the election of right-wing deputies, the Kadets made a creditable showing: 54 seats. Theoretically the government could count on a two-thirds majority on most issues, and not surprisingly, unlike its predecessors, the Third Duma was allowed to last out its full term of five years.

And yet from the very beginning of this experiment in what might be called emasculated constitutionalism,* there were clear signs that the emperor's regime and parliamentary institutions of any kind were essentially incompatible. Part of the trouble lay in the fact that prior to 1907 Russia had been ruled not only autocratically but also conspiratorially with just a handful of people, sometimes only the emperor and a few advisers, privy to what was going on in the government. Now, no matter how tame the Duma, it could not help but subject the government's decision making and the activities of its officials to public scrutiny. The very fact that it was not a real partner in the government and that its members could not, except in very exceptional cases, aspire to ministerial portfolios, made this assembly in some ways a much more censorious critic than the

---

*The Almanach of Gotha described Russia as a constitutional monarchy, with an autocratic sovereign.

all-powerful parliaments of Britain and France. It is one of the most striking paradoxes of modern Russian history that it was the emasculated Duma, the institution so carefully devised to assure its submissiveness to the regime that helped, as much if not more than all the revolutionary propaganda, unwittingly to undermine the prestige and authority of the crown. In the end, it was this ill-begotten assembly which delivered the coup de grace, not only to the autocracy, but to the monarchy itself.

This paradox has seldom been expounded on by historians. The conventional view of Russian parliamentarism has stressed that it had not been given enough time to establish itself in the national life. For all of its shortcomings, its limited powers and unrepresentative character, the Duma, it is said, provided the country with an experience of nationwide representative institutions. Its mere existence was an introduction to the give and take of political life. It did provide in a modest way a brake on the arbitrariness of the absolutist system, served as a continuous lesson, so needed by Russian society, that politics is the matter not only of moral absolutes and ideological incantations but also of the prosaic business of legislation and budget making. Quite aside from having the rudiments of parliamentarism, never before or since has Russia come as close to being an open society, to achieving both freedom and stability as during those years, 1907 to 1914. Russia was still a police state, of course, but a police state with a difference, where one could write or say almost anything touching on politics with little fear of untoward consequences. Autocracy was in retreat, this time not before a revolution, but because of the logic of social, economic, and educational progress. But time ran out before the country could be set firmly on the path leading to freedom and democracy. The strains of war reopened the wounds of the Russian body politic, and the cataclysm of the revolution and civil war swept it onto a different path, which ended in a new form of autocracy.

It is as fascinating as it is useless to speculate what Russia's destiny would have been had the war come some years later (few students of international politics would hold that Europe could have avoided it indefinitely). It is just as unrealistic to view the seven years preceding it as the dawn of a new era which, except for the cataclysm of 1914, would have exorcised from the Russian scene the twin phenomena of autocracy and revolution.

The main dilemma of Russian politics of the period was pointed out sharply at the very first meeting of the Third Duma. Ostensibly the regime had every reason to be pleased with its handiwork. Unlike the membership to the first two Dumas, who shocked the court by their appearance and manners as much as by their politics, this one, or at least its great majority, promised to be as punctilious in their dress as loyal in their sentiments. It seemed then a felicitous idea, the prime minister suggested, for the emperor to give the deputies a reception. The emperor's reaction was unenthusiastic and portrayed well his notion of the legislature's role. "It is still too early to invite them. They have not as yet demonstrated their attitude, whether they will justify My hopes and be willing to cooperate with the government. One must avoid untimely and precedent-making initiatives on My part."[4] Nicholas's caution proved justified. The Duma, whose election cost the government a great deal of trouble and expense (the local officials had been instructed to use their influence and government funds to help elect the right, in both senses of the word, people), demonstrated at the outset that any Russian assembly, no matter how conservative, indeed reactionary, its composition, was bound to be disputatious and a troublemaker. Unlike its rebellious predecessors, the new body proposed to begin its activity by a message of homage to the tsar, but its members launched immediately into a petulant quarrel as to how the recipient should be styled. "To His Majesty, Lord Emperor, All Russian Autocrat," proposed the extreme right. No, objected the Kadets and their allies on the moderate left (the extreme left would not of course have anything to do with the whole business), "Autocrat," must be omitted. Autocracy was a thing of the past, and the message should emphasize it by including in its text the word *constitution.* After a tempestuous debate, the emperor found himself receiving not one but two messages of loyal greetings. The version voted by the majority, composed of the Octobrists (who thereby sadly disappointed the expectations reposed in them by the government) and the Kadets skipped both contentious terms. The right, 114 strong, stuck to the word *autocrat.* "The emperor was greatly indignant that the Duma, for whose loyalty Stolypin had personally vouched, could put to a vote—and reject!—His title as established by the Fundamental Laws."[5] To the majority address he responded drily, "I am ready to believe in the feelings you express. I expect from you fruitful labor." He was more gracious, after his manner, in replying to those who retained *Autocrat* in their greeting: "I firmly believe that the Duma, which I created, will engage in constructive work and that by strictly observing the Fundamental Laws which I have promulgated, it will justify My expectations."[6]

The outcome of this battle of the address led to great jubilation among the liberals. The very same people who a few months before would have no traffic with the regime, unless it introduced forthwith a most thoroughly democratic constitution reducing the monarch to a figurehead, now saw a great victory in the elimination of one word in the majority message to the tsar. It was a historic event, a tangible proof that Russia *was* a constitutional state, proclaimed a Kadet newspaper, oblivious for the moment of what had happened to the constitutional guarantee that only the legislature could enact a new electoral law. Correspondingly intense and preposterous was the discomfiture of the far right. What the majority of the Duma did, bewailed a reactionary journalist, was part of a veritable plot to rob the Russian people of their inalienable right to be governed autocratically. Defeated in their frontal attack on the system, forces of the left were trying to outflank it, to emasculate it while feigning loyalty to the throne.

At first the whole incident might appear humorous and the attitude of the concerned parties peevish and unrealistic to the point of absurdity: a twentieth-century ruler insisting on speaking and being addressed as if he were Peter the Great, the Kadets exulting in their trifling victory, the right espying portents of national doom in the omission of one word, so offensive in its implications to the dignity of a civilized country.

But there was a serious side to the dispute. It was symptomatic of what was to become the master cause of the revolution of 1917, the erosion of the sense of political legitimacy in Russian society. Prior to 1905 no Russian, whatever his political persuasion, could have any doubt as to what was the ultimate seat of political authority. Where a West European used the word *state*, a nineteenth-century Russian would most frequently use *autocracy*, a peasant still more specifically *the tsar* in describing the source of his obligations and rights, the institution charged with the protection of the people's well-being or, conversely, that which was responsible for their sufferings. Now Russia had ceased being an autocracy without becoming a constitutional state. It would have been difficult in any case to accustom the Russian political mind to the notion that there is no single supreme source of authority, to a system of constitutional checks and balances. It was not a group of hotheaded revolutionaries, but people led by some of the country's most eminent experts on law and history who, when the tsar in exercising his indubitable right dissolved the First Duma, called for a campaign of civil disobedience. But after 1907, despite the return of relative political calm, the situation became even more perplexing: a quasi-autocratic system coexisted uneasily with a spurious parliamentarism. The revolution had loosened the traditional moorings of Russian society without replacing them with new ones. When another storm came, the ship of state was bound to founder.

No one was more conscious of the impermanence of the system than the man to whom it fell to preside over the tsar's government between 1906 and 1911, and who, had he been given more years of life and power, might have softened the impact of the coming cataclysm, if not avoided it. Far from being a mere defender of the absolutist status quo, Stolypin strove with a sense of urgency to build a new Russia that would be able to withstand the next crisis, which he believed was inevitable. His philosophy was well summarized in a speech to the Duma, where he defended the regime's repressive policies as a necessary but temporary expedient.

We in the government have raised but a scaffolding behind which you can go on with the work of erecting a new edifice. Our enemies claim that the scaffolding is but a protective shield for tyranny, and are furiously engaging in trying to bring it down. And inevitably one day it will collapse, and it well may be that we too will be buried under its debris. But when it happens, let the edifice be ready—a new reborn Russia, free in the truest sense of the word. Russia, where poverty, ignorance, and lawlessness have been eliminated and where the whole nation as one man stands united in its devotion to the Sovereign.[7]

Stolypin's vision was anachronistic—some of its elements behind, others ahead of his time. There was an echo of Slavophilism: the tsar and his people. But the ancient formula was to be translated into the idiom more akin to the post-World War I nationalist movements than to the Slavophiles' autocracy and orthodoxy. The tsar was to be a national leader rather than an autocrat, the people not a mass of peasants absorbed in their communal affairs, worshipping the God's anointed and trusting in his wisdom, but modern, active citizenry, vocal and active in public affairs.

There was thus palpable, even though grandiose, unrealism about the task Stolypin set before himself and the regime. One could not imagine Nicholas II transmogrified into a charismatic political leader. Parliamentary institutions were a vital element in Stolypin's scheme. His parliament was not like the Assembly of the Land of the Slavophiles' imagination, summoned occasionally to offer its advice to the tsar, then whatever his decision, accepting it and meekly trooping home. It was to be a real legislature, representative of the people and passing laws on their behalf, yet somehow never clashing with the emperor's prerogatives, a fantastic idea under any, let alone Russian, conditions. In fact the notion of real parliamentarism was incomprehensible to most of Stolypin's colleagues, not to mention the emperor. "Thank God, we don't have a parliament in Russia," a tsarist minister told the Third Duma, to its face. Yet even though unrepresentative of the nation and severely circumscribed in its powers, the Duma was light years away from the Supreme Soviet or Hitler's Reichstag. In one respect it was very much like other true parliaments: it made life difficult for the government of the day. Indeed Russians, even of the most conservative views, could not be expected, when given the freedom to criticize their government, to be inhibited from so doing. Its members, whether on the left or the right, fell with some gusto to baiting elderly bureaucrats who never before had had to face a public forum, to scrutinizing the regime's mistakes and abuses, and to prying into the hitherto sacrosanct activities of the imperial family and the court. Stolypin, whose gift of eloquence would have made him a formidable parliamentarian under any system, could usually dominate the unruly assembly. But for his imperial master and most of the officials it was at best a nuisance, at worst a malignant excrescence on the body of autocracy, to whose existence they would never really become reconciled.

Stolypin's edifice was then being built upon rather shaky foundations. But its principal flaw lay in what for many was its most appealing feature. It was to be explicitly a national Russian state, where the rights of other ethnic groups would be subordinated to the needs and interests of the dominant nation. Half of the population of the empire was now non-Russian. Under the old type of autocracy the dominant role of the Russians was obscured, if not softened, by the general absence of civic rights. But Stolypin's vision was that of a society no longer backward and passive. This was the age of burgeoning nationalism. One could not expect that in a modernized literate society, half of its population would acquiesce to the status of second-class citizens. Once again, but this time more drastically, the national interest in the broader sense of the word was bound to clash with Russian nationalism. How could Russia "great and united" be also free? It was a question to which Stolypin, no more than the Decembrists, Alexander II's liberal ministers, or for that matter, the typical Soviet dissenter of today, could ever find an unambiguous answer.

The enlightened reformer within him often clashed with an authoritarian nationalist. In 1907 the government felt constrained to restore the restrictions on the Jews' admission to the universities, which Stolypin had abolished only one year before. In 1910, to the dismay of his more moderate supporters, he pushed through the Duma a law curtailing the autonomy of the Grand Duchy of Finland, thus violating the solemn pledge of every ruler since Alexander I. "Juridical considerations," the premier bluntly told the legislature, must not stand in the way of the higher interests of the state.[8]

The State Council, now also the upper chamber of the legislature, was a thoroughly conservative body, half of its members nominated by the emperor, practically all of them former or actual officials of the regime. All the greater the shock produced by its rejection in 1911 of a piece of legislation warmly sponsored by Stolypin. In line with his policy of encouraging civic participation in public affairs, he proposed to extend local self-government to the Western provinces of the empire where it had not existed before; most of the landowners there were Poles, and he feared they would dominate the local zemstvo councils. Stolypin proposed to avoid this danger by instituting two separate constituencies, Polish and Russian, and to guarantee the latter a preponderance of the seats on the council. The Duma, its majority even more unabashedly chauvinist in sentiment than Stolypin, passed the measure. But among the older bureaucrats on the State Council there was still a lingering feeling for legal norms and proprieties. Being conservatives in the traditional sense, they felt closer to Poles of their own class —the bulwark, as they saw it, of the social order in the Western provinces—than to their peasant masses. For Stolypin, himself an estate owner in Lithuania, his fervent nationalism took precedence over the class viewpoint. "We are trying to protect the interests of the Russian majority, weak as it is economically, against the Polish minority, superior economically and culturally," he said, revealing the typical blind spot of Russian nationalism.[9] The bulk of the peasant population of the area was not Russian, but Ukrainian, Byelorussian, and Lithuanian.

Personal pique, joined with anger at what he viewed as the Establishment's lack of patriotic fervor, made Stolypin for once forget his political skills. He could have reintroduced the measure and with some manipulating could have easily carried it through. Instead, by threatening to resign, he forced the reluctant emperor to promulgate the contentious measure into law by decree. He also exacted from him an agreement that the two men whom the premier blamed for the defeat of the contentious measure in the State Council be commanded to leave the capital for the balance of the year, an exercise of autocratic power which even Nicholas found anachronistic and distasteful.

Even Stolypin's staunchest supporters were outraged by his actions. Though the blow had been directed mainly at the upper chamber, most Duma members felt that it struck also at the prestige and self-respect of the legislature as a whole. There was, of course, gleeful rejoicing among the opposition. "How it will look to the West" had always been an important element in society's assessment of the regime's actions. And now the regime had behaved as if this were sixteenth-century Muscovy, instead of a supposedly civilized state. How astounded must the foreigners be when they read that senior public servants for speaking their mind could be dealt with like the serfs of yore! exclaimed a Kadet deputy. The Duma, hitherto his obedient tool, passed what amounted to a vote of censure on the prime minister.

Insignificant as the whole incident might appear in the sequence of events which led to 1917, it still exposed the inherent incongruity of the political system between the two revolutions. Its main architect had hoped that autocracy and parliamentary institutions could coexist, indeed impart additional strength to each other. In fact their unnatural coexistence was undermining the prestige and viability of both.

Yet their inherent incompatibility seemed to offer little consolation for a revolutionary who hoped for a forcible overthrow of the regime. For a Marxist, for whom politics is but a product of economic and social forces, the general trend of events after 1907 could not have been very encouraging. Socially and economically the country was becoming modernized, the population's standard of living, though still behind the West, was rapidly rising. Statistical indices testified to the rapid economic growth. Steel, iron, and coal production increased by 50 percent between 1909 and 1913 and the rate of industrial growth for the period compared favorably with that of the United States, with horse power per industrial worker surpassing that of France by 1908.[10] In St. Petersburg alone in 1907 there were fourteen factories with over five thousand workers; in all of Germany there were only twelve such factories.

Superficially these signs of receding economic backwardness should have been hailed by a Marxist, for it was accompanied by a corresponding increase in the numbers of the industrial proletariat. But a revolutionary of 1910 believed, just as had his predecessor in the 1860s, that Russia's salvation lay in her backwardness, which would make the coming revolution more elemental, more radical than in the West.

From the viewpoint of someone like Lenin, the most disturbing feature of the social change was the rapidly evolving picture of the countryside. By making it possible for the peasant to leave the commune and to become an independent land holder, Stolypin laid the foundations for a rural middle class imbued with the sense of private property, hence a formidable barrier against revolution and socialism. The beginning of this process, as in the case of every great social experiment, was bound to be attended by strains and dangers. As critics on both the left and the right pointed out, the traditional commune, for all of its palpable defects, provided some, even if in most cases quite minimal, forms of economic security for its members. Freed from its tutelage, the inefficient or improvident cultivator might fail and swell the ranks of either the rural and urban proletariat or the unemployed. But whatever the travails or risks involved in his scheme, they were in Stolypin's eyes well justified by its eventual goal.

Isn't it clear that the [present] system of communal and family ownership keeps ninety million people in actual and bitter servitude? In legislating one should not only have in mind the interest of those who are weak and incapable of taking care of themselves. . . . when we make laws for the whole country, we make them for the benefit of the prudent and strong, not the weak and dissolute.[11]

The same feeling of urgency was imparted by the masterful statesman to the government's drive to appease the peasant's land hunger, the prime cause of social unrest in the countryside. During the first fourteen months of the program, more land was purchased from the gentry and turned over to the peasants than had been done during the past twenty-five years.[12] The rapid transition under government aegis (through the Land Bank which extended credit to the peasant purchasers) from large- to medium- and small-scale land holdings had its potentially negative side effects. It still threatened to lower, at least temporarily, productivity of Russian agriculture. New areas were being opened for cultivation; 2.5 million peasants moved to Siberia between 1906 and 1910. All in all a grandiose feat of social engineering, but one which would have required at least the "twenty years of peace" so fervently desired by its architect to accomplish its goals and to immunize rural Russia against a revolution.

To a radical another, deeply disquieting, development on the social scene were the signs of changing attitudes on the part of the intelligentsia. No matter how much his ideology and his hopes centered on the worker or peasant, no revolutionary could exclude the intelligentsia from his calculations. It had traditionally carried the banner of dissent and from its ranks came the leaders of his movement. There was little danger that the intelligentsia as a whole could be won over by the regime, which found its popular support, however much there was, among the semieducated element in society, and among those for whom the mythology of the benevolent autocracy still retained some validity. But were the intelligentsia to abandon its traditional attitude of at least friendly neutrality toward the revolutionary cause, to recognize that, as some liberals had urged, there were enemies on the left, the next national crisis might culminate in a real constitutional solution rather than a real revolution.

Such unpleasant possibilities were highlighted by the appearance in 1909 of a collection of essays entitled *Vekhi* (Landmarks, or Signposts) written by a number of leading contemporary philosophers, political publicists, and literary critics, some former adherents of Marxism, all more recently in the liberal camp. Without necessarily repudiating their political views, the authors subjected the traditional ethos of the intelligentsia and its customary stance on philosophical and political issues to a severe critique. What the typical intelligent saw as a bold defiance of the conventional values was, one contributor asserted, but shallow conformism. "He who professes devotion to truth or beauty is suspected [by the intelligentsia] of being indifferent to the people's welfare and censored for disregarding social needs in favor of imaginary values, or self-indulgence; he who seeks God appears as nothing more or less than a people's enemy."[13] The widely accepted notion that religion is an ally of reaction has been a product of prejudice and ignorance. What is undeniable is that true religiosity is incompatible with moral nihilism or with a purely utilitarian attitude toward life's problem. The ostentatious moralism of the Russian intelligentsia expresses its basic amorality.

Another participant in this symposium of self-criticism sought to spell out political consequences of the intellectual's loss of moral sensitivity. "Conventional morality must not stand in the way of any ideal or pursuit. If my ideology demands it, I have the right to decide not only whether someone else should own property, but whether he lives or dies. In your extremists you will often find petty Napoleons of anarchism or socialism." What happened during the revolution with its armed robberies, its mass incidence of terror and other outrages was a direct consequence of this unrestrained self-indulgence, allegedly for the sake of an ideal.[14] How demoralizing is this psychology of the educated class for society as a whole! Yesterday the intelligentsia was ready to see a hero in every terrorist. Now that the mood had changed, should anyone be surprised at the prevalence of cynicism and pornography or "at the very epidemic of suicides which is falsely attributed to political reaction and the sad condition of Russian life"?[15] And so the intelligentsia should give up its fruitless moralism and adopt a creative religious humanism.

Great was the indignation in the proverbial progressive circles at this collective breast beating of some of the leading representatives of the class which they so mercilessly criticized. The chorus of protests ranged from Lenin to Milyukov; accusations from that of a betrayal of the noble traditions of Herzen and Chernyshevsky to one of abject surrender to the powers of darkness, that is, the unspeakable regime and the contemptible Established Church. Years later Lenin, who indeed turned out to be a Napoleon, although far from a petty one, of Russian socialism, was to reveal the alarm with which the left viewed the book. "This shamefully notorious book, *The Landmarks,* has been having a great success among the liberal bourgeois society which is filled with renegade sentiments. It has evoked but an unsatisfactory response and insufficiently deep analysis from the camp of democracy."[16]

The essays were widely read, having gone through several printings the very first year, and their message undoubtedly had an impact on the class they described and to which they were addressed. In the years just before the war a new spirit grew up among the intelligentsia. As had the regime after 1905, so had its traditional enemy grown more tolerant. Leading representatives of the intelligentsia now admitted the possibility that a man may be honest and enlightened and hold ideas on politics and religion which diverge from what we would today call ritualistic liberalism. Again, as in the case of the regime, the change did not go far enough and was unaccompanied by a greater understanding of the realities of Russian political life. Also it was late for those hostile powers—the regime and society—to find a common language. There would be a brief truce between them at the beginning of the war; then they would follow separate paths to their common doom.

His standing impaired with the tsar, who could not forgive him his domineering ways, discredited in the eyes of the moderates, appalled by his reliance on the xenophobic and anti-Semitic elements in the Duma, Stolypin was on the verge of being dismissed when an assassin's bullet spared Nicholas the embarrassment. At a gala performance in Kiev on September 1, 1911, a police agent—and a revolutionary—Dmitri Bogrov, whose admission to the closely guarded theater has never been adequately explained, inflicted a mortal wound on the prime minister. Bogrov could have easily shot the tsar, but if indeed he was acting as a revolutionary, he chose by far the more logical target. Though in disfavor and on the way out, Stolypin in all likelihood would have been called back in Russia's next hour of trial. With this dynamic man rather than some bureaucratic nonentity in power during the war, events might have taken a different course. In some ways a typical nobleman from the provinces, Stolypin lacked Witte's broader horizons especially when compared to the latter's on the nationality problem and his realization that autocracy had had its day. But, unlike his predecessor Goremykin, a quintessential bureaucrat, Stolypin had a capacity for national leadership. Equally enamored of power, Stolypin had little of Witte's envious careerism in his makeup and no illusion as to what power would eventually bring him. "Let me be buried where they kill me," he said long before he met Bogrov's bullet.[17]

Imperial Russia was to have five more prime ministers, but none of them was a real replacement for Stolypin. His immediate successor, Vladimir Kokovtsov, long minister of finance, typified both the virtues and deficiencies of the old school. The happiest days of his youth, he recounts engagingly in his reminiscences, were spent as a rising officer of the Main Prison Administration. From this quiet haven he moved eventually to the financial branch of administration, first as Witte's protégé, then as minister, the target of his former boss's unremitting hostility. Kokovtsov was a man of probity. His first steps as premier were to insure that Bogrov's shot—he came from a rich Jewish family—would not be followed by pogroms. The extreme right was indignant at this undue solicitude for the Jews, and soon it had other reasons to be displeased with the new premier. Unlike his predecessor, he was reluctant to have its organizations subsidized by the government, which led to attacks in the Duma and the press accusing the prime minister of insufficient patriotism. He was equally insistent in trying to stop another custom of even longer standing: from grand dukes and ministers to dashing young officers, people temporarily in financial trouble but with influential friends at the court took it for granted that the government would give them some assistance, just as an official who had negotiated a foreign loan expected a percentage of the proceeds as a reward for his labors. Such practices were normal in less censorious times, before the Duma closely scrutinized state expenditures. Kokovtsov's stand earned him the enmity not only of the disappointed petitioners but also of their powerful sponsors, including on at least one instance, the empress herself. There was, however, one such request that the prime minister and his imperial master felt unable to refuse. Witte, once his benefactor, now his political enemy, wrote the emperor pleading that unless he was given two hundred thousand rubles, he would be unable to live on a scale befitting a man who had rendered such services to his country, or equally unthinkable, he would be constrained to seek private employment. He received the money, which did not inhibit Witte in the slightest from continuing to intrigue against Kokovtsov and to speak scathingly about the tsar.

Although such tales tell much of the mores of tsarist Russia, it would be wrong to assume that corruption among officials was more widespread there than in some other continental states. The fundamental flaw of the bureaucratic machine was not corruption, but inefficiency. The Council of Ministers was set up in 1905 to provide unity and a sense of direction to the government's operations and policies. But Nicholas II found the cabinet system as difficult to understand and work with as he did the legislature. Under a man as masterful as Stolypin the system worked tolerably well, but with him gone, it began to break down. The emperor had always held that foreign affairs and defense were not within the province of the prime minister's powers, but his own responsibility. And now other ministries, too, began to revert to the status of separate fiefdoms, their chiefs perfunctorily acknowledging the prime minister's authority, but going instead directly to the emperor, and working at cross-purposes. Kokovtsov was thus put in an impossible position. Whatever influence he had came mostly through his office as minister of finance rather than as head of government. The emperor would at times disregard his views in appointing or dismissing ministers. Faithful to his public servant's code, Kokovtsov would not resign but kept remonstrating with his sovereign, who finding it irksome, eventually dismissed him shortly before the war. His replacement was an elderly bureaucratic nonentity.

Compared with the country's brisk social and economic development, the government of the post-Stolypin period was one of bureaucratic stagnation and once war came the stagnation gave way to progressive paralysis. Even before the revolution struck, the central machinery of the regime had to all purposes disintegrated.

Authoritarian in its ideas, often venal and inefficient, imperial bureaucracy still had had individuals of ability and character, and in times of national emergency it seldom failed to produce men capable of coping with it, such as the remarkable group of officials of Alexander II's reign, and in more recent times Witte and Stolypin. But none remotely like them would emerge after 1911. There is a curious air about the epigones of old Russia's ruling class. The ministers, governors, and others of Nicholas's last years shuffle across the stage as if in a dream, and indeed the first stirrings of the revolution would make them vanish like phantoms.

The decline of the role and quality of the ruling bureaucracy was closely connected with the situation in which the regime as a whole found itself after what, for all of its sins of omission and commission, had been the period of resurgence, 1907–11. The pattern of coexistence between autocracy and parliamentary institutions, between the bureaucratic government and a now almost fully emancipated public opinion became subject to increasing strains centered around the lynchpin of the whole system, the monarch.

The Rasputin story has been exploited so much in popular literature and told with such garish sensationalism that it is difficult for a historian not to overreact and try to minimize its significance. Yet it is significant. The annals of the imperial house had always been filled with scandals and unedifying tales of the monarchs' favorites. Some of the latter had played a far more important part in the country's politics than the Siberian peasant, allegedly a holy man, who exercised such sway over the empress Alexandra and through her on her husband. But all previous incidents of that sort took place when autocracy was firmly entrenched and when a scandal or resentment over the monarch's behavior might occasionally lead to a palace coup but would never imperil the system itself. But now Russia's status—neither a constitutional state nor an absolutist monarchy— made the ruler's personality and behavior both more important politically and more visible to the nation. Stories, often scurrilous, of what went on at the court and within the imperial family circle could no longer be confined to a few aristocratic drawing rooms. The press and the Duma alluded to the subject with a freedom which would have been inconceivable in contemporary Britain, with its House of Commons and uncensored journalism.

Prior to the war, Gregory Rasputin's actual influence on political appointments and related matters was virtually nil. Yet even then his position and activities were harmful to the reputation of the imperial couple and the morale of the officials. Kokovtsov, for one, always remained convinced that his disfavor with the emperor dated from the day he read a stern lesson to the charlatan and tried to get him to leave St. Petersburg. Even more damaging than the largely untrue but widespread gossip was the atmosphere surrounding the ruler, of which the Rasputin affair was partly a cause, but mostly a symptom.

It is usually assumed that the emperor, an exemplary family man, tolerated Rasputin because of his devotion to his wife. The latter's infatuation with the holy man is in turn explained exclusively by her anxiety over her hemophiliac son, whose incurable illness was, she believed, alleviated by Rasputin's ministrations and prayers. Yet Rasputin was but the latest of a number of such spiritualist faith healers who had gained access to and influence over the imperial family. The empress with her neurotic disposition was always prone to religious exaltations and hysteria. As with so many foreigners brought up on a superficial reading of Dostoyevsky and travellers' accounts, for her Russia always remained an exotic land where millions of muzhiks bowed worshipfully before their Father Tsar, where saintly monks and beggars wandered around working miracles and dispensing folk wisdom, a country utterly alien and unsuited to the constitutional contraptions of the materialistic West. Her transformation from a princess at a minor German court into the wife of the Autocrat of All Russia, and her conversion into the Orthodox faith, which she embraced with the avidity of a cult follower of today, strengthened Alexandra's immersion in a blend of mysticism and obscurantism.

All of this would have been of no political importance except that the empress's influence over her husband strengthened somewhat similar notions in his own mind. More sober in his religiosity, Nicholas still believed that he was divinely ordained to pass on in full the autocratic power to his heir, that unlike the small minority corrupted by non-Russian ideas, the bulk of the population saw in him God's Anointed (how he wished he could eliminate the word *intelligentsia* from the language, he once told a minister). Ill-at-ease and awkward in their public appearances, eschewing contact with anyone beyond the narrow, unrepresentative, even of the aristocracy, court circle, the imperial consorts were thus an easy prey for one who in his appearance and manner epitomized the legendary simple Russian folk with its abiding faith and devotion to the throne and whose presence and prophecies were so soothing and reassuring. The fact that meddlesome ministers, the insolent Duma, and the impossible press agitated against "Our Friend," as the couple referred to him, was in their eyes a presumptive proof of his righteousness. They feared this holy man who told the tsar what the people really felt. In a strange way Nicholas in fact did share some of the prejudices of his lower-class countrymen: he was anti-Semitic; for all of his family ties, anti-British—"The English are just like the Yids," he once told Witte—and though mostly German by his ancestry, prejudiced also against that nation.

As for his wife, her superstitiousness and credulity could hardly be matched by that of an illiterate peasant woman. He should not forget, Alexandra wrote the emperor during the war, that before making a decision or participating in a conference, he must smooth his hair with a special comb given to him by Rasputin. The Duma was about to assemble, and Alexandra expostulated with her husband that he [Rasputin] urges that it be postponed as long as possible. "They [the deputies] should be all busy in their own localities, now they will start meddling and passing judgment on all kinds of things which are not their business."[18] And her concepts of how the emperor should rule:

Oh, my darling, when will you finally bang your fist on the table and shout at Djunkovsky and others, who are acting so wrongly?* No one is afraid of you and they *should* be, they must tremble before you, otherwise they will make trouble for us. . . . Oh, my boy, make them tremble before you; it is not enough for you to be loved. They must be afraid to make you angry or not to do what you desire. . . . Be more severe, this cannot continue.[19]

*Djunkovsky was deputy minister of the interior, who following a drunken brawl caused by Rasputin in a fashionable restaurant had him detained. As illustrated also on other occasions—he had a Bolshevik Duma deputy who was a police agent lay down his mandate—Djunkovsky was a man of probity and energy, exactly the kind to revive the sagging morale of the bureaucracy. Following the incident with Rasputin, he was discharged.

The Rasputin affair was thus but the most vivid manifestation of the general malaise afflicting the doomed monarchy. Despite their usual prudishness (the letters are not free of intimate allusions) and their doctrine of minimizing the importance of individuals in determining historical events, the Soviets, who saw fit to publish the correspondence, displayed a sounder instinct than many foreign historians. The unhealthy atmosphere surrounding the last Romanovs was an important link in the chain of events which led to 1917.

The bizarre doings at the court were all the more damaging because they were affecting the attitude of circles traditionally loyal to the throne, and entirely immune to anything smacking of revolutionary or even reformist ideas. The military and bureaucratic caste as a whole had in all previous crises always taken the side of the regime. While neither the left nor the liberals had reasons to be surprised or pained by the widely circulated stories of the "dark forces" behind the throne, they struck the right in its most vulnerable spot, its identification of autocracy with Russia's national interest. Rumors impugning the honor of the empress and her husband's rationality could be dismissed for what in fact they were, idle gossip. But the mere fact of their wide dissemination was a sign of the crumbling of imperial authority and prestige. The next national emergency would thus find the regime's last line of defense already breached, its traditional defenders too demoralized and confused even to attempt to rally to its aid. While itself crippled and incapable of fulfilling its historic function as the guardian of the nation's unity and greatness, the autocracy in its decline blocked all efforts at erecting another institution which might have assisted in the task or taken it over.

The air of bigotry and superstition emanating from the highest levels may have proved contagious. In 1911 Russian society had fresh proof that there were indeed dark forces in various nooks and crannies of Russian life, not excluding what had hitherto been the most enlightened branch of government, the judiciary. During the subsequent two years, the healthy part of society and the civilized world watched with incredulity and revulsion an attempt by a twentieth-century state to prove the practice of ritual murder among the Jews. Without the slightest evidence connecting him to the case, a Kiev workman, Mendel Beilis, was arrested and charged with the killing of a twelve-year-old Christian boy whose body, covered with a number of stab wounds, was discovered in the vicinity of a Jewish-owned factory. The obscenity and absurdity of the charge was too much even for some of the most right-wing and usually anti-Semitic public figures. One of them, writing in a reactionary journal, exploded with anger, recounting how the prosecution pressed the investigators to falsify their testimony, impressing upon them that the important thing was not whether the accused was guilty or innocent but to prove the existence of the opprobrious practice. "It is you who are trying to sacrifice a human life at your altar," he threw in the teeth of the authorities. The issue of the paper containing the attack was confiscated, and its author charged with defaming judicial authorities.[20]

The whole affair could not be taken as reflecting merely on the local authorities. It was within the power of the minister of justice to chastise the unspeakable prosecutor and to order a search for the real culprits, evidently members of a local robbers' gang. Instead the highest judicial officer of the empire actively encouraged the witch hunt. Efforts were not spared to find academic and clerical experts, whose training and knowledge, reinforced by generous payments from the police fund, made them attest at the trial that indeed "some Jewish sects" indulged in ritual murder of Christian children. Speeches for the prosecution virtually ignored Beilis, expanding instead on the theme "The Jews are ruining Russia." There was apprehension among the sane elements of society about the possible verdict. The jurors' bench was a microcosm of the lower-class Russia: peasants, craftsmen, one postal clerk, from an area where anti-Semitic feelings ran strong. Though befuddled by the so-called experts and refusing to repudiate unambiguously the prosecution's main theme, these uneducated people still showed themselves, unlike the high officials, endowed with simple human decency. Beilis was acquitted. "Russia has suffered a great defeat," lamented a reactionary spokesman.

The prosecuting team could find some consolation in a telegram addressed to its members by a number of right-wing notables, including two high Orthodox Church prelates and this incredible minister of justice. It saluted the "heroes of the Kiev trial" and hailed their "noble civic fortitude and high moral standards worthy of the incorruptible intransigent spirit of true Russian people."[21] Apart from its other aspects, the Beilis affair was a vivid illustration of how thin was the regime's veneer, of rationality and civilized behavior, and how lamentably Russia's political life had failed to keep pace with her enormous social and economic progress. It is fair to say that even in the heyday of absolutism, no minister of justice would have permitted, let alone abetted, a sordid affair of this kind.

In ancient Greek mythology Sisyphus was condemned by the gods to be forever pushing a heavy boulder up a steep hill, the burden always slipping from his grasp just as he is about to ascend the top. The myth is expressive of Russia's political history, never so much as between the two revolutions. To a liberal the fulfillment of more than half a century's strivings must have seemed quite close after October 17, 1905, but then it receded, to fade again into the distant future. There had been a less ambitious dream of the enlightened bureaucrat: Russia while retaining the autocratic framework would become what the Germans call Rechtstaat, her government under the rule of law. Even such modest expectations were rudely dealt with by incidents like the unmasking of the double agent Azev, with the lurid light it threw on the activities of the secret police, and the government's wanton disregard of law in the Beilis case.

No less frustrating had been the experience of a man of the right. For a little while after 1907 it might have seemed that Russia was on the threshold of a new era, when autocracy would be revitalized through a close collaboration between the government and the Duma and where the state's rebuilt and strengthened social foundations would render it immune from any liberal or revolutionary assault. But by 1912 no perceptive conservative could be confident any longer that such a new edifice was in fact being raised, that if, as Stolypin had phrased it, the scaffolding of repression were dismantled, the structure behind it would be able to stand on its own. One essential support of the structure, the emperor's personal authority, was being undermined. The other intended support, the Duma, designed to provide the link between the people and the crown, was neither a true spokesman for the former nor a reliable friend and helper of the latter.

The regime's predicament with the parliament on which it had expended so much trouble and money in order to shape it exactly to its specifications would have been amusing, except that it typified the impossible dilemmas of Russian politics and presaged their eventually tragic consequences. After June 3, 1907, it became easy for the government to prevent the election of the kind of Duma it did *not* want, one with a liberal-left majority, but it still remained virtually impossible to have any Duma, once elected, behave the way the regime desired. Part of the trouble sprang from the inherent incompatibility between the Russian bureaucratic mind and parliamentarism of any kind, part from the political immaturity and volatility of the deputies. The Third Duma proved a disappointment. Its right wing was, even from the government point of view, too much so. Any official measure of a faintly progressive character was bound to be branded by the reactionaries as a Jewish and/or liberal plot. On the other hand the Duma's moderates proved too independent—they would not keep quiet about the government and the dark forces. And as for the left . . .

The Fourth Duma, the one destined to deal the coup de grace to the tsarist regime and then through its suicidal self-effacement to Russian parliamentarism as well, was elected in 1912, after its predecessor had completed its term. The elections mirrored the growing disarray of the regime and of political life in general. The prime minister, Kokovtsov, insisted that his government should not repeat Stolypin's gross interference in the elections. Still, considerable latitude was left to local governors as to how they might protect voters from making wrong choices. The less finicky among them scorned indirect methods and simply purged electoral rolls of the names of those known for their political unreliability. The procurator general of the Holy Synod did not share the prime minister's squeamishness. At his urging and at the bishops' orders, virtually every parish priest was mobilized to insure that his flock would not vote for God's and the tsar's enemies. Due to the nonaccidental peculiarities of the law, many rural electoral colleges found themselves filled with clergymen, so that at one point of the multistage election it appeared that about half of the Duma's membership would be composed of Orthodox priests. Fearing ridicule, the government made some hasty last minute readjustments and the number of "little fathers" among deputies was not allowed to become embarrassingly large. The law did provide for appeals against fraudulent practices, but such complaints could be considered only after the electoral process had been completed and could not undo the results.

Alas, for all that labor, the government still did not get the kind of legislature it wanted. There were only thirteen socialists, among them six Bolsheviks, and about fifty Kadets, but that was enough to guarantee tempestuous antiregime oratory and the deputies prying into every real or alleged government malfeasance. Many deputies elected, or perhaps more accurately selected, on the strength of their political dependability, priests among them, soon began in the heady atmosphere of the assembly to display signs of liberal and even radical proclivities. The Octobrists, representatives of the moderate element among the gentry and the bourgeoisie, now on occasion voted with the liberal-left opposition. There was, to be sure, a solid majority for the government on most issues where it could invoke the national interest. But Stolypin's dream—the regime and parliament working together, endowing each other with added strength and legitimacy— seemed farther away than ever. In view of its origins, the Fourth Duma could hardly be said to represent the people of the empire. It still spoke for them when by a majority vote it adopted a resolution calling upon the regime "to enter firmly and openly upon the task of implementing the principles of the October 17 Manifesto, and introducing the rule of law."[22]

There had been other signs that the period of deceptive political calm was drawing to its end. In 1910 the death of Leo Tolstoy was followed by widespread student demonstrations, an infallible portent of coming political turbulence. The demonstrators protested the government's refusal to join in honoring the great writer's memory, a decision understandable in view of Tolstoy's attitude in politics and his excommunication by the Holy Synod, still stupidly insensitive of society's and the world's feelings.*

Then in the spring of 1912 there came a clash between the authorities and workers which shook Russian public opinion almost as much as had the massacre of January 9, 1905. This time it was in distant Siberia, in the Lena gold fields

---

*The emperor did not issue a public statement, but noted on the report of the death, "May he [Tolstoy] be judged mercifully by God."

that troops opened fire on a crowd of striking miners, killing over two hundred. There was an outburst of indignant questions and condemnations of the massacre in the Duma, the most fiery among them focusing public attention for the first time on a young radical attorney, Alexander Kerensky. Public indignation was brought to its highest pitch by an explanation by the minister of the interior that when a crowd's attitude becomes menacing, the police and soldiers have no other recourse but to shoot with live bullets: "Thus it has been done before, so it will be in the future."[23] The government was forced to open an investigation which established that the mining company and the local authorities dominated by it had indeed treated the miners inhumanely. They were to all practical purposes indentured serfs, working for eleven to twelve hours per day, standing frequently in icy water up to their knees, their hardships compounded by the terrible climate and their isolation from the outside world for most of the year. The uproar was all the greater as the company was mostly foreign owned. There were belated steps at remedying the situation and appeasing public opinion. The Russian managers of the enterprise were removed, the local police chief fired and prosecuted. But the harm had been done. A wave of sympathy strikes, student protests, and manifestations spread throughout the country.

The Lena massacre marks the beginning of a sharp upturn in industrial strikes, many of them partly political in nature.* Soviet historians have credited this upsurge to the effectiveness of Bolshevik propaganda among the working masses. In fact for the average worker, especially outside the two capitals, there was still little perceptible difference between the various branches of the socialist movement. He would not necessarily strike because the Bolsheviks, Mensheviks, and the Socialist Revolutionaries told him to do so. He reacted to the prevailing political climate where he encountered sporadic repression, where the regime could on occasion be brutal and arbitrary, but was usually on the defensive, and where political parties and unions were partly tolerated and partly subjected to police chicaneries. All of which contributed to a mood of frustration and unrest, more noticeable when it came to the workers, but hardly less pronounced among other segments of Russian society. Once again, as before 1905, the regime was felt to be not so much tyrannical as unintelligently and anachronistically oppressive. Even when potentially beneficial, its measures were greeted by society with irritation and derision. Shortly before the war the government decided to launch a temperance campaign, oblivious to the futility of such efforts in the past and unmindful of the words of St. Vladimir, founder of the Russian state: "In Russia

---

*Thus the figures for the number of strikers for 1912, 1913, and 1914 are respectively 725,000, 877,000, and 1,377,000 (in 1914 strikes virtually ceased with the coming of the war), as against a mere 46,000 in 1910. Quoted in Leopold Haimson, "Social Stability in Urban Russia, 1905–1917, Part I," *Slavic Review* (December 1964), p. 627.

there can be no joy without drinking." This happened also to be a pet project of the emperor. It was proposed to reduce sharply the number of government-owned liquor stores, something the critics argued realistically would only lead to an increase in illegal manufacture of alcohol and deal a blow to state revenues, heavily dependent on the monopoly of spirits. The campaign was greeted with universal ridicule. The Duma turned down the government's proposal for state subsidies for abstinence societies. Russia first had to become free before you could hope for the curse of alcoholism to abate, one deputy argued eloquently, but, alas, unrealistically. The announcement that liquor sales would be prohibited during the Easter week caused workers in several St. Petersburg factories to go on strike. The ban, they protested, would deprive them of the Russians' immemorial right "to spend the holidays in the customary manner."

It was not only when it came to such rude interference with ancient traditions that the Duma was proving obstreperous. In the last prewar session it voted down several government sponsored measures, including part of the budget of the Ministry of the Interior, an unprecedented act since 1907.

Clearly the country was headed for a new political crisis whose nature and eventual outcome were unknown. It would seem that within the past decade Russia had tried and found wanting every conceivable political option. The old style autocracy had failed. So had the experiment in constitutional government between October 17, 1905, and June 3, 1907. Revolution had come and gone. The edifice of new autocracy planned by Stolypin stood unfinished, its instability obvious to all. A strong admirer of Stolypin and fervent believer in his vision of Russia's future, Alexis Guchkov, leader of the Octobrist party, gave a succinct assessment of the current condition of the regime. A true patriot, he said, must fight to protect "the monarchy against those who should be the natural upholders of the monarchical principles [the emperor and his entourage], the Orthodox Church against its bishops, the army against its commanders, the authority of the government against those who actually govern."[24] The Octobrists, the only respectable party of the right, was now seen by the regime as hardly better or more reliable than the Kadets.

If there was near despair among the more intelligent of the regime's supporters, then similar feelings of discontent about their own leaders agitated other political camps. Liberalism was stuck in dead center, the Kadet party as uncompromisingly hostile to the regime (though now for better reasons than in 1905–07), as fearful of renewing its ties with the left. The latter attitude was seen by some of the more impatient party members as unreasonable and bound to condemn Russian liberalism to permanent impotence. For them the most dynamic force on the political scene was obviously the industrial proletariat, and it was foolish for the liberals not to try to come to an understanding with its professed leaders, the Socialists.

Indeed in the spring of 1914 soundings were made by a number of more radical Kadet leaders to establish contacts with the Bolsheviks and Mensheviks.[25] Once burnt, twice shy has seldom been an enduring attitude of liberalism in Russia, or for that matter in some other countries. Some Kadets had personal links with a few more moderate representatives of the left, Alexander Kerensky among them, through their common affiliation with Freemasonry, and this connection would be of political importance in the first weeks after the 1917 revolution. For the time being any meaningful connection between the Kadets and the left was precluded, among other things by the fact that the latter was also divided and like every other political force in Russia in those first months of 1914, appeared to be drifting, waiting upon the events.

The last point would be hotly disputed by most Soviet historians. The Bolsheviks, they assert, were just then on the point of forging the working class's unity and of leading a new revolutionary upsurge. The most vivid proof they adduce is the great strike which seized the capital in the very last days of peace. In response to the police dispersal of a meeting called to express solidarity with the striking Baku oil workers, the Bolshevik local committee on July 3 called upon the St. Petersburg proletariat to stop work.

Turbulence in the workers' quarters assumed dimensions reminiscent of the fall of 1905. By July 7 more than one hundred thousand people were on strike. Public transportation was immobilized, barricades were being erected, and there were attacks upon the police. By the ninth, out of five hundred tramway cars, only forty were still in circulation.

But though politically inspired—and all the socialist factions joined in it—the strike clearly did not have any specific political goals. Unlike 1905 no soviets were formed. In fact no one thought of calling for them. Also unlike 1905 the workers' turbulence did not spread to other segments of the population. While the factory sector of St. Petersburg was in a virtual state of siege, the center of the city was witnessing festivities attendant on the state visit of President Raymond Poincaré of France. By the tenth the Bolshevik committee called off the strike, yet by its very momentum it continued (showing, incidentally, how little the Bolsheviks were in control of the working masses), and the situation in the capital and in a few other urban centers, such as Riga, remained tense until the very day of the outbreak of war.

The strike was but the most dramatic demonstration of the political malaise which had affected society as a whole during the last prewar years, rather than part of any thought-out political campaign or a prelude to a revolution. Russian society was angry and frustrated over the political impasse yet unable to see clearly any way out of it. The revolutionary camp was divided more basically and, insofar as its leaders were concerned, more hopelessly than ever before. The major share of responsibility for this lack of unity which prevented the extremists from turning the revolutionary potential inherent in industrial strife into revolutionary activity rested on one man: Lenin. It was his activities since 1907 which frustrated all attempts at a reunion of the revolutionary forces, and any coalition with the radical bourgeoisie and liberals. Stung by epithets like "liquidators" and "Stolypin's labor party," those who refused to accept Lenin's dictation were as incapable of mounting a united front of the working class as they were verbally terrorized from seeking an accommodation and joint action with other enemies of the regime. The Bolsheviks' role as unwitting helpers of the government was well understood and highly prized by the secret police. Having its agents at the very top of the Bolshevik home organization, notably in the person of Roman Malinovsky, a Duma deputy and Lenin's confidant, the Okhrana could have easily put every Bolshevik activist under lock and key. In fact it remained selective in its arrests, wisely feeling that with Lenin's followers at large, the radicals' unity, except for sporadic strikes, would remain unattainable. Secret police agents within the revolutionary movement were instructed not to worry about strikes and demonstrations but to keep in mind "the impermissibility of union of those organizations and especially of a reunion between the Bolsheviks and the Mensheviks."[26]

On the eve of the war the country's mood represented a curious blend of exasperation and apathy. The regime chafed under the glare of publicity which the Duma and the press, for all the restrictions on its freedom, could turn on its sins of omission and commission. The liberals lived with the hope of some miraculous event which would make the magic term *constitution* become a reality. From his place of exile in Austrian Poland, Lenin subjected his sorely tried partisans at home to a ceaseless stream of instructions of how they were to unmask the liquidators and conciliationists (those Bolsheviks who tended to stray from the path of unremitting hostility toward other socialist factions) before the workers and how in general to keep making life impossible for the Mensheviks. The latter in turn could only pray for something happening which might rid them and Russian socialism of that impossible man. And there was a ray of hope: the Second International was to have a congress in August. Having warned Lenin repeatedly to cease his obstructionist tactics, the International might now expel the Bolsheviks from its ranks.

And then came an event, which though long anticipated with dread, still gave the politicians reasons to believe that it held answers to their prayers. War! For an unreflecting conservative, this was a veritable blessing in disguise, the national crisis would silence the critics and scoffers, military triumphs would restore glory and prestige to the autocracy. An equally short-sighted liberal had seemingly more sophisticated reasons to be hopeful: while fighting and winning the war on the side of the great democracies of the West, Russia was bound to win also her own freedom. And to Lenin, whom the July crisis caught vacationing in the Tatra Mountains, came a flash of inspiration which soon would harden into an irrefutable conviction: this was a prelude not only to Russian but also to world revolution. All his previous worries and uncertainties gave way to a new vision. "From the point of view of the working class . . . of all the nations in Russia, the least evil would be a defeat of the tsarist monarchy and its armies. . . ." It was clear what had to be done: "Our slogan must be a civil war."[27]

Chapter 5

WAR AND

REVOLUTION

IN THE AFTERNOON of July 19, following Germany's declaration of war, the tsar addressed an assembly of notables gathered in the Winter Palace. "Calmly, and with dignity, has our great Mother Russia met the news. And I am convinced that with the same resolve, come what may, we shall carry out the war until the end." Alas, his propensity for malapropism did not desert Nicholas even on that historic occasion. He chose to repeat the famous pledge of Alexander I after Napoleon had invaded Russia in 1812: "I solemnly promise not to conclude peace until the last enemy soldier leaves the soil of Russia." There were no enemy soldiers on Russia's soil at the time, and the Russian army proposed to carry war into the enemy's territory, but such incongruities were overlooked in the drama of the occasion. That exaltation which seized other belligerent nations at the beginning of this attempt by Western civilization to commit collective suicide was also prevalent in Russia. From early morning crowds began to flow toward the palace from every quarter of the capital, including those devastated in recent riots. This time, unlike January 9, 1905, there were no Cossacks or police to bar their way. On the appearance of the imperial couple on the balcony the crowd filling the Palace Square fell on their knees. All joined in singing the national anthem, its motto to assume in the years to come such a direct and tragic meaning, "God Save the Tsar," and an equally portentous religious hymn, "Have Mercy, oh Lord, on Thy people." This was the moment, one onlooker felt, for the emperor to come down among his people and to speak to them, as undoubtedly some ancestors of his would have done under the circumstances. Instead, after bowing to the multitude, Nicholas and his family retired and left the capital for their summer residence.

Still most foreign observers were impressed. This was a convincing demonstration of national unity and a refutation of all those predictions that Russia could not risk a war because of her internal divisions. For a French diplomat the scene revealed the true spirit of the people, that legendary Slavic soul, which made them in a time of danger gather around their Father-Tsar. Their grievances and lack of freedom were forgotten as they bowed to the will of their crowned leader. But even a more knowledgeable and skeptical observer was impressed. Though very much a man of the left, the historian and publicist Michael Lemke testified about the mood of those July days: "Today they began to call up the reservists. What a contrast to the picture in 1904 [the Japanese war]. [Now] one senses a general uplift and fortitude. . . . The people are ready to sacrifice and overlook personal inconveniences."[1]

The war had been preordained by the breakdown of that delicate mechanism which governed international relations in the nineteenth century and that was replaced then by the system of alliances which ranged the great powers in two competing camps. All this made it almost inevitable that one of the international crises which had racked Europe with increasing frequency would not be resolved by a localized conflict but would lead to a general war. There had been statesmen, notably Witte, who had felt that quite apart from the lunacy of a European war, Russia's alliance with France portended under those conditions if not a military then a political catastrophe for the country. And war would not wait until Russia put her house in order. Had the shots of Sarajevo not been fired, or missed their target, it is still unlikely that Germany would have for very long overlooked another pretext for opening hostilities. For the German general staff time was running out. Russia's rapid industrial growth, the proposed improvements and extensions of her railway network threatened within a few years to make her war machine much more formidable; her army would soon be able to utilize to the full her tremendous advantage in manpower. Stolypin may have been overoptimistic when he said in 1910 that twenty years of peace would bring domestic stability, but he was not far off the mark in implying that they would render Russian arms well nigh invincible.

Had a prudent statesman like Stolypin or Witte been at the helm in 1914 he would have also remembered that every war conducted in the past one hundred years had placed autocracy in jeopardy. The triumphs of the Napoleonic wars begat the Decembrists. What it viewed as an unsatisfactory peace after the defeat of Turkey in 1878 made society more tolerant of the revolutionary and terrorist activities which culminated in the assassination of Alexander II. It is superfluous to repeat what had been the domestic consequences of the Crimean and Japanese wars. This conflict was going to test much more strenuously not only the military might but also the political and social fabric of every belligerent state. With millions of people hurled into the fray, amidst enflamed national passions and hatreds, the coming war would be fought under quite different circumstances than those of the past. Courts and statesmen would not be able to stop it and conclude a negotiated peace before the international order and their societies suffered irreparable damage.

Even the patriotic elan with which the news of the war was greeted held some ominous implications for the regime. For the people this was a struggle against Germandom and its arrogant aspirations to subjugate not only the "Slav brothers" of the Balkans but also all of the Continent. At the same time most educated Russians still felt there was something distinctly Germanic about their own government, a legacy of Peter the Great's reform of the autocracy in the bureaucratic mold he copied from Prussia. German titles and appellations of court military and civil functions still grated on the Slavic ear, as did the German names of so many high officials, even though coming from the Baltic nobility their bearers had been Russian for generations. For the moment this Germanophobia was not directed against the imperial family, the tsar being acclaimed as the nation's leader. But the fact remained that in the male line he was descended from a Holstein Gottorp princeling, Romanov being a polite fiction, and without exception (Nicholas's mother, though daughter of a Danish king, came from an originally German family) the rulers' wives had for a century and a half, down to the present and already unpopular empress Alexandra, been procured from what had been Europe's largest mart of eligible non-Catholic princesses.

A remarkable preview of the consequences of Russia's involvement in war was contained in a memorandum submitted to the emperor a few months before the outbreak of war by a former minister of the interior, Paul Durnovo. The main burden of actual fighting, he warned, would very likely fall upon the Russian army, her allies expecting it to be used as a battering ram against Germany, with all that it would mean in terms of expected casualties.

Military setbacks, even if let us hope temporary, and deficiencies in equipping the armed forces will be inevitable . . . and in view of the extreme excitability of our society, it is bound to exaggerate their significance. . . . From the beginning military defeats will be blamed on the government. The latter will be subject to violent attacks in the legislature. . . . There will be revolutionary disorders throughout the country. . . . The army, having lost its dependable professional cadres, pervaded for most part by the peasants' elemental striving for [more] land, will become too demoralized to protect law and order. The legislative institutions and the opposition parties recruited from the intelligentsia will have lost authority in the eyes of the population and will be unable to contain universal disorders which they themselves had provoked. Russia will be plunged into an unmanageable anarchic turbulence, the outcome of which defies prediction.[2]

Yet such Cassandra-like warnings went unheeded. In all fairness to Nicholas II and his government, had they failed to pick up the German challenge and abandoned "little Serbia" to her fate, public opinion would have exploded against them, with liberals and most conservatives leading the charge against the regime which had dishonored the nation and betrayed its interests. In a strange way autocratic Russia's foreign policies had since 1855 been more responsive to popular pressures and passions than those of many a democratic state.

Patriotic fervor seemed to mute political antagonisms of the past. The Duma, summoned on July 26, approved war credits and other emergency measures with no vote cast against them, and with but the Social Democratic deputies (of both factions) abstaining. In fact the war fever and anti-German feelings ran high even among those on the extreme left. The rank-and-file Mensheviks and Bolsheviks hastened to enlist under the colors. Many political exiles joined in supporting their country's stand. The patriarch of the Russian radical movement, pacifist and anarchist prince Peter Kropotkin, proclaimed this to be a crusade against Prussian militarism. Few among the revolutionaries were as deeply immersed in Germany's culture, as closely linked, both ideologically and personally, with her leading Socialists, as was the father of Russian Marxism, George Plekhanov. News of the war brought from him quite a different reaction than that of his most famous pupil. To one who argued Lenin's point of view, Plekhanov replied boisterously: "So far as I am concerned, if I were not old and sick I would join the army. It would give me great pleasure to bayonet your German comrades."[3] Even the man who in three years would be one of the two main architects of the Bolshevik revolution was at the moment far from sharing Lenin's opinion that his country's defeat would be a lesser evil, if not indeed a blessing. It was Germany, wrote Trotsky in an emigré paper, which headed the camp of reaction, hence a Socialist must not wish for Russia's defeat. Patriotism for those who had often spent their lives fighting the regime was not confined to mere words. Milyukov's son, long estranged from him, now sought him out to resolve a personal dilemma. He had just been commissioned, and it was within his choice whether to be assigned to a unit in the Far East or one at the front. His heartbroken father gave what he felt was the only possible advice. Young Milyukov was among many who gave their lives during the terrible retreats of 1915.

Universal though the patriotic fervor was, it did not guarantee that the old political wounds might not be reopened, and rather soon. For many, future victories would be Russia's, defeats the fault of the regime. A wise government would have known how to minimize the danger: call upon society's representatives to join it, speak to the nation in the kind of language which would sustain its will to fight and sacrifice even after the initial euphoria had vanished in the wake of setbacks and casualty lists. No one could expect the tsar to speak in the accents of a Clemenceau or Churchill. But even in a predemocratic age another autocrat, Alexander I, was able to infuse Russian society with the belief, illusory though it was to turn out, that it was fighting not only for the tsar and country but also for freedom. But Nicholas's words at the beginning of the war did not give the slightest indication that after all its travails and sacrifices the nation could expect at its conclusion anything different from what it had before 1914. In 1941 Stalin, whose power dwarfed that of the most absolute tsar, had the inspiration to begin his speech to the people over whom he had tyrannized, "Brothers, sisters, I speak to you, my friends." How insensitive and pallid in comparison the words of Nicholas II to members of the legislative bodies, hence to the nation: "I am convinced that each of you and everyone else manning his post will assist Me to sustain this God-willed burden, and that all of us, starting with Myself, will do our duty until the very end," an eighteenth-century style speech to begin a twentieth-century war.[4]

Though it manifested an exemplary loyalty and willingness to overlook past animosities, the Duma was prorogued after one day, the government, evidently not intending to summon it again until after the war and only under pressure, promising to have another brief session by February 1915. It could not have said more plainly that the conduct of the struggle in which millions must fight and die was to remain an exclusive prerogative of the monarch and his advisers with even the civilian side of the war outside the purview of the legislature.

It did not seem to have occurred to him to appoint some leading politicians to his cabinet; nevertheless, the emperor could have at least purged it of those who were clearly not up to the gruelling tasks ahead, as well as being discredited in the eyes of society. The septuagenarian prime minister, Ivan Goremykin, had a richly deserved reputation for incompetence and indolence. There were at least two others whose continuation in office at a time like this was most offensive to public opinion. Ivan Shcheglovitov, minister of justice, was compromised by his part in the Beilis affair and his subsequent persecution of the lawyers and journalists who had decried that attempt at judicial assassination. Nicholas Maklakov was known to have advised the emperor to curb still further the Duma's powers, if not to get rid of it altogether. They stayed on, as did the other ministers, for most part gray bureaucratic figures whose names meant little to the public. No ministerial changes were made for more than a year.

This incomprehension of what the moment required in the way of political change resulted from the emperor's conviction, unshaken by all that happened during his twenty years' reign, that he was closer to the real Russian people than any politicians and that he would be failing in his duty to God and country by inviting those quarrelsome people into the government. This belief was assiduously fostered by the one person who enjoyed his full confidence, the unfortunate empress. But there were people in his entourage who, though sensitive to the need for a government of national unity, felt it to be a danger almost as great as that of German victory: the war must not become the means for a constitution and real parliamentarism stealing into Russian life.

During the first months of the war, there was no disposition on the part of various political parties to claim a share in its management. Public opinion would have been considerably cheered if those obnoxious to it were dismissed; and the retention of the decrepit Goremykin was increasingly felt to be a scandal. But the old syndrome—fear of responsibility—was still strong among Russia's parliamentarians. Born of that mutual reluctance to tamper with the political status quo was a peculiar arrangement whereby the regime licensed extraofficial bodies to engage in civilian activities essential to the war effort. During the Japanese war the Association of Zemstvos performed functions supplementing those of the Red Cross. In August the government gave its permission for the creation of the All-Russian Union of Zemstvos for the Relief of Wounded and Sick Soldiers and of a parallel organization of municipal self-governments, the All-Russian Union of Cities.

From the beginning there were considerable misgivings in some court circles as to the advisability of delegating to society functions which logically should have been assumed by a state agency or ministry, all the more so since leaders of these two unions were people with liberal views, most notably the Zemstvos' president, Prince George Lvov, who had long-standing ties with the Kadets.

In the course of the war, both organizations greatly expanded the scope of their activities. Amalgamated in 1915, they assumed, in addition to their original philanthropic function, the role of supplying the armed forces with a variety of necessities, including munitions. The zemstvo-city union and its offshoot, the Central War Industry Committee (which included representatives of the workers, something which would be of crucial significance in February 1917), sponsored by the beginning of 1916 almost eight thousand local branches which assisted in all facets of the war effort, some actually running factories whose personnel ran into the hundreds of thousands. The money for all those multifarious activities came mostly from the state treasury. That the regime, for long so jealous of its powers, so suspicious of private initiative in anything which might encroach on its prerogatives, not only permitted but also financed this huge network of voluntary organizations, is a proof of its bewilderment when dealing with the economic and administrative aspects of the war. Every warring country had to face a hitherto unprecedented multitude of social and economic problems, but most of them responded by improvising new techniques of planning and administration, creating new ministries of supply, labor, food. In Russia, as the war progressed, so did the administrative, as well as political, paralysis of the machinery of government.

All this still does not fully explain the collapse of the system, which precipitated rather than was caused by the revolution. A knowledgeable observer could not have predicted in 1914 that Russia would be the first casualty of war among the great powers. Most of the gloomy (or from the liberal and revolutionary point of view, hopeful) predictions of what the war would do to the regime touched on its aftereffects. Compare the situation in which other powers found themselves at the outset of the world conflict. Britain had been widely believed to be standing on the brink of a civil war over the Irish question. The Habsburg Empire was an anachronistic and artificial mosaic of nationalities, most of them chafing under the rule of the Viennese and Budapest bureaucrats, who themselves were divided as to the war's conduct and aims. Germany had the most efficient army but also the most powerful and best organized socialist movement in Europe, its republican and radical tendencies bound to revive in the wake of military reverses. France was militarily most vulnerable of all, and in the past the enemy's presence on its soil had always enflamed the country's political and social divisions.

As for Russia, a student of history had to believe that no matter how unpopular and inefficient her regime, it was still safe for the duration. For the masses and even for most of the intelligentsia the monarch was still the only possible focal point and symbol of national unity and patriotism. Many who in 1917 would demonstrate under the slogan "Down with Autocracy" were undoubtedly among the throngs who on July 20, 1914, dropped to their knees on the appearance of the emperor and sang "God Save the Tsar." Where else in Europe was such a spontaneous gesture of veneration of the ruler conceivable? This was not, as poor Nicholas believed, a sign of his personal popularity. The fact was that for all, except the most hardened Marxists, Russia without a tsar in wartime was simply unthinkable. As long as he faced the enemy and the traditional pattern of military and political control continued, the peasant soldier would be immune to political agitation. Military defeats by themselves were unlikely to destroy the patriotic feeling which shielded the monarchy. Unlike 1904–05 this was felt to be a national war. If forced to fight on his own soil, the Russian soldier would do so with even more than his usual tenacity. For all the political vicissitudes of the past, the war reestablished the bond between the throne and Russian nationalism. Only when this bond was snapped, when the monarchy's cause would appear to be divergent from the nation's, would the regime collapse and the nationalism which had sustained it become temporarily submerged underneath political and ideological passions.

The oft-quoted simile of the Russian colossus with feet of clay misses the real point of its weakness. Its feet, the country's human resources, especially in war, were firm and formidable. It was its brain, the ability of the political and military leaders to plan, to improvise, to sustain the patriotic fervor, which progressively atrophied and brought the downfall.

Signs of atrophy were visible from the beginning. In February 1914 there appeared in a St. Petersburg paper an officially inspired article, allegedly written by the minister of war, Vladimir Sukhomlinov himself, under the defiant heading "Russia wants peace but is ready for war." The author sought to refute foreign (that is, mostly German) insinuations that "Russia is not taking the possibility of war into account, is not prepared for its contingencies." On the contrary, declared the writer, "We can proudly say that the time we had to heed foreign threats has passed." Public opinion could rest confident that come what may, the Russian army would prove "not only huge in numbers, but excellently trained and armed, fully equipped with everything called for by the most up-to-date military science."[5]

The first test of these brave words came all too soon. Having mobilized in the first five months of the war upward of six million people, the Russian high command discovered it had but five million rifles. The boastful minister had assured the public that "in future battles, Russian artillery will never suffer from a shortage of shells. Our artillery has not only large reserves but a foolproof system of supply."[6] This was going to be, everyone assumed, a short war. But within six weeks of its start, generals were complaining of crippling shortages of artillery shells. They were being expended at the rate of a million per month; the vaunted "foolproof" system of supply was producing but one hundred thousand.

Russia's industrial development was still not at a stage where she could fully cope with the enormous and unanticipated voraciousness of the great war. The problem was compounded by her landlocked situation; hence difficulties in getting arms and supplies from her allies. Still deficiencies such as the number of rifles were inexcusable. In general, especially at first, the country's manpower permitted it to mount a vast army without unduly interfering with its essential economic activities. Conscription in the beginning claimed but one male per family. Unlike the situation in France, for example, workers in armament factories were not subject to the call. As the war progressed and casualty lists swelled, however, Russia was bound to experience what every other belligerent power did: shortages of labor, food, and other goods. Still it is incredible to read that in January 1916 one-fourth of all soldiers on the western front lacked even one pair of shoes. Undoubtedly the government handled the economic side of the war effort more incompetently than did the other European powers, and the consequences, political and psychological, were all the more devastating because unlike under a parliamentary regime, the ultimate responsibility for this state of affairs rested with one person.

To the great relief of his ministers, the emperor did not choose to exercise personally the supreme command of the army. "Reasons of state," proclaimed an imperial rescript, precluded him "for the time being" from assuming the post to which he appointed his first cousin once removed, Grand Duke Nicholas Nikolayevich. With his imposing stature of six feet six inches, stentorian voice, and martial air, the grand duke had all the external characteristics of a great commander and in the first flush of bellicose enthusiasm was avidly accepted as such by the nation, long starved for military heroes. In fact he was not much different from the bulk of those World War I generals whose ideas of strategy went little beyond throwing wave after wave of troops against the enemy's entrenched positions, who billeted far behind the front lines, and who when setbacks came would blame them on civilian leadership and deficiencies of the home front.

This was not the first time that because of his birth and, one assumes, physical attributes Nicholas Nikolayevich was considered for a position of great importance. In 1905 the tsar had thought seriously of bestowing on him dictatorial powers to quell the revolution. But the grand duke said that he would rather shoot himself than assume the task and implored his cousin to accept Witte's proposals. The Empress Alexandra never forgave "Nikolasha" for thus helping to foist the Duma on her husband or for the fact that he and his meddlesome wife,* having introduced Rasputin to the imperial couple, became subsequently his great enemies. His one moment of liberalism over, the grand duke gravitated toward the extreme right.

Had it been led with imagination and intelligence, the Russian army could have, for all its material deficiencies, dealt at the very outset a crippling blow to the enemy. Germany's war plan called for the bulk of her army to be thrown against France, with but light forces protecting the eastern front. After scoring a lightning victory in the west, the kaiser's general staff then proposed to turn its full attention on the Russians. This much-celebrated Schlieffen plan was in fact a relic of the nineteenth-century military mentality and, as such, extremely risky under the actual conditions. It assumed that France could be knocked out of the war by one major blow and the occupation of Paris, something which had

---

*Grank Duchess Anastasia (not to be confused with the more celebrated bearer of the name) was the daughter of that notorious sponger on the Russian treasury, the king of Montenegro; hence she and her sister were referred to in the family's correspondence as the "black women."

not been quite true even in 1870, when, unlike in 1940, Germany had only one front to cope with. For all of its defects the Russian army in 1914 was much quicker in its ability to mobilize and more formidable than in 1898 when the Schlieffen plan had been conceived.

As the German army poured across Belgium and into France, an opportunity appeared for Russia, one which would never occur again, to respond by an equally daring coup of sending the gross of her forces across the lightly defended heart of Germany straight for Berlin! True, such a move would have exposed the army's lines of communication to attacks from two sides, for Russian Poland was geographically a huge bulge, with Austrian Galicia to the south and German East Prussia to the north of it. But both flanks could have been protected with relatively light forces. The East Prussian force was not strong enough to mount a major attack, the Austro-Hungarian army was little respected as a fighting force (one of the few pre-1914 military prognoses which the experience of the war was to confirm.)

But to concentrate on striking for Berlin would have clashed with the inherent conservativism of the Russian military mind—one does not attack with one's flanks vulnerable—and more importantly with what was conceived to be the war's primary political aims, the liberation of the "brother Slavs" of the Habsburg Empire. Hence the major part of the Russian army was committed against the Austrian forces to conquer Galicia. The eastern part of the province was settled very largely by the Ukrainians, hence in the nationalist nomenclature an essentially Russian land, the western part was solidly Polish. In the old days it had been thought unsporting to try to subvert the enemy's subjects, but now such scruples were thought obsolete. Therefore Grand Duke Nicholas issued two proclamations, one beginning "Brothers" was addressed to the Russian people of Galicia, and the other was "to the Poles." The commander-in-chief assured "our Russian brothers who are being liberated" that "you will all find a place in the bosom of Mother Russia," and urged them "to turn your swords against the enemy and your hearts to pray for Russia, for the Russian Tsar."[7] Most Ukrainians, even if anti-Austrian, in fact preferred greatly the status quo to finding themselves under a government which did not even acknowledge the existence of their nationality and was known to be hostile to their religion, most of them adhering to the Greek Catholic rite rather than the Russian Orthodox. As the Russian armies advanced, the Ukrainian nationalists, including high prelates of the Uniate church, were being rounded up, their reunion to "the bosom of Mother Russia" taking the form of deportation to the interior of the empire, a pattern which would recur on a much larger scale after the Soviets occupied Eastern Poland in 1939.

The problem with the Poles was even more delicate. Under the lenient rule of the Habsburgs they enjoyed freedoms their brethren under the Romanovs had not had since 1831. Hence the grand duke, or rather the writer of the manifestoes to which the commander-in-chief put his name, felt it necessary to assure Poles everywhere that their unfortunate nation was on the eve of a new era. "Poles . . . a century and a half ago, the living body of Poland had been cut up into pieces, but her soul never died. It has lived in the hope that there will come a time of resurrection and of a brotherly reconciliation with Great Russia. . . . Let the frontiers which cut into the body of the Polish nation be erased. Let it be reborn as one under the sceptre of the Russian Tsar."[8] Because the last point was unlikely to be greeted with wild enthusiasm by any Pole hitherto under the scepter of the Habsburgs and the Hohenzollerns, the writer hastened to describe the boons the Russian tsar had in store for his new subjects: they would be free insofar as the practice of their religion and the use of their language was concerned, they would receive self-government. All of which was rather vague, but enough to alarm a diehard Russian nationalist for whom a reunited Poland loomed as a much greater danger than the moribund Austro-Hungarian Empire. However, the promises were being made in the name of the commander-in-chief, not quite the same thing if the pledge had been solemnly proclaimed by the tsar. (He balked later when pressed to do so by the allied ambassadors: "We have been a bit too hasty with the Poles," said Nicholas II to a minister.) The proclamation did have some effect in countering similar moves by Austria in regard to Russia's Poles. But for the unhappy divided nation the main hope for independence had to lie in a contingency which in 1914 seemed the most improbable of all: a simultaneous collapse of the three empires.

Though not very sophisticated in their execution, Russia's propaganda moves augured this new type of war in which political subversion and the nationality problem would be almost as important as armies and weapons. Both would play an important role in bringing about the demise of the Russian Empire.

That motley crowd of Czechs, Croats, Poles, Hungarians, Germans, et cetera, which was the Austro-Hungarian army did reel under the first onslaught of Russia's military might; but during those hectic August days of 1914 Galicia was a sideshow. The world's attention was riveted on the battlefields of France. The Germans, having moved through Belgium, were rapidly advancing, sweeping the French ahead of them in a vast enveloping movement and in a preview of the 1940 blitzkrieg, seemed almost certain to conquer Paris. The Western Powers' pleading with the Russian government and high command assumed a frantic character; with Britain having entered the war with a small army and no conscription, there seemed to be no force available to arrest the German juggernaut. The only hope the panic-stricken French statesmen and generals saw lay in a massive Russian move which would compel the Germans to detach troops from the west for the defense of their homeland. Some demands on the Russian government bordered on the ludicrous. The British proposed that three or four Russian corps be dispatched directly to the western battlefield. However, in view of the available communications facilities and with Archangel in the far north the only conceivable port of departure, this operation would have required months. Nor was there any mention of how this force was to be transported and where it could be landed! (The situation was to be neatly reversed in World War II when Stalin, in the first catastrophic weeks of the German invasion, asked for some twenty-five to thirty British divisions to fight on Russian soil.)

Both common sense and the tsar's feeling of loyalty toward his allies urged a major attack on Germany. But here the imprudence of Russia's war plans became evident: forces allocated to the northwest front against Germany were not adequate, it was felt, for an offensive push all along the western frontier of the empire. Because of the inadequacy of the railway network, the plan of mobilization envisaged that the full combat force of 3.5 million could be assembled in the theater of operation only two months after the beginning of hostilities. The only practical way of striking a blow at Germany, therefore, was to invade her East Prussian salient, vulnerable to Russian thrusts from both east and south. Hastily assembled, the two Russian armies entered Germany's easternmost province. During the first few days they scored local successes, pushing the enemy before them and confronting the German force with the threat of encirclement.

The news of this invasion of the fatherland had its intended effect on the German general staff; it lost its nerve. Two army corps were detached at the crucial point of the battle of France and sent to East Prussia. New commanders were dispatched to the embattled province, Erich Ludendorff, who had distinguished himself as a brilliant staff officer and by a daring coup during the Belgian campaign, and Paul von Hindenburg, sixty-seven years old, freshly recalled from retirement. In view of Ludendorff's lack of military seniority, Hindenburg would serve, largely nominally, as commander-in-chief in the east and would soon become Germany's number one war hero. It was Ludendorff who made the tactical dispositions which in a few days changed the whole complexion of the campaign. Noting the apparent lack of communication between the two enemy forces and the slow pace under which the First Russian Army under General Paul Rennenkampf was advancing from the east, he shifted the bulk of his forces southward against General Alexander Samsonov's Second Army, which on the contrary was rushing headlong into what soon turned out to be an encirclement. The result was the battle of Tannenberg, which ended in the annihilation of the Second Army, the Germans capturing one hundred thousand prisoners, and Samsonov shooting himself. A few days later came Rennenkampf's turn. In the battle of the Masurian Lakes his army was decisively beaten, its remnants forced to withdraw from East Prussia.

The East Prussian campaign, calamitous though it was for Russia, accomplished its larger purpose. By forcing the Germans to detach forces from the west, it made possible "the miracle of the Marne," the French victory which saved Paris and frustrated the Schlieffen plan. All hopes on both sides for a lightning war were now gone. Had it been the nineteenth century, Tannenberg, in conjunction with Marne, would have persuaded the warring powers that the time had come for negotiations, that the conflict, which had already claimed casualties on the scale of the Crimean and the Franco-Prussian wars, would be long and in its ultimate results hardly less costly to the victors than the defeated. But within a few days of the two battles, Russia and her allies reaffirmed their intention to carry on the war, each pledging not to sign a separate peace.

Russia had been a great military power long before the rise of a united Germany. Thus the effect of the defeat of the Russian armies by a German force half their size had to be traumatic. It implanted in many Russians that awe of the German war machine which even the fall of Germany in 1918 would not obliterate and which would be dissipated only in the winter of 1943 with the victory at Stalingrad. Guchkov, who played such an important role in February to March 1917 and in the events leading to the revolution, had concluded that the war was lost in August 1914. Perhaps of equal importance was the fact that no lessons were drawn from the defeat, and no reassessment was made of the command structure and procedures of the Russian army. Of course, Rennenkampf and the commander of the northwest front, on whom lay the responsibility for coordinating the activities of the two armies, should have been court-martialed. In fact the former retained his command, and the latter was merely shifted to another post.

The impact of the news from East Prussia was somewhat softened by Russian successes in the south against the Austrians. Eastern Galicia, with its capital, Lvov, were captured toward the end of August. Soon the tsar's armies were poised at the Carpathian mountain chain threatening, as they had in 1849, to pour into the Hungarian plain and to deal a fatal blow to the ramshackle Dual Monarchy. Another thrust was developing into western Galicia toward the ancient Polish capital of Cracow. Once they crossed into the patrimonial Habsburg lands, the Russians could indeed expect some support from the local populations: the Slovaks and Ruthenes resented the rule of the Hungarian magnates, Russophile feelings were strong among the Czechs, possibly because they never had had an occasion for a closer acquaintance with their Slav brothers (and so they would remain until 1948, to disappear completely in the wake of the Soviet invasion of 1968).

It was now the turn of the German high command to become the recipient of urgent appeals for help from its ally. There was a real danger that under the continued hammering from the Russians, the multination Austrian army might disintegrate. The German general staff now had to abandon its hope that even after the failure of the Schlieffen plan, it could concentrate on fighting the war in the west, while leaving the main burden of containing the Russians to the Austro-Hungarians. The latter would now have to be bolstered militarily on a large scale. Therefore, in the fall of 1914 the Germans had to improvise a series of offensive actions on the eastern front. One of them almost ended in a Tannenberg in reverse, several divisions finding themselves in a trap near Lodz. It was only the utter confusion among the Russian commanders, as well as the already alarming shortage of arms and ammunition (several thousand soldiers at a crucial segment of the front found themselves without rifles, some artillery units were being rationed to five shells per day's firing), which enabled two German corps to escape what would have been an annihilating encirclement.

At the end of the fateful year, the struggle in the east had still not settled down, as in France, to trench warfare. The tsarist armies' position appeared, deceptively, quite satisfactory. They held their own against the Germans, they still cut deep into Galicia. Yet casualties had already been tremendous; about one million men, killed and wounded, had been lost. To compensate for their deficiencies in equipment, Russian generals were lavish in expending manpower. The losses depleted the professional core of the army. Society, which had greeted the war in an almost festive spirit, had become sober and anxious. Prowar enthusiasm was never felt as much in the countryside as in the cities and towns. It was, of course, the peasants upon whom fell the main burden of providing recruits. To an average villager, the war's professed aims could not have the same meaning as to an intelligent; he cared little about "heroic Serbia," the "German threat" was something vague as long as the fighting continued far away from home. News from the front was not only about deaths and wounds but also about soldiers having to fight with their feet wrapped in rags because there were not enough boots, insufficient rations, and the grim, unsanitary conditions. For the moment the peasant soldier would endure all the hardships with his traditional stoicism, but his relatives at home were beginning to grumble. "Peasants now talk a lot about politics, something which was rare between 1906 and the beginning of the war," noted a police report.

In general, patriotic feelings still ran high. "Your people bow low before you Oh, Great Sovereign," bombastically declared the president of the Duma, Michael Rodzianko, when it assembled briefly at the end of January 1915. As yet there was not a whisper of organized antiwar propaganda; the opposition's grievances, stated with circumspection, touched on the government's derelictions on the home front. It was significant, however, that on this occasion the Duma Mensheviks voted against the war budget, while the Trudoviks, the labor group, abstained.

Where were the Bolsheviks? At the beginning of the war, following Lenin's directives,* they committed themselves to what amounted to an act of political self-immolation. The five Duma deputies and Lev Kamenev, the exiled leader's personal representative in Russia, were ordered to issue a manifesto endorsing his "war theses," that is, the call for a civil war. They did so at a supposedly secret meeting and were promptly arrested on November 4, 1914. The intended declaration was palpably treasonous. "The grandiose slogans of Panslavism and the liberation of nations from under Austria and Germany are deceitful and intended in fact to bring those nations under the Russian whip. . . . Organize the masses. Prepare them for a revolution. Don't waste time. *The* day is near. Remember what happened after the Russo-Japanese war." (Thus by implication even the Bolsheviks did not firmly believe in the possibility of a revolution during the war.) There was considerable danger that the whole group would be turned over to a military court, in which case there could have been only one possible verdict and sentence. Fortunately for the Bolsheviks, they were in the end tried before a civilian court. Here a team of lawyers, headed ironically by Alexander Kerensky, managed to save them from the gallows, and they were sent to exile in Siberia. In no other country at the time would an open appeal for treason have been dealt with so leniently.

But the harm to the Bolshevik organization in Russia was enormous and seemed irreparable, as paradoxically enough was recognized by Lenin himself. ". . . The work of our party has become a hundred times more difficult," he wrote about this consequence of his implicit order.[9] And indeed the party lost its main avenue of propaganda, as well as its only remaining prestigious leaders still at home, after Malinovsky's work had led to the imprisonment of such as Stalin and Jacob Sverdlov. It is not surprising that in the first weeks of the 1917 revolution, the Bolsheviks' role, as compared with that played by the Mensheviks and the Socialist Revolutionaries, would be quite minor.

It was not, however, the revolutionaries who particularly worried the secret police and authorities in general. It was society as represented by the Kadets and increasingly even politicians on the right, which was growing increasingly critical of the government—the regime was not doing its part in trying to preserve that sacred national unity proclaimed at the beginning of the war. Elsewhere in Europe national danger had thrust to the fore new leaders responsive to their embattled nations' sentiments. In view of what had been happening and what

---

*The outbreak of the war found him in Galicia. Interned as an enemy alien, he was soon released, thanks to the intercession of the Austrian socialists.

undoubtedly lay in store for the country, it seemed incongruous that the government should continue to be headed by the decrepit and lackadaisical Goremykin. Everyone remembered the prewar assurances by the military bureaucrats that the army was excellently equipped and ready for all contingencies. Yet the man mainly responsible for that complacency and unpreparedness, Minister of War Vladimir Sukhomlinov was still at his post, still assuring the Duma and the public that everything had been thought of, everything was going according to the plan. Sukhomlinov was being blamed not only for his own transgressions but also those of the high command, whose head was in reality strongly at odds with the war minister.

Like most commanders-in-chief of this war, Grand Duke Nicholas was in fact a figurehead run by his staff, primarily its chief general, Nicholas Yanushkevich. The latter was obsessed by the idea that Jews in the theater of operations represented a danger to the Russian armies, since for reasons which did not have to be spelled out, they were bound to sympathize with Russia's enemies, serve them as spies, et cetera. He ordered a wholesale deportation of that alien element from occupied Galicia, as well as from the areas contiguous to the front. This in turn brought protests not only from among the progressive circles but also from governors of the provinces where the unfortunate people were being forcibly settled. It was likewise pointed out that the regime, having appealed so eloquently to the Poles to help Russia, was doing nothing to implement its promises. The Polish deputies in the Duma had at the outset proclaimed their fidelity to the Russian throne, but now they waited, and in vain, for at least some of the boons, such as autonomy, promised in the grand duke's proclamation to their nation to be put into practice. The emperor's attitude on the Polish question was characteristic of his approach to politics in general: were they to grant really extensive rights to the Poles, they might after the war turn out to be embarrassing to Russia. Were they to fob them off with some minor concession, that ungrateful people might become disheartened and mutinous. Better to wait.

What equally perturbed the liberals and society in general was the continuation in office of the minister of the interior, Maklakov, known to be a reactionary of the deepest hue, whose chicaneries against the press infuriated even many conservatives. It was not only Maklakov's political views that endeared him to Nicholas II. The youngish minister had a talent for mimicry, could parody his elderly colleagues and imitate animal sounds, all of which was greatly enjoyed by the emperor and distracted his mind from the burdens of his office.

In 1915 forces were set in motion which hastened the collapse of the monarchy. The year's military catastrophe was to be felt all the more acutely because it was preceded by a great victory: in March the great Austrian fortress of Przemysl capitulated after a four-month siege, and more than one hundred thousand enemy soldiers were captured. Eastern Galicia was now considered as having been definitely secured, and without waiting for a peace treaty, the tsarist government proceeded to organize it as a Russian province, intensifying the persecution of the Ukrainian nationalists and Jews.

But on April 18 at Gorlice a tremendous artillery barrage ushered in a massive offensive of combined German and Austrian forces which broke through the Russian lines and sent the tsar's armies into a hurried retreat. On May 21 the enemy retook Przemysl, whose capture two months before had brought such great hopes and patriotic celebrations all over the country. On June 9 Lvov fell, only a few weeks after Nicholas II had graced the capital of his new province with a triumphant entry. Eastern Galicia was now swept clean of Russian troops and would return to what in the meantime had been transformed from "Mother Russia" into the "Socialist Fatherland" only in 1939 and then, after another hiatus caused by the Germans, in 1944. The debacle suffered by the Russian armies in the spring and summer of 1915 was catastrophic, though not nearly so great in terms of the territory yielded to the enemy as that experienced by the Red Army between June 22 and December 1941. But the number of casualties incurred on each occasion was fairly close, about three million. With the German-Austrian armies pushing ahead in the south and the enemy simultaneously attacking in the north, Russian Poland became untenable. Warsaw was evacuated on July 22. At the end of the summer, though Russian resistance stiffened, there were fears that a similar fate was in store for Riga on the Baltic and the "mother of Russian cities," Kiev.

At home the defeats brought among other things mob violence, which though patriotic in its inspiration carried grim portents for the future. The most serious disorders erupted in Moscow toward the end of May. There was a regular pogrom, with the crowds attacking and looting shops, commercial enterprises, and even private houses whose owners, in most cases Russian by citizenship and nationality, happened to have German-sounding names. Rumors were already circulating among the masses that the government had "sold out" to the enemy, and the local authorities thought it prudent not to interfere unduly with the mob's actions. Grand Duchess Elisabeth, a German princess by birth like her sister the empress, had her carriage stoned and was spat upon.

Defeat and danger dissipated much of the regime's complacency but failed to endow it with a new sense of purpose or the ability to encourage the nation in the hour of danger. At an even more critical period of Russia's history, in November 1941, with the front lines not far from Moscow, Stalin found the right words to sustain his countrymen's spirits and to imbue them with the resolution to keep fighting the seemingly invincible foe: "May you be inspired . . . by the gallantry of our great ancestors"; and he then listed the heroes of Russia's past, beginning with Alexander Nevsky, who in the thirteenth century defeated the Teutonic Order, and ending with Michael Kutuzov, who sent Napoleon's armies in a headlong flight. How appropriate would similar language have been in the mouth of one who was in fact a descendant of Alexander Nevsky and who, for all his sins of omission and commission, was still viewed by the majority of Russians as a living link with the glorious past. But it did not occur to Nicholas even to address the Duma or to make another imaginative gesture which would establish him as the nation's leader rather than just the head of state.

The regime did feel constrained to try to appease society but did not do it very felicitously. Dropped were those ministers thought particularly obnoxious to public opinion, such as Sukhomlinov, Maklakov, and Shcheglovitov. But their replacements were other bureaucrats, their personalities hardly such as to inspire much public enthusiasm or confidence that they could deal effectively with the emergency. The only previous administrative experience of Prince Nicholas Shcherbatov, minister of the interior, had been as director of the state stud farms. One popular appointment was the new head of the war ministry, General Alexis Polivanov, known for his liberal sympathies and reputed to be a good administrator. Like most half-measures, in a crisis this one had consequences contrary to those intended. The regime did partially capitulate to society but thereby only whetted its appetite for more fundamental changes and increased its exasperation with the man who, incapable of being either an autocrat or a national leader, kept temporizing and hesitating. As a biographer friendly to Nicholas comments on the changes,

There arose a [basic] misunderstanding between the Sovereign and society. The Sovereign believed that it was necessary in wartime to keep all power in his hands and to govern through people in whom He had complete trust. For Him the consideration whether his ministers were or were not popular with society was, though a factor, but of secondary importance. "Society," on the other hand, now received the impression that it was within its power not only to "overthrow" but "to appoint" ministers.[10]

This increased self-confidence, or, as the emperor undoubtedly considered it, brazenness of society became evident at the session of the Duma which he felt necessary to recall, and which assembled in July amidst the continuing grim news from the battlefield. (Despite his wife's various objections. "Our friend," she remonstrated with Nicholas, "said that recalling it will bring nothing but trouble. Russia, thank God, is not a constitutional state, but those creatures [Duma members] are trying to play a political game and interfere in matters they ought not be permitted to touch. Don't let them pressure you. How awful!—if you make a single concession, they immediately become insolent."[11])

The legislature sought to deal with the emergency by establishing a new network of councils designed to plan war production and related activities. They were composed partly of parliamentarians and representatives of various public bodies, the whole structure topped by the Defense Council, which included ten representatives from each legislative chamber. Under the circumstances this merely duplicated the functions of the already existing ministries and organizations and was a blueprint for further confusion rather than a more fruitful way of cooperation between the government and society.

Otherwise, the session of the Duma went far to confirm Empress Alexandra's gloomy prognostications. The majority of the legislature led by the Kadets and the Octobrists formed itself into the so-called Progressive bloc, its main postulate, formation of "the government of public confidence." The actual meaning of the phrase was somewhat ambiguous. As some Kadet leaders tried to elucidate it, they did not actually want a government composed of politicians and technically responsible to the Duma. Rather, they envisaged their goal as that of a cabinet, still mainly bureaucratic in its composition, but with its actual members enjoying the confidence of the nation, that is, acceptable to the Duma and deferring to its wishes. Here then was another manifestation of the original sin of Russian liberalism: its fear of political power. Some defenders of the regime suspected, not without reason, that the real implications of the Progressive bloc's formula would be a government still bearing the main burden of dealing with Russia's grievous problems, with the parliament free to criticize and veto the ministry's policies. It would then have been a situation somewhat analogous to that which would arise between March and October 1917, when Russia would have two governments, the official one, of which the hapless Kadets would at first constitute the core, and the Petrograd Soviet which would arrogate to itself the right to tell the bourgeois government what it could or could not do. Still it is fair to acknowledge that the intentions of the Progressive bloc were genuinely patriotic, and had it been confronted with a government of officials whose honesty and competence they could trust, they would not have refused it their support. Besides, nothing kept the regime from calling the Progressive bloc's bluff and inviting some of its representatives to join the imperial administration.

The opposition was unconditionally committed to carrying on the war to a victorious end. Though the Kadets were its mainstay, it included people hitherto far to the right. All the more remarkable that among the Progressive bloc's postulates were of a kind as hitherto had been associated with the left: a broad amnesty for political crimes, autonomy for Poland and Finland, an end to the persecution of the Jews and the Ukrainian nationalists. Some ministers were indeed in favor of meeting the bloc halfway in order to further national unity, but the emperor would not hear about it. "All those problems," [raised by the bloc] declared the emperor, "may be politically important, but they are not relevant to the needs of the hour." To free himself from further bother, Nicholas ordered the Duma to be prorogued on September 3.

Even before that date he took another and major step toward his doom. Empress Alexandra had for long importuned her husband to dismiss the grand duke-supreme commander. Her letters are full of insinuations about "Nikolasha": he acts and talks as if *he* were emperor; his closest collaborators are reputed to be German spies [!]; he tries to lower the emperor's prestige in the eyes of the army. "Visit the front, not telling Nicholas about it in advance. . . . Since when is he your guardian? Make the soldiers happy by your precious presence. I beg you in their name—*lift up their spirit,* show them for whom they are fighting and dying—not for Nicholasha but for you."[12] Apart from her fears for the throne, to which the hysterical woman seriously believed the emperor's cousin aspired, her hostility toward the grand duke was also being fed by Rasputin. When the charlatan had expressed his wish to visit the field army in order "to bless the troops," the usually indecisive grand duke's reaction was forthright: if Rasputin showed himself anywhere near the front, he would have him hanged!

But the emperor's decision to assume personally the post of commander-in-chief did not stem primarily from his wife's and Rasputin's intrigues. It was generally recognized that the grand duke's closest assistants, who in fact ran the high command, were incompetent and acted irresponsibly. Always a slave of an ill-conceived sense of duty, Nicholas II did believe that his assumption of command would uplift the morale of the army at the moment of crisis. He was, finally, heartily sick of the political side of his job and the atmosphere which surrounded him in, or rather near, Petrograd, as it was now called (the imperial couple never liked the city, and never stayed if they could help it in the traditional home of the tsars, the Winter Palace, their chief residence being in the suburb of Tsaskoye Selo), and was naive enough to think that in Mogilev, the seat of Supreme Headquarters, far from the capital, he would find a quiet refuge from politics (as well as, one ventures to think, for all his love and unabating physical passion for her, from the empress).

When the tsar's intentions became known, they alarmed his ministers. The minister of war reported to his colleagues:

I allowed myself to emphasise [to the tsar] how dangerous it was for the Head of the State to assume command at a time when the army was demoralized and depressed in consequence of continuous misfortunes and a long-lasting retreat. . . . It is horrible to think what impression would be made on the country if His Majesty were to give the order for the evacuation of Petrograd, or God help us, Moscow, in his own name.[13]

"It is impossible to conceal the fact that, abroad, there is little confidence in the Emperor's firmness of character, and there is apprehension about the influences which surround him," chimed in the minister of foreign affairs. According to Alexander Krivoshein, minister of agriculture and probably the ablest member of the cabinet, "The people have considered His Majesty as unlucky and unfortunate for a long time, from the time of Khodynka and the Japanese campaign."[14] (Khodynka was the site of a catastrophe during a popular celebration of Nicholas II's coronation. The stands' collapse threw the crowds into a panic, and several thousands were trampled to death.) According to the minister of finance, the emperor must be apprised of the fact that "a change in the Supreme Command, in view of present circumstances and of the internal complications which may follow it, will worsen our foreign credit, which has already fallen to a point unbelievable for a great power." Fears were expressed that the grand duke might not accept his dismissal quietly and that there were people in his entourage capable of attempting a military coup. To read the record of the proceedings of the Council of Ministers during July and August of 1915 is to wonder how the system managed to survive another year and a half.

Eight ministers signed a letter to Nicholas II begging him to reconsider his decision. But his mind was made up and the change in the Supreme Command was officially announced on August 4. Superficially the consequences were not as grave as had been expected. Though the grand duke retained, for some unfathomable reasons, the reputation of a great commander, General Yanushkevich, his chief of staff, who was removed at the same time, was widely considered to be one of those responsible for the military disasters. In addition, it was he who through his treatment of Jews in the war zone had incensed liberal public opinion both at home and in the allied countries. ("We are not strong enough to fight both the Germans and the Jews," said one of the ministers in discussing the shift.[15]) Rather than staging a military coup, as some expected and a few hoped he would do, however, Nicholas Nikolayevich meekly accepted his new post as commander-in-chief in the Caucasus, against the Turks, taking along with him the unspeakable Yanushkevich. The tsar's military experience had been limited to the parade grounds and the mess of a Guards' Regiment when a very young man, so there was another sigh of relief at the announcement that General Michael Alexeyev, a competent, if unimaginative, officer, would serve as his chief of staff and presumably run the operations.

And in fact the emperor's role at the Stavka, as the high command was called, would be largely that of a kibitzer at staff conferences, signing orders and dispositions prepared by Alexeyev, all of which he could have done perfectly well while remaining in the capital. But compared with the routine at home, Mogilev was an oasis of political tranquility. Nicholas took long walks, swam and boated on the river. There was a pathetic incongruity in the presence amidst all those generals and staff officers of one member of the family the tsar could not bear to part from, his ailing little son. Tragically, the tsarevich's condition seemed to symbolize that of Russia; being a hemophiliac, the slightest accident might bring a fatal crisis.

In the public mind there had always been a distinction drawn between the government and the highest power, that is, the tsar. The most dangerous, from the regime's point of view, consequence of the tsar leaving the main battlefield of politics for the seclusion of the high command headquarters, was to blur that distinction: the emperor had seemingly abandoned the country to his ministers, semiabdicated, so to speak. Worse still, society had long bruited about the "dark forces around the throne," meaning in the main the empress-Rasputin connection and its ramifications. But now with the emperor's departure, it would be increasingly believed that the dark forces had stepped into the vacuum and that Russia was being ruled by the German-born empress and the unsavory Siberian peasant who had conquered her mind. It is a considerable exaggeration to say, as do some Soviet historians, that the last phase of the autocracy was characterized by "the rule of Rasputin." But at the time many believed that it was so, and others who knew better still stood appalled at the extent of the foolish woman's and Rasputin's meddling in purely political and even military affairs.

It was only after the revolution and the publication of the intimate correspondence of the imperial couple that one could arrive at a balanced view of Alexandra's personality and the role she actually played in influencing her husband's decisions. The letters explode the myth, believed at the time by so many, that the empress was engaged in treasonous activities or was pressing her husband to conclude a separate peace with her country of birth. (It is not only unfair, but, to say the least, incongruous for Soviet historians to allege that this was so. The war was, from their point of view, an imperialist one, and the emperor and his wife should be praised, rather than blamed, if indeed they were trying to end it by a negotiated settlement. It was not the Romanovs, but Lenin, who eventually concluded a separate peace.) Alexandra Fedorovna had become a fervent Russian patriot, and there is not as much as a hint in her letters that she could have urged the tsar to do something that clashed with his notions of duty and loyalty to his allies.

There is no question, however, that her influence on her husband on other issues was considerable and most unfortunate. The tsar must have realized, even if subconsciously, that his wife was not well mentally; still he found it impossible in many cases not to defer to her wishes, especially to her often hysterical pleas, both in her letters and one assumes when he was at her side, as to which officials should be dismissed, appointed, et cetera. This constant bombardment was interspersed with the empress's communiqués about her usually precarious health: she believed that her heart at times became enlarged and only "drops" would return it to the normal size, noted scrupulously her migraine headaches and feminine indispositions, as well as those of her daughters and even close friends. Delicacy in general was not Alexandra's strong point: his former mistress, she informed the tsar, was now living with a grand duke in charge of ordinance and was rumored to be taking bribes from the army's suppliers.

Though it meant long separations from the man she passionately loved, her husband's assumption of the supreme command made Alexandra exult:

> I cannot find words to express what my heart feels. You have, finally, shown yourself master, a real autocrat without whom Russia cannot exist. . . . The only salvation is for you to be firm. I realize how hard this is for you, and I suffer with you. . . . I know your exceptionally mild disposition, and now you have overcome it and won, alone against all of them. . . . God [sic] anointed you at your coronation, destined you for your place, and now you have *fulfilled* your obligation. Be assured He does not forget His anointed. Our Friend daily and nightly offers prayers for you, and the Lord in His heaven hears them. . . . Everything will turn out for the best, says Our Friend, the worst is behind us.

For all her exultant mood, the empress's feelings toward the man her husband had superseded had not softened. The grand duke was to be sent to the Caucasus forthwith before he had time for any new intrigues: "You *trusted* him and now you can see how right was Our Friend when he kept telling you months ago that he [the grand duke] is disloyal to yourself, your country and your wife." She herself, wrote the empress, was quite ready to handle politics at home.

> Don't worry about what you have left behind. It is necessary to be severe and to put an end to all that business [presumably the Duma, et cetera]. Dear, I am here, and don't you laugh at your silly, old, wifey, but I can wear trousers and can make the old man [Prime Minister Goremykin] act vigorously. Tell me what to do, use me whenever I can be of service. At such times the Lord gives me strength, because our cause is right, and we are struggling against evil.[16]

The emperor had enough sense left not to entrust his wife with any formal powers in his absence. Yet inevitably she became his main channel of communication with the capital, received the ministers and other public figures, et cetera. Her main yardstick in judging them was, needless to say, their attitude toward Rasputin. "The enemies of Our Friend are our enemies." Some of the recent ministerial appointments had thrown Alexandra and Gregory (as he is also referred to in the correspondence) into despair. Their special *bête noire* was Alexander Samarin, the new procurator general of the Holy Synod, a man of probity who proposed to deal severely with Rasputin's pals among the church hierarchy. Hence the empress's alarm.

I beg you at the first opportunity speak firmly to Samarin—do it, my love, for the sake of Russia. I am convinced that Russia will not be blessed by God, if her monarch allows His man to be persecuted. Speak to him severely, tell him in a firm and decisive tone that you forbid any intrigues or gossip concerning Our Friend, and that you will fire him [if he does not stop them].... Don't laugh at me, if you could see my tears you would realize how important this is—not some womanly silliness, but sheer naked truth.[17]

And, not long afterwards, "Samarin continues to intrigue against me. I expect soon to have a list of suitable names ready for you, and I believe I can find [Samarin's] successor before he does more harm."[18] Samarin's tenure of office was less than three months.

His dismissal was due not only to the empress's urgings but also to the fact that he had been one of the eight ministers who protested the tsar's assumption of the supreme command and that he also was one of those who pleaded for cooperation with the Duma and the Progressive bloc. Samarin spoke for most of them when, protesting Prime Minister Goremykin's supine attitude toward the emperor, he declared that "the government cannot be useful to the Emperor and the Motherland without the confidence of the loyal mass of society." And he added words significant for one whose whole past and family tradition had been that not only of a monarchist but of a believer in autocracy, "If the Tsar acts to the detriment of Russia, then I cannot follow him submissively."[19] His like-minded colleagues were later also dismissed or allowed to resign. Among them was Krivoshein, a longtime collaborator of Stolypin and probably the only one among the current crop of bureaucrats capable of filling his shoes. Their replacements for the most part were mediocrities or worse. Alexis Khvostov who succeeded to the all-important Ministry of the Interior is best characterized by the following tale related uninhibitedly by Alexandra in one of her "reports" to the tsar:

Khvostov and many other loyal people think that [Minister of Finance Peter] Bark is not up to his job. In any case he does not help Khvostov. They have for long asked him [Bark] for money in order to bribe partially [sic] The New Times.* ... [But Bark is reluctant] and as a result the papers are being bribed by Guchkov and the Jews.... They [Khvostov and his ilk] believe that a clever minister of finance could easily trap Guchkov and render him harmless by cutting him off from the Jewish money.[20]

Guchkov was of course the archenemy of the empress and Rasputin, having broached the subject of Rasputin in public. Alexandra Fedorovna then suggested her own candidate for the Ministry of Finance, a man whose qualifications consisted of his being a cavalry officer and the fact that he "both knows and deeply respects Our Friend, and has excellent relations with Khvostov."

*A very conservative newspaper which had turned recently against the government.

The emperor did not replace Bark by the exemplary cavalry officer, and Khvostov very soon was to prove to be a great disappointment to the empress, and almost fatally so, to Rasputin.

The emperor, though at times resisting his wife's suggestions and insinuations, could not bring himself to put an end to this public scandal which was rapidly eroding the little respect remaining for the throne. He failed to see that his domestic situation had become a national disaster and that even if useful for reasons of domestic diplomacy, the tone of his letters strengthened Alexandra's delusions that she was rendering a great service to him and the country: "I have no greater joy than my pride in you, and I have been so proud during those last few months when through constantly pestering me and imploring me to be firm you made me stick to my resolve."[21]

The prevailing impression of those last months of the doomed regime is not so much that it was intellectually and morally obtuse as that it was impotent. For all the imperial couple's detestation of Guchkov, for all the reports that the ambitious Moscow industrialist spoke almost openly of the necessity of getting rid of the empress and perhaps even her husband, the regime did not feel strong enough to remove him from his quasi-governmental and influential position as chairman of the Central War Industry Committee. No matter how reactionary, the new ministers soon after their appointment would come to realize the almost impossible predicament of their position vis-à-vis society. The government's indecisiveness tended in turn to make society exaggerate the stature and repose exaggerated hopes in the most prominent figures of the opposition. Guchkov and the head of the Zemstvo Union, Prince George Lvov, were viewed, on rather insufficient evidence, as statesmen of the first rank upon whom must sometime fall the task of saving Russia's honor and greatness, whether asked to do so by the emperor or not.

But people wondered when this sometime would come. If the government was afflicted by intrigues and a certain sense of impotence, then the opposition, as represented in the main by the Progressives, suffered from a feeling of frustration and indecision. By conviction, practically all of its members and followers were staunch Russian patriots, and as such, also monarchists. Russia without a tsar was for them inconceivable, particularly when there was an imperative need for national unity to repel the enemy. But by the end of 1915 there were already voices urging that it was unrealistic to expect the present incumbent of the throne to understand the problem and to appoint a government which would enjoy society's confidence and could be counted on to persevere and carry the war to a victorious end. There was plenty of solid evidence to support such arguments: the whole record of the emperor's twenty-year reign, his isolation from and incomprehension of politics, et cetera. But purely rational arguments are seldom resorted to or thought persuasive in a crisis. Hence the readiness of some of the regime's opponents to hint that what stood in the way of the country's salvation might be something more fundamental than the emperor's incapacity and the unhealthy atmosphere at the court—intentional duplicity or even treason.

Among the first to voice such insinuations was not a radical agitator, but one of Russia's richest industrialists, Peter Riabushinsky. While entertaining a group of opposition politicians and Duma members in his palatial residence in Moscow, the millionaire liberal bared his suspicions that the dynasty (he meant in the narrower sense the emperor and his immediate family) desired to conclude peace in short order because then the regime could cope more easily with proconstitution and revolutionary forces than after a lengthy, even if victorious, war. Another variant of the theme was more indulgent to the emperor himself: he was a prisoner of those dark forces that were pressing for a separate peace with Germany, since victory in the war would inevitably bring with it a diminution of the imperial prerogatives. There was little rhyme or logic in all this. His whole record proved poor Nicholas II incapable of such Machiavellianism; he would not be in his present straits if he were. It was also not clear why the sinister dark forces should seek a separate and of necessity humiliating peace: nothing else would bring the monarchy down as rapidly.

The dominant theme of the opposition was still one of restraint: the government, not the monarch, was the enemy. This was the gist of the resolution passed in September 1915 by the Congresses of the Union of Zemstvos and Cities. Their respective presidents, Prince Lvov and the mayor of Moscow, Michael Chelnokov, then sought an audience with the emperor but were rebuffed and told to see instead the minister of the interior. Representatives of the most influential independent bodies in the empire which with the government's blessing were assisting in the war effort were thus treated in a manner befitting a group of petitioners from a provincial town. Deeply resentful of the snub, Prince Lvov refused to discuss the situation with the minister, handing him instead a somewhat melodramatic letter addressed to the emperor in which he warned that "the government has brought Russia to the brink of an abyss. In your hands lies her salvation."[22] There was no reply.

The so-called voluntary organizations, the zemstvo-city and war industries' committees networks, with their thousands of members represented a potentially powerful political force, especially because of their association and the similarity of their political outlook with that of the Progressive bloc in the Duma. Behind them stood the bulk of the intelligentsia, the business community, and progressive gentry. Had the Russian bourgeoisie been as purposeful and selfish as depicted by Soviet historians, had the opposition's leaders been as villainous and greedy for power as various apologists for the old regime have argued, then the coalition of forces over which they presided could have *made* the decrepit government listen to it. But in fact, as 1917 was to demonstrate, the leaders of this society were strong on oratory and weak on practical politics. Their patriotism inhibited them from an open challenge to the government; their fear of assuming the burden of responsibility for the country's governance kept them from that single-minded and ruthless pursuit of power which has often been ascribed to them. Even the most meticulously researched argument for the existence of a liberal conspiracy against the regime, such as presented in George Katkov's book,[23] manages to prove, rather than any definite plots, only the existence of what might be called a conspiratorial atmosphere—a campaign of gossip and insinuations directed against the regime, talk at various private meetings, usually monitored by the secret police, that "things cannot go on the way they are," attempts by people like Lvov and Guchkov to persuade various military and political figures that "something must be done," putative lists of ministers for "when and if." Like their predecessors one century before, the opponents of the tsarist regime mostly talked and waited for something to happen, and only then they proposed to act. But even more than the Decembrists, they were in a quandary as to what that something might be and what to do when it happened.

There were some impatient voices, especially among the Kadets, urging an alliance with the revolutionary left and recalling the experience of 1905 when a workers' revolt spurred the regime's acquiescence in liberal changes. But unlike the fall of 1905, Russia was now at war, and by inciting the masses they might be indirectly contributing to what they feared the most. Don't fall for the government's provocations, Milyukov told some hotheads among the Kadets early in 1916; it would welcome political disorders to use them as a rationale for signing a separate peace.

Some wondered if the masses could be used to force the government to capitulate to society. Until the end of 1916 it hardly seemed so. The rising cost of living, the shortages of goods, the lengthening casualty lists, and the calling of new classes of conscripts under colors, all contributed to the growing disenchantment with the war, but even among the workers of the major industrial centers, who had long been imbued with socialist ideas, the revolutionary impulse seemed for the duration to be in abeyance. There had been some major strikes, alleged but never proven to have been the work of enemy agents. The dominant attitude among even the radical segment of the working class was still "defensist," which was the current terminology for "we must defeat the foreign enemy before attending to the domestic ones." Pacifist feelings were obviously gaining ground but not those Lenin hoped for when he wrote, "Our slogan must be a civil war." A liberal who wanted to activate the working class in order to force concessions from the regime thus faced a dilemma: how to do it without hampering the war effort. One ray of hope was the workers' group within the Central War Industries Committee, whose head, Menshevik Gvozdev, rationalized their participation in this government-sponsored "bourgeois" institution by saying that it was necessary for "the struggle against the aggressor Germany, but also against our terrible internal enemy, the autocracy."[24] But for the time being, neither he nor other like-minded socialists could see how in practice the two struggles could be conducted simultaneously.

In distant Switzerland, Lenin could only fret at the ineffectiveness of Bolshevik propaganda at home as well as at the meager success of his campaign to turn the international socialist movement toward greater militancy. After a year and a half of the slaughter, pacifist feelings were growing stronger among the Socialists of all countries. But even those in the left wing of their respective parties who joined Lenin at the antiwar conferences in Zimmerwald (1915) and Kienthal (1916) in Switzerland rejected by a large majority Lenin's slogan to turn the imperialist war into a series of civil ones and opted instead for simple pacifism, a peace without annexations and indemnities. Lenin's reaction was one of bitterness: "And objectively, who profits by the slogan of peace? Certainly not the revolutionary proletariat. Not the idea of using the war to speed up the collapse of capitalism."[25] His notions of what was going on behind the scenes at home were at times as unrealistic as those of the most antiregime members of the Progressive bloc. It is only logical to believe, he wrote, that the German and Russian courts were secretly negotiating and might conclude not only a separate peace, but an alliance. Or another fantasy: the tsar would *pretend* that he was about to conclude a treaty with Germany and extort billions and all sorts of other concessions from the British and the French.[26] Had poor Nicholas II and his pitiful gaggle of courtiers and ministers been capable of such guile, there would have never been an occasion for Lenin to leave Switzerland.

None of the main figures in the drama which was unfolding had a clear idea of how and when it would be ended. The man who occupied the center of the stage was blissfully unaware of the degree of unrest in the domestic situation. Nicholas's inspections of military units, where he was invariably greeted with tumultuous "hurrahs" and expressions of personal devotion on the part of officers and men, kept reinforcing the conviction which would stay with him until the eve of his abdication that the army, hence the people, were behind him and that the crisis of confidence existed only in the imagination of a small number of troublemakers, as usual mostly from the intelligentsia, centered in the Duma and the political drawing rooms of Petrograd and Moscow. The troublemakers, for their part, were becoming frantic over their inability to change the political course which in their minds was leading Russia to an irretrievable catastrophe, if not during the war then surely after it ended.

The crisis was compounded rather than lessened by the improvement in the military situation. As of September 1915 no one knew where or when the enemy could be stopped. But then the German offensive on the eastern front ground to a stop. With a major action being planned in the west at Verdun, the German army was simply incapable of shouldering the burden of casualties of simultaneous offensives on both fronts. And with Italy now on the side of the Entente and engaging their armies in the south, the Austrians were even less able than before to help effectively their allies. The front line between the Russians and Germans now became stabilized and in general was to remain so until the revolution. The munitions situation, the Achilles heel of the Russian war machine during the 1914–15 campaign, was in the course of 1916 to improve considerably: production of weapons, equipment, and ammunitions of all kinds was to rise impressively by the end of the year. Perhaps neither the government nor the voluntary organizations could claim much credit for this achievement; the overall organization of the economic side of the war effort remained chaotic. But then Russia did have a considerable industrial base which when harnessed to the patriotic feelings and strivings was bound to make a difference.

Yet short of a complete military collapse, nothing is so pernicious to the morale of a nation as a war which is being neither won nor lost, especially so in Russia's case. The immediate danger had passed, but recriminations over the defeats had not stopped, and the frustration with the present unsatisfactory situation only grew. Had the enemy reached deep into the heart of the country, it is quite conceivable that the regime and society would have momentarily composed their differences, the emperor's sense of duty would have stirred his sluggish intelligence toward a gesture befitting the emergency, and the regime's opponents might have found themselves occupied by sharing the direction of their country's policies rather than by impotently and irritably criticizing them from the sidelines. But the impasse tended to reinforce each side in its usual attitudes. Even more important, this new kind of war was bound to have a lasting and in the long run depressing effect on the morale of the nation as a whole. The front ran from Latvia and the Baltic in the north alongside the borders of Galicia in the south. (With Rumania's entrance into the war, it would soon continue through that country down to the Black Sea.) Militarily the war had suddenly become quite distant to most, certainly to the ethnic Russians who were not at the front. There was neither a sense of imminent danger nor victories, and yet in every other respect it was affecting everybody's life more and more.

War weariness was not confined to Russia. By 1916 it became the prevalent mood in every belligerent country. Elsewhere the emergency thrust to the fore leaders capable of sustaining the nation's will to fight. In Great Britain it was the eloquence of David Lloyd George at the head of a government representing all the major parties that imparted a new dynamism to the country's war effort. In France the bloodletting of Verdun was followed by unrest and mutinies among the front-line troops on a scale that Russia's troops were not to experience until well after February 1917. But in Henri Pétain the French army found a commander who by a mixture of severity and persuasiveness was able to subdue the defeatist spirit just as an elderly radical politician, Georges Clemenceau, was to galvanize the patriotic spirit of the nation as a whole. A realistic analysis of the situation, especially the manpower data, should have been sufficient to establish that after the end of 1915 and barring a near miracle such as a real revolution which would force Russia to withdraw from the war, Germany could no longer hope to prevail. It was the myth of military infallibility of the Hindenburg-Ludendorff team, appointed in the summer of 1916 to the supreme command, which kept in check the rising political and social ferment and antiwar feelings in Germany.

No such morale-building legend or heroes appeared in Russia as she was entering the third year of the world conflict. The enormous fund of patriotic feeling which in wartime had traditionally sustained even the most oppressive rulers of Russia was being frittered away by the tsar and his government. In the course of 1916 many Russians would become convinced that it was the opponents of the regime who were the true defenders of the country's honor and interest and the government its covert enemy. Even an otherwise feeble propaganda machine should have known how to capitalize on the fact that the enemy offensive had been stopped within a few weeks after the tsar had assumed active direction of the supreme command, that there were considerable military successes by the Russians in the course of 1916 against the Austrians and the Turks, that the supply situation was vastly improved, et cetera. But the government's ineptitude when it came to propaganda made all those achievements inconsequential as against the ever-spreading tales about the dark forces behind the throne and of actual treason in its ranks. How some of the regime's strongest proponents proposed to recoup its prestige is well illustrated in the following tale. General Alexander Spiridovich, head of the imperial family's personal security, while on a visit to Odessa dined with some of his fellow courtiers as well as some local right-wing politicians. Over coffee, one of the latter launched into a political tirade: "He spoke eloquently about how to strengthen the government and the regime: one should immediately start organizing pogroms, first of the Germans, then of the Jews. This would in his opinion raise the people's spirit and help the war effort." Spiridovich, hardly a flaming liberal, was taken aback, as were many of his fellow diners. But the most effective counterargument to the speaker's proposal that they could muster was that "in its time, the Kishinev pogrom did so much harm to the regime and reflected unfavorably on the prestige of the

Monarch. . . . We parted amicably, but one felt that here in the south the atmosphere was very provincial."[27] With people of such moral and intellectual horizons as the regime's friends, it is hardly surprising that the stories about the dark forces behind the regime were gaining ever-wider currency.

Ironically those very forces, that is, Rasputin, contributed to the tsar's decisions which in the beginning of 1916 seemingly created for a few weeks a climate of detente between him and society, or more precisely, the Progressive bloc. There was a profound relief among the latter at the news that Nicholas II finally acceded to its pleas to discharge the senile prime minister. To be sure the opposition's contentment over any official action was usually short lived, and in this case there were sound reasons for it being so. The new man, Boris Sturmer, had one solid advantage over Goremykin—at sixty-eight, he was ten years younger. This advantage (in fact Sturmer's physical vigor was hardly superior to that of his predecessor; he would fall asleep in the middle of a conference) was largely offset by the embarrassment of having a man with a German name at the head of the government. There was some speculation that he might change it to a Russian-sounding one, but Rasputin, who unbeknownst to society, had been a warm sponsor of the elderly bureaucrat, felt that it would be ridiculous and counterproductive. What was a more serious deficiency of Sturmer's was his utter incapacity to instill a new spirit in the imperial administration, as well as his ineffectiveness as a parliamentarian at a time when the Duma debates would become increasingly important in swaying public opinion.

It was also very largely on Rasputin's advice that the tsar decided not only to recall the Duma into session but also, unprecedentedly, to grace its opening with his presence. (At the inauguration of the First Duma, he had received it in the Winter Palace; now he came to its residence.) It is a measure of all the opportunities he had and would continue to squander that even at this late date, one year before the fall, the emperor's gesture evoked a warm response on the part of the great majority of the deputies; only a handful on the extreme left absented themselves from the ceremony. Unremarkable as the tsar's speech was, and couched in his usual style ("Let the love of the country help you and serve as the guiding star in the discharge of your duties toward the Fatherland and Myself."), it was nonetheless greeted with applause. The chamber's president, "the fat Rodzianko," as the emperor called him among his intimates, declared in his reply that the emperor's visit ". . . has strengthened the bond of union between Yourself and Your loyal people, the union which will assuredly clear the path to victory. . . . Long live the Great Sovereign of All Russia." Again, an ovation and long lasting "hurrahs" followed by the singing of the imperial anthem.

Rodzianko then introduced the legislature's leading members to the monarch.

Though this Duma had been in existence for over three years, it was the first time that Nicholas had met most of them! Almost anyone else in his profession, and he had ruled for over twenty years, would have found a few bantering or complimentary words for those people who would soon determine his, and his dynasty's, fate. But the tsar, obviously ill at ease, shook their hands in silence. Still Rodzianko had an inspiration, "Sire, use this glorious moment and tell us right here that you will grant a responsible ministry," he claims to have told the emperor on the occasion. "I'll think about it," said the tsar. It was February 9, 1916, the only time in history when Russia's sovereign visited his people's elected representatives. How considerable still the residue of awe which imperial presence could inspire even in a convinced enemy of the regime is suggested by Milyukov's account of the occasion. During the reception he noticed the emperor looking fixedly at him. "For a few moments I withstood his gaze, then unexpectedly for myself, I smiled and lowered my eyes." He did so, wrote the Kadet leader toward the end of his days, because he suddenly sensed that the man was doomed and was sorry for him.[28] But possibly the passage of time and events had distorted Milyukov's recall: the real reason was probably quite different.

Favorably as society had received the visit, its soothing effect was not allowed to last long. Having discharged an unpleasant obligation, the tsar hoped to resume his tranquil existence in Mogilev: daily briefings by the generals, religious devotions, playing dominoes with his aides, reading sentimental French and English novels recommended by his wife, walks and boating. But soon his peaceful routine was shattered by a new crisis, which necessitated his return to the capital. This time, when the true facts of the latest chapter of the Rasputin saga became known to the public, it was not only scandalized; it became firmly convinced of what hitherto could be held as gossip and rumors. There were indeed sinister dark forces not only behind but also within the regime.

By now, it would seem, there was little that the government could do which would surprise society. Still it had to have come as a shock to learn that none other than the official guardian of law and order, the minister of the interior, had been caught at planning a murder. Ironically, the culprit had until recently been a close friend of his intended victim. Alexis Khvostov had been appointed to his job largely because of his connection with Rasputin, and hence Alexandra Fedorovna's pleadings with the tsar that the "tail," as she called him endearingly,* should receive the post. Once in office, Khvostov became disenchanted with his benefactor and former boon companion. For one, the relationship compromised him in the eyes of society, for another, he had set his sights still higher—on

---

*After the English meaning of the stem of his family name.

becoming prime minister—and Rasputin had thrown his influence behind Sturmer. The ambitious and unbalanced minister then concocted a variety of schemes, all of them to misfire, to get rid of the charlatan.

First, he tried to enlist the help of the notorious Iliodor. One-time monk and a fervent acolyte of Rasputin, this worthy had already some years before the war become disillusioned with Rasputin and convinced that he was possessed by the devil. To cure him of this affliction, Iliodor and a similarly disillusioned bishop lured him to the latter's residence, where they proceeded to beat him and, according to Rasputin's version, had he not freed himself from their grasp and bolted, would have castrated him. Iliodor was then defrocked and locked up in a monastery, but he fled abroad where he initiated the vast literature about Rasputin, with an exposé entitled *The Holy Devil*. Now Khvostov dispatched a special emissary to Norway, where the demented ex-monk currently resided, to seek his advice about people who might be willing to dispose of the Rasputin problem in an even more drastic way than he, Iliodor, had attempted. But Khvostov's activities were being watched warily by his deputy, Serge Byeletsky, who was charged by the tsar with the responsibility for Rasputin's safety, and he managed to frustrate his chief's Iliodor gambit.

Khvostov then tried to persuade Rasputin's bodyguards to have him poisoned. Rebuffed again, Khvostov turned to Byeletsky, asking him to organize the assassination: he would be doing the country and the tsar a great favor—the holy man was a German spy. Byeletsky kept finding excuses; apart from other reasons, he suspected that once the deed was done, his chief would try to place the blame on him, if not for the actual murder, then for being negligent in protecting the precious life of the imperial couple's mentor.

With so many people involved, the whole story finally reached Rasputin's entourage, and the intended victim ran in panic to his protectors. Early in March the tsar dismissed both Khvostov and Byeletsky. Amazingly enough, no further action was taken against them. Even more amazingly, it did not occur to anyone to demand that such action be taken against a man who had planned a murder and another one who had taken his time in revealing the plot. If it was hoped thereby to avoid further disastrous publicity, all such hopes were soon dashed, for both discharged dignitaries gave their own versions of the affair to the press.

"Am so wretched that we, through *Gregory*, recommended *Khvostov* to you —it leaves me not peace," wrote the empress in her picturesque English to her husband. It is unnecessary to describe the impression the whole sordid business left on society. But it is fair to say that for most educated Russians, it destroyed the last vestiges of that nationalist mystique which surrounded the person of the tsar. Hitherto most of them still hoped that the needed reforms could be achieved through him and felt that as long as the war lasted, it would be unpatriotic and divisive to attack the emperor, as distinguished from his entourage and ministers. Now many Russians would see Nicholas as the main obstacle to the country's successful pursuit of the war, and their patriotic duty would urge them to rid the throne of its unworthy incumbent.

In reality Rasputin was undoubtedly a factor, but not a very important one in the sequence of events which caused the downfall of the monarchy, and thereby ushered in the Russian Revolution. Granting the personalities of the tsar and his spouse, it is hard to resist the conclusion that if Rasputin did not exist, someone like him would have inevitably found his way to their entourage, and even without a holy man at their side, their attitudes toward the Duma, autocracy, reforms, et cetera, would have been pretty much the same. Rasputin was a product, and then became the focus, of not so much the dark but obscurantist influences around the court. They in turn were a national consequence of the court's isolation from what was vital and rational in society. It was quite a gallery of characters. The imperial couple's and Gregory's closest friend was another religious maniac, Anna Vyrubova, whose name achieved a notoriety almost equal to that of the charlatan. There was the latter's usual ally, though occasional rival, Peter Badmayev, a russified Buryat, practitioner of so-called Tibetan medicine, and on the side a business entrepreneur who advised the imperial couple and highly placed officials on subjects ranging from foreign policy in the Orient to the most efficacious ways of soothing the holy man's frequently ruffled feelings and keeping him out of trouble. Another friend of Our Friend was Prince Michael Andronnikov, a well-known pederast and political busybody. With Vyrubova acting so to speak as its chief of staff, Rasputin's entourage included a number of women worshippers, shoddy financiers, and the like. But it is more than doubtful that any of them were actually enemy agents.

By the time the war came, Rasputin was a victim of his own success and abandoned whatever prudence and restraint he had observed before. Like most successful charlatans, the barely literate Siberian peasant had come to believe that he had indeed supernatural powers. According to one version, hypnotic powers had been bestowed on him collectively by a group of "black occultists." Belying his sturdy peasant heritage, he now got drunk easily (a consequence possibly of his having abandoned the traditional native brew for the delights of champagne and madeira) and then tended to become indiscreet, his tales soon becoming the talk of the capital.

One should admit that when sober he would not say much, but give him a bottle of port or madeira, and then he would. . . . They would take Rasputin to a restaurant, pour a bottle of madeira into him, and then he would describe his visits to Tsarskoye Selo. I must say that he talked very disrespectfully about the person of the former emperor, but praised highly the former empress, called her very clever, another Catherine the Great. . . . The way he talked about the former emperor embarrassed the [police] agents whose duty it was to report on him. He usually called him [the emperor] "papa." "I come," he says, "to Tsarskoye. I see papa sitting gloomily. . . . I pat his head and say, 'Why are you sad?' He says, 'Nothing but scoundrels all around. No shoes, no weapons, we are to start an offensive, but how can we?' "

Since the story, as related to the Provisional Government's investigating commission comes from Khvostov, it has to be taken with a double grain of salt, but there is no doubt that Rasputin did tell similar tales.[29]

But Rasputin could not have been a tool in anyone's hands nor, in the real sense of the word, a seeker after political power. His interventions with the empress usually touched not on policies* but on political and ecclesiastical appointments, where he simply pleaded the case of persons who befriended him and criticized those who he had reasons to believe were his enemies. While this undoubtedly helped to secure the appointment of nonentities or worse, it is unlikely that the empress by herself would have made a better counsellor to her husband or, ultimately, that the latter, even if entirely on his own, would have made better choices. In brief, Rasputin was a tragicomic, rather than sinister, figure.

Whatever the actual harm done by the man, it pales in comparison with that wrought by his legend and its ramifications. This legend, which magnified his importance, and attributed treasonous intent to him, the empress, and their entourage, struck at the regime's last line of defense, the allegiance of the professional officer corps, the rank and file of bureaucracy and of the other traditionally monarchist elements in society. Few lent full credence to the rumors of German spies among the associates of the charlatan and of the Empress Alexandra's complicity in seeking a separate peace with the country of her birth. But the mere existence and widespread circulation of such rumors was bound to undermine the morale of the regime's last partisans. Some of the staunchest monarchists would soon conclude that the interests of the country and the dynasty could be best served by deposing the emperor. Others, though balking at the idea, would at the crucial moment be unable to summon the will to defend the regime which had been so deeply compromised.

The impact of the Rasputin legend on the moderate left was more complex. It was politically convenient for the Kadets and their allies, enabling them to lash out at the government without any inhibitions that by doing so they might appear in their own as well as others' eyes as unpatriotic and undermining national unity in wartime. Paradoxically, though never sentimental about the dynasty, the

---

*Paradoxically, he was a strong supporter of the campaign against alcoholism. His rare advice on military affairs was totally disregarded by the emperor. Elsewhere one detects an occasional glimpse of peasant common sense amidst the habitual nonsense of his opinions and prophesying—he warned repeatedly about the problem of food shortages, and the danger they posed for the country.

liberals were more apprehensive about the damage being done to the emperor's prestige than some of the die-hard conservatives. They could see a palace coup having consequences going quite beyond the removal of Nicholas, "the German woman," and their guru. They feared for the country, but also for themselves: with the monarchy irreparably damaged, the burden of power and of coping with anarchy might prove too heavy for their shoulders.

For the extreme left, the whole Rasputin affair was a pleasing confirmation of their image of the regime; a Bolshevik wrote.

Opportunities for easy money and for corruption brought together such disparate characters as the Jewish banker Rubinstein, the avowed anti-Semite and inciter to pogroms [Metropolitan] Pitirim, the bribe taker, Manusevich-Manuilov, and the prime minister, Sturmer. They all found shelter and protection under the aegis of the court prophet Rasputin. The war cast a glaring light on the complete rottenness; all the vices and debauchery of the court of the last tsar.[30]

The theme of the dark forces was common to the opposition along all the points of the political spectrum, echoed among the grand dukes and generals, as well as the socialist agitators. As 1916 progressed, the focus of the political crisis and universal resentment tended to shift from the government to the person and family of the emperor.

Yet the regime which was so universally and vehemently criticized could hardly be called repressive. It would be incongruous to characterize Russia of the time as a functioning autocracy. In fact, in no other country at war did the government seem so helpless in dealing with what ranged from dissent to outright subversion. Censorship existed, but it seemed powerless to stop the constant stream of criticism and insinuations, often scabrous, about the imperial family and ministers which emanated from the Duma and the press. Organizations subsidized by the government and playing an important part in the war effort were headed by avowed enemies of the regime. Opposition politicians felt free to seek support, fairly openly, from generals on active service and from allied envoys to Russia.

Indicative of the regime's disastrous loss of self-confidence was the decision to arrest and put on trial the former minister of war, Sukhomlinov. (The retreat of 1915 brought in its wake a spy scare, and one of its victims was an ex-aide of Sukhomlinov, Colonel Serge Myasoyedov, who was hurriedly and without any solid evidence convicted of being a German agent and executed.) Now, retrospectively, the past year's defeats were being attributed to treason in high places, and Sukhomlinov, widely unpopular during his tenure of office, was in the public's eyes the main culprit. The emperor and the more level-headed officials knew that the charge was absurd. The elderly general had incensed his subordinates and irritated his colleagues by his levity and boastfulness, and proved to be a poor administrator, but was certainly not a traitor. Merely to admit such a possibility in regard to the man who for a number of years had been the sovereign's principal military adviser was deeply discrediting and humiliating to the regime and certainly would not quell but rather intensify similar rumors about even more highly placed personages. Still the emperor could not summon enough courage to challenge public opinion by ordering the proceedings against his old servant quashed. Nor did he feel it possible to intervene to save the elderly and ailing man from being incarcerated in the Petropavlovsk fortress while the investigators were rummaging for nonexistent proofs of his crimes. It was only the empress's compassionate pleading, one of the infrequent occasions when Alexandra Fedorovna is seen in a favorable light, which persuaded Nicholas to order Sukhomlinov released and placed under house arrest while awaiting his trial.

In March the tsar compounded the unfortunate reverberations of the Khvostov affair by discharging one of the few officials who still enjoyed some popularity and managed to maintain good relations with the Duma, the minister of war, Alexis Polivanov. His main sin, in the emperor's eyes, as the latter told him bluntly in the notice of dismissal, were Polivanov's close ties with the war industries committees, ". . . whose activities do not inspire My trust and whose supervision by you has not, to My mind, been sufficiently firm."[31] The chairman of the Central War Industries Committee was Guchkov, whom the emperor heartily disliked and who returned the compliment and was, as Nicholas knew, involved in all sorts of intrigues with the Progressive bloc and the generals. But what a bizarre situation, and what a light it throws on the politics of this allegedly autocratic system! The regime felt powerless to dismiss the man known to be a personal enemy of the ruler and thus allowed him to continue as the head of a semiofficial, state-financed organization. Instead the popular minister of war, generally acknowledged as capable, whose duty it was to maintain good rapport with such bodies, was sacrificed to the emperor's displeasure. His successor was an obscure military administrator unlikely to enjoy any following among the politicians or prestige within the army. (Polivanov was to be one of the many tsarist generals who after the revolution offered their services to the Soviet government.)

In July yet another of that dwindling group of regime figures who enjoyed a measure of public confidence was dismissed. Serge Sazonov had been foreign minister for over six years. The immediate cause of his dismissal was Sazonov's insistence that the Russian government make a specific statement on the Polish issue before Austria and Germany did, detailing the extent of Poland's postwar autonomy and borders, a step considered as urgent by the Progressive bloc and even more so by Paris and London. Germany and Austria were strenuously courting the Poles and about to set up a quasi-independent Polish state under their own auspices. But Nicholas too refused to commit himself on the issue; he felt, with some justification, that it was incompatible with the dignity of the imperial government to have its policies dictated by its allies. Militarily, no one could accuse Russia of not being willing to bear a heavy sacrifice in the common cause: again and again, in answer to the allies' please, her armies would be sent on the offensive, often ahead of their timetable, to relieve the enemy's pressure on the western front.

Whatever the merits of the case, Sazanov's departure was bound to lend further plausibility to stories about the dark forces plotting to conclude a separate peace, especially since the person who took over his job was none other than the prime minister with the unfortunate German-sounding name. It must remain a source of wonder that anyone could credit the feeble Sturmer, easily frightened by the Duma, with the ability to conceive, let alone execute, such Machiavellian designs. But the stories of his Germanophile sympathies and of plotting with the empress were widely circulated not only among the regime's opponents, who had worked themselves to the point where they could believe almost anything about its malevolent intentions, but also among the presumably more dispassionate British and French diplomats. After all, Lenin, whose general assessment of Nicholas II was realistic and unflattering, was at times ready to credit him with schemes worthy of Talleyrand.

Logically, such slanderous rumors should have been silenced by the allegedly treacherous government's determination to pursue the war effort in a manner which hardly suggested any behind-the-scenes contacts with the enemy. In May 1916 the Russian army opened an offensive all along the Austrian front, and as usual, *against the Austrians* its efforts were crowned with success. During the summer, the southwestern army group, under Russia's most renowned field commander, Aleksey Brusilov, captured huge quantities of prisoners and equipment, once again pushed into Galicia and conquered Bukovina. Victories also attended Russian armies in the Caucasus, with the Turks being routed and forced to retreat, yielding some of their territory. But for the public, those were victories achieved by the Russian soldier, despite rather than reflecting credit on the government and the supreme commander-in-chief.

Yet at the end of the summer, and with the fighting reverting to trench warfare, the end of the war loomed no nearer. The human cost of the campaign had been prodigious, some 1.2 million Russian soldiers killed and wounded, over two hundred thousand taken prisoner. By the end of the year, the figure of casualties since the beginning of the war would surpass 5 million, with the empire having mobilized about 15 million men.[32] Manpower needs led the government to try to conscript the Moslem inhabitants of central Asia, who had traditionally been exempted from military service. This led to a veritable uprising in Turkestan, in the course of which reputedly upward of two hundred thousand natives were killed, many others fleeing across the border into China. The rebellion was quelled, but the region was more or less pacified only after the government revoked the conscription order for much of the area.

It is characteristic that the uprising, which claimed many more lives than were to be lost during all the revolutionary disturbances of 1917, was hardly acknowledged in Russia proper, nor did it influence in the slightest the overall political situation. It is a reminder that over most of the immense expanse of the empire, autocracy still lived in the minds of the people, and even large-scale revolutionary disorders could be put down in a manner reminiscent of Nicholas I's time. It was only the heart of the country, notably in the two capitals, which was beating to a different rhythm. Eroded at the center, the tsar's authority still held sway over the vast multination country and as such was irreplaceable. That is why when the regime collapsed, it would leave behind not only a political vacuum at the center but also a crumbling empire, which those who eventually stepped into the vacuum—the Bolsheviks—would not so much inherit, but would have to reconquer.

Yet few of those who were aiming or preparing their blows at the ghost of tsarist absolutism gave thought at the crucial moment to what had traditionally stayed the hand of the regime's enemies: that ". . . if you did not have autocracy, you would not have the great Russian empire." For the extreme left, notably the Bolsheviks, the dissolution of that empire was in itself a desired goal, and so it would remain until power was theirs. Lenin spoke for all the Marxists when he called Russia ". . . a prison house of nationalities." But other enemies of the autocracy had come to believe that they could have both freedom and the empire. For them the nation's cause and that of the regime had, since at least 1915, parted company. Russia's greatness and unity required that the war be carried to a victorious conclusion, hence the regime had to go. Militant nationalism remained the most prevalent political passion, underlying all others. The Kadets shared with the extreme right the conviction that it was Russia's manifest destiny to implant her flag over Constantinople and the Bosporus Straits. Unlike their conservative allies in the Progressive bloc, the liberals combined imperialist aspirations with democratic ones: their Russia of the future would be generous to its non-Russian citizens, the Jews being accorded full civic rights, Poland, a far-reaching autonomy (but not full independence), et cetera. But militant nationalism provided the unifying bond among the forces opposed to the regime, their most visible manifestation the Progressive bloc, including 300 out of 442 members of that Duma, which when elected in 1912 had been assumed, and correctly so, to be predominantly right-wing and monarchist in its character. Outside of what now could be called the opposition Establishment were the die-hard partisans of autocracy, who could not accept either the legend of the dark forces and other slurs on the monarchy or an alliance with the liberals, and the left, represented in the Duma by a handful of Mensheviks and the Labor (Trudovik) group with its ties to the Socialist Revolutionaries, whose most prominent member, the rising star on the political firmament, was thirty-five-year-old Alexander Kerensky.

The opponents of the regime were virtually united in the desire to carry on the war until victory. (Though they would not believe it, so were the ruling circles. It would have astounded those who gave credence to the scurrilous rumors about the empress to read Alexandra's letter to the tsar in which she spoke ecstatically of the day when with Constantinople "liberated," that is, Russian, a cross would rise once again over the basilica of St. Sophia.) Among the people at large, however, it was becoming increasingly evident that antiwar feelings were spreading and growing in intensity, as there seemed no end in view to the grim struggle.

Logically the rumors, so widely circulated and believed at all levels of society, that the regime was secretly seeking a separate peace with Germany should have brought the putative peace makers popularity rather than obloquy. But logic is not always a reliable guide in analyzing political sentiments. In Russia in 1916 the widespread exasperation with the war, whatever its manifestations—the soldier's reluctance to become cannon fodder, his fellow villager's fear of being called up, the urban dweller's discontent at food shortages, the rising cost of living and other hardships—was incongruously combined with a revulsion at the idea of a separate peace with Prussian militarism and the execration of those who were allegedly scheming to bring it about. The war, the masses felt, was insufferable; but news that it had been ended by a separate deal with Germany would have triggered military mutinies and urban uprisings dwarfing in their extent and intensity those which would actually take place in February and March 1917.

This paradox which would affect the first phase of the revolution finds its explanation in the peculiar nature of antiwar feelings as they crystallized in the last months of the old regime. Pacifism in the strict meaning—sheer revulsion at blood shedding—never played an important role in them, rather surprising in a country which produced Leo Tolstoy and where to the numerous religious sectarians bearing arms for the state was in itself sinful. Actual opposition to the war was at first predicated upon ideological reasons. The class-conscious worker could be expected to balk at fighting or producing arms in a cause which was not his, but his exploiters' and oppressors'. At first such scruples were silenced by instinctive patriotism, which a Marxist could rationalize by believing that he was fighting not for the tsar and the bosses but against the Kaiser and the German capitalists. That theme was reinforced by another one: victory over Germany would also defeat autocracy at home. Hence Lenin's precept that ". . . from the point of view of the working class . . . the last evil would be a defeat of the tsarist monarchy and its armies" was so contrary to the workers' sentiments that anyone trying to propagate it among them would have been lynched as a German agent. As late as the eve of the revolution the Bolsheviks' leader in Russia, Shlyapnikov, described their tactics as planning street demonstrations under the slogans "of the necessity of struggling against the war, the high cost of living and the absolutist monarchy, and for an eight-hour working day and land to the peasants."[33] Nothing about turning "the imperialist war into a civil one," as Lenin had been preaching from Switzerland, not even an unambiguous plea for immediate peace.

Even so, the Bolshevik's covert defeatist propaganda failed to influence the great majority of the urban proletariat. Insofar as the mood of politically conscious workers was concerned in the waning days of the regime there were two main attitudes. First, what might be called a modified defensist position: the war must be carried on, but the general peace which will come at its end ought to eschew annexations and indemnities, must be a people's peace rather than one which serves the interests of this or that group of militarists and exploiters. The second attitude, found in the non-Bolshevik activists among the workers, was the growing conviction that far from requiring a political truce, successful conduct of the war did in fact demand revolutionary changes—a conclusion undoubtedly suggested by liberal propaganda about the dark forces and the government having brought Russia "to the brink of an abyss," but especially attractive for those who like the numerous Mensheviks and Socialist Revolutionaries collaborating in the war effort were thus able to reconcile patriotic impulses with their ideological convictions. Already in February 1916, a secret police report tells that workers' delegates from twenty cities attending a closed meeting of the war industries' committees, who joined in telling their bourgeois colleagues that "the existing political situation must be changed rapidly and thoroughly," called the regime "criminal" and pleaded for "a real parliament and responsible government." Only then the country shall be able to "enter the path that will lead to a peace without annexations and indemnities, and one which would enable the enslaved nations to decide their destinies."[34]

The shift in the workers' attitude toward the war, or at least toward its side effects, was noticeable already in 1915. During the six war months of 1917, the total number of striking workers was thirty-five thousand; in September 1915 alone the number was one hundred fourteen thousand. In 1916 strikes grew even more frequent.[35] Practically all the strikes were due to purely economic grievances. Yet they reflected a deepening malaise, especially of the industrial proletariat, one which required only a fortuitous happening to turn it into political turbulence. Oldenburg, a writer usually eager to attribute an unduly large share of responsibility for the events leading to the revolution to the Bolsheviks, has the following explanation.

The country's mood in the fall of 1916 was one of gloom and apprehension. The main and perhaps decisive cause was the feeling of weariness with the war which had spontaneously afflicted the masses. Fear of famine, grief over the huge losses, that desperate feeling "one can see no end to the war"—they all led people quite apolitical to become increasingly hostile toward the government responsible for the conduct of the war.[36]

For the regime's foes, the nation's mood offered yet another justification, as well as a potential weapon, in their unrelenting campaign against the incompetent and perhaps treasonous government. Unless the situation was mended, unless the unworthy ministers and favorites were replaced by men enjoying the nation's confidence, the country might become the scene of vast social upheavals. The latter in turn could provide the regime with an excuse to conclude an infamous peace. At the same time some were beginning to view the possibility of popular disturbances not so much as a danger but as the ultimate weapon with which to force the obdurate tsar to change the political course. They may have to appeal to the street, said Guchkov during one of those frequent and not-so-secret conclaves at which leaders of the Progressive bloc along with those of the voluntary organizations vented their indignation and fears over the situation and racked their brains for ways to save Russia. The more adventurously inclined among the Kadets urged renewed ties with the left and drawing into their semiconspiracy against the regime people like Kerensky and Nicholas Chheidze, chairman of the Menshevik Duma group, reputedly the two most prestigious names among the working masses. But others, notably the party's most influential voice, Milyukov, recoiled at the idea of making common cause with those whose ultimate goal was revolution and a republic rather than winning the war and a constitutional monarchy. The Kadets remembered what happened in 1905 when the street had been summoned to assist in conquering constitutional freedoms and instead plunged the country into anarchy. For Milyukov and his adherents, it was the Duma which remained the preferred site of the duel with the dark forces, and the fiery indictments of the corrupt and incompetent ministry which then resounded all over Russia their chosen weapon. For the liberals this was a return to the Jericho strategy of 1904–06: with shouts and incantations they would circle the now plainly crumbling walls of the autocracy. This time they would succeed, the walls finally and utterly collapsing, but so would much else.

For all the heightened drama and future sufferings they portended, the last six months of the regime appear also in some ways as a tragicomedy. In September Nicholas II once more demonstrated his almost unerring instinct for making disastrous appointments by choosing Alexander Protopopov to be minister of the interior. Outwardly there seemed much to be said in favor of the new incumbent of an office so important in a police state. He should have been acceptable to society, having been a deputy to the Duma, indeed its vice-president, and a member of the Progressive bloc, the first (and last) such to be appointed to a high government position. Protopopov had just headed a delegation of Russia's parliamentarians to Britain and France, where his speeches and general demeanor had been well received. His leadership of a mission which included such notables as Milyukov was a sign of the esteem in which he was held by his colleagues, so sensitive to the impression Russia's budding parliamentarism should make in the "cultured West." This then could be taken, as the emperor hoped, as a propitiating gesture toward the Duma, perhaps a harbinger of other ministers being drawn from its midst and of a government of "public confidence," if not indeed one responsible to the legislature, the ultimate goal of all progressive thinking Russians.

Alas, as poor Protopopov himself was to say much later, his entry into the government "was more than a mistake, it was a disaster," both for himself and everyone else concerned. Society's initial approval soon turned to dark suspicions and condemnations: wasn't the government trying to subvert the Progressive bloc by luring one of its members with a ministerial portfolio? Had it been some other post, perhaps it would not have been so bad. But the Ministry of the Interior, with its infamous secret police, was something no decent man should have accepted so long as the regime as a whole remained the way it was. His erstwhile colleagues now reflected on certain personal characteristics of Protopopov's which until then had not been allowed to stand in the way of his popularity. He was unusually fond of drinking; something which had been seen as quite normal in a Russian of his class was now perceived as a clear sign of the moral decadence of an impoverished nobleman. He had been in bad health, occasionally somewhat erratic and at times incoherent in his speeches; obviously the original ailment had been syphilis, and the current symptoms those of progressive paralysis.

In fact Protopopov's past and then his behavior in office gave some plausibility to that diagnosis. His appointment was brought about not only because the tsar wished to please the Duma. Protopopov had been sick and a long-time patient of the so-called Tibetan healer, Badmayev. It was through the latter that he established contacts and made a favorable impression on Rasputin. Not surprisingly he was then warmly endorsed by the empress, and once in office her favorite minister and trusted counsellor. Apart from his deference to Our Friend, now his constant adviser, his greatest asset in the imperial couple's eyes was Protopopov's cheerfulness, such a contrast to the prophecies of gloom and doom they now heard from everybody. There was nothing, he kept assuring them to the very end, to all those rumors about the trouble brewing in Petrograd. He had the situation well in hand. Protopopov was easily the most incompetent in the rather remarkable, in that respect, galaxy of wartime ministers.

Ostracized by his former Duma colleagues—as he later described, he had been verbally flagellated and figuratively spat upon by society—the unfortunate minister became all the more dependent upon and drawn to the empress. He not only kept Alexandra informed about all the official business which passed through his hands but also found it soothing to discourse with her on a variety of philosophico-historical subjects. "She was a very cultured person and it was very interesting, for example, to talk with her about the Physiocrats."[37] Within weeks other ministers were clamoring for Protopopov's dismissal, and it dawned even on the emperor that there was something wrong with the man. "He keeps jumping from one idea to another and cannot make up his mind about anything. . . . They say that a few years ago he was not quite normal after a certain illness," Nicholas II wrote his wife, adding what was perhaps the greatest understatement of his life: "It is risky at a time like this to leave the Ministry of Internal Affairs in the hands of such a man." The emperor begged his wife not to drag Rasputin into the business. He was determined to make a new appointment. All in vain! Alexandra Fedorovna would not have her favorite removed and Our Friend slighted. "I entreat you, don't go and change Protopopov now; he will be all right. . . . He is *not* mad. . . . [Only] vile *Petrograd and Moscow* speak against him."[38] She rushed to headquarters and had her way. Thus, fittingly and symbolically, Alexander Protopopov passed into history as the last minister of the interior of the tsarist regime.

For the opposition, Protopopov's appointment became a signal for an all-out assault on the government. The Duma was to open its session on November 1, but even before it assembled, the foes of the regime brought their heaviest guns into action. Chairmen of the Unions of Zemstvos and Cities addressed letters to the Duma's president, Rodzianko, containing the most intemperate attacks to date upon the government. Prince Lvov, widely considered the leading candidate to head the Ministry of Public Confidence when and if it should materialize, wrote,

[His constituents] reached a unanimous conclusion that the present government, which is openly suspected of being under the influence of dark forces hostile to Russia is no longer worthy to rule the country and has set it on the path of ruin and dishonor. . . . they support the struggle of the State Duma to create a regime which would be capable of uniting all of the nation's vital forces and bringing victory for the Fatherland.[39]

Lvov and his opposite number in the Union of Cities were emphatic that time was running out if the crisis was to be solved peacefully. "The hour of decision has struck, any delay is impermissible." One year before Lvov had tried to carry his message to the emperor and had been rebuffed. Now in his letter to Rodzianko there were no ritualistic references to drawing "His Gracious Majesty's" attention to this or that, in fact no direct reference to the tsar, and a clear insinuation that he was a prisoner of the dark forces. In its substance, the appeal to the Duma stopped just short of calling for a coup d'etat. In the not-so-distant past a message of this kind would have earned its writer a trip to Siberia. But now the disintegrating regime could not summon enough resolution to stop the purveyors of patriotic sedition, let alone arrest them.

The next and devastating blow to fall upon the regime was to be delivered in public. At the very first session of the Duma, on November 1, Milyukov launched into a philippic which, as he was to write modestly, became known as the "first battle cry of the revolution," indeed as its real beginning. That is something of an exaggeration. But the speech was undeniably instrumental in setting the style of revolutionary rhetoric and politics, that style of bombast, demagoguery, appeal to irrational fears and unsubstantiated suspicions, which certainly helped give another push to the tottering tsarist system but was even more important in bringing about the downfall of the cause for which he, Milyukov, and his fellow liberals had stood and fought. The speaker could have made an excellent case for the argument that the regime was not merely incompetent but preposterously so, not only unpopular but completely out of touch with any significant element of Russian life. And that was how he began: this was the worst government in modern Russian history.[40] But very soon he changed: a liberal brought up in the nationalist tradition and a historian accustomed to assess carefully the evidence before him yielded to a demagogue operating by innuendo.

> . . . if our own government wanted deliberately to set for itself the task, or if the Germans wanted to employ their own means for the same purpose [of disorganizing Russia] through propaganda and bribing—they could not do better than to act as the Russian government has acted. . . . How are you going to deny the possibility of such suspicions, when a handful of sinister individuals, for personal and base motives, direct the most important affairs of State.[41]

Then Milyukov's flight of rhetoric carried him on to endorse the theme so depressingly familiar in revolutionary propaganda, and which became a frequent motif in Soviet criminal justice: when it comes to treason one does not need concrete proofs, the nation's healthy instincts are sufficient to establish who are "the people's enemies," as in the case of the former war minister. "At the time we accused Sukhomlinov we did not possess the facts which were brought to light by the investigations. We had only . . . the instinctive voice of the whole country and its subjective certainty."[42] (Of course, the investigation of the Sukhomlinov case was still proceeding, and no facts had or would be found to justify the charges.)

The speaker listed several actual and alleged sins perpetrated by the government, punctuating the recital with the ominous phrase "Is this stupidity or treason?" As he was later to write, somewhat shamefacedly, "The audience by its applause signified its support of the latter explanation, even in those cases about which I myself was not fully convinced."[43] Purported evidence consisted of variations on the Rasputin theme, scraps of tendentious articles in the foreign and domestic press, and sensational data allegedly obtained from sources the speaker intimated he was not free to divulge. But he did not hesitate to quote remarks critical of the regime which the British ambassador had made in private and confidentially to him and other opposition figures, something deeply embarrassing to the diplomat and astoundingly tactless for a man who aspired to become, and would soon briefly be, Russia's foreign minister.

Most of the venomous shafts were directed at Sturmer, whom Milyukov explicitly accused of working for a separate peace with the country from which his ancestors had come and, by insinuation, of treason. Needless to say, the speech did not spare Protopopov. But the most dramatic moment came when the speaker, reading hurriedly in German so that the presiding officer who did not know the language could not stop him, quoted an article from a Vienna paper, which named the empress herself as the guiding spirit of the pro-German camarilla, a charge which even the most radical enemy of the regime would hitherto not have dared to repeat in public.

The speech was noisily applauded by the great majority of deputies ranging from the Mensheviks to many on the extreme right. In that Duma, once so reactionary, few were left who would defend the government from the opprobrious accusations. When not drowned by the majority's cheers, their interjections of "Slanderer" and "Where are the proofs?" were sternly silenced by the presiding officer.

In one version of the speech the orator concluded, "No, if you please, gentlemen, it seems too much to be explained just by stupidity." Those who followed Milyukov spoke for the most part in a similar vein, if not quite matching his level of vituperation, joining in the demand that the government which had forfeited the nation's trust must go and be replaced by one which the Duma could accept.

The autocracy, if not yet dead, was in a coma. There is no other interpretation of the regime's lame reaction to having been vilified in public and to the charge that the ruler's wife and his principal ministers were virtually enemy agents. The pitiful Sturmer argued for reprisals against his tormentors, but his ministerial colleagues would not listen to him. He finally announced that he would sue Milyukov for slander, the statement provoking general merriment. The authorities did prohibit the papers from printing the seditious stuff. But within days the speeches became known to practically every literate Russian. Leaflets carrying their unauthorized, often "improved," texts rolled off private and even government-owned presses, with millions of copies being passed from hand to hand in the streets, villages, and at the front. For many Russians it now became an established fact that the empress and several ministers were German agents. Even the staunchest monarchist had to feel shaken in his allegiance to the ruler who could not keep his wife from meddling in the affairs of state nor, conversely, protect her name from slander.

On November 10 Sturmer, now a target of as much ridicule as of execration, was dismissed. His successor as premier, Alexander Fedorovich Trepov, had shown considerable energy as minister of transport, and ordinarily, despite all the associations his name evoked,* he would have been accepted as a considerable improvement on his predecessor. But public opinion could no longer be appeased by token concessions. On his first appearance before the Duma the new prime minister was greeted with boos and catcalls from the left and with silent disdain on the part of the Progressive bloc. The chamber then picked up its battle cry, passing a resolution calling for an end to the influence of the "dark irresponsible forces," and for "a cabinet which would rely on the Duma and carry out its majority's program." The State Council, for all its predominantly bureaucratic membership, concurred in the sentiments of the other branch of the legislature.

He would perhaps be allowed to govern, believed the prime minister, if he demonstrated that he could remove or limit the influence of the dark forces. He tried to get rid of Protopopov, but his efforts were foiled by Alexandra's hysterical pleas on behalf of her favorite. In desperation Trepov tried to tackle an even more formidable problem. An intermediary offered Rasputin a handsome bribe on the condition that he should leave and permanently stay away from the capital. But one should not tempt a saint, and in this case there was no real temptation. All of Rasputin's needs were being taken care of free of charge by his numerous, especially female, admirers and protégés. It was naive to expect him to abandon his divinely ordained mission, as well as all the lures of high life, and to return permanently to his Siberian village and the company of his long-suffering wife. The unworthy offer was promptly brought to the attention of the empress, with immediate results, as shown in the sick woman's letter to the tsar: "He [Rasputin] *entreats* you to be *firm*, to be the Master and not to give in to *Trepov*. You know much better than that man, [still you let him lead you] and why not Our Friend, who leads through God."

Rasputin's murder, which took place in the early hours of December 17, did not still the furor about the dark forces. His assassins, who included a grand duke and the emperor's nephew by marriage, acted from what they believed were patriotic motives. The man who inspired and helped carry out the killing was

---

*Son of the Trepov who became notorious as governor of Petersburg under Alexander II for ordering a political prisoner flogged, for which he was shot and wounded by the famous Vera Zasulich; brother of Dmitri, the "dictator" of 1905.

Vladimir Purishkevich, a well-known eccentric and reactionary, notorious for his anti-Semitic oratory. It was he who in a Duma speech two weeks before the murder identified Rasputin as the main cause of Russia's ills and bombastically implored the ministers to go to headquarters and "throw themselves at the Tsar's feet," thus to beg him to remove the charlatan and save the country.

Rasputin was a symptom rather than the cause of the regime's disarray and ill repute, and after the initial and macabre rejoicing which had greeted the assassination, most thinking Russians reached the same conclusion. But the murder and its sequel were yet another symptom of that moral and intellectual disequilibrium which often characterizes a society on the eve of a revolution. What lesson could be drawn by an ordinary citizen or soldier from the sordid end of the Rasputin affair? People from the highest rungs of society and the political world (several politicians had been made privy to the assassins' intentions, and if some of them demurred, none informed) committed a deliberate murder for which they were warmly applauded by society, something which, though Rasputin was widely loathed, was bound to undermine any lingering respect for the law and public morality. The murdered man had been known to be venerated by the emperor and had been allowed to influence the highest appointments in the state and the church, yet the perpetrators of the crime were allowed to remain virtually unpunished. After a brief house arrest, they were told to repair to their estates.*

Trepov was now allowed to resign. The new prime minister was Prince Nicholas Golitsin, bearer of one of Russia's most historic names. One Golitsin helped to rescue young Peter the Great from the intrigues of his sister Sophia, whose lover and adviser was another member of the clan. But the last premier of the old regime was quite unlike his famous forebears: an amiable and obscure nonentity, formerly head of a charitable organization, his part in the tumultuous events which were to unfold was so insignificant that he was barely noticed by his contemporaries or mentioned by most historians. Yet he deserves to be remembered, if only for this story: asked by a friend why he, a man with no political ambitions or experience, agreed in the evening of his life to assume so hazardous a post, the elderly nobleman replied, "Ah, to have yet another pleasant memory."

In fact the personalities and activities of the moribund government's members were now of little interest to society. The only exception was Protopopov, who with Rasputin gone was now cast in his dead mentor's role as the visible embodiment of the dark forces, and became next to the empress the most unpopular person in the country. In reality the unbalanced man had practically given up administering his department; most of his time, when not quarrelling with his

---

*One of them, the tsar's young cousin, was ordered to join a regiment in Persia, and this alleged punishment (which probably helped to save the young man's life during the Revolution) led to an indignant collective protest to the tsar by the other grand dukes.

colleagues, was spent in meditating about and trying to commune with the spirit of Rasputin. While no one could replace the latter in the heart of the disconsolate empress (though she was comforted by the thought that where his soul now was, Our Friend would be an even more effective advocate before God on behalf of the imperial family and Russia), she naturally tended to lean all the more on her favorite minister. With such backing, Protopopov felt he could disregard his colleagues' hostility and the public's jeers. "Society," he said to a subordinate, who delicately drew his attention to all the unfavorable publicity he was getting, "I spit on society."

The air was now heavy with rumors of plots and conspiracies. Enemies of the regime now recognized that it was almost immaterial to scrutinize actions in terms of "Is this treason or stupidity?" In either case, unless something drastic was done soon, Russia would explode. A few still hoped to persuade the tsar this time not only to change his ministers but also to do something about his wife: send her away to the Crimea, or even shut her in a convent. But most people realized that such expostulations would be in vain. Similar suggestions, though in more circumspect form, had been made to the emperor on a number of occasions and by persons close to him and invariably had been rebuffed. The man himself was stubborn and unteachable, blind and deaf to what was happening around him and in the country. It was he who would have to go.

The atmosphere was quite similar to that between 1821–25, except now the plotters were to be found among gray-bearded politicians rather than young Guards officers, and their plots were being hatched not amidst "friendly banter" and between "claret and champagne," but in sober and strained discussions. A palace revolution? But this was the twentieth century and not a time when politics was something of interest to at most a few hundred people, the rest hardly noticing how or why a ruler was changed. A veteran Kadet, Prince Paul Dolgorukov, jotted down his reflections on the subject, and they soon reached not only those for whom they were intended but also the secret police, the Okhrana, now seemingly the only government agency functioning normally and fairly efficiently. "If the sovereign does not agree voluntarily to a government responsible to parliament, then, judging by the current mood of the Romanov family, we will be facing the danger of palace revolution, carried out by those who do not wish to remain in the power of an unbalanced woman who dominates the emperor."[44]

But, noted the prince, whose family's lineage was considerably more ancient than that of the ruling house, a palace coup would be a catastrophe because no other Romanov could be an improvement on the present occupant of the throne. A palace coup then would force "us monarchists by conviction to turn into republicans."

Another noble conspirator, Prince Lvov, was less pessimistic about the possibility of finding a suitable replacement. His thoughts naturally turned to the Romanov who literally towered over the rest of the clan. On Lvov's instructions, an associate sounded out the viceroy of the Caucasus, Nicholas Nikolayevich, as to whether he would agree to replace his cousin. But "Big Nicholas" was not quite ready to lend his hand to the overthrow of "Little Nicholas," as they were familiarly known in the army. He was quite low on the ladder of succession to the throne, but more fundamentally, the grand duke felt that the army would not understand or approve such a step in wartime. He evidently thought that the average soldier still was bound by his oath of allegiance to the sovereign. All the more remarkable that he himself, an imperial prince as well as a soldier, felt little inhibited by the same oath. Instead of having his interlocutor arrested the minute he made the disloyal proposition, Nicholas Nikolayevich asked amiably for some time to consider it. Then, while rejecting the offer, he was rather apologetic about his inability to join in the plot against "His Majesty's Sacred Person." To be sure, in addition to more altruistic reasons, the grand ducal clan had a clear, one might call it professional, interest in a palace coup, which would forestall a revolution.

But what a topsy-turvy world the Russian political scene was in the expiring months of tsardom! The conspiratorial itch was felt most strongly among the traditionally conservative and monarchist circles. Practically everybody believed that a revolution was imminent, except the revolutionaries themselves. In a talk he gave as late as January 1917, Lenin concluded, "We of the older generation may not see the decisive battles of this revolution."[45] He was still in Switzerland, but his sentiments were shared by leading Marxists and radicals at home. Nicholas Chheidze, head of the Mensheviks in the Duma, was emphatic in denying the possibility of anything resembling a revolution happening until it did.

Lenin's suspicious mind, however, did detect a conspiracy in the offing: at the behest of its French and British capitalist masters, the bourgeoisie would try to seize power to prevent a separate peace. There was some superficial evidence to support his hugely oversimplified diagnosis. The British and French ambassadors in Petrograd behaved in a fashion which in normal times would not have been tolerated by the government of any self-respecting state, let alone a great power. They maintained close links with the opposition, were indiscreet in their comments upon leading regime figures, and on several occasions attempted to lecture the emperor on the necessity of appointing a government agreeable to public opinion. Their importunities, as well as constant demands that Russia should do more in the common cause—at one time it was demanded that Russia should send four hundred thousand soldiers to the West—would have exhausted the patience of any other head of state. But Nicholas's character was a strange mixture of stubbornness and docility. As he himself wistfully and with a tragic presentiment noted, he was born on the day the Orthodox Church consecrated to the biblical Job. Much as it was generally doubted, his loyalty to Russia's allies in the war was unshakable, and all such doubts should have been dispelled by the Order to the Army of December 12, when in answer to the Germans' public proposals for negotiations between the warring powers, the tsar proclaimed, "It is unthinkable to consider peace until the final victory over the enemy, who brazenly believes that just as he began the war, so it is up to him to decide when it should end," and he repeated Russia's war aims: Constantinople and the Straits and (this time heeding the allies' and domestic opposition's demands) a united and free Poland.

But by now such declarations could no longer dispel the fears of the regime's enemies nor put an end to their plotting. Whatever the assessment of the tsar's intentions or the ability to withstand pressures of the dark forces, this became secondary to the conviction that a continuation of the political impasse must bring a catastrophe. What most frightened and incensed them was not the ghost of autocracy which still stalked the land, not so much the government's real and alleged misdeeds, but the breakdown of any sense of authority in society, a phenomenon which in Russian history augured invariably not only a revolution but anarchy. For liberals, especially, there came the realization that what they had struggled against for so long—autocracy—had in fact ceased to exist. But now what appeared to some as its most likely successor was not an orderly constitutional system but what Pushkin had called "that Russian kind of revolt with no thought behind it, save of wanton destruction." A perceptive police agent reported that some Kadets were afraid "of being swept overboard by the revolutionary tidal wave which is inevitably approaching," hence they urged their party to ally itself with the extreme left, thus to get some measure of control over the coming events.[46]

As 1917 arrived, few politically minded Russians were willing to concede that the existing regime would or should be able to last through the year. That the present situation could not continue was evident even to two people perhaps most isolated from the political currents of the day: the tsar and the tsaritsa. Alexandra intensified her epistolary pressure on her husband; he must become a real autocrat, follow in the footsteps of such of his predecessors as Ivan the Terrible, Peter the Great, the Emperor Paul. (Her knowledge of her adopted country's history could not have been very extensive. She evidently ignored how or why Paul I met his end.) People like Milyukov, Guchkov, Lvov, should be hanged or at least dispatched to Siberia. "Crush them all." Her fantasies brought assurances from her "poor little weak willed hubby," as he pathetically signed the letter, that he intended to be "strong and firm." More specifically, Nicholas was convinced that his tempestuous coexistence with the Duma could not go on. He entrusted his old favorite, Nicholas Maklakov, to prepare the draft of a law which would reduce the legislature to complete impotence.

Yet for practically everyone else, it was the Duma which offered the last fading chance of avoiding a violent overthrow of the regime. Apart from the tottering throne, this was the only national institution with a claim to legitimacy. Furthermore, its performance during the last two years made many Russians forget, or forgive, the fact that the Duma had been chosen on the basis of a very restrictive franchise and in somewhat fraudulent elections. The trouble was that the Duma itself, or more properly the liberal nucleus of its leadership, could not forget and felt inhibited by its sinful and undemocratic origins. The liberals had no hesitation in believing that they spoke for the nation when they chastised the regime, and demanded that it reform itself or depart. But when it came to the question of who should step into the vacuum and snatch power when it finally slipped from the feeble grasp of its nominal holders, the Kadets and their allies were still afflicted by the usual ailment of liberalism, fear of power and harrowing doubts whether they, members of the propertied and educated class, had the right to speak and act for the people. "Why does not the Duma seize power?" asked someone of Milyukov on the eve of the revolution. He answered with what at the time he believed was a joke: "Fetch us two regiments and we will seize power."[47]

The legislators' diffidence was sensed and exploited by the left, which in a manner that had become traditional tried to make the liberals do its own work. They kept pressing them toward a confrontation with the regime while intermittently denouncing them for their pusillanimity and class origins. "The workers," said a socialist, "have little use for the Duma and its bourgeois deputies, but they need the Duma for it creates an atmosphere in which they can breathe more freely."[48] The meaning of this apparent self-contradiction was plain: once the workers could breathe completely freely, that is, once tsarism had been overthrown, then it would come the turn of the Duma.

The concept of "the government of public confidence" neatly skipped the whole problem of direct power for the legislature, for it assumed a government composed essentially of bureaucrats, of a different caliber to be sure than the present ministerial group, headed by a popular figure, possibly a prestigious general, and responsible to the legislature. But by 1916 such a solution was no longer thought practical. Duma politicians realized, their sense of patriotic duty and in some cases personal ambition overcoming their usual fears and scruples, that they might have to shoulder directly the burden of government. The country's mood was such, they believed, that only a genuinely parliamentary regime stood a chance of convincing the people that there had been a real change and definite break with the autocratic past. If not convinced of it, Russia was headed for disaster. Still there was little competition for ministerial portfolios in the "Duma government." The list of putative ministers drawn up by the Progressive bloc early in 1916 was virtually identical with that which actually materialized as the first Provisional Government after the February 1917 explosion. The pomp and appurtenances of power held little attraction for people who made their careers as critics and censors of the regime. They still felt, as a Kadet pamphlet phrased it in 1906, "It is much easier and more convenient to criticize than to assume the burden of responsibility associated with power," and that the opposition, by stepping into the gap, would "bare its breast to the blows of malicious and ruthless criticism. . . . it would risk losing most of the prestige it had accumulated by its unyielding struggle against the old order."[49]

To agree in principle to bear the cross called for considerable self-sacrifice from people whom most apologists for the old regime as well as later Soviet historians would portray as ruthless and unscrupulous seekers of power, but who in fact and quite presciently saw it as a calvary. But once "ministers" were selected how were they to be put in office? The liberals were learned people, some of them professional historians who must have remembered that in the French Revolution the Estates General, also not a very democratic assembly, declared themselves a constituent assembly and forced the monarch to heed their wishes. But the prevailing tendency within the Progressive bloc was to wait for something to happen or for someone else to save them from such a precipitous step. That something might be the emperor finally and unexpectedly understanding the situation and appointing the people they wanted. Then there were those conspiracies being bruited about in Petrograd's drawing rooms; the regime's more enterprising enemies, such as Guchkov and Lvov, were known to be plotting with the generals and grand dukes. An invariable feature of those rumored conspiracies was that someone else, rather than the politicians, should do the dirty work: thus the approach to Nicholas Nikolayevich, the story about the naval officers ready to seize the imperial couple and place them on a warship and pack them off to England, et cetera. Practically all variants of the proposed or imagined plot envisaged Nicholas's successor pledging to rule constitutionally and agreeing to be guided by the Duma.

Yet there was an element of implausibility in all this talk. For all their grumbling about "Cousin Nicky" and "that woman," which Romanov would be willing to ascend the throne after its previous incumbent had been forced to abdicate or killed? The very shock of such a coup might trigger what it was supposed to prevent, a popular revolution. Most high-ranking generals were fed up with the situation, and quite willing to support a parliamentary regime which would restore national unity and strengthen the war effort. But with their armies facing the enemy and soon to go on the offensive, they would not risk taking the initiative in a coup, which even if successful and popular, might still deal a devastating blow to the morale of their troops. Patriotism was turning many on the highest rungs of the Establishment into would-be-conspirators, but the same patriotic feeling kept them hesitant to strike. This was not the eighteenth century, when a handful of people had been able to replace one autocrat by another with the country at first barely noticing the change. Now a palace revolution might injure irreparably the fragile fabric of Russian society.

Similar considerations appeared to rule out a republican solution. In 1905 a Kadet pamphlet stated the case for a constitutional monarchy in terms which were still valid, though less so, in 1917: the very word *republic* was incomprehensible to the peasant masses. It was held—and in view of what soon was to happen who can say mistakenly—that if the monarchy were abolished, the masses would take it to mean that there was no longer any legitimate central authority in the land. *State* to the Russian ear was a legal term and as such devoid of any emotional, almost any political, connotations. Even at the nadir of its power and prestige, the monarchy was a symbol of not merely national but also supranational unity of the empire. Would something so artificial and alien sounding as *the Russian state* or *republic* convey the same feeling of authority to an average Russian, let alone a Pole or Georgian? Whether they were Kadets, Octobrists, et cetera, all leading figures at the moment, save those at the extreme left, were fervently nationalist. That is why none of them, no matter what his personal feelings about the ruling house and where it had brought the country, could, without serious qualms, envisage the liquidation of the monarchy.

The logical solution of the dilemma would have been for Nicholas II to abdicate in favor of his twelve-year-old son, with the emperor's brother Michael becoming regent. Michael was little known to the public, which in a grand duke was rather reassuring. He had never displayed an interest in politics or personal ambition, and he had a creditable war record. Thus the grand duke would make an acceptable constitutional ruler. He was not regarded favorably by other members of the imperial family on account of his morganatic marriage to a commoner and a divorceé, but no one else could worry about such things at a time like this. As the near future was to show, it would have been easier to persuade Nicholas to abdicate than to become a constitutional monarch. He clung to what shreds of autocratic power were still his, not out of personal ambition, still less because he enjoyed the role, but out of an anachronistic concept of his duty before God and Russia. No one believed that it would have been possible to induce the emperor to step down as long as the empress remained in the picture. So the plotters continued to weave their designs, and the politicians kept waiting, though with growing impatience.

But was the country at large as restive, as revolution minded, as those who had declared war on the regime at once hoped and feared? Superficially what was to happen in February and later ought to answer that question. Yet the historian's judgment must be balanced between the proverbial "it could not have happened otherwise" and "what might have happened if only." It was inevitable that the autocracy, stripped of the protective shield of nationalism and thus virtually defenseless, should prove vulnerable to a sudden new onslaught; it had been crumbling under its own weight. But the actual timing and character of the February and March events was far from preordained. It was not the grim forces of history but administrative incompetence of the local authorities which sparked the Petrograd riots. It was the rioting mob which frightened the Duma politicians into initiating a coup d'etat, something they could, and should, have done on their own. It was the generals who completed the coup, by inducing the tsar to abdicate, again a move, which in view of their virtual unanimity on the imperative necessity of his abdication and the ease with which it was actually brought about, might well have been risked weeks, months, before Petrograd erupted.

Would a timely palace coup and/or the introduction of constitutional monarchy have forestalled the February drama, i.e., appeased the people, or in the Communist nomenclature, the masses? Here it is important to be more specific as to what the situation was among the various components of the population. Insofar as the urban proletariat was concerned, especially in the capital, the invaluable secret police reports, the closest thing to a public opinion poll, portray it as restive and in a potentially rebellious mood, not so much about politics as the economic side effects of the war. "Attempts by the extreme left to stir up bread riots might find a favorable response [among the workers]," the police department informed the Ministry of the Interior in January and early February of 1917.[50] The report's authors then suggest some concrete steps, a central organ which would regulate the supply and distribution of foodstuffs, rationing, and price controls, but their suggestions went unheeded by the sluggish administrative machine, both at the central and the local level. The workers' mood can then be characterized as one of passive hostility toward the authorities but a chance event might turn it into militancy.

Among the bulk of the front-line troops, morale stood quite high. The rate of desertions had not varied very much since the beginning of the war, about sixty-three hundred per month,[51] a figure which in view of the immense size of the field force, seven to eight million at any time, and the relative ease with which a soldier on leave could disappear within the vast country, hardly suggests an army in the process of decomposition. As Bolshevik memoirists acknowledge, their revolutionary and defeatist propaganda efforts among the front-line troops made no headway prior to the February revolution.

But in the rear the morale situation was quite different. Very unwisely the authorities turned large urban centers, such as Petrograd, into military depots for reserve and training units. Soldiers were crowded into barracks designed for a fraction of their number and penned in there like virtual prisoners by the commanders who were fearful of the dangers, political and otherwise, that city life held for young men freshly conscripted from their villages. Their officers were for the most part nonregulars or those thought unfit for front-line duty, and quite a few had been political radicals in their civilian past. Should a political fire start in their vicinity, garrison troops might turn into combustible material. Even more explosive was the situation among the sailors of the Baltic fleet, who were drawn mainly from the working class and who, in view of the German navy's domination of the sea, were pent up at their bases, condemned to demoralizing inactivity.

Thus, there was plenty of potential for revolutionary trouble, regardless of whether or not Nicholas II continued on the throne and whether the government did or did not become responsible to the Duma. Still it is unlikely that this would have added up to a nationwide revolution as long as the country was at war and in the main convinced that it must be carried on until victory. The army—"peasants in uniform"—as Bolshevik writers dubbed it, stood as a whole ready to obey orders as long as there was someone with the right to issue them. As events were to demonstrate, the Petrograd riots turned into the Russian Revolution only when the nation and the army began to realize that there was no longer any legitimate central authority in the land.

In January 1917 the autocracy's coma began to be interrupted by convulsive spasms. On the twenty-seventh the police arrested several worker-members of the Central War Industries Committee. This was the government's answer to the worker groups of the committee issuing a call to the Petrograd proletariat to stage street demonstrations on February 14 in support of the Duma and against autocracy on the occasion of the legislature's return from its recess. The workers were to march to the Tauride Palace, the Duma's home, demanding a "government of national salvation" and denouncing the existing one "which is strangling the country."

Issued at the behest of some members of the Progressive bloc, the appeal was somewhat ambivalent as to what should be the workers' attitude toward it as well as toward society in general. "The current struggle of bourgeois society against the regime creates favorable conditions for an intervention by the working class [because] this conflict between the Duma and the government offers an opportunity for the people to strike a decisive blow at the autocracy."[52] Even more ambiguous was the appeal's stand on the war: "The conflict's end and peace are eagerly desired by our war-weary country, but peace will not rescue the people from their present calamitous situation unless it is brought about not by the autocratic regime but by the nation itself." And such a peace must be "acceptable to Russia's, as well as the other countries', proletariat." This was certainly far from the attitude of the Progressive bloc, which thirsted for victory and could not care less what would or would not be acceptable to the German proletariat.

As Shlyapnikov, the Bolshevik author who cites the document, notes, the Menshevik leaders of the working group tried both to go along with the mood of the working masses, weary of the war, somewhat suspicious of the Duma and its bourgeois majority, and at the same time to help their friends in the Progressive bloc to pressure the regime. Despite Shlyapnikov's allegations, the appeal's ambivalence was genuine, rather than contrived, and as such it reflected the similarly ambivalent feelings of Petrograd workers: they desired peace, but not at any price; they wanted the regime out, but were quite confused as to what could or should take its place.

The Bolsheviks' influence in the capital was quite weak. This is reflected in the fact that their local committee felt it impolitic to try to counter the pro-Duma appeal with one of its own. Instead, it prepared an instruction guide for its agitators, explaining why the workers should not march on February 14. Such a demonstration, individual agitators were to explain whenever they found listeners, would only play into the hands of the bourgeoisie, which wanted to strike a bargain with the regime and prolong the imperialist war indefinitely. Upon tsarism's collapse the socialists should aim for political power to pass not to the bourgeoisie, but to "the workers and poor peasants represented by the Provisional Revolutionary Government, which by summoning the Constituent Assembly will secure both political freedom and peace."[53] The document offers an interesting hint of the authoritarian idea already germinating in the Bolsheviks' mind. Traditionally for Russian radicals of all varieties, it had been the people rather than one class who should inherit power upon the autocracy's collapse. Why not summon the Constituent Assembly and "secure political freedom" right away? Isn't "workers and poor peasants" a euphemism for the one party which really defends their interests, the Bolsheviks themselves? But equally remarkable is the fact that even at this late hour, the Bolsheviks' agitation plan does not call explicitly for revolution or an immediate end to the war.

The arrest of the workers' group brought a defiant protest from the industrialists' and officials' sector of the Central War Industries Committee, which included some of the country's leading capitalists. Their public statement, put out on January 31, identified the arrested as belonging "to the so-called Mensheviks, one of the more moderate tendencies among the Russian workers."[54] Uninhibitedly, the statement concluded, "While differing from the Workers' Group, insofar as our political and social views are concerned, the Committee associates itself with the group's appraisal of the current political regime and the government's policy and considers the regime as incapable of securing Russia's victory over the foreign enemy."[55]

In their exasperation over the regime's obduracy—for a year and a half they had been trying without success to soften its attitude—some opposition leaders had forgotten their declared objective: to effect constitutional changes so as to prevent a revolution. Perhaps, with all those palace coups being talked about and not materializing, an aroused working class was the only means capable of forcing a change. It was rather late for Milyukov to talk about the danger of unleashing the mob's passions, but the veteran Kadet leader now became frightened at the growing inclination among his fellow liberals to appeal to the street for help in their campaign. At a meeting of several leaders of the voluntary organizations and Duma deputies, called to discuss the arrests, Milyukov, to the amazement of others, declared that the war industries committees, the *zemstvos*, et cetera, should not be concerned with politics and that no single class undertake by itself to defy the government and indulge in attempts or agitation to overthrow it. "Only the State Duma ought and can tell the country how to fight the regime. . . . Apart from the Duma, no group of the population, no social organization, has the right to proclaim its own slogans and to launch on its own, a struggle."[56] Others present, who included, unprecedentedly in a conference of the constitutional opposition, such leaders of the left as Kerensky and Chheidze, derided Milyukov's sudden scruples and cautions. With this attitude he risked, said Chheidze, finding himself one day left behind by events. The gathering, attended by a secret police agent masquerading as a worker representative, then fell into discussing various ways of drawing the masses into the struggle: a special conspiratorial circle to direct the effort and an underground journal to inform the people of what was really going on. The last item can only be viewed as entirely superfluous, considering the ease and speed with which antigovernment propaganda of all kinds, leaflets, proclamations, et cetera, could circulate throughout the capital. Considering what was going on and what would happen in about three weeks, it was the regime which should have been preparing to go underground.

If the would-be-conspirators were going about their business in such a leisurely way, it is not too surprising that the main figures of the regime remained so complacent in the face of the growing critical situation. February 14 came and went without anything of what for those days could be considered as an unusual commotion. Prior to it the military governor of the city warned the workers against demonstrating: by striking they would be betraying their brothers at the front. He cautioned further that the city had the status of a war zone, and he would not hesitate to use the force of arms should disorders break out. Astounding his liberal friends, Professor Milyukov seconded the commandant's appeal. In his letter to the papers he urged the population to remain calm and not to fall for provocations "emanating from a most sinister source . . . by actions which would play into the enemy's hands."[57] Whatever the reason, there were but sporadic strikes, and, contrary to what had been feared, no mass gatherings and workers' processions like January 9, 1905.

There were some demonstrations, mostly by the students. In reporting on them, a secret police observer stumbled upon a portent of the coming storm: "The sight which attracted general attention was what might be described as mass participation [in the demonstration] by officers, predominantly ensigns in rank, who along with the students, and with great enthusiasm, sang the 'Marseillaise.'"[58] (Ensign was the lowest officer rank; "Marseillaise," the traditional hymn of Russian radicals, the "Internationale" remaining little known until well into the revolution.) Another ominous sign was the junior officers' hostile attitude toward the police whom they would greet with shouts like "You should be at the front, and not fighting your battles here, you fat bellies."

But the very atmosphere of crisis contributed to a somewhat complacent feeling that nothing extraordinary was likely to happen soon. Strikes, calls for manifestations, clashes in the Duma, rumors about the conspiracies were now such common and expected occurrences that in a way one did not take them too seriously. The sense of an impending catastrophe had been with Russia for very long—in fact, since 1855, except for the years of hope, the late 1850s to mid–1860s, and of resignation, the 1880s. At other times, if one listened closely to what society was saying, there seemed to be a monotonous chant, its theme, "This cannot go on," "We are standing on the edge of an abyss."

As the dismal Petrograd February dragged on, there suddenly seemed to be less tension in the air than during the preceding fall. The British and French ministers, who had visited the capital for an interallied conference, returned home rather reassured by what they had seen and heard. Stories about an imminent domestic crisis were greatly exaggerated, they reported to their governments. True, the tsar, as they had tried to hint to him, would do well to heed the opposition's quite reasonable and moderate demands. But the Russian nation was united in its determination to see the war through. Russia's industry of late had performed prodigiously in stepping up the output of weapons of all sorts and munitions (and so in fact it had). The army was now well equipped and quite ready to launch an assault on the Germans, which was being planned for April, at the same time that French and British troops were scheduled to open their offensive in the west.

The growing feeling that those who had been in the forefront of the battle against the regime were beginning to back down was conveyed by Kerensky's speech to the Duma on February 15. The young lawyer was now seen more and more as the leader of the left; such Socialist luminaries as Lenin and Trotsky, et cetera, and their equivalents among the Socialist Revolutionaries were either abroad or in exile and almost forgotten by the workers, if not their party comrades. Kerensky taunted leaders of the Progressive bloc with just teasing the nation with their antigovernment oratory. Why don't they *do* something, rather than prattle endlessly about the dark forces, German influence at the court, et cetera? He was quite explicit as to what he and his friends thought was the main source of the country's miseries and hinted broadly that not only the tsar but also the monarchic principle would have to go. Also, the Progressive bloc should realize that the people did not share its war aims: "You gentlemen are united in your goal of imperialist conquests; you suffer from national megalomania, just as much as those who rule us."[59]

At the time, Kerensky had a good ear for the urban masses' mood. He was also that rarity on the Russian political scene: a politician who really craved power. Therefore, if, as he alleged, the Kadets, et cetera, tried to exploit the workers' grievances for their own ends, Kerensky in trying to shame the liberals into a more radical stance was not without some personal calculations of his own.

A premonition that something might be in the offing struck, however, those two usually unperceptive persons, the tsar and his wife. As if unwittingly trying to flee from the coming catastrophe, the tsar was eager to leave the capital, or more precisely, his suburban residence to which he had hastened two months before in the wake of Rasputin's murder, and to get back to the quiet of headquarters. This time his hurry was uncharacteristic, for he would have to leave behind the little tsarevich, sick with measles, and it was hard for him to part even for a little while from his beloved son. Alexandra, though passionately fond of her husband, was usually glad to have him away, vacationing, as it were, in Mogilev, especially since in Petrograd he was subject to the importunities from politicians and his imperial relatives, all now solidly hostile toward herself. This time she asked him to delay his departure.

There were some apprehensions even in Protopopov's muddled mind. Repeated warnings from his secret police subordinates made him draw the emperor's attention to the unsatisfactory condition of the Petrograd garrison. Some one hundred sixty thousand strong, composed of raw recruits and convalescents, it could not be relied upon if there were serious trouble among the civilian population. It would be desirable to bring up some disciplined battle-hardened units to back up the police, whose numbers, about ten thousand, were hardly adequate in a city of two and a half million. In general, the minister of the interior was reassuring. There were detailed contingency plans to deal firmly with any possible riots, and he had the situation well in hand. However, perhaps the emperor could stay around for a few more days, just in case. But Nicholas would not. Of course the Duma was in session, and that might open up all sorts of unpleasant possibilities. But—again his whole pattern of behavior seemed to suggest a semiabdication—he thought he provided for various contingencies by leaving a signed rescript proroguing the Duma with the date for the proclamation to be filled in whenever Prince Golitsin and his colleagues decided it was necessary. On February 22 the imperial train pulled out of Tsarskoye Selo. When he next returned, Nicholas II would be a prisoner.

For some days there had been labor unrest in the huge Putilov factory. Some workers had demanded wage rises of between 20 and 60 percent. When refused, they entered upon a sit down—it was then known as an "Italian-type"—strike. On the twenty-second most were ready to resume work, but the management fired the instigators and ordered a lockout, which affected thirty thousand workers.

Interestingly enough, during all of this the underground socialist organizations had been trying to prevent the strike movement from spreading. February 23 was a radical holiday, International Women's Day, but no demonstrations were being planned for it. Trotsky, a meticulous historian when personal or ideological considerations did not interfere with his reconstruction of events, noted: "Not a single [underground socialist] group called for stikes on that day. What is more, the most militant Bolshevik committee, that of the Vyborg area, which was entirely proletarian in its character, was in fact calling on the workers not to strike."[60] The reason, according to Trotsky, was its conviction that a strike would turn into street manifestations, which would be easily subdued by the authorities, with needless sacrifices among the workers. ". . . The time for street fighting had not yet come. [Our] party was not strong enough. There had been but little rapport between workers and soldiers."

To be sure the Bolshevik leader in Petrograd at the time, Shlyapnikov, affirmed the opposite: he and his friends had wanted to provoke street fighting and to make the army shoot at the workers. "We hoped to involve them by pushing the struggle to its most intense phase, street fighting, with all the bloody sacrifices that it required."[61] But this was obviously a very subjective post-factum attempt to claim clairvoyance for the local Bolsheviks. And even Shlyapnikov confessed that he and his committee had nothing prepared for the day in question and were taken by surprise by what actually happened.

One group, however, for some days had been calling, if not explicitly for strike, then for some kind of violent action on International Women's Day. As Shlyapnikov wrote vaguely, "There had been circulating around the city a leaflet of the 'Interfaction' committee devoted to the day."[62] The "interfaction" socialists were those who like Trotsky (then of course in America) professed themselves to be neither Mensheviks nor Bolsheviks but working for the party's unity, and at the time they were even weaker among the Petrograd proletariat than the Bolsheviks. The actual leaflet which Shlyapnikov adduced was not signed by them, nor does it contain any reference to the interfactionalists. It bears the imprimatur of the "Petersburg International Committee" of the Russian Socialist Party, and insofar as is known, no such body existed in the capital.

The leaflet has several characteristics which distinguish it from the bulk of contemporary revolutionary propaganda appeals. It is much more violent in its general tone: "The workers' blood is being spilled at all the fronts, the empress herself is trafficking in the people's blood and is selling Russia piece by piece [*sic*]. Soldiers, practically unarmed, are being sent to their deaths. And at home, capitalists and industrialists want to turn the workers into their serfs." Ostensibly addressed to "comrades, women workers," the appeal stresses the hardships on the domestic front: "Prices are terribly high and rising, hunger knocks on every door . . . in the villages they requisition for the war your last piece of bread, your last head of cattle. We stand in queues for hours." The appeal is fairly unique for the time in expressing solidarity with the proletariat of the enemy countries, a theme hitherto treated rather gingerly in socialist agitation:

Do we have to kill millions of Austrian and German workers and peasants? The German workers also did not want to fight. Our dear ones, don't go to the front because they want you to. Neither do the workers in Germany, Austria or England. . . . It is the government which is guilty: it started the war and does not know how to end it. . . . The capitalists are guilty. The war lines their pockets. It is high time we told them: enough! Down with the criminal regime and its gang of thieves and murderers. Long live peace! The day of retribution is near. . . . In every country the people's wrath is rising.[63]

The appeal, issued at a time when all the known underground socialist organizations were, by their own admission, trying to restrain the workers and to confine the celebration of International Women's Day to "meetings, speeches . . ."[64] was unrestrainedly inflammatory in its tone. Furthermore, its message was uncompromisingly defeatist: the war ought to be ended right away, something which even the most radical Bolshevik appeals had eschewed until this time, their slogan, "Down with the war," usually accompanied by an admonition that only the Constituent Assembly could secure peace. There is, thus, the possibility that the propaganda missive to "comrades, women workers" was in its genesis the work of enemy agents.

For conducting subversive and defeatist activities within the Russian empire, the German government had a very competent adviser, Dr. Alexander Helphand, who under the sobriquet of "Parvus" or "Fatty" had been active in the Russian revolution of 1905, and who with Trotsky had authored the famous theory of permanent revolution. Now a millionaire and German subject, but still something of a Russian revolutionary at heart, Helphand put his great knowledge of his native country's internal conditions at the disposal of the kaiser's government. Some of the money which the latter was spending for fostering subversion in the enemy territory undoubtedly did find its way to Russia, with Dr. Helphand acting as the conduit and his agents operating through neutral Scandinavia. At the same time, it is equally certain that prior to the revolution, none of the major Russian socialist groups received financial help from Germany or was connected with Helphand and his designs. In 1916 he approached Lenin in Zurich, but at the time the latter would have nothing to do with him or his money. But it is quite possible that an occasional antiwar pamphlet or incitement to revolutionary disorders in 1916–17 may have had its ultimate source in Helphand's ingenious mind.

However, it would be unreasonable to see the February events at any stage as having been organized or guided by enemy agents. An author who makes a valiant but unconvincing case for the German hand behind the uprising writes, "Why should such a movement have occurred then, and only then in Petrograd? Neither before nor since have the Russian masses shown any such capacity for 'spontaneous' action."[65] This last statement is hardly correct. There had been a quite spontaneous mass action in the Moscow anti-German riots of 1915. On January 9, 1917, in commemoration of Bloody Sunday, one hundred sixty thousand Petrograd workers had laid down their tools. And there had been street demonstrations in the capital; one in the workers' quarter in the fall of 1916 which had to be dispersed by the Cossacks, and rather minor ones on February 14.

Therefore what happened at first on February 23 was not too unusual. Women textile workers went on strike to celebrate their day. They sent delegates to other factories, asking for support. The underground socialist committees, starting with the Bolshevik one, decided, though with "a heavy heart," as one of their members was to write, to join in the action. Altogether some ninety thousand workers were on strike that day.[66]

From the middle of the month heavy snowfalls had disrupted communications with the capital and slowed down the supply of flour and other foodstuffs. Some bakeries had to shut down. There were shortages and rumors that bread would soon become completely unavailable. And so crowds composed mostly of women, some with children, poured into the streets, demonstrating with shouts of "Give us bread." This in conjunction with the Women's Day strikes triggered the revolutionaries' resolve to give the manifestation a political character. "Once you have a mass strike, then you call upon everybody to come out into the street and set yourself at the head of the movement," wrote a Bolshevik activist of the day.[67]

Thus there began to appear placards proclaiming "Down with the war," "Down with the autocracy." Army patrols were summoned to help the police to disperse the demonstrators, but as yet there was no shooting, no major clashes. At the end of the day, no one had realized that this had been the first day of the revolution. The strike might last another day, at most three, was the general feeling in the underground socialist circles.

Then on February 24 two hundred thousand workers were on strike. The crowds' behavior grew more unruly. They were beginning to assault policemen, twenty-eight of them were beaten up. The Cossacks still rode their horses into the mob, forcing it to disperse, but they only regrouped elsewhere. Some Cossack units displayed less than exemplary diligence in performing their tasks. One unit rode quietly in a single file through the path opened by the crowd without any attempt to push it back or to chastise any of the demonstrators. Such incidents were immediately and widely reported throughout the city, creating a sensation. "The Cossacks were traditionally considered that part of the army which was most alien to the working class and the revolutionary movement."[68] They served as the Praetorian guards of the regime; their traditional tactic when ordered to disperse an unruly crowd was to ride into it or even charge in a battle formation, dealing out blows with their famous *nagaikas* (long whips) or even sabers. Now those incidents which showed the Cossacks' restraint and presumably their reluctance to obey orders had to have a powerful and uplifting effect on the workers.

For some former tsarist officials, when they later gloomily pondered the past, the incident with the Cossack squadron epitomized what to their bureaucratic mentality appeared as the prime reason why the bread riots escalated into the revolution: the chaotic state of Petrograd's administration and the utter incapacity of those charged with preserving public order. Nobody was quite sure who was responsible for watching over the capital's food supplies; the city council or the regime's officials. In dealing with public disturbances, the lines of authority and communication were snarled, with several people issuing orders, the military governor of the city, its police chief, the commandant of the Guards, as well as several regimental commanders, each of them responsible for a given district. For all the contingency plans, none of them appeared to know what to do in the sudden emergency. Thus it may not have been initially any sympathy for the demonstrators which made the Cossacks behave in such an unusual way but simply the fact that they had been told not to use arms, and someone had forgotten to equip them with the *nagaikas,* their usual instrument of "persuasion" in dispersing mobs. One man should have been in charge of coordinating efforts of the various authorities, the minister of the interior. But Protopopov first minimized the importance of the whole business as not worthy of his attention and then completely lost his head.

On Saturday, the twenty-fifth, there were, however, signs that the roots of the trouble went deeper than just administrative inefficiency and the inexperience or stupidity of some officials. In one place, a crowd of some six hundred workers had its path barred by detachments of Cossacks and dragoons. Then a few policemen appeared on the scene. "After the arrival of the police, the Cossacks and dragoons turned around and rode away. This deliberate departure of the soldiers at the appearance of the police emboldened the crowd to the point of attacking the latter. The police colonel was pulled off his horse and beaten into unconsciousness." Elsewhere "a platoon of police horsemen with drawn sabers was about to disperse a crowd. At the same time there appeared a Cossack squadron, commanded by an officer, which forced the police to leave. . . . The crowd loudly cheered the Cossacks."[69] As yet this ominous insubordination was confined mostly to Cossack units. When some demonstrators shot at policemen in another part of the town, soldiers opened fire on the crowd, killing several people.

For some days the Council of Ministers had been engaging in stormy deliberations, but not about what was happening practically under their windows. They were debating what to do about the Duma and themselves. Most of the ministers, including Prince Golitsin, his hopes of "yet another pleasant memory" cruelly dissipated, felt that their position had become untenable, not because of street riots but because the Duma was making their life impossible. At the last session when the food problem was discussed, the minister of agriculture burst into tears when a deputy asked how he, a decent man, could work alongside someone like Protopopov. The majority of the council was quite ready to lay down their invidious burden and to implore the emperor to appoint people who could get along with the irate legislators. But the minority argued obstinately that the tsar would never agree to a responsible cabinet and that it was the ministers' duty to remain until it pleased him to relieve them. What was finally and unanimously decided at the cabinet session late that Saturday night was, under the circumstances, the equivalent of throwing a stick of dynamite into the fire. The prime minister filled in the date of the imperial rescript: as of Monday, February 27, the legislative session would be terminated. The Duma was to reassemble, "not later than April, barring unforeseen circumstances." The rioting workers may not have cared very much about the Duma, but to those officers and soldiers who still hesitated as well as to the deputies themselves, the government's action suggested that it might try to stage a coup of its own and get rid of the Duma altogether.

There was a direct telephone line between the emperor's headquarters in Mogilev and the capital. Yet at a time when every hour counted, both the tsar and the officials in Petrograd chose to communicate by telegraph and a primitive type of teleprinter, the so-called Hughes apparatus. Late in the evening of the twenty-fifth, headquarters had already been apprised of the riots, but the telegraphic messages concluded reassuringly, "The military have taken energetic steps. . . . by the twenty-sixth the trouble should be over." Another man might have rushed back to the capital or picked up the phone to keep in touch with the situation. Instead Nicholas wired the military governor an order, which in view of what was happening was reminiscent of the story of King Canute and the sea, "I command that the disorders be put down tomorrow without fail. They are utterly intolerable at a time when we are at war with Germany and Austria."

"Tomorrow" was Sunday, February 26. After the revolution, the unfortunate military governor was to describe his reaction to the emperor's command: "It put me in a state of shock. . . . 'Tomorrow,' no matter what, it said. . . . What could I do, how could I put them [riots] down? . . . But the tsar commands; so we have to start shooting."[70] Whether in fact those were his feelings or not, General Serge Khabalov now told his subordinates to use firearms if, after having been warned, the demonstrators should still press on. Until now they had been instructed to shoot only if shot at. The uprising could have been crushed immediately if troops had been allowed to shoot from the very beginning, a police official wrote subsequently.[71] But it is difficult to follow his logic of shooting at a crowd composed mostly of women, who were protesting food shortages.

An order to use firearms indiscriminately would have led to trouble even among well-disciplined soldiers, not to mention the kind currently in the Petrograd garrison. This was wartime. They had been called under arms to defend the country, not to shoot their countrymen. What compounded the psychologically disastrous effects of the order was that while the demonstrators' behavior was not exactly peaceful (some shops had been looted, streetcars immobilized) and the slogans displayed were certainly subversive, what had been happening until now could be described as revolutionary manifestations, but certainly not an organized attempt at revolution. No government buildings had as yet been seized or appeared to be endangered. The average soldier could thus hardly have a clear idea of what or whom he was defending and would be, therefore, susceptible to the revolutionary agitator's argument that the regime was the real aggressor by ordering him to fire at his unarmed working-class brothers. Shlyapnikov, in his memoirs, credits himself with restraining his more impatient party comrades from acquiring arms and using them in the street clashes, and indeed widespread armed resistance by the workers would have been both suicidal and counterproductive from the viewpoint of propaganda.

On Sunday morning the city appeared deceptively calm, but in the afternoon, crowds began to assemble and march again, one thousand in one place, five thousand in another, et cetera. Their behavior was defiant; after a salvo from the troops, they would break up, hide in neighboring houses, and then reform. Firing was heard all over the city, with the number of killed and wounded civilians running into hundreds.

These initial shootings were the first harbinger of the coming mutiny. A reserve battalion broke out of the barracks to which it had been confined. Seizing rifles from the armory, fifteen hundred soldiers ran wildly through the streets, firing into the air and occasionally at passing policemen. Surrounded by other still loyal units, the battalion was finally persuaded by its commander and the regimental chaplain to lay down their arms and to surrender the instigators of the incident and to return to barracks.

At the day's end, several left-wing politicians assembled in Kerensky's apartment were almost ready to concede that the government had carried the day: obeying orders, soldiers did shoot and the workers were now talking about ending the strike. About one hundred socialist activists had been arrested, and the leaders had good reason to suspect that the secret police, well aware of their meeting, proposed to pay them the same compliment.

"The revolutionaries were not ready, but the revolution was," an eye witness would write.[72] But this begs the question because even if one believed that it was approaching, no one could have predicted the kind of revolution. And then February 27 gave the answer: it was several revolutions combined into one. There was Pushkin's spontaneous "Russian revolt with no thought behind it," as yet not "ruthless." It was the "bourgeois democratic revolution" of the Marxist jargon; the uprising by the masses shocked the Duma leaders into taking power, or at least its external appurtenances, into their hands. Very soon came what was essentially a palace revolution; the generals forced the emperor to abdicate. Add yet another, a socialist revolution; for the leaders of the left, hitherto outpaced by events, proclaimed the rule of "revolutionary democracy," represented by the Petrograd Soviet of the Workers' and Soldiers' Deputies, to coexist and watch over the "liberal bourgeois" regime.

The revolutionary avalanche started Monday morning with the uprising of one of the regiments which had been involved in Sunday's bloody clashes. Now its soldiers, led by a young sergeant, a former student and a professor's son, burst out of their barracks, killed an officer who tried to stop them, and rushed toward the working-class district of the city, joined on the way by soldiers from other units, as well as many civilians. There was sporadic resistance in some regiments, but it was soon overcome, their officers subdued or running away. At noon what was now a huge crowd of soldiers and workers moved to the center of the capital, wrecking police stations, setting fire to some public buildings. This was no longer a mutiny in the strict sense of the term, for the Petrograd garrison had dissolved into an armed mob. The city had not been seized but rather flooded by the

revolution. There remained a few islands of government authority still guarded by loyal troops, but their numbers were fast dwindling. For all the excesses, the mood prevailing among the revolutionary mob was festive rather than vengeful, one of inebriation with the moment of liberation and not yet of class hatred. While shots and shouts reverberated over much of the city, some residential quarters remained undistrubed, many Petrograd inhabitants learning quite late in the day that what had been going on was more than just another demonstration. "I agree with those who affirm that all you needed to suppress the February uprising was one or two fully dependable battle-tested battalions," wrote a prominent participant in the events, one who as a revolutionary could not be accused of being biased.[73] But no such battalions could be found in all of Petrograd, and what was more, there was no one to lead them.

Anxious Duma deputies who had made their way through the crowds to the Tauride Palace met with another shock, the announcement of the chamber's prorogation. To avoid any appearance of openly defying the imperial order, deputies assembled for a "private meeting" in one of the conference rooms, rather than in the main hall. Leaders of the Progressive bloc hesitated as to what course of action was indicated. It appeared unthinkable to obey the imperial order and to disperse meekly. Furthermore, they might not be allowed to; the soldier-worker mob, having brushed aside the guards, was now pouring into the building. At first it was not clear what was on the invaders' mind: mayhem or to seek protection and guidance from the official representatives of the Russian people. The deputies' deliberations were given a new turn by Kerensky's intervention. Playing to the fullest his habitual role of the tribune of the people amidst the representatives of the bourgeoisie, he now declared that he had to inform his radical friends and the masses in general whether the Duma was with them and would set itself at the head of their movement. That far the legislators were still not ready to go as of 3:00 P.M., though they would be in a few hours. For the moment they engaged in what might be called a semirevolutionary act. As Milyukov explained: "I propose to wait until it becomes clearer what is going on, and for the time being to create a provisional committee of the Duma 'for the restoration of order and for maintaining liaison with persons and institutions.' "[74] This casuistry, which was intended to avoid any impression of the Duma openly superseding the government, proved acceptable to the majority. The committee was duly constituted. Headed by Rodzianko, it had eleven additional members, nine from the Progressive bloc, including Milyukov, and Kerensky and Chheidze representing the left.

At the time the surrogate government was making its timid bow, the old tsarist one had finally faded away. The Council of Ministers had been meeting for some hours, deliberating frantically what could be done in view of the emperor's message forbidding them to resign, when late at night they were informed that a crowd was approaching. Lights in the building were hurriedly extinguished, and the ministers stole away, except for two of them who, afraid to brave the street, hid in the servants' quarters. Soon the palace housing the Council was occupied by a mob.

Among the revolution's other conquests that day were the city's two prisons, whose inmates were, of course, released. Among them were various revolutionary activists detained during the last few days, as well as those five worker-members of the war industries committee arrested one month before. And it was on the initiative of the latter group that there occurred what, in retrospect, was *the* event of the day, one which would have the most far-reaching consequences: the formation of the Petrograd Soviet. The freed labor leaders quickly summoned their friends and activists of the various socialist factions, not merely the workers but also the intelligentsia, and when some forty to fifty of them assembled, they proclaimed themselves the representatives of the Petrograd proletariat. The problem of housing the new organ was solved very simply: it occupied several rooms in the Duma building, already filled with hundreds of soldiers and workers settling down for the night, some to sleep, but most to hold those interminable political meetings which were to become such a prominent feature of the revolution. Rather symbolically, the Provisional Committee of the Duma had to move into somewhat cramped quarters in one wing of the huge palace.

As can be judged from Shlyapnikov's account of the Petrograd Soviet's birth, the idea did not arouse much enthusiasm at first among the Bolsheviks. The initiative had come from the Menshevik defensists, and they were bound to dominate the Soviet's organization and decisions. Even when the original self-appointed group would be enlarged through genuine elections by the workers, the Bolsheviks would constitute a small minority. The Mensheviks and the Socialist Revolutionaries were currently more influential among the Petrograd proletariat and had leaders with national reputations, such as Chheidze and Kerensky, as against Shlyapnikov, as yet little known, and his equally obscure collaborator, Vyacheslav Molotov, who would one day be famous.

As yet the organizers of the Soviet were too much filled with the exaltation and urgency of the moment to hold a grudge against the Bolsheviks and to remember their previous vilification of fellow Socialists of other party persuasions. Thus the majority of this pell-mell assembly ("Nobody examined credentials of those present. . . . But then who could verify them and how?"[75]) elected the Bolsheviks' representative to the eleven-member Executive Committee. But Chheidze was slated to become its chairman, and another Menshevik, Michael Skobelev, and Kerensky, then identified with the SRs, its vice-chairmen.

Unlike that other child of the revolution, the Provisional Committee of the Duma, the Executive Committee did not propose to wait on events. Emissaries were dispatched the very same night to every working-class quarter of the city to tell its inhabitants of the rebirth of the Soviet after those twelve years, and to call upon them to elect their representatives. By the next morning the Soviet's organ, *Izvestia,* appeared in the capital's streets. (Because of the strike, it was the first newspaper put out in four days.) The Soviet set up various commissions, and it is noteworthy that the one charged with examining the food situation discovered—after four days of strikes and so-called bread riots, ". . . that insofar as the [food] supplies were concerned . . . various social organizations . . . and government institutions disposed of considerable quantities of them. . . . The overall picture was far from catastrophic."[76] Also set up that hectic night was the Military Commission of the Soviet which within twenty-four hours would produce the celebrated Order No. 1, an event almost as pregnant with consequences for the future of the revolution as the mutiny which triggered it.

The Petrograd Soviet, as of March 1, of the Workers' and *Soldiers'* Deputies, would quickly grow into a huge unwieldy body, fluctuating between two and three thousand milling members, with the Executive Committee enlarged to almost one hundred. Though it would acquire some quasi-parliamentary rules of procedure, it would never lose the somewhat bogus atmosphere of its organizing meeting, "with people wandering in and out, with mandates, God knows from whom," as an eyewitness would write. But unlike on that first night, the Soviet would become much less businesslike and addicted to the most common feature of all revolutions: endless, usually bombastic, oratory.

Following the day of triumph and debauch, the revolution appeared to be sobering up. There was now, on February 28, a government of sorts, the Provisional Committee of the Duma, which proclaimed that "it has found itself compelled . . . to take into its own hands the restoration of state and public order" and asking the help of the civilian population and the army "in the difficult task of forming a new government in accordance with the desires of the people."[77]

An average Petrograder must have been confused by a simultaneous proclamation by the Soviet that *it* "has set . . . as its main task to organize the popular forces and to fight for the consolidation of political freedom and popular government," calling upon "the entire population of the capital to rally at once to the Soviet. . . ."[78] More specific than the Duma's, the Soviet's proclamation promised to fight "to wipe out completely the old government and to call a constituent assembly on the basis of universal, equal, direct, and secret suffrage."

But despite those fiery proclamations of the Soviet, its socialist leaders recognized that, as Marxism taught, Russia was not as yet ready for socialism, for the proletariat taking over power in a predominantly peasant country. This was, their doctrine unmistakeably instructed, the time for "a bourgeois democratic regime." Their rhetoric, the call upon the workers to arm themselves, et cetera, reflected not so much their ambitions but their fears. There was still a lingering suspicion that the bourgeoisie might betray the revolution, and the Provisional Committee of the Duma might try even now to make a deal with what remained of the imperial regime. Up to now this had been a Petrograd revolution. The tsar was still in the picture, and what was much more important and alarming, there were the generals with millions of loyal troops under their command.

The other fear, more acute, was that the Duma committee might in effect say, and this would be in line with Marxian logic, that there was no room for two rival governments in the capital, that the Soviet was by definition a strike and/or revolutionary organization, that with the revolution having been won and the strike over, there was no further need for it. Marx had never said that the bourgeois democratic regime should have a soviet looking over its shoulder!

February 28 might have been a propitious day for the Duma leaders to issue such an ultimatum. To the Soviet's anguish, the population of the city, both civilian and military, appeared to recognize the Provisional Committee of the Duma as the legitimate successor of the old regime. Somehow, most of the armed rabble of the day before sought now to return to being soldiers. Regiment after regiment, with their officers leading them, would march in perfect order to the Tauride Palace to pledge allegiance to the Provisional Committee. Members of the latter had by the day's end shouted themselves hoarse from perorating to the warriors, praising them for their disciplined behavior, reminding them that the war was still on, and raising cheers for Mother Russia.

The soldiers were opting for the Duma, among other things, because of the instinct for self-preservation. The Provisional Committee was the only organ which would be able to complete peacefully the transfer of power and thus save them from punishment. Who else stood any chance of making the tsar abdicate or of being recognized by the generals and by the country at large as the legitimate government? Were the Soviet to take full charge, the most that could be expected was a civil war, but more likely some army corps would move on the rebellious capital and subdue it without much resistance. Strangely enough, no one within the Provisional Committee perceived the strength of its position vis-à-vis the extremists, or foresaw the horrendous consequences of its continued coexistence with the Soviet. And for two of its members who were also on the latter's Executive Committee, it would have been difficult to take sides.

It was the awareness of its vulnerability which prompted the Soviet on March 1 to issue Order No. 1. Its language was probably intentionally ambiguous. Some of those who voted for it may well have thought that the order applied only to the garrison of Petrograd, yet most must have sensed that they were striking a blow at the morale of the whole Russian army. The order commanded all military units to form their own soviets. Every company, warship, division, et cetera, was to be under the authority of its own soldiers' council and ultimately under that of the Petrograd Soviet. The soviets were to control all the weapons, *"which under no conditions are to be handed over to the officers,* even if they request them."[79] Any grievances of the rank and file were to be adjudicated by the soviets. The old forms of saluting and address between soldiers and officers were abolished. Confusingly and somewhat humorously, the order stipulated that when discharging military duties, every soldier should observe the strictest discipline.

An appeal of this kind, unless quickly countermanded, was bound to undercut any effort to reintroduce order in the capital's garrison and in due time to destroy the morale of the entire army. But the Provisional Committee of the Duma was in no mood, or as its members believed, in no condition, to seek a confrontation with the Soviet. It might still have a struggle on its hands on another front.

As of March 1 there still had to be some fear of the emperor ordering loyal troops to reconquer the capital. Up to and through February 27 Nicholas II had remained deaf to all the appeals and anguished warnings that the salvation of the regime, of the dynasty itself, required the immediate appointment of a man trusted by the public, such as Prince Lvov, with a free hand to form the cabinet. He had remained deaf to the frantic pleas and messages pouring into headquarters from Rodzianko, Golitsin, his brother Grand Duke Michael, even the empress, who telegraphed "concessions are necessary." Instead he ordered an elderly general at the head of a single battalion (larger units were to be detached from the front and join him later) to go to Petrograd, there to assume dictatorial powers and crush the uprising. Only at 5:00 A.M., February 28, did the tsar himself, his main concern now the safety of his family, set out from Mogilev by train for Tsarskoye Selo.

The prospect of Nicholas II returning to the capital while still tsar alarmed the Provisional Committee. More reasonably, they had to be apprehensive about the possibility of front-line units, no matter how small, arriving in Petrograd. On behalf of the committee, railway authorities were instructed to prevent all trains from headquarters from reaching the city's vicinity. At 3:00 P.M. March 1, without any mishap, the imperial train reached a railway station with the ominous and infuriatingly symbolic name Dno (in Russian "bottom"). Here the emperor and his entourage were told that it would be dangerous for them to try to continue to Tsarskoye Selo. After some hesitation on Nicholas's part, the train was rerouted to Pskov, three hours away and headquarters of the Northern Army Group commanded by General Nicholas Ruzsky.

The general had been in touch with Rodzianko, the president of the Duma and head of its Provisional Committee. Immediately upon the emperor's arrival, General Ruzsky made it clear to him that the situation brooked no delay: he must appoint a responsible ministry headed by Rodzianko. The pressure was reinforced by General Alexeyev's message in the same vein, the chief of staff thoughtfully enclosing the text of the rescript in which Nicholas should announce his decision. Now utterly broken in spirit, the tsar agreed to the measure, which if put in effect one week before, would at least have delayed the fall of the monarchy. Now it was much too late. The Provisional Committee was already transforming itself into a government, and it was not the emperor's approval that it felt it had to secure. When late at night Ruzsky called Rodzianko with the news, the latter informed him that in view of what had been happening, Nicholas could not be allowed to retain the throne.

March 2 marked the end of the three-hundred-year-old dynasty. From Mogilev General Alexeyev contacted all the commanders-in-chief, including Grand Duke Nicholas in the Caucasus. They all concurred with him in the absolute necessity and urgency of the emperor abdicating in favor of his son, Alexis, with Grand Duke Michael as regent. By now the erstwhile autocrat of All Russia needed little persuading and in the early afternoon indicated to Ruzsky his agreement to step down in favor of his little son.

Even so, an announcement to this effect could not be made for the emperor was informed that two emissaries had been dispatched from what was now the Provisional Government to obtain his resignation in writing. While awaiting their arrival, Nicholas rethought his original decision. He inquired of his personal physician whether there was any chance of Alexis ever being cured of his ailment —Rasputin had assured him that once the tsarevich survived to a certain age, his hemophilia would disappear. The boy might indeed live longer than either of them, the doctor answered, but his disease was incurable. The idea of parting with the sick child—Nicholas could hardly expect to retain Alexis around him, or indeed to remain in Russia after he abdicated—was intolerable to the father. Therefore, when the emissaries arrived that same evening, he announced his resolve to resign also on behalf of the boy, with the throne going to his brother Michael. The envoys were dumbfounded; there was no precedent for the sovereign renouncing the throne and bypassing the legitimate heir. What was more to the point, the Duma envoys, both fervent monarchists, hoped that the idea of a boy emperor might assuage the Soviet, which had been proclaiming noisily its intention to be done with the Romanovs and the monarchy altogether. But this, for him supreme, sacrifice, Nicholas would not make. Later, back in Mogilev, the patriot prevailing over the father in him, the deposed emperor wanted to reverse his decision and to agree to Alexis's succession, but by that time the whole issue became irrelevant. The throne passed to Michael whom the Abdication

Manifesto, hastily composed in headquarters and signed by Nicholas, called upon "to govern in union and harmony with the representatives of the people according to such principles as they shall see fit to establish." There was one more favor his visitors sought. The Provisional Committee of the Duma had now given birth to the Provisional Government of Russia, and they were eager to preserve the fiction of a legal transfer of power. The ex-tsar agreed to appoint Prince Lvov as premier and Grand Duke Nicholas Nikolayevich as commander-in-chief, and the nominations were dated so as to make them appear to have been made prior to the abdication.

Returning from what in their view was a tragic mission,* the emissaries met with another shock. The revolution had not remained still during their brief half-day absence from the capital. Right there at the railway station they hastened to inform the assembled crowd that Russia now had a new emperor, Michael II. The crowd, composed mostly of workers, reacted indignantly, and Guchkov and his companion barely escaped being beaten up. Even before, when informed by telegrams from Pskov of what had happened, a majority of their Duma colleagues had decided that Michael should not be allowed to rule. It is difficult to decide how genuine and deep were the antimonarchist feelings amongst the urban masses. What mattered most was probably the soldiers' feeling that a link, no matter how tenuous, with the old regime might lead to their being held accountable for the revolt.

The issue was decided, like everything else in those days, in a hectic manner, at a hastily improvised meeting between the Grand Duke Michael—"tsar"—and the leading politicians. Only Milyukov and Guchkov were ready to argue the case for monarchy. From a politician, sometime demagogue, the former reverted to being a historian, pleading passionately that the country's whole past taught that Russia could never be ruled by a committee, "I was arguing that to stabilize the new order we needed a firm government, such as could be provided only by the regime shielded by that symbol of authority to which the masses have grown accustomed."[80] Without that symbol—monarchy—the Provisional Government would not survive. Others present remained silent, or hinted to the grand duke that his life (and very likely, they felt, their own) would be endangered should he accept the invidious burden. It was his duty to accept, shouted the professor, pleading that if need be, the government should leave Petrograd for Moscow or for the army headquarters.† Yet it was obvious that no matter how brave, the grand duke would not be able to undertake to reign with figures as influential as Kerensky and Prince Lvov resolutely set against it.

March 4 brought the official announcement of both renunciations. There had

---

*Despite the fact that one of them, Guchkov, had had a personal vendetta against Nicholas.
†Moscow, as of March 1, had been conquered by the revolution.

been a spirited debate among the Duma leaders whether Michael could abdicate in view of the fact that he had never reigned. Finally it was agreed that his manifesto should state that he refused to assume the throne. In any case, his renunciation, or whatever it was, proclaimed that he was willing to rule only when and if the Constituent Assembly, democratically elected by the people, should decide to offer him the crown. Until the Assembly materialized, obviously a distant prospect under war conditions, he called upon the citizens "to obey the Provisional Government," which rather unrealistically the document described as "being invested with full power by the State Duma."[81]

It took nine days to bring about the downfall of the political system which in some of its essential characteristics had remained the same since the end of the Mongol rule over Russia, more than four centuries before.

What kind of regime was it then as of March 4? Certainly not a monarchy, nor yet a republic. Its essential characteristic was expressed in the first part of its title: "Provisional."

Legitimacy and leadership are the two main ingredients of any viable form of government. From the beginning there was very little feeling of legitimacy surrounding this new strange creation. "Who elected you," Milyukov was asked when at a public meeting he read the names of new ministers. The only answer he could think of was "We were elected by the Russian Revolution."[82] If nine days of riots had elected ministers, then a few other days might overthrow them. He could have answered "the State Duma" and thus tried to grasp some shreds of legitimacy still lying around after the old regime had been smashed. But for Milyukov and for his party, the Kadets, who constituted the nucleus of the Provisional Government, the Fourth Duma had been born in sin: it represented mainly the propertied class and not the people. Still, why not keep it going until the Constituent Assembly could take over? After all, it had been, and very much so, part of "the Russian Revolution." Apart from their feelings of guilt about their class origins, the liberals could not help suspecting that the originally very conservative majority of the Duma might, despite their recent and quite revolutionary behavior, again become so. Better the hazards of coexistence with the pesky Soviet than that.

The Provisional Government added up to a very unusual political organism; a council of ministers with no head of state (which would prove embarrassing when ministers had to be changed or reshuffled) and with no legislature.

When it came to leadership, it would seem that the Provisional Government and its followers were abundantly endowed. Here were the fighters for freedom, politicians of practically all persuasions who over the past decades had become known to the whole nation, eminent lawyers, professors, businessmen, the elite of Russian society. Having been in the forefront of the liberation struggle, the intelligentsia were now in the seat of power. Alas, they had always talked and written, often brilliantly, about government and politics but never practiced it. Nothing in their background had prepared them to take over the reins of power in a country where most of the traditional forms of authority had or were visibly crumbling, a country that had never experienced real freedom and hence the self-discipline it requires, a country that was at war.

There was Kerensky. His photographs circa 1917 suggest an actor in the title role of a modern dress *Hamlet.* But at the moment his histrionic gift enabled him to come closest to being universally acknowledged as the leader of the revolution. They all—monarchists, Bolsheviks, liberals—crowded around the man in those days. Later on most of them would remember him with hatred or scorn, but at the moment he was seen as the hope of the revolution and of the nation. It was Kerensky who galvanized the hesitant Duma into action on February 27. Then, when mutinous soldiers began to arrest and drag to the Tauride Palace the old regime's ministers and satraps, it was he who protected them from being lynched by the mob. An eye witness described the scene: "[Kerensky] was terribly pale, his eyes burning . . . his upraised arm . . . warning the crowd. . . . They all recognized him, parted, making a path for him, obviously frightened of the apparition. . . . [Addressing the armed soldiers about to attack Protopopov] he shouted, 'No one dare touch this man.' " The victorious revolution does not shed blood, Kerensky then proclaimed, more calmly to the cowed crowd. And that day he saved many others.[83]

In the first Provisional Government Kerensky accepted the post of minister of justice. This ran against the Soviet's previous decision that its members—Kerensky was its vice-chairman—should not expose themselves to the ideological pollution inherent in being a member of the "bourgeois-democratic" regime. On March 2 Kerensky appeared before the Soviet to explain his action. His speech on the occasion, while tempestuously applauded, must have stirred doubts in some people's minds whether the orator was in fact cast for the role of Russia's savior.

Comrades, in my hands are the representatives of the old regime, and I have resolved to keep them in my hands. [Loud applause. Shouts of "Right"] . . . Once I became minister I ordered the release of all political prisoners. . . . [Loud applause turning into an ovation] . . . Since I became minister of justice . . . I hereby resign as deputy chairman of the Soviet of the Workers' Deputies. But comrades, I cannot live without the people, and I am ready to resume the post [of deputy chairman] if you think you need me. [Shouts: "We ask you to."] Comrades, though I am in the Provisional Government, I remain what I have always been, a republican. In my office I need the people's support. . . . Can I trust you as I trust myself? [Loud applause, shouts of "Comrade believe in us."] It is unthinkable for me to live without the people's support, and when you no longer trust me, kill me.[84]

This was typical of Kerensky's style during the few months that he dominated the revolutionary scene. And the style was contagious; revolutionary Russia was being launched and would continue to be swayed by powerful gusts of hot air.

Its official leader, Prince Lvov, had more in common with his last tsarist predecessor, Golitsin, than just an ancient title. There was an air of unreality surrounding both men, so that for most people the eight months separating the February revolution from its October sequel are known, and rightly so, as the Kerensky period even though the great orator was not to replace Lvov as prime minister until July. Ideally suited to head an eleemosynary institution which was essentially what he had been doing or to be president of a peacetime constitutional regime, the prince was unable to cope with a job and a situation which would have taxed the ingenuity of a political genius. If there was something surrealistic about Kerensky's style, then Prince Lvov exuded an air of abstraction far beyond the grasp of an ordinary mortal.

How marvelous is the Russian Revolution in its grandiose and tranquil [sic] progress. What is wonderful about it is not merely the fairy-like quality of its arrival, nor its gigantic uplift, not the strength and speed with which it stormed and seized power, but principally the essence of its leading idea. The freedom which revolution brings is permeated with elements characteristic of the whole world, nay, the universe. The ideas which have grown from small seeds planted in the fertile soil of a half-century ago have blossomed to express the interests not only of the Russian nation, but of the whole world. The Russian people's soul has revealed itself as being democratic in all its aspects. It [the soul] is ready not only to merge with the democracy of the whole world, but to forge ahead of it, and to lead it along the path of mankind's progress, according to the great principles of freedom, equality, brotherhood.[85]

Here then were the leaders who were respectively the new regime's strong man and its official head. Yet it still took eight months to reduce this regime to a state somewhat reminiscent of that of the tsar's before its fall. What held it up? The government kept functioning, and for the first few weeks not too badly. The army did not run away. Desertions to be sure increased fivefold following the revolution, but as late as October an army of five million still held the front against the Germans and the Austrians.

The explanation must be sought beyond the politicians, parties, the soviets. The revolution brought a tremendous explosion of freedom, freedom such as the Russian nation had never known in its history. Even in its decrepitude old Russia had been a police state, with arbitrary arrests, censorship, the oppressive, often brutal, officialdom. Now came freedom, and with it the resurgence of patriotism and of the sense of civic obligation. In March 1917 Russia became, the words come not from a Menshevik or a liberal, but from Lenin, the freest country in the world. That is why the preposterously unworkable political system born out of the revolution appeared at first so full of vitality and hope. But then Russia's freedom, like its government, was to be "temporary."*

*The Russian word for *provisional* also means *temporary.*

Chapter 6

"THE FREEST COUNTRY IN THE WORLD": RUSSIA, MARCH-OCTOBER 1917

PARADOXICALLY, the immediate impact of the revolution was more bewildering for those who had lived and worked for it for years than for the average citizen. The latter, though not quite clear in his mind how it happened, still knew, and for the moment this was all that he cared about, that on February 27 Russia had been an autocracy, and then on March 3, she became—free. But for the former, it was a dream and the revolutionary activists even now were not sure that this dream had really and fully come true. "As everyone knows, revolution is a vision and not something which really happens" was the way one of them described his initial reaction to the February events.[1]

For educated Russians, March 3 marked not only the end of the old regime but an abrupt collapse of the whole world of political concepts and verities with which they had lived for generations. Chief among these was the belief that political life was an unending struggle between autocracy and society, with autocracy embodying the nation's power, and society its intelligence and conscience. Though antagonistic, their relationship, and this was the sudden revelation which dawned on many in those first days of March, was also in a curious way symbiotic. For *society,* and its near synonyms *public opinion* and *the intelligentsia,* could not be defined as merely an aggregate of lawyers, doctors, progressive capitalists, landowners, but principally as a force pressing upon the autocracy to persuade it to reform itself. The revolution in that scheme had been thought

304

of as a covert or at times an open ally of society. If attempts at persuading the autocracy to mend its ways would continue to remain unavailing, then there was always the threat of revolution or just enough of it, as in 1905, to force it to capitulate. It would surrender not to a class or, what would be even more absurd, to some political party, but to the people, that is, to the ideas of democracy and freedom for which society had fought and suffered. The greatest harm done by the autocracy to Russia was that by denying or perverting popular participation in government, it had accustomed the nation to think of politics in terms of high historic and moral abstractions rather than as a mundane humdrum occupation.

This fatal habit was to persist beyond the February revolution. Political pragmatism would come into its own only with October.

For the moment in those early March days the bewildered victors felt as their most urgent priority not the reconstruction of the crumbling machinery of government but a reformulation of their own shattered *Weltanschauung*. Autocracy had evaporated. How then could there still remain a society, that amalgam of liberals, radicals, near revolutionaries, and of late also many conservatives and nationalists whose only common characteristic lay in their opposition to the government? Whom or what did the new government represent? One could not eschew such perplexing questions by saying that *society, the people*, had been convenient political abstractions, and that now there was no further need for them but rather for some very practical measures to hold the country together. Nor would many Russians of that generation be satisfied if someone pointed out that the Provisional Government was composed of distinguished public figures and the important thing was not what class or principle it embodied but whether it would be allowed to, and how well it could, govern. Such answers from practically every point of the political spectrum would have been decried as cynical, the kind of philistinism one might have expected from a tsarist bureaucrat and not from a representative of new Russia.

The ideological rationale for what had happened was constructed, like everything in those days, hastily, partly by improvisation, and partly out of various elements which in their origin can be traced to John Stuart Mill, Karl Marx, Nicholas Chernyshevsky, et cetera. The English liberal would have been pleased by the proclamation, in wartime at that, of unconditional freedom of expression and by the fact that after originally balking at the idea, the Petrograd Soviet licensed the publication of papers of even the most reactionary hue. The sage of Russian populism would in turn have approved the attitude of the people (occasional mayhem by armed sailors or workers) which made expression of reactionary views risky and rare and which in general displayed a healthy disregard for Western-legalism and scruples, as was soon to become evident in events such as the peasants seizing and partitioning the landlords' estates.

Russia's Failed Revolutions

Karl Marx, the philosopher of history and economic determinist, played a rather inhibiting role in the beginning, and it was only with the return in April of his most eminent pupil that Marx the revolutionary surged to the fore. But even before Lenin's appearance on the scene, Marxism, or more properly its curious by-product, the Soviet, had become an integral part of the picture. The clandestine socialist parties, the Mensheviks, the Socialist Revolutionaries, and to a lesser extent the Bolsheviks, played a vital role in the revolutionary events and in setting up the Soviet. Yet the bizarre system of dual power—the Provisional Government and the Soviet—and the whole philosophy of revolutionary democracy (ultimately fatal for these institutions), emanating not from the workers but from the minds of a small group of intellectuals not formally connected with any of the socialist parties, was initially much more decisive in determining the role of the Soviet than any of the official socialist leaders.

Here again is an illustration of how seemingly small accidental things can affect great historical events. Most of the great figures of the revolution were in those days almost uninterruptedly on their feet, either perorating or running from one end of Petrograd to another for their speaking engagements, to calm the soldiers, arouse the workers, reassure the officers and other categories of the population.* For some this feverish activity followed not only the pace of events but reflected their temperament. Kerensky's sobriquet in the secret police files had been "Swifty." He was famous for his ability to throw off a police agent trailing him by jumping in and out of moving tramcars.

Mao notwithstanding, power in the first days of the revolution came not so much out of the mouth of the gun, as out of the mouth—oratory—and from the printed page. Every group tried to be the first with a fiery proclamation, appealing to the aspirations and fears of the multitude, by publicizing its own version of events, and by providing an elegant theoretical explanation of what was happening and what must follow, one which would be intelligible to the worker and convincing to the intellectual. The Kerenskys, Shlyapnikovs, and their like were constantly on the move, or burdened with committee meetings where one talked and argued without end. So the bulk of the theoretical and literary work of the Soviet was delegated to a handful of intellectuals who despite all the excitement around them were still capable of sitting down and drafting those resolutions, appeals, and articles which for the moment were the main weapons in the hands of the revolutionary democracy. What they wrote was quickly and often without any discussion—there was no time—approved by the Executive Committee or the Soviet as a whole.

*The problem was complicated by the fact that public transportation, paralyzed on February 26, did not resume until the second week of March. Automobiles and horse carriages were hard to find. And it was thought not quite proper for a revolutionary leader to resort to them.

One such accidental maker of history was Yuri Steklov, entrusted by the Soviet with editing its organ, *Izvestia,* which for a few days was the only paper appearing in the capital. As such this litterateur and essayist who had oscillated between the Bolsheviks and Mensheviks became the official spokesman for revolutionary democracy, as influential, if not more so, than its titular leader, the uncharacteristically phlegmatic Georgian, Chheidze. Russia being the freest country in the world, it did not occur to Steklov that what he wrote should be bound by the wishes of his employer, the Executive Committee of the Soviet. The latter was and would remain for a long time predominantly defensist in its attitude. Steklov was strongly antiwar and his editorials were inflammatory in their explicit attacks upon the Provisional Government and the army hierarchy. "He talked about counterrevolution, about the counterrevolutionary generals at Headquarters, that one should have them chained and ruthlessly sentenced; [or] proclaim them outside the law, so that anyone could with impunity kill them."[2] At the time even the Bolsheviks did not indulge in the kind of demagoguery Steklov was spewing from the columns of *Izvestia.* The majority of the Executive Committee found itself in a quandary concerning Steklov: he was clearly misrepresenting the Soviet's position and endangering its already strained coexistence with the Provisional Government. But one could not fire a man just because he was farther to the left. In order to discredit their troublesome collaborator, his Socialist colleagues dug into his past and uncovered a scandal. His real name was Nahamkis. It was quite usual and felt proper for a Jewish revolutionary to adopt a Russian-sounding name for his party work, e.g., Trotsky, Kamenev, and many others. But Nahamkis-Steklov had applied to the tsarist authorities to have it legally changed, a shameful un-Socialist attempt to conceal one's Jewish origins. He was not fired from his job as editor of the Soviet's organ, but he became nonetheless much more circumspect in what he wrote.

Another accidental and temporary leader of revolutionary democracy who, however, left a lasting imprint on the whole tone of its activity was Nicholas Sokolov. Before February he had been a well-known lawyer with wide contacts in liberal circles, his apartment on the Okhrana's list as one of the gathering places for activists of the left. His profession notwithstanding, Sokolov became one of the main organizers of the Petrograd Soviet of Workers' Deputies, indeed at its first meeting arrogated to himself the role of its leader. "He ran around issuing instructions, telling the deputies where to sit, et cetera. With an air of authority, though no one had authorized him to do it, he was telling those present which ones among them had the right to vote, who was there in an advisory capacity, and who had no business to be there in the first place."[3] He was soon replaced as the leader of the Petrograd proletariat by Chheidze, also a somewhat incongruous choice since the latter, though a Socialist member of the Duma, had been elected from Georgia. But the victorious revolution paid no heed to such details.

Sokolov's place in history is secure. He drafted the celebrated and fateful Order No. 1, which marked the beginning of the end of the Russian army. "N. D. Sokolov was sitting behind a writing desk. He was surrounded, they were virtually glued to him, by soldiers, some standing, others sitting or sprawled on the desk; they were telling, if not dictating to Sokolov what to say. He kept writing."[4]

The most interesting of the trio of gray eminences in these early days of the Soviet was undoubtedly Nicholas Sukhanov. He typifies the air of unreality in which Russia and the revolution were swathed. We have become accustomed to seeing such people in our own time; otherwise it would be hard to believe that a man like that really existed and said the things he did, rather than being a fictional character in a satire from the pen of a latter-day Dostoyevsky.

How typically unreal had been his existence already under the old regime, or rather how unreal the regime under which such an existence was possible! As early as 1914 Sukhanov was banned by the police from residing in Petrograd for his radical writings. Sukhanov continued to live there, not quite illegally, for he worked peacefully under his real name, Nicholas Himmer, in the Ministry of Agriculture. By profession a statistician and economist, he attended conscientiously to problems of agriculture and irrigation of Russian central Asia. The bureaucrat Himmer was at the same time the revolutionary publicist Sukhanov, the name under which he published cautiously subversive articles in Maxim Gorky's *Chronicle*, which provided shelter for radical intellectuals of all varieties. (Gorky's literary renown, as well as his connections in high society—he associated with grand dukes almost as easily as with the Lenins and Chaliapins—kept the paper, for all of its distinctly revolutionary tinge, from being shut down.) The Sukhanov-Himmer mode of life involved one inconvenience: he had to change occasionally his lodging for the night, but then most Russian intellectuals, even if only casual acquaintances, would consider it an honor to offer hospitality to one allegedly hunted by the secret police for his political beliefs.

Like other revolutionaries, Sukhanov may not have been ready for the revolution. But at the very hour it happened he was ready with an answer to the question always so perplexing to Russia's radicals: what is to be done? More quickly than Lenin, Kerensky, and others, he saw what a true democrat, revolutionary, and a representative of the working class (all of which Sukhanov believed himself to be) must strive for: to force the bourgeoisie to take over power. His reasons may seem bizarre and unwittingly humorous, but to the majority of Russian Marxists they had the ring of compelling logic. And if we are tempted to smile at Sukhanov's torturous reasoning, we should remember that the scenario he sketched did in fact become the first act of the revolutionary drama, not only for Russia but also for several other societies since.

Revolutionary democracy, so began the argument, was utterly incapable of ruling Russia. "It could not cope with the technical side of government, especially under the present desperate conditions, it could not overcome the [remaining] forces of the old regime, nor those represented by the bourgeoisie, both hostile to it [i.e., the proletariat-revolutionary democracy]."⁵ Therefore, "Soviet democracy should hand over power to its class enemy, the bourgeoisie."

So far this has been just a variation on the old Marxist theme that Russia, not having completed her capitalist cycle, was not ready for socialism, and hence every orthodox Marxist, painful though it might be, must acquiesce in a "bourgois democratic" regime, which in due course, probably decades, will be destroyed by its then fully grown offspring, the class-conscious proletariat. But here Sukhanov introduces an interesting and fairly innovative variant: "The power handed over to the class enemy, must be the *kind of power* which would afford democracy *the fullest freedom of struggling* against the enemy, that is, the holder of power. And *the conditions* under which power is given [to the bourgeoisie] must be such as would assure Soviet democracy of fully vanquishing the bourgeoisie in the near future." The capitalist government then is to be used as a very temporary expedient, a tool for hastening its own destruction. Its power is to be attended by so many restrictions and reservations that it would amount in fact to the right of a prisoner under a death sentence to make dispositions for his funeral.

If Sukhanov's phrasing was fairly original, he did not invent the formula. It was a fatuous idea whose time had come: a glimpse of it can already be seen in Trotsky's and Parvus's theory of "permanent revolution" of some years before and which was implicit in the whole arrangement of "dual power"—the Soviet and the Provisional Government. But the credit for creating an elegant Marxist theory to explain the unworkable arrangements, or if one prefers, of being embarrassingly candid about its real purpose, belongs undeniably to this man.

Inherent in his formulations there was also, undoubtedly, a strong personal motivation. Sukhanov represented the breed of Russian intelligent of whom it has been said that they knew about everything and could do nothing. It is perhaps not quite fair to say this of Sukhanov, evidently a competent statistician, a profession he would again pursue in Soviet Russia until like so many others of his background, he disappeared in the purges of the 1930s. Sukhanov became the Boswell of the revolution, producing, at a time when one could still write honestly about it, an invaluable chronicle of the events in which at first he had played an important part. Yet it is impossible to imagine him doing something in politics, rather than talking and writing about it. Trotsky's judgment of Sukhanov is not far off the mark: "a conscientious observer rather than a statesman, a journalist rather than a revolutionary . . . capable of standing by a revolutionary conception only up to the time it becomes necessary to carry it into action."

It is thus not surprising that Sukhanov acknowledged that his formula had one potential weakness: "Would the capitalist class in Russia accept power under those conditions," and agree to embark cheerfully upon digging its own grave? Hence the most difficult task for revolutionary democracy lay in "forcing the capitalists to accept power, compelling them to embark upon, for them, this risky experiment."[6] It was with trepidation that Sukhanov watched as Milyukov (whom he considered the key man on the enemy side) threatened at times to go on strike so to speak, and when confronted with a particularly outrageous demand by the Soviet, would warn that he might resign from the Provisional Government and take his Kadet friends with him. How typical of the perfidious bourgeoisie to try to undo the revolution by forcing the proletariat, that is, its Socialist leaders, to assume full powers, inevitably making a mess of things, and thus discrediting themselves and Socialism in the eyes of the masses!

The prospect of having to govern, instead of remaining a half-government, terrified not only the Sukhanovs and Steklovs, but even the more responsible spokesmen for the Soviet. Indeed, at the time even the Bolsheviks were not serious when they declaimed against the Provisional Government and in favor of a truly proletarian revolutionary regime. The official stance of revolutionary democracy was that having won the revolution, it displayed great magnanimity and self-denial in letting those capitalists form a government, and then allowing it some powers, and protecting it from the masses. In fact, in March and April, at least, it was the Provisional Government which provided a shield behind which the Soviet could indulge in its revolutionary pyrotechnics, without as yet having to worry about the resultant fires. A completely socialist government would not have been accepted by the army, in fact by most of Russia outside the two capitals. Indeed, without the presence, at once soothing and irritating, of the bourgeois ministry which interposed itself between the Soviet and public opinion, it is doubtful whether the former would have survived the outrage over such actions as Order No. 1, or even (excluding the possibility of some general moving with his troops to liquidate them forcibly) whether the Soviet's leaders could long have retained the confidence of their constituents.

Here was another pathetic aspect of revolutionary democracy's reluctance to be associated with the actual business of governing; its leaders were not only diffident about their abilities but also fearful that once their administrative incompetence was revealed their followers would quickly become disenchanted and melt away.

One possible way out of the impasse would have been for the Socialist notables to participate in the Provisional Government, and this is what Prince Lvov was to propose at the end of April, when dual power had already and amply demonstrated its disastrous consequences. The Soviet's leader, Chheidze, then recalled how he had been offered a ministerial portfolio (of labor) on the morrow of the revolution but had refused because "I was in the evening of my life [he was in his early fifties] and did not feel that I possessed the necessary qualifications." In any case the Executive Committee of the Soviet then decided that its members as a rule should not become ministers.

The decision I believe was correct. By remaining outside the government the Soviet, in the eyes of the masses, gained authority, which enabled it to organize them and to establish democracy throughout the country. When we defend a bourgeois rather than our own government from attack and say that no conceivable government could establish peace and carry out basic reforms right away, then the masses trust us and see that under such circumstances the socialists should not become ministers. But were we to enter the government *we would arouse among the masses the kind of hopes and expectations which in fact we would not be able to fulfill.* [7]

Here an outsider, even one most sympathetic to the non-Bolshevik left, is bound to lose his patience with these people and wonder why in Heaven's name when they would not and could not govern themselves, they had first set out to overthrow tsarism, and then made life impossible for the first Provisional Government.

In all fairness to revolutionary democracy, it is most doubtful whether the Provisional Government would have been more successful had it been entirely on its own, rather than constantly and suspiciously chaperoned by the Soviet. The latter was not invariably obstructive, nor unsympathetic to the bourgeois democratic regime, at times indeed it attempted to bolster the government's authority and tried to restrain the rising tide of anarchy. The relationship of the two half-governments might be compared to that of a pair of shipwrecks trying to row a leaking boat to safety. They are constantly arguing as to the direction to be taken, which one ought to steer while the other bails out, but both derive some comfort from the other's presence.

Having acted as the midwife of the new and bizarre regime, the Duma was informed that its services were no longer needed. Rodzianko made a valiant argument that if not the chamber as a whole, then its Provisional Committee might still perform a useful function, but no one knew what it could be: it was bad enough to have two governments without adding another body which might have ideas on that score. There was also a legal technicality—the Duma had been prorogued by the former emperor. No one could now summon it into session. Nor could it be dissolved; that would have been an act of parricide on the part of the

Provisional Government. So the last real parliament of Russia continued its shadowy existence, its members not meeting as a body but collecting their monthly checks, until the end of its appointed term, a few days before the Bolshevik coup in October.

In concrete terms and eschewing all the euphemisms, such as *revolutionary democracy* and *democratic bourgeoisie*, the post-February revolutionary government resulted from a bargain struck by two groups of intelligentsia, the liberal one, as represented by the Provisional Government, and the radical one, for that was the intellectual and political milieu from which most leaders of the Soviet came, Chheidze, Skobelev, and Kerensky, not to speak of the Sokolovs and Sukhanovs. The dichotomy of bourgeoisie versus proletariat, which the two groups allegedly represented, was also very largely a fiction insofar as their social and economic backgrounds were concerned, for there was nary a real proletarian in the high command of the Soviet and few real capitalists in the first Provisional Government. Milyukov, currently on the right, was an architect's son; Kerensky's father, the director of a high school, a post of considerable social prestige in tsarist Russia, which usually brought with it a title of nobility.* Noble titles in Russia were not always a reliable guide to their possessors' economic or even social status: Prince Lvov was actually a moderately well-to-do landowner and in every other respect a fairly typical liberal intelligent. Among members of his cabinet Alexander Konovalov, minister of trade, could be classified as an industrialist, and Guchkov, minister of war and navy, came from a well-known Moscow merchant family. But the only minister who fitted the popular stereotype of a capitalist was the minister of finance, Michael Tereshchenko, a sugar magnate from the Ukraine.†

The leading figures of both the Soviet and the government had been brought up in the ethos of the intelligentsia, an ethos which exalted opposition to the powers that be, rather than the acquisition of the skills and habits needed to govern Russia at that decisive hour of her existence. Politics, the intelligentsia's creed urged, was simply a matter of following the right principles or enacting the right kind of laws. Democracy, though it might be differently defined by the radicals and the liberals, was for both groups a universal salve for all social and economic problems.

It was thus characteristic that the initial declaration of the Provisional Govern-

---

*One of Fyodor Kerensky's prize pupils in the Simbirsk gymnasium was Vladimir Ulyanov, who as Lenin would cut short his (Kerensky's) son's political career.

†"Who is Tereshchenko?" were the shouts from the crowd when Milyukov read the list of ministers, all the other names well known and meeting, supposedly, the standard the Provisional Government set for its members. Tereshchenko's past public activities had been mainly those of a patron of music. The twenty-nine-year-old millionaire was probably chosen because of his Masonic connection with Kerensky and Konavalov, rather than, as Milyukov replied to the crowd, because "his name is famous in southern Russia."

ment setting out its program of action had nothing to say about such pressing problems as inflation, food shortages, and the need to preserve public order in a country which had just experienced the traumatic shock of seeing the traditional foundation of all authority overthrown within a few days. The fullest possible freedom and democracy were to be the solution to all those ills and dangers. Under the circumstances it was natural that an "immediate and complete amnesty" should have been considered the first priority but another revolutionary regime might have hesitated in extending it in *"all* cases of a political and religious nature, including terrorist acts, military revolts, and agrarian offences, et cetera."[8] Russia after all was at war. Agrarian offenses obviously included such things as the burning of landlords' residences and crops, while "military revolts" included not only the mutiny of the Petrograd garrison, but other cases of military insubordination even if they did not have anything to do with politics. Were those imprisoned for participating in anti-Jewish pogroms to be released if their crimes had been politically motivated?

Ironically the amnesty was proclaimed on March 6, the same day that, at the insistence of the Soviet, the ex-emperor and his family were ordered placed under arrest to be imprisoned in Tsarskoye Selo. Several of the old regime's officials would continue in jail, despite the amnesty and the fact that from a legal point of view, there was no case against them. At the same time, murderers, arsonists, the expropriators of public and private funds, in many cases ordinary rather than political offenders were being let loose upon society. And so were the sailors in Kronstadt who, having seized the base during the revolution, massacred over forty captive officers.

The Kadets, who constituted the core of the new government, had long been committed to a fully democratic legislature. Hence the declaration that a Constituent Assembly would be elected on the basis of universal (including women), equal, and direct suffrage by secret ballot. Few at the time would have objected publicly to this formula, though it would give Russia, much of whose population was still illiterate, the most democratic franchise of all the major countries in the world. As a matter of fact most of the secret misgivings on the subject were felt on the left, for no one was as yet sure how the peasant masses might vote, and whether a right-wing, indeed a monarchist party, would not still command a considerable following in the countryside.

The most ominous of the Provisional Government's original promises was its pledge to substitute a people's militia for the police "with elective officers responsible to the organs of local self-government." While reasonable for a country with long-standing traditions of local self-government, in the case of Russia this was a clear prescription for anarchy. True, the old policemen or gendarmes symbolized the autocracy, but to dispense with them this abruptly in a society where political power and administration had from time immemorial been highly centralized and where the tendency toward lawlessness and peasant *Jacqueries* was so widespread, was not liberalism, but simply foolishness.

In fact the way Prince Lvov proceeded in his other capacity, as minister of the interior, might have entitled him to claim that he was putting in practice the slogan, soon to be made famous, "All power to the Soviets." The latter indeed were already mushrooming all over Russia: workers', peasants', soldiers', while with a few strokes of a pen the prince virtually abolished the principal tool of any government, the civil service. On March 5 he dismissed by telegraph all the provincial governors and deputy governors. Their place was taken by the "commissars" (Lvov could thus lay the claim also to having invented the title later employed so widely by the Bolsheviks)—special commissioners drawn at first from presidents of the local zemstvo boards. If that were not enough, Lvov refused to stipulate the new officials' powers beyond the helpful suggestion that unlike the old tsarist governors, the commissars were not to be chief administrators of their provinces, but merely "mediating links between the central power and the local organs of self-government." It was anachronistic, said Lvov in an interview, to think of the central government as making decisions concerning local matters. Let the population of the provinces, cities, et cetera, regulate their own affairs through their freely elected representatives. The prince refused to go into the details concerning respective spheres of responsibility, launching instead into his famous rhetoric, "We are extremely fortunate to live at this great moment, happy to be able to contribute to the forging of the nation's new life, not by telling the people what to do, but by working together with them. In these historic days our nation is demonstrating its genius."9

With the government announcing in advance its hands-off attitude, much of provincial Russia was plunged into complete chaos. The existing local government institutions suffered from the same flaw as the Duma. They had been elected on the basis of class and property qualifications. Hence in many instances they were pushed aside or rendered impotent. In their place there sprang up bodies often less representative of the population at large than the old ones. A handful of radical activists would proclaim themselves the local soviet or some other institution representing the people's will. It was usually not difficult for them to "mobilize the masses," real workers, if available, if not, a random mob, to seize government buildings, disarm the demoralized police, and put old officials under arrest. Already on March 5 for example something which called itself the Executive Committee of the City's Social Organizations declared itself to be the highest civilian authority, not only for the city of Saratov, but also for the whole province.10

The unravelling of authority proceeded in the provinces at a much faster pace than at the center. If the tsarist government was by February but a phantom of its former self, then by October, on the eve of the Bolshevik coup, Russia's government was like a house hit by repeated bombings: of the once huge edifice, only the front was still standing, the rest was debris.

With the new government unwilling and/or unable to assert its authority, it is small wonder that many in the provinces found it difficult to understand why Prince Lvov's and his colleagues's actions and statements should influence the course of events in Tambov or Saratov. The new order of things appeared to have a certain logic if one lived in Petrograd or Moscow, where the Socialist leaders could control their followers and explain up to a point the intricacies of the dual power system. But in the provinces what the population saw was that the tsar was gone, and the local government and police chief had been chased out or put in jail. Why then should one pay any attention to what a group of capitalists in Petrograd, calling itself the Provisional Government, was decreeing or forbidding? If it was a revolution which was taking place, why did landlords and manufacturers still keep their ill-gotten gains and why were workers still supposed to obey their bosses? Anarchic impulses had always lain close to the surface of Russian life, and now there were no police, no whip-swinging Cossacks to keep them from erupting. At first the national jubilation over the new freedom helped keep excesses to a minimum, and the example and influence of the Petrograd Soviet tended to restrain local revolutionary democracies from launching into violence and lawlessness. But the revolution brought to the fore not only the relatively disciplined followers of Marx but also a variety of ultra-left sects and movements, some tracing their geneaology to Bakunin, who had once said, "In Russia it is the criminal who is the only real revolutionary," or Tkachev, with his slogan, "A revolutionary does not prepare a revolution . . . he makes it." Now partisans of such views could propagate them openly among the landless peasants, among the dregs of the urban masses and other elements for whom all that had happened seemed like a very pale preview of a real revolution.

Some anarchists probably were primarily responsible for an incident which, though on its face rather humorous, was a portent of many similar but more serious episodes which would afflict the country for years. On April 26 the capital press announced that the Schlusselburg district, not far from Petrograd, had been declared an independent republic by its soviet. The latter, proclaiming itself the provisional revolutionary government, ordered all former officials arrested and decreed nationalization of land and all other means of production. The Petrograd Soviet hastened to send a commission to the rebellious district to find out what had happened and if need be to stamp out the insurrection by the usual weapon of the revolution: speeches. As it turned out, the story had been somewhat exaggerated. The local soviet was about to, but had not yet declared its independence. If the government continued to be run in the old bourgeois ways, its spokesman explained, they might as well set up their own proletarian republic. After considerable oratorical efforts, the visitors, headed by Chheidze himself, were able to persuade the Schlusselburg people to return to Mother Russia, and to await with her the dawn of real socialism. Before October there would be several similar incidents, nor would they cease with the new revolution. The Bolsheviks' slogans contributed mightily to the flowering of every conceivable separatist movement, and after coming to power they would not only have to struggle against counterrevolution but also to undo the effects of their propaganda and to reconquer the country piece by piece.

The dual power formula was thus a blueprint for anarchy. In the early days of revolution one might have hoped that the very unworkability of the scheme would prove to be Russia's salvation. Surely it was logical to expect that one or the other of the half-governments would find the situation intolerable and force its partner to abdicate its claims. But politics in Russia defied logic and the alleged laws of political science. Unable to govern effectively, the Provisional Government used the existence and claims of the Soviet as a convenient excuse and a comforting rationalization for its failures. Unwilling to rule, in fact frightened by the prospect, revolutionary democracy found the presence of the bourgeois ministers greatly reassuring, and the stern watch over their activities and the occasional countermanding of their moves was as much power as it wanted.

Historically a situation of this kind has usually called for the appearance of a Cromwell or Bonaparte. But here again Russia in March 1917 seemed an exception. The possibility was very much on everybody's mind, especially radical intellectuals like Sukhanov, who had been weaned on the histories of the French and English revolutions. But after a close scrutiny of the scene, it was impossible to find a convincing candidate for the role. Nobody in his right mind could accuse Prince Lvov of the slightest proclivities (or abilities) in that direction; his personality was so self-effacing, his language so other-worldly, that the government which he headed was referred to as the Milyukov-Guchkov cabinet by those who wanted to stress its bourgeois character, or as the Kerensky after its most visible member. Kerensky's own case presented yet another paradox of this paradox-laden era. The more popular he became, and the higher he rose in the official hierarchy, the less seriously he was being taken as a leader. It was becoming clear to even his most envious enemies that it was not political power which the younger lawyer craved but office and public adulation. The first identified him increasingly with his fellow bourgeois ministers, among whom he now felt more at ease than with his erstwhile revolutionary comrades. The latter led Kerensky to expend his energies in continuous oratory, rather than in building an administrative machinery or a body of devoted followers as behooved a real candidate for dictator.

The danger of "a man on a white horse" was felt acutely by the left, one reason among others for Order No. 1. But where in the current crop of generals could one spot a likely Napoleon? Napoleon had been a child of the French Revolution; the Russian generals on the other hand all owed their careers to the old regime, and the best known among them were renowned for their skill in effecting retreats rather than for victories, of which the Russian army had had so few. The Soviet had forced Prince Lvov to revoke the appointment of Grand Duke Nicholas Nikolayevich, and the acting commander-in-chief was General Alexeyev, a conscientious military administrator, who far from having any political ambitions, kept imploring revolutionary democracy to leave him some authority over the army.

But if not a Napoleon or Cromwell, then perhaps a Robespierre? Here again the field was most unpromising. The head of the Soviet, Chheidze, was the model of an impartial chairman. It had not even occurred to the Menshevik and Socialist Revolutionary leaders of revolutionary democracy to try to keep the Bolsheviks, their vilifiers of yesterday, from places on the presidium of the Soviet. Nor did they react with more than just mild complaints to the Bolsheviks' new attacks on them for having allegedly sold out to the bourgeoisie by supporting the Provisional Government. For all their violent rhetoric, most of the Socialist leaders, not excluding as yet those on the Bolshevik side, were humane and genuinely idealistic politicians. Their revolutionary ethos made them tolerant of excesses, if spontaneously perpetrated by the masses, but restrained them from using violence as a means of solving any ideological or political quarrels within their own camp. One could not expect the revolution to pass without violence or be too surprised by instances of savagery by the sailors and soldiers or by the peasants—the people had suffered so much and for so long. But the victorious revolution must not sully its hands with blood. And it was entirely unthinkable that one should resort to force against one's fellow revolutionaries, no matter how profound their political mistakes and harmful to revolutionary democracy their activities.

There was one man who was known to scorn such niceties and to deem them unworthy of a real revolutionary and who, from afar, had let loose bolts of vituperation against his fellow Socialists for their temporizing with the class enemy. Lenin's arrival from Switzerland was being awaited with some apprehension not only by his opponents but also by quite a few Bolsheviks. His articles, which had been appearing in the revived *Pravda,* showed little understanding of what was happening in Russia, or of the current mood of the left at home. But surely once here even Ilyich would come to understand that the old controversies between the Mensheviks and the Bolsheviks, perhaps even between both of them and the Socialist Revolutionaries, had after the revolution lost their importance and that continued wrangling between the proletarian parties would only help their common enemy. In any case, other Socialists believed, even if Lenin tried, he could not stop the movement toward unity of the socialist parties, or deflect them from their present stance on the Provisional Government and the war. He was a willful and occasionally unscrupulous man, but still a Marxist. It was laughable to think of him as a would-be-dictator. No Socialist could aspire to become a dictator, and if Lenin somehow developed any ideas in that direction, his own followers, not to mention the workers at large, would soon show him!

The convoluted relationship of the Provisional Government with the Soviet was subject to constant strains, which were but little relieved by a special liaison committee between the two bodies. The Provisional Government expressed or feigned indignation at the Soviet's usurpations, the Soviet watched suspiciously for any signs that the ministers were trying to elude the restraints of revolutionary democracy. What was of special concern to even moderate Socialist leaders was any manifestation of popular support for their partners and class enemies. The bourgeois regime was supposed to govern, but not to be popular. Thus a fairly typical incident: since everyone else was doing it, high school students in Petrograd decided to demonstrate in honor of the revolution. Skipping their classes, a crowd of young people marched to the Tauride Palace carrying placards with seemingly innocent inscriptions appropriate to the hour, "We greet the Provisional Government," "Make way for young Russia," "Long live the free schools of a free country," "Keep producing shells and munitions." Nothing about the Soviet! This proved too much even for the phlegmatic Chheidze, who appeared before the youth to read them a lesson:

> I see on your banner "We greet the Provisional Government," but you must know that many of its members on the very eve of the revolution trembled and argued against it. And you hail it! Evidently you believe that it will hold high the new [revolutionary] banner. If so, go on believing it. We ourselves support it as long as it observes democratic principles. But we realize that our government is not democratic, but bourgeois. And so watch vigilantly what it does. We shall support those of its measures which are for the people's welfare, but we shall unmask those which are not, because Russia's fate is at stake.[11]

Much later Lenin was to write that when cooperating with bourgeois or reformist parties, the Communists should support them, "the way a noose supports a hanging man." Chheidze and his friends did not believe in complete strangulation of their bourgeois partners, just once in a while jerking back the leash.

What at first enabled the strange dual power arrangement to function at all was the very thing which was eventually to contribute to its downfall: the war.

It is necessary to repeat, since this point is so often ignored by historians, that this had also been a *patriotic* revolution, brought about by the general feeling that the tsarist regime was not only incapable of pursuing the war to a victorious end, but also that some within it were scheming to conclude a separate peace with German militarism. Now that Russia had shed the decrepit and treasonable autocracy, her free warriors would match, it was exultantly proclaimed, the exploits of the armies of the French Revolution, carrying on their bayonets the ideas of freedom and democracy.

This outburst of patriotic feeling was a revelation and a source of apprehension to those on the extreme left who during the February riots had seen crowds demonstrating under placards proclaiming "Down with the war." It now became clear that although the masses of soldiers and workers were indeed weary of the war, once the autocracy had fallen, they were resolutely opposed to a peace without victory. No one could have suspected soldiers of the Petrograd garrison of burning with impatience to face the foreign enemy. Those who like the Bolsheviks had convinced themselves that the Russian soldier was through with the imperialist war had been considerably cheered when at the soldiers' insistence the Soviet exacted from the Provisional Government the pledge that those units which took part in the revolutionary events of February would not be withdrawn from Petrograd without their own permission. But on the morrow of the revolution, this crowd of marauders and mutineers was seized by what seemed to an "internationalist" Socialist such as Sukhanov an incomprehensible and deplorable chauvinist passion. As he plaintively recorded, "It was easier to talk with them [the soldiers] about starting an offensive than about peace. . . . In those first weeks the soldier masses of Petrograd would not listen, let alone allow anyone to argue for peace. They were ready to bayonet those incautious enough [to talk about peace] as 'traitors' and 'people willing to open the front to the enemy.' "[12] Indeed, the Bolsheviks as well as non-Bolshevik defeatists like Sukhanov had to watch their step lest the bourgeois government mobilize this patriotic feeling against them, by picturing the extreme left and the Soviet as a whole as an unwitting ally of the enemy. Fortunately for revolutionary democracy the Milyukovs and Guchkovs had well nigh exhausted their resources for demagoguery in their campaign against the dark forces of the old regime, and Kerensky, though himself transformed within a few days of revolution from a defeatist into a defensist would still not allow any impugning of his old comrades' patriotism.

Very soon even the Bolsheviks decided that it was preferable to incur the wrath of the still-distant Lenin than to risk that of the masses by continuing to expound that this was an imperialist war. On March 12 Stalin and Kamenev arrived from their Siberian exile—another piece of luck so characteristic of Stalin's political career. He had been exiled originally in a distant location, six weeks travel from the nearest railway line. Late in 1916 he was transferred to a place only four days by train from Petrograd. Had he arrived there some weeks later, he probably would have been dispatched on party work to his native Caucasus. They had seniority over the local Bolsheviks, Stalin as a member of the party's central committee, Kamenev as its former agent in Russia. So, despite their vigorous protests, Shlyapnikov and Molotov were shoved aside, the newcomers taking over *Pravda* and Stalin replacing Molotov on the Executive Committee of the Soviet. To Lenin's horror as he read them in Switzerland, *Pravda's* editorials now became quite moderate and defensist in their tone. No, Russia could not conclude the war by signing a separate peace, wrote Kamenev, "When an army faces an enemy, it would be the most stupid policy to make it lay down arms and go home. That would be a policy not of peace but of self-enslavement, which the free nation rejects with contempt."[13]

Whether they resulted from conviction or political calculations, Kamenev's and Stalin's relatively moderate position and essentially defensist views saved the Bolsheviks from a lot of trouble. Even four months later, in July, when the popular mood on the war had undergone a considerable change, accusations that the Bolsheviks were in effect doing Germany's work would deal the party a very serious blow. Had the Bolsheviks in March followed the line urged upon them by Lenin—antiwar, anti-Provisional Government, and hostility to the other Socialist parties—their own survival would have been threatened and their headquarters and paper would have become a very likely object of a pogrom at the hand of the indignant soldiers. Stalin, as editor of *Pravda*, quietly censored or simply refused to publish Lenin's articles sent from Switzerland whenever their language passed beyond what was deemed acceptable. He thus tactfully excised his leader's characterization of Chheidze and other figures of revolutionary democracy as "scoundrels and traitors to the cause of the proletariat, peace and freedom." Lenin's reference to the Provisional Government as being composed of "robbers" was softened to "annexationists."*

---

*Whether out of personal pique or ideological reasons, Shlyapnikov and Molotov continued to intrigue against the people who superseded them. They instigated the Petrograd Committee of the party to pass a resolution describing Stalin as unfit for leadership "in view of certain personal characteristics of his," ditto for Kamenev because of his past behavior, allegedly unworthy of a revolutionary (there would soon be rumors that Kamenev had been a police spy). All this in vain. Insteading of leading the local Bolsheviks, Shlyapnikov had to spend much of his time defending his party's action in "expropriating" the luxurious residence of the celebrated ballerina Matilda Kshesinskaya for its headquarters. At the time such seizure of private property by a Socialist party was quite unprecedented, and the famous dancer complained loudly and tearfully to the Soviet. Shlyapnikov, rather embarrassed, defended his comrades' action on the ground that the residence "had served as a haunt for high society debauchery, and a trap for young and comely girls, with the old ballerina serving as a procuress," a statement which does him little credit as a diarist. At the height of her fame and generously provided for by a succession of grand dukes, Kshesinskaya did not have to live by others' labors. For all of the Soviet's appeals to observe socialist legality, the Bolsheviks held on to the house until July.

The patriotic groundwork of the first postrevolution days had to be of concern not only to the Bolsheviks but also to revolutionary democracy as a whole. Its leaders were for the most part doctrinaire Marxists. Even if convinced of the necessity of continuing the war, they had to feel uneasy over the nationalist fervor of the soldiers. For all the apparent lack of pretenders to dictatorship, no one familiar with history could exclude the possibility of a "man on a white horse" making a sudden entrance on the scene.

The soldiers' susceptibility to patriotic appeals had another disquieting side. The average soldier came from and reflected the psychology of a class which as yet had not had its say in the revolution—the peasants. Seventy percent of Russia's population belonged to this class. It was easy for the typical Marxist to indulge in ritualistic oratory about the main threat to the revolution coming from the class enemy, the capitalists. But coming from a middle-class background, he had good reasons to know the Russian bourgeoisie's weaknesses and that by itself it was incapable of reversing the course of the revolution. But the Russian countryside was, to the Marxist, a veritable kingdom of darkness, for unlike the Populists, he had never believed in the people being a repository of socialist virtue and thus viewed the villager's mentality with a mixture of puzzlement and apprehension. The peasant accepted the fall of autocracy with equanimity, thus dissipating the radical's fear that the rural masses had never quite been weaned from their faith in the Father Tsar. But as Marx had warned, the peasant was in his economic and political thinking essentially petty bourgeois. He would support the revolution up to a point, that point being his realization that socialism might threaten his property and subjugate his country's interests to those of the international proletariat. Sukhanov, much of whose value lies in his naive candor concerning subjects his fellow Marxists pretended to ignore or dealt with by circumlocution, saw peasant Russia as the main threat to socialism. The peasant lads with rifles held the future of the revolution in their hands. "This was unfortunate and [potentially] disastrous. The Revolution had on its agenda a number of fundamental and difficult tasks which lay beyond the peasant's power of comprehension. Those could be accomplished only if peasantry were neutralized, if it would not stand in the way."[14]

Stand in whose way? In the way of doctrinaire Marxists like most of the current leaders of both Marxist parties, Lenin included, who saw what had just happened in Russia as but a prelude to a general European revolution. If backward Russia with its numerically puny proletariat had overthrown the tsar and his minions, how could anyone in his senses doubt that the German workers, brought up for generations in the philosophy of Marx and Engels, would soon follow suit, that the French would awaken to their famous revolutionary traditions, that the masses everywhere, having bled for three years for the benefit of their exploiters, would fail to seize the chance of taking their destiny in their own hands. What is most startling to a modern reader of Sukhanov's chronicle and Trotsky's history of the revolution (and this is typical of most accounts written by the left-wingers) is their apparent unconcern with what might be called the human side of the events. The leading political figures are dealt with at length, but otherwise real human beings are obscured by causes and ideologies. People en masse are not groups of creatures made of flesh and blood but signposts of Marxian taxonomy: "the proletariat," "the peasant masses," "imperialist plutocracy." There are no national peculiarities, people don't express joy or grief because of what happened to them as Russians, Poles, and Jews. They indulge in chauvinism or rise above their narrow national self-identification because of their class interest or according to the degree of their class consciousness.

This mechanistic approach to revolutionary politics was often, as in Sukhanov's own case, accompanied by genuine idealism and humanitarianism. For many convinced Marxists the war was detestable not only because they saw it as imperialist in its nature or were afraid that if allowed to continue it might turn the peasant masses against them. They felt, as did many people of quite different political persuasions, a genuine revulsion at the senseless slaughter to which there seemed no end and that tended to brutalize every aspect of life. Only for a few, most notably Lenin, was the humanitarian side of the question *completely* secondary to the political one and pacifism, as such, laughable. For most Russian Marxists to end the war was a goal in itself, and a European revolution, while also sought for its own sake, was mainly a means of securing peace. For Lenin it was that revolution which was the goal and the demand for peace but a slogan to further its coming.

The Soviet's first official statement on the war was contained in its "Proclamation to The Peoples of The World," adopted on March 14. The work of the left wing, with Sukhanov taking a prominent part in its drafting, the manifesto sought to serve two somewhat inconsistent purposes. First it sought to demonstrate that revolutionary democracy unlike the bourgeois government would strive staunchly for a peoples' peace, serving the interest of the world proletariat and humanity at large with no nationalist aims. The second aim was to still the accusation that the left was in fact working for the enemy and would seek to have the Russian army lay down its arms. Hence "comrades, proletarians, and workers of all countries," were told that "Russian democracy, conscious of its revolutionary strength announces that it will by all means resist the policy of conquest pursued by its ruling classes and calls upon the peoples of Europe for concerted and decisive action in favor of peace."[15]

The manifesto then went on to address specifically "brothers, proletarians of the Austro-German coalition, above all the German proletariat." It was understandable that they had supported the war, for their government had represented it as the struggle to defend Europe against Russian autocracy, hence "Asian despotism." But now that despotism had been overthrown, free Russia can no longer threaten civilization. Won't they return the compliment and overthrow their own semiautocratic system, get rid of their "kings, landowners, and bankers" and together with their Russian brothers put an end to the shameful butchery!

So much about the war from the class point of view. But to deflect accusations that the tone of the document was bound to demoralize Russia's fighting forces still further, its authors included some qualifying sentences. "We will firmly defend our own freedom from all reactionary encroachments, from within as well as without. The Russian Revolution . . . will not allow itself to be crushed by foreign military force." Yet some within the Soviet objected that this was hardly enough. The manifesto made good sense to a socialist intellectual, but would a simple soldier understand its subtle differentiations? The soldiers in the trenches across from him were obviously not German "bankers and landowners," but more likely "brother proletarians"; was he to fire at them? Also it would be difficult for an unsophisticated mind to discern from the declaration whether and to what extent a "foreign military force" constituted a greater danger to the revolution than "the policy of conquest of our ruling classes." To clear up the possible misunderstanding, Chheidze added a common sense gloss to the document: all the proclamation said, he observed, was that if the German proletariat overthrows William II, then we will talk about peace. Until then war! This reassured the doubters and the manifesto was almost unanimously approved by the Soviet. But Sukhanov was furious about Chheidze's intervention. The manifesto, though he does not say so outright, was supposed to mean different things to different people, and to insinuate to the soldier that their own government was as much the enemy as the Germans. And now the chairman of the Soviet had obfuscated this masterful insinuation by his defensist interpretation. "Chheidze's comments were not only illegal [sic], they were extremely harmful."[16]

The condition of the Russian army in the first weeks after the revolution mirrored the mood of the nation. It was at once radical and patriotic. This incongruous combination was epitomized by the placards borne by the units of the Petrograd garrison in their currently continuous visitations to the Tauride Palace, still the seat of those discordant twins: the Provisional Government and the Executive Committee of the Soviet. Some of them proclaimed political and economic themes highly agreeable to a socialist—demands for the eight-hour working day, for the democratic republic, for land for the peasants. But along with such slogans the soldiers would display others greatly depressing for those on the left of revolutionary democracy: "We shall defeat the enemy or die,"

"Down with German imperialism," "War until full victory." One carried by a detachment of Cossacks must have been simply horrifying to every believer in proletarian internationalism. "We shall wash our horses in German blood." Perhaps equally ominous, though unwittingly humorous, was the sight of demonstrating warriors carrying a banner inscribed "Soldiers to the trenches—workers to their factory bench."[17]

As Chheidze's comments show, most of the responsible leaders of the Soviet (and until Lenin's arrival, this remained broadly true of the Bolsheviks) were far from wishing that the army should disintegrate or be crippled as a fighting force. If they perceived but dimly that declarations such as those of March 14 were bound to have a deleterious effect on the soldiers' morale, this was because they dwelt in the realm of ideological abstraction and were ignorant of military affairs, not because they wished for their country's defeat. But if Chheidze and other relatively moderate Mensheviks and Socialist Revolutionaries deferred for the moment to the Sukhanovs and Steklovs (who represented no one but themselves), this was because of their common fear that this veritable explosion of martial zeal and patriotism might spell the end of dual power, if not of revolutionary democracy itself. Indeed there were portents of danger. Throughout the latter part of March, a number of front-line units kept sending messages to both half-governments in Petrograd urging that the successful prosecution of the war required unified direction of state affairs. "Soldiers and workers, we beg you not to complicate our task, but to help by providing us with weapons and munitions. We ask you to reject [the concept of] dual power" was a fairly typical message from the soldiers of the Minsk garrison. Representatives of thirty-one front-line regiments were even more outspoken in their message to the minister of war, Guchkov: "We are not deceived by the naive chatter about the German proletarians being allegedly led by the nose by the Junkers. . . . We firmly support the Provisional Government and pledge to protect you against any threat or attack no matter from what quarter it might come."[18]

The soldiers' argument, as indicated in one of their statements, "in unity lies strength, 'dual power' leads to a catastrophe," was, at least during the first weeks of the revolution, quite convincing even to some workers. The telegram of the Union of Railway Employees in the south addressed to Minister of Transport Nicholas Nekrasov on March 26 said, "We . . . acknowledge only the Provisional Government as the sole authority in the state. We shall not tolerate any interference with its activities. On the war issue we consider a full victory as imperative, because only if the German war machinery is fully shattered will our freedom and that of the world be made secure."[19]

Even the most moderate Socialists must have been troubled by signs that the worker-soldier alliance, the very basis of the Soviets' power, was showing strains.

In principle, the workers' goals, such as the eight-hour working day, were warmly supported by their military comrades. But at the same time the latter were also grumbling increasingly that the workers were shirking their duties and that demands for a shorter labor day and strikes, especially in the munitions factories, represented a stab in the back to those at the front. Sukhanov attributed all such dissonances to vicious capitalist propaganda and to the "imperialist plutocracy's" organized effort to turn the army against the Soviet. Yet by his own account one could frequently hear soldiers in those March days threatening to go into the factories, and, with their rifles if need be, persuade their proletarian brothers to work harder.

This is not the picture one receives from most other accounts by contemporaries; their usual verdict is in line with Trotsky's. "Nobody wanted to fight any more, neither the army nor the people." But both Bolshevik and anti-Bolshevik narrators usually have their own axe to grind when they present the Russian soldier on the morrow of the revolution as being resolutely opposed to the continuation of the war. For a Bolshevik historian and memoirist such a picture confirms the soundness of Lenin's analysis. For an opponent of the Bolsheviks, the soldier's demoralization provides an explanation and justification of the Provisional Government's inability to assert itself and to shake off its crippling dependence on the Soviet.

To be sure, this period of patriotic uplift was relatively short lived; by the middle of April the situation began to change, and quite drastically. But politics is very largely the art of timing. Had the Provisional Government been composed of skillful and realistic politicians, they might well have used this brief period for exploiting the nationalist sentiment to put the Soviet in its place so it would not interfere with their governing the country. Most of its members were not politicians, however, but liberals who had been taught that rational argument was bound to prevail in a political dispute. Far from indulging in Machiavellian schemes against the Soviet or trying to stir up the masses against it, as Sukhanov would have his readers believe, members of the Provisional Government kept pleading, patiently at first, then with mounting exasperation, with their Soviet guardians and censors, pointing out the impossible position in which the government was placed, the danger to the country, and so on. Some of them might have been expected to do more than plead. Guchkov, who as minister of war had the most frustrating task of all in dealing with revolutionary democracy's encroachments on the army, had long before earned the reputation of a dynamic and resourceful politician, not averse to demagoguery, not shrinking from conspiracy. But now the erstwhile challenger and tamer of the dark forces appeared to be the most helpless of all the bourgeois ministers. At those meetings between the representatives of the Soviet and the Provisional Government designed to adjudicate their disputes, Guchkov, once so spirited and voluble, sat usually in silence, at times fighting back tears.

If not promptly channelled into restoring the army's esprit de corps, the soldiers' patriotic zeal could not be expected to endure for long; it would be replaced by apathy, which then might turn to defeatism. Though in the main patriotic and resistant to subversive propaganda, the soldiers had, to put it mildly, been disoriented by the revolution. The old military ethos, epitomized by "For the Tsar and Fatherland," was dead. To restore military discipline another supreme and unquestioned authority and/or a rallying cry like the French Revolution's "The Fatherland is in danger" was needed. The country was in danger, with the enemy occupying a large area of the Russian state, if not of ethnic Russia. But the Soviet and its offshoots would not espouse such so-called chauvinist slogans. Socialist agitators urged the soldier to be on guard not only against the foreign but also against the domestic enemies of the revolution, and among the latter there might be his officers, even some bourgeois ministers. Guchkov hoped to still criticism from the left by dismissing several generals, allegedly die-hard partisans of the old regime. Needless to say, this only served to increase the demoralization of the officer corps, without in the slightest stopping the attacks. The *unwitting* subversion of the army by revolutionary democracy, and the Provisional Government's incapacity to counter it, thus prepared the ground for the quite open preaching of defeatism and sedition which would be launched by the Bolsheviks after Lenin's return. Inept and divided in its own councils, the Provisional Government failed to exploit the period of nationalist enthusiasm which followed the revolution, and which might have enabled it to stop the Soviet's interference in military affairs and thus save the army and perhaps along with it, Russia's freedom, for it was the demoralized and disintegrating army which was to become that freedom's gravedigger.

There were socialist leaders who at least half-realized that a disciplined armed force was a necessary prerequisite of democracy, whether revolutionary or any other kind. On March 18 Irakli Tsereteli came back from his exile to a tumultuous welcome by the Petrograd Soviet. At twenty-six he had been the leader of the Socialist faction in the Second Duma, and then along with some of its other members was sentenced to hard labor, followed by settlement in Siberia. A born orator, and amply endowed with great charm, the ebullient Georgian soon became the dominant voice on the Executive Committee of the Soviet, though his indecisive countryman and fellow Menshevik, Chheidze, stayed as its official head. Unlike the latter, Tsereteli undertook to combat vigorously the influence of the likes of Sukhanov, whom he described acidly, though not unfairly, as a "dried out, nervous and bilious doctrinaire, completely alien to the real life politics into which he has been thrust." Even before Lenin's return, the spirited Georgian saw how the Soviet's early policy on peace and the army question played into the hands of the most irresponsible elements. "We must not consider the defense of the country as something which does not concern us . . . something we don't want to talk about. [On the contrary] it should be for us one of the basic tasks of the Revolution without which we would not be able to achieve a democratic peace and to preserve the achievements of the Revolution," he said soon after his return.[20] This was startlingly new language for a Russian Marxist.

Though greatly lamented in doctrinaire and extreme left circles, Tseretelli's position was still close to the sentiments of the rank and file of the army. This became evident at the conference of representatives of the workers' and soldiers' soviets from all over the country and the front held at the end of March. Nobody could accuse such a body of being prone to "bourgeois chauvinism," yet it adopted a resolution drafted by Tseretelli, which unlike the Soviet's statement of March 14, was unambiguous in calling for an all-out war effort. There was, of course, the ritualistic phrase about a peace without annexations and indemnities. But then the conference called upon Russian democracy "to mobilize all of the country's energies and resources, in every sphere of national life for the purpose of strengthening the front." It went on to warn that "any effort to weaken the army's cohesion, strength, and ability to carry out offensive operations would be a treacherous blow against the cause of freedom and the country's vital interests."[21]

Though Lenin was still outside the country, the Bolsheviks were again edging toward his position on the "imperialist war." But a resolution along these lines proposed by Kamenev received only 57 votes against 325 for Tseretelli. It was the representatives of *front-line soldiers* who were most eager that the conference endorse as strongly as possible the need for a cohesive and disciplined army. Those who wanted to subvert and demoralize the soldiers, they told Tseretelli, were insinuating that the sole duty of the army was to fight back if and when the enemy attacked. The purpose of the insinuation as propagated by anarchist and Bolshevik agitators was clear: to persuade the soldiers to disobey their officers when ordered to advance beyond defensive positions. Certainly the fact that such agitation could be carried on at the front has an eloquence of its own, but an army in which the soldiers themselves pleaded to be allowed to obey their officers and to fight was still quite far from being in the process of dissolution, as most Soviet historians would have us believe. Even Trotsky, who was eager to present that army as being "incurably sick," was forced to admit that desertions declined substantially in the first weeks after the revolution.

Yet had the Russian army after March been composed of ancient Spartans rather than simple peasant lads befuddled by all that had been happening, it still could not have preserved its cohesion and fighting spirit indefinitely. It was being subjected to virtually unhampered subversive and defeatist propaganda, and in wartime such agitation cannot be counteracted by persuasion and by passing resolutions while forswearing any sanctions against the agitators. Here then was the paradox: Tseretelli and his fellow democratic socialists had the defects of their virtues. Much as they understood the Bolsheviks' game, it was still almost inconceivable for them to deal with their opponents through repression. The latter, for all their misguided and harmful activities, were after all their fellow Socialists. Courts-martial, bans on antiwar agitation? Certainly not! Russian democracy would only disgrace itself by reverting to such authoritarian practices. It would have been a repudiation of everything they had stood for to admit that the masses were being manipulated by unscrupulous demagogues. The people's healthy instincts were bound to warn them off the Bolsheviks' insinuations and make them see that the path advocated by Tseretelli and his circle was the only one which would secure the gains of the revolution and free Russia. Prisoners of their own ideology, inheritors of the Populists' mystic faith in the people, the democratic socialists would thus be unable to deal resolutely with the force which they would allow to grow until it destroyed them and Russia's freedom.

The Provisional Government's ineptitude combined with the democratic socialists' scruples added up to a perfect prescription for anarchy. For anyone not equipped with ideological blinders it had to be evident after the first month of the revolution that the Russia which had emerged could not endure. If the revolution's overriding goal—freedom—was to be preserved, Russia had to have a government. It had two squabbling half-governments. If a coup from the left or the right was to be avoided, there had to be a disciplined army; an army which held together and in which subversive propaganda could not be carried on with impunity. If a multination state was to be kept together, there had to be a generally recognized central authority and symbol of statehood. In its absence signs were growing that ethnic groups, such as Poles, Ukrainians, Finns, would not remain content to share in Russian freedom but would, in varying degrees, demand freedom from Russia.

The diffusion of power and the growing chaos argued against the appearance of a force capable of mastering the revolution. The political system, if it could be described as such, instituted on March 2 was obviously unworkable. Someone had to put all the pieces together and reestablish a real state, with a real government and a real army.

Though no one would have suspected it, the solution to this quandary materialized on April 3. At 11:10 that night, the train carrying Vladimir Ilyich Lenin arrived at Finland Station in what was officially Petrograd, but what the Bolsheviks alone continued perversely to call St. Petersburg.*

"Our tactics: complete opposition, no support whatever for the new regime—we suspect especially Kerensky. . . . The only guarantee, the immediate arming of the proletariat . . . no rapprochement with other parties," Lenin had written on March 6.[22] Like everyone else not present in Russia during those hectic days, he was incapable of fully realizing what was happening: not only the autocracy had been overthrown but also the whole centuries-old fabric of Russian statehood and society was being shattered. In the first of his "Letters From Afar," which Kamenev and Stalin found so embarrassing that they either censored or withheld them entirely from *Pravda*, Lenin groped at fitting the events into some comprehensible Marxian pattern. At times it seemed very simple: the bourgeoisie at the orders of its British and French masters carried out a coup, so as to continue the imperialist war.

> The Guchkov [*sic*] government . . . serving the interests of the capitalists is compelled to continue the robber war so as to preserve the capitalists' enormous profits, the landowners' property, and to restore the monarchy. . . . Under the pressure of the starving masses, the government feels itself constrained to lie . . . and to try to gain time by all sorts of proclamations and promises.[23]

As he poured laboriously over the British and French press reports from Petrograd (to add to his fury at being unable to leave Switzerland, mail from Russia virtually stopped until late March) Lenin could only seethe at the concept of dual power, and the acquiescence of the Soviet's Menshevik and Socialist Revolutionary leaders in the Provisional Government's continued existence. The crying need of the hour, he kept insisting in his epistolary diatribes, was to arm the workers. He was cheered by any news of mob violence against the old regime's officials and referred with implied approval to the lynching of an admiral and a number of naval officers by the sailors of the Baltic fleet. This was again in startling contrast to the stance of his followers at home, who as yet eschewed any endorsement of summary "people's justice," well aware that in the prevailing mood of the masses, their approval of wanton violence would only increase the Bolsheviks' unpopularity and isolation within revolutionary democracy.

Lenin's impatience to get back and to take his followers in hand was increased by his fear that if his return were much delayed, he might find himself a leader without a party. To his horror, preparations were taking place for a reunion of the Bolsheviks and the Mensheviks. Again, as in 1905, the rank-and-file workers

*They refused to accept the tsarist regime's "chauvinist" renaming of the city in the beginning of the war.

could not understand why at a time like this, the two main branches of the Marxist movement should be fighting each other rather than working for the common cause; in some provincial centers, the two factions had already merged into one organization. Kamenev and Stalin, current leaders of the home forces, were leaning toward a partial reunion. They did not, whether out of conviction or fear of their irascible leader, seek unity with the Mensheviks on the right, people like Plekhanov and Tseretelli who stood solidly behind the war effort. But for them the Mensheviks who took the internationalist position (that is those who demanded a speedy and negotiated peace with no annexations and indemnities), as well as nondenominational socialists on the left like Sukhanov and Steklov, belonged in the same party with the Bolsheviks. How far most Bolsheviks were as yet from divining what was in Lenin's mind is best shown by what Stalin was writing and saying at the time. To merge with other socialists would make, according to him, good sense. Otherwise the Bolsheviks would find themselves isolated and weak when the Constitutent Assembly was eventually convoked. That the victorious proletariat would unceremoniously dispense with that assembly was something that no one, except for one man still in Zurich, even suspected. Therefore, Stalin vigorously urged the case for reunion: "We ought not to look too far ahead and foresee disagreements. There can be no party life without disagreements. Within a [united] party we would overcome mild disagreements. . . . We ought to seek a meeting [with the Mensheviks] without presenting any preconditions."24

The effect on Lenin of arguments such as Stalin's, if and when they were communicated to him, can only be imagined. A few more weeks and the Bolsheviks would become virtually indistinguishable from "traitors" and "scoundrels" like Chheidze and Skobelev, like them willing to be led by "the loudmouth Kerensky," ready to pass up the opportunity for a real revolution which in turn would ignite a European one.

It was undoubtedly the alarm he felt at the spread of the democratic and pacifist contagion among his followers that helped persuade Lenin to undertake a step he had eschewed until the revolution: to accept German help. He needed the permission of Kaiser William's government to pass through Germany, as none of the Allied countries would facilitate the passage home of a notorious opponent of Russia's continuance in the "robbers' war," and Lenin would have risked being interned had he tried to travel through France or Britain. Other antiwar revolutionaries such as Julius Martov, leader of the Menshevik internationalists, proposed to wait for an official authorization by the Soviet before they undertook the potentially compromising trip through enemy territory. But everything the Soviet did, except for issuing manifestoes, took a long time, and Lenin was in a hurry.

The decision to accept money from the Germans was also influenced by his reading of the situation at home. As it looked from Zurich in March–April 1917* Lenin had no assurance that once back (1) he could resume his virtually dictatorial sway over his followers and (2) even if he did, the Bolsheviks, still a poor third behind the Socialist Revolutionaries and Mensheviks in their influence among the soldier and worker masses, would be able to carry out an armed coup, which he (at the time practically alone in the socialist camp) saw as necessary to keep the revolution from settling down into a bourgeois democratic mold, or conversely, and more likely, to keep the country from lapsing into utter anarchy where no political party would be able to retrieve the legacy of the tsars. Russia's being the world's "freest country" was both an opportunity and a danger. "We need revolutionary *power* . . . we need the *state,*" he wrote as early as March 11 (o.s.). The Bolsheviks, or a new revolutionary party he would have to create if a majority of the Bolsheviks rejected his leadership, would advocate and promote anarchy only up to a point where it would render both half-governments helpless. As of 1914 Lenin was renouncing the party's name—"social democratic" should be abandoned like a "soiled child's garment," he had written, and "Communist," recalling the earliest, most militant, phase of Marxism, adopted in its stead.

In either case, money, a lot of it, was needed. The Bolsheviks' prodigious growth in membership and prestige between March and October, from about ten to fifteen thousand members to close to three hundred thousand, would reflect not only the skill of their leaders and the popularity of their slogans but also their superior resources. They would be able to spend freely on newspapers, full-time agitators, and arms for their private army, the Red Guards. Their most effective organ of subversion, *Pravda of the Trenches,* would be distributed at the front free of charge. Conversely, their opponents, most notably the Mensheviks whose membership and influence would decline catastrophically during the same period, would be strapped for funds. The Petrograd Soviet itself, piquantly enough, was subsidized by the Provisional Government, which initially allocated ten million rubles for its expenses.

Granted Lenin's premises, his decision to take German money was perfectly logical. Both he and the Kaiser's government wanted another and violent installment of the revolution and hence the destruction of the Russian army as a fighting force. The idea of playing into the hands of the German militarists and capitalists may at first have troubled the Bolshevik leader, but he firmly believed that an example of a socialist revolution in Russia would prove irresistible to the German working masses, while the prospects of soviets springing up in France and especially in Britain were much more distant. True, the February revolution

*The Western calendar was still thirteen days ahead of the Julian one, the Western usage to be adopted by the Bolsheviks as of February 1, 1918.

failed to find an echo in Berlin and Vienna, but then this was understandable because the German worker saw that those who overthrew Nicholas II did so because he did not want (or know how) to conduct a successful war. But a Bolshevik revolution had to be "the spark which will set off the conflagration." To do Lenin justice, it is unlikely that *at the moment* he craved power for its own sake. After their coup, the Bolsheviks might not be able to hold on to power for very long. In March 1917 he would have thought it most unlikely that Russia would be able to endure as the only Communist* state in Europe. But even if it lasted a few weeks and then succumbed to a counterrevolution, Communist Russia would set the world proletariat on the march, first in Germany then elsewhere, and with the worldwide revolution, Communism would eventually return to its birthplace. In view of such splendid possibilities how silly to have scruples about accepting money from the Junkers and thus letting them subsidize their own, as well as the other capitalists', eventual demise.

For its part, the German government and high command viewed the whole transaction in a coldly practical way. Lenin and his people, they were told by their Russian experts, would accelerate the momentum of internal disorder and hence the decomposition of the Russian army. Germany was no longer capable of an all-out effort on both fronts, especially with America about to enter the war. After the February revolution Germany refrained from exploiting the confusion in the enemy camp by launching an offensive in the east. It was thought, and wisely so, that time was working for the Kaiser's armies, a few more weeks of the soviets and the morale of the Russian soldier would be completely undermined. But the danger remained that with the current configuration of political forces the Russian army might not only preserve but also enhance its fighting capacity. The Soviet's slogan, "Peace without annexations and indemnities," could give Germany's rulers little comfort; they still hoped for a quite different kind of peace, and the slogan itself was having some unsettling effects on their own socialists, hitherto for the most part staunch supporters of their official war policy. Hence the decision to intensify political subversion within Russia by subsidizing its most promising propagator, Lenin's party.† "Since it is in our interests that the influence of the radical wing of the Russian revolutionaries should prevail, it would seem to me advisable to allow transit to the revolutionaries, . . ." minuted State Secretary Arthur Zimmermann to Imperial Headquarters on March 23 (N.S.). And on April 1 the German Foreign Ministry drew 5 million marks for "political purposes in Russia."[25]

---

*Though his party would not adopt this name until March 1918, it is not anachronistic to begin using the term now.

†Needless to say, the Bolsheviks were not the sole recipients of German funds, money from the same source reached some branches of the Ukrainian, Finnish, etc., separatists as well as, one assumes, outright German agents. Dr. Helphand was the general impressario of the enterprise.

While Lenin's and his suite's passage through enemy territory was grudgingly accepted as necessary by revolutionary democracy in view of the Allied countries' attitude, it is fair to say that the idea of his taking money from the Germans would have been as repugnant to the average Bolshevik in Russia as to any other socialists. It is characteristic that the people chosen by him to be the contact men in the business were all non-Russians: Karl Radek, born in Austrian Poland, Jacob Furstenberg-Hanecki, a member of the Polish Socialist Party, and Vaclav Vorovsky, with long-standing Bolshevik connections but a Pole by birth, all resident currently in Sweden, all having business connections with the ubiquitous Dr. Helphand. It was only after Lenin's return that some of the home Bolsheviks were let in on the secret. For the mass of the party membership, the story of German money would remain an outrageous slander, even when as in July 1917 strong circumstantial evidence appeared substantiating it.

But it was not the unthinkable notion of Comrade Lenin being beholden to the Kaiser that made so many friends and foes alike nervous about his return. For almost a generation this one man had stood as the main obstacle to the unity of the Russian Social Democracy, vilifying his opponents, scandalizing and terrorizing his partisans. What was he going to do now? Indeed that very night of April 3–4, Lenin demonstrated that he would continue to be a divisive force, and that the triumph of the revolution, far from mellowing him, had made him only more doctrinaire in his views, more violent in his rhetoric. He was given a festive reception by the Petrograd Soviet, whose officials spent much of their time in ceremonial welcomes of returning revolutionary heroes of all political persuasions. But only someone who did not know Lenin could think that he would be mollified by the sailor's guard of honor which presented arms as he stepped out of his carriage or that he might be propitiated by Chheidze's conciliatory remarks and his fatuous expression of hope that he would now work alongside others within revolutionary democracy. Completely ignoring the man he referred to as "the Menshevik scoundrel Chheidze," the new arrival addressed the "soldiers, sailors, and workers," he made clear that for him the revolution was just beginning and that its path was to be quite different than that proposed by revolutionary democracy. Possibly to soften the jarring effect of his having travelled through the enemy's territory, but also with evident conviction he spoke about the coming revolution in Germany. "Not far away is the hour when at the call of our comrade Karl Liebknecht, nations will turn their weapons against the exploiters. . . . In Germany everything is boiling." Here the snubbed Chheidze might well have interjected that Karl Liebknecht was currently in jail and that Lenin had come to Russia through the courtesy of the government which had put him there. But that would have been uncomradely and a breach of socialist etiquette.

Outside the station, standing on an armored car, Lenin again gave a short speech in the same uncompromising vein. Then at the Bolshevik headquarters, in Kshesinskaya's once luxurious palace (in a bow to "bourgeois legality" its current occupants had allowed the ballerina to remove most of its sumptuous furniture) Lenin continued his furious oratory. Anxious that their returning champion should be, as befitted a leader, surrounded by worshipping masses, the Petrograd Bolsheviks had in spite of the late hour conscripted a number of workers and soldiers to gather around their headquarters and call for another speech. Addressing them from the balcony, Lenin reiterated his *leitmotif:* the ruinous war was being continued solely in the interests of the robber capitalists. "The [alleged] defense of the Fatherland means in fact the defense of one band of exploiters against another." Here, despite the select nature of the audience friendly to the Bolsheviks, there were shouts of disapproval from the soldiers. A man guilty of such unpatriotic sentiments should be lifted up on bayonets, shouted some of them; let him just come down among them and they would show him . . .

The usually platitudinous "turning point of history" describes precisely the significance of Lenin's return. For all the historian's predilection to ascribe great events to social and economic causes transcending personalities, the course of the revolution was indeed determined by the qualities and deficiencies of a handful of people. What if Grand Duke Michael had been cast in the mold of Nicholas I of December 14, 1825? What if Kerensky's oratorical magic had been matched by his political skills? The whole complexion of the Soviet and, for the moment, of revolutionary politics was transformed by the appearance on the scene of Tseretelli. What if the percipient Georgian had been endowed with the same drive for power as the new arrival, if he had behind him, as would Lenin in a few weeks, a united and disciplined party?

And Lenin came back just in time! Literally, one more day and the Bolsheviks would have been setting in motion the machinery of reunification with the Mensheviks. Even their half-hearted opposition to the war was in danger of being swamped by the still-rising tide of revolutionary patriotism. "The spirit in the army is for the time being excellent, the soldiers all want and expect us to attack," wrote General Brusilov, Russia's outstanding military leader and the commander of the southwestern front. "But the moment had to be seized, for continued passivity at the front could destroy the mood, would disillusion the soldiers and undermine their faith in their officers, and by providing an opening for subversive propaganda, would lead to the disintegration of the army."[26] All of Lenin's calculations hinged on subverting the Russian soldier. With the army on the march and even with minor military successes, *his* revolution would recede beyond the horizon.

In *Lenin in Zurich,* Solzhenitsyn portrays the father of the Communist state as possessed by an obsessive hatred of his own nation, a view which is both oversimplified and unjust. *Once in power* Lenin would amply demonstrate, even if unconsciously, that he was one of those Russian Communists of whom he himself said, "Scratch them and you will find Russian chauvinists." But for the moment his unconscious nationalism was subdued by the vision of a world revolution. To start it he meant to destroy the Russian state in its present form and hence to anesthetize the force which had always held this state together and might enable it to survive even under the current grotesque dual power regime: Russian nationalism.

To achieve his initial aim, Lenin had to call upon another elemental force which has intermittently made its appearance throughout Russian history: anarchy. To follow the path of orthodox Marxism, the one from which he had never explicitly departed before 1914, would have meant to acquiesce in the existence, and for a long time to come, of a bourgeois and parliamentary Russia, a prospect more hateful to Lenin than the restoration of the autocracy. From April 3 until October 25 the main thrust of his policies would be to destroy all elements of social, economic, and political stability and to plunge the country into complete anarchy. It was only as heirs to anarchy that his Bolsheviks could come to power. But more than that: at times, as in July 1917, Lenin's craving to overthrow the existing form of political authority almost seemed stronger than his conscious desire for power. He would flirt with the idea of insurrection, even at a time when it appeared likely that the Bolsheviks themselves would be submerged by the tide of anarchy they had been trying to create.

That the erstwhile leading Marxist theoretician had for all practical purposes become an anarchist was indeed the conclusion of most who listened to Lenin's two speeches on April 4, which passed into history as the famous April Theses. The main discourse was delivered before a joint session of the Bolsheviks, Mensheviks, and nonaligned Socialists convened to start the reunion of the Russian Marxists. From the beginning Lenin rejected the whole concept of dual power, hitherto accepted even by his most faithful followers in Russia. "No parliamentary republic . . . but a republic of the soviets of workers, rural laborers, and peasants throughout the whole country at all levels—the abolition of the police, army, officialdom." (An abbreviated, somewhat toned down version of the Theses was published on April 7, the initial reaction to them persuading the author to be more circumspect in his language, especially when he touched on the problem of peace.)[27] It is almost superfluous to add he opposed any idea of support, no matter how conditional or temporary, for the Provisional Government. As for the war, he was by now sufficiently impressed with the soldiers' behavior the night before not to urge an immediate end to the war, but what he did argue speaks for itself: the need for intense educational propaganda among the soldiers, demonstrating "the organic connection between capitalism and the imperialist war, and that *one cannot* achieve a democratic peace without overthrowing capitalism." This argument should be widely propagated in the front lines where the soldiers were encouraged to fraternize with the Germans and Austrians in the opposite trenches. For the complex agrarian-peasant problem, Lenin offered a simple solution: immediate confiscation of all private estates and control of the land fund by the poor and landless peasants' committees.

It would have been difficult to imagine a more perfect blueprint for creating instant chaos and paralyzing the country's political and social life. Though after what he had just said Lenin hardly needed to stress the point, he rejected emphatically any possibility of reunion with the Mensheviks or even with radical nondenominational Socialists like Steklov. The name Social Democracy had been disgraced and sullied by the behavior of most Socialist leaders throughout Europe, who sold out to their respective capitalists and supported the war. Militant Marxists should choose Communist as the name of their party and of the new International.

As the speech progressed, the initial shock of incredulity gave way to angry interjections like: "But this is nonsense" and "This is insane." Although deeply embarrassed by his performance, the Bolsheviks present felt duty bound to applaud the speaker when he finished. This brought new turmoil, shouts of "Shame" and "How can you call yourselves Marxists?" They had just heard a call for a civil war against democracy, declared one of the subsequent speakers—what Lenin had spouted represented the most primitive kind of anarchism. Rather than reply to his critics, Lenin thought it prudent to disappear. Only some of the Bolsheviks followed him. But others joined in the resolution for reunification and in the election of a committee to prepare for a congress representing all Socialist factions.

No one could have had any doubts of what Lenin's program meant. If his view prevailed among the Bolsheviks, Russia would have in addition to the two half-governments a party working openly for the destruction of both and for the dissolution of the Russian army. Lenin's position was thus in the true sense of the term counterrevolutionary, for he proposed to destroy the whole framework erected by the February revolution.

Many at the time, as well as some future historians, were taken in by his slogan, All power to the soviets. Didn't he then propose that all power should pass over to Tseretelli, Chheidze, et cetera? Wasn't this an act of political abnegation on his part, for the Bolsheviks were as yet a small minority within the Petrograd Soviet and even weaker in most of the provincial and army ones? Yet from his point of view, there was an excellent logic behind his slogan. In the first place, no one acquainted with the scene could really believe that the soviets could rule.

They were good at passing resolutions and telling the Provisional Government what *it* must *not* do. But how could anyone seriously think that a body of two or three thousand people, which was the Petrograd Soviet, its membership fluctuating almost daily,* would be able to function as a parliament or that its Executive Committee of eighty or ninety might make a reasonable facsimile of a government? In any case there was as yet no all-Russian congress or executive of the soviets, and even when it emerged in June, it would be almost incomprehensible to most people that anyone sitting in Petrograd could or should issue orders to the Samara or Irkutsk soviet. "All power to the soviets" meant in effect no central political authority at all. And when there appeared a possibility that somehow the soviets might improvise such an authority, Lenin and his Bolsheviks would rapidly abandon the slogan and would revert to it only once they had the soviets in their grip.

But its use was a masterful psychological stroke, one of the most notable examples of the Communists' skill when it comes to verbal magic—those formulas and slogans which render their enemies confused and then helpless. No Socialist could oppose in principle the idea that all power should be in the hands of the workers, soldiers, and peasants, operating through their own representative bodies and not through some distant western-type parliament. To the Russian people, soviets were now becoming synonymous with what is today called grass roots democracy. Who indeed would not like a "government" in which one participated not by casting a ballot every four or five years but which was right there on the spot, and to which one could repair in person and speak one's mind! In addition to passing resolutions and hosting festive receptions, the soviets' main business consisted of receiving endless streams of delegations from every conceivable type of organization.

That behind the fanatic there was also a shrewd politician was evident in the one anarchist postulate Lenin refused to endorse: the workers' ownership and management of factories. His theses stipulated that the soviets should only *control* production and distribution, thus rejecting the anarchists' demand for immediate expropriation of all industrial and commercial enterprises. Any attempt by the workers to dispense with managerial personnel and to try to run factories by themselves would inevitably lead to a breakdown of production, and the resultant unemployment and shortages would be blamed on Lenin and his party and thus compromise them in the eyes of the proletariat.

The next two weeks were the crucial time in Lenin's political career. To every clear-thinking person it should have been evident as of April 4 that this man

*Workers' and soldiers' deputies could be recalled by their constituency at any time. Lenin was to denounce as grossly undemocratic the proposal that there should be a set term of two or three months!

represented a much greater threat to the revolution than all those dignitaries of the old regime still kept under lock and key. It was unthinkable in the prevailing atmosphere that a left-wing politician should be imprisoned or otherwise prosecuted, but had it been endowed with any sense of self-preservation, revolutionary democracy would have roundly denounced Lenin and declared him an apostate from socialism. That in turn would have made his position untenable even among the Bolsheviks. The latter were well aware that their leader's position threatened them with an irretrievable catastrophe. The April Theses, when published on April 7 in *Pravda,* aroused universal indignation. There was a serious possibility that what the soldiers and workers did to the tsarist authorities on February 27 would now be replicated in an anti-Bolshevik pogrom. His party comrades' nervousness was reflected at the meetings of the Central Committee Bureau on April 6 and the Bolshevik Petrograd Committee on the eighth. At the latter, only two votes were cast in favor of Lenin's position, thirteen against.

Lenin was saved, not for the last time, by his enemies. Revolutionary democracy, that is, those very same Mensheviks and SRs he vilified and would soon destroy, interposed itself between the masses' wrath and the man who would render his country defenseless against the enemy. Already on April 4 the Executive Committee of the Soviet, at Lenin's personal request, issued a declaration justifying Lenin's trip through Germany. It was all the fault of the Provisional Government the committee declared; it had failed to facilitate his return through Allied territory, thus leaving him no other route to his country.

Even so, the attitude of the masses remained threatening. The soldiers' sections of both the Petrograd and Moscow soviets denounced Lenin's defeatist propaganda. Hostile crowds kept gathering every evening around the Bolshevik headquarters, and on a couple of occasions Lenin himself appeared on the balcony and amidst boos and catcalls tried to defend himself from the accusations. The sailors who had formed the honor guard on Lenin's arrival addressed a public letter, whose torturous prose was a sure sign that it came from the rank and file. "Having learned that Mister* Lenin came to Russia by permission of His Majesty, the German Emperor and King of Prussia, we express our deep regret that we participated in his solemn welcome to Petrograd."[28] Had they known the route which he had taken, they would have shouted, they declared, "Down with you, go back to the country through which you come to us." This from the Baltic fleet sailors, already the most unruly element in the armed forces, who in three months would become the shock troops of the Bolsheviks.

Much of the anti-Lenin campaign was being inspired of course by the right-wing, that is, mainly Kadet, press. (Such was the rapid transformation of Russian

*Under the circumstances, an insulting term; if not "Comrade," it should have been at least "Citizen."

life following the revolution, that from being considerably left of center, the Milyukov faction of the Kadets was now on the right insofar as the spectrum of political forces which really counted was concerned.) But not even Sukhanov, who saw the sinister hand of plutocracy behind the agitation, could deny that among the people at large, the anti-Bolshevik feeling ran high during those April days. The high point of the campaign came on April 17. Accustomed to demonstrations of all kinds, the inhabitants of Petrograd were still startled and moved by this most unusual one: filing through the streets toward the Tauride Palace, still the seat of both half-governments, was an enormous crowd, estimated at more than fifty thousand, of wounded and mutilated veterans of the war, the blind led by their comrades, amputees and cripples in trucks and carriages. They were not protesting the imperialist war which had cost them so dearly. The signs they carried proclaimed "Down with German militarism," "Our wounds call for war until victory." But the main purpose of the macabre procession was to ensure that those seeking to subvert the country's army be silenced and punished. In front of the palace, the demonstrators were addressed by Tseretelli and Skobelev. Lenin had described the two as "the social chauvinists . . . a group which *objectively* has sold out to the bourgeoisie . . . helping the latter to rob and oppress small and weak nations." Yet they now staunchly defended the man who sought their destruction. They begged the demonstrators to disperse peacefully: the majority of the Soviet understood and shared their sentiments, but the revolution must not be sullied by mob violence and lynchings. The crowd was not appeased. There were shouts that Lenin was a spy and provocateur and must be imprisoned. It finally took the intervention of the "arch-reactionary" Rodzianko to calm down the infuriated veterans and to persuade them to return to their hospitals and dwellings.

This was probably the closest that Lenin came to becoming a victim of "the people's justice," which once in power he would endorse. If one can understand revolutionary democracy's humane though suicidal impulse to protect its enemies on the left, it is more difficult to account for its virtual eulogy of its tormentor and slanderer. Defending Lenin from the alleged libels of the bourgeois press, an editorial in the Soviet's *Izvestia* spoke indignantly of how shameful it was that in a free country like Russia, one could even conceive of resolving a political dispute "not through an open debate but by using forcible measures against a man who has devoted his whole life to the working class, has always served the interests of the oppressed and exploited."[29]

If his avowed enemies protected Lenin and paid him such handsome compliments, how could the Bolsheviks continue to reject his lead? Their initial nervousness now quickly dissipating, they had to admire their comrade who had sized up the situation so masterfully and who, as so often in the past, while others were lost in doubts and hesitations, knew precisely what had to be done. It would be unfair to credit Lenin's recovery of control of his party just to his opponents' pusillanimity. He towered intellectually over other Bolsheviks and, insofar as audacity and strength of will were concerned, over other figures on the revolutionary scene. Almost completely isolated within his own party, on April 4, with even his closest lieutenant and fellow traveller from Switzerland, Gregory Zinoviev, opposing his plans as impractical, Lenin by the end of the month had bent the majority of the Bolsheviks to his will. At the All-Russian Party Conference that opened on April 24, his proposals on most issues carried the day. True, there remained disagreements on such temporary academic questions as whether backward Russia was ready for a socialist revolution, and whether the party should adopt a new name and establish a new Third International. But the important thing was the Bolsheviks' endorsement of every conceivable issue which might contribute to the overthrow of the existing revolutionary regime and the destruction of the Russian state. The peasants would be encouraged to seize the landlords' estates, the soldiers to fraternize with the enemy, the workers to press the soviets to liquidate the Provisional Government.

On the explosive nationality issue, Lenin also hastened to embrace the most divisive slogan advanced already in his theses. "On the national question, the proletarian party must support, above all, the proclamation and the *immediate realization* of the rights of *all* nations . . . forcibly annexed and forcibly retained within the [Russian] state."[30] At the conference he was more specific, "Why should we Great Russians, who have oppressed more nations than any other people, refuse to acknowledge the right of independence of Poland, Ukraine, and Finland?" At the time the most that the Finnish and Ukrainian nationalists demanded was a far-reaching autonomy. To argue for full unconditional rights of independence, especially of the Ukraine, was to outrage the deepest feelings not only of the average middle-class Russian but even of his own Polish-born and Ukrainian followers. The latter were well aware that their countrymen, once they were really free from Russia, were not likely to opt for Lenin's, or quite possibly for any other, kind of socialism, and did not Marx say: "Workers have no country"?

Lenin could not say, perhaps he was not fully aware of it himself, that all his extreme slogans carried with them an unspoken proviso. "Valid only until power is ours." And indeed interspersed throughout his anarchist manifestoes was what might be called the Marxist small print. The Bolsheviks were not anarchists; they believed in the state. They were not pacifists; if necessary, they would conduct a *revolutionary* war. They were Marxists, hence believers in closer links among nations, and once free, the Polish and Ukrainian workers would not necessarily want to separate themselves from their Russian brethren. Of course, scientific socialism taught that small-scale agricultural production was uneconomical and that it is the state and not the workers which should run industry. But all such qualifications, while they assuaged the doctrinaire scruples of the faithful, were unlikely to be deciphered by the masses. For them Lenin's party offered what they craved most: peace, land, national freedom for those who were non-Russians. It did not occur to them that the people who promised such a splendid future, once power was theirs, might start reneging on the freedoms they had sponsored so vigorously against the bourgeois state.

What of Russian nationalism which only so recently had risen like a tidal wave threatening to engulf the Bolsheviks and sweep Lenin from the scene? Insofar as the mass of workers and soldiers was concerned, the danger inevitably subsided after the Soviet certified Lenin and his comrades as good and loyal *Russian* socialists, misguided in their views on some issues to be sure, but absolutely innocent of any actual or intended wrong doing. Hence the amazingly schizophrenic strain in the Bolsheviks' references to Tseretelli, Chheidze, and other leaders of revolutionary democracy. At one point in a speech or article, they were branded as betrayers of the cause of socialism and as such repudiated by every honest proletarian. Next page they were identified as universally trusted and revered leaders of the working masses who denied all those absurd rumors about Comrade Lenin's connections with the Germans. The slandered man himself wrote about the impugning of his patriotism more in sorrow than in anger. Soldiers of the Fourth Motorized Battalion passed a resolution requiring an inquest into the circumstances of his trips through Germany, and branded him and his fellow travellers as traitors. How sad, mused Lenin in *Pravda,* that they did not pay attention to *Izvestia,* Number Thirty-two, of April 5, with its announcement that the Executive Committee of the Soviet had fully exonerated him of all the opprobrious charges. "Is it honorable, is it wise, to disregard this vindication and to indulge in agitation for repression? . . . Isn't this anarchism to *try to undermine the authority* of members of the Executive Committee who have been elected by the workers and soldiers."[31] It was true that he was advocating the overthrow, or rather removal, of the Provisional Government, but then he was also urging the German workers to overthrow their government, and while in Switzerland, he and Zinoviev wrote a pamphlet to that effect, which was translated into German!

His powers of equivocation, always formidable, were now breathtaking. It was another slander to allege that the Bolsheviks were inciting a civil war, he wrote in *Pravda.* Almost simultaneously another article of his, this time in *Soldiers' Pravda,* was aimed at the peasant soldier's most vulnerable spot: "No freedoms are of any use to the peasants as long as the gentry owns millions of acres. . . . And in order that the peasants take over immediately all the landowners' land,

and be able to do it while observing perfect order [!] and without damaging the property they need the assistance of the soldiers. . . . Soldiers help workers and peasants to unite and arm themselves."[32] One may well imagine the effect of such appeals on a peasant lad in the trenches: perhaps in his native village the local peasants had already expropriated a neighboring estate, and he was not there to get his share! If people like Tseretelli and even Rodzianko defended Lenin's right to write such things, an unsophisticated mind had to conclude that after all, there might be something to what he was saying. The number of desertions from the front units rose dramatically in the course of April.

The growing confusion in the soldiers' minds was also reflected in the action of the soldiers' section of the Soviet. It denounced the Bolsheviks' subversive tactics. But the resolution added that as long as the Bolsheviks confined themselves just to propaganda, no attempt should be made to repress them. Lenin quoted this resolution with approval. He did not mean to disorganize the army but was merely in favor of peaceful persuasion and urged soldiers to fraternize with the Germans. It was the minister of war, capitalist Guchkov, who was really undermining Russia's military machine by threatening and reprimanding those army units which had fired their old officers and elected new ones. There was very little in fact that the military authorities could do but reprimand and threaten; the death penalty had been abolished as early as March 12. Fraternization was becoming a common occurrence all along the front. Russian officers were virtually helpless in trying to stop it, while on the other side, German soldiers who participated in these friendly chitchats with the enemy were carefully selected by their commanders.

All in all it was certainly a miracle that the field army still preserved a modicum of morale and discipline. A meeting of the front-line soviets which gathered in Petrograd at the end of April condemned by an overwhelming majority the Bolsheviks' position on the war and the army. Such was the mood of the gathering that Lenin, though invited to address it in person, felt it prudent to avoid a face-to-face confrontation with the warriors. He was devilishly busy with his party's conference which dragged out all day and night, and much as he wished to, he simply could not find the time to come, he wrote in answer to the invitation.[33] A rather lame excuse: the Bolshevik conference concluded its labors on April 29, the soldiers' not until May 4.

The non-Bolshevik left thus could continue reassuring itself that the proverbial healthy instincts of the masses made them see through the Bolsheviks' game and that they recoiled from Lenin's subversive and adventurist advice. But they were living in a fool's paradise. Lenin was not interested in majorities, votes. While publicly he continued chastising the Provisional Government for not summoning the Constituent Assembly, privately he already intimated to his associates that if things went the way he planned, the Assembly would not be needed. His principal concern was to speed up the process of political and social disintegration of the state and to build an army of followers strong and cohesive enough, never mind the numbers, to pick up the pieces when the tottering structure of dual power finally collapsed. And he was getting the kind of party he wanted. On the eve of the revolution, the number of Bolsheviks in Petrograd, according to an official party source, was (and this is probably exaggerated) about fifteen hundred. Now, at the end of April, it stood at sixteen thousand.[34] The newcomers were people attracted by the promise of action and power, not like those in the Menshevik and Socialist Revolutionaries ranks whose notion of party membership consisted mostly of going to meetings, listening to speeches, and voting. One speaker who undoubtedly touched Lenin's heart at the party conference confessed that he did not understand this whole business of dual power and the fuss over the Provisional Government. Where he came from, the industrial town of Orekhovo, the workers had already pushed aside the official organ of administration.

All power in Orekhovo is in the hands of the workers. Nobody is allowed to own or carry arms without the soviet's permission. The peasants work hand in hand with the workers. Church lands are going to be expropriated. . . . We told the capitalists that unless they provided the workers with fuel and enabled them to work, we were going to take over the factory. Every delivery of goods has to be approved by the soviet.[35]

In fact the activist momentum Lenin imparted to his party carried with it certain dangers. People were joining the Bolsheviks because unlike their Socialist rivals, they did not propose to sit with their arms folded until the Constituent Assembly and the war's end. Many of the zealots, however, wondered why if Lenin's slogan "All power to the soviets" was correct, they should not set out to put it into effect immediately.

What happened a few days before the party conference was illustrative of the danger of this revolutionary impatience which Lenin instilled in his followers. On April 18, May 1 in the West, the Socialists of all colorations celebrated the day of international proletarian solidarity. Its talent for mistiming its actions being now on the level of the late tsar, this very same day was chosen by the Provisional Government for addressing a note to Russia's allies, the contents of which were bound to strike revolutionary democracy in its most sensitive spot. On its face the document was quite innocuous and reasserted the government's determination to carry on with the war and to eschew any separate peace. But in speaking of the Allied Powers' war aims, the note referred to their joint determination "to obtain those guarantees and sanctions which are indispensable for the prevention of sanguinary conflicts in the future." When published in the press on April 20 this seemingly innocent sentence caused a veritable explosion. "Everyone," that is, the Soviet, knew that the note's author, Foreign Minister Milyukov, was an unregenerate imperialist, and on that occasion a historian is bound to agree with the verdict of revolutionary democracy. Sanctions and guarantees were simply euphemisms for those territorial aspirations traditionally dear to the heart of Russia's nationalists, primarily Constantinople and the Straits. But whatever one thinks of "historic rights" and "a cross over St. Sophia's" as goals in themselves, Milyukov's note was, under the prevailing conditions, a piece of unnecessary foolishness. It was as if Lenin had declared that in fact he did not care for the soviets and his aim was really a one-party state. People like Tseretelli had recently been trying to establish the concept of what might be called revolutionary patriotism, under whose flag Russians of most diverse political opinions might unite, and which would have had a fair chance of saving the army from the assaults of the Bolsheviks and other subversive elements. The cardinal tenet of revolutionary patriotism was that Russia was fighting for her own and other nations' freedom and therefore abjured any goal of annexations or other forcible conquests. And here was Milyukov baring his lust for the Dardanelles and providing grist for the Bolsheviks' mill.

All Socialists were indignant, but for the Bolsheviks this was a wonderful opportunity to distract the masses' attention from Comrade Lenin, his unfortunate trip through Germany, et cetera. The Bolsheviks' City Committee on the afternoon of April 20 organized street demonstrations. Crowds poured from their stronghold, the Vyborg district, with placards proclaiming "Down with the Provisional Government" and "Kick out Milyukov." Along with the workers there were many adolescents in the mob, who if the principal object of the demonstrators' ire is to be believed, had been paid to march and shout.[36] The workers were soon joined by soldiers. The Finland Regiment, led by a Bolshevik noncommissioned officer, surrounded the Marinsky Palace, the seat of the Provisional Government, and was followed by some other military units in full battle order. The soldiers were told by the agitators that they were marching to arrest Milyukov and other bourgeois ministers. As Sukhanov, who in general saw the demonstration as a positive phenomenon, noted disarmingly, "The arrest of the Provisional Government transgressed the rights and competence of any party. In addition, such an act, though quite easy to accomplish, would not have corresponded to the views of the Soviet nor would have been appropriate to the needs of the hour."[37]

Once again the leaders of the Soviet interposed themselves between the masses and the object of their wrath with the usual oratory: the revolution must not be sullied by violence, and so on. It is not clear whether it was the oratory which saved the day or news that the commandant of the Petrograd district, General

Lavr Kornilov, was dispatching cavalry and cannon to protect the ministers. He too was persuaded by the Soviet to desist from such drastic measures. Having calmed passions on both sides, the Executive Committee of the Soviet launched on an all-night session. The Bolshevik minority within it (the Bolsheviks and Mensheviks should have exchanged their names) was arguing that they were missing a splendid opportunity to start a civil war, but the majority sternly reproved them and decided merely to demand that the Provisional Government should clarify its position on the war.

Even so there were armed clashes on April 21. The Kadets now mounted counter demonstrations, the participants carrying signs hailing Milyukov and his fellow ministers. There were some armed clashes and casualties, but the emphasis was still on speechmaking. Addressing his partisans, the foreign minister struck a pose worthy of an ancient Roman: "When I saw the sign 'Down with Milyukov' I trembled not for myself, but for Russia."[38] The Executive Committee of the Soviet finally put an end to the disorders. It informed the military units in the capital that only its members had the right to give them orders (which led to General Kornilov's resignation as the city's commandant), and it banned all street demonstrations for two days. Looking to the future, the Executive Committee implored fellow citizens to remember that "your guns are for the protection of the revolution. You do not need them for demonstrations and meetings." No one was charged with instigating riots and trying to lay hands on the government: Russia was the freest country in the world.

Three lessons emerged from the April days, as the hullabaloo became known: the Provisional Government was in disarray and virtually impotent; the prestige of the Soviet still stood high; the Bolsheviks, though prone to mischief making, were still weak. Except for the first, such conclusions were deceptive. The leaders of the Soviet were confirmed in their fatal delusion that rhetoric could always stem violence and protect the democratic character of the revolution. The Bolsheviks had suffered a setback. But a retreat, if the enemy does not exploit it, is not necessarily a defeat; in fact it may set the stage for a future offensive. If at first you do not succeed, try and try and try again might well have been Lenin's guiding motto; it has certainly become that of the Communists, whether in their domestic or foreign policies. There would be the June days and the July days, and on each occasion the Bolsheviks would inch a little further toward a coup d'etat. Since in neither case their attempts resulted in real reprisals, they would finally be ready for *the* day in October. One Bolshevik agitator was able to arouse a whole regiment and to persuade it to try to seize the Council of Ministers, the soldiers being but dimly aware of what they were about. Was it really to be so different in October?

Lenin is usually represented as having been deeply shocked by some of his followers' attempt to carry out a coup. Indeed a few days after the events at the party conference, he was full of chagrin that because of unauthorized actions by a few individuals, the whole party could be held responsible for such un-Marxist and undemocratic doings. His talent for speaking out of both sides of his mouth was never more in evidence.

> We say that the slogan "down with the Provisional Government" is adventurist, because *right now* one should not overthrow this government, and therefore we were just for peaceful demonstrations. We wanted only to carry out a *peaceful reconnoitering* of the enemy's forces, but not to offer battle. But the Petersburg Committee [of the Bolsheviks] went *a wee bit too far,* which in this case was a major crime."[39]

The correct line, he went on to shout, is "Long live the soviets," and not, God forbid "Down with the government." His spell over his audience must have been considerable, for no one rose to ask what happened to *the* slogan "All power to the soviets." And many must have remembered what he had said only two weeks before in one of his rare appearances before a group of soldiers (to be sure not from the front, but from the garrison): "Having started the Revolution we must strengthen and expand it. . . . All power in the state from below to the top . . . must belong to the soviets of workers, soldiers, peasants, and farm hands."[40] And what precisely was the meaning of his final reflection on the April days: "Did we make mistakes? Yes, we did. Only he who does nothing makes no mistakes. It is not easy to organize things well."

The humiliated Provisional Government (who now remembered that seven weeks before it had been endowed with "the plenitude of all state powers") entered upon a ministerial crisis, which in fact was to be its perpetual condition until the very end. It was obvious that Milyukov had to be sacrificed as a peace offering to the offended revolutionary democracy. The minister of war, Guchkov, was eager to be relieved of his impossible job; the man who once had taunted with impunity the Autocrat of All Russia was as a result of his experiences in office close to a nervous breakdown. The Provisional Government did meekly explain that its war policy was not motivated by territorial greed; where its note talked about "guarantees and sanctions" it meant such laudable objectives as the limitation of armaments, an international court, and so on. But quite apart from changes in personnel and declarations, something had to be done if dual power was to hobble along, if Russia was to have as much as an appearance of a government. Again there were threats that the bourgeois ministers would go on strike.

At a festive occasion which filled in the time between riots and crises, this one on the eleventh anniversary of the summoning of the First Duma, an old right-winger, Vasili Shulgin, departed from the usual decorum at such gatherings and instead of expatiating on the evils of the past and the blessings of the revolution, complained bitterly about the ludicrous position in which Russia's government found itself. Instead of governing, it was a prisoner of the Soviet, the latter in effect telling the people: "We must keep guard on the ministers for they are capitalists."[41] A man like Lenin could go on preaching sedition, but no one warned the people against him, all of the Soviet's stern vigilance was directed against the unfortunate government.

This was too much even for Tseretelli, who erupted with a spirited defense of Lenin, one he must have often reflected on in the years to come, when Lenin's party first made him flee Russia and then robbed him of his homeland. (In 1921 the Red Army invaded Georgia, until then independent, and overthrew her Menshevik government, of which Tseretelli was a member. He was to die in New York in 1959.) But emotionally Tseretelli's outburst was understandable. People like Shulgin had cheered when he was imprisoned in 1906 and sent into Siberian exile which lasted until the revolution. It was slanderous, he said, to accuse Lenin of exciting to excesses and undermining the army. He himself disagreed with the Bolshevik leader but had to grant that Lenin was a man of principles and an idealist. Hence even if mistaken, Lenin assumed that Shulgin's views represented those of the Provisional Government and the bourgeoisie at large and saw the only solution in the soviets taking over. Were Tseretelli convinced that Lenin's premise was correct and a voice like Shulgin's not an isolated one, he would join with his Bolshevik opponent in urging the dictatorship of the proletariat, even at the price of a civil war.

And so the heated debate went on, the problem of what was to be done obscured by that other perennial problem of Russian modern history: who is guilty? But something had to be done, and after much soul-searching and violent arguments pro and con, the Soviet decided to sanction what might be described as a trial marriage between revolutionary democracy and the bourgeois government. Prince Lvov still remained the head of the ministry, though by now he had become such a shadowy figure that his name was usually skipped in the Bolsheviks' attacks upon the regime. Kerensky took over the war and navy ministry, and there were now five other Socialists in the cabinet. Tseretelli was given posts and telegraph, Skobelev, the ministry of labor. Another recent returnee from political exile abroad, Victor Chernov, became minister of agriculture. This seemed like a logical choice because Chernov was the acknowledged leader of the Socialist Revolutionaries, the peasants' party, though there was already a widespread feeling that nobody could equal him in the length and tedium of his speeches, for those days a remarkable achievement.

On paper this was a government of national unity, and since it included the most prominent members of revolutionary democracy, its formation should have stilled the call for "All power to the soviets." The new minister of foreign affairs, Tereshchenko, would now carefully eschew any hint of imperialist aims.

In fact, however, the new government represented a merger not of strengths, but of weaknesses. The remaining non-Socialist ministers brought to it their growing unpopularity, the six Socialists their administrative inexperience. Except for Kerensky, they treated their participation in the government as symbolic; the business of their ministries was run by their assistants, in most cases as incompetent as themselves. The Bolsheviks came up with the slogan "Down with the ten capitalist ministers" and portrayed the Socialists who joined the coalition as traitors to their class. Dual power of course continued, for the Executive Committee would not abandon its role as the watchdog over the government just because some of its members now sat in it. The fortunes of the government turned very largely on its real head, Kerensky. Still the most popular figure in the country at large (the fact reflected in the rather moderate tone of Lenin's attacks upon him), he turned his oratorical talents to instilling the revolutionary élan in the army, without at the same time doing anything to stop the flow of propaganda which was sapping its morale. The new war minister issued on May 9 a declaration of the rights of soldiers and sailors which sanctioned all forms of political propaganda and activism in the armed forces. When not on duty, that is, engaged in actual combat, every soldier was free to engage in politics, enlist in any party he wished. The declaration thus extended the principles of Order No. 1, this time on behalf of the government to the whole army. In a way the statement largely ratified the status quo, but it widened the breech between the officers corps and the regime. Entirely alien to military matters, still fearful of a "man on a white horse," the non-Bolshevik left remained oblivious to the fact that a democracy, especially in wartime, cannot afford to have its army politicized and turned into a discussion club. "The soldier will trust you if he understands you are not enemies of democracy," Tseretelli told the generals.

As was the tsarist regime throughout 1916, so the revolutionary regime was visibly disintegrating. Revolutionary patriotism was still a potent force, but if it was not channelled into the restoration of a generally accepted national authority, it could no more save the revolution than the formula For the Tsar and Fatherland had been able to keep Nicholas II on his throne. Kerensky's perorations before soldiers' meetings were wildly applauded, the Bolsheviks' and anarchists' objections usually shouted down. But with the war minister or other patriotic orator gone, the soldiers would often revert to discussing whether their officers could be trusted and what should be their attitude if and when they were ordered to go on the offensive. Characteristically, most of the surviving veterans of the revolutionary struggles of the 1870s and 1880s now took a strongly prowar and anti-Bolshevik position. Among them were such legendary figures as Katherine Breshko-Breshkovskaya, the "grandmother of the Revolution," who upon her return from exile and in her seventies set out to organize women's battalions to fight the enemy and Nicholas Chaykovsky, the pioneer of Populism, whose views on the war's aims echoed those of Milyukov. Nicholas Morozov, who in the late 1870s represented the extreme terrorist tendency within The People's Will and then endured twenty years of solitary confinement in tsarist Russia's most dreaded prison, toured the front-lines by plane, calling upon soldiers to be ready to sacrifice themselves for their country. The father of Russian socialism, George Plekhanov, was unstinting in his support of the war and in exposing, virtually alone among the Marxian Socialists, the harm being done by the Bolsheviks and the danger they presented to the Revolution.

Granted that no objective observer could feel optimistic about the survival of the regime born out of the revolution, it would have been equally difficult for him to imagine the manner of its demise, except as a consequence of Russia dissolving completely into anarchy. There seemed to be no political force or party capable of putting an end to the growing chaos or to exploit it by seizing power and establishing a real government. The soviets stood as an immovable barrier to Russia being governed in the real sense of the word, and they precluded the possibility of a successful coup by a general or a party. This was another reason for the complacency of revolutionary democracy in the face of both the Bolsheviks' propaganda and the growing indiscipline of the army. If there was a lurking danger, it lay in the unlikely possibility of the army becoming too disciplined and at the behest of some reactionary general sweeping away the main safeguard of democracy: the soviets. But apart from such an eventuality, what else could endanger the revolution? Suppose that the Bolsheviks could muster a few regiments to carry out a coup against the government. In the first place the soldiers would very likely desist from their mutiny once the situation was explained to them by the Soviet. But even if by some quirk Lenin and his people did succeed, what would they have gained? Just Petrograd, and that not for very long, for soon they would have all of Russia against them. Could the soviets themselves be won by the Bolsheviks and their allies? Only if their legitimate leaders, that is, the Mensheviks and the Socialist Revolutionaries, departed from the path of socialist virtue and thus gave the masses reasons to believe that by reintroducing discipline in the army, curbs on the freedom of speech, too vigorous a prosecution of peasant disorders, et cetera, they were in effect betraying their interests and siding with the camp of reaction. Short of being convinced of such a betrayal, how could the majority of class-conscious proletarians embrace the adventurist and un-Marxist policies of the Bolsheviks? In fact if the latter had any deeper scheme behind their wild talk and irresponsible moves, it was to provoke the democratic left into supporting repression and thus discrediting itself in the eyes of the masses.

Bizarre as it seems in retrospect, this convoluted thinking had at the time a certain degree of logic. In the late spring of 1917 Lenin's formula for undermining dual power and destroying the political and social fabric of the post-Revolution settlement was obviously meeting with success. At the same time there remained even for him the perplexing question of exactly how the Bolsheviks were going to seize power and more fundamentally, how they could cling to it after the initial coup. Originally this question did not appear overly important. Lenin came back to Russia to start a *European* revolution, and if the Bolsheviks were to be swamped by revolutionary anarchism that they had instigated, it would be a small price to pay for the larger goal. But with his continued immersion in domestic politics, his attitude began to change. He now craved not only to lead his people into the wilderness but to see the promised land of power and socialism.

In the middle of May some readers of *Pravda* must have rubbed their eyes in disbelief, for here was Lenin warning about the danger of an economic depression and criticizing the Menshevik minister Skobelev for his demagogic attacks upon the capitalists. Skobelev had just declared that all profits and dividends should be taxed away. If there were pressing reasons for it, Lenin was able to turn himself into an anarchist, but he was not an economic illiterate, as was the Menshevik minister who said in a public speech, "If the capitalists want to preserve the bourgeois economy, let them work without profits. . . . We should introduce compulsory labor for all those bankers, shareholders, and manufacturers." Lenin was hugely amused, and indeed with people like that as ministers, how could the regime survive even if there was no war and all the Bolsheviks were in jail? But in his derisive comments on the nonsensical statement, one suddenly glimpses the real Marxist Lenin, and not the one who had been arguing, and would intermittently continue to argue, for everything conducive to anarchy. The Bolsheviks, he wrote, repudiate any such wild and unscientific schemes bound to ruin the national economy. They did not plan to expropriate industry or to abolish profits. Their state would establish *centralized* control over banking and industry. And the capitalist would have a place in *his* Russia; if loyal to the socialist state, he would be able to work both honorably and profitably. "One should above all seek and choose talented administrators. They are to be found among *all* classes and elements of the population, without in the slightest excluding the capitalists, especially since *right now* they have the needed [managerial] experience."[42]

The nation was rich in talent. Let but economic and political life be organized properly and it would emerge from the mess caused by the government's idiotic policies. He had been explaining that All power to the soviets meant that every community "from the most backward village to a district in Petrograd" would rule itself. But in May he added, incongruously, that, yes, the Bolsheviks believe that the state must be strong. Though his followers might be incredulous or confused, there was no real inconsistency insofar as Lenin was concerned between his anarchist rhetoric and his blueprint of Marxian statism. One was for before, the other was for after. But there might not be an after if, as the result of the Bolsheviks' efforts and the regime's unwitting strivings toward the same goal, the state was utterly shattered. Here was one potentially fatal political weakness of Lenin's: he was a great strategist, but not a tactician of revolution. He preached constantly the importance of organization, yet he himself was not a good party manager, having no head for details. The party had a handful of capable organizers: Jacob Sverdlov, who would act as its unofficial secretary until 1919, and Stalin, who was already earning the reputation of a hardworking and unobtrusive activist. But what the Bolsheviks needed above all was someone to manage the coming revolution, and in May he appeared on the scene.

Fortune again smiled on the party, for Trotsky's talents neatly complemented those of Lenin's. He was unmatched as a revolutionary orator and agitator, while the older man, despite the subsequent legend, was not at ease addressing crowds and was at his best before closed party gatherings. Lenin, though somewhat mellowed of late, still tended to be harsh and abusive in political argument, often alienating even potential allies by his undisguised contempt for his intellectual inferiors and political waverers. Trotsky was as yet largely free of that arrogance and visible vanity which eventually would contribute to his political downfall in Soviet Russia. At the time he radiated joviality and amiability. "One could talk to Trotsky" was the general verdict among the Mensheviks and the Socialist Revolutionaries, and few among them would have asserted the same about Lenin. The future ruthless war commissar was an ideal person to soothe the fears of the Bolsheviks' opponents, and to make converts among the undecided.*

Most important of all, Trotsky was endowed with a revolutionary practicality. Lenin's impatient temperament would push him toward what he himself described as adventurism, such as a premature armed uprising. He tended to follow Napoleon's motto: *on s'engage et puis on voit*—one should plunge into the fray and then see what happens. Without Lenin there would have been no Bolshevik revolution, without Trotsky it might have happened prematurely and failed.

On his arrival Trotsky was not as yet a Bolshevik. He was associated with the small group of Interfaction Socialists who already worked closely with Lenin's

---

*Strange how the roles and temperaments of the two men were reversed after the Bolshevik Revolution when Trotsky became renowned for his arbitrary ways and haughty attitudes while Lenin often seemed tolerant and conciliatory by comparison.

party and would join it officially in July. Few would have predicted that the two men would be able to forget their past differences and work so closely together. Prior to 1914 no other Russian Socialist had been denounced by Lenin as often and as scathingly as his future brilliant second-in-command. And as early as 1903 Trotsky accused his future leader of being possessed by dictatorial ambitions unworthy of a true Social Democrat. But now they saw each other as indispensable to what they both desired above all.

There was another old enemy of Lenin whose return in May was to help the Bolshevik cause, though in a strange and indirect way. Julius Martov had been an early political associate and close friend of the young Lenin. Their paths parted following the Bolshevik-Menshevik split, and yet, uncharacteristically, Lenin must have retained a trace of personal affection for him; Martov was one of the very few people outside his family circle Lenin ever addressed by "thou."* He never wrote of him in the vituperative language he often used for Trotsky and other political foes. Martov, for his part, retained few illusions about the friend of his youth. Lenin, he declared before the war, was not a politician but the leader of a Mafia-like organization within the Socialist party, bent upon establishing his personal dictatorship over it.

But for the anti-Bolshevik left, the consequences of Martov's return were catastrophic. Although he was universally liked and respected for his probity and absence of personal ambition, unlike his old friend-turned-enemy, even his great admirer, Sukhanov, admitted that Martov's personality and policies contributed greatly to the destruction of democratic socialism. The diarist, himself a good illustration of how a keen psychological insight may still be combined with political naivete, wrote perceptively, "Martov was too intellectual to succeed as a revolutionary. A brilliant theoretical mind like his often proves to be a disadvantage in the moment of struggle, in an elemental clash of wills and passions. . . . The consequences of his errors were to weigh heavily on the fate, if not of the Revolution, than on his party's and his own."[43]

The Menshevik leader clearly saw through Lenin's game, yet to the very last, with the Winter Palace about to be seized on October 25, Martov would insist that one must not use force or any kind of repression against a proletarian party.

Martov found his political home among the so-called Menshevik internationalists, hitherto a small and uninfluential left-wing of the party. These were in fact ideological stragglers, unwilling to side either with Lenin or Tseretelli, decrying in one breath both the Provisional Government and the war, and the Bolsheviks' undemocratic and adventurist ways. Now though they remained weak in numbers, they had a prestigious and popular leader and would wield influence out of

---

*Except when speaking to a social inferior, a mark of intimate friendship in old Russia.

proportion to their size. Again and again they would stay the hand of revolutionary democracy when it was raised against those who would destroy it and opposed as undemocratic any measures for the restoration of civil order and military discipline.

The disintegration of the Russian state would thus be accompanied by a parallel disintegration among the democratic left. For a few weeks after the revolution, the Menshevik and Socialist Revolutionary parties loomed like giants on the political scene. In comparison, the Bolsheviks' following among the urban masses was puny, and in rural areas was virtually nonexistent. Now the two parties dissolved into warring factions and it became increasingly difficult for the average worker or soldier to understand what they stood for. Tseretelli's Mensheviks supported the Provisional Government, in fact some of them were in it, and yet they continued to castigate the actions and attitudes of their bourgeois colleagues. Martov's internationalists virtually echoed the Bolsheviks' complaints about dual power and the war, but it was unclear what they wanted to do about them. Then there was the Menshevik center, headed and epitomized by Chheidze, critical of the positions of both the left and the right, its own political stance impenetrably obscure.

The situation was even worse among the Socialist Revolutionaries. In any nationwide elections they would undoubtedly have received a majority, as they would even after the Bolshevik coup in the November voting for the Constituent Assembly. But this simply reflected the fact that Russia was a peasant country, and in the absence of competition, the average peasant saw the heirs of the Populists as *his* party. Yet it was difficult to consider this conglomeration of actions and personalities as a real political party. The range of views among the SRs spread from a position considerably to the right of the government Mensheviks to one to the left of the Bolsheviks and verging on outright anarchism. Nor was it possible to locate their political leadership. This strange political movement had an assortment of big names from the revolutionary past and present but no single man with the kind of following enjoyed by Tseretelli or Martov, let alone Lenin. Kerensky, though listed on the party rolls, was still not considered a true Socialist Revolutionary. It was difficult for a movement with its roots in semianarchic populism, its instinctive impulse to be against any power that be, to admit that anyone so closely identified with the government was a bona fide Socialist Revolutionary. Like the soldiers, his party comrades were ready to applaud him more than anyone else, but as with the former, it was more than doubtful that they would follow where he would lead them. Victor Chernov had a long party record and, unlike Kerensky, was not too much compromised by his participation in the government, since it was known that he spent most of his time quarrelling with his fellow ministers. He was also, next to Lenin, the favorite *bête noire* of the bourgeoisie, both because of his strong antiwar views while in exile, and because he looked tolerantly at the growing lawlessness, the peasants' seizure of estates, et cetera, in the countryside. But it was hopeless to expect Chernov, famous for his long-winded speeches and hesitant manner, to pull the various wings of his movement together.

Compared to this disunity and disarray in the camp of revolutionary democracy, the Bolsheviks presented a picture of cohesion and discipline. It would be erroneous to see here anything approaching the future totalitarian Communist party. Lenin was far from being a dictator. His views were quite often opposed, and the argument might at times grow as unruly as at a Menshevik or SR meeting. But eventually he would almost always prevail. His opponents' usual refrain was: This is too dangerous; it will not be understood by the masses, and will bring upon the Bolsheviks' heads reprisals from the Soviet, the government. Then, when his proposals were acted upon and there were no reprisals, while the party membership continued to grow, even the most timid had to admit that he had again been right and must have some unique gift of foresight.

The motto "All power to the soviets" had been proclaimed by Lenin in order to facilitate the decomposition of all authority, and not because he expected that the Bolsheviks eventually would come to power through the soviets. "Eventually" might take a long time; there could be a dramatic turn in the war, or even worse, there might be peace, which would be a veritable catastrophe for it would rob the Bolsheviks of any chance to seize power and start a worldwide revolution. "We shall know how to wait," he said to his followers at one point in April. But by June he and his party were getting impatient. There appeared a disquieting possibility that Russia might get a central state authority other than the crippled Provisional Government and the dormant Duma. (There were periodic calls from the right for its resuscitation, but they were stoutly resisted by revolutionary democracy. While the Duma was slumbering, its offshoot, the Provisional Committee, along with the Soviet, was pulled back on the stage to give a formal seal of approval, whenever there was a change of government, an absurd procedure, but unavoidable since there was no head of state.)

The First All-Russian Congress of the Workers' and Soldiers' Soviets met in June. Out of the 777 members of the assembly with party affiliations, the Bolsheviks had over 100, and their allies, the Interfaction Socialists, about 30. Lenin emerged for the occasion from the editorial offices of *Pravda* and delivered what was even for him an unusually violent and demagogic speech. Tseretelli had said that there was no single political force willing or ready to take power by itself. Nonsense, said Lenin, "our party is ready at any moment to do that." But what created a general shock was his call for revolutionary terror, something he had hitherto carefully eschewed. What the country needed immediately was to arrest fifty to one hundred of the most substantial capitalists and to force them to reveal the clandestine intrigues that kept the Russian people at war and in misery. The blinders would then fall from the eyes of the masses, food shortages and inflation would disappear. Even the majority of the Bolshevik delegates were stunned by this blatant demagoguery. For once the "windbag Kerensky," as Lenin called him, proved equal to the task. What they had just heard, he declared, was something he had never expected to hear from a man who called himself a Social Democrat, something even the old tsarist police would not have dared to do in its heyday: to arrest and grill people just because of their social status or origin. And turning to the Bolshevik benches: "Who are you, Socialists or common bullies?" It was a moment of supreme discomfiture for Lenin, and he who scorned the bourgeois amenities of political discourse shouted to the chairman, "You should call him [Kerensky] to order." It was just a metaphor, explained the presiding officer, who happened to be, in Lenin's parlance, a "Menshevik scoundrel." But in the future, and wisely, Lenin would eschew oratorical duels with the "windbag Kerensky" and others of his ilk.[44]

It fell to Trotsky to try to dissipate the fatal impression created by his leader's performance. No one, he assured them, meant to resort to violence or, even more absurd, to seize power against the will of the soviets. However, with the socialist ministers doing such a good job, why did they need any capitalist ones? But Trotsky still was absent from the Bolsheviks' inner councils. On the ninth of June their Central Committee issued a proclamation calling upon soldiers and workers to take to the streets to demonstrate against the government, described as a tool of the class enemy. The "ten capitalist ministers" had to go. Kerensky's recent and extravagant charter of the soldiers' rights was described as a gross violation of their civic freedoms. The masses were to demand an immediate peace, but with the German workers, and not capitalists.

The demonstration was to be peaceful: "State your demands calmly and convincingly as behooves the strong." But who could believe it? Thousands of armed soldiers and the Bolsheviks' armed partisans, the Red Guards, would be marching on the government's residence.

Confronted with the threat, the Congress of Soviets reacted with unexpected vigor. It banned all demonstrations. Leading figures of revolutionary democracy were dispatched to barracks and factories to explain the Bolshevik game. Pro-Menshevik and SR military units were alerted. On the morning of June 10 the Bolshevik Central Committee called off the demonstration.

"What the Bolsheviks are doing now has nothing to do with propaganda; it is a plot," thundered Tseretelli on the morrow of the aborted demonstration. "People prattle about the danger of capitalist counterrevolution. Well, there is a clear and present danger of counterrevolution, but it does not come from the capitalists. Measures must be taken to prevent the recurrence of danger, the Bolsheviks' private army, the Red Guards, must be disarmed." That far revolutionary democracy was unwilling to go. Tseretelli's discovery—a few weeks ago he was the one who pleaded that Lenin was a man of principle and believer in peaceful persuasion—was vehemently assailed by Martov's faction. How could one even talk about disarming the workers? Who would defend the soviets? The Congress's resolve melted in the heat of ritualistic oratory. The Bolsheviks paraded their injured innocence. In calling for an armed demonstration all they had tried to do was keep the outraged masses from perpetrating mayhem. And they did submit to the majority, even when the latter had grievously slandered their intentions. The congress passed a resolution stressing the inadmissibility of armed demonstrations and violence . . .

Even so Lenin began to have doubts about "All power to the soviets." The masses seemed to take it literally. It was also becoming difficult to persuade them to take seriously the danger of capitalist counterrevolution. The Provisional Government did not even try to intervene in the crisis of June 9. It was the soviets which barred the way. And so, he reflected, if the soviets took all power and tried to interfere with the Bolsheviks' agitation, as he called it, whether in the capital or at the front, his party would not submit but rather would go underground like the old times.

For the time being the soviets' bark proved much worse than its bite. Hopes that the congress would mark the birth of a new central authority which the country needed so desperately had to be set back by the decision that its standing organ, the Central Executive Committee, would be composed of 200 members, with, of course, the Bolsheviks and Martov's Mensheviks represented on it* and the ineffective Chheidze its chairman.

By the last days of June, the traditional lament of Russian politics, "We are standing on the edge of an abyss," would have seemed a wildly optimistic understatement. But its twin dirge, "Things cannot go on the way they have," was precisely correct. Even if the Bolsheviks are forgotten for the moment, the whole fabric of national life, not to mention the government, was unravelling. The capital and some other cities were plagued by anarchists of all varieties. One faction comprising obviously criminal elements occupied a large private residence in Petrograd, leading to one of those agonizing discussions in the Soviet as to the propriety of using force against people who, though lawless, were motivated by a genuine ideology. (Freedom of the press was felt to be in a different category than property rights; when another gang seized a right-wing newspaper and smashed its plant, the Executive Committee dispatched its champion orators to

*Lenin, an elected member, never attended.

threaten the culprits with grave consequences.) Occasionally prisons would be taken over and their inmates released. The countryside was seething with marauding gangs of army deserters. The peasants' congress held in May passed some very radical resolutions including one that called for the expropriation of estates and, somewhat incongruously, also demanded strong police measures to protect the peasants from the pillaging deserters. Of what use would land reform and a Constituent Assembly be, said one delegate plaintively, if they might not live to see either.

Separatism grew apace with anarchy. In the Ukraine the local nationalists escalated their demands from a measure of autonomy in March to near independence in June. Their council, or *rada,* presumed to speak for the nation as a whole and demanded that the Provisional Government not pass any laws affecting the Ukraine without its approval. The Finns, always jealous of their autonomy, now carried on a continuous struggle with Petrograd, and there were stirrings among other ethnic groups. The government could only offer its usual answer to every social and political demand, "Wait until the Constituent Assembly." But most nationalists were as impatient as Lenin, and they proceeded with the creation of quasi-governments of their own. Perhaps because most of their tiny country was occupied by the Germans, a group of Lithuanians proclaimed itself to be the national diet and demanded full independence and permanent neutrality for the Baltic land. As on almost any other issue, revolutionary democracy was of two minds about national self-determination: in theory, yes, but in practice it proposed to wait. Even such people as Sukhanov felt vague stirrings of Russian nationalism when confronted with the danger that the Russian state might soon be pushed back, at least in Europe, to its mid-seventeenth century boundaries. They rationalized their reluctance by the argument that the separatist agitation usually came from the bourgeois circles. But Lenin, whatever his inner feelings, held sternly to the slogan of unconditional independence for any non-Russian nationality which asked for it.

It was under such circumstances that the Provisional Government ordered the army to start an offensive in the second half of June. The decision was motivated mainly by two reasons. First, and above all, a military victory was needed to arrest the momentum of political and social disintegration. Second, it was believed that inactivity was having a disastrous impact on the army's morale and discipline. Two months before an offensive might have been crowned with success and had a salutary effect on the overall situation. Now it was foolhardy and could be explained only by the fact that General Brusilov, the commander-in-chief, was an incurable optimist and that Kerensky, who was mainly responsible for the order, fell victim to his own fiery oratory. The persuader-in-chief, as he was ironically dubbed by some officers, toured the front lines, and the enthusiasm with which he was greeted by the soldiers convinced him that the Russian army, like that of the French Revolution, would carry freedom on its bayonets.

What in fact did happen is vividly illustrated by some excerpts from the postmortem on the operation by General Anton Deniken, commander of the southern front.

After extraordinary efforts by the commanding staff, the Tenth Army finally moved forward, but under what circumstances! Forty-eight battalions refused to engage in combat. . . . I was present when the Pota regiment was handed a red banner and its soldiers swore on it to fight until death. One hour before the attack the regiment fled to the rear, stopping only after fifteen kilometers.[45]

Bands of deserters, the general continued, would manhandle their officers, pillage the countryside, and inflict all kinds of atrocities on their own civilian countrymen. The soldiers had by now lost any conception of military discipline. Even units which fought well had had to be argued with prior to the attack. He, commander of an entire front, had been summoned by an army's soviet to explain the whys and mechanics of the offensive and had to spend his time lecturing about what a breakthrough was, what reserves were at his disposal, et cetera.

The soldiers' behavior becomes more understandable if one remembers that not only was there no death penalty for desertion or any other offense but also because a few days before the attack Kerensky had thought fit to abolish courts-martial altogether. They were replaced by regimental courts composed in equal proportions of officers and soldiers, elected by the given regiment. All that one risked in running away was presumably to be judged by one's fellow deserters!

Amazingly, along some sectors of the front the offensive at first went well. This can be explained by the Russians' enormous numerical superiority and the fact that the Austrian army, the target of the initial thrust, was not in much better shape than they. In one area, Deniken was able to concentrate 138 battalions against the Austrians' 17, employ 900 artillery pieces against the enemy's 300. Though on occasion the soldiers had to be lectured on why they should pursue the retreating enemy after they had broken through, Brusilov's forces again cut deep into Galicia and Kerensky's telegrams from the front grew ecstatic.

All the more shattering the blow when in the beginning of July German reinforcements were thrown in, and the Russian advance gave way to retreat, then in many segments to a headlong flight. It was only the Germans' deficiencies in manpower that enabled the Russians to reestablish the front lines where they had been before their ill-omened offensive.

Yet in all fairness to Kerensky and his military advisers, the picture should be put in perspective. Had the home front held firm, it is just possible that the initial successes could have infused a new spirit in Russia's armies. The armies of the

French Revolution also did not distinguish themselves in their first battles. Nothing that happened to the Russian armies until *after* the Bolshevik coup in October was as catastrophic as the fate which befell the Soviet forces in the first weeks following the German attack in June 1941. But in both cases the government of the day proved strong and ruthless enough to restore discipline and to start turning the situation around. Reporting to his civilian superiors on the debacle, General Deniken refused to blame it *primarily* on the Bolsheviks rather than on the general politicization of the army by revolutionary democracy. "The Bolsheviks," he said, "are vermin feeding on the festering wound."

He was doing Lenin's party an injustice in minimizing its role in demoralizing the soldier. The Bolsheviks viewed the prospect of even a partial success in the campaign as a grave danger to their plans and goals. Toward the end of June, with the offensive's fate still in balance, they had to consider seriously undertaking a preemptive strike. They made little secret of their intentions. Between June 15 and 24 there took place a conference of the military affiliates of the party. Its one hundred sixty delegates represented twenty-six thousand members of Bolshevik cells from more than five hundred regiments. It is remarkable even for those days that the delegates, most of them soldiers on active duty, felt no compunction to endorse, unanimously and in public, the call to sabotage the offensive, and almost as explicitly to call for an armed uprising against both the government and revolutionary democracy.

> More than ever it is incumbent on revolutionary social democracy . . . to persuade the masses that the current offensive gravely imperils the Russian and world revolutions. . . . The danger springs from the policies of the Menshevik and SR parties; they are trying to deceive the masses, make them follow the counterrevolutionary bourgoisie. The [Bolshevik] Military Organizations have to marshal their forces and lead a mass movement which would confront the bourgeois government and the ruling Menshevik and SR parties, demand the ejection of the government and a thorough turnabout in domestic and foreign policies.[46]

Pravda reported approvingly how Regiment X refused to fight and Division Y, after pushing the enemy back, would decide to stop, because to advance further "would serve the interests of the Russian, British and French bourgeoisie." Even the Menshevik internationalists were shocked by the Bolshevik organ's gleeful account of how Sokolov, of Order No. 1 fame, who in his capacity as one of the Soviet's envoys was urging the soldiers to do their duty, was set upon by them and beaten into unconsciousness.

The Provisional Government responded to the emergency by disintegrating; on July 2, four Kadet ministers offered their resignations in protest against their colleagues' approving a wide measure of autonomy for the Ukraine. The Executive Committee of the Petrograd Soviet was currently preoccupied by what its left felt was a case of police brutality. (There were no police in the strict sense of the word; progovernment soldiers were serving as a voluntary militia.) A private villa, long occupied by the anarchists, was finally cleared of them, some of the inhabitants allegedly manhandled in the process.

The chaos was compounded by more than the usual turmoil within the Petrograd garrison. Some of its units had just been informed that they would be sent to the front. One of them, the First Machine Regiment, a hotbed of Bolshevik and anarchist influence, voted that the order was counterrevolutionary. Its leading spirit, Ensign Semashko,* then organized on July 3 a musical matinee interspersed with political speeches. After listening to Bolshevik orators, among them Trotsky, the regiment decided to demonstrate for "All power to the soviets." Joined by other soldiers and the striking workers from another Bolshevik stronghold, the Putilov Works, they took to the streets. There were random shots and clashes as the procession wound its way toward the Tauride Palace, which having been vacated by the Provisional Government, was now the seat of both the Petrograd Soviet and the Central Executive Committee, as well as of their innumerable offshoots, the Workers' Section of the Soviet, the Bureau of the Central Executive Committee, et cetera, the revolution ever sprouting new limbs from its eviscerated body.

Up to now the Bolsheviks had *incited* but not yet assumed leadership of the manifestation. Some of its moves, obviously, were being synchronized by them. Among the demands presented by the demonstrators to the Soviet was, in addition to the sacramental "All Power . . . ," one for the suppression of the bourgeois press. At the same time in the Workers' Section where the Bolsheviks and their allies attained a temporary majority, Zinoviev was hectoring the Soviet leaders on the same subject: "You have left the monopoly of the press to the capitalists who use it to subvert [*sic*] the countryside. Why haven't you taken from them that destructive weapon?"[47]

Informed of the situation, Lenin cut short his vacation in Finland and returned to the capital. But his party did not need his physical presence to embark on the now well-rehearsed tactics: to proclaim loudly that the manifestation should not lead to violence, while preparing for the eventuality that the expected violence should be crowned with success. Its Petrograd (not Central) Committee called for the intensification of the demonstrations, so that the people's will should be heeded and the capitalist ministers chased out. A special military commission was appointed to supervise the uprising, should it somehow materialize despite all the Bolsheviks' public pleas against it. None of the party's leaders was on the commis-

*In Communist Russia he would be shot as a common criminal.

sion—if the enterprise failed, it could be blamed on the unauthorized actions of a few hotheads. Some such unauthorized individuals tried and failed to intercept Kerensky as he departed from the railway station to summon front-line regiments to the defense of the capital and the revolution.

On July 4 the Bolshevik high command had to recognize that its forces consisted largely of an unruly, armed but panicky and looting mob. Trucks filled with armed soldiers and Red Guards coursed through the main thoroughfares of the city, their passengers shooting at random into shop and apartment windows behind which they allegedly spotted "agents of the bourgeoisie." The ministers hid in Prince Lvov's private apartment, while the other half-government, the Central Executive Committee of the Soviets, was continuing its session and issuing proclamations. Its usual remedy for disorders, sending orators to the mutinous regiments, could not be used for there were few volunteers for the mission which involved running the risk of being lynched by the brutalized soldiers.

Feeling that the situation was getting out of hand, the Bolshevik Central Committee called upon what they hoped would be a more disciplined element, the Kronstadt sailors. Their leader asked Stalin by telephone whether they should bring along their rifles. It was up to them, a celebrated story has Stalin replying. He, a writer, always carried his weapon, a pencil, with him. Twenty thousand strong, fully armed, with military bands playing, the sailors marched first to the Bolshevik headquarters, where several party luminaries addressed them on the theme of "All power . . ." Only in answer to insistent demands did Lenin himself emerge on the balcony to repeat the refrain and to hail the sailors as "the pride and glory of the Russian Revolution." Then on to the Tauride Palace. But their arrival there was delayed by looting and armed clashes on the way. By the time they arrived the Bolshevik high command had had second thoughts. There were rumors that indeed some progovernment military forces were hastening toward the capital. If so, there was no question but that the pro-Bolshevik armed rabble would run away. As Lenin said, "The front line soldiers, deceived by the liberals, might come and slaughter the Petrograd workers."

One version of the Bolshevik scenario had the mutinous soldiers and sailors arresting the leaders of the Soviet, at the same time they were handing it "All power . . ." But when the sailors finally arrived before the Tauride Palace and tried to seize Chernov, who came out to calm them (one of them shouted, "Take power, you son of a bitch, when we give it to you"), Trotsky intervened to save the Socialist Revolutionary leader from what might have been a lynching, with incalculable consequences for the future course of events. Confused, the sailors' leaders led them away. Most of them, rather than wait for the Bolsheviks to make up their minds, fled back to Kronstadt. The same night the Bolshevik Central

Committee called off the enterprise, declaring, "The demonstration achieved its goal. The leading forces of the working class and the army presented their demands in a dignified and inspiring manner."

The morning of July 5, Lenin left his apartment in search of a hiding place. Now that the danger had passed, it was apparent that there were quite a few units in Petrograd ready to defend dual power. With their so-called army melted away, the Bolsheviks' eagerness to suppress the counterrevolutionary press now became understandable. Stories appeared in the Kadet papers linking Lenin to German money and correctly naming the intermediaries. The Bolshevik headquarters was occupied, *Pravda*'s printing plant smashed. The outcry against the party was now universal. This time it had suffered, almost everyone was sure, an irretrievable disaster. The Bolshevik leaders who still dared to appear in public kept imploring their Menshevik and SR "comrades," as they suddenly had become again, to suppress and repudiate the scandalous libels about Lenin and to save them from the reactionaries' vengeance. On July 7 a warrant was issued for the arrest of Lenin and his chief lieutenant Zinoviev. Some other Bolsheviks, including Trotsky, let themselves be arrested, rather than follow the example of their leader. This was not necessarily a proof of their craving for martyrdom. They were safer in prisons, some of them guarded by pro-Bolshevik soldiers, than at large. Groups of officers and military academy students were on the lookout for "German agents." Reaction, Sukhanov noted sadly, was triumphant.

Revolutionary democracy, however, was already having second thoughts about its narrow escape. "This is how a counterrevolution always begins," shouted Martov when loyal troops arrived to defend the Soviet from the pro-Bolshevik mob. It was disgraceful that a Socialist, even if an erring one, could be accused of taking money from the Germans. It would reflect on the movement as a whole. What was worse, the Socialists who were in the government must have known (though neither then nor after the October Revolution would they admit it) that there was at least a prima facie case for the accusations. From his hideouts, Lenin kept addressing letters to Menshevik journals, protesting that he hardly knew those agents of Parvus who allegedly had supplied him with money. He had met Hanecki only once in 1907. This must have given a jolt even to some Bolsheviks, aware that Hanecki had been in Lenin's entourage during his prewar years in Galicia. At the same time the Ministry of Justice had in its file copies of Lenin's recent letters to Hanecki and another intermediary in Stockholm, Radek, in which he urged them to be "extra cautious in their connections" and acknowledged the receipt of a considerable sum from their contact in Petrograd, another Polish Socialist, Vorovsky.

Hence, no real attempt was made to apprehend Lenin. He was hiding first in the apartment of a well-known Bolshevik and then between July 11 and August

8 on a farm twenty miles from Petrograd. It would hardly have required a Sherlock Holmes to track him down, because he was frequently visited in both places by Bolshevik notables who had not been arrested and by members of his family. A commission was appointed to investigate the charges against Lenin, but evidently it was never shown that dossier in the Ministry of Justice, and it never completed its investigation.

The same logic dictated that no attempt be made to finish off, or in fact to interfere seriously, with the Bolsheviks. The party operated in what Communist historians describe as a condition of semilegality, which meant in practice that the Bolsheviks pretended to hide from the authorities, and the latter pretended not to notice them. Lenin's followers, according to this reasoning of revolutionary democracy, had finally discredited themselves in the eyes of the masses, and hence represented no danger even though their membership kept growing. To persecute them further would merely play into the hands of reaction. "If they arrest Lenin, tomorrow they will take me," said Chheidze. Already as a result of the July days the Kadets and the generals had become less supine in their attitude toward the soviets. Many officers and junkers—students in the military academies—were now banding in patriotic societies for the defense of Russia against internal and external enemies. There was talk of a military dictatorship; as history infallibly taught, a threat to the revolution could only come from the right . . .

Toward the end of July, the Bolshevik party held its Sixth Congress in Petrograd. The Bolshevik press announced that it was taking place, but not where. Of course, neither the government nor the Soviet seemed able to discover where some 270 people assembled and deliberated for eight days. The congress's work was guided by Stalin and Sverdlov, who were in daily communication with their absent leader and imprisoned comrades. The congress gave its formal blessing to the merger of Lenin's and Trotsky's Interfaction groups. The party, for all its alleged persecution and renunciation by the masses, was flourishing. Its membership tripled in three months and now stood at two hundred forty thousand, with about fifty thousand in each of the two capitals.

Many of the delegates could not understand why Lenin and Zinoviev were still hiding, a good testimony of how the Bolsheviks attracted men of action rather than those unduly given to reflection. Were they to give themselves up, some delegates held, their trial would be a splendid vindication of the party's honor and a repudiation of the capitalists' scurrilous slander.* But the more realistic,

---

*Some food for thought was offered by the very cursory financial report at the congress. The party during the previous three months, it was affirmed, had spent 50,000 rubles out of its income of approximately 71,000. Yet *Pravda*'s printing plant cost 260,000 rubles. And where did the money come from for The Red Guards' arms, etc.? *The Sixth Congress of the Russian Social Democratic Workers' Party (Bolsheviks)* (Moscow, 1958), pp. 38–42.

and presumably more knowledgable, party leaders persuaded the congress that their leaders could not count on being accorded a fair trial by the government, now committed to a course of reaction and suppression.

Acting on Lenin's instructions, the Bolsheviks now dropped the old battle cry of "All power to the soviets," an obvious reaction to the fiasco of those July days. But in reporting to the congress, Stalin thought it prudent to omit the absent leader's accompanying reflection that "The peaceful period of the evolution of the Revolution has ended," (There had been several hundred killed and wounded on July 3 and 4), and that they ought to come out explicitly for an armed uprising. The new formula called for the transfer of all power to the revolutionary proletariat and the poor peasants. How this was to be done was not specified, but, added Stalin, they did not propose to undertake anything which smacked of illegality. It was, after all, due to their exertions that the masses during the July days did not get out of hand, and the bourgoisie's provocation did not result in wholesale slaughter!

Superficially the abortive coup and the popular reaction to the breakdown of the army should have strengthened the hand of the right. Yet the latter had virtually disappeared as an organized force, and as political parties, in the wake of March 2. Monarchism which had been its cementing link had simply evaporated as a political sentiment. There remained an inchoate feeling of outraged nationalism, but the various patriotic leagues and other veterans' and officers' organizations had no political movement to turn to. The crisis ought to have strengthened the Kadets, the only party which had been warning about the consequences of destroying the fabric of political authority. But for most conservatives it was the Kadets who were the main culprits in the situation: having contributed mightily to the destruction of old Russia, and incapable of creating a new one, they were now hostages of revolutionary democracy, and all they could do was to bewail the results of their handiwork.

More essentially, the Party of the National Freedom, to give it the official name, was still the victim of the feeling which had plagued it since its birth, that it was for the people, but not of the people. The Kadets had never tried to expand their political base from the intelligentsia and the propertied class to the workers and peasants, and now it was too late. It was felt quite natural that anarchists of all varieties should have access to the soviets; a workers' or soldiers' deputy who proclaimed himself a follower of the Kadets would have been considered a wonder of nature. The "bourgeois" label affixed to the party was all the more ironic because by West European standards the Kadets were considerably left of center. They had always stood for the compulsory purchase and parcelling out of large estates to appease the peasants' land hunger, favored a progressive income tax, and were ready to accept far-reaching government controls in industry. Their "capitalist" character was evident only in their helpless pleas that radical reforms should be carried out with due observance of the law, rather than through "the initiative of the masses." And their "chauvinism" lay in their devotion to Russia's greatness and unity, and even there they were ready to go farther in recognizing the Poles' right to self-determination than many from revolutionary democracy, who feared that an independent Poland would be run by priests and aristocrats. (The left thus endorsed the Russian reactionaries' traditional argument against Polish independence.)

The party was still torn by policy disagreements and indecision, something that had handicapped the Kadets before 1917, but which in a revolutionary situation was simply disastrous. Some members were beginning to see the only possible salvation in a military dictatorship. But it was difficult for the standard bearers of Russian liberalism to commit themselves wholeheartedly to such a solution. From being the "revolutionary bourgeoisie" (somewhat similar to "honorary Aryans") in the parlance of the soviets, it would be turning itself into a counter-revolutionary one, thus confirming what the Bolsheviks had always been saying.

By July a few among the more realistic Kadets were ready to concede, if only in private, that the war's continuation was bound to end in disaster. But they hesitated to come out openly for a separate peace. Russia's allies, torchbearers of democracy in the world, who were barely defending their own positions, would surely be crushed by the German army, one-third of whose strength had hitherto been tied up in the East. And the prospects were dim for Russia's, democracy's, future in a Europe dominated by Prussian militarism. Furthermore, were the government to enter upon negotiations with the enemy, revolutionary democracy and the Bolsheviks would unite in crying treason: peace was to be made with the German and Austrian workers and soldiers, not with their ministers and generals.

The only remaining option for the Kadets was to continue to cooperate with the moderate wing of revolutionary democracy. Like panic-stricken swimmers, the two would cling to each other, both to be pulled down eventually by the revolutionary whirlpool.

Even so, it was not easy to overcome the ministerial crisis which began on July 2 and continued until the eighth. Yielding to the generals' indignant expostulations, Kerensky felt constrained to promise them the restoration of the death penalty for desertion and other crimes committed by the military as well as to curb the circulation of subversive (that is, Bolshevik) literature at the front. To sweeten this bitter pill for the left, the Socialist ministers proposed to proclaim Russia a republic and to ban all commercial transactions in land, unless approved by the local land committee and the appropriate ministry, thus virtually presaging the nationalization of landed estates. To everyone's surprise, Prince Lvov, at this point, chose to emerge from the shadows by announcing that he was resigning as prime minister. In principle, he said, he approved of both measures, but it was up to the Constituent Assembly to make decisions so fundamental to the future of the country. There could be no question as to his successor. Few historical figures have had as precipitous a rise and fall as Kerensky. In February he was about to be arrested by the tsarist police, by November he would be hiding from the Bolsheviks.

Now at the highest rung of the official ladder, Kerensky had but a fraction of the power he had in the beginning of the revolution. As prime minister, he retained the portfolio of war, an obvious hint that his mind was turning to the possibility that the revolution might have to be defended through means other than rhetoric. But his hopes of building a base of support in the army were bound to be disappointed. As he himself said pathetically, "With the support of the masses and the army, the government will save Russia and forge unity. If the appeal to reason, honor and conscience will not suffice, it will have to be done so through blood and iron. . . . But the question is, would it work?"[48]

The new prime minister courted the officer corps, but like everything he tried, the results were to be opposite from what he expected. He chose as his main assistant in the war ministry Boris Savinkov, a celebrated revolutionary terrorist in the prewar era and now, like most of his ilk, a staunch supporter of war until the end, but not a fortunate choice for the role of intermediary with the generals, some of whose colleagues he had helped dispatch to the next world. The officers had another reason to be disgruntled with Kerensky: after the Soviet had condemned the reintroduction of the death penalty, Kerensky in his hopeless fashion intimated that he meant to quash all such sentences. After dismissing Brusilov, who had blamed the government for the failure of the July offensive,* Kerenski selected General Lavr Kornilov to be his commander-in-chief. Truly a people's general, of humble birth, with legendary war exploits and known for his whole-hearted acceptance of the revolution, the new head of the armies seemed to be exactly what Russia and Kerensky needed. Such a combination of virtues also made many feel that here finally was a man who might save the country from the politicians. But Kornilov's utter lack of political sophistication, another trait which influenced Kerensky in his choice, made him both susceptible to the temptation of becoming the country's savior and unlikely to succeed in what would have been a herculean task.

If toward its end the tsarist regime seemed like a man in a catatonic trance, then dual power in its final phase resembled a manic depressive. The accelerating process of political and economic disintegration became momentarily interrupted

*In 1920 he would volunteer his services as military adviser to the Communist regime in the war against Poland.

by a mirage of social reconciliation and national unity, the mood of despair punctured by outbursts of optimism and nationalist exaltation.

Kerensky was still living up to his prerevolution police sobriquet "Swifty"; always on the run, devising new ministerial combinations, improvising fresh consultative and quasi-legislative organs. Depending on his audience, he thundered against the propagators of anarchy with whom his government now proposed to deal firmly and without any sentimental regard for their past revolutionary services; or he threatened draconic penalties against those who would try to restore the monarchy or entertained senseless dreams of a rightist coup. The Kadets and what remained of the right-wing press fumed and warned: let revolutionary democracy put its house in order and be done with the Bolsheviks, or the people's patriotic wrath would sweep them away. In the Soviet and the Central Executive Committee, the majority of the Mensheviks and Socialist Revolutionaries defended the policies, if that be the proper word, of the Provisional Government, though with growing embarrassment and hesitations, and implored their left-wing comrades not to fall for the Bolshevik strategems. But the Menshevik internationalists and left-wing Socialist Revolutionaries would have none of that: there could be no danger from the left. The Bolsheviks' popularity reflected the masses' disgust with undemocratic actions of the government, its persecution of people who had given their entire lives to the revolutionary cause, while closing its eyes to the plots by capitalists and monarchists, of Kerensky hobnobbing with the generals, and his authorizing the death penalty for political dissent in the army.

In the meantime inflation kept growing, rural violence (now in many cases directed against well-to-do peasants and those who had opted for individual farmsteads under Stolypin's reforms, as well as landlords) became endemic in many areas. Industrial strikes and urban disorders were an everyday occurrence. The flood of oratory and resolutions continued, but whether emanating from the government or the Central Executive Committee or the Soviet, it was powerless to stop the process of social disintegration.

Neither the liberals nor the democratic left were ready to surrender the belief bred by the decades of struggle between the government and society that oratory and intellectual persuasion were magic weapons of politics. They had been so effective in breaching the walls of autocracy in 1905–6, then in bringing them down altogether eleven years later. Russian politicians did not stop to consider that if indeed the walls of Jericho were brought down by such means, there was no biblical authority for holding that propaganda and manifestations would be effective in building another line of fortifications. Confronted by the ever-worsening situation, dual power decided that what was needed was another and bigger talk feast.

It materialized in the form of the State Conference held in Moscow between August 12 and 15. The spectacle was supposed to unite all the vital forces of Russian society in a grandiose manifestation of national unity. The Duma awoke from its slumber for the occasion, its deputies joined by those of the central organ of the soviets, representatives of the peasants, Cossacks, and of the learned professions and the venerable veterans of the revolutionary and liberation movements in their individual capacity. The assembly represented all shades of political opinion, except the Bolsheviks, banned for their recent misbehavior, and the more unruly anarchists.* Moscow, where the whole apparatus of dual power migrated for the three days, was chosen in the expectation that its atmosphere, calmer than that of the younger capital, and its historical associations would help to imbue the gathering with a sense of dignity and national rededication, expectations somewhat dampened when the local unions under the Bolsheviks' prompting proclaimed a day's general strike to protest the undemocratic character of the conference. Another jarring note was the appearance of General Kornilov, whom Kerensky had hoped to keep away for fear that some intemperate remark of his might enrage revolutionary democracy and break the spell, and who indeed aroused suspicion from that quarter even prior to gracing the conference with his presence by his well-publicized appearance at a religious shrine.

The prime minister's speech was equal to the occasion. "Those who raise their armed hand against the people's government . . . will be stopped with iron and blood. . . . Only by taking our lives could the body of the great Russian democracy be torn and destroyed. . . . There is no will and authority in the army higher than that of the Provisional Government."[49] He had called his colleagues, he said, to acquaint them with all the economic disasters which had befallen the country, and the threat of famine, but his own peroration ended on a positive note, "We shall move . . . with all the strength of the state wherever there is violence and arbitrary action."

As usual the spellbinder was repeatedly interrupted by applause in which the whole audience joined. That much of the apparent unity was superficial could be seen during the subsequent speech by Kornilov. At his appearance, all except the representatives of revolutionary democracy rose to their feet, with the ensuing turmoil punctuated by shouts of "Scoundrel" and "Have the decency to stand up" from the right, and countershouts of "Lackeys." The general's plea for restoring the army's discipline, his recounting of the drastic measures he had adopted on his own to deal with desertions and hooliganism among the soldiers, again brought cheers from the right and protests from the left. If his proposals for healing the army were not heeded, he said, Russia would face further defeats.

*The patriotic ones were represented by the aged Prince Kropotkin and some veterans of The People's Will.

Even an early peace would not save Russia, for once demobilized, the undisciplined mob "would destroy the country in a torrent of outrages."

One could have foreseen that this meeting which threw together three thousand representatives of revolutionary democracy and what still considered itself society, but in the eyes of the former was simply the bourgeoisie, would only widen the chasm between the two. The soviets' representatives could not but experience renewed stirrings of class antagonisms when exposed to the others' schoolmasterish warnings and the implied threats that the soviets must learn to behave or the generals would teach them a lesson. Those professors, lawyers, and industrialists, all erstwhile followers of the Liberation movement, were for their part visibly shaken by the left's insensitivity to the nation's plight, its failure to understand that ideological incantations and phrase mongering could not arrest the momentum to disaster. History was repeating itself: one year before (though it seemed like a century) it was the liberals who were being beseeched not to undermine the government and who were being warned that if they succeeded, it would be the forces of anarchy which would gain the upper hand. Now the Milyukovs, Maklakovs, and others, were cast in the role once held by tsarist bureacrats, while the left kept repeating the refrain they once had used, "You must trust the people and eschew repression of any kind. . . ."

Despite their growing unhappiness with each other, neither revolutionary democracy nor the progressive bourgeoisie could afford to break off their liaison. Their bond was reaffirmed in the best theatrical manner when a representative of industrial managers called upon Tseretelli to demonstrate their determination to work together for Russia. To the thunderous applause of the whole audience, the two shook hands. Perhaps fearful of being upstaged by this symbolic embrace between capital and labor,* Kerensky rose to new heights in his closing address: "I will cast away the keys to this heart that loves the people and will think only of the State." Such hyperboles were by now deeply embarrassing to many politicians on the left and exasperating to the right. But the gallery was still responsive to the traditional revolutionary bathos: some cried, others implored the orator not to let his heart harden against his countrymen. The speech ended on a note of euphoric incoherence.

The Bolsheviks' surge towards power continued. Five days after the Moscow theatricalities, their slate scored spectacular gains in the elections to the Petrograd city council, receiving one-third of all votes. The Mensheviks' support declined catastrophically. While the Socialist Revolutionaries came out slightly ahead of the Bolsheviks, and the Kadets, though down, received 20 percent of the vote, the results were an unmistakable sign that Lenin's party, as behooved

---

*Actually, like practically all socialist leaders, Tseretelli came from a well-to-do family.

its name, had behind it a majority of the urban proletariat and would soon control the soviets, with the right-wing Mensheviks, hitherto the mainstay of revolutionary democracy slated, as Trotsky would put it on the night of October 25, for "the rubbish heap of history."

The stage was being set for the last act of the drama. Late in July the Provisional Government, defying superstition, moved to the Winter Palace, the Central Executive Committee of the Soviets abandoned the splendor of the Tauride Palace in favor of the more austere premises of the Smolny Institute, until recently a finishing school for noble-born damsels. These were to be the two focal locations of the October coup.

But before the last act a tragicomic interlude intervened. General Kornilov's relations with Kerensky had from the beginning been somewhat analogous to those between the Provisional Government and the Soviet. Whenever he visited the capital to report to his civilian superiors, the commander-in-chief felt it prudent to take along his Turkomen bodyguards, personally devoted to him in view of his long service in central Asia.* Fully armed and deploying machine guns, the tribesmen camped around their chief's residence, not a reassuring symbol of the state of military-civilian relations.

Rumors of an impending military coup were now as rife as before the revolution, and this time the dark forces to be eliminated would be not only the Bolsheviks but also some other Socialists, allegedly connected with the enemy.† Scenes from past revolutions were floating enticingly before the minds of many Russians, including not a few Kadets, Cromwell marching into Parliament at the head of his Ironsides and saying, "By the bowels of Christ, you have sat here too long. Go;" or, Napoleon's grenadiers prodding with their bayonets the delegates of the French assembly, thus to persuade them to accept the Consulate. How delightful if something similar could be reenacted in Smolny!

Since July the German high command had eschewed offensives, awaiting, though with increasing impatience, the enemy's total disintegration. But in the second half of August, after a probing attack in the north met with little resistance, the Imperial army stumbled into occupying Riga. With the capital now thought to be endangered, the Petrograd Military Region was placed under the commander-in-chief. Insofar as the capital's garrison was concerned, this was a purely academic exercise. Words like *subordination* and *command* had become

---

*Before the war Kornilov had carried out a number of daring intelligence missions in Afghanistan, Chinese Turkestan, and British India.

†Kornilov would subsequently claim that Kerensky had warned him not to discuss military secrets before the cabinet since he suspected that the minister of agriculture, Chernov, was a German agent. This would have been absurd on two counts, since the SR leader, for all his antiwar past, was impeccably loyal, and what military secrets were there to betray? By diligent reading of the Russian, and not only Bolshevik, press, the Germans could learn everything they needed to know about the army, war plans, etc.

anachronistic; various units, depending on their political colorations and attitude in a crisis, might decide to follow the Soviet or the Bolsheviks, but certainly not some reactionary general.

Now Kerensky himself began to contemplate—it is hard to believe he could ever have decided upon—a military coup of his own. Savinkov was dispatched to Mogilev to dissuade Kornilov from having any ideas of his own on the subject and to persuade him to dismiss several suspicious persons in his entourage. At the same time the ex-terrorist was to apprise the supreme commander that Kerensky indeed wanted him to concentrate a cavalry corps near the capital so as to move in at an opportune time and crush the Bolsheviks.

The subsequent story of the intrigue is blurred since each of its main partici-pants was to accuse the other of lying. But this is the most likely interpretation: Kerensky must have read how Napoleon as First Counsul had cleared his path to dictatorship by using a political crisis to crack down impartially on both the left and the right and had imprisoned and deported both the partisans of the Bourbons and the Jacobins. Therefore, Kerensky would avoid a right-wing coup by inveigling Kornilov to squash the Bolsheviks, and then he might appease the left by sacrificing the overzealous commander-in-chief, and so emerge as the savior of the revolution. Kornilov, a "man with the heart of a lion and the brains of a sheep," as a fellow general characterized him, appears to have been befuddled throughout the whole affair, pulled to and fro by various adventurers in his entourage and by his loathing of Kerensky and his sense of duty as a soldier and patriot. At this point a veteran political intriguer, Vladimir Lvov (no relation of the former prime minister), offered to act as an intermediary between Kerensky and Kornilov and on the prime minister's behalf (entirely on his own, according to the latter's version), he presented himself in Mogilev to draw out the supreme commander. Kornilov evidently expressed himself as willing to accept any solu-tion which would lead to the squashing of Bolshevism and to the country acquir-ing a real government. At Lvov's prompting he admitted that one such solution might be for him to become dictator. (Kerensky might stay on as minister of justice.) Seeing himself as the gray eminence of the future regime, Lvov trium-phantly hurried back to Petrograd and on August 26 informed the prime minister that he was the bearer of an ultimatum by Kornilov: he must hand over all power to the general, and to assure his own personal security while the capital was being purified of subversion, he should repair forthwith to headquarters.

Kerensky then called Mogilev on the Hughes teleprinter* and asked Kornilov whether what he had just heard from Lvov was true. Without asking what it was that he was supposed to have said, the poor general said yes. Kerensky promised

---

*Again a strong reluctance to use the telephone.

to visit him soon and rang off. Great was Kornilov's surprise when next day he received a telegram from the prime minister ordering him to lay down his command. After some further hurried long-distance negotiations, Kornilov refused, issuing instead a call to the Russian people "to awaken from the foolish blindness and realize . . . the depths to which our country is sinking" under the pressure of "the Bolshevik majority in the soviets," (at the time this was not true) and the Provisional Government's complicity, (whether it was intentional or unwitting was not made clear) with the German General Staff's plan to undermine the army, something which was both untrue and politically foolish to say, since it tied the hands of the Kadet would-be-supporters of Kornilov.[50]

Kerensky now donned the armor of the savior of the revolution. He denounced the general and his counterrevolutionary enterprise and called upon the soviets and the people to ward off the danger.

Within two days the attempted putsch expired. The mainstay of the expeditionary force against Petrograd was to be the so-called Savage Division, composed of Moslem highlanders from the Caucasus, who it was assumed would not be able to understand any prosoviet oratory directed at them. The ruse was parried by the Soviet, which found a number of revolutionary highlanders among the city garrison and sent them to tell their countrymen of the generals' perfidious schemes. The expedition was moving slowly—railwaymen were tearing up the tracks—and during one of the stops, the agitators succeeded in persuading the soldiers of the counterrevolutionary character of the enterprise.

The Kornilov affair was over. Its main hero was persuaded to let himself be arrested as were several generals who had expressed sympathy with him.

There ensued the inevitable ministerial crisis. Kadet ministers, though dissociating themselves from the attempted coup, resigned, accusing Kerensky of having entrapped Kornilov. Not being able to find a general to serve as the latter's successor, the persuader-in-chief appointed himself commander-in-chief. That Kerensky still hoped to put into operation some elements of his original scheme is shown by his attempts to exploit the emergency. Petrograd was placed under martial law, and he also moved against the Bolsheviks. Their organ, *The Proletarian*, was banned, only to appear the next day as *The Worker*. It was proposed to shut down the left Menshevik newspaper *New Life*, which specialized in ridiculing the prime minister. He should pay no attention to the government order, a friend told its editor, Sukhanov, but hire some twenty or thirty sailors to guard the paper's premises and chase away anyone who tried to interfere with its publication.

The whole affair turned out to be a boon for the Bolsheviks. At the moment of alleged danger, their Menshevik and Socialist Revolutionary foes implored them to forget bygones and join in the defense of the revolution. The Central

Executive Committee authorized the issuance of arms to the Red Guards. From his hideout Lenin approved that his party succour revolutionary democracy in its hour of need, but in a manner which would further discredit Kerensky and his allies.

He ought not to have worried; the prime minister continued to be his own worst enemy. He told the soldiers that the rebels would be swiftly and ruthlessly punished. At the same time he tried to recoup some ground among the officer corps by protecting Kornilov and his people and placing them under a very lenient arrest. Most officers had come to view their new supreme commander with feelings they had hitherto reserved for Lenin, and Kerensky's pleas that now they must trust and obey their commanders met with the expected response. (At the height of the crisis, a crowd of sailors in Vyborg seized and drowned nine officers suspected of being Kornilovites.)

What would have appeared utterly fantastic one month before—the Bolsheviks assuming power in an entirely peaceful manner—seemed a real possibility by the beginning of September. The emergency led to the release of the Bolshevik leaders imprisoned in the wake of the July days. Lenin still stayed away,* his colleagues fearful not only about his safety but also that with him in their midst, they might be driven into another rash undertaking, and things seemed to be going too well for the party to risk a repetition of the July fiasco. In the beginning of the month the soviets in both capitals received a pro-Bolshevik majority and Trotsky became the chairman for Petrograd. It was only a matter of time before a new Congress of the Soviets would replace the current Menshevik and SR-led Central Executive Committee with a Bolshevik dominated body. One by one a peaceful revolutionary democracy was surrendering its bastions. The other half-government, the Council of Ministers, was hardly worth bothering about; when the Bolsheviks took over the central organ of the soviets it would collapse like a house of cards. So there was no need to try to rush things.

But for Lenin such complacent thoughts bordered on treason, and the idea of an entirely peaceful takeover of power threatened, he felt, his entire life's work. He was well aware that his colleagues had not emancipated themselves sufficiently (and would not do so entirely until well after October 25) from their baneful social democratic traditions. Without him, most Bolsheviks would opt for a coalition with other socialist parties. But how could Russia, indeed any country at any time, be ruled with the likes of Martov in the government! To think in terms of majorities, et cetera, was for his party suicidal. The Bolsheviks might be able to control the soviets with their worker and soldier constituency, but they

*On August 8 at the first rumors about the possibility of a military coup, he moved to Finland. In Helsingfors where he stayed until September 17, his host was a Bolshevik sympathizer who happened to be the city's chief of police.

could never hope to achieve a majority in the Constituent Assembly where most of the peasants' votes would go to the right Socialist Revolutionaries. Originally scheduled for September, the elections were now slated for, and would take place, in November. Their postponement was another piece of bad luck as well as foolishness on the part of the Provisional Government, granted all the technical difficulties of holding a nationwide vote in wartime. Had the Assembly been in existence in October, it would have enormously complicated, quite possibly barred, the Bolsheviks' road to power. In January when it actually did meet, it was just a nuisance and as such quickly chased out. What was needed was a dramatic act of force which would finally sever the party's umbilical cord from the old social democracy with its claptrap about such things as majorities, and the inviolability of this and that. Without such an act the Bolsheviks would never be able to retain power even if it fell into their lap. And they had to hold on to it long enough to start a European revolution.

There were other reasons for the desperate (hysterical, in his comrades' view,) tone of the messages with their refrain "To wait is to die," "Now or never," which he addressed to the Central Committee, and his threats of denouncing the committee and going to work among the rank-and-file Bolsheviks to agitate for an immediate uprising. He could now almost taste power; yet if they waited much longer there would be no power to seize, the anarchy he and his party had helped to foment would sweep them away just as it was now sweeping away the Provisional Government and revolutionary democracy. There was no point to a coup d'etat if there was no state to speak of.

What seemed to be happening was that while outwardly following a party, most Russians were putting in practice the precept urged by Tolstoy, saying to themselves, "For me there is no state." It was inertia which kept six million soldiers at the front, rather than following the example of the two million who had deserted, that made government and private employees keep office hours, kept workers at the factory bench when they were not striking or holding meetings, and the majority of peasants still tilling their land, rather than raiding and looting landlords' estates or their more prosperous neighbors. But there was no way of knowing how long could this go on. Many in this fall of 1917 had come to believe that indeed what awaited Russia was the literal fulfillment of All power to the soviets, every city and hamlet would become a law unto itself, a little republic. How could you then suddenly turn things around and start creating the centralized socialist state, which the Marxist in Lenin, now awaking from an anarchist trance, sought?

Indeed, much of the apparent complacency in the face of the approaching Bolshevik insurrection becomes understandable in view of the well-nigh general belief that Russia, for the foreseeable future, could not be governed by anyone.

374

Let the Bolsheviks try to start ordering the soldiers around, persuade the workers that their inordinate wage demands cause inflation, the peasants that the country was going to suffer famines unless they stopped their outrages. They might last two weeks. Many, whether on the left or the right, who in the past had extolled the people for their socialist and democratic, or conservative, virtues, now were experiencing a striking revulsion against their erstwhile idol. No, it was not the Kerenskys, Milyukovs, or even Lenins who were mainly at fault for the nation's shameful condition. It was the beastly masses. In the past they had tolerated uncomplainingly their slavish and degrading status, and one should have known how they would use freedom when they got it. Now their previous trust in the Father-Tsar had been replaced by an equally idiotic faith in all kinds of ideological mumbo jumbo, the former battle cry of society's scum, "Beat the Jews and the intelligents" replaced by an equally enlightened "Down with capitalists and landowners." Some on the extreme right viewed the prospect of a Bolshevik takeover with a kind of masochistic glee: what a joke it would be on the liberals and the democratic left, and eventually on the Bolsheviks themselves! After it was all over and the masses had learned their lesson, then one could start building a new Russia, but along those principles which in the past had made her great.

Though he was blissfully unaware of it, this covert antipopulism which turns upon itself was a strong element in Lenin's own makeup and would become his enduring legacy to the movement and state he created.

For the time being, however, he could not infuse his leading comrades with his own sense of urgency for a decisive blow. Some, like Kamenev, were timorous by nature and averse to violence of any kind. Others believed that Lenin grossly underestimated the difficulties inherent in the undertaking. It was true the Bolsheviks could count on a number of military units in Petrograd. But as the lesson of the July days showed, they could be counted on up to the prospect of real fighting at which point they were likely to run away. The government was not entirely defenseless: there were the Cossacks, who did not like Kerensky, but liked the Bolsheviks even less; there were students of the military academies, who while they would not fight for Kerensky and revolutionary democracy, would fight if persuaded it was for Russia and against those rumored German agents, finally a division or two might be conjured up from the front if the soldiers became convinced that they were defending not the Provisional Government, but the revolution. Then there was the Railwaymen's Union, where Bolshevik influence was virtually nonexistent and which, even if the Bolsheviks managed to secure Petrograd and Moscow, could isolate and eventually starve out the insurrection.

The great curse of the Russian liberation and revolutionary movement—fear of actual power—was not entirely absent among the Bolsheviks. They would actually have to run a ministry. They were pledged to make peace, not with

William II and his generals but with the German workers. They would have to deliver on their promises of "peace, land, and bread." As they approached the fateful hour of decision, one notices greater and greater nervousness and hesitation among those people, who in their own and most historians' accounts are represented as exemplars of revolutionary audacity and decisiveness, but who left to themselves were not as yet so different from the Martovs and Chheidzes.

It is thus not surprising that Lenin employed his exile for theoretical work designed to reassure his followers (and undoubtedly himself) that running the government after the revolution would be quite easy. *State and Revolution* largely written (but never completed) during this period of hiding was probably one work Lenin would have liked to forget once he became chairman of the Council of the People's Commissars. It was meant to appeal to the anarchist mood of the moment and at the same time to convince the faithful that he was not leading them into a trap. The bourgeois state would be smashed, but within twenty-four hours after the overthrow of capitalism, ordinary workers would be able to control production, rank-and-file soldiers to run the army, et cetera. Administration was not some mysterious art which it took generations to acquire; it consisted simply in "watching and bookkeeping." But in his articles written at the time, Lenin felt constrained to be more pragmatic. In one entitled, "Will the Bolsheviks Succeed in Keeping Power?" he pointed out that tsarist Russia had been ruled by a relative handful of landowners and bureaucrats; the party now had two hundred forty thousand members. Sensing that some might still remain unconvinced, he used a more reassuring argument: "We will make capitalists work for us." In his mind there was no logical inconsistency between his condemnation of dual power for tolerating capitalists in important positions and his dictatorship of the proletariat being staffed and guided by the same noxious breed.

To be sure there were already quite a few industrial managers and even generals who thought that perhaps the Bolsheviks were the only way out of the madhouse which was currently Russian politics. They were but an advance guard of that phalanx of bourgeois specialists who would play such an essential role in saving the Communist regime during the Civil War, 1918–21.

But that was for the future. The overwhelming problem facing the Bolsheviks in the fall remained whether and when to seize power. Lenin demanded a clear commitment to armed rebellion, with none of the euphemisms and double talk attending such efforts in the past. Contrary to what is generally believed, the Bolsheviks *as a party* never committed themselves unequivocally to an uprising. Only on October 10 did the Bolshevik Central Committee say in effect "In principle, yes." As to when, the party officials never gave a clear-cut answer. In fact they took special pains to assure that if an uprising materialized and failed, as it had in July, they could claim that it was all done by some hotheaded members carried away by the revolutionary zeal of the masses.

Throughout September the prevailing feeling among the Bolshevik hierarchy was to await the Second Congress of Soviets which would enthrone them as the legitimate representative of the Russian workers and soldiers by replacing the lame-duck Central Executive Committee with one they would dominate. The target date was October 20, though it was to meet five days later. In the meantime revolutionary democracy, seeing control slipping away, decided to improvise another talking shop where it could hold sway even if the soviets were conquered by the enemy. This was an *omnium gatherum* of representatives of soviets, trade unions, municipal councils, journalists, midwives, cleverly designed so that neither the right nor the Bolsheviks could challenge its domination by the forces of democracy, the right and center Mensheviks and Socialist Revolutionaries. The Democratic Conference assembled on September 14, and after six days of tumultuous oratory gave birth to another, this time a standing body, the Council of the Republic. This was supposed to provide dual power with something it had hitherto lacked, a quasi-legislature, which it was hoped might keep the patient alive until the real parliament, the Constituent Assembly, took over.

As of the beginning of September, Russia had been proclaimed a republic by Kerensky, which evoked a protest from another assembly few realized still existed. The Senate, theoretically, as under the tsars, the highest judicial and administrative tribunal, solemnly declared that the Provisional Government had no right to prejudge the country's future constitution, a startling sign of life from the venerable body whose members continued to attend its sessions dressed in frock coats and uniforms with the old imperial emblems. On its institutional side, Russian politics came to resemble a junkyard: various prerevolution bodies in different states of disrepair lying side by side with brand new pieces of government machinery produced since February 1917, but not functioning properly.

Bolshevik participation in the Democratic Conference brought another outburst from Lenin. He lashed out at the Central Committee's dilatory tactics: "It would be naive to wait until the Bolsheviks achieve a 'formal' majority, no revolution has every waited for that."[51] The conference met on September 14, with Kerensky in his usual form: ". . . we will remain the same defenders of freedom of our native land, and of the happiness of the people as we have been hitherto. . . . Anyone who dares to plunge a knife in the back of the Russian army will discover the might of the Revolutionary Provisional Government." On September 15 the Bolshevik Central Committee discussed Lenin's letter with its unflattering admonitions. ("You are nothing but a bunch of traitors and nincompoops unless you surround the conference and arrest those scoundrels.") The

Bolshevik notables were appalled by the outburst. Stalin suggested diplomatically that the party's local organizations be acquainted with the contents of the letter, but that the decision on the uprising be delayed until another meeting. It was finally decided to burn all copies but one of the dangerous document and to keep the party's partisans from any rash steps. Lenin was ordered to keep away from the capital, and Zinoviev, who had become separated from his chief, was instructed to rejoin him forthwith. With his notoriously unheroic disposition, he was felt to be a good, restraining influence on that demonic force.

On October 3, with a heavy heart, the Committee finally authorized their leader's return and as of the seventh he went into hiding in the Vyborg region of the capital. Few were likely to be looking for Lenin; attention was riveted on the Council of the Republic which began its brief and ephemeral existence the same day, in the luxurious premises of the Marinsky Palace. It was only by a narrow majority that the Bolsheviks, entitled to sit in it (as delegated by the various soviets), decided to boycott the council, thus avoiding another fearful eruption from their chief. After a provocative speech by Trotsky, the Bolshevik contingent stalked out to shouts of "Scoundrels," "Go to your German friends." Freed from their indecorous presence, the council launched into the now all too familiar pattern of revolutionary discourse: stirring appeals for national unity, anguished pleas for order and social discipline from the right, bitter retorts from the left that only further and thorough democratization could save the country, heartening declarations by Kerensky that finally the government had the situation well in hand. Most revolutionary dramas unfold to the accompaniment of effusive oratory, but the February revolution is the only one which literally talked itself to death.

Lenin's pleading now took on a clearly hysterical tone: "Now, now, or it would be too late!" A cogent argument in one letter would be followed by ideas verging on incoherence.

The Bolsheviks have no right [*sic*] to wait for the Congress of Soviets. They must *seize power* right now. It is only thus that they would save the world revolution (otherwise there is a danger of the imperialists of all countries . . . making a deal and *uniting against us*) also the Russian Revolution (otherwise the wave of anarchy may become stronger than we) and the lives of hundreds of thousands at the front. To procrastinate with the rising is criminal. To wait until the Congress would be a silly game, a shameful game at formalities and a betrayal of the Revolution.[52]

If they are afraid to start the business in Petrograd, let them begin with Moscow. Let the latter's soviet take over the city, banks, newspapers. It (that is, the Moscow soviet) would have a "gigantic base of support." Kerensky would then surrender. The revolutionary regime would make concessions to railroad and postal workers (two crucial labor unions whose hostility to the Bolsheviks was being used as an argument against the uprising), proclaim an *immediate* peace, an *immediate* distribution of land to the peasants. Then in conclusion, what to the recipients of the message must have appeared as bordering on lunacy, "Victory is assured, and there is a ninety-nine percent chance that it would be bloodless."

To begin with Moscow would very likely have been a serious mistake; even after Petrograd had been conquered the Bolsheviks would have a hard time in the older capital. But *not* to wait for the Congress of Soviets with its pro-Bolshevik majority was a clear blueprint for disaster. The congress would throw a cloak of revolutionary legitimacy over the Bolshevik coup, maximize the Mensheviks' and Socialist Revolutionaries' indecision and paralysis, and stay the hand of those military units, most notably among the Cossacks, who would have reacted violently to another Bolshevik adventure but would have become confused when one half-government obviously sanctioned the enterprise. It was fortunate for Lenin and his party that his impetuous counsels were rejected.

On October 10 the Bolshevik Central Committee, or rather twelve of its twenty-seven full members, held a clandestine meeting with Lenin present. With Zinoviev and Kamenev dissenting, the assembled voted, ten to two, "that the armed uprising is inevitable and that the moment for it is ripe [and] the Central Committee orders all party organs to be guided by this consideration in connection with the practical problems."[53] This was far from what Lenin wanted; the crucial "when" was not settled and the committee of seven elected to guide the enterprise included Zinoviev and Kamenev, who made it clear their hearts were not in the business. More precisely, they were scared to death. They would all get shot, pleaded Zinoviev. He wanted to wait not only for the Congress of Soviets but also for the Constituent Assembly, where the Bolsheviks with luck should get one-third of the seats, an argument which must have brought Lenin close to an apoplectic stroke. The danger of such a stroke (which in fact took place five years later), was compounded within a few days when the two leaders leaked the news of the resolution and of their dissent from it to *New Life*, published by Maxim Gorky and which in the spirit of left Menshevism was critical of everybody: the Provisional Government for its policies, the right Mensheviks and the SRs for their support of the former, and the Bolsheviks for their undemocratic ways. Lenin, quite beside himself, now demanded that the guilty duo be excluded not only from the Central Committee but also from the party as well. But the other leaders (except for Trotsky who hated his brother-in-law Kamenev) were for forbearance. Stalin, throughout 1917 the voice of moderation, proposed that the two, both his future victims, be just reprimanded if they promised to mend their ways. And so it was done.

Again, what a strange partiality of providence for the Bolsheviks. Instead of putting everybody on alert, Zinoviev's and Kamenev's revelations had the opposite effect and served as kind of a sedative on dual power. How could one be too concerned about a party, two of whose most prestigious leaders announce in advance that it might stage an insurrection and who oppose it as bound to end in failure?

No other successful coup d'etat had ever been so widely advertised in advance, none had seemed to be of as little concern to the authorities against which it was being quite openly prepared. By the middle of the month, everyone was talking about it, but no one was acting to prevent it. On October 14 Theodore Dan, who in Tseretelli's absence (sick and dispirited, he went to recuperate in his native Georgia, another piece of luck for the Bolsheviks) was the leading figure among the non-Martov Mensheviks felt curious enough to ask about the rumors in the Executive Committee of the Soviet. "I demand that the Bolshevik party give us a straightforward answer: yes or no."[54] It fell to David Ryazanov, one Bolshevik universally liked and respected for his Marxian scholarship, to answer that embarrassing question.* Indeed his answer displayed great dialectical skill. No proletarian party, certainly not the Bolsheviks, could contemplate anything so un-Marxist as a putsch—Dan should know that. But the uprising is preparing itself, as the masses cannot endure the effects of the Provisional Government's repressive and undemocratic policies. And should the masses rise and call for the Bolsheviks to join and guide them, a proletarian party could not refuse. The dialectical correctness of the formula could not be faulted. But four days later Trotsky was asked a similar question and gave a similar answer, with a variant. It was obviously the bourgeoisie that was preparing a coup and the Bolsheviks could not be blamed for preparing to resist it. He, Trotsky, was being asked why as president of the Soviet he had authorized the issuance of five thousand rifles to the Bolshevik sympathizers. Didn't the Mensheviks recall that it was they who during the Kornilov affair had demanded that the workers should be armed?

It fell to Trotsky to devise the formula for the uprising, one which would at least partly appease his party colleagues' apprehensions and at the same time go far in satisfying Lenin's frenzy for action. The Bolsheviks would stage the insurrection but through and on behalf of the Soviet. On October 12 the latter created the Revolutionary Military Committee, ostensibly to guard against a coup from the right and to organize the defense of the capital, which the Provisional Government was preparing to evacuate and move to Moscow, partly because of its vulnerability to a German attack, partly because it might thus decapitate the revolution. There was some substance to the rumors, but as usual Kerensky could

*A man of independent spirit and great courage, Ryazanov would be continuously in trouble with the party leadership after the Revolution and eventually would disappear in Stalin's purges.

not make up his mind. Having in fact proposed the creation of the committee, the Mensheviks and the right SRs refused obligingly to participate in its work, leaving the field free to the Bolsheviks and their allies, the left SRs. One of the latter, an eighteen-year-old youth, was the titular head of the committee, but its actual leader was Trotsky, and for his aides he enlisted members of his own party's military organization. Emissaries of the committee were dispatched to the city's military units to remind them that they were under direct control of the Soviet which thus superseded both the city commandant appointed by the Provisional Government and their officers. Some units agreed, others declared they would remain neutral in any clash between the Provisional Government and the Soviet. The lame-duck Central Committee, shrewdly suspecting that the Bolsheviks would synchronize their move with the assembly of the Second All-Russian Congress of Soviets, postponed the latter from October 20 to the twenty-fifth, thus giving Trotsky and his group more time for their work among the soldiers. It was crucial for the success of the uprising that the insurgents should be able to secure the Petropavlovsk fortress with its large stocks of arms. But practically up to the last moment its garrison refused to commit itself and kept chasing out the emissaries sent by the Revolutionary Military Committee. On October 24 Trotsky went there himself, and after listening to him the soldiers decided to cast their lot with the insurrection.

He hoped the Bolsheviks *would* try something was Kerensky's usual reaction to warnings about what was about to happen. Besides, the government was facing yet another ministerial crisis. In the wake of the Kornilov affair the prime minister, unable to persuade any of the better-known generals to take the job, appointed a very junior one, Alexander Verkhovsky, as minister of war. On October 20 he reported to the Council of the Republic on the state of the army. Much of this report was encouraging. There were to be sure two million deserters at large, but six million soldiers still held, in a manner of speaking, the front, tying down one hundred thirty enemy divisions. "Ideological Bolshevism does not exist among the soldiers." But then Verkhovsky dropped a bombshell: an army of that size could no longer be fed or clothed, and some units were unlikely to stay in the trenches once cold weather set in. The government ought to announce immediately that it was seeking peace. It is not clear whether Verkhovsky, whom some considered to be mentally unbalanced and whose speech was rather incoherent, was pleading for a separate peace, or whether he believed that an announcement that one was in the making would buoy up the army's morale and enable it to fight more effectively against both its foreign and domestic enemies. In any case there was a great outcry at his suggestion, followed by the announcement that in view of his health he had to go on leave. Now Kerensky in addition to being supreme commander and prime minister also took over the war ministry, an unprecedented combination of offices, but which one day would be held by a man quite different from the hapless persuader-in-chief, Joseph Stalin.

Everything was now in place for the great day. Or so it seemed. But among the future victors there was still anxiety and apprehension. Their behavior did not betray an overwhelming faith in their success. On October 24 Lenin, still in disguise, sporting a wig and with his face bandaged, worked his way to Smolny. Arriving there in the evening, he erupted furiously with reproaches against his hard-working followers. Did they really mean to wait twenty-four hours until the wretched Congress assembled? Once it met who knows how it might vote. He felt, and with reason, that the "democratic superstition" was still not dead among his followers and many, especially provincial Bolshevik delegates, might fall for some coalition scheme with the Mensheviks. "To wait is to die." He was calmed by Trotsky who assured him that Bolshevik armed units were on their way to seize the strategic points, the telegraph and telephone exchange, and to guard the bridges. Smolny presented an incongruous appearance: headquarters of the insurrection, of the Revolutionary Military Committee, it still housed in a different wing of the building, the ghost of revolutionary democracy—the lame-duck Central Executive Committee which on the next day was to surrender its functions to one elected by the new congress.

The Bolshevik Central Committee which met a few hours before Lenin's arrival in Smolny was still ambivalent. It is significant that its official protocol does not mention terms like *insurrection, armed uprising.* Were it to fall into the hands of the authorities following an unsuccessful uprising, it would be difficult to prove that the Bolsheviks had been planning anything but to defend themselves against an attack from the right! There was discussion about where the Bolsheviks ought to place alternate headquarters should the forces of reaction seize Smolny. Kamenev proposed to place them on a Bolshevik man-of-war, the famous *Aurora,* but his less timorous colleagues decided on the Petropavlovsk fortress. All armed activities were to be led by Bolsheviks of lesser standing, none of them from the Central Committee. Without special authorization, no member of the latter was to leave Smolny. All of which hardly adds up to an iron-clad alibi, but should the insurrection collapse, some leaders might be spared and, as in July, begin to rebuild the party.

In retrospect, such precautions must seem superfluous. Revolutionary democracy cheerfully continued on its suicidal course. The same day, the twenty-fourth, Kerensky appeared before the Council of the Republic with sensational news. He now had definite proof that the Bolsheviks were up to no good. He had given them every opportunity to back off from this foolish venture. "I prefer in general that authorities act more slowly but surely, and when the time comes move resolutely." But now "let the population of the city know that it is dealing with a resolute and determined government."[55] He demanded that the council declare formally its support of his stand. It was not in the style of dual power assemblies to act hastily, so there ensued a long discussion. Martov reiterated his argument: of course they opposed a coup d'etat, but if it takes place, it will be because of the Provisional Government's insensitivity to the masses' demands. With Tseretelli away, the democratic left became even more confused and indecisive. Dan argued that the Bolsheviks could not be subdued by force, the only solution was for the government to declare immediately that it would seek a general peace and that all land would be turned over to the peasants. Only then could the masses be made immune to the Bolshevik allurements. Kerensky had been loudly cheered, but when it came to voting, the majority of the council followed Dan's position, refusing to give the government its unconditional support. Enraged, Kerensky declared first that he might resign but then stalked out of the council, declaring haughtily that this was the time for deeds rather than declarations.

One such deed might have been for the government to seize Smolny. A detachment of a few hundred men could have grabbed the entire staff of the uprising, since the building was virtually unprotected up to the evening of October 24. But on the government's side, no one even thought of occupying Smolny. That would have been a provocation, a palpable proof that it was the bourgeoisie which was embarking on a coup designed to prevent the meeting of the Congress of Soviets. Instead, detachments of military cadets were sent to shut down the Bolshevik papers. After they sealed off the premises and posted guards, pro-Bolshevik soldiers arrived, chased off the guards, and the newspapers were back in business.

"The resolute and determined government" spent most of the night trying to persuade various armed units to come to its defense. The Cossacks first said "Maybe," then "No." They had helped in the past and were promised that the Bolsheviks would be crushed once and for all and look what was happening. The only volunteers were found among students of the military schools, and among that innovation of the revolution, the women's battalions. Even so, no attempt was made to organize the progovernment units into a cohesive force and to place an experienced officer in overall command.

The previous day Kerensky had declared that members of the government preferred "to be killed and destroyed rather than to betray the life, honor and independence of the state." But as of the morning of October 25, he was on the move. He was leaving the city to collect a force with which to crush the uprising, he told his colleagues. In the meantime they had to hold the fort, and they took it in the literal sense, gathering in the Winter Palace still composing declarations and issuing appeals while the city was being taken over by the Bolsheviks.

It would have made more sense for the ministers either to order and direct armed resistance, or failing that, for the government to leave Petrograd as a body for a safer location. Instead they huddled in the palace, sending out broadsides which under the circumstances sounded ludicrous. "Members of the Provisional Government are staying at their posts and will continue to work for the good of the country." They could have called upon the considerable body of civilian supporters of their parties to arm themselves and to offer resistance to the usurpers, but all they asked was for the population "to hinder the madmen who have been joined by all the enemies of freedom and order."

In fact the population of the metropolis preserved remarkable equanimity during that most momentous day in the country's history. The takeover of the city by the Revolutionary Military Committee which began before dawn proceeded quite peacefully, shaming those Bolsheviks who had predicted a repetition of the July days or worse. No one tried to hinder them, hardly a shot was fired as the motley crowd of soldiers, sailors, and Red Guards proceeded to occupy the strategic points—the power station, telephone exchange, headquarters of the military district. Like most of the garrison, the civilian population stayed neutral, displaying neither enthusiasm nor any visible opposition to what was going on. No panic, no multitudes shouting as on so many occasions in the past eight months, "Shame" or "Down with . . ." In fact it was something of an anticlimax.

The expiring revolution kept on talking. The Council of the Republic assembled in the morning, its various factions discussing what should be their attitude toward the hardly unexpected turn of events.

The deliberations were interrupted by the arrival of armed soldiers who asked the deputies to vacate the premises. Some were for courting martyrdom by defiantly staying in session, but a motion to that effect was defeated. So the representatives of the Russian people adjourned after having passed a resolution denouncing this gross interference with their activities.

The Petrograd city council displayed more spirit. No one thought of interfering with its session, so they continued to protest until the evening, when it was decided to march in a body to the Palace Square, there to lend moral support to the besieged government. But a sailors' detachment barred the councillors' way, and they had to return to speech-making.

Early in the afternoon the Winter Palace remained the only island of lawful authority amidst the rebel-controlled city. It had a garrison of sorts, a few companies of junkers—officers' candidates—and a women's "death battalion." The huge edifice with its many entrances could hardly be turned into an impregnable fortress, and as it grew dark some of its defenders, disgusted by the ministers irresolute attitude, departed. The headless government kept on deliberating but could not make up its mind on the question of the moment: to give up or not. As one of its members was to write, "We could not order them [the defenders] to fight until the last man because by now we might be defending just ourselves. . . . nor could we order them to surrender because as yet we did not know whether the situation was hopeless."⁵⁶

Although vastly superior in numbers, the insurgents did not try to take the palace by assault. Their leaders felt, with some justification, that if real shooting started, their troops might run away, and then, who knows, as in July some hitherto neutral military units might come out to defend dual power. They tried persuasion: if the palace did not surrender, the ministers were told it would be bombarded by the cruiser *Aurora* and from the Petropavlovsk fortress. The ultimatum was not heeded and the guns thundered, but to little effect. Those of the fortress were defective, their shells falling far from the target. *Aurora's* gunners not trusting their marksmanship fired blanks, the only casualty being a member of the crew. Hours passed. The bolder among the besiegers tried infiltration and pushed by little groups into the building. Some were chased away with shots, others captured and disarmed, in the process haranguing the junkers about the futility of their efforts.

The delay in capturing the last redoubt of reaction was greatly embarrassing for the Bolshevik high command. The scenario had called for the whole business to be over by noon when the Congress of Soviets was to assemble and enthrone the new masters of Russia. Yet with the palace still unconquered, Lenin was fearful about what might happen at the assembly. The Bolsheviks and their allies had a solid majority, some 390 out of about 650 delegates who had already reached Petrograd. But many, especially among the Bolsheviks from the provinces, were not privy to Lenin's and Trotsky's complex designs or shared their conviction that soviet must mean in fact Bolshevik power. Someone might offer a motion for a truce and negotiations with the government and it might carry! Or out-of-town military units might suddenly appear and ruin the whole game.

To put the provincials in the right mood, it was felt safer to begin with the meeting of the Petrograd Soviet. The session was opened at 3:00 P.M. by Trotsky, who announced that "the Provisional Government of Kerensky was dead and awaited only the broom of history to sweep it away."⁵⁷ Then Lenin ascended the tribune to a standing ovation. He spoke of the new revolution as an accomplished fact, and repeated the magic formula designed to win the minds of waiverers: immediate peace, land, bread.

With the rehearsal a success, it was decided to go ahead with the main show. There was one potentially troublesome feature about the mechanics of the congress which opened in Smolny around 11:00 P.M. Officially it had to be inaugurated by the Central Committee elected in June, hence predominantly Socialist Revolutionary and Menshevik in its composition. Common sense, not to mention political considerations, should have urged the Central Executive Committee to declare that under the circumstances, no democratic assembly could function properly, and it must be postponed until some semblance of order were restored. No doubt the Bolsheviks would have gone ahead and opened the congress, but the fact that it was being held illegally might have had a great psychological effect and just possibly drawn the thousands who still followed the Socialist Revolutionaries and Mensheviks out of their passive attitude.

Yet revolutionary democracy proceeded uncomplainingly with the arrangements for its own funeral. The proceedings were opened on behalf of the Central Executive Committee by Theodore Dan. He would not treat them to a long discourse, announced the Menshevik leader. His party comrades who were fulfilling their duty were currently under siege in the Winter Palace, and so it was no time for political speeches. Yet one cannot help feeling that if Dan was not going to do anything about it, then a political speech was precisely what was indicated.

Meekly the Central Executive Committee turned its powers over to the new Bolshevik-dominated presidium of the congress, with Kamenev its chairman. Lenin's party had become the official representative of Russia's workers and soldiers. It was only now that the Menshevik and right-wing Socialist Revolutionary minority of the congress erupted with futile protests. The revolution was being violated and disgraced, an end must be put to the outrages. They must call off the fighting and find a negotiated settlement to avoid a civil war. If the Bolsheviks did not agree, Martov declared, the opposition would walk out. They were answered by Trotsky, ". . . a compromise is no good here. . . . You are pitiful isolated individuals, you are bankrupt; your role is played out. Go where you belong from now on—the rubbish heap of history."[58] Had such a challenge been thrown in their teeth by a representative of the bourgeoisie, these veteran revolutionaries would have stormed the podium, gone among the workers and soldiers to stir them up to fight the usurpers. But now they obediently trooped out.

The other half-government capitulated about the same time. At two o'clock at night the weary ministers told their young defenders to lay down their arms. The armed multitude burst into the palace. "Members of the Provisional Government submit to force and surrender in order to avoid bloodshed" was the exit line of the regime, as the Bolshevik Vladimir Antonov-Ovseyenko burst into the ministers' conference room where they stoically awaited their oppressors.[59] It was now discovered that Kerensky had fled, and many in the mob wanted to vent their frustration by lynching his colleagues. It was with some difficulty that Antonov and the more disciplined among the workers managed to protect the ministers and to convey the group to the Petropavlovsk fortress where they were placed in the cells which under the tsars had housed generations of revolutionaries.

The announcement of the Winter Palace victory was received by the congress with elation. (Figures for the actual casualties during the siege vary from zero to six.) But there were individual voices protesting that while it was all right to place the capitalist ministers under lock and key, it was inappropriate in the case of those who belonged to socialist parties—a preview of the trouble Lenin would have with the survival "of social democratic superstitions" among his followers.

The Second Congress of Soviets marks the beginning of the Communist regime in Russia and constitutes the official foundation of the state which is known as the Union of Soviet Socialist Republics. The people who thus at least nominally opened a new era in Russian and world history appeared ill suited to the historic occasion. Accustomed as he was to the fairly sophisticated Petrograd workers, fastidious Sukhanov was disenchanted with the appearance and mood of the congress delegates. The mass of them impressed him as being "gray and non-descript people who have crawled out of the trenches and slums, their [alleged] devotion to the Revolution reflected but anger and despair, their 'socialism' was the product of hunger and of eagerness for peace."

The congress reassembled the evening of October 26 to open what is known as the Soviet era. It assumed the sovereign power in the state. The new Central Executive Committee elected Lev Kamenev as its chairman. The mild-mannered, bookish Bolshevik became the closest surrogate of a head of state, successor to Nicholas Chheidze and Nicholas Romanov, though as if to underline the relative unimportance of the office, another dispute with Lenin would in a few weeks lead to Kamenev's being unceremoniously dismissed from the office. To avoid the title Minister, with its tsarist and bourgeois connotations, the new executive was christened the Council of the People's Commissars, all fifteen of them Bolshevik, with Lenin as chairman, Trotsky in charge of foreign affairs, and Joseph Djugashvili-Stalin as commissar of nationalities.

The Bolsheviks had conquered Petrograd; Russia still remained to be won, hence two steps taken the same night. Lenin read to the congress the Decree on Peace, calling upon all the warring nations and governments to enter into immediate negotiations for a peace without indemnities and annexations. How many soldiers would now be willing to follow those who attempted to reconquer Petrograd and seize power from the only people who pledged an immediate end to the disastrous war? Then the Decree on Land proclaimed the immediate transfer without compensation of all land, previously owned by landlords, et cetera, to the working peasants. This was aimed to neutralize the pro-Socialist Revolutionary and anti-Bolshevik sentiments among the peasant masses; it would not be easy to stir up the latter against a government which though not viewed with favor in the countryside still gave the peasant, with no ifs and buts (so it seemed at the time) what he most wanted. The land decree was abhorrent to the spirit of

Marxism, which advocates large-scale, scientifically organized agricultural production and considers individual peasant proprietorship as economically ruinous and dangerous to socialism. But that could and would be taken care of later on.

Having given birth to a new epoch in history, the Second Congress of Soviets was adjourned—the talking period of the revolution was over.

Official nomenclature is a very deceptive guide to the underlying realities of Russian politics. If things were to be called by their right name, then October 25–26 marks the beginning of a *counterrevolution*. Practically all the political goals that the revolutionary parties and movements had striven for ever since the Decembrists, and which were, even if partially and foolishly, put into effect between March and October would be utterly destroyed during the next three years. The most insistent slogan of the almost hundred-year-old tradition of protest against the autocracy had been that the people should determine their own destiny and for the democratically elected Constituent Assembly. The Council of the Commissars instituted on October 26 was to be, according to the resolution which authorized it, but another provisional government "until the meeting of the Constituent Assembly," which did meet on January 5, 1918, its majority anti-Bolshevik. After one day's session, armed sailors, acting on orders of "the provisional government," dispersed the only free and democratically elected parliament in Russia's history.

Those freedoms secured so laboriously and at the cost of so much sacrifice by Russian society ever since the 1860s, then so profligately abused during the few months of the revolution, began to be abrogated on the very morrow of the coup. The bourgeois newspapers were shut down on October 27. "To tolerate the existence of bourgeois papers means to cease being a Socialist," Lenin said soon afterward.

On December 7, 1917, there was reborn the kind of institution that the February revolution was supposed to have done away with forever. A decree of the Council of the Commissars established the Extraordinary Commission to Combat Counterrevolution and Sabotage, Cheka for short. By its own admission, the Cheka during its first year of existence executed summarily, without trials sixty-three hundred people. The total number of executions for political crimes in the course of the *entire nineteenth century* in Russia had been something on the order of two hundred.[60] The Cheka's successors would be variously named the OGPU, NKVD, and today the KGB. But all of them in the scope of their activities, number of victims, and the fear they have inspired in the ordinary citizen would far surpass the tsarist Okhrana.

The most ironic aspect of post-1917 history touches on the Communists' appropriation of the institution and symbolism of the Soviet. It became the name of the state, society, and nation they had conquered. In fact October 25–26 marked the beginning of the end of the soviets' role as a vital force in politics, whether at the state or local level. As a slogan and symbol, Soviet power would serve the Communists well and would provide one of the keys to their victory in the Civil War. To many the name still carried the connotations of grass roots democracy, and obscured the encroaching reality of one-party dictatorship and the police state. Until 1921 some dissidents, a stray Menshevik or Socialist Revolutionary, were still tolerated in the soviets, the latter playing some, though progressively diminishing, political role. But after that they became and remained a purely ornamental part of the state machinery.

Prior to October 25 few Bolsheviks, including those closest to their leader, would have suspected, let alone approved, the full extent of repression their regime would visit upon their unhappy country. Indeed some of the most difficult challenges encountered in the first few days came not from partisans of the old regime,* but from Lenin's own followers. Many opposed the idea of a purely Bolshevik government, some balked at the suppression of the freedom of speech and press.

Lenin's ability to infuse the Bolsheviks with the authoritarian spirit reflected his own standing in the party; not only the political leader, but a veritable prophet and magician, with a few formulas he had conjured away all that had stood in the way and brought his followers into the promised land. But more fundamentally, it was the nature and magnitude of the task facing the victors which turned the erstwhile Social Democrats into repressors of freedom and democracy. Once in power they discovered that it was not merely the bourgeois state which had been smashed, but the very idea of state and authority. They had to compress into three years, the period of the Civil War, the work which had taken Russian rulers centuries to accomplish: to build the modern state. The worldwide socialist revolution receded into the distant future.

It was to Russian nationalism, seemingly eroded by the year of anarchy and their own ideology, that the Communist regime felt constrained to appeal in its struggle for survival. When the peace negotiations at Brest Litovsk broke down and there appeared the threat of the Germans advancing on Petrograd, the Council of Commissars headed its call for resistance with "The Socialist Fatherland is in danger." In commenting upon the appeal, Lenin skipped the adjective: "This shows at once the change of 180 degrees from our defeatism to the defense of the Fatherland."[61] Though muted by Marxian semantics, the nationalist theme becomes an essential ingredient of the Communist effort to rebuild the Russian state and empire.

---

*Kerensky's pitiful attempt to stage a comeback with a few hundred Cossacks, all that he had been able to muster, collapsed on the approaches to Petrograd. The only serious armed resistance to the Bolshevik takeover in Russia proper occurred in Moscow, not subdued until November 2.

So does the autocratic principle, as the Communists discarded one by one those anarchic postulates under which they had surged to the top: no secret police, no regular army, no professional bureaucracy. In defending the Treaty of Brest Litovsk, Lenin read this lesson to those who recalled his own pledge of no peace "with the imperialist robbers." "Learn to be disciplined, to introduce severe discipline, otherwise you will be under the German heel . . . until the nation learns to fight, until it will create an army which will not run away, but will be able to endure the most extreme hardships."[62] He who had called Imperial Russia "the prison house of nationalities" would see nothing incongruous in Soviet Russia imposing Moscow-dominated Communism on the Ukraine, conquering socialist Georgia, attempting the same with respect to Poland.

In March 1918 the seat of the government was transferred to Moscow. Ostensibly the change was made because of the danger that the Germans, even after the peace treaty, might be tempted to seize Petrograd. But also the atmosphere prevailing in the "cradle of the Revolution" was felt to be uncongenial to the new order. Armed bands of sailors and demobilized soldiers, some proclaiming themselves anarchists, others just plain criminals, roamed the city, posing a real danger to the regime they had helped to power a few months ago. It was for fear of provoking those elements that the decision and the date of departure of the government organs was kept secret until the last moment. The Communist regime was fleeing from the revolution.

The relocation of the government, although originally dictated by purely practical considerations, can be seen in retrospect as prophetic in its symbolism. The capital founded by Peter the Great had epitomized Western influence on Russian life. That influence manifested itself in the city which now bears Lenin's name, becoming the birthplace and center of activities of practically every reform and revolutionary movement in the country's modern history. The Kremlin evoked another much older tradition: of autocracy in its pristine, pre-Petrine form, of the grand dukes and tsars of Muscovy. In their fanciful view of the old autocracy, the nineteenth-century Slavophiles portrayed it as a uniquely Russian system and philosophy of government, a harmonious blend of absolutism and popular participation. To the tsar belonged the plenitude of powers, and yet a wise ruler would listen attentively to the voice of the people conveyed by the occasional Assembly of the Land. And the form of government of which Lenin dreamed in his last years, when disenchanted with the growth of bureaucracy in the Communist state, and fearful of dictatorial ambitions of his would-be-successors, such as Stalin and Trotsky, he groped for some never-never land where the dictatorship of the proletariat could be combined with popular participation, was in a strange fashion reminiscent of the old Slavophiles' historical fantasy. The party leadership would be, as in fact it had already become, the Autocrat. The masses would speak their mind through the party and Soviet congresses—a government for the people, but not by the people. Yet while the Slavophiles' populistic autocracy never in fact existed, so Lenin's "democratic centralism" broke down even before his illness, and then death, removed him from the scene.

As the autocrats of old, the Communist rulers would see the state's power as their deed of legitimacy and teach their people to accept it as a surrogate for freedom. So the question and moral posed by most recent Russian history is still the same as a chronicler of the Decembrists derived from their fate: "And when will our national consciousness be rid of that fatal confusion [between the state's power and national welfare] that has brought so much falsehood into every sphere of national life, falsehood that has colored our politics, our religion, education?"[63]

Chapter 7

WHO IS GUILTY AND WHAT IS TO BE DONE: STALINISM AND AFTER

WHO, even the most incurable optimist, would have prophesied on that night (October 25, 1917) the full extent of their victory, reminisced Lenin before his comrades on the third anniversary of the occasion. Indeed, against all the odds and historical laws, the Communist regime had managed not only to survive in this peasant land but also to cling to the major share of the tsars' old empire. And, continued the miracle's chief conjuror, they had launched their struggle in the firm conviction that it could succeed only if it triggered a world revolution; without this conviction they would have never embarked upon their struggle. This is, perhaps, a correct reconstruction of his own thoughts on that memorable night, but for one whose ideology presumes to transcend national boundaries and loyalties it was strange to rejoice because history played a bad joke on "scientific socialism." The Bolsheviks set out to find the passage to Karl Marx's promised land and instead stumbled upon the not-so-new-world of absolute power in their own "backward and semi-Asiatic country," in the traditional parlance of the Russian Marxists.

As yet there seemed to be no reason for the Communists to believe that their rule as the modern "gatherers of the Russian lands"* was incompatible with that

*The name bestowed on the grand dukes of Muscovy who in the fifteenth-sixteenth centuries laid the foundations of Russian greatness.

of the apostles of a worldwide movement. But there was already an element of national pride in the fact that Moscow rather than Berlin or Paris was the seat of the Third International, destined to usher in a new era in the story of mankind.

A universalist creed had stood also at the cradle of the old tsars' Russia. To bolster the stature of the grand dukes of Muscovy, the Orthodox Church formulated the legend of three Romes destined in turn to rule over the civilized, that is, Christian, world. Old Rome fell because it harbored a heresy. The second—Constantinople—was seized by the infidel Turks. And so it was Moscow that became and would remain forever the center and arbiter of the true faith. "For two Romes have fallen, but the Third stands and a Fourth shall never be," wrote a sixteenth-century monk to Grand Duke Basil III.[1]

Lenin and his comrades would have been scandalized by such parallels. Theirs was not a musty ethnocentric and superstitious creed, it was the finest flowering of modern science and internationalist spirit. But the comparison would soon suggest itself to many, and there would come a day when their Chinese coreligionists would refer to the Kremlin's masters as the "Soviet tsars."

"The time has passed when Russia served the interests of the Third International: now the latter is beginning to serve as a mighty weapon in the achievement of Russia's national goals."[2] This was not written in Stalin's Russia during the thirties. In 1921 a group of exiles published a collection of essays affirming their belief in the essentially Russian character of the Soviet state, and calling upon their fellow émigrés to come back and collaborate with their country's new masters. The title, *Changing Signposts,* was an explicit link with the theme of the *Signposts* (or *Landmarks*) published in 1909. The earlier symposium's authors, many ex-Marxists and radicals, had called upon the intelligentsia to reconsider its traditional attitude toward the public order and moral and political values, since as shown in 1905–06 it had done incalculable harm to the nation's cause. But *Changing Signposts* urged the Russians in exile to capitulate in deed and in spirit to the Communist autocracy, something their predecessors never urged the Russian intelligentsia to do in regard to the tsarist one.

The argument of the repentant exiles touches not only on Soviet Russia as it emerged from the Civil War, presumably more tolerant now and less doctrinaire. Nor are they—once liberals—content to plead that it is every Russian's duty, no matter what his political opinions, to assist in the gigantic task of healing the nation's wounds, of helping his fatherland whose fifty years of economic and cultural progress had been virtually undone through the ravages of the foreign and civil wars. The crux of the authors' argument lies in their identification of the Soviet regime as the fulfillment of the national ideal, the surest path to Russia's greatness, something that neither the decrepit monarchy nor the disorderly post-February 1917 democracy could secure the nation, "The hundred million strong Russian people so rich spiritually, so redoubtable in its physical might, has been reborn in the revolutionary storm, and now for the first time as a nation it can embark upon its historical mission."[3] There is no doubt as to the nature of that mission: conquest and domination. "The very internationalism of the Soviet power is in fact deeply nationalist in its thrust, it fits that 'universalism' of the Russian nation described already by Dostoyevsky as a necessary characteristic of a truly great people." Communism is just an ideological veneer over Russian nationalism, but much more useful to the latter than old-fashioned autocracy or equally obsolete Western democracy.

This was 1921, when the Soviet regime was still a fragile and precarious experiment: it had just suffered a military defeat at the hands of Poland and the country was in the throes of one of the worst famines in its history. And yet a *Changing Signposts* author perceives astutely, though a bit prematurely, how international Communism serves as an instrument of Soviet, that is, Russian expansionism: "Communism in Moslem countries—that is but an impossible dream. . . . But Russian influence in Asia Minor, Iran, to some extent in India . . . the Russian military instructors on 'the roof of the world' in Afghanistan, that is a concrete fact, a major historic achievement for Russia."[4]

The author's stance was hardly characteristic of the postrevolution emigration, but it was not a case of a few eccentric individuals whose appeal found no echo. If some two million Russians, the bulk of them from the professional and former privileged classes, fled, or were forced to leave their country between 1918 and 1922, then quite a few stayed, often by choice, enduring persecutions and privations, famines and epidemics. Some who had left would return during the deceptive thaw which lasted from the end of the Civil War to the beginning of forced collectivization and other horrors at the end of the decade. The survival of the Communist regime during the earlier period owes much to the devoted labor of these bourgeois specialists, for they provided the necessary scientific and technical cadres. Many of them persevered in their labors though they had no illusions about the regime they served. "The Bolsheviks have subjected Russia to the kind of experiments I would not try on a frog," said the great physiologist Ivan Pavlov, one of those scientists who because of their world renown received (at Lenin's personal order) very special treatment from the government. Others, whose roots lay in the non-Bolshevik left, continued to hope that one day their Communist rulers would revert to the true socialist path. Many former tsarist officers who had cursed Kerensky enlisted in the Red Army, providing as Trotsky himself acknowledged, a key ingredient in its success. Some to be sure did so under compulsion, their families held hostage to their loyalty, but quite a few, including the army's principal commanders, did so out of a sense of patriotic or professional duty.

It was a new Russia, and yet until the late twenties it continued to function in many ways on the human capital of the old one. This then is what allowed these people to retain not only their old ideals, but dreams of the future. Whether in exile in Paris or Berlin, or at home working in some Soviet institution, a former Nationalist, Kadet, or Menshevik could still find reasons for hope that the present was but an aberration and a charade; *his* Russia must soon come out from behind the current Communist mask. The ballast of foreign ideology will drop off, leaving behind a mighty nation state. Or, once the people became educated (and no one could deny that the campaign for universal literacy was the one electoral promise the Soviet regime has kept) how could they fail to see through the absurd doctrine and demand real Western freedoms. And finally, from an unreconstructed non-Communist leftist: the working class has not spoken its last word, soon it will demand *real* socialism.

All these varieties of wishful thinking could in the Russia of the 1920s be bolstered by some solid evidence. And yet in sum they amounted to a great illusion which sprang from the failure to recognize that Communism, though it had many facets, still added up to something entirely new in Russian life and as such was not going to revert to the old nationalism, real socialism, or democracy. Its main characteristic was a cult of political power on a scale unprecedented in modern history. Communism simply would not tolerate anything which might interfere with the omnipotence of the state, and within it of the Communist party. Even Russian nationalism which from the thirties on the Soviet rulers would, under the euphemism of "Soviet patriotism," make the main psychological prop and title deed of their power, would be their servant and not master.

It was thus a great misunderstanding of the nature of Communism, inexcusable even in 1921, to write: "One cannot fight for Russia and its great historical mission without working together with the Russian intelligentsia and the Russian revolution."[5] Even more pathetic is another prognosis of *Changing Signposts:* "From now on one has put an end for a long time or forever, to all kinds of revolutionary extremism, whether in the 'broad' or 'narrow' sense of the term, and to bolshevism."[6] It was a tragic illusion to believe that the Soviet regime could tolerate the rebirth of the intelligentsia in its pre-1917 form, that the Communist autocracy, like its tsarist predecessors between 1855 and 1917, would accept the coexistence of government and society. As it emerged from the Civil War, Communism had been stripped entirely of its social democratic moorings and could not and would not tolerate any even potentially independent social or intellectual source of influence.

That the regime should leave any sphere of social or intellectual life free from control and regimentation was incomprehensible to Lenin, even in his last years when he grew disillusioned with some aspects of Soviet reality. A rather eccentric party member wrote to him suggesting that the bureaucratic abuse he had publicly deplored could be remedied by allowing a measure of freedom to the press. In his reply Lenin implied that his correspondent must have fallen prey to a nervous disorder, "My advice is don't give way to despair and panic."[7]

One can argue indefinitely whether Stalinism was an inevitable step in the evolution of the Communist system or a historical accident. But there can be hardly any room for dispute as to whether Russian Communism could have evolved away from its utter intolerance not only of any actual opposition to its rule but also of any social and intellectual force it could not control. That being the case, it is clear that even Lenin's "democratic centralism" had to give way to a much more tightly centralized and controlled rule of the party itself, whether by a single dictator or an oligarchy. A society of some 150 million people could not be tightly controlled and hermetically sealed off from actual and potential dissent, if the instrument of this control, a few hundred thousand members of the Communist party, were divided by political, personal, and ideological disputes. It was a hopelessly romantic idea which Lenin thought up during his last and fatal illness: some fifty rank-and-file workers to be coopted to the Central Committee, there to keep a stern watch on the leaders and to arbitrate any disputes between Stalin, Trotsky, and Zinoviev. Had the formula by some miracle been put to the test following his death, the Communist party would have soon become as quarrelsome and long winded as revolutionary democracy of recent memory and would have undoubtedly come to share its fate. Another of Lenin's deathbed illusions was that there could be an authoritarian centralized state where, as he himself had written some years before, "We don't believe in 'absolutes.' We laugh at 'pure democracy,' " and which yet would not be nationalist, indeed Russian chauvinist, in its orientation. The general thrust of Soviet nationality policy under Stalin's aegis, he wrote *in 1923* (in retrospect the most liberal period in Soviet history, insofar as nationality policies were concerned), made him feel that the non-Russians were not being protected "from invasion of their rights by this typical Russian man, the chauvinist, whose basic nature is that of a scoundrel and oppressor, the classical type of bureaucrat."[8] Had the spirit of Lenin's deathbed musings been observed by his successors, the Soviet empire would have found itself in a condition reminiscent of Russia under the Provisional Government, when in addition to the disintegration of authority at the center, the country was afflicted by every conceivable kind of national and local separatism.

Stalinism represented the extreme of intolerance and repression. Had someone else emerged as the leader very likely the regime would have been more humane and would have exacted far fewer human sacrifices in its quest for power. But whoever the leader, it is hard to imagine the Soviet state allowing any segment of its society the kind of autonomy and freedom which even the old autocracy felt constrained to grant after 1855 in those spheres of social and cultural activity not touching directly upon its prerogative. Tsarism at its most authoritarian required obedience; Communism at its most liberal demands conformity.

Terror, as a deliberate state policy, had ceased to be in Lenin's time merely an instrument of self-defense and class war and became a regular administrative technique. It was used not only in the fight against actual or potential subversion but also in dealing with economic problems, such as securing foodstuffs from the peasants, in keeping the bureaucracy alert, et cetera. "Shoot," "Threaten to shoot" were recurrent motifs of Lenin's instructions when dealing with problems ranging from recalcitrant military commanders to a faulty telephone connection. A badly printed Marxist classic without an index made him recommend that the publisher be given six months in jail.[9]

That was *revolutionary* terror and was rationalized in terms of the fearful anarchy the Bolsheviks faced after October. But when the revolution and the Civil War were over, the secret police were not, as the name might have supposed, abolished, but merely renamed; the word *extraordinary* in its title was dropped. It became and remains a very ordinary Soviet institution.

The year 1927 was the high point of the New Economic Policy of postrevolutionary normalcy. Stalin, though the acknowledged leader, was not as yet the absolute dictator, and his partners in power Nicholas Bukharin and Alexis Rykov were reputed, and with some justification, to be among the most humane of Lenin's disciples, exponents of what today is called "socialism with a human face." Yet in the wake of some setbacks abroad for the USSR, the regime felt it necessary to give proof of its revolutionary vigilance and sternness. The secret police rounded up and shot twenty peaceful citizens whose only crime was that they had belonged to the prerevolutionary nobility and upper bourgeoisie. The sole objection raised in the party circles touched on the impression this wanton cruelty would have on foreign public opinion. Stalin answered those timid protests: "The shooting of twenty 'noblemen' met with approval and understanding on the part of the millions of workers in the USSR and in the West. . . . To hell with those liberal-pacifist philosophers and their 'sympathy' for the Soviet Union."[10]

With Stalin in full command, terror ceased being just a technique of governing and became an essential ingredient of official ideology. The closer to socialism, the sharper must become the character of the class struggle was Stalin's formulation of this new contribution to Marxism. In practical terms this meant that all the current and future victories of socialism would only increase rather than diminish the need for vigilance and repression. Treason then became a constant companion of victorious socialism. The task of the state's security organs became not only to suppress subversion but also, so to speak, to manufacture it.

The above may seem irrational to the point of madness. Traditionally authoritarian regimes strive, at least in public, to minimize the extent of hostility and resistance it arouses in its own society. The secret police may have professional reasons for occasionally inventing a plot, for destroying some innocent people. But it is not pressured by the highest authority to keep finding new cases of treason, fresh lists of the people's enemies! Not so under Stalinism. At the height of the purges, it would have been suicidal for a Soviet official to assert that subversion was not lurking everywhere in the party and state apparatus, industrial management, among the intellectuals. Had anyone dared to assert that having been repeatedly purged of the "Trotskyites," "Bukharinites," et cetera, Soviet society was now foolproof against subversion of any conceivable kind, this would have been considered a prima facie case of his own treacherous designs.

In post-1956 Soviet references to Stalin, the surrealistic horror was blamed on the dictator's "inordinate suspiciousness" and "cult of personality." A most unsatisfactory explanation. An ordinary despot certainly has to be inordinately suspicious; otherwise he would not keep his job very long. Few of the breed are free of vanity and the conviction that they are endowed with special qualities entitling them to be worshipped by their subjects. Yet it certainly would not have entered the mind of Nicholas I, for example, to have his chief of secret police dismissed or executed because several months had passed without a new conspiracy being uncovered. To look for an explanation of the terror of the 1930s just in Stalin's irrational characteristics is to postulate that he was entirely mad, an assumption that his ability to retain absolute power for twenty-five years renders quite absurd.

It is more reasonable to assume that terror on such a scale was the product of a deliberate design, the only way the tyrant could reconcile his twin objectives of absolute power for himself and maximizing the power of the state over which he ruled. Terror allowed him to appear indispensable, for the people had been taught to believe that even his closest associates and would-be-successors were not immune to treason. Were he, by some quirk, forcibly removed, he would bring the whole Communist edifice down with him. Terror was part of the educational campaign to convince the nation that all horrors which attended forced collectivization, such as the famine which claimed five million lives, that all the privations and sufferings consequent upon hurried industrialization resulted not from the government's policies, but from sabotage by the people's enemies. Terror, in brief, was necessary not only to make the people obey but, even more so, also to make them believe. It bridged the gap between reality and fiction, between the most tyrannical regime on earth, which the Soviet one undoubtedly was in

1936–37, and the Soviet constitution adopted during the same years, which was described, and insofar as its text was concerned quite correctly, as "the most democratic in the world."

The beginning of the era was marked symbolically enough by an assault on what remained of the old intelligentsia. "From now on . . . one has finished with revolutionary extremism of all kinds," some of its representatives in 1921 had written when justifying their decision to collaborate loyally with the Soviet regime for the sake of Russia. Many of the breed then placed their skills at the service of the Communist state, discarding their previous Kadet, Menshevik, or other party allegiances. But how could the great crusade to remake Russia's economy and society be launched, its sacrifices and initial failures be justified, without rekindling the fires of the class war? The masses had to be presented not only with the grandiose goal of remaking peasant Russia into an industrial power but also with a visible enemy whose betrayal and guiles would induce in them a kind of creative hysteria, redouble their enthusiasm and efforts, make them submit to privations unparalleled since the Civil War. There could be no better candidates for the role initially than those thousands of bourgeois experts who seemingly reconciled themselves to Soviet reality, but who because of their class origins and convictions were bound to sabotage the building of socialism. In trying to impede the realization of the Five Year Plan, bourgeois economists would falsify plans and statistics to make the leadership's goals appear foolhardy and unrealizable. These managers and engineers would cause accidents in the plants and mines, produce defective machinery and inferior products, so that the worker consumer would blame it on the party and begin to develop doubts about the leader's wisdom and foresight. Thousands of these wreckers and saboteurs were seized by the secret police. In 1960 Khrushchev's de-Stalinization campaign was in full swing, but a Soviet author could still write: "In the course of 1928–31 wrecking organizations were uncovered in the following industries: coal mining, defense, textiles, machine, chemical, rubber, oil in transport, retail trade. Wreckers penetrated into the most important key institutions of the national economy . . . the Supreme Economic Council and the Planning Commission."[11] Most of these traitors were disposed of by the secret police itself, sent off to a forced labor camp or worse.

But the educational side of the enterprise required that those with identifiable political backgrounds (for example, the celebrated chronicler of the revolution, Sukhanov) confess their sins in public trials, recite obediently fantastic tales of treason and sabotage in which they had engaged at direct orders of exiled Menshevik politicians and anti-Communist White generals, foreign espionage agencies . . . These tales had to be so complex and vivid that the average citizen could hardly conceive that they had been wholly invented. The fertile imagination of the secret police illusion-makers made whole counterrevolutionary parties spring into existence, only to be unmasked and annihilated through the vigilance of the security organs, such as the Industrial Party, whose hard-core, former Octobrists and Mensheviks had wormed their way to high posts in management and economic planning. Another mirage was the Working Peasant Party, which specialized in sabotaging collectivization and supporting the kulak (rich peasant) in his struggle against the regime's wise and benevolent designs to bring efficiency, prosperity, and social justice to the countryside. "The smashing of the wrecking counterrevolutionary kulak-PR group laid the basis for a speedier construction of socialism in the countryside, removed serious difficulties in the way of construction of the rural economy."[12] The unmasking of yet another criminal organization, entirely Menshevik in its members' antecedents, made the party spell out explicitly rather than just hint at the desired lesson of the whole business. "The more successfully the proletariat of the Soviet Union conducts its offensive, the more the counterrevolutionary elements inside the country . . . placed their wager on the attack of foreign imperialists against the USSR. The answer of workers and peasants must be an ever more resolute socialist offensive all along the front."[13]

Compared with the great purge trials of 1936–38, when the prosecution's motif would be "Shoot them like the mad dogs they are," those of 1928–31 appear rather subdued in their inhumanity. Though the workers' mass meetings would usually call for death for all the accused, many of the latter, especially if endowed with technical skills which might make them useful in the future, were merely sentenced to jail. One of them, Professor Ramzin, lived not only to be pardoned, but to become head of an institute and to be awarded a Stalin prize! An occasional accused, whether by design, through stubbornness, or simply because he forgot the script, would plead innocent. And a few were actually acquitted, which in 1936–38 would have been unbelievable.

In general the pogrom of the intelligentsia, while breathtaking in its extent and mechanics, was a fairly mild affair when compared to the ferocity with which Stalin attacked the peasants in the early thirties and then proceeded to decimate the Old Bolsheviks, the officer corps, and the security organs themselves.

Stalin called writers "the engineers of the human soul," and so it was natural that the purge of the pre- and revolutionary intelligentsia, having started with real engineers and economists, would then extend to all of its segments: writers, artists, scholars. A contributor to *Changing Signposts* had painted a rapturous picture of the future of Russian culture under Communism: "If prerevolutionary Russia with its inert masses and rotting at the top [still managed to produce] geniuses who have inspired whole centuries and nations—Tolstoy, Dostoyevsky, Mendeleyev, Moussorgsky, Scriabin—then what marvels will the freed Russian soul contribute to world culture." In Stalin's Russia probably all of them, except perhaps for Mendeleyev, would have been dispatched to a camp or at least constrained to observe the canons of "socialist realism" in their writings and compositions. Even the scientific community, so prized in theory by Communism, was dealt a devastating blow, the logic of terror and the requirements of the national economy and defense being reconciled by those prison research institutes set up for scientists thought too valuable to be shot or sent to the camps.

The climate of terror of the 1930s made it inconceivable that any class or segment of society should be exempted. The mechanics of the purges, the high premium put on denunciation—and that to refrain from it entirely meant to incur the suspicion of disloyalty—made it quite natural that scientific, esthetic, and professional disputes and rivalries would keep furnishing ever-new victims of terror. Yet the attack upon the intellectual community bore also a very specific character and is important for understanding not only Stalinism but also the Soviet state and society, both before and after him.

Lenin's attitude toward the class from which he himself had sprung bore a deeply ambivalent character. More than any other, a socialist society must prize its intellectual elite, in fact insofar as its material conditions of life are concerned, must treat its intellectual and professional people as a privileged class. But no other segment of society is to be watched as carefully and suspiciously by the Communist state. In the early postrevolution days, Maxim Gorky often expostulated with Lenin about the chicaneries and indignities which so many intellectuals suffered at the hands of the secret police and other state agencies. After all, some of those people had helped the Bolsheviks and served the cause of the revolution. Lenin replied:

Yes, excellent people, kind-hearted people, and that is why we search and investigate them . . . because they are excellent people and kind hearted. They sympathize with the downtrodden, they don't like persecution. And what do they see now? The persecutor is our Cheka, the persecuted the Kadets and the SRs who run away from it. . . . And we have to catch the counterrevolutionaries and render them harmless. Hence the moral is clear.[14]

The Russian intelligentsia created and nourished the revolutionary movement; for all of its garrulity and sentimentality, it had been the key factor in undermining and then overthrowing a powerful authoritarian system. Unless kept under strict supervision and discipline, this perverse breed would do the same to Communism.

For Stalinism, to submit the intelligentsia to occasional humiliations became clearly insufficient. Nicholas II had said that if he could, he would erase the accursed term—*intelligentsia*—from the Russian language. Stalin went much further. He turned the intelligentsia into a caricature of its former self. Under the empire its role was that of the social critic, or at least the articulate part of the nation. Lenin would have been content to have the intellectuals shut up and work for the state; it was up to the party to discuss and criticize. He would let the artist alone as long as he kept away from political themes; he was enough of a man of the old school to view with distaste the various kinds of proletarian art spawned in the wake of October. In fact his attitude was not dissimilar from that of Nicholas I: the latter did not want a philosopher or writer to praise autocracy any more than to criticize it; it was simply none of their business.

With the 1930s the intellectual was again called upon to speak up for the whole nation to hear. But not with his own voice. All branches of the arts, literature, historical scholarship, and even science became one vast sounding board proclaiming the theme of victorious socialism and the cult of the Leader. In the 1860s and 1870s society tended to be hard on a writer who avoided political themes, those who believed in art for art's sake, scientists who kept away from public affairs, historians who wrote of Russia's past, concentrating on monarchs and wars rather than on the people. Now such detachment became not only unpopular, but dangerous: it threatened not only one's professional or artistic life but also often physical survival. One had to demonstrate his positive, that is, euphoric, attitude toward Soviet reality not only through one's work but also by speaking out on politics, for example, joining in the chorus of praise for the Stalin constitution and the latest Five Year Plan, signing one's name to petitions urging death for the latest batch of unmasked traitors and diversionists. Hypocrisy, toadyism, even one's internal as well as external conformity were far from being absolute guarantees of security. As in other spheres of Russian life during the period, one might get caught in the net because of a relative, an incautious remark, or an informer's malice. But the intellectual found it more difficult to swim with the current than most. His lifetime research might be turned into the evidence of treason by a sudden shift in the ruling doctrine in historiography, economics, agronomy . . . The Leader himself might develop an interest in a field of science or aesthetics, and the hitherto prevailing orthodoxy on the subject would be brusquely overthrown with its exponents scurrying with recantations and condemnations of their former views and work. The name of Constantine Pobyedonostsev epitomizes what was most reactionary and intolerant in old Russia, yet by the standards of Stalin, he was fairly liberal. He had Leo Tolstoy anathemized by the Holy Synod, but it would not have even entered Pobyedonostsev's mind that the writer, unless he recanted publicly his views on politics and religion, should be arrested and all of his books banned from circulation. It is the normal Communist state which demands conformity from its intellectuals; Stalin's in addition required self-abasement.

In the immediate context the technique proved highly successful. Dissent was not only silenced, it became unimaginable.

> We live without feeling the ground under our feet.
> Ten paces away and our voices cannot be heard.
> But everywhere one hears the voice of the Kremlin mountaineer,
> The destroyer of life and the slayer of peasants.

wrote Osip Mandelstam in the poem about Stalin which was to cost him his life. The poem was heard by just half a dozen people to whom the poet read it individually, and of whom at least one denounced him to the secret police.

"From where did you acquire your independent way of thinking?" was a standard question addressed by the tsar's inquisitors to imprisoned Decembrists. Stalin's subjugation of the intelligentsia made it certain that very few Soviet citizens growing up in the thirties and forties were likely to acquire this habit, and most of their elders, if they wanted to survive, had to try to erase it from their minds. It was not only a devastating blow dealt to a class and a tradition but also virtual annihilation of that spiritual and intellectual autonomy of the individual without which a society cannot even begin to struggle for freedom.

With Stalin's death dissent ceased to be a manifestation of an irrational and suicidal impulse and became again something which required merely considerable courage. Many outside observers believed that Russia's professional and intellectual class, so much larger now than in the prerevolutionary times, would revert to the habits and tradition of the old intelligentsia, thus forcing the regime to evolve toward greater political freedom. But the numbing effect of Stalinism has still not worn off. The regime has become more humane, but not more tolerant. Individual dissent has indeed reappeared, but it has not assumed the critical mass of the prerevolutionary intelligentsia. Insofar as one can penetrate the real thinking of educated Russians, it would seem that most of them still live with the memories of Stalinism, and still have not overcome their feeling of relief that all that is required of them now is to conform.

Prerevolutionary society was not an invariable opponent of autocracy. At times, as during the Great Reforms, their relationship was one of cooperation. But in general, the educated class in old Russia served not so much as an enemy as a critic, the scorekeeper, so to speak, of the government's policies. The old autocracy was tempered not only, as the saying has it, by assassinations and corruption, but also by statistics. The twin refrains "Our country is backward," and "Things are not being done in Russia the way they ought to be in a civilized state" were heard and often heeded by the government, even during the most reactionary periods. It is clear that the Communist regime could not permit its intelligentsia to become a social critic any more than it would tolerate it as a political rival. It was the modest hope of the intellectuals and artists who had declared their intention to collaborate with the Soviet state that at least in their work they would be allowed to observe the intelligentsia's prerevolutionary ethos: to adhere to the truth, whether in evaluating an economic plan or portraying life in a village.

But it was not only in literature that Stalinism replaced objective reality by socialist realism. In order to present collectivization as a great success, the regime embarked upon a systematic falsification of data about agricultural production. Terms like *inefficiency, poor planning,* and *accident* virtually disappeared from the official vocabulary, their place being preempted by *wrecking* and *sabotage.* Viewed from the Kremlin, Soviet society was composed of two categories of people: enthusiasts and the people's enemies. There was no middle ground, certainly not for those who by virtue of their work must speak and write, evaluate and plan. Solzhenitsyn's story about a factory director who was sent to a camp because during an ovation following the mention of Stalin's name at a public meeting he was the first to stop applauding and sit down epitomizes the spirit of the times. One could never be sure that it was safe to stop cheering, not only at a meeting but also in writing a book or preparing a technical blueprint.

This phantasmagoric design was crowned with considerable success, and it has continued to affect Soviet life to this very day. To believe, and not merely to pretend to, in the official version of reality became an important factor in assuring not only one's safety but also at times one's sanity. If one refused to believe that Trotsky was connected with the German and Japanese espionage agencies or that a person one had known all one's life had, for much of the time, been a diversionist and a wrecker, then one had to conclude that the country's rulers were not simply criminals, but mad. In the memoirs by the rehabilitated victims of the purges, one still finds traces of this indoctrination through terror: the author writes indignantly about his own ordeal, vouches for the innocence of those victims he personally knew or worked with but does not question that there were others, a lot of them, who did spy, sabotage, and wreck, and who were justly punished.

Terror was a powerful educational force. How deep and lasting the effect of that education can be judged from the words of one of the most perceptive students of contemporary Soviet reality, exiled scientist and writer, Alexander Zinoviev, who tries to portray how a fairly skeptical Soviet citizen reacted to the terror, and how he himself views it in retrospect.

In the consciousness of the people Stalin was not so much a villain as a symbol of a great historic development. This development went beyond a handful of scoundrels subjecting a kindly, deceived nation to cruel outrages. The people were not deceived. Do not forget that millions of ordinary people rendered active assistance in the mass purges which claimed millions of other ordinary people as victims. And often the erstwhile executioner would in time become a victim himself. The purges resulted from a spontaneous initiative of the masses. It is now very difficult to establish who was more guilty, the villainous elite headed by Stalin, or those supposedly deceived masses.[15]

For an outsider this is hard to understand; he has no difficulty in deciding who was more guilty. But the above passage provides a good explanation why after 1964–65 the Soviet regime felt constrained to stop telling the truth about the past and why Stalin's legacy still weighs so heavily on today's Soviet Russia. He has made a whole nation his accomplice, he has beguiled the minds of even some of the most resolute and clear-thinking opponents of the Soviet system.

The main reason for this beguilement is similar to that which led many Western analysts to be rather ambivalent in their verdict on Stalinism. The man himself, all agree, was obviously a bloodthirsty tyrant, and, as is sometimes added, paranoid. Yet in his reign, the Soviet Union advanced from a backward, predominantly rural society to the status of an industrial and military superpower. The Georgian was capable of evoking the vast power of Russian nationalism on behalf of the grandiose feat of social engineering. Under his leadership, the Soviet Union recovered from defeats unprecedented in Russian history, to proceed to a victory also unprecedented in the country's annals. Thus, it is said, it would be a hollow moralism to begrudge him the title to greatness or to deny that in some ways his brutal and violent methods were redeemed by his achievements.

There is a major fallacy underlying this argument. It may be best seen by recalling the stance taken by Khrushchev and his associates when they embarked on de-Stalinization. Far from expressing any contrition because of the supine attitude of the Communist party in the face of Stalin's excesses, as they were delicately termed, they claimed that, on the contrary, it was a proof of the party's strength and vitality that it had survived and was now correcting those—another euphemism—"mistakes and violations of socialist legality."* The argument, rather unconvincing when the party is concerned, can with much greater justice be applied to appraise Stalin's historical role. It was the strength and vitality of Russian society which enabled it to survive and make a stupendous advance despite and not because of Stalinism. His own greatness consisted mainly in the ability to hold on to power despite errors of judgment and crimes which would have toppled lesser tyrants. Modernization and industrialization required terror only if they were combined and subordinated to another goal: absolute power for

---

*In closed party circles, another, more, but still not completely, truthful, answer was given. A story has Khrushchev recounting before an official gathering the horrors of the thirties in much more vivid detail than he did in public. "And why did you not do away with him?" shouted a listener. "We were all afraid," replied the first secretary and then burst into tears.

one man. "Give us twenty years of peace and you will not recognize Russia," Stolypin had said in 1908. He meant that the very momentum of the country's social and economic growth would carry it, barring an internal or external cataclysm, to the forefront of the community of nations. Few experts would question that all moral considerations aside, less drastic methods of modernization would have made Russian industry and especially agriculture much more productive, the country militarily stronger, and the average citizen considerably better off than was the case on the eve of the German invasion in June 1941. Terror hampered and delayed industrialization. But the crux of the matter is that if one wanted both modernization and the nation united, servile, and enthusiastic, terror was the only way.

Similar caution must be observed before describing Stalin as a Russian nationalist. In his speech at the Victory Day celebration in 1945 he offered a special toast to the *Russian* nation, singling it out for praise over and above the other nationalities of the Soviet Union. The government, he said, had made many mistakes before and during the first phase of the war—both a huge understatement and the only time when he even indirectly acknowledged his own errors of judgment. Any other nation, he continued, would have made short shrift of such a government. Not the Russians! A singularly left-handed compliment, but a revealing statement of the extent of Stalin's nationalism—he loved the Russians above all other people because he had been able to forge them into a pliable instrument of his tyranny.

Indeed if the redeeming quality of his leadership is allegedly found in his passion to make Russia—the Soviet Union—great, one is hard put to explain, again laying aside all moral considerations, his policies of the thirties. Collectivization led to the death of millions who could have continued as productive workers or served as soldiers. The purge of the party might be rationalized as having removed the potential troublemakers—people who, when the invasion came, would have harped on those mistakes which Stalin alluded to in 1945, dwell on the past, and hold the regime responsible for the military disasters of the initial phase of the war. But then if Russia's defense against the would-be-aggressor was the dominant consideration in the dictator's mind, it does not fit in with the slaughter of the Red Army's officer corps perpetrated between 1937–39.

The main rationale of Stalin's policies was not the nation's security and strength but considerations of personal power. The peasants had to be subdued because the regime did not choose to negotiate with them through the price mechanism to exact foodstuffs but wanted to be in a position to requisition them. Talented generals, officers, had to be purged and dishonored as traitors so that the rest would be completely cowed, and when the war came would identify their allegiances to the country with that to the Leader. He destroyed every alternative to his despotism, every source of independent thinking in society so effectively that when the blow did come, he was the only institution standing in the way of complete chaos, the only man above the possible imputation of treason. His associates must have been sorely tempted to get rid of Stalin when the news of the invasion threw him into a nervous shock which for more than a week kept him disabled. But they probably realized that the nation would not understand, and that what was already a military disaster would, with Stalin exposed and gone, turn into a national catastrophe.

In brief, Soviet patriotism, that is, Russian nationalism, was like every major theme of his dictatorial reign—"socialism in one country," the struggle against international fascism, world Communism, et cetera—something to be manipulated for his self-aggrandizement rather than a goal pursued for its own sake. Whether and to what extent he himself understood that it was so is a question of great psychological interest but not relevant to our argument.

It is thus a distortion of Stalinism to describe it as Trotsky did as the Thermidor of the Russian revolution. If the revolution had a Thermidor it happened almost immediately after October, with the victors' decision to recreate a centralized and bureaucratic state. Stalin's achievement was much more massive. It might be compared with one of those grandiose nature-mastering schemes conceived during his years; planting a forest belt to change the climate of a whole region, reversing the course of a river so it would flow in the same bed but in the opposite direction. Thus, with terror acting as the dam, the course of development of a whole society was blocked and reversed, so that it would not follow its natural route, but one desired by the regime. As old Russia became more educated and civilized, her society grew more vocal and insistent in its demands for political reform, and for the right of the individual to dissent from the official orthodoxy. Modernization, universal literacy, the acquisition of professional and intellectual cadres many million strong in Stalin's Russia were made to produce a society which applauded, not only outwardly, its unfreedom and the intellectual whose most urgent need was to be accepted as a conformist and true believer.

Much of the debate over whether Communism as practiced in the Soviet Union has followed the pattern and logic of Russian history or, on the contrary, has been entirely the product of a foreign and alien creed and thus distinctly un-Russian, is therefore beside the point. Communism as practiced in the Soviet Union developed quickly into a cult of power with its high priests ready to sacrifice to any god, nationalist or ideological, as long as their offerings promised to assure them of remaining its sole possessors.

Before and during the war, it was the Russian god who was propitiated most strenuously to the point of slighting the Marxist one. No part of the patriotic ritual was neglected: at the height of the wartime danger, the Orthodox Church, until then the target of execration and persecution, became a recognized and valued national institution; Panslavism, hitherto scorned as an offshoot of Great Russian chauvinism, was resuscitated and encouraged; reactionary tsars and generals were rehabilitated and joined the pantheon of patron saints of the Soviet state. With the myth of the regime's infallibility shattered by what had happened during the first months of the war, another one was hastily contrived: the regime had undergone a genuine change of heart and it was truly a national one; from now on it would truly trust the people; the victory will bring a better and freer life for everyone. To nourish such hopes, the camps and prisons released many surviving victims of the great terror, proving incidentally how artificial and mendacious had been its rationale. Some of them went directly to high commands in the army, or returned to important posts in industry and even the government. The shackles of socialist realism were removed and writers, hitherto silenced, were encouraged to write and publish. Genuine, not hackneyed, literature and art were especially needed to foster the belief that the terrible but heroic present would not be followed by a return to what was now seen as the terrible and sordid past.

The vocabulary of class war and Marxism virtually disappeared from the official language. It was not by "Comrades" that Stalin addressed his people in wartime; "Brothers and sisters," "My friends," "Fellow countrymen," he began his speeches to the country where practically every family had yielded a victim to his terror. And Russia was allied with the democracies of the West, and surely that portended if not freedom then surely an end to terror.

The regime's performance was very persuasive. It convinced even its inveterate enemies, political émigrés in the West, that a different and better Russia would emerge from the war. Some of them who during World War I had stoutly opposed the government's imperialist designs and pleaded for a peace without annexations and reparations now found quite natural the Soviet regime's territorial claims against Poland and its emerging imperial role in East and Central Europe.

The god of power was a jealous god, and with the war's end the worship of Russia had to be subordinated once more to his demands. "Long live and flourish our Fatherland. . . . Glory to our victorious nations," said Stalin on September 2, 1945, the day of Japan's official capitulation. On February 9, 1946, the pre-June 1941 Stalin reappeared. He began his speech with "Comrades" and he chose to tread hard on any wartime hopes and illusions which may have still remained. It was no longer the Russian, or even the Soviet, *nation* which won the war. "Our victory means above all that our *social* system has won. . . . Our *political* system has won."[16] Stalinism had won and would remain.

Nationalism in wartime had been used to create an impression of partnership between the regime and the people. Now again it became a rationale and force for oppression. For all the horrors of the war, it had brought with it a sobering sense of reality in the place of the phantasmagoric one which had prevailed ever since the late twenties. The enemy was real: the Germans and their collaborators, and not the people's enemies, "the Trotskyites," etc. The war had put a stop to the nation's division into the hunted and the hunters when in Nadezhda Mandelstam's words, "We were set on our fellow men like dogs, and the whole pack of us licked the hunter's hand squealing incomprehensibly."[17]

In 1946 the lights dimmed again, and society reverted to being a vast stage where the audience sees just what the producer allows: the bulk of the people working strenuously and happily to frustrate new designs of the imperialists—erstwhile allies; and flitting among the shadows, but revealed whenever the spotlight was turned on them the new emanation of the people's enemy, the cosmopolites—purveyors of foreign influence, proponents of decadence and pessimism, denigrators of great Russian culture and tradition. Once more the camps filled up, not only with those who had really collaborated with the invader but also with soldiers who through no fault of theirs had been taken prisoners of war. More than ever before in its history, the Soviet Union was sealed off from the outside world, whatever had trickled in through wartime friendship and intercourse with the West had to be extirpated. In the familiar manner, fresh, sudden blows were dealt to various segments of society, as Mandelstam had written in his poem about Stalin: "He hammers in decree after decree/Like horseshoes to be flung out:/This one is to be struck on the head,/This one in the groin/,This one in the eye." The peasant, whom collectivization had turned back into a serf (he no more could leave his place of employment without permission of the collective farm's chairman than his ancestor before 1861 could without the landlord's) found his work norms raised and much of his wartime savings confiscated. Jewish intellectuals were singled out as constituting the hard core of "rootless cosmopolites." Non-Russian writers who wrote with even modest pride in their native culture and tradition were branded as bourgeois nationalists. But even those who wrote in the language of the master nation were not immune from scabrous attacks when their poetry or prose struck a false individualistic note, when, as did the country's greatest poet, Anna Akhmatova, they chose to express themselves—to quote a resolution of the Central Committee—in "empty idealless poetry, foreign to our nation" suitable to one who was "half nun and half whore."[18] The atom bomb had made the physicist as important as a marshal of the Soviet Union, and like the latter he would be pampered but strictly watched and chastised if he revealed himself a "follower of Einstein and Planck." Treason was unmasked in high places within the party and state apparatus.

All of which was obviously a preliminary to another educational campaign through mass terror. A moment was coming, the nation braced itself for it, when all the disparate strands of treason—the "murderer doctors," "cosmopolites," "agents of American imperialism," would be tied into a whole and the people's wrath would be unleashed, the main blow to fall—one could not be sure—upon the party apparatus, the Jews, or, as in 1936–39, indiscriminately upon all elements of society. As the arrangements were being completed, on March 5, 1953, Stalin died.

Many, including some of his victims, cried at the news. Like the aged Decembrist who wept when Nicholas I died, they could not conceive of Russia without the man who had caused so much suffering, but who must have been great because he made the country great and feared. "Death closed those eyes which had looked so far into the future," wrote Alexis Surkov, a court poet.

The dictator's closest subordinates and successors could not afford to indulge in such masochistic sentimentality. (According to one version, informed on the night of March 1 that he had suffered a stroke and was unconscious, they delayed summoning medical help until the next morning.) Their immediate reaction was one of relief and panic. Relief because some of them, no one was sure which ones, were slated to be among the victims of the coming purge; panic because much of the edifice of tyranny would have to be dismantled, and they were all fearful that in the process, the Soviet system itself might topple. As Khrushchev wrote poignantly, "We were scared—really scared. We were afraid the thaw might unleash a flood, which we wouldn't be able to control and which could drown us. How could it drown us? It could have overflowed the banks of the Soviet riverbed and formed a tidal wave which would have washed away all the barriers and retaining walls of our society."[19] They were afraid of the people and of each other.

But fears made the continuation of terror culture—this was the basic characteristic of Soviet society between 1930–41 and 1945–53—inconceivable. The vast network of forced labor camps began almost immediately to disgorge its inmates. Another numerous category of people now allowed to return to normal life were those "exiled without deprivation of freedom," that is, not in the camps, but confined to a specific, usually Siberian, locality. Amnesties in old Russia had been proclaimed on occasions of official rejoicings such as the tsar's coronation or birth of an heir to the throne, and since 1917 on the major anniversaries of the revolution. This one coincided with the period of mourning for "Comrade Stalin whom we all have loved so much and who will live forever in our hearts." It is safe to say that the amnesty of March 27 affected more people than any previous one, possibly more than all of them together. Among the crimes whose perpetrators were now freed were such as lateness to work, alleged inefficiency in production, desertion as proved by having been a prisoner of war. The criminal code's provisions concerning such crimes were to be revised, for the most part abolished, within one month. In the old Duma, a Socialist deputy once declared that it was nonsensical to talk about the tsar granting an amensty for a category of political crime. As long as autocracy continued, all of Russia was one vast prison. What had been a hyperbole in 1906, came by 1953 to describe fairly accurately Russian society. The law of March 27 and accompanying measures were thus more in the nature of a summary absolution than amnesty. The imputation of guilt, under which the whole population from a peasant to a Politburo member had hitherto lived, was lifted: to commit a crime from now on one had actually to do, say, or write something which was prohibited.

De-Stalinization did not put an end to unfreedom, but it enlarged considerably the area of reality. Society still remained tied down, so to speak, but it was no longer anesthetized by mass terror, individuals began to experience normal reactions, in some cases to speak up. Political courage had virtually ceased to be a meaningful concept in Stalin's Russia. Any manifestation of it would have been not merely suicidal but also senseless and unconscionable: one's voice or example would not carry beyond one's immediate circle. Moreover, it was not only the perpetrator who suffered for an act of defiance or non-conformity but also his family and friends. The height of heroism was to intercede on behalf of a victim of terror one knew to be innocent or to refuse to sign a petition calling for death for the latest batch of the people's enemies. It is only with 1956 when the shock of relief had largely worn off that *protest, dissent, civil courage* began to be meaningful terms even for an intellectual.

The process of de-Stalinization, as it unfolded between 1953–64, both through the government's policies and in the people's minds, demonstrated that a large part of what is known as Stalinism had become firmly embedded in the Soviet system and could not be dislodged without endangering this system. As Khrushchev has disarmingly phrased it, "We wanted to guide the process of the thaw so that it would stimulate only those creative forces which would contribute to the strengthening of socialism."[20] (And if he had been given to introspection, he might have added, "and my own position in the party and the state.") The party wished to get rid of mass terror, but not of the police state; it moved quickly to improve the material conditions of the peasant, until then the most exploited member of Soviet society, but would not tamper with the collective farm system. As Khruschev inimitably puts it, "Of course we wanted a relaxation of control over our artists, but we might have been somewhat cowardly on this score."

In brief the question at each step was how much in the way of controls was needed. No controls at all would have been inconceivable to the most liberal-minded member of the ruling oligarchy. As for political freedom, the question never arose. The rulers did not understand what it meant and would not have known how to bring it about even if they did. The issue dividing Khruschev and the Molotov-Malenkov wing of the party was not that of reform versus Stalinism, but principally (apart from personal factors) how much reform and liberalization the Soviet system could stand without undermining its basic, essentially Stalinist, characteristics. It was only in his last two years in power that Khrushchev began moving in a direction which might eventually have loosened the party oligarchy's iron grip on society. But it is unlikely that he realized what he was doing, and he fell prey to the conspiracy of his fellow oligarchs who did see the danger.

The enduring effects of the Stalin era could also be noted in the people's reaction to official revelations of its true nature. To a Westerner it is almost incomprehensible that Khrushchev's secret speech in 1956 and later his much more explicit and public avowals about the crimes of the past did not lead to widespread riots, to a spontaneous revulsion and revolt against the system which had produced and tolerated such horrors. Equally difficult to understand for a foreigner is the fact that when Khrushchev became the victim of his colleagues' maneuverings, the removal from power of the man, who for all his considerable faults and limitations presided over changes which increased the average citizen's security and well being, was received with such remarkable indifference by the people.

It has often been said that throughout their modern history the Russian people have displayed little concern or real understanding of political freedom or, conversely, that the popular notion of freedom is so extravagant and anarchic to them that any effort to achieve it is bound to end in a new autocracy. As Maxim Gorky wrote in his reflections on the Civil War, "The Russian peasant has for centuries dreamed of some never-never state which would have no right to bind the individual's will, no right to regulate his activities—a state with no power at all over the individual."[21] And Gorky (who, after criticizing Bolshevism during the revolution, made his peace with Lenin, and became the patron saint of Soviet literature under Stalin) quotes a nineteenth-century historian: "Opposition to the state has always existed among the masses but with the wide spaces of the country offering the opportunity, it expressed itself by people fleeing from its reach. They fled from the burdens which the government imposed upon them rather than staying and struggling against it."[22]

Both theses seem to point to the same conclusion: whether out of a servile or anarchic instinct, the Russian people have found it impossible to govern themselves.

Yet such vast generalizations about national character are seldom convincing when submitted to historical scrutiny. It is not some innate characteristics of the Russian soul, but specific historical and social circumstances which hampered the struggle for freedom in the last century and a half. By the time Western ideas percolated into Russian society, the state was both too strong and too weak to begin to evolve along Western lives. Too strong in the sense that the institution and classes which contributed to the curbing or overthrow of absolute monarchy in Britain and France were about to or just developing in Russia; too weak because any parliamentary institution and advance in political freedom threatened the unity of the multinational empire. Even so the liberation movement did force the government to move away from the autocratic model, and only the catastrophe of 1914 stopped this evolution. Except for the war it is inconceivable that the democratic revolution of 1917 would have led to October and all that followed.

What history had done to Russian society as it entered the nineteenth century, the Communist regime accomplished by design; between 1921 and 1953 it destroyed all those social and cultural institutions and influences which might threaten or impinge upon the authoritarian state. One feels that the Soviet rulers have studied the past, especially with the view of ascertaining what it was that forced the old autocracy to retreat after 1856 and eventually to disintegrate, so as to make sure that history would not repeat itself. Hence what Communism had to destroy most thoroughly was the Russian revolutionary tradition. "Look," said Stalin, to an associate in 1934, "if we bring up our children on stories of The People's Will, we shall make terrorists out of them."[23] Discussion, scholarly and otherwise, of the revolutionaries of the 1860s and 1870s was strictly curbed forthwith. But much more effective than banning the tales about the revolutionary past has been its distortion: all the revolutionary and freedom movements of the nineteenth century are shown as leading organically to and finding their fulfillment in Leninism. And as to the present: the bureaucratic state ruled by an oligarchy, still watchful over, if no longer terrorizing, every sphere of social activity, is officially proclaimed as revolution on the march!

All of which goes far to explain not only why Khrushchev's and his colleagues' fears that de-Stalinization "might unleash a flood . . . which could drown us" proved unfounded, but also why there are no revolutionaries today in the Soviet Union. Unfair as it might be, those who dislike a person tend to be suspicious of his relatives and friends. Someone who abhors the Soviet regime cannot feel much sympathy or desire to emulate the example of, say, Chernyshevsky, Plekhanov, and perhaps even Herzen since all were, even if unwittingly, forerunners of Lenin and Stalin. This guilt by historic association is then extended to the idea of revolutionary violence: again where did the heroic strivings and sufferings of so many finally lead to? Were it possible (which it is not) to create a revolutionary organization within the Soviet Union, it would have to be at least as conspiratorial, elitist, and intolerant as the regime it sought to overthrow. There is then no point to restarting the old cycle of stirring up the masses, of terrorist acts, et cetera. One hundred fifty years of history seem to prove that at least in Russia, violence cannot be a successful midwife of freedom.

The modern dissident, even if he finds himself in exile in the West, does not call for bombs, popular uprisings, and the like. His main concerns and weapons are moral and ideological. And here, of course, there is a thread of continuity between the old liberation movements (in the broader sense of the term) and modern dissent. The former tried—and largely succeeded—to impart to the people, beginning with the upper classes, the belief that the existing system, autocracy, was not only unjust but absurd, that it not only acted arbitrarily but also did not live up to its own laws, that it disgraced Russia in the eyes of the civilized world, and was harmful to the national interest. And so the modern dissident—through personal example, by writing and speaking out—seeks to strike at the regime's legitimacy, and self-assurance, tries to expose its ideological and nationalist pretensions. Like a revolutionary or liberal publicist of old, he has to believe that when enough of his fellow citizens come to share his convictions, the walls of Jericho will start crumbling, and perhaps even some in the garrison —members of the Communist party—would see the necessity at least partially of dismantling them.

But the mere listing of similarities between the old and the modern dissenter shows how enormously more difficult and dangerous the latter's task is. Tsarist autocracy was, at least after 1855, much more tolerant of criticism, as well as incomparably less severe and efficient in dealing with it. But what is even more important, a nineteenth-century autocracy could merely preach and punish. A modern authoritarian system is capable of mobilizing vast propaganda and indoctrination resources in order, so to speak, to outshout dissent. Tsarist authorities tolerated, indeed as time went on, were pleased, when prominent writers and intellectuals remained neutral in the contest between the government and society. But such a neutral stance in Soviet Russia, even though no longer as in Stalin's days frought with dire danger, can still prove costly to the individual who takes it; the regime's motto, especially concerning intellectuals and artists, remains: "Who is not with us, is against us."

In its inception, dissent was a foster child of official de-Stalinization. Here again there are clear parallels to the prerevolution past: young Alexander I, with his liberalism, stimulating the ideas which were to inspire the Decembrists; his nephew's Great Reforms encouraging the radicals of the 1860s and 1870s. For both ideological and power reasons the Khrushchev wing of the party hierarchy welcomed independent support for their assault on the Stalin myth. The first secretary and his lieutenants little thought that by fighting Stalinism they were opening a Pandora's box whose contents would plague them and their successors. They hoped that by telling part of the truth they could stem the clamor for all of it, that by ventilating the political scene they would bring a new ideological elan to the Communist party and, incidentally, complete the rout of Khrushchev's rivals. To some extent their calculations were justified. The country had applauded the executions of Lavrenti Beria and his cohorts, "violators of socialist legality," just as it had of those whom Beria had liquidated as the people's enemies. And few thought it incongruous that Khrushchev, who for most of his career had been a faithful executor of Stalin's orders, should now brand such men as Molotov and Malenkov as diehard Stalinists and accomplices of the tyrant's crimes. The party's morale was undoubtedly improved, and the average citizen, in addition to breathing more freely, had the satisfaction of seeing at least some who had oppressed and lied so atrociously now the recipients of similar treatment.

"Don't keep looking behind you. Something might be catching up with you." This wise saying of that American homespun philosopher Satchel Paige might well have been the feeling of Khrushchev's colleagues as he kept dipping into the well-nigh inexhaustible depository of past crimes and deceptions. And by the early 1960s the official version of Stalinism started to sound hollow. There were people who felt compelled to initiate their own search for the truth, seek their own answers about the real lesson of the past and what it meant for the present.

Prior to 1861 an educated Russian tended to view serfdom as the root evil of the whole system. But could the responsibility for the perpetuation of serfdom be attributed solely to the emperor's fear of reform or even to the autocratic system as such? Wasn't a part of the blame to be attributed to the upper classes, or even beyond them to something in the national character which made the mass of people endure supinely their servile condition? The inquiry became the genesis of all the reform and revolutionary movements, which continued and intensified after the degrading institution had been abolished.

Similarly the problem of responsibility for the Stalinist terror in the fifties and sixties became the starting point of an inquest by society upon itself, of a vast self-analysis of which official revelations, scholarly reevaluations, and even the numerous memoirs and biographies by rehabilitated victims constituted but a small part.

As in the nineteenth century, one must look to fiction to sense the moral dilemmas involved in this reappraisal. One frequent theme encountered there is that of silent complicity: a rehabilitated victim returns from a camp to confront a friend or professional colleague who kept silent while he had been denounced and victimized; a returnee's wife and children rethink their feelings toward the man whom they renounced and maybe publicly denounced once he was swallowed by the *Gulag;* then the victim's own feelings when he relives his confessions about imaginary crimes, perhaps his false testimony about equally innocent people. This of course goes beyond anything which had happened in the prerevolutionary past. The Decembrists' friends and families could solicit on their behalf without any fear they might endanger themselves, or even their high position in society. Could all such inhumanity result from just one man's actions?

The answer the regime expected and prompted was, of course, yes, it was one man, occasionally a few sadistic subordinates who had caused the havoc. There are many accounts both fictional and in recollections, some undoubtedly sincere, where the victim even when in a camp or before his death reasserts his faith in the party. Rather preposterously the regime in the late fifties took to boasting of how many innocent victims were being rehabilitated, and how no other system could have matched such magnanimity, such honesty and frankness about its past errors.

Less dramatic, but for a believer in Communism probably even more shattering, were the historians' and statisticians' unemotional accounts exposing the alleged rationale of all those human sufferings: that somehow they were necessary for reshaping and industrializing the country, a high but inevitable price paid for national greatness. The brutal and hasty character of collectivization crippled Soviet agriculture for a generation. "Many kolkhozes experienced great difficulties with provisionment. There were mass cases of people swelling up from hunger and dying." This was an aside in a technical article with a highly approving view of collectivization and of the regimes' policies in the thirties.[24] Or, from a novel about a Ukrainian village during the famine of 1933, which otherwise eulogizes the socialist experiment in the countryside: "The men died first, then the children, then the women."[25] Military historians were allowed, up to 1965, to expose the legend that such sacrifices still enabled the country to prepare for war and assure the victory. On the contrary, the purge of the military and industrial management personnel, the chaos caused by the whole imbroglio, lowered the morale and efficiency of the armed forces, contributed to the initial defeats, and increased immeasurably both the human and material costs of the war.

As long as the momentum of de-Stalinization continued, the feelings of guilt, revulsion, and bewilderment were not likely to build into an open and articulate dissent. Apart from the obvious reasons, there was always the hope that the regime would prove capable of self-reform. To have attacked the Soviet system and its premises, it was believed, and with some plausibility, would have meant to play into the hands of the conservative element within the leadership, eager to discredit Khrushchev and other liberals. Especially among the intelligentsia, there was an awareness of where hopes and demands for perfect freedom had led in the past, hence the willingness to wait and see. Let the situation just keep on getting better.

The poet Alexander Tvardovsky was the leading literary exponent of this, one might call it, liberal orthodoxy; the magazine he edited, *Novyi Mir* (New World), its main organ. Tvardovsky's famous poem about Stalin captured the mood of those who clung to the vision of a better, yet Communist, future. The tyrant "had hovered over us like a dread spirit." Yet

> Who amongst us is fit to judge
> Who was right and who was guilty?
> We talk of men,
> And is it not men
> Who for themselves make gods?[26]

And then (echoing Khrushchev's motto of de-Stalinization: Back to Lenin)

> Great Lenin was not a god,
> Nor did he teach us to make gods. . . .[27]

With Stalin's death "The might of sacred truth reclaimed its limitless rights," so "in things great and small follow in Lenin's steps."

But Lenin's Russia seemed as distant from the realities of the 1960s as that of Alexander II. The romance and ordeal of the revolution could appear vivid and inspiring to people like Khrushchev, who had joined the party in 1918 and somehow never quite lost the faith and enthusiasm of that generation of Communists. But even for them it was palpably impossible to follow Lenin whether in great or small things. Leninism could provide little guidance for dealing with the danger of nuclear war, for the growing disunity of the World Communist movement as illustrated by Yugoslavia in 1948, Hungary in 1956, and above all the growing and ominous tension between Moscow and Peking. For the hard core of the party leadership, Leninism, even if viewed with the nostalgia one feels for his youth, was simply an official rite, the observance of which assured them of their jobs and privileges. And the great majority of their subjects had grown as tired of Communism as they were of ideologies in general. "I see present day Soviet society as being marked . . . by ideological indifference and the cynical use of ideology as a convenient facade," Andrei Sakharov was to write, and with a great deal of truth.[28] After two generations of Communism, the result was pretty much what Maxim Gorky had prophesied: "not the [proverbial] 'kind hearted and enchanting Russian people,' but one which is practical, distrustful and indifferent to anything which does not have a direct bearing on its needs."[29] This cold-blooded practicality and ideological agnosticism of the average Soviet citizen must be even more disturbing to an activist opponent of the Soviet regime than it is to a Communist official.

Khrushchev attempted to combat this indifference by domestic and foreign policy pyrotechnics: the people were to be compensated for their past sufferings and present-day hardships by a sense of participation in grandiose schemes of social and economic construction, such as the reclamation of the virgin lands, surpassing the United States in production of the basic foodstuffs. By 1980, the socialist stage would be completed, and society would enter upon the communist one. (When it came to details as to what it would mean, the First Secretary could offer only free public transportation and as a harbinger of "the withering away of the state," the abolition of the State Committee on Sports.)

But his acrobatics, or as his successors uncharitably characterized them, "hare-brained schemes," began to misfire. Some of the freshly cultivated virgin land was turning into a dust bowl. There were food shortages which led to public riots, something unheard of for a long, long time. The conflict with China came out into the open. Khrushchev's devious scheme of cajoling the United States into a partnership with the Soviet Union brought instead the confrontation and humiliation of the Cuban crisis. In his last two years in power, the intermittently ebullient and choleric innovator felt increasingly trapped. He responded by fresh antics and slogans: reshuffling the party apparatus, throwing open the meetings of the Central Committee to outsiders (and just before his fall he proposed to do the same with the Presidium's), so that his fellow oligarchs would be inhibited from opposing his policies. The most basic canon of Soviet politics—secrecy of decision making—was being threatened, and the bureaucrats' fears that their boss was moving, even if unwittingly, toward some kind of populist, participatory dictatorship was further intensified by his latest formula: the Soviet Union was becoming "the state of the whole people." For the historically minded among them, it must have brought memories of revolutionary democracy of 1917, sending shivers down their spines. So he went. The final public act of this fantasist, probably the last Soviet leader who really believed in Marxism-Leninism, was fittingly a message he addressed to the Soviet cosmonauts circling the earth, of greetings.

"He never carried anything to its conclusion—least of all the fight for freedom," Solzhenitsyn was to write a bit unfeelingly about the man who by authorizing the publication of *One Day in the Life of Ivan Denisovich* allowed the voice of free Russia to be finally heard. And that has been a real, if unintended, achievement of Khrushchev. In 1933 Mandelstam had written that a free man's voice could not carry ten paces away. From the 1960s on such voices would be heard both in the Soviet Union and throughout the world. Nor is it likely they can ever be entirely silenced. Those who speak out may be exiled and imprisoned, but even if abroad, theirs is an authentic echo of new, Soviet society and not, as in the case of the exiles after the revolution, of old Russia.

Eugene Yevtushenko, that political weathervane of Russian literature, wrote in 1962 a powerful, if artistically awful, poem[30] in which he appealed to the

Soviet leadership "to double, triple the guard over Stalin's tomb,"* lest the dead tyrant's spirit reemerge. With Khrushchev's dismissal in 1964, Yevtushenko's fear became more than a fantasy. The new leaders were determined to retain and perpetuate those elements of Stalinism that they judged essential to the Soviet system and which in their view had been jeopardized by the excessive garrulity and innovations of their predecessor. The party, the regime had nothing to apologize for or even to explain; hence the decision to stop talking about things which made people imagine it did. The regime was going to be discreet about the misfortunes of the past and would impose the same discretion upon others —writers, historians, survivors—who had already talked too much.

The debate about Stalinism served between 1956–64 as a kind of surrogate for intellectual, and perhaps in a tiny way, also for political, freedom. The regime's course had been erratic, intermittently brutal, as when it reimposed the death penalty for economic crimes (such as pilfering), occasionally vulgarly repressive with the intellectuals, as with Boris Pasternak, but generally it had seemed pointed in the right direction. Now the outlet had been shut off. Beginning with 1965 one has had to face the stark reality: the Communist regime would not keep moving forward, in some spheres it would try to move the clock back. Mass terror could not return, because it runs against the logic of what is now a fully matured oligarcho-bureaucratic system where the elite is unlikely to entrust itself again to the mercies of one man and the secret police. But what under Khrushchev had been an erratic pattern of chicanery against dissent and nonconformism was with Leonid Brezhnev and Aleksei Kosygin replaced by a systematic one. The very appearance and style of the successors carried with it a kind of warning. In high party circles Khrushchev's jovial vulgarity had long been regarded as quite unfitting for one in his position; he lacked that awe-inspiring quality which the Russian people allegedly prize in their ruler. Brezhnev's usually stern expression and Kosygin's bilious one, both in their behavior reminiscent of masters in a reform school, conveyed the message to their subjects "Now then, there will be no more nonsense."

Punishment and persecution were soon the lot of those who spoke out of turn. The handful who prior to 1965 had pushed their criticism of Soviet life a bit beyond the line set by the party had been shouted at and vilified, but seldom punished severely. For publishing *Doctor Zhivago* abroad, while having been banned at home, Pasternak had been yelled at and humiliated. (The novel's theme runs against the whole Communist-Leninist ethos. Hence Khrushchev, who had not read the book, felt justified in banning it while authorizing the publication of *One Day*, which *on the face of it* is just an indictment of Stalin-

---

*His earthly remains had the year before been demoted from the Mausoleum next to Lenin's to the Kremlin wall.

ism.) But for the same transgression, Andrei Sinyavsky and Yuli Daniel, once the secret police penetrated their literary aliases, were arrested in 1965 and in 1966 condemned to seven and five years respectively in strict regime labor camps. They were sentenced under a law which makes it a criminal offense to engage in anti-Soviet agitation and propaganda, a prohibition so broad and loosely worded that it could apply literally to everyone who ever spoke or wrote about Soviet life.*

The Sinyavsky-Daniel trial was probably the crucial event that led the dissenters into taking the path of protest and defiance. Hitherto many of the individuals whose names would appear in public protests and trials of the next few years could still entertain a modern version of the good tsar—bad counsellors notion of the nineteenth-century reformers: whatever changes in the leadership, the party as a whole could not flaunt society's changed condition and expectations. Here they were faced with an unambiguous signal by the government that it was done with playing games with dissenters. As for society . . . "in 1966 about three hundred leaflets calling for freedom were pasted on walls and dropped into the mailboxes in various districts of Moscow (by two teenage girls). . . . The majority of the citizens who received leaflets turned them over to the KGB."[31] Before those whose hopes had been shattered there arose the old dilemma of the Russian reformer and revolutionary: what is to be done? During the next fifteen years, various individuals and groups would work out different answers to the question.

The overwhelming majority of that small minority within society who consider themselves active dissenters has eschewed the conspiratorial path. The average dissenter has operated openly by trying to draw the regime's attention to his protest; or semiopenly, by engaging in activities like circulating forbidden literature, which, as he fully realizes, must lead sooner or later to an interview with the secret police, loss of his job, perhaps exile or a camp. In most cases it is not a craving for martyrdom, but a rational design which lies behind such tactics: to make the regime come out from behind its protective screen of ideology and "socialist legality." Unlike his nineteenth-century predecessor, the modern dissenter is informed by somber realism. He knows that neither his own example and preaching nor the authorities' repeated acts of arbitrariness will lead the people to rise in revolt or even to approve of his actions. But what he does hope for is, first, to enlarge the people's awareness of how their government really operates and to increase their uneasiness and inner embarrassment at the kind of system under which they live. While he has learned the futility of appealing to his rulers' sense of justice and fair play, he has not given up hope that there are some within the Communist establishment who can be swayed by common

*Including Lenin and Stalin, who in their speeches often berated officials' abuses and inefficiency.

sense. Surely they must see that it is preposterous for the mighty Soviet state to persecute a handful of religious sectarians, ban nonobjective art; to consider a writer who satirizes the bureaucracy as a dangerous enemy. Surely such practices injure the Soviet Union's image abroad (an argument which since Stalin's death has ceased to be completely ineffective), and they feed that silent alienation from the system, especially among the intelligentsia and the young, which is of real concern to the regime. An inveterate Stalinist would attribute the rise in crime and alcoholism to the still excessive toleration of baneful Western influences, and the still inadequate enforcement of social discipline, but a more intelligent official must at least suspect there are other reasons as well.

One battlefield chosen by dissent has been that of the Soviet law. The Soviet Constitution of 1936 had hitherto stood as a grandiose monument to despotism. It listed an impressive array of individual and political rights, yet no Soviet citizen in his right mind would have thought of invoking them. Even under Khrushchev the past violators of socialist legality, for example, Beria and his group were themselves disposed of with but scant regard for the letter of the law. Not so with his successors. They have employed judicial procedure as one of the main weapons of political chicanery but have taken great care to observe outward proprieties. Political trials have been open, though in the most delicate cases, the KGB agents would preempt most of the seats, leaving no room for outsiders. The accused, except for an occasional provocateur thrown in, have been allowed to plead innocent, their lawyers really to defend them.* To be sure, the judges run the trials and render their verdicts as instructed by an appropriate party or state organ. In brief, a decorous rather than hitherto macabre travesty of justice.

The regime's gambit provided a natural opening for dissent. Here was an issue which could unite its most diverse strains, from those loyal to Marxism-Leninism but deploring the way it was being practiced to the allout opponents of the whole rationale of the system, demanding that the Soviet regime live up to the Soviet law. In 1968 four people were tried and sentenced for disseminating *samizdat,* that by now considerable body of literature ranging from fiction to documentary evidence and political tracts, written, translated, and circulated in contravention of censorship. The conduct of the trial provoked some three hundred Soviet citizens, most of them from the intellectual community, to address a formal protest to the attorney general of the Soviet Union (copies were sent to Brezhnev and Kosygin): "The trial was characterized by an even more gross and senseless violation of the law [than some previous trials]. . . ." Constitutional guarantees had been violated both procedurally and in substance, the signatories went on.

---

*In the great purge trial of 1938, a "defense" lawyer usually began his speech to the court by confessing that like the prosecutor, he stood appalled by the magnitude and depravity of his clients' crimes.

There was no answer from the highest judicial officer of the state, nor is it likely that one had been really expected. The way the regime and to some extent society answered can be best seen in the story of Valerie Gerlin, which epitomizes current Soviet life better than many much more dramatic and widely known critical accounts.

For signing her name to the petition, Valerie Gerlin was fired as a teacher of Russian literature in a high school. Again the formalities were being observed: not an administrative fiat, but a proposal by the local party committee that she be excluded from the local teachers' union, which would also bar her from teaching anywhere else and presumably leave only physical or clerical labor as a means of securing her livelihood.

To the meeting of fellow teachers which was to decide, formally, her case, Gerlin recounted her background. Her father, a party member, was shot as a "people's enemy," and her mother received the usual punishment in such cases, an eight-year camp sentence, so that she became an orphan at the age of seven. As was also customary for children of people in that category, Gerlin herself was arrested upon reaching her maturity in 1949 and sent into exile. After 1953 she was reunited with her mother, and the young woman pursued her professional career. That is why she could not remain insensitive to an injustice. Her action, Gerlin declared, was entirely open, with no hint of disloyalty to her country and the government. She did not, as some others did, try to publicize the "trial of the four" abroad. She did not even question the verdict in the case. "This would not be within my competence, I am not a judge. But that the law be observed strictly and honestly is of importance to every honorable person. In each law-abiding state, hence especially in our Soviet one, anybody who is accused, be he a murderer or a rapist, ought to be tried according to the law and only thus."[32]

Here she was interrupted by one of her colleagues. "According to you, people who are anti-Soviet should also be judged according to the law." And when Gerlin replied, "Yes, absolutely, everybody," the same person continued incredulously and incredibly. "But they are our enemies. How can one intercede for an enemy? They do harm to society and we are supposed to observe the law when dealing with them. . . . If you insist on justice, you would have to acquit the whole gang." The accused woman's reply could not be faulted for lack of Soviet patriotism. "Have you no shame? What you just said is unworthy of a teacher, of any, even the most ignorant human being. . . . Our law is strong and stern enough to punish any transgressor without resorting to injustice. And if we do not observe the law of our land, how different are we from the enemies of our state?"

During the discussion-inquisition which followed, it became clear that Gerlin's "anti-Soviet" act was not an isolated incident. She taught her students, a colleague revealed, the poetry of such as Akhmatova and Nicholas Gumilev (a noted poet executed early in the Soviet era for alleged counterrevolutionary activities), whose decadent writings, while no longer banned, were certainly not in the curriculum, certainly not what the young should read. "Before she came to us, no one ever heard, not to mention discussed [these writers]. . . . Now students, even in other teachers' classes . . . read their poetry, copy their poems, and on the school typewriters, if you please."[33]

Some colleagues pleaded cautiously in the woman's defense: a very good teacher they testified. All the more dangerous was the usual rejoinder. Several found Gerlin's tale of her tragic childhood in bad taste. She has known quite a few people, one speaker said, who had spent years in the camps, and not like the culprit just in exile, and yet they were staunchly loyal and would not dream of signing a petition besmirching Soviet justice and defending slanderers of the state and the party. How could she have done what she did, exclaimed another zealot, at a moment when the whole "camp of socialism" was being threatened by the capitalist enemy as demonstrated by what was happening in Czechoslovakia. (This was taking place during "the Prague spring" before it was cut short by the Soviet invasion.) "If a teacher is not convinced in his state's absolute righteousness, he is not fit to be an educator. . . . And what does Gerlin's personal story have to do with anything? All that was needed has already been said about the past. It is useless to keep rehashing it."[34]

Along with such contributions, questions were being fired at the brave and unfortunate woman in a style quite reminiscent of a past which supposedly had been left far behind. Who persuaded her to sign? How many of the other signatories did she know personally? Did she realize that the petition was being used by the capitalist press, featured on the BBC? Though the drift of the discussion was unmistakable, the director of the school, who next to the culprit had probably most to lose from the affair ("How could he have allowed his institution to become a hotbed of subversion," he was probably told by a superior), chose to serve notice on those who visibly wavered or expressed sympathy for Gerlin: "We are warning them in plain language: think twice before you cast your vote. . . . She should have been fired a long time ago."[35] Despite such subtle hints, the vote was not unanimous: thirty-seven for expulsion, five against, one abstaining.

Six people chose deliberately to place their own careers and jobs in jeopardy. It is not known whether and to what extent Valerie Gerlin's faith in the Soviet state's ability to remedy its own abuses and injustices has survived her ordeal. But at least some among those who condemned her must have reached fresh conclusions on that count.

This small tableau of Soviet life in 1968 is still relevant and instructive for 1980. Such occasions when the juggernaut of the system clashes with the human conscience of a few and the sense of decency among a more numerous minority are not an everyday occurence, but not too unusual either. In their sum they are probably as damaging, if not more so, to the moral authority and legitimacy of the Soviet system as those cases of protest and persecution which attract world-wide attention.

In the moral and intellectual sphere, the achievement of the relative handful of dissidents has already approached that of the Russian intelligentsia in the 1860s and 1870s: it has put an oppressive political system on the defensive. The Soviet autocracy is incomparably stronger, more ingenious and less given to scruples than the tsarist one. It has displayed considerable sophistication in combating its opponents and critics. Some, in whose case more brutal methods of repression would have been counterproductive in terms of public opinion at home and abroad, have been expelled or allowed to emigrate. Many others have been incarcerated, some declared insane, a practice for which there are perhaps two precedents in the entire tsarist period, and placed in asylums under the care of KGB doctors. A few have been left at large (though closely watched and occasionally threatened), as proof of the regime's forbearance and humanity.

Indeed in the official view, there is no such thing as political dissent, but only the antisocial activities and attitudes of a few. Many dissidents tell stories of interviews with security officers who have, often in fatherly tones, implored them to give up their senseless and dangerous activities. Stalin's secret police wanted its customers to confess, Brezhnev's, for the most part, to desist. Those who don't are then classified and punished as abnormal, or parasites and hooligans, and therefore attracted by the West's licentious ways, or finally as outright agents of some anti-Soviet organization abroad.

With their new self-image of respectability and with mass terror impracticable, the rulers find it inconvenient to detain within the Soviet state large numbers of those who openly disagree with both its ideological and nationalist premises. Hence the government's decision, reached around 1970, to license a sizable exodus of Jews, a decision which would have been unthinkable under Stalin, and hardly less so under Khrushchev. It is erroneous to ascribe the chief reason for such a change in attitude to pressures from abroad. The decision marked a shift, this time almost explicit, from ideology to nationalism as the principal rationale and line of defense of the Soviet regime. Why keep a large number of people who because of their ethnic origin are bound to be at least divided in their allegiance? That leaving the Soviet Union is not made easier for the Jews, indeed that the government does not order their expulsion en masse (as some within the oligarchy undoubtedly wish it could) is due not only to the lingering ideological scruples and needs, and reluctance to lose valuable human skills, but to yet another factor. The government cannot afford to establish the precedent that anybody who feels oppressed and wants to leave may do so, or that exile abroad should be the chief predictable consequence of one's disloyal activities and sentiments. The current stand on emigration offers on the contrary some tangible political advantages to those in power: officially it can be defended as being entirely free of any racist or xenophobic motivations; on the contrary, it is those who leave who have fallen under the spell of a reactionary and nationalist philosophy—Zionism—being in that respect completely unrepresentative of the bulk of the Soviet Jewry. Unofficially the policy is designed to appeal to the still considerable residue of anti-Semitism among the people and to utilize it in the struggle against dissent. In pre-1917 Russia the camp of extreme reaction purported to see Jewish influence behind every conceivable form of revolutionary and liberal organization and agitation. Now by its stand on the Jewish question, the government tries to insinuate a somewhat similar theme: whatever the nationality of a critic of the Soviet regime, whatever the issue to which he addresses himself, he in essence echoes the Zionists' slanders about the Soviet land and its people.

Despite such stratagems, dissent has made its main point: most thinking Soviet citizens over forty have not been brainwashed into forgetting what Stalinism was or into ignoring how heavily its legacy still pervades Soviet life.

But having established in the people's minds the answer to "who is guilty?" the dissenter is faced with the other part of his self-proclaimed mission: to indicate some ways out of the present situation. Here he finds himself in an infinitely weaker position than his predecessor in tsarist times. The nineteenth-century revolutionary or reformer was seldom at a loss when it came to recommending what should be done to cure the country's ills. The answers were obvious if widely divergent: organize a revolutionary conspiracy; educate the people about socialism; work alongside the liberal element within the ruling establishment for a constitutional parliamentary monarchy; coerce or persuade the regime to summon a constituent assembly. . . . Terms like *democracy, liberalism, socialism* had in that simpler age a clear-cut, concrete meaning, with neither their advocates nor foes in doubt as to what they would be in practice.

For the contemporary Russian advocate of freedom, the problem of actually changing the system is enormously complex. Where and how does one begin to lighten, let alone to lift completely, the enormous weight of the Communist state which presses upon the body of the nation? Is that state now so firmly engrafted upon society that it cannot be removed or seriously altered without destroying the latter? Can anything but a centralized, authoritarian government hold all the nations of the USSR together, or must any democratization or real liberalization lead to full independence for some of them? If all the above were by some miracle resolved, what feasible form of government for the people who for sixty years were systematically taught to forget all the lessons in freedom and self-government they had learned before?

Messianic thinking and striving, so common among the nineteenth-century's opponents of autocracy, has been conspicuous by its absence among the critics and enemies of the Soviet system. Nor is there much hope among them that mechanistic contrivances—constitutions, parliaments—have in and of themselves much relevance to the future of the country. There is on the contrary a considerable dose of apocalyptic feeling, epitomized by the title of one projection into the future by Andrei Amalrik, *Will the Soviet Union Survive until 1984*, the feeling that the militaristic and expansionist state is inexorably committed to a course which leads to a national as well as worldwide catastrophe.

Most of the thinking about the future is characterized, however, neither by exuberant hopes, nor visions of nuclear or other cataclysmic disasters. "We do not urge the destruction of those values which the October Revolution brought into our life and that of the whole world. We urge their renewal and purification, further development and fulfillment." The writer then takes Leninism as his point of departure, to urge "a gradual and systematic development of socialist and party democracy."[36] Such a democracy, Medvedev argues, would mean toleration of dissent and/or outright opposition to the regime, but not an end of the Communist party's monopoly of power. Other, non-Marxist, parties and movements which would spring into existence would lack a mass basis and hence pose no threat to socialism or the party's rule.

It is an ingenious scheme and perhaps not entirely unrealistic. But it would certainly upset Lenin. Most Soviet citizens, one suspects, would find the suggestion that their rulers might entrust their jobs to really free elections as rather humorous. If they remember Marx, they must recall one of his most perceptive observations: no ruling class is likely to surrender voluntarily its power.

Alexander Solzhenitsyn's proposals-reflections-prophecies are diametrically opposed to Medvedev's neo-Leninism. The basic evil of the Soviet system, the most resonant voice among those opposed to it argues, lies precisely in the ideology. Not because it is widely believed or really relevant to what is going on in the Soviet state. In fact in today's world the doctrine is clearly anachronistic, and not even the rulers, let alone the vast majority of the people, find it relevant or convincing. But it is this pretended worship of the false gods of Marxism-Leninism which is the main source of moral corruption of the regime, the master cause of that falsehood and inhumanity which afflicts every sphere of social life and vitiates the humane and constructive impulses and energies of the Russian people.

In his writings Solzhenitsyn has not confined himself to moral preaching and exposing the Soviet past but has also displayed a considerable political acumen. The Kremlin's most effective argument in selling Communism has been that it is indissolubly bound up with the unity and greatness of the Soviet-Russian state. Quite the opposite, says the writer. Communism has already and immeasurably harmed the nation, claimed huge and needless human sacrifices, and warped its traditions and moral health. Its main psychological effect on the alleged practitioners of the doctrine is that it fills them with an unquenchable craving for power, on whose altar they are ready to sacrifice their peoples' welfare as well as any other considerations. The Soviet rulers' proprietary rights on the cult have indeed enabled them to maximize their power and project it into every corner of the world. But in so doing they conjured up the greatest threat as yet to the Russian nation and the Soviet Union, one which dwarfs the alleged dangers presented by the capitalist West. Non-Communist China would have been a tolerable neighbor of the USSR and a peaceful member of the world community. But it is in the nature of Communism that it cannot tolerate two centers of power, two competing sets of high priests. Besides the same psychological mechanism is at work in the mind of Peking's rulers as in that of their Kremlin coreligionists: it pushes them toward militarism and territorial expansion. Mao in 1964 laid claims to vast areas of the Soviet Far East and Siberia. The Chinese colossus, a billion strong, once industrialized, which under Communism is synonymous with militarization and readiness to embark upon conquests, will present a mortal danger to the Soviet state. The danger can be avoided or lessened by the Russian people giving up the wretched ideology which has caused them and the world so much harm and which must be fully exposed and checked before it plunges the whole world in a nuclear catastrophe.

This variant of the nationalist argument is probably the most effective case to be made against the continuation of the Soviet system since it appeals to the widespread, if inarticulate, anxiety of the Soviet people—the menace from the East. Many must have silently reflected why capitalist Japan presents no real threat to their future, while it is the greatest triumph of Communism since 1917 which stands like an ominous shadow over their lives. Is this merely, as the regime keeps insisting, because of the "dogmatism and sectarianism" of a handful of the leaders in Peking (and since Mao's death such labels have been difficult to sustain), with whose removal the two nations would resume their fraternal relations? It is safe to say that this Chinese version of the cult of personality gambit finds even less credence among the masses than it is believed by those in the Kremlin. The Communism-national interest nexus hitherto the most effective rationale of the Soviet regime has thus become its Achilles heel.

Solzhenitsyn's musings about Russia's future and his jeremiads about the West have led some to classify him as a neo-Slavophile, as authoritarian, reactionary.

Yet it is impossible and unfair to try to fit him into such political categories. He preaches no political ideology, and indeed his insistence on the moral responsibility of the individual makes him according to his lights unable to do so. Let the Soviet leaders continue to rule autocratically, provided they give up the lie which is Communism, a statement which does not reflect Solzhenitsyn's penchant toward authoritarianism, but his anti-Communism as well as, one suspects, the feeling that once stripped of its ideological pretense, the authoritarian system would soon collapse. If the writer severely criticizes the West for its craven posture vis-à-vis the USSR, and its preoccupation with material values, it is not because like a nineteenth-century Russian radical he affects to reject the whole complex of Western values. On the contrary, it is the West's declining faith in those values, the growing reluctance to stand up for them and against the onslaught of Communism and other forms of modern barbarism, which fills him with anger. The current posture and condition of the Western world, Solzhenitsyn senses, is one of the greatest obstacles to the cause of freedom in his own country. A note so familiar among the nineteenth-century enemies of autocracy that despite, but also because of, its sufferings the Russian nation is somehow spiritually superior to Europe, corrupted by materialism and hedonism, is intermittently echoed by Solzhenitsyn. But such echoes are more than balanced by a sober view of his own society as when he writes, "The majority of young people could not care less whether we have been rehabilitated or not, whether twelve million people are still inside [the camps] or are inside no longer; they do not see that it affects them. Just so long as they themselves are at liberty with their tape recorders, and their dishevelled girl friends."[37]

Many who admire Solzhenitsyn as a writer and a voice for freedom have still felt estranged by the nationalist and traditionalist idiom in which his reflections on politics are expressed. The typical Western liberal feels more at home and less disturbed by the views of a dissident like Andrei Sakharov. There he discerns a more hopeful note: the inevitability of the Soviet system shedding its irrational and oppresive excrescences, evolving toward a real social democratic kind of society. The logic of modern technology and economy, the distinguished and persecuted physicist believes, is bound to prevail over ideological incantations and imperialist impulses. Yet like most visions of Russia's future, this one also falters when it comes to the key problem of power. The school of convergence, which Sakharov's views by and large represent, may be, probably is, quite correct in assuming that with the passage of time the habits of thought and aspirations of the typical Soviet scientist, engineer, and worker have become increasingly like those of his opposite number in the West. But in the Soviet state decision making is vested in the hands of a small elite; its members are trained and habituated to worship power as the highest goal and to see its tangible expressions not merely in the rate of economic growth and well being of their subjects but mainly in their ability to manipulate their society and to project the might of the state abroad. There is as yet no evidence that convergence works insofar as the Politburo of the Communist party of the USSR, and the mentality of its present and putative future members, is concerned.

But how long can any, even the most despotic, system resist pressures which are building up around it and permeating its society? The Soviet economy is visibly faltering. The declining birthrate among the Russians, combined with the stirrings of nationalism among the other ethnic groups, the growing numerical strength of the Moslem-Turkic element of the population—will they not eventually assume a critical mass which will force the regime to undergo basic changes or face an explosion?

Here the story as recounted in these pages offers an instructive if not exactly reassuring answer. It is mainly by draping itself with the national interest, appealing to Russian nationalism (and *Soviet patriotism* is but its synonym in an ideological guise) that autocratic regimes from Nicholas I's to Brezhnev's have sought to withstand pressures for liberalization and the demand for freedom. In the nineteenth century this argument that if the country was to remain united and great it had to have a strong government grew increasingly unconvincing, first to the intelligentsia, then to the people at large, finally to many within the ruling class. What was happening in the outside world was a vivid demonstration that, on the contrary, national power and well being are promoted by free institutions. Russia's relapse into autocracy after two generations of political progress came only after another vivid demonstration, this time of the failure of liberal institutions and democracy. They had proved incapable of preventing or promptly terminating the war which undermined the whole fabric of European civilization and social order.

Since 1945 the Soviet regime has, at least with partial success, taught its people another lesson opposite to that offered by the nineteenth century: liberal and democratic institutions make for national weakness. Its other claims to legitimacy exposed or tarnished, the Communist state has placed its wager on the competitive advantages which its denial of freedom offers in today's world. Now that the unity of the Communist movement is irretrievably lost, and the doctrine itself has become discredited or irrelevant insofar as its own people are concerned, the regime strives to demonstrate its viability and vitality by its enhanced power and influence throughout the world; whatever its shortcomings, it is under Communism that the Soviet Union (for the most part Russia) has steadily advanced in power and influence, while the democracies for all their alleged freedoms and riches have been in retreat. The defeats and humiliations suffered by the West serve as a kind of negative indoctrination for the Soviet citizen. Whatever his discontents with what he finds at home, can he really believe that the other system has a future?

There is little that can be described as uniquely Russian about the country's pattern of political development in the last century and a half, just as there is nothing exclusively Western about the ideas of democracy, intellectual freedom, the rule of law, socialism, which affected so deeply that development, even if their cumulative effect in 1917 was so shatteringly different. The ideas continue to express universal human aspirations, but their future fortunes depend on whether they continue to bring along with them power and progress, or spiritual and political decline. So it is the worldwide reputation of freedom which will determine largely its future in Russia.

REFERENCES

Chapter 1

1. A. S. Pushkin, *Works*, V (Moscow, 1957), p. 213.
2. Pushkin, *Works*, V, p. 212.
3. *The Decembrist Uprising Materials*, III (Moscow, 1927), p. 52.
4. Pushkin, *Works*, IV (1934), 803.
5. Pushkin, V, 209. This was written by the poet several years after the emperor's death and reflected at least partly his personal grudge. In 1820 Alexander banned him from the capital for having written some politically indiscreet poems which were widely circulated in St. Petersburg's drawing rooms.
6. Nicholas K. Shilder, *Emperor Alexander I* (St. Petersburg, 1905), p. 344. His language on the occasion was both vague and could not but hurt Russian national pride. The level of education prevailing in Poland allowed him, said the emperor, to grant her a constitution. While for long he had had a similar boon in mind "for other dominions which Providence has entrusted to his rule," they were as yet not quite ready for it.
7. Pushkin, *Poems, 1814–1825*, I (Moscow, 1934), p. 284.
8. A. Karamzin, *A Memoir on Ancient and Modern Russia*, ed. Richard Pipes (Cambridge, Mass., 1959), p. 43.
9. Karamzin, p. 73. The writer disregarded the fact that their present status did not preserve them from either.
10. Karamzin, p. 74.
11. Karamzin, p. 40.
12. M. V. Nechkina, *The Decembrist Movement*, I (Moscow, 1955), p. 204.
13. Quoted in M. V. Dovnar-Zapolski, *The Secret Society of the Decembrists* (Moscow, 1906), p. 44.
14. Nechkina, I, pp. 207–213.
15. Shilder, p. 430.
16. Baron Vladimir Steingel, quoted in A. Borozdin, *Letters and Depositions of the Decembrists* (St. Petersburg, 1906), p. 62.
17. *Notes, Articles, Letters* (Moscow, 1951), p. 35.
18. E.g., Nechkina, I, pp. 304–33.
19. *Materials*, IV, p. 102.
20. *Materials*, IV, p. 159.
21. *Materials*, I, p. 32.
22. *Materials*, XIII (1975), p. 218.
23. Cited in I. I. Gorbachevsky, *Notes and Letters* (Moscow, 1963), p. 23.
24. The text of the constitution in *Materials*, I (1923), pp. 109–132.
25. *Materials*, IV, p. 92.
26. *Materials*, VII, (1958), p. 189.
27. *Materials*, VII, p. 189.
28. *Materials*, VII, p. 174.
29. *Materials*, VII, p. 185.
30. *Materials*, VII, p. 139.
31. *Materials*, VII, p. 144.
32. *Materials*, VII, p. 146.
33. *Materials*, VII, p. 149.
34. *Materials*, VII, p. 230.
35. *Materials*, VII, p. 230.
36. *Materials*, VII, p. 204.
37. *Materials*, VII, p. 207.
38. *Materials*, VII, p. 160.
39. *Materials*, I, p. 324.
40. *Materials*, I, p. 178.
41. *Materials*, IV, p. 160.

References

42. *Materials,* IV, p. 92.
43. *Materials,* IV, p. 92.
44. *Materials,* IV, p. 103.
45. *Materials,* IV, p. 104.
46. *Materials,* IV, p. 118.
47. *Materials,* V (1926) p. 28.
48. Quoted in Gorbachevsky, p. 28.
49. Gorbachevsky, p. 30.
50. Gorbachevsky, pp. 33–34.
51. Gorbachevsky, p. 35.
52. *Materials,* I, p. 167.
53. *Materials,* IV, p. 407.
54. G. S. Gabayev, "The Guards in the December Days of 1825" in A. E. Presnyakov, *The Fourteenth of December, 1825* (Moscow, 1926), p. 197.
55. Shilder, p. 435.
56. *Materials,* II (1954), p. 250.
57. *Materials,* IV, p. 125.
58. Nechkina, II, 397.
59. Borozdin, p. 22.
60. Borozdin, p. 81.
61. *Materials,* III, 124, 128.
62. *Materials,* V, p. 100.
63. Pushkin, *Works,* III (1949), 7.
64. *Poems and Letters* (Moscow, 1934), p. 117.
65. Serge Volkonsky, *The Decembrists—Family Recollections* (St. Petersburg, 1922), p. 96.

Chapter 2

1. Quoted in N. D. Brodsky, ed., *The Early Slavophiles* (Moscow, 1910), p. 19.
2. V. S. Belinsky, "Letter to Gogol" in B. G. Guerney, *A Treasury of Russian Literature* (New York, 1947), p. 243.
3. Brodsky, p. 89.
4. Brodsky, p. 91.
5. Brodsky, p. 69.
6. Brodsky, p. 86.
7. Brodsky, p. 92.
8. Brodsky, p. 94. Another conservative writer of the period, Michael Pogodin, expressed his reservation about the Russian peasant with less restraint: he was a wonderful human being, insofar as his potential was concerned, but in actuality the masses were "base, horrid and beastly."
9. Brodsky, p. 286.
10. Alexander Herzen, *Works,* ed. Michael Lemke, VI (St. Petersburg, 1919), pp. 456–57.
11. S. S. Tatishchev, *Emperor Alexander II,* I (St. Petersburg, 1903), 302.
12. Tatishchev, I, 314–16.
13. I. S. Turgenev, *Works,* III (Moscow, 1961), 187.
14. P. A. Zayonchkovsky, *The Abolition of Serfdom* (Moscow, 1968), p. 87.
15. Zayonchkovsky, p. 69.
16. Quoted in Vladimir Burtsev, *One Hundred Years* [in Russian] (London, 1897), pp. 19, 21.
17. *The Bell,* August 1, 1857.
18. *The Bell,* February 15, 1857.
19. N. G. Chernyshevsky, *Works,* V (Moscow, 1950), 165.
20. Chernyshevsky, V, 65.
21. Chernyshevsky, V, 70.
22. Chernyshevsky, V, 70.

23. Brodsky, p. 85.
24. Chernyshevsky, V, 647.
25. Chernyshevsky, V, 649.
26. Chernyshevsky, V, 653.
27. L. F. Panteleyev, *Memoires* (Moscow, 1958), p. 166.
28. Tatishchev, I, p. 369
29. *The Bell*, March 1, 1860.
30. *The Bell*, March 1, 1860.
31. Tatishchev, I, p. 407.
32. The text of the proclamation in Michael Lemke, *Political Trials in Russia of the 1860s* (Moscow, 1923), pp. 62–80.
33. The text of *The Great Russian*, Nos. 1–3 in Michael Lemke, *Studies in the Russian Liberation Movement in the 1860s* (Moscow, 1908), pp. 359–68.
34. F. Dostoyevsky, *The Possessed* [in Russian] (Paris, 1969), p. 416.
35. The text of the proclamation in Michael Lemke, *Political Trials*, pp. 508–18.
36. Herzen, *Works*, IV, p. 111.
37. *The Bell*, August 15, 1861 (Author's italics).
38. B. I. Gorev and B. P. Kozmin, *The Revolutionary Movement of the 1860s* (Moscow, 1932), p. 12.
39. Gorev and Kozmin, p. 18.
40. *The Bell*, July 1, 1861.
41. The text in Chernyshevsky, XVI (1953), 947–53.
42. *The Bell*, November 8, 1861.
43. Chernyshevsky, X (1952), 487–88.
44. Peter Tkachev, *Works*, III (Moscow, 1933), 225.
45. Tatishchev, I, p. 491.
46. *Letter to Soviet Leaders* (London, 1974), p. 53.
47. S. Nevedensky, *Katkov and His Times* (St. Petersburg, 1888), p. 170.
48. Chernyshevsky, VI (1949), p. 337.
49. Quoted in N. A. Lyubimov, *Michael Katkov and His Historical Achievements* (St. Petersburg, 1889), p. 100.
50. *The Bell*, June 15, 1864.
51. George Plekhanov, *Works* (Moscow, 1924), V, p. 115.
52. Tatishchev, I, p. 523.
53. Tatishchev, I, 534.
54. M. M. Klevensky and K. G. Kotelnikov, eds., *The Karakozov Attempt*, I (Moscow, 1928), p. 8.
55. M. N. Katkov, *Collected Editorials for 1878* (Moscow, 1898), p. 154.
56. *Historical Papers* (St. Petersburg, n.d.), p. 386.
57. O. V. Aptekman, *The Society of Land and Freedom of the 1870s* (Petrograd, 1924), p. 178.

Chapter 3

1. See A. Ulam, *In the Name of the People* (New York, 1977), p. 361.
2. See Ulam, *Name of the People*, p. 360.
3. See A. Ulam, *The Bolsheviks* (New York, 1965), p. 341.
4. S. Witte, *Memoirs*, II (Moscow, 1960), 305–06.
5. Witte, II, 165.
6. Dostoyevsky, *Collected Works*, X (Moscow, 1958), 453.
7. *The Diary of Yegor Peretz* (Moscow, 1927), p. 37.
8. P. Z. Zayonchkovsky, *The Crisis of the Autocracy* (Moscow, 1964), p. 38.
9. V. A. Maklakov, *Memoirs*, I (Paris, 1937), 13.
10. Maklakov, I, 13.
11. Quoted in Samuel Galai, *The Liberation Movement in Russia, 1900–1905* (Cambridge, England, 1973), p. 25.

References

12. Galai, p. 26.
13. P. B. Struve, *Collected Works*, ed. Richard Pipes, [in Russian] III (Ann Arbor, Michigan, 1970), 80.
14. Struve, III, 81.
15. Struve, V, 2.
16. E. D. Chermensky, *The Bourgeoisie and Tsarism in the First Russian Revolution* (Moscow, 1970), p. 32.
17. Lenin, *Works*, 4th ed., V (Moscow, 1941), 347.
18. *Autocracy and the Zemstvos, Confidential Memorandum of S. I. Witte*, ed. P. Struve (Stuttgart, 1903), p. 15.
19. Jeremiah Schneiderman, *Sergei Zubatov and Revolutionary Marxism* (Ithaca, New York, 1970), p. 104.
20. Dmitri Sverchkov, *George Gapon* (Moscow, 1930), p. 37.
21. Quoted in George Fischer, *Russian Liberalism* (Cambridge, Mass., 1958), p. 190.
22. Fischer, p. 194.
23. Maklakov, II, 331.
24. Quoted in Maklakov, II, 339.
25. Sverchkov, p. 81.
26. Sverchkov, p. 81.
27. Sverchkov, p. 90.
28. Lenin, *Works*, VIII (1949), 93.
29. Sverchkov, p. 113.
30. Chermensky, p. 52.
31. Sverchkov, p. 95.
32. Sverchkov, p. 95.
33. Quoted from *The Third Congress of the Russian Social Democratic Party* (Moscow, 1955), pp. 63–64.
34. Lenin, *Works*, VIII, 353.
35. Lenin, *Works*, VIII, 370.
36. *Third Congress*, p. 62.
37. *Third Congress*, p. 65.
38. S. Maklegiladze and A. Yavidze, *The Revolution of 1905–07 in Georgia* (Tiblis, 1956), pp. 141–42.
39. S. Gusev, *1905 Materials and Documents—The Fighting Section of the Socialist Party* (Moscow, 1927), pp. 19–21.
40. Chermensky, p. 57.
41. Chermensky, p. 58.
42. P. N. Milyukov, *Recollections* [in Russian] I (New York, 1955), 302.
43. *Letters of Nicholas II and His Mother* (Paris, 1929), pp. 76–77.
44. Cited in Sidney Harcave, *First Blood, the Russian Revolution of 1905* (New York, 1964), p. 196.
45. Milyukov, I, 309.
46. Milyukov, I, 309.
47. Milyukov, I, 329.
48. Chermensky, p. 134.
49. Quoted in *1905*, ed. M. N. Pokrovsky, III, (Moscow, 1925), 42.
50. N. Volkovicher, "The Sebastopol Uprising," *1905*, p. 103.
51. Witte, III, 31.
52. Milyukov, I, 329.
53. Maklakov, III, 466.
54. Quoted in Chermensky, p. 175.
55. *The Correspondence of Nicholas II*, p. 139.
56. Quoted in D. Izgoyev, *P. Stolypin* (Moscow, 1917), p. 64.
57. S. S. Oldenburg, *The Reign of Nicholas II* [in Russian] I (Belgrade, 1939), 351.
58. Oldenburg, I, 357.
59. A. A. Kizevetter, ed. (St. Petersburg, 1906).
60. Kizevetter, p. 8.
61. Kizevetter, p. 63.

62. Oldenburg, I, 340.
63. *The State Duma,* Stenographic Account, II (St. Petersburg, 1907), 1558.
64. Oldenburg, I, 383.
65. Oldenburg, II (Munich, 1949), 52.

Chapter 4

1. Lenin, *Works,* 4th ed., XXXIV (Moscow, 1952), 288.
2. S. G. Strumlin, *From My Past* (Moscow, 1957), p. 213.
3. S. S. Oldenburg, *The Reign of Nicholas II* [in Russian] II (Munich, 1949), 13.
4. Oldenburg, II, 14.
5. Oldenburg, II, 15.
6. Oldenburg, II, 16.
7. Oldenburg, II, 43.
8. Quoted in Oldenburg, II, 69.
9. Quoted in Oldenburg, II, 70.
10. G. A. Arutiunov, *The Workers' Movement in Russia, 1910–14* (Moscow, 1975), pp. 30–31.
11. Quoted in Oldenburg, II, 34.
12. Oldenburg, II, 31.
13. *Landmarks Collection of Essays About the Russian Intelligentsia* (Moscow, 1909), p. 151.
14. *Landmarks Collection,* p. 45.
15. Lenin, *Works,* XVIII (1948), 285.
16. *Landmarks Collection,* p. 32.
17. D. Izgoyev, *P. A. Stolypin* (Moscow, 1912), p. 111.
18. *The Correspondence of Nicholas and Alexandra Romanov,* III (Moscow, 1925), 224.
19. *Correspondence of Nicholas and Alexandra,* III, 236.
20. Oldenburg, II, 102.
21. P. Y. Shchegolev, ed., *The Fall of the Tsarist Regime,* II (Moscow, 1925), 395.
22. Oldenburg, II, 93.
23. Oldenburg, II, 90.
24. Quoted in P. N. Milyukov, *Recollections* [in Russian] II (New York, 1955), 164.
25. Haimson, "Social Stability, Part II," *Slavic Review* (March 1965), pp. 7–16.
26. M. A. Tsiolovsky, ed., *Bolsheviks, 1903–1916. From the Files of the Former Security Department* (Moscow, 1918), p. 148.
27. Lenin, *Works,* XXI (1948), 4.

Chapter 5

1. *Two Hundred Fifty Days at the Imperial Headquarters* (Moscow, 1920), p. 6.
2. Quoted in S. S. Oldenburg, *The Reign of Nicholas II* [in Russian] II (Munich, 1949), 133.
3. Samuel H. Baron, *Plekhanov* (Stanford, 1963), p. 324.
4. Oldenburg, II, 15.
5. Lemke, p. 5.
6. Lemke, p. 5.
7. Lemke, p. 13.
8. Quoted in Lemke, p. 14.
9. *The Lenin Collection,* I (Moscow, 1924), 198.
10. Oldenburg, II, 172.
11. *The Correspondence of Nicholas and Alexandra Romanov,* III (Moscow, 1925), 244.
12. *Correspondence of Nicholas and Alexandra,* III, 243.

References

13. Quoted in *Prologue to Revolution,* ed. Michael Cherniavsky (New York, 1967), p. 77.
14. Cherniavsky, p. 80.
15. Cherniavsky, p. 65.
16. *Correspondence of Nicholas and Alexandra,* III, 215–54.
17. *Correspondence of Nicholas and Alexandra,* III, 219.
18. *Correspondence of Nicholas and Alexandra,* III, 269.
19. Quoted in Cherniavsky, pp. 160–61.
20. *Correspondence of Nicholas and Alexandra,* III, 501.
21. *Correspondence of Nicholas and Alexandra,* III, 267.
22. B. B. Grave, ed., *Bourgeoisie on the Eve of the February Revolution* (Moscow, 1927), p. 60.
23. *Russia 1917, The February Revolution* (New York, 1967), especially pp. 163–87.
24. Grave, p. 68.
25. *The Lenin Collection,* I, 202.
26. Lenin, *Works,* 4th ed., XXIII (Moscow, 1949), 121.
27. A. P. Spiridovich, *The Great War and the February Revolution, 1914–1917,* II (New York, 1960), 84.
28. Oldenburg, II, 190.
29. P. Y. Shchegolev, ed., *The Fall of the Tsarist Regime,* I (Leningrad, 1924), 21.
30. A. Shlyapnikov, *Year 1917,* I (Moscow, n.d.), 13.
31. Quoted in Oldenburg, II, 202.
32. Nicholas Golovin, *The Russian Army in the World War* (New Haven, 1931), p. 97.
33. Shlyapnikov, I, 17.
34. Grave, p. 150.
35. A. I. Sidorov, *The Economic Situation of Russia During World War I* (Moscow, 1973), 95.
36. Oldenburg, II, 213.
37. Shchegolev, I, 140.
38. *Letters of the Tsaritsa to the Tsar,* ed. Bernard Pares (London, 1924), pp. 439–40. (The orthography and grammar as in the original.)
39. Grave, p. 145.
40. F. A. Golder, *Documents of Russian History, 1914–1917* (New York, 1927), p. 155. The text in this compendium is a translation of a greatly expurgated version of the original as eventually passed by the censor.
41. Golder, p. 156.
42. Golder, p. 162.
43. P. N. Milyukov, *Recollections* [in Russian] II (New York, 1955), 277.
44. Grave, p. 160.
45. Lenin, *Works,* XXIII, 56.
46. Grave, p. 176.
47. Milyukov, II, 282.
48. Grave, p. 178.
49. A. A. Kizevetter, ed., *Accusations Against the Party of National Freedom* (St. Petersburg, 1906), p. 8.
50. Grave, p. 190.
51. Golovin, p. 123.
52. Shlyapnikov, I, 225.
53. Shlyapnikov, I, 28.
54. Cited in Shlyapnikov, I, 225.
55. Shlyapnikov, I, 225.
56. S. P. Melgunov, *On the Paths Towards a Palace Revolution* (Paris, 1931), p. 209.
57. Shlyapnikov, I, 42. By *enemy* the professor meant the government, specifically Protopopov, whom he credited with diabolical designs. Shlyapnikov, rather self-consciously, took him to refer to German agents.
58. Grave, p. 187.
59. Cited in Oldenburg, II, 237.
60. L. Trotsky, *History of the Russian Revolution, Vol. I: February Revolution* [in Russian] (Berlin, 1931), p. 126.
61. Shlyapnikov, I, 18.

62. Literally "interborough." Shlyapnikov, I, 61.
63. Shlyapnikov, I, 240.
64. Trotsky, I, 126.
65. Katkov, p. 256.
66. Shlyapnikov, I, 40.
67. Cited in Trotsky, I, 126.
68. Shlyapnikov, I, 73.
69. From an official report cited in Shlyapnikov, I, 248, 250.
70. Schegolev, I, 190.
71. Spiridovich, III (1962), 123.
72. Vasily Shulgin, *The Days* [in Russian] (Berlin, n.d.), p. 68.
73. I. Yurenev, *The Interfaction 1911–1917 in the Proletarian Revolution,* II (Moscow, 1924), 193.
74. Milyukov, II, 292.
75. Shlyapnikov, I, 119.
76. Shlyapnikov, I, 121.
77. Golder, p. 281.
78. Golder, p. 288.
79. Shlyapnikov, I, 174. Italics in the original.
80. Milyukov, II, 316.
81. Golder, p. 301.
82. Milyukov, II, 305.
83. Vasily Shulgin, *The Days* (Berlin, n.d.), p. 190.
84. Cited in D. F. Sverchkov, *Kerensky* (Leningrad, 1927), p. 20.
85. Cited in Irakli Tseretelli, *Recollections of the February Revolution* [in Russian] I (Paris-Hague, 1963), 114. This is a literal translation.

Chapter 6

1. Nicholas Sukhanov, *Notes About the Revolution,* I (Berlin, 1922), 5.
2. Sukhanov, II, 231.
3. Sukhanov, I, 126.
4. Sukhanov, I, 265.
5. Sukhanov, I, 231.
6. Sukhanov, I, 231.
7. Quoted in Irakli Tseretelli *Recollections of the February Revolution* [in Russian] I (Paris-Hague, 1963), 128–29. My italics.
8. P. N. Milyukov, *Recollections* [in Russian] II (New York, 1955), 306.
9. Quoted in Milyukov, II, 335.
10. V. A. Osipova and G. I. Sukhareva, eds., *1917 in the Saratov Province* (Saratov, 1957), p. 618.
11. Quoted in N. Avdeyev, *The Revolution of 1917* (Moscow, 1922), p. 114.
12. Sukhanov, II, 140.
13. Quoted in A. Shlyapnikov, *Year 1917,* II (Moscow, n.d.), 185.
14. Shlyapnikov, II, 140.
15. Frank A. Golder, *Documents of Russian History, 1914–1917* (New York), p. 325.
16. Sukhanov, II, 236.
17. Sukhanov, II, 216.
18. Sukhanov, II, 298.
19. Sukhanov, II, 299.
20. Tseretelli, I, 47.
21. Avdeyev, p. 197.
22. Lenin, *Works,* 5th ed., XXXI, (Moscow, 1969), 7.
23. Lenin, *Works,* XXXI, 36.
24. Quoted in *Problems of the History of the Communist Party of the Soviet Union,* No. 6 (Moscow, 1962), p. 140.

References

25. Z. A. Zeman, *Germany and the Revolution in Russia, 1915–18, Documents from the Archives of the German Foreign Ministry* (London, 1958), pp. 24, 26.
26. Quoted in Shlyapnikov, III, 288.
27. Lenin, *Works,* XXXI, 113–19.
28. Sukhanov, III, 109.
29. Sukhanov, III, 116.
30. Lenin, *Works,* XXXI, 78. My italics.
31. Lenin, *Works,* XXXI, 236.
32. Lenin, *Works,* XXXI, 266.
33. *The Seventh All-Russian Conference of the Social Democratic Party (bolsheviks) April 1917* (Moscow, 1958) p. 364.
34. *The Seventh Conference,* pp. 200–201.
35. *The Seventh Conference,* p. 134.
36. Milyukov, II, 362.
37. Sukhanov, III, 262.
38. Milyukov, II, 363.
39. *The Seventh Conference,* p. 111. My italics.
40. Lenin, *Works,* XXXI, 187.
41. Tseretelli, I, 151.
42. Lenin, *Works,* XXXII, 111.
43. Sukhanov, IV, 34.
44. Sukhanov, IV, 37.
45. Quoted in *The Red Chronicle,* No. 6 (Moscow, 1923), 21.
46. Quoted in Vera Vladimirova, *The Revolution of 1917. Chronicle of Events* III (Moscow, n.d.), 299.
47. Vladimirova, III, 136.
48. Sukhanov, V, 48.
49. Quoted in Paul Browder and Alexander Kerensky, eds., *The Russian Provisional Government,* III (Stanford, Calif., 1961), 1458–62.
50. A. S. Lukomsky, *The Memoirs of General A. S. Lukomsky* [in Russian] I (Berlin, 1922), 245.
51. *Central Committee of the Russian Social Democratic Workers Party (bolshevik) Protocols, August 1917–February 1918* (Moscow, 1958), p. 57.
52. Lenin *Works,* XXXIV, 390.
53. *The Central Committee Protocols,* p. 85.
54. Sukhanov, VII, 51.
55. Sukhanov, VII, 133.
56. P. N. Maliantovich, "In The Winter Palace, October 25–26," *The Past* (Moscow, 1918), Bk. 6, No. 12.
57. Sukhanov, VII, 185.
58. L. Trotsky, *History of the Russian Revolution, Vol. II: February Revolution* [in Russian] (Berlin, 1931), p. 377.
59. Maliantovich, "In the Winter Palace."
60. M. Latsis, *Two Years of War on the Domestic Front* (Moscow, 1920), p. 75.
61. L. Trotsky, *Lenin* (New York, 1926), p. 137.
62. *Seventh Congress of the Communist Party (bolsheviks) Protocols* (Moscow, 1923), p. 34.
63. Serge Volkonsky, *The Decembrists—Family Recollections* (Petersburg, 1922), p. 96.

Chapter 7

1. See Robert L. Wolff, "The Three Romes" in *Daedalus,* No. 2 (1955), 291.
2. Lenin quoted in L. Trotsky, *History of the Russian Revolution, Vol. II: February Revolution* (Berlin, 1931), p. 662.
3. *Changing Signposts* [in Russian] (Prague, 1921), p. 173.

4. *Changing Signposts*, p. 177.
5. *Changing Signposts*, p. 33.
6. *Changing Signposts*, p. 49.
7. Lenin, *Works*, 4th ed., XXXII (Moscow, 1950), 479.
8. Lenin, *Works*, XL, 356.
9. Lenin, *Works*, XXX, 338.
10. Stalin, *Works*, X (Moscow, 1950), 46.
11. I. Trifonov, *The History of the Class War in the USSR* (Moscow, 1960), p. 153.
12. Trifonov, p. 167.
13. *The Communist Party of the USSR in Resolutions*, IV (Moscow, 1958), 506.
14. *V. I. Lenin and A. M. Gorky* (Moscow, 1961), p. 21.
15. See Zinoviev, "About Stalin and Stalinism" [in Polish] in *Kultura*, January 1980 (Paris), p. 65.
16. Stalin, *Works* [in Russian] III (Stanford, Cal., 1965), 7. My italics.
17. *Hope Against Hope* (New York, 1970), p. 107.
18. *The Communist Party in Resolutions*, II (1953), 1028.
19. *Khrushchev Remembers, The Last Testament* (New York, 1974), p. 79.
20. *Khruschev*, p. 79.
21. M. Gorky, *The Russian Peasant* [in Russian] (Berlin, 1922), p. 6.
22. Gorky, p. 7.
23. Quoted in S. I. Volk, The People's Will (Moscow, 1966), p. 31.
24. I. Zelenin, "The Political Department of the Machine Tractor Stations, 1933–35," *Historical Notes*, No. 76 (Moscow, 1967), p. 47.
25. Ivan Stadnyvk, *People Are Not Angels* (Moscow, 1966), p. 79.
26. "Horizon Beyond Horizon" in A. T. Tvardovsky, *Collected Works*, III (Moscow, 1967), 205.
27. Tvardovsky, p. 208.
28. In *Kontinent, An Anthology* (New York, 1976), p. 6.
29. Gorky, p. 44.
30. Printed in *Pravda*, Oct. 21, 1962.
31. Victor Chalidze, *To Defend These Rights. Human Rights and the Soviet Union* (New York, 1974), p. 170.
32. From a report in *Documents of Samizdat* [in Russian] I, No. 42 (New York, 1972), p. 3.
33. *Documents* I, 7. That noxious literature should be typed on "socialist property" was evidently thought especially heinous.
34. *Documents* I, 10.
35. *Documents* I, 16.
36. Roy Medvedev, *On Socialist Democracy*, [in Russian] (Amsterdam, 1972), p. 400.
37. A. I. Solzhenitsyn, *The Gulag Archipelago Three* (New York, 1976), p. 452.

INDEX

Abdication Manifesto, 299
Accusations Against the Party of National Freedom (pamphlet), 191
Afghanistan, Russian influence in, 394
Aksakov, Constantine, 73–74, 84
Akhmatova, Anna, 409, 422
Alaska, 36*n*, 45
Alexander I, Tsar, 7–13, 17–23, 67, 208, 226, 230; death of, 48–50; in Napoleonic wars, 5, 80, 226; Pestel and, 38; plot to assassinate, 26, 40
Alexander II, Tsar, 49, 71, 73, 91–92, 123, 135, 142, 153, 165, 208, 214, 272*n*, 417; ascent to throne of, 70; assassination of, 127–28; 130–31; 228; attempts to assassinate, 122, 124; Polish issue under, 106, 109, 116, 119; serfdom abolished by, 75–76, 78–84, 88, 94–95, 106, 109; status of Jews under, 134; suppression of dissent by, 114–15
Alexander III, Tsar, 128, 132–34, 145, 147, 159, 185
Alexandra, Empress, 228, 234, 244, 265, 271; and events leading to 1917 revolution, 276, 279, 285, 297; opposition to Duma of, 244; Protopopov and, 268, 269, 272–74; Rasputin and, 215–16, 234, 247–50, 257, 260; Sukhomlinov and, 262
Alexeyev, Gen. Michael, 246, 298
Alexis, Tsarevich, 298
All-Russian Congress of Soviets, 131

All-Russian Party Conference, 340
All-Russian Union of Cities, 231, 251, 269
All-Russian Union of Zemstvos for the Relief of Wounded and Sick Soldiers, 231, 250, 251, 269
Almanach of Gotha, 203*n*
Amalrik, Andrei, 426
Anarchists, 356, 360; Lenin and, 335–37; Moscow State Conference and, 368; in 1917 revolution, 315; Tolstoy as, 130
Anastasia, Grand Duchess, 234
Andronnikov, Prince Michael, 259
Anti-Semitism, 35; of Nicholas II, 216; Plehve's use of, 154; of Purishkevich, 273; of reactionary populists, 187; Witte's opposition to, 184
Antonov-Ovseyenko, Vladimir, 386
Apraxin market fire, 112
April Theses (Lenin), 335, 338
Arakchevey, Alexis, 11, 18, 20, 21, 23
Armenia, socialists and, 163
Assembly of the Land, 72, 74, 207, 390
Association of Zemstvos, 231
Aurora (ship), 382, 385
Austria: in alliance with Germany, 149; 1848 revolution in, 69; Hungarian uprising against, 69; Polish autonomy urged by, 118; in World War I, 235, 236, 239, 242, 254, 255, 262, 263, 291, 302, 336, 358
Azev, Yevno, 141, 155, 164, 218

Index

Index

Index

Nicholas I (continued)
pression under, 66–67, 105, 114, 146, 264; Stalin compared with, 398

Nicholas II, Tsar, 129, 145, 183–90, 332, 348, 387, 401; abdication of, 154, 296–99; Alexandra's influence on, 247–50; arrest of, 313; Bulygin Duma and, 171, 173; and events leading to 1917 revolution, 274–79, 281, 285, 291; First Duma dissolved by, 193; in Galicia, 242; Maklakov and, 241; military strategy and, 237; during 1905 revolution, 169–73, 175; 1916 visit to Duma of, 256–57; October Manifesto of, 177, 183, 186–88; Protopopov appointed by, 267, 269; Rasputin and, 215–16, 256–61; response to Germany's declaration of war, 226–27, 229, 230, 232; Riabushinsky on, 251; Russo-Japanese War and, 149, 151; Sazonov dismissed by, 262–63; status of Jews under, 195; Stolypin and, 205–8, 212, 214; Sukhomlinov and, 262; and Supreme Command of army, 234, 244–48, 253, 255; Union of the Russian People and, 187; wartime change in ministers by, 243; Witte and, 148, 149, 183–85, 189; zemstvos petition rejected by, 135–36

Nicholas Nikolayevich, Grand Duke, 246, 248, 298, 317; and plot for palace coup, 275, 278; in Supreme Command of army, 234, 235, 241, 245, 299

1905 revolution, 14, 129–98, 279, 305, 367; First Duma and, 188–93; Gapon and, 155, 160–65; Helphand in, 287; impact of, 199–200; liberal-revolutionary alliance in, 155–58; Marxism and, 138–45; 1917 compared with, 252; police unionism and, 137, 152–54; repression to end, 186–87; Russo-Japanese War and, 149–51, 172–73; soviets in, 166, 175–77, 180

1917 revolution, see February revolution; October revolution

Nizhni-Novgorod uprising (1612), 31

NKVD, 388

Northern Army Group, 297

Northern Society of Decembrists, 25, 29–31, 38–40, 45–49, 51

Nosar-Khrustalev, 177

Notes About the System of Governance (Pestel), 36

Novyi Mir (magazine), 416

Obolensky, Prince Eugene, 54

Obruchev, Nicholas, 107, 111, 112

Obruchev, Vladimir, 103, 107

October Manifesto (1905), 177, 183, 184, 186–88, 220

October revolution, 129, 200, 312, 362, 397, 413, 426; Bolshevik seizure of power in, 384–89; events leading to, 370, 373–84

Octobrist party, 185, 196, 203, 205, 220, 222, 279, 400; during World War I, 244

Odessa: general strike in, 154; 1905 uprising in, 172; police unionism in, 153

Odoyevsky, Prince Alexander, 51, 64, 143

Ogarev, Nicholas, 80, 96, 105–7, 110

OGPU, 388

Okhrana, 137, 141, 274, 307, 388; Bolsheviks infiltrated by, 224; labor movement and, 152

Old Believers, 119, 133, 195

Oldenberg, S. S., 266–67

One Day in the Life of Ivan Denisovich (Solzhenitsyn), 418, 419

Order No. 1 of Petrograd Soviet, 295, 296, 308, 317, 348, 359

Orekhovo soviet, 343

Organization (underground group), 123–24

Orlov, General, 187

Orlov, Count Michael, 19–20, 24

Orthodox Church, 11, 26, 119, 136, 222, 235, 276, 393, 407–8; Alexandra and, 215; Duma and, 220; Holy Synod of, 132; labor movement and, 153; in Poland, 117; proselytizing policies of, 133

Pacifism, 265

Paige, Satchel, 415

Panslavism, 408

Panteleyev, 87

Party of National Freedom, see Kadets

Parvus, see Helphand, Alexander

Pasternak, Boris, 419

Paul I, Tsar, 10, 12, 276

Pavlov, Ivan, 394

People's Justice, The, 125n

People's Will, The, 127–28, 130, 134, 141, 142, 144, 152, 349, 368n, 413

Permanent revolution, theory of, 104, 288, 309

Pestel, Paul, 24–27, 30, 32–41, 46, 81, 98, 109, 130; arrest and imprisonment of, 56, 59; in assassination plots, 26–27, 40–41; execution of, 4, 62; in Union of Salvation, 6; in Union of Welfare, 18, 24

Pestel, Vladimir, 62

Pétain, Henri, 255

Peter the Great, 68, 69, 82, 84, 88, 206, 273, 276, 390; death of, 10; form of government devised by, 30, 72, 74, 80, 86, 177, 228

Peter III, Tsar, 10

Petrashevsky circle, 67, 92

Petrograd (St. Petersburg): factories employing more than five thousand workers in, 210; anarchists in, 356; demonstration by high school students of, 318; Kornilov putsch against, 372; Lenin's return to, 329; during 1905 revolution, 163–65; strikes in, 161, 223, 286–92; Protopopov on rumors of trouble in,

Index

Index